Inside
Today's Home

Inside Today's Home

Fifth Edition

the late **Ray Faulkner**

Stanford University

LuAnn Nissen

Education Member ASID, IDEC
University of Nevada—Reno

Sarah Faulkner

Holt, Rinehart and Winston

New York   Chicago   San Francisco   Philadelphia   Montreal   Toronto
London   Sydney   Tokyo   Mexico City   Rio de Janeiro   Madrid

Publisher: Susan Katz
Acquisitions Editor: Karen Dubno
Picture Research: Sybille Millard
Design Supervisor: Gloria Gentile
Sr. Production Manager: Nancy Myers
Special Projects Editor: Jeanette Ninas Johnson
Designer: Caliber Design Planning, Inc.
Line art: J. Dyck Fledderus
Composition and camera work: York Graphic Services, Inc.
Color separations: The Lehigh Press, Inc.
Printing and binding: R. R. Donnelley & Sons Co.

Library of Congress Cataloging-in-Publication Data

Faulkner, Ray Nelson, 1906–1975
    Inside today's home.

    Includes bibliographies and index.
    1. Interior decoration. I. Nissen, LuAnn.
II. Faulkner, Sarah. III. Title.
NK2110.F38 1986   747   85-17711

Printed in the United States of America

ISBN 0-03-062577-7

CIP 8 9 039 9 8 7 6 5

Preface

When the first edition of *Inside Today's Home* was written some years ago, the objective was to create a book that would inform and pleasantly stimulate the senses of its readers while building on a foundation of sound interior design principles that would endure the test of time. In the interim, styles, materials, and some standards have changed, but the principles remain the same. The fifth edition has adapted those timeless principles to the changing lifestyles and needs of today.

With the ever-increasing complexities of our lives, it is becoming even more important that our homes provide not only a structure to meet our physical needs, but also an environment to meet our emotional and psychological needs. We hope that *Inside Today's Home* provides direction to those ends.

As with any subject whose trends change periodically, home design is a field that requires timely update to keep abreast of current style and technology. We have attempted to retain the rich influence of the past, present the reality of today, and offer a hint of changes to come while paying special attention to both function and aesthetics.

In an effort to aid the reader in understanding and appreciating the complexity of the field of interior design, the fifth edition has been given a more professional focus. The broad background of design information is retained but the chapters have been reorganized for more logical use and additional, more technical information has been added and pertinent research in the field of environmental design has been cited where applicable to enable the professionally oriented student of interior design to work effectively with the many other specialists involved with interior space.

Part I, "Space for Living," begins with the concept of the home as a lifespace which protects, nurtures, and fulfills our physical and psychological needs. Subsequent chapters detail the process of planning space for social, work, and private activities. Control of environmental factors such as heating, cooling, ventilation, sanitation, acoustics, and lighting, and alternatives for satisfying them are presented in a final chapter in Part I.

The enduring elements and principles of design are examined in Part II, "Design." Design theory is presented as basic background for making aesthetic decisions, and the individual elements and principles are discussed specifically as they apply to planning and furnishing a home. The goal of these chapters is to aid in providing some guidelines for putting all the various parts of home design together to form a cohesive, pleasing whole.

Part III, "Materials for Interiors," explores the characteristics and qualities of the many materials used in homes today. With an understanding of and respect for the distinctive qualities of each material, the best use can be made of each. "Interior Components and Treatments" constitute Part IV. Here each aspect of residential interior design is studied individually in some detail. Lighting is the topic of a new chapter both because it is vital to the aesthetic quality of design and because new technology has changed and improved lighting in the last decade.

Finally, Part V, "Interior Design Today," briefly chronicles the history of furnishings and interiors from roughly the Industrial Revolution to the present in order to provide an understanding of past accomplishments and their relationship to interior design today. The interior design profession, including career opportunities and educational requirements, forms the subject of a new concluding chapter for the fifth edition, a reflection of the continued growth in demand for the services of qualified professionals in the field of interior design. The book concludes with a new Appendix of Designer Symbols and a Glossary of important terms.

No discussion of *Inside Today's Home* would be complete without acknowledging the influence and contributions of Ray Faulkner to the book's birth and life. From the inspiration that gave rise to the first four editions, Ray Faulkner's involvement and influence will always be evident.

The fifth edition has been a collaborative effort on the part of LuAnn Nissen and Sarah Faulkner. LuAnn Nissen feels as though she has come of age professionally with *Inside Today's Home*, having used the book first as a student, then as an educator, and finally, in writing the fifth edition.

Our work has been prodded, assisted, supported, and cheered on by the helpful staff at Holt, Rinehart and Winston. We are grateful to Karen Dubno, Acquisitions Editor, who with skill, perseverance, and endless patience saw the manuscript through the writing stages, a long and tedious process. A number of interior design educators throughout the country, through their replies to a questionnaire, alerted us to the needs, design attitudes, and concerns of students and teachers today. In particular, we would like to thank the following for their in-depth comments on the fourth edition or detailed reviews of the fifth edition manuscript as it progressed: Sheila Baillie, Western Kentucky University; Mary Ann Baird, University of Wisconsin—Stevens Point; Barbara Cannon, Kansas State University; Genevieve H. Cory, Cañada College; Curtiss Cowan, Cañada College; Carla D. Dumesnil, The University of Utah; Sandra J. Evers, North Dakota State University; Brenda M. Focht, Riverside City College; Dorothy L. Fowles, Iowa State University; Herbert Gottfried, Iowa State University; Agnes Hartnell, Phoenix College; Jan Jennings, Iowa State University; Christine Wilson Kesner, Indiana University of Pennsylvania; Nancy Kwalleck, University of Texas at Austin; Gary McCurry, formerly of The University of Tennessee; Karen Moerman, California Polytechnic State University; Lee A. Muse, Indiana State University; Cheryl R. Myers, Central State University; Fran Newby, Kansas State University; Carolyn B. Nuetzel, Southern Illinois University at Carbondale; Mildred Roske, California Polytechnic State University; Betty McKee Treanor, Southwest Texas State University; Margaret Weber, Oklahoma State University.

Jeanette Ninas Johnson, Special Projects Editor, and Gloria Gentile, Design Supervisor, guided the book through the actual design and printing processes with great sensitivity for the subject matter and the final result.

Special recognition must be given to Sybille Millard for her help in searching for and securing the illustrations in the fifth edition, for gathering permissions, and keeping track of the myriad details of the picture program. In any book dealing with as graphic a subject matter as interior design, the selection and quality of the illustrations is vitally important. Sybille's contribution to this task has been invaluable. Our thanks also go to the individuals whose pictures do so much to illuminate the text, illustrating the points we wish to make and providing an overview of the best in residential interior design today. In particular we appreciate the work of Morley Baer; Karen Bussolini; Centerbrook; Alfredo De Vido; Esto; Charles Farrell; Michael Graves; Norman McGrath; Richard Meier; Philip Molten; Norman Petersen; Robert Perron; Tim Street-Porter; Venturi, Rauch & Scott Brown; Paul Warchol.

Finally, we wish to acknowledge the personal contributions of those near to us. LuAnn expresses her deep appreciation for the continual support and assistance of her husband, Howard Goodman. Together they discussed style and content, and his help in composition and editing is reflected throughout the book. And as always, Sarah's sons provided the day-by-day strength to see another edition through to its rebirth.   •

LuAnn Nissen   Sarah Faulkner
University of Nevada—Reno

Contents

For my parents . . .

LuAnn Nissen

And for my sons . . .

Sarah Faulkner

Space for Living

Space for living—a pavilion overlooking Long Island Sound. Ungers & Kiss, architects. *(Photograph: © Karen Bussolini)*

1

Lifespace

Today's home plays a critical role in our lives, perhaps more than at any other time in history. It not only shelters and protects us from physical harm but also nurtures our growth, enhances our development, insulates us from the stress of the outside world, provides a feeling of control over at least a small segment of our environment, fosters development of our individual potential, and serves as an outlet for our need for creative self-expression.

The concept of home as a *lifespace*—the space we call our own, within which a good portion of our social and private living takes place—is a constant in our rapidly changing world. The physical facility and geographic location may change many times during each of our lives. But the idea of the home as a lifespace where our basic needs are fulfilled will remain unchanged.

And, in spite of the diversity of types and locations of living spaces available today, we all have common biological needs and are subject to certain ecological, cultural, and psychological influences that guide our choices in designing our personal dwellings.

4

Biological Needs

Physical lifespace needs are, of course, basic: protection from the elements and from intruders, a safe place for bodily rest, and nourishment. These needs are our most immediate and are easy to understand. We must have food and sleep and we cannot endure without protection when exposed to the extremes of climate or to other living things that might harm us. But ways of meeting these needs have long been diverse and imaginative and are conditioned by ecological, cultural, and psychological influences.

Ecological Concerns

Concern for the environment has become increasingly important in our lives in recent years. Fewer homes are being built without regard for terrain or climate, in part because building and energy costs are soaring as our finite resources are depleted. Our growing knowledge of the effects we have on our natural environment, and it in turn has on us, has led us to a greater respect for the contributions that environmental awareness can make in the design of homes. (Ecological economy is discussed in detail later in this chapter; energy-efficient design is considered in Chapter 6.)

We are also learning the value of preservation of both our natural and our built environments for all living things, for their beauty and for the feelings of self-renewal we derive from them. More than ever before we are reusing our homes—rehabilitating, remodeling, and restoring them—to provide living quarters for today and to preserve our heritage for the future.

Cultural Influences

The complex term *culture* refers to the system wherein a group of people—a society—shares certain values; that is, there are common ways of doing things, common notions of right and wrong, common ideas of how things ought to be, even fairly common perceptions of what is beautiful or ugly. These shared values are passed from generation to generation and often preserved when people immigrate to a new country. Many diverse cultural groups in the United States have been quite persistent in maintaining their separate identities, resulting in neighborhoods in many cities known as Chinatown, Little Italy, The Barrio, and the like, where respect for tradition maintains a collective and accepted way of life. Architect Amos Rapoport[1] notes that even for primitive people, the house was more than just a physical shelter.* It was a symbol of the ideal life, a culturally controlled concept, and it took its form primarily because of the common goals and values of the people, with climate, materials, and technology having less influence.

Even today our attitudes toward eating, bathing, privacy, and relaxation have a definite impact on the form and use of eating areas, bathing facilities, and sleeping spaces within the home. The culturally established norms of behavior we take for granted dictate that in our homes we sit in chairs and sleep in beds, whereas Japanese people sit and sleep on objects close to the the floor; Irish bathtubs are traditionally much shorter than American bathtubs because, in Ireland, bathers are not used to stretching out.[2]

In general, Western dwellings consist of a *multipurpose house* with *single-purpose rooms*. Traditionally in our culture, all the functions of daily life except

*Notes are grouped at the end of each chapter.

1–1 The classic Japanese house has sliding doors and panels that can be closed or opened to structure the interior spaces as needed over the course of the day. *(Photograph: © Paul Warchol)*

working are performed within one structure—sleeping, preparing food, eating, bathing, entertaining, and so on. Yet within this multipurpose structure, we have most often assigned specific regions to each activity and call them bedroom, kitchen, dining room, bathroom, living room. As activities or needs change, people must shift location from one room to another, or even from one structure to another when our jobs take us to the office or factory "working house." In other cultures, quite different arrangements are seen as normal.

The classic Japanese home, for example, is a multipurpose house with multipurpose rooms. Spaces are not demarcated permanently by walls; instead, screens or sliding panels that can be closed or opened easily adapt the space to changing needs over the course of the day. What is by day the "eating room" or the "living room" becomes at night, with the addition of mats, the "sleeping room." The same *place* thus serves different functions and *changes* with needs. Conversely, in our own culture, a shift in needs requires that people change location; we sleep in a bedroom and move to the living room for social gatherings. In parts of the South Seas, in contrast, we encounter single-purpose houses; the principal family dwelling serves for sleeping, while cooking and eating are done communally in a separate "cooking house."

In recent years more and more households in the United States have broken free of the boxes-within-a-box formula to create lifespaces suited to their individual needs. The studio apartment or loft is not very different in concept from the Japanese house and embodies the same goal in its planning: the most flexible possible utilization of space.

Psychological Effects

Psychologist Robert Sommer has studied the effects of the physical environment upon the attitudes and behavior of the people who use it. Architecture, Sommer says, must be functional in terms of user behavior and satisfaction; "not only must form follow function, but it must assist it in every way."[3] In other words, a space should contribute positively to the comfort and efficiency with which activities take place within it. In a living room, obviously, furniture should be arranged to promote social interaction in an easy, friendly conversational grouping; in the bedroom adequate provision for privacy and light control will contribute greatly to the effectiveness of the space.

Concern with the behavioral effects of the physical environment, and our ability to design our surroundings for our greatest benefit, has led to the ever-widening interdisciplinary field of study known as **environmental design** or **environmental psychology.** Professionals in this field combine scientific disciplines of psychology, sociology, biology, anthropology, geology, and ecology with the practitioner disciplines of architecture, urban and community planning, interior design

1–2 Sliding fiberglass shoji screens of Oriental inspiration temper the light and divide the space in this long L-shaped loft, creating privacy without being permanent. Katja Geiger, designer. *(Chester Higgins, Jr./NYT Pictures)*

of both home and workplace, and landscape architecture. The approach is both humanistic and holistic rather than purely aesthetic or narrowly specialized. Environmental design emphasizes the dynamic ecological view that we have an active role in creating our own environment, suggesting that we need to become more aware of the possibilities for using and shaping our personal environs in a positive, effective manner.[4] We are often unwilling to reshape our immediate surroundings actively; rather, we seem passive, tending to adapt to even the most undesirable spaces and furnishings. In fact, our ability to adapt may be the reason we tolerate so much poor design—uncomfortable chairs or closets that have not been planned in terms of actual use. A good user-environment "fit,"—body/chair, clothes/closet— is the desired outcome in the environmental design process.

Social psychologist Irwin Altman has examined how people can and do use the environment to shape social interaction with others in terms of four behavioral concepts: *privacy*, *personal space*, *territoriality*, and *crowding*. He suggests that "privacy is a central regulatory process by which a person (or group) makes himself more or less accessible and open to others and that the concepts of personal space and territorial behavior are *mechanisms* that are set in motion to achieve desired levels of privacy." Crowding occurs when these "mechanisms have not functioned effectively, resulting in an excess of undesired social contact."[5]

Privacy

The home provides privacy from outsiders with walls that protect us from physical, visual, and various degrees of acoustical intrusion. Windows provide some flexibility between total seclusion from and total exposure to the outside world.

1–3 Vertical blinds provide privacy, protecting the occupants of this studio apartment from visual intrusion. Scott Kurland, architect. *(Photograph: © Peter Aaron/ESTO)*

1–4 Large windows open and extend interior space. This Mondrianlike window composition with its small sections of colored glass not only frames an outward view but also provides a focus of interest itself. Dmitri Bulazel, architect. *(Photograph: © Peter Aaron/ESTO)*

They can be large or small, placed for outward views but shielded from inward observation, whether open or closed, curtained or not, as desired.

Inside the house, the floor plan first sets the privacy levels at which the home functions. A very open plan might satisfy a single person; internal privacy and access are controlled by the owner. A larger family group would probably be happier with some spaces that can be closed off as the need for seclusion arises. Closed doors establish off-limits boundaries in our culture and secure privacy for those behind them.

Personal Space

Each person moves within an area or bubble of personal space that expands and contracts according to individual needs and social circumstances. Its size varies with personality, age, and cultural background. The size of our space bubble determines our perception and experience of a particular space; people with large space bubbles use furniture arrangements to create physical barriers between themselves and others and perceive a tightly arranged space as crowded and uncomfortable.[6] Any intrusion into our invisible space bubble is viewed as threatening, creating stress and a sense of malaise. **Proxemics** is the study of our personal and cultural spatial needs and our interaction with surrounding space.

Edward T. Hall has identified four *interpersonal distances* (each with a near and far phase) as closely related to personal space and the regulation of privacy and social interaction.[7] *Intimate* distance ranges from zero to 18 inches and stimulates all the senses in unmistakable involvement with another person. In some cultures, intimate distance among adults is accepted only in the privacy of the home. *Personal* distance of 18 inches to 4 feet generally coincides with the invisible bubble of space that can literally be physically dominated by an individual. It can be likened to keeping someone at "arm's length," or the relationship between two people may be indicated by how close to each other they stand or sit. *Social* distance (from 4 to 12 feet) is maintained for impersonal business, casual social gatherings, or formal interactions. Furniture arranged for easy conversation in the home should not exceed this distance between pieces. Finally, *public* distance ranges from 12 to 25 feet and implies decreased warmth and individuality of interaction. These categories of relationships and the activities and spaces associated with them hold generally true for Americans and Northern Europeans. Other patterns exist in other parts of the world. What is intimate in one culture might be personal or even public in another.

By studying these proxemic patterns, the designer can plan a living room in which a conversational grouping will be successful; people will be close enough to hear each other, see each others' faces and expressions, and get cues from them but not so close (or far) that they will feel uncomfortable. Individual family members can also be provided with personal spaces ranging from intimate to social, as an extension of their personality and physical self and to suit their varying needs.

Territoriality

The concept of territoriality in humans is closely related to the attainment and protection of privacy. A territory is a specifically defined area owned or controlled and personalized by defensive boundary markers such as fences, signs, nameplates, or sometimes behavioral cues as simple as a cold stare. Symbolic of our psychological identification with "our" place are our attitudes of possessiveness and arrangement of objects and furnishings within it. Within our territory we feel safe and comfortable, our self-image and sense of well-being are enhanced, and we feel in control. Often this is the only space in our lives we feel we can exert control over, and, as such, it satisfies our need to be creative, to express our individuality. Because our home is considered a retreat or haven from the unwanted stresses of everyday life, we protect it and defend it from intrusion without invitation.

Not only does each household establish a territory of its own; each individual in it should also have a particular territory that remains inviolate. In an affluent household, each member may claim rights to an entire bedroom and may express unhappiness or discomfort if forced to share or exchange. But even in shared spaces, individuals are typically territorial about those portions that are theirs, such as furniture, closets, drawers, and play or work spaces. Boundary markers such as closed doors are usually not crossed without permission. Even in very small quarters, one chair often belongs to one person and that person only. Places at a family dinner table may be so firmly allocated that any change in the seating plan brings protests from a young child deprived of his or her usual place. Such territorial habits seem to smooth day-to-day life, with all family members having "places."

Crowding

Many studies have shown the adverse effects of crowding on animals, but similar studies of humans have yielded conflicting results.[8] Perhaps that is because adverse effects such as stress generally build up over a period of time, and in some situations density is desirable. We tolerate being crowded in an elevator, even though it is unpleasant, because we know it is a temporary condition and we have learned many coping mechanisms for dealing with invasions of personal space on a short-term basis. On the other hand, we often seek out a crowded dance floor or sports arena: the density is part of the fun. In either situation, however, psychological discomfort is instantly introduced if we are confined. If we are unable to leave a stranded elevator or packed dance floor, stress builds up and panic may set in.

We can relate this concept to selecting and arranging furniture in our home. For example, a person seated in the middle of a 6-foot sofa may feel vaguely or even acutely uncomfortable. Penned in by the people on either side and often trapped by a coffee table in front, the unfortunate prisoner may long to escape. A more com-

above left: 1–5 A home office can be delineated by built-in furnishings yet still remain accessible to life around it. Peter Samton, architect. *(Photograph: David Hirsch)*

above right: 1–6 A child's nook for privacy is a feature many adults would treasure. Architect Murray Whisnant designed his home with many windows, soaring ceilings, and private spaces for all family members. *(Photograph: Gordon H. Schenck, Jr.)*

1–7 A small sofa, chairs that can pull up, and two small coffee tables form an intimate conversation area with easy access in designer Stanley Barrows' Manhattan apartment. *(Photograph: Gene Maggio/ NYT Pictures)*

11

1–8 A conversation pit provides seating for many around the perimeter of a small space. Les Walker, architect. *(Photograph: © Peter Aaron/ESTO)*

fortable arrangement might incorporate smaller seating pieces such as love seats and individual chairs that allow more freedom of movement on the part of each occupant. Other people may be drawn to large sofas or heaps of floor pillows on which they can congregate as closely as they wish.

Crowding appears to lead to territorial behavior. Controlling a territory reduces the stress and *overstimulation* of crowding. The more affluent and socially powerful we are, the larger the space we usually claim for ourselves to insure against feeling crowded.[9]

Planning a Lifespace

The person or persons involved in designing a home may be the individual home-owner or family, an architect, builder/contractor, professional interior designer, consultant in a retail store, or a friend with interest and ability to assist. In some cases, several of these people work cooperatively; in many cases the owners enter the picture only after construction is complete, with spatial arrangements, floor coverings, and fixtures already determined (no more than 5 percent of all structures in the United States are custom designed). Most people select a home that most nearly suits their space needs and then begin to personalize it with their own selections of furnishings, colors, patterns and textures, sometimes with and sometimes without the help of trained interior designers, retail consultants, or others.

Whoever bears the main burden, or fun, of deciding on the actual furnishings and their placement needs a background of information to make the result a workable, comfortable, reinvigorating, and aesthetically pleasing home. This knowledge will range from the psychosocial and behavioral implications and effects already noted to a familiarity with design principles; from all the practical considerations that enter into choosing furniture and materials to an understanding of the people who will be living there. (Who are they, what are their likes and dislikes, how do they see themselves, how do they interact with others?) Factors to be considered in creating a successful lifespace include the people and their lifestyle, mobility, and tastes; their psychological reactions; the location and orientation of the home; and the resources available. An analysis of these factors should be made before a home is rented or purchased in order to achieve the most harmonious relationship between people and their living environment.

People

The people who will live in the home are the most important planning factor because they are not only the reasons for the home and the basic ingredient in the mix of elements but are also the final judges of how well the home functions. Initially, some period of time should be spent gathering as many facts as possible about the inhabitants of a home, getting an idea of who they are and what they like. This information may be acquired informally by communication among family members or between family members and an interior designer or consultant. More formal interviews may also take place with an interior designer who may utilize a detailed questionnaire or *client profile* covering as many topics as the designer thinks necessary to assist in the design program. Questions such as the following are pertinent:

Who will live in the home?   The number, ages, sex, sizes, activities, and relationships of people who make up a household must be a primary factor in planning a lifespace in order that the special needs and interests of each individual, and of the group as a whole, can be met. Anthropologist Paul Bohannan defines the household as "a group of people who live together and form a functioning domestic unit. They may or may not constitute a family, and if they do, it may or may not be a simple nuclear family."[10]

Clearly, this definition encompasses a great variety of living arrangements:

- The single-person household, which comprises nearly one-third of all households today
- Two or more people who may or may not be related; more than half of U.S. households consist of no more than two people
- The child-free married couple
- The nuclear family of husband and wife and their children
- The single-parent family
- The extended family, including grandparents and/or uncles, aunts, or cousins
- The aggregate family consisting of divorced parents who remarry and their children from previous marriages as well as their own
- Groups of the elderly, ethnic minorities, or other nonfamily units who come together to share communal living spaces
- Long- or short-term guests

Alvin Toffler reports that 93 percent of the United States population no longer fits the formerly prevalent nuclear family model. No single family form now dominates as the extended and nuclear families of the past did. Families of the future, "third wave families," will be characterized by diversity of form and might even include families "expanded" by unrelated outsiders who, with the advent of home computers, might join the household in a modern-day version of cottage industry.[11]

Whatever the type of household, the ages and the stage in the life cycle of household members are determining factors in planning pleasant, efficient, and flexible spaces for various activities. Consider a young childless couple both with professional careers, who might use a room with a pleasant view, sun exposure, and access to the kitchen and living areas for a home office or study. If children are planned, the same room might become first a nursery, then a playroom, and then a family room while they are being reared. When the children leave the family home, the room's use might again be changed, this time to a large bedroom suite for the older, perhaps retired couple—or for their parents. Other unused bedrooms might be rented to provide companionship and additional income. Safety needs may also vary over the life span, influencing choices for types of furniture, floor coverings, lighting, and hardware. Optimally, the home planned for more than one person would provide just the degree of privacy and interaction with others that each member desires.

What is their lifestyle? For the purposes of planning a lifespace, lifestyle is the amount of time devoted to various activities in the home. This definition includes entertainment habits: large or small, formal or informal gatherings of friends or relatives; types of social activities such as meals, music, games, or television viewing; and the location of these activities within the home—living room, family

left: 1–9 A dining room designed by Richard Meier creates an airy setting for social activities. *(Photograph: © Ezro Stoller/ESTO)*
right: 1–10 A family room provides a comfortably informal space where family members and friends can congregate. *(Courtesy: Armstrong World Industries, Inc.)*

room, kitchen, library, or patio. Closer, more detailed study could also be made of cooking habits, eating patterns, study and work needs, and the family's approach to housekeeping. Some families prefer a very clean and neat home while others have a casual attitude toward housekeeping.

The family itself and the way in which the members regard their home must also be considered. Are they a close-knit family, playing, studying, working, and eating together, or a loose-knit family with members who pursue individual interests? The first family might have a considerable home life and regard the home as the center of activity while the second household might view the home simply as a base of operations—a place to eat and sleep—with all other pursuits undertaken elsewhere. Expectations and values conditioned by ethnic and cultural backgrounds which should also be considered will undoubtedly emerge from these explorations.

Any such delving into people's lifestyles should include not only how they live but also how they would like to live in the future. Many remodeling projects are undertaken to improve the *ergofit*—the user–environment fit—between physical structure and desired lifestyle.

How long will they stay in the home?   In a day when mobility is a fact of life, this is an important consideration. It is easy to see that a studio apartment rented for a few months in the city is a different proposition from a three- or four-bedroom home finally purchased in an outlying suburb, but today even a house is apt to be only one in a series. As the cost of housing has risen, many families view their first home as an entry-level position in the housing market, to be "traded up" several times, each time more closely approaching the ideal satisfaction of their needs and tastes.

Whether "home" is an apartment, townhouse, or single-family detached house, people's attitudes toward it are often affected by how long they plan to stay there. Research has shown that longer-term occupants tend to personalize their homes more than those who have only a short-term residency and who may regard the home as temporary.[12] In addition to practicality, this response to stability versus mobility may account for the number and type of furnishings and personal possessions a family accumulates. A young couple in their first rather tentative home may well furnish it with a few lightweight, collapsible furnishings that can easily be moved or even replaced. Sometimes, furniture is rented in a temporary residence until decisions are reached about a more permanent location.

The family who owns a houseful of traditional furniture certainly might not want to throw it all out and start afresh upon moving into a modern home. The challenge then becomes one of making the old furniture fit gracefully into a new environment. Plate 1 (p. 23) shows how one family accomplished this adjustment. The house itself is strikingly contemporary, with varied heights and a bright airiness enhanced by broad areas of glass; the furnishings are a mixture of antiques and modern classics. Yet there is no jarring sensation of incompatibility. Rather, the two elements settle together comfortably and in such a way that each heightens the drama of the other.

What are the tastes of the household members?   Taste, the particular likes and dislikes of an individual or of a family, is perhaps the single most important abstract factor in determining what a home will look like. It expresses the personality and values of the home's occupants. We often learn more about an individual or a family by visiting their home than after many conversations in less personal environments such as the office or school. At home, they surround themselves with furnishings of their own choice that express and extend their personality, offering a broader and more intimate view of who they are.

right: 1–11 A cozily cluttered loft gives the feeling of having all the accumulated possessions of a lifetime at hand to enjoy. Peter Stamberg, architect. *(Photograph: © Paul Warchol/ESTO)*

below: 1–12 Reflective and transparent materials help floors, walls, and ceilings seem to disappear in a renovated Manhattan apartment, focusing attention on the antique furniture, carpets, and art objects in the living area. Paul Rudolph, architect. *(Photograph: Robert Levin)*

A comparison of Figures 1-11 and 1-12 shows how dramatically personal rooms can be because of the tastes of their owners. The loft in Figure 1-11 is an extravagant feast for the eyes, a bazaar of objects of various shape and texture filling every possible corner. Obviously, the owner of this house feels most at home surrounded by the comfort and clutter of "things" left out in view. Many people share such a taste for objects that carry special associations or that simply delight the senses.

An opposite pole of taste created the stripped-down living space in Figure 1-12. Walls, floors, and ceilings are all minimally treated. Even the furniture, which has been reduced to the barest essentials, is simple and streamlined.

These two examples are extremes; many people would not want their homes to be either so stark or so rich. Nevertheless, these rooms do illustrate how important a role personal taste plays in designing a lifespace that is successful for the individuals who will occupy it. If we were to transpose the owners of these two homes—if we could persuade them to exchange environments—each would certainly feel uncomfortable.

Taste is not a constant, unvarying phenomenon but may change considerably over the lifetime of an individual. The home one furnishes at the age of forty will probably look quite different from the one planned at twenty. It would be an oversimplification, however, to assume that personal taste gradually "improves," becomes increasingly refined, and perhaps becomes more conservative with advancing age. A great many factors—daily experiences, travels, friends, cultural and ethnic backgrounds, status consciousness, and fashions in general, to name but a few—affect the development of taste.

Although related to the earlier discussion of psychological reactions to environment, taste involves a conscious level of decision-making. Questions about personal tastes usually bring forthright answers: a taste for traditional over modern, a preference for blue, a dislike of highly ornamented furnishings.

A study of illustrations in magazines or books, or a file collection of appealing ideas, will reinforce subjective expressions of taste and allow objective decisions. "Good" taste is developed through study, experience, discrimination, and judgment. It is the selection of furnishings and accessories that meet the needs and suit the personalities of the individuals involved as well as have properties of good design and construction.

above: 1–13 An appreciation for the heritage of the past led to the restoration of this 18th-century house in Durham, Connecticut. *(Photograph: © Karen Bussolini)*

left: 1–14 A contemporary taste for open space may include a reference to tradition, as in this Chicago renovation with its fluted column. Kenneth Schroeder, architect. *(Photograph: © Peter Aaron/ ESTO)*

What are household members' psychological reactions to the surrounding environment? Much of this information may be hard to come by directly. Most people are only dimly aware of why they respond positively or negatively to a certain room or color. They may be drawn toward the room because it is traditional in style, or they like the red color of the sofa; this is easy enough to understand. But more subtle nuances—the fact that the traditional style is reminiscent of a childhood home, for instance, or that the color harmonies in the room as a whole are pleasing—may cause reactions only at a subliminal level.

Here, too, a collection of illustrations of rooms or objects that appeal to the family members may be helpful. Not only does such a file show individual taste, it also gives an unconscious overview of basic responses to many environments. By studying the illustrations we can begin to understand whether a person might feel most at home in a busy environment or is a very private individual who would like small, quiet areas in which to enjoy seclusion. A room with the furniture widely spaced might alert us to an individual whose personal-space dimension requires a certain distance from other people in order to feel comfortable. Of course, many clear questions should be asked to supplement these silent cues.

Location and Orientation

The importance of location and orientation lies in the way climate can affect the architectural design of a home, calling for more or less insulation; fewer or more strategically placed windows; a pitched, domed, or flat roof; and the interior choices of materials, colors, and furniture arrangement. Although the concern of this text is primarily the interior, Chapter 6 addresses climate-sensitive design and orientation for energy efficiency.

Where is the home? A city or country location does not dictate the type of interior design but does often suggest or even strongly indicate the type of furnishings that might be suitable. A seaside summer cottage is an obvious candidate for cool, casual, cleanable furnishings. A ski lodge might also imply informal furniture, but of a kind that promises warmth, comfort, and protection from the elements.

A city apartment occupied on a permanent basis lends itself more readily to traditional, relatively expensive furnishings than does a vacation home. But no rules demand that such an apartment be formal or that a house in the woods necessarily be rustic.

The living room in Figure 1-15 forms part of a basement apartment in central Chicago. Previously a commercial laundry, the space was filled with pipes, electrical lines, water meters, and gas mains. To dispel the industrial image and create a more human atmosphere, the owner filled the room with mellow old furniture, soft textures, and a profusion of growing plants. Exposed brick walls and wood beams (which conceal the pipes) augment the rustic quality.

Figure 1-16 illustrates a contemporary, rather sophisticated interior that might be found in a townhouse or city apartment. Actually, it is located in the country.

Both of these examples would seem to controvert the quality of their locations. A house in Nevada, however, exploits to the fullest the character of the Old West, with thick adobe walls, rough-hewn beams, and unfinished brick floors (Fig. 1-17). Furniture and artifacts reflect the dual influences of Southwest Indians and Spanish missionaries. Regardless of the approach—harmonious contrast or true authenticity—location will nearly always affect the mood of a home.

left: **1–15** A rustic, country atmosphere defies what might have been a depressing location in a Chicago basement apartment designed by Don Konz. (*Photograph: Hedrich-Blessing*)

below: **1–16** If it is thoughtfully planned, a country house can be as elegant and sophisticated as the owner wishes, yet still blend with its surroundings. Myron Goldfinger, architect. (*Photograph: © Norman McGrath*)

left: **1–17** A reflection of the architectural heritage of the old Southwest, this modern adobe house is well suited to the high-desert landscape of Nevada. Maurice J. Nespor & Associates, architects; Diana Cunningham, interior designer. (*Photograph: Hyde Flippo*)

19

What is the climate of the area and the orientation of the home? A home can be designed and constructed to maximize and/or minimize the effects of climate. Walls that face hot sunlight or a cold wind can shield the interior of the house from uncomfortable temperatures and drafts. Windows can be oriented to collect warmth and provide ventilation.

These structural considerations reduce the amount of energy required to maintain comfort inside the home and thus help conserve precious nonrenewable resources. Interior treatments can also assist in this effort, either complementing structural design or (when necessary) providing temperature control even in poorly oriented homes. For example, wide window walls may need draperies to insulate rooms from excessive heat loss or west-facing windows may need sun control to prevent heat gain. Floor and wall materials can be selected to store natural solar heat or to insulate against cold.

Beyond these specific physical considerations, it is possible to create an *atmosphere* of warmth or coolness, snugness or airiness. A home containing light colors and broad areas of uncluttered space will make its owners *feel* cooler to the point that they actually *are* cooler. People who live in chill, wet climates may choose to counteract the depressing psychological effects of the weather by choosing warm colors—reds, oranges, yellows—and patterns and colors that delight the eye and bring the quality of sunshine indoors regardless of its presence or absence outside. Texture can also add to the psychological effect: smoother surfaces feel cooler while thick, plush, and rough textures add warmth so that people feel less in need of heat or air conditioning.

1–18 Heavy-beamed ceilings, enclosing spaces, plush upholstery, patterned rugs, and the earthy texture of wood and plants help establish a feeling of warmth in an interior that adds to its comfort. CBT/Childs Bertman Tseckares & Casendino, Inc., architects. *(Photograph: © Nick Wheeler)*

1–19 Webbed chairs look and feel cool in a summery pavilion home. Alfredo De Vido, architect. *(Photograph: © Norman McGrath)*

Resources Available

Both human and financial resources should be taken into account. An inventory of present possessions can help household members decide what should be kept and what is needed. The individuals' skills, hobbies, and creative abilities should be taken into consideration for the addition they may make as well. For example, old pieces of furniture may be refinished, some new furnishings may be built, and home crafts can provide many personal accessories at less than retail cost.

1–20 Recycled materials belie their age in a contemporary New Haven apartment designed by Andrus Burr and Peter Rose. The old table top rests on a new base of heavy plywood, chairs get a fresh coat of bright paint, and empty wine bottles without labels serve as accessories. *(Photograph: John T. Hill)*

The amount of time and energy family members have or wish to devote to the upkeep and maintenance of the home is also important. Materials should be selected to provide a balance between care required and aesthetic qualities desired. Hardwood floors, for example, can be treated for minimum care while still maintaining the warmth and beauty of the wood.

Costs—both original and continuing—can never be ignored. A realistic evaluation of how much is available for spending over what period of time is necessary. This is most often the area where compromises must be made and a clear look taken at both probabilities and possibilities. What expenditures will give the greatest satisfaction? With new construction costs soaring (they tripled in the last twenty years), many people are concentrating their expenditures on interior design and renovation of existing structures.

Planning Objectives

In discussing the factors that influence the planning of a lifespace we emphasized the specific needs, desires, and reactions of the individual or group. How do we translate the information gathered about the particular people–environment interrelationships into a satisfying home? What are the qualities that constitute "good" home design? They are the same as those required in an individual object.

A chair, for instance, is well designed if it:

- gives comfortable support, thereby fulfilling its requirement of *utility*
- is ecologically conservative and is worth the original cost, plus the time, energy, and money necessary for its maintenance; if it is *economical*
- gives pleasure when seen or touched; if it is *beautiful*
- suits the individual or group so well that it "belongs" in the home, yet at the same time has special qualities of its own; if it has *character*

Transferring these four qualities of utility, economy, beauty, and character to the design of a home, they become four goals that should be considered the cornerstone of good design when making planning and purchase decisions.

Utility

Everyone wants space and furnishings that "work" effectively, that serve the purposes for which they are intended. This includes space that is planned for the intended activities, furniture that is the right size for the expected user, storage that is convenient and accessible, and lighting that provides adequate illumination without glare.

An increasing amount of research is being undertaken to give the interior designer helpful data that will aid in functional planning. *Ergonomics* or *human*

1–21 The Jefferson lounge chair and accessories, designed by Niels Diffrient, incorporate the human comfort factors of ergonomics in an innovative, adjustable design suited for a variety of tasks in a high-tech environment. *(Courtesy Sunar-Hauserman. Photograph: Bill Kontzias)*

left: **Plate 1** Old and new furnishings are blended in a very contemporary house set in the midst of the changing tableau of nature. John M. Johansen, architect. *(Photograph: Pedro E. Guerrero)*

below: **Plate 2** The renovated home of architects Robert Venturi and Denise Scott Brown reflects their philosophy of variety, complexity, and symbolism in design. *(Photograph: © Paul Warchol)*

above: Plate 3 A uniquely designed partial wall separates living and working spaces in a one-room house. Colorful textiles cover the floor, wall, and furniture and express individuality. Lazlo Kiss and Simon Ungers, architects. Robert Hobbs; interior designer. *(Photograph: © Karen Bussolini)*

below: Plate 4 A partial greenhouse brings nature indoors and opens up the interior of a house designed by Joe D' Urso. *(Photograph: © Peter Aaron/ESTO)*

factors engineering combines anthropometric (human body measurement) data, physiology, and such psychological factors as personal space to improve the relationship between users and their environments. For example, in *Human Dimension and Interior Space*, Julius Panero and Martin Zelnik, both architects and interior designers, provide a wealth of information concerning "the actual physical fit, or interface, between the human body and the various individual components of interior spaces."[13] Responses to temperature, sound, and illumination, combined with anatomical measurements, help form standards for the design of both humanistic and functional spaces, equipment, and furniture.

Economy

Economy refers to the management of human, material, monetary, and natural environmental resources. **Human resources** consist of abilities, plus time and energy. Because each person's productivity is influenced by the environment in which he or she works and relaxes, sound economy makes this environment as pleasant as possible. Certainly a well-planned kitchen allows those who cook to work effectively and efficiently while making the best use of individual abilities; a private, well-secluded study or studio is usually a necessity for anyone who works at home. Labor-saving devices have contributed much to conserving time and energy for life-enhancing avocations. This advantage can nevertheless be negated by poor planning, such as arranging a kitchen so that preparation of a meal requires twice as many steps as necessary. The time required for maintenance of the home, performed by humans at least until household robots are readily available, must also be balanced against time desired for other activities.

1-22 "Hubot" is already busy providing entertainment. *(Courtesy Hubotics)*

Material resources begin with the space-for-living itself and include the furniture and all the things that have been acquired over the years. These need to be inventoried and decisions made about their use. A decision may have to be made whether to remodel an old house or build or buy a new one. Furnishings also must be scrutinized to decide whether or not to repair and refinish an old table that is of better quality than one in the affordable price range today. Even such miscellaneous odds and ends as a collection of seashells may be turned into an attractive accessory.

The economy of **monetary resources** will vary widely among households, but a system of using money wisely justifies the little time it takes to plan and follow. Remember that cost is both original and continuing. A long-wearing, easily maintained carpet with a high price tag may be a better investment in the long run than a less expensive one that is not durable or easily cleaned. Similarly, the advantages of wall-to-wall carpeting must be weighed against the possibility of moving to new quarters, in which case the carpet would probably have to be left behind.

Concern over ecology, the conservation of nonrenewable **natural resources** and the harnessing of renewable energy sources, is growing rapidly as we become aware of our great and too often unthinking impact on the environment. Ecological economy should underlie all our decisions and may well change our way of life fundamentally in the years ahead. We have much to learn about this field, and wise choices are not always easy to make.

It is hard to decide whether a chair, for example, should be made of wood or plastic. Wood objects have a long life, can be refinished many times, and when no longer useful are readily reabsorbed into the environment; but our forests are being depleted, and for the first time in the history of the United States wood has become scarce and expensive. Plastics are relatively inexpensive to produce but are derived from petroleum; also a plastic object can be both beyond repair and indestructible: that is, *nonbiodegradable.*

Such ecological factors will concern us at all levels of home planning—from choice of materials in furnishings and accessories to kind and amount of heating, cooling, and lighting we should use, to the components, types, and placement of our housing. Because these concerns for a sustainable society have just begun to attract widespread attention, and because the choices are so basic and controversial, we can point out only some of the issues as we discuss other aspects of creating a home.

As already suggested, one type of conservation—sound economy from both a financial and an ecological point of view—consists of giving things a second life, making old objects serve new purposes. This principle can apply at many different levels, from accessories and furnishings to whole houses. However, because of the element of personal choice, efficiency (whether functional or economic) is not the sole criterion for decision making.

Beauty

The concept of beauty is subject to highly individual interpretation. By definition, beauty is that which pleases the senses and lifts the spirits. To one person it may be the precision of machine-made objects while to another the variation found in natural or hand-crafted articles has aesthetic appeal. Like taste, beauty is conditioned by time and culture. We have only to glance at photographs from another time or place to realize its diversity.

1–23 An old Chicago factory has been transformed into an unconventional living space. Two LeCorbusier sofas echo the angle of the stair tower, and old wood columns found in a salvage yard but cut down to size support the tower. Part of one column supports the glass table top. Kenneth Schroeder, architect. *(Photograph: © Peter Aaron/ESTO)*

26

Everyone has an inborn need for the sensory stimulation beauty provides, and efforts of humans to beautify their surroundings are evident in the earliest archeological sites. Both the process and the result bring pleasure. The home is often the only environment that allows the freedom to explore and express a uniquely individual idea of beauty. Together with a working knowledge of design elements and principles (see Chapters 7 through 9), which will serve as a guide to achieve beauty and evaluate choices, the supportive role of the home can help to build confidence in one's aesthetic decisions. (See Plates 2, 3, and 4, pp. 23, 24.)

Character

The quality that differentiates one home from another and expresses the personality of its owners is vital. While we can analyze a room to determine the components of its beauty, in the end the real determinant is the people it serves. No one wants a home to have the generalized aura of a hotel bedroom or lobby. Individuality—and therefore character—ensues almost automatically when a home is allowed to grow naturally from its inhabitants' needs, interests, and preferences. It develops most convincingly from fundamental lifestyles, not from acquiring the latest fashion in accessories. A home will have character if it is imbued with the individual qualities, tastes, and personalities of its inhabitants by their active participation in its development.

left top: 1-24 The individual character of this living room is derived largely from the owner's selection and display of accessories on table tops and bookshelves. Paul R. Pugliese, architect. *(Photograph: © Karen Bussolini. Reprinted by permission of* House Beautiful's Home Remodeling *© 1982. The Hearst Corporation.)*
left bottom: 1–25 In homes such as Forth House near Livingston, New York, a brick manor house built in the 1760s, restoration of traditional character is the design goal. Lead rosettes ornament door and window frames and a Federal table rests on an Aubusson rug beneath a crystal chandelier. *(Photograph: Robert Levin)*
1–26 The beauty of instruments placed individually on Oriental rugs sets the character of an apartment for music lovers. *(Photograph: © Paul Warchol)*

Utility, economy, beauty, and character are as closely related as the warp and filling of a textile. One cannot be completely dissociated from the others and retain full significance. On the other hand, it is difficult to consider all these factors simultaneously. In choosing certain items, such as rugs or chairs, function and economy might take precedence. Once these points have been established, beauty and character can be taken into account. However, in selecting purely decorative objects, beauty and character will probably be the first consideration. Each goal must be balanced with the others to achieve the objective of good design.

The Planning Process

Having acknowledged all the qualities that go into creating a successful lifespace, we may well wonder where to start. Like any problem, that of planning a home to satisfy all the elements described above can be approached by segmenting it and dealing with a single aspect at a time. One possible system for approaching the design process is to follow the steps used by professional designers: programming, design, construction, use, and evaluation.[14]

Programming is the identification of all the facts, criteria, objectives, and constraints previously discussed in relation to the people who will inhabit the space, its location and orientation, and the resources available for it. Chapter 2 provides more detail on the specific elements contained in the program in addition to the client profile outlined earlier in this chapter. This crucial preliminary analysis provides a statement of purpose, a clear description of the design problem.

Design is, of course, the development of a specific plan to achieve the desired end product. All the information gathered in the program—including the household members' psychological and behavioral reactions and interactions, together with technological knowledge of materials, wiring, plumbing, structure, and so on—must be synthesized in order to create a workable plan. A good design is the result of methodically working through the sequence of steps in the planning process so that all aspects of the problem are addressed. The design step combines and balances creative ability with scientific knowledge. The solution to the problem is conceived graphically and presented with floor plans and other drawings, paint schedules, color boards showing materials and furnishings, and any other necessary illustrative devices. Furnishings, colors, textures, and patterns are chosen, coordinated, and located. Any construction or remodeling is detailed and the design should be checked to verify that all objectives in the program have been met, an early evaluation measure.

Construction is the actual work of building or remodeling the structure; plastering, painting, papering; and purchasing and installation of furnishings.

Use begins when the inhabitants move in, when the home starts to work as a lifespace. This is the true test of the success of the previous steps as the users experience the space.

In the case of the individual home, **evaluation** is rarely a scientific process but shows up in both behavioral and structural adjustments necessitated by the demands of daily living or the desires of the occupants. Evaluation is a measure of how well the user-environment fit (ergofit) of the home satisfies the original programming goals, focusing on the people who *subjectively* use the space rather than on the designer who *objectively* planned it.

The first four steps in the planning process are used more or less consciously by anyone designing a space. Professional interior designers and architects find the last step, evaluation, a final analysis of the work done and its efficiency, a useful tool for future work. Designers can effectively judge the results of their work by observing user behavior and satisfaction. And, since relatively few people have the opportunity to design and build a dwelling from the ground up, the individual homeowner can also profit from a conscious evaluation of pre-existing lifespaces, making improvements or rearrangements that will add to the pleasure and potential of the living space.

People in their environmental context are the measure against which all decisions are made in designing a home. The home is not a painting to be looked at and admired in short glances; it is a living place, constantly changing, interacting with the people who live in it, having an impact on the natural world and on those who share it with us. Only by taking into consideration the influences, factors, objectives, and processes discussed in this chapter can the outcome be successful. We can exercise control over the quality of our homes, both in the initial choice of a space and in the shaping of it. Carried to the fullest extent, we can create homes that are, in the words of architect Richard Neutra, "soul anchorages."

Notes to the Text

1. Amos Rapoport, *House Form and Culture* (Englewood Cliffs, NJ: Prentice-Hall, 1969).
2. William H. Ittelson, Harold M. Proshansky, Leanne G. Rivlin, and Gary H. Winkel, *An Introduction to Environmental Psychology* (New York: Holt, Rinehart and Winston, 1974), p. 354.
3. Robert Sommer, *Personal Space: The Behavioral Basis of Design* (Englewood Cliffs, NJ: Prentice-Hall, 1969), p. 5.
4. Ittelson et al., p. 5.
5. Irwin Altman, *The Environment and Social Behavior: Privacy, Personal Space, Territory, Crowding* (Monterey, CA: Brooks/Cole Publishing Company, 1973), p. 3.
6. Joanne Henderson Pratt, James Pratt, Sarah Barnett Moore, and William T. Moore, *Environmental Encounter: Experiences in Decision-Making for the Built and Natural Environment* (Dallas, TX: Reverchon Press, 1979), p. 105.
7. Edward T. Hall, *The Hidden Dimension* (New York: Doubleday, 1966), chap. 10.
8. Irwin Altman, Amos Rapoport, and Joachim F. Wohlwill, *Human Behavior and Environment: Advances in Theory and Research.* Vol. 4: *Environment and Culture* (New York: Plenum Press, 1980), chap. 4, by John R. Aiello and Donna E. Thompson.
9. Albert Mehrabian, *Public Places and Private Spaces: The Psychology of Work, Play, and Living Environments* (New York: Basic Books, Publishers, 1976), p. 107.
10. Paul Bohannan, *Social Anthropology* (New York: Holt, Rinehart and Winston, 1963), p. 86.
11. Alvin Toffler, *The Third Wave* (New York: Morrow, 1980), chap. 17.
12. Altman, *The Environment and Social Behavior*, p. 131.
13. Julius Panero and Martin Zelnick, *Human Dimension and Interior Space: A Source Book of Design Reference Standards* (New York: Whitney Library of Design, 1979), p. 12.
14. Altman, *The Environment and Social Behavior*, pp. 197–201.

References for Further Reading

Hartwigsen, Gail Lynn. *Design Concepts: A Basic Guidebook*. Boston: Allyn and Bacon, 1980, Unit 1.
Maslow, Abraham. *Motivation and Personality*. New York: Harper, 1954.
Maslow, Abraham (ed.). *New Knowledge in Human Values*. New York: Harper, 1959.
Meeks, Carol. *Housing*. Englewood Cliffs, NJ: Prentice-Hall, 1980.
Naisbitt, John. *Megatrends: Ten New Directions Transforming Our Lives*. New York: Warner Books, 1982.
Sommer, Robert. *Design Awareness*. San Francisco: Rinehart Press, 1972.

2 Planning Space

A floor plan may seem an innocuous and sometimes hard-to-read two-dimensional drawing, but its importance in determining the kind of life possible in any given space can scarcely be overestimated. It not only establishes the basic character of a particular structure but also seriously influences the lifestyle that can flourish there. For example, an open space with minimum floor-to-ceiling partitions might be suitable for a family or group of people who enjoy the easy contact and group interaction such a plan engenders. Conversely, people who desire a certain amount of privacy—and prefer their interaction with others be confined to certain life rituals such as dining together or social entertaining at prescribed times—will be happiest in a lifespace that provides designated, separated areas for the various functions of living.

Almost everyone lives in spaces that have defined limits, with doors and windows puncturing the surrounding walls, with light switches and outlets, heating and cooling vents that must be accessible and unrestricted. Few people have the opportunity to design their own homes from the ground up. To a greater or

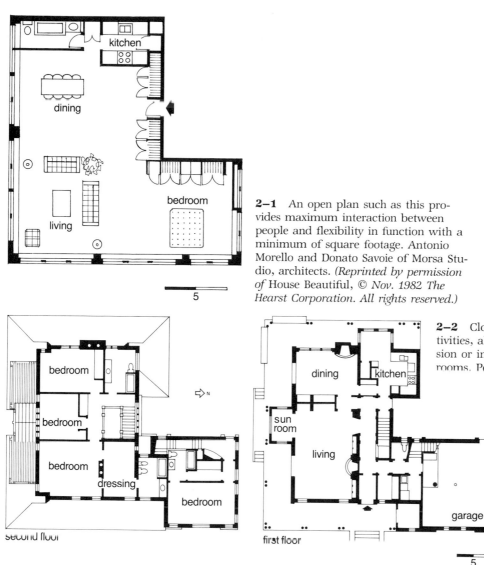

2–1 An open plan such as this provides maximum interaction between people and flexibility in function with a minimum of square footage. Antonio Morello and Donato Savoie of Morsa Studio, architects. *(Reprinted by permission of* House Beautiful, © *Nov. 1982 The Hearst Corporation. All rights reserved.)*

2–2 Closed plans differentiate activities, allowing individuals seclusion or interaction through choice of rooms. Peter Rose, architect.

lesser degree, most do what they can to make the space available to them as habitable and pleasing as possible. An ability to read house plans and recognize the architectural symbols used will aid in this endeavor. A little experience in drawing simple plans will also help determine furniture arrangements. For the professional designer, expertise in reading and drawing plans is an integral part of the design process. As a means of communicating with other professionals such as architects and contractors, a way of explaining ideas to the client, and to be certain that the finished space will work for its intended uses, plans are a valuable graphic tool.

Reading Plans

The floor plan is an outline of space, delineating the structural elements that physically limit and enclose the spaces in which we live. It is drawn from a bird's-eye view, looking straight down upon and into each floor level as though the roof and/or each higher level were removed. Each level of a multiple-story home is drawn separately and must be envisioned "stacked" when reading the total plan. Usually the drawing indicates walls, floors, and other dividers that shape the spaces for living, eating, and resting as well as major built-in cabinets and appliances. Furniture is often drawn in place to help in understanding the way in which the house functions and in creating an accurate estimation of the amount of space allotted for the various furnishings and activities.

So that all aspects of the space are represented in accurate size relationship to one another, floor plans are always drawn to *scale*. This means that, while the plan on paper will, of course, be much smaller than the actual house itself, the proportions will remain the same. Everything is reduced in size so that a fraction of an inch on the plan represents a foot of actual space in the physical structure of the house. The scale ¼ inch equals 1 foot is standard for house plans. A wall that is actually 20 feet long would thus be drawn 5 inches long on paper, and a closet 5 feet wide would be 1¼ inches on the plan. Any scale may be used to accurately represent the space(½″ = 1′, ⅛″ = 1′) so long as everything is drawn to the same scale.

One purpose of drawing a living space is to illustrate it simply, without requiring verbal explanation. For this, symbols are very useful. They indicate basic structural features such as walls, windows, stairways, and doors as well as specific types of windows and doors, appliances, cabinets, storage facilities, and electrical fixtures. The precisely drawn floor plan acts as a guide for the builder as well as a useful tool for the designer and homeowner. The architectural, electrical, and furniture symbols commonly used for these purposes appear on pages 530-534.

Developing the Plan for a New Home

Chapter 1 outlined the steps in the planning process, starting with programming, the identification of all the elements that should be considered. The program is further explained here because the more detailed the analysis, the more likely it will be that all the needs of those who do design their own home will be met.

The Program

When the designer first touches pencil to paper to draw a plan, a number of decisions should already have been made. In fact, most good architects and interior designers have a carefully worked-out program identifying the requirements of a home long before the graphic stage of planning is begun. The elements of this program include:

- Functional goals
- Equipment needs
- Space requirements
- Desired character of the space
- Site analysis
- Cost

Functional Goals

The way in which the home functions should be determined by the values and lifestyle of the family for which it is being planned. If reduction of human energy expended in the operation and maintenance of the home is desired, a home computer could be installed to control and monitor utilities and household inventories, even to command a household robot to perform routine chores. The increased leisure time thus made available might result in special consideration being given to a media room equipped with video and sound systems that demand careful planning for the lighting and acoustical qualities of the space, its reflective and absorptive characteristics. Other functional goals could include a home office with separate access, maximum energy efficiency, or barrier-free design for an elderly or handicapped person, to name just a few. The activities of each household member as well as group interaction should determine planning objectives.

Equipment Needs

Basic mechanical requirements such as plumbing, electricity, heating and cooling units, telephone wiring, and television cables are an obvious consideration. Particular needs must also be met: safety and security devices, sound and video systems, home computers, or a power workshop, for example.

Space Requirements

Spatial requirements are based on careful study of the activities, behavioral patterns, developmental needs, values, and desires of the occupants as discussed in the client profile questions posed in Chapter 1. First, general area size and shape are indicated to accommodate activities, furnishings, and open spaces, then a corresponding allotment of square footage is determined. Of course, space for storage, utilities, walls, and traffic corridors must be estimated as well. Overall, the home should provide each person with a minimum of 200 square feet, although 300 square feet per person would be better and 500 would allow for truly comfortable living. These figures represent gross area, including walls, partitions, and all service spaces.

Character

In describing the character of the proposed spaces, aesthetic goals are established. This part of the program concerns itself with the emotional impact of the spaces and their design upon the occupants of the home. Window area, ceiling height, room size, and the choice of color and pattern establish the character of a home.

While vision plays an important part in our perception of character, other senses contribute as well. The tactile sensation of walking across a soft carpet produces quite a different response from that experienced in touching a polished marble floor. Also, the manner in which voices and other sounds are reflected or absorbed by an enclosed space gives us clear messages about the qualities of that space—messages that may elicit feelings of well-being, comfort, uneasiness, awe, safety, or fear.

Site Analysis

An analysis of the site provides descriptive information regarding size, shape, location, topography, wind and sun directions, views, relation to the street, and natural features such as trees on the lot chosen for construction. Local building codes and zoning limitations must also be known. These restrictions will affect the orientation of the house, type of plan, allowable height, placement on the lot, methods and materials of construction, and energy-conservation possibilities for the structure. Even styling may be influenced, either by other homes in the area or by deference to environment.

Cost

Costs are critical to planning. A house is usually the largest single purchase a family will make. In 1981 first time home buyers spent nearly 40 percent of their monthly income on housing compared to the 25-percent maximum traditionally recommended. Home prices are rising faster than median household income, resulting in a reduction in the size of the average new home to less than 1400 square feet.

When either building or remodeling, an accurate estimate of cost is essential. Some rooms, such as kitchens and baths, are more expensive to build or remodel than others because of their special equipment, built-in cabinetry, and plumbing and wiring needs. Other areas, such as basements, porches, and garages or carports, are less expensive to construct. Several steps can be taken during planning to limit costs, both initially and over the life of the structure.

A simple shape encloses the maximum amount of space for minimum construction costs. The more the house deviates from a square shape, the more lineal feet of wall and foundation are required. Even a rectangle increases costs. The addition of ells in L-, U-, and T-shaped plans increases lineal feet, number of costly corners, and expense of roof framing, without necessarily increasing square footage, as can be seen in Figure 2-3.

Utilities can be centralized to help reduce expenditures. For example, plumbing fixtures can be located back-to-back in adjacent rooms or stacked above one another in multiple-story plans; all utilities can be located in a central core; fireplaces can use a single chimney stack.

2–3 The more complex the shape of a plan, the more expensive it is to construct, without necessarily increasing square footage of interior living space. (*Adapted from* Architecture: Design-Engineering-Drawing *by William P. Spence, p. 101.* © *1979 McKnight*)

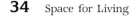

40'0"
1600 sq. ft.
4 corners
160 lineal ft.
wall & footing
40'0"

20'0" 20'0" 20'0"
20'0"
1600 sq. ft.
8 corners
200 lineal ft.
wall & footing
40'0"
60'0"

60'0"
1620 sq. ft.
4 corners
174 lineal ft.
wall & footing
27'0"

60'0"
20'0"
1600 sq. ft.
6 corners
200 lineal ft.
wall & footing
40'0"
20'0"

80'0"
1600 sq. ft.
4 corners
200 lineal ft.
wall & footing
20'0"

20'0" 20'0" 20'0"
10'0"
1600 sq. ft.
8 corners
200 lineal ft.
wall & footing
30'0"
60'0"

2–4 Plywood paneling, arranged in sections at different angles, creates dramatic linear patterns in a prefabricated house. *(Courtesy American Plywood Association)*

Further economies in materials and labor can be realized by using modular planning (a standard unit of measure of construction material, such as a 4- or 6-foot module), standard milled items (doors, window frames, stairways, cabinets), and readily available native materials. Long-term costs can be minimized by taking advantage of climate to reduce heating and cooling costs, selecting materials and equipment that will have a long life with low maintenance, and designing for flexibility and change rather than permanence. Good design costs no more than poor design and its value often increases with time.

Much of the information needed in the program can be derived from the client profile questions outlined in Chapter 1. It is the architect's and interior designer's task to analyze and synthesize the data collected with their own professional training to develop a holistic design that can become a home flexible enough to respond to the changing needs of individual occupants over their life span.

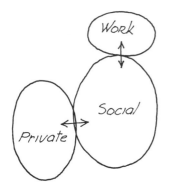

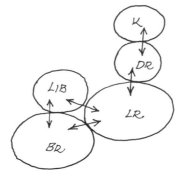

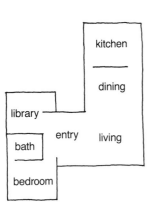

5

The Schematic Diagram

Planning moves naturally from discussion of an overall program to the first graphic stage—the schematic diagram. Here activities are grouped and conceptually organized into loosely drawn circles or free-form bubble shapes that roughly outline different space uses or zones. In their proportion to each other the circles show the relative size and importance of each general activity area. The schematic diagram also establishes relationships between the various spaces and activities by means of connecting lines. Arrows on the diagram signify ingress and egress as well as general circulation patterns. The schematic diagram may be redrawn several times to establish the most desirable configuration that meets specific planning goals. The number of bubble shapes corresponds to major activity areas grouped according to zoning principles.

Zoning

From the smallest living module to the largest house, space divides itself into *zones* that group similar kinds of activities and separate incompatible uses according to the degree of privacy or sociability each requires. The three primary zones in the home encompass social, private, and work activities. Transitional zones or semi-public and semi-private spaces, including entries, exits, and circulation routes are used as control points and buffers between major zones. The purpose of zoning as a planning tool is simply to assist in the arrangement of blocks of space so that relationships between them are functional and practical.

top left: 2–5 A schematic diagram is the first step in deciding on a house plan and/or its furnishing. An initial rough diagram shows possible zones of activity.
top right: 2–6 The diagram is easily redrawn to indicate living spaces.
bottom left: 2–7 A rough sketch of possible room placement comes next.
bottom middle: 2–8 As the plan evolves more details are added.
bottom right: 2–9 Finally the plan itself takes shape. Hugh Newell Jacobsen, architect.

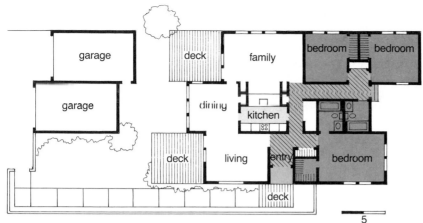

above: 2–10 This plan clearly separates activity zones with circulation routes buffering private areas from the noise and the view of social and work zones. Donald MacDonald, architect.

right: 2–11 Furniture placement alone can establish zones for different activities. Dining space, a library-study, and a conversation grouping all borrow from the surrounding areas without intruding on them. A low-walled bedroom-balcony further extends the feeling as well as the actuality of space. George C. Oistad, Jr., architect.

Social Zone This is the public and semi-public area of the home where social activities take place. The design of these spaces is discussed in detail in Chapter 3; here we are concerned with the way in which these spaces relate to the overall home plan.

The living zone relates closely in function to the work area of the kitchen and to access from the main entrance. It may also be oriented toward a view or outdoor living areas such as terraces or balconies. This requires shielding from the view of passersby, accomplished by facing windows away from the street or by means of protective fencing, shrubbery, or earth berms.

Living spaces that accommodate more than one group activity can be subdivided architecturally by room shapes that offer alcoves or ells for different activities without sacrificing a visual sense of spaciousness and freedom, by careful placement of furnishings, or by a change in floor levels or ceiling heights (perhaps between dining and conversation areas). In many homes the provision of two or more completely separated group spaces helps maintain harmony in the household or simply gives a choice of the kind of room in which to gather for various activities. A playroom opening off either the kitchen or children's bedrooms is a good solution in a one-story house. The latter arrangement also gives older children a degree of privacy and room to expand. When children are small and need fairly constant supervision, the kitchen–family-room connection may be ideal. This solution also creates a relaxed entertainment center for adults and teenagers. A private study gives the seclusion needed for two or three people to meet away from the larger group for quiet conversation. In homes with more than one story, a secondary multipurpose space on an upper or lower floor allows some isolation.

Work Zone Chapter 4 details explicit planning for the utility, service, or operative "nerve center" in the home.

2–12 Two separate social areas provide flexibility or permit diverse kinds of social activities at the same time. Sam Davis, architect.

The spaces and facilities labeled work zones include those for cooking, laundry, heating, cooling, and storage. During the last several decades the amount of space devoted to these functions in the home has been shrinking steadily—partly because of inflated construction costs and partly because of streamlined equipment. To reduce the size of homes, square footage is first eliminated from these service areas because they can sustain a cut without apparently reducing the living standard. Much of the equipment itself is smaller, cleaner, and less noisy: a closet often suffices to house heating and air-conditioning equipment, a second closet to hold laundry appliances.

2–13 An open stairway provides circulation between two stories of a row of townhouses and indicates division of areas on the lower level without shutting them off from each other. The inset bands of closets, bathrooms, and kitchens between units result in an unusual degree of privacy for this type of housing. Ralph A. Anderson, architect.

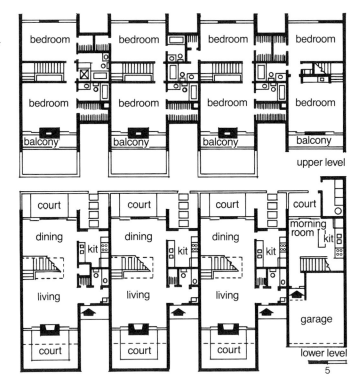

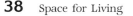

For maximum efficiency, service areas and utilities should be centrally located in the house plan. This reduces the length of all sorts of umbilical cords that thread through the house to distribute energy in various forms. The shorter the run of the hot water supply, the sooner hot water appears at the faucet; the closer the kitchen to the various dining areas, the greater the likelihood of food being the desired temperature and appetizing when it is placed on the table.

The **utility core** is a refinement of this idea. A predesigned industrial module, it contains all the equipment necessary for basic support functions: cooking, laundry, bathing, space heating, air conditioning, and water heating. Utility cores can be produced in standard sizes, shipped to the site in one piece, and installed with unskilled labor.

Often it is possible to merge one of the service areas with the group space. As cooking becomes more of a family operation and less the exclusive province of a single member, this function can be more completely integrated with other family activities. Thus we find the lines that separate kitchens from major group spaces becoming increasingly blurred.

Private Zone The rest or sleeping areas of the home are the private and semi-private spaces, discussed in detail in Chapter 5. The primary consideration in locating private spaces is to ensure that they truly are private. A common error in house planning is placement of the bathroom—surely the most private of sanctums—in a position that offers a vista from hallways or even the living space. Various possibilities exist for isolating private spaces, the most obvious being their segregation in a separate wing of the home. In the so-called binuclear plan developed by Marcel Breuer, a house divides into two wings, one for group living and work spaces, the other for private space. An entry area that serves both wings connects them.

When bedrooms and baths are placed on a second floor, the desired seclusion results automatically. Sometimes (perhaps with a hillside topography) an upside-down solution is better, with the private spaces underneath the group living area.

In the best of circumstances, private spaces are easily accessible from the cooking and eating areas. The heart of the home continues to be the food center, and all members of the household will tend to converge there.

The schematic diagram of spaces, zones, and relationships may be reworked many times, with considerable adjustment and balancing of priorities. After these initial decisions have been made, the process of organizing space as a more precise two-dimensional drawing begins in earnest.

The Finished Floor Plan

The floor plan depicts the exact dimensions of rooms, either as they exist or will be built, and the placement of walls, doors, windows, and other structural elements, as well as built-ins and various outlets. It shows both the constraints within which the designer must work and the challenges and possibilities. It is a useful tool in determining the placement of furnishings both for social interaction and for individual comfort. In addition, consideration must also be given to orientation, circulation, efficiency, storage, and safety, including the avoidance of architectural or furnishing barriers.

Orientation

Referring to the relationship between dwelling and environment, orientation is the compass location of various rooms to make best use of sun, topography, wind, and views. A **solar orientation** provides large southern exposures to collect

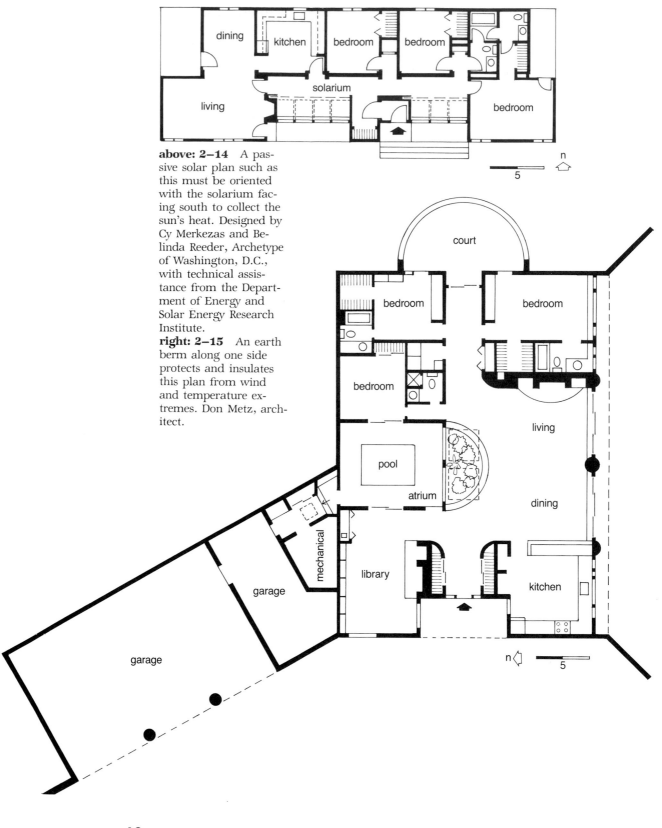

above: 2–14 A passive solar plan such as this must be oriented with the solarium facing south to collect the sun's heat. Designed by Cy Merkezas and Belinda Reeder, Archetype of Washington, D.C., with technical assistance from the Department of Energy and Solar Energy Research Institute.

right: 2–15 An earth berm along one side protects and insulates this plan from wind and temperature extremes. Don Metz, architect.

heat, and morning and afternoon sun where desired. **Topographical orientation** refers to design that takes full advantage of the contour of the land (a split-level or multiple-story house on a sloping lot, for example). **Wind orientation** captures desirable summer breezes while blocking winter winds. **View orientation** allows both pleasant vistas from major rooms and privacy from outsiders.

Circulation

When economy is a factor, the barest minimum of square footage is allotted to passageways into and within the home—entry halls, corridors, and stairways. Minimum hall width is 3 feet, but Edward Hall's "hidden dimensions" of interpersonal space reveal that two people passing in a 3-foot hallway might feel a psychological infringement on each other's personal space; one would probably wait for the other to come through the corridor, particularly if the two were not well acquainted. Average hallways in the home are usually 3½ feet wide (which accommodates a wheelchair more comfortably), with the central hall often 4 feet or even wider. The longer the hallway, the wider it should be so as not to seem like a dark tunnel. Stairways are part of the circulation system and must be a minimum of 3 feet wide, but 3½ to 4 feet is more desirable for heavy traffic and for moving furniture.

In any plan, paths of circulation should be economical of space: short, direct, and as free of turns as possible, radiating from the principal entrance, and connecting zones without directing traffic through them. All rooms should be conveniently accessible without going through another room, with some occasionally permissible exceptions: the family room, which is often the nucleus of activity; the dining room, which is used only at specific times of the day; and the kitchen, which may also be the hub of family activity, but only if it is large enough so that traffic does not interfere with food preparation. Bedrooms, the ultimate private territory, should not be traffic routes. When rooms are used for circulation, they should be planned so that the most direct route is across a corner or along one side of the room in order not to interrupt activities in progress.

Besides major circulation routes through the house, determined by architectural structure, each room will have its own minor traffic paths, influenced heavily

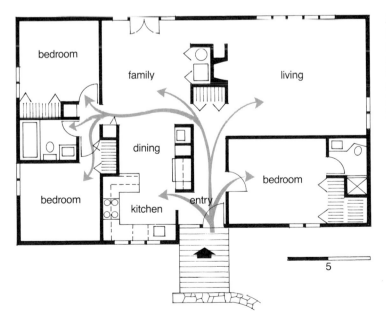

2-16 An efficient circulation system helps this 1185-square-foot plan seem much larger than it really is, with a minimum of space used for traffic. G. Hugh Tsuruoka, AIA, architect.

by furniture placement and the space needed to perform tasks, the ergonomics or human factors engineering mentioned in Chapter 1. Various furnishing arrangements can be tried on the plan in order to analyze circulation paths to other rooms, to doors and windows, heating/cooling vents, electrical switches and outlets, and major pieces or groups of furniture. The most frequently traveled routes, both major and minor, should be the shortest. A good circulation plan avoids causing fatigue (inconvenient routes), conflict (invasion of privacy), and accidents (traffic crossing work areas).

Efficiency

The efficiency of a plan is the percentage of area that is actually usable, livable space; it does not include space taken by halls, walls, closets, stairs, or utilities. Although these are all necessary, they need be kept to a minimum; hallways should occupy no more than 10 percent of the total area in the efficient house, while approximately 75 percent of the total area should be occupied by rooms with floor area sufficient for furnishings and activities.[1] Usable space is increased by good zoning, a convenient relationship among rooms, minimum traffic through rooms, rooms that permit good furniture arrangement, and livable outdoor areas.

Storage

Closets and other storage facilities should be located where needed throughout the home, and should be abundant. The floor space occupied by all storage areas in the house, including kitchen cabinets, should amount to 10 percent of the total square footage. Well-designed storage makes maximum use of minimum space; closets, especially walk-ins, may have one third less storage potential than a storage wall of equal square footage.[2] Flexible storage (movable clothes rods and shelves) also allows more efficient use of space. General storage principles advise storing items where they are used, storing at convenient heights (light, small objects in higher places; heavy, bulky items lower), storing similar things together, and storing objects where they are easy to see and easy to reach.

Safety and Architectural Barriers

Architectural barriers create unnecessary difficulty in day-to-day living and generally limit the safety, security, comfort, and convenience of *all* people. It is the designer's responsibility to acquire and apply hazard-reduction knowledge for the safety of all users. The most opportune time to apply this critical knowledge is during the planning process.

There are three major hazard areas in the home: stairways, baths, and kitchens. And there are three groups of people who need special consideration: children, the elderly, and the handicapped. With some forethought, many functional features can increase the safety of the home without affecting cost or aesthetics.

Stairs Changes in level are hazardous to everyone and are the most frequent location of home accidents. A slight change in level such as a platform should be at least two steps above or below the main level, and the change in the horizontal plane should be clearly marked by a railing, plants, or furniture. Stairways should have *uniform* riser heights (7″ is recommended) and tread depths (11-12″ for low-risk), a slope of 33-40°, sufficient head room, handrails, adequate lighting with switches at top and bottom, and enough contrast between the stair and its surroundings for accurate perception. The total length of run (tread less nosing) for a flight of stairs that rises the average 9 feet from floor to floor is approximately 13 to 14 feet, depending upon exact tread depth, and contains 15 risers and 14

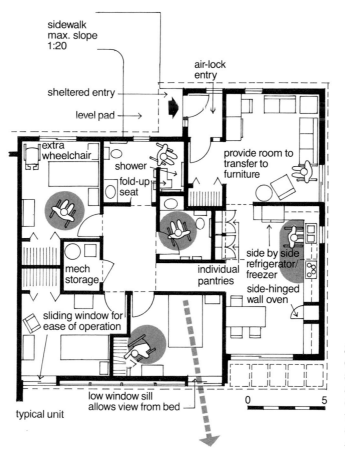

sidewalk
max. slope
1:20

air-lock
entry

sheltered entry →

level pad →

extra
wheelchair

shower

fold-up
seat

provide room to
transfer to
furniture

mech
storage

individual
pantries

side by side
refrigerator/
freezer

side-hinged
wall oven

sliding window for
ease of operation

typical unit

low window sill
allows view from bed →

0   5

2–17 Designed for the disabled, this 1240-square-foot plan can accommodate a family or two individuals living with a personal-care attendant. Juster Pope Associates, architects.

treads. (As riser height increases, tread depth must decrease for a normal stride.) Unnecessary steps can be eliminated in planning by considering the extra energy expended by locating laundry facilities either up- or downstairs from bedrooms and baths.

Bathrooms Bathroom equipment should, of course, be chosen with safety in mind. In some cases, wheelchair access will determine types, widths, heights, and locations of bathroom fixtures. Grab bars may be necessary in tub and shower enclosures and near toilet fixtures. For specific positioning, consult the *American National Standard Specifications for Making Buildings and Facilities Accessible to and Usable by Physically Handicapped People* (ANSI A117.1-1980). In addition, doors that open outward instead of inward allow someone to enter the bathroom in case of a fall or need for assistance, and slipfree surfaces should be specified for floors and fixtures. Various bathroom plans are detailed in Chapter 5.

Kitchens Cooking areas, discussed in detail in Chapter 4, can be designed so that frequently used utensils and foods are stored within easy reach, eliminating the need to climb on a chair to reach things, risking a fall. For someone who needs to sit down while working or for a child or short person, a pull-out work surface below standard counter height can be installed. (Too many changes from standard measures should be avoided unless necessary, as they can have a negative effect on resale value.) Cabinet and appliance doors should not swing into pathways where they can cause accidents.

All through the House Other areas needing attention to safety are lighting, bedrooms, and traffic paths. In general, illumination should be sufficient and without glare or abrupt changes in lighting levels. Three-way switches at both ends of hallways or stairs, night lights, automatic timers, and exterior lighting add security. Both switch and outlet heights can be adjusted for easy access.

In the bedroom, storage position and access are important, as in the kitchen. Adjustable shelves and closet rods allow flexibility. A window positioned for view while reclining is desirable, whether for someone confined to bed permanently or for occasional illness. A light switch near the bed takes the hazard out of night walking; a telephone within reach is another safety precaution.

Traffic paths should be convenient, unobstructed, and safe, with trip-proof, nonskid, durable floors. For barrier-free design, doorways between rooms do not need sills, which can trip anyone who walks unsteadily.

Safety, security, comfort, and convenience in home design are important in producing a positive self-image and reducing the expenditure of human physical energy for everyone. The three groups of people who need special consideration in planning—children, the elderly, and the handicapped—have some unique problems and some that are common to all. It is important to keep in mind that we all belong to each of these groups at some time during the normal course of our lives; even some of the physical limitations of the handicapped are experienced for brief periods as we endure broken or injured limbs, illness, or pregnancy.

Children The young have the problem of undeveloped body coordination and strength, and insufficient experience with and knowledge of their environment.[3] For their safety, play areas must be located within range of sight and sound of adequate supervision, stairs may require toddler gates and should have railings with banisters no more than 4 inches apart, and storage facilities for toxic substances must be provided beyond reach. Bathroom wash basins, light switches, door handles, and closet rods are difficult for small children to reach. Some fixtures can be designed for flexibility and change to keep pace with growth (adjustable height storage); others may require temporary measures such as a step stool to accommodate small statures. Lever-type faucet and door handles are easiest for children to operate, as they are for the elderly and handicapped.

The Elderly As we grow older, we experience difficulties caused by diminished strength, size, and speed of reaction as well as impaired senses. By the end of this century it is estimated that the elderly may comprise 18 percent of our total population;[4] at present, there are nearly 20 million Americans over the age of sixty-five. Most prefer to remain independent in their own homes as long as possible. Some of their problems include maintenance, stairs, hard-to-reach storage, and too much space for decreased energy levels and mobility. As vision dims, more light is needed, glare becomes a confusing problem, and greater color contrast is needed for clarity. Resilient floor coverings reduce the severity of injuries from falling, a frequent type of home accident. (See Table 2-1 for additional guidelines in adapting housing to the needs of the elderly and handicapped.) As the aged are confined more to their homes, it becomes increasingly important that they feel secure and able to function in this environment.

The Handicapped The physically limited constitute an even larger percentage of the total population than the elderly, and include many elderly. An estimated 20 percent of the population is handicapped, not including the aged with limited mobility.[5] Whether the impairment is limited or extensive, temporary or permanent, it handicaps the individual in his or her ability to function. Many standard and accepted architectural features such as stairs and narrow passageways can become barriers to the disabled. Some can be avoided during initial planning: doorways that are 32 inches wide can accommodate a person using a wheelchair, crutches, or a walker. Others may require adaptation, such as ramps or remodeling of kitchens and bathrooms. Many devices are also available to assist the disabled. (See Table 2–1 for specific adaptive recommendations.) Responsible designers are aware of the problems of this group and sensitive to their needs; they provide supportive lifespaces that facilitate a positive self-image.

2–18 In this home, designed by architect Alfredo De Vido, doorways are wide enough for wheelchair access. The door between the kitchen and dining area slides easily and has no sill to impede passage. (*Photograph: © Daniel Cornish*)

Design Feature	Wheelchair Confined	Ambulatory	Visually Impaired	Hearing Impaired	Hand Impaired
bathtub	bottom flat and slip-resistant built-in seat 2 accessible sides	bottom flat and slip-resistant built-in seat 2 accessible sides			
climate control	shield radiators controls 2–4' high	shield radiators			
counter	28"–34" high recess 27" high, 30" wide, 19" deep pull-out boards continuous counter	pull-out boards continuous counter			pull-out boards continuous counters
dishwasher washer/dryer	front loading combination washer/dryer front controls	top loading combination washer/dryer front controls	controls raised or color coded		combination washer/dryer pushbutton controls at front
door	32" wide (minimum) interior door pressure 5 pounds exterior door pressure 8½ pounds top-hung sliding doors kickplates bathroom door open out lever knob knob 3' high	top-hung sliding doors door pressure 8 pounds bathroom door open out lever knob	color contrast on frames door open against wall		interior door pressure 5 pounds exterior door pressure 8½ pounds lever knob
faucet	thermostatic control spray attachments; swing spouts at side of sink	thermostatic control spray attachments; swing spouts at side of sink	single control lever thermostatic control		single control lever thermostatic control spray attachment; swing spouts at side of sink
floor	slip-resistant cork or wall-to-wall low pile (½") carpeting	slip-resistant cork or wall-to-wall low pile carpeting	slip-resistant low gloss changes in material hard enough to echo	muffle sound	
floor plan	single story level open plan wide halls L-kitchen; 5' between counters	single story level open plan parallel kitchen	level open plan with clearly divided sections	open plan	
grab bar	slip-resistant support 250–300 pounds 1¼"–1½" diameter extend 1½" from wall	slip-resistant support 250–300 pounds 1¼"–1½" diameter extend 1½" from wall			slip-resistant support 250–300 pounds 1¼"–1½" diameter extend 1½" from wall
kitchen storage	2'2"–4'6" high 1' deep open storage revolving and pullout shelves vertical storage pegboard	2'2"–6'4" high 1' deep open storage revolving and pullout shelves vertical storage pegboard			2'2"–6'4" high 1' deep open storage revolving and pullout shelves vertical storage pegboard magnetic catches bar handles 3–4" long at 45° angle

Table 2–1 Guidelines for Adaptive Housing

Table 2–1 *(continued)*

Design Feature	Wheelchair Confined	Ambulatory	Visually Impaired	Hearing Impaired	Hand Impaired
lavatory	wall-hung 3–7″ deep shallow front 2′5″ high, 19″ deep recess pipes insulated				
lighting	pull-down fixtures increase at changes in floor level	pull-down fixtures increase at changes in floor level	increase illumination increase at changes in floor level		pull-down fixtures
mirror	3′ high or slanted				
oven	wall oven with pull-out board beneath side opening controls on front	wall oven with pull-out board beneath side opening			wall oven with pull-out board beneath side opening
range	2′6″–3′ high burners straight or staggered burners flush with counter	burners straight or staggered burners flush with counter	burners straight or staggered		burners straight or staggered burners flush with counter
refrigerator	upright, vertically divided non-tip, swing out and revolving shelves	upright, vertically divided non-tip, swing out and revolving shelves			upright, vertically divided non-tip, swing out and revolving shelves
shower	eliminate curbs at least 3′ × 3′ 17″–19″ high hinged shower seat curtains	eliminate curbs 17″–19″ high hinged shower seat curtains			
sink	4″–6½″ deep sink and pipes insulated				
stairs		uniform dimensions riser 6–7″; tread 11″ non-projecting nosing handrails extend 1′6″ at ends handrails 1¼″–1½″ diameter handrails support 250 pounds	uniform dimensions non-projecting nosing handrails extend 1′6″ at ends riser and tread contrasting color		handrails 1¼–2″ in diameter handrails extend 1′–1′6″ at ends handrails support 250 pounds
storage	midpoint height sliding doors low clothes rods (54″)	midpoint height sliding doors			midpoint height sliding doors
switches and outlets	switches 3′ high 3-way switches outlets 1′3″ high	3-way switches	3-way switches		rocker switches
threshold	flat, ½″ high, or polyethylene	flat, ½″ high, or polyethylene	flat contrasting color if raised		
toilet	wall-hung 17″–19″ high built-in spray and warm air dryer backrest	built-in spray and warm air dryer backrest			built-in spray and warm air dryer
walls	smooth	smooth	smooth right angles at corners	sound absorbent right angles at corners	smooth
window	sliding 2–3′ high	sliding	large window area spaced to avoid contrasts of light and dark		sliding cranking controls

Source: Marilyn Dee Casto and Savannah S. Day, "Guidelines for Adaptive Housing for the Elderly and Handicapped," *Housing Educators Journal/Housing and Society,* Vol. 4, No. 2, May 1977, pp. 34–35 (with minor modifications based on ANSI 117.1 1980).

2–19 A floor plan can combine open and closed spaces. The living and dining rooms and kitchen occupy the large open second level; bedrooms and studio are distinct spaces separated by changes in level. Alexander Seidel and Jared Carlin, AIA, architects.

Types of Plans

The two basic determinants in shaping a plan—the intended occupants and the space available—can be interrelated in countless ways. Family size, resources, ages of members, and way of life indicate the amount of square footage desirable and economically feasible, as well as the disposition of space for satisfactory living on one level or two, compacted or spread out. The size, shape, contour, and environment of the space, in turn, suggest whether a given amount of square footage can be contained in one story or will need more than one, whether the plan should be a square or rectangle or can be expanded into an L or T shape or a cruciform, and perhaps whether an inward-turning court plan would be better than one that opens outward to a nonexistent view, to a street, or to nearby neighbors.

Over the centuries the concept of space within the home has fluctuated between two basic arrangements: a single large, undifferentiated area in which most of the homelife took place and a series of tightly segregated rooms with minimum intercommunication. In the late nineteenth and early twentieth centuries, specialized rooms meant for designated activities appeared in the house plan. The terms *card room*, *drawing room*, *music room*, and even *smoking room* suggest the compartmentalization of a time now past. This century has witnessed changing lifestyles that in turn are reflected by more open space planning, with slightly demarcated but expansive spaces flowing into one another. As modern life became less marked by formality, elaborate social rituals, and rigid distinctions, so our homes changed in response to these demands. People with active, mobile, informal lifestyles today often find a combination of the two plans, with one part of the home more open and another more closed, most responsive to their needs.

Closed Plans

The closed plan divides space into separate rooms for specific activities. It has several points in its favor and still appeals to many people because it affords privacy for different age groups and pursuits. A closed plan allows modulated levels of upkeep: for instance, children's play space does not necessarily have to be neat at all times, but adults often prefer a situation at least moderately ordered. Conflicting activities can take place simultaneously without interference. Furthermore, it is possible to close off certain portions of the house so that only those spaces in constant use need be heated or cooled at a given time—an important energy-conserving feature. The house shown in Figure 2-20 exhibits such a plan as it is conceived today. If desired, the downstairs rooms can be totally or partially shut off from the rest of the house and left unheated; levels of heat throughout the house can also vary according to need.

One disadvantage of closed plans is the division of space into many separate cubicles that may be quite small unless the house is very generous in size. Another is the possible segregation and lack of communication that may be fostered among family members.

Open Plans

An open plan provides a minimum of fixed, opaque, floor-to-ceiling partitions and a maximum of flexible group space. Instead of being tightly closed into boxlike rooms, space is organized as a continuous entity, flowing from one section to another and from indoors to outdoors, all of which greatly expands the potential of any one area. The advantages of open plans include a sense of spaciousness beyond actual dimensions, diversified use of space, and recognition that family or group

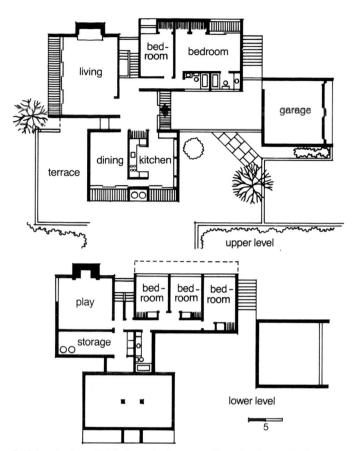

2–20 A plan divided vertically as well as horizontally into group and private, quiet and active zones is easily encompassed within a two-story format. Willis Mills, architect.

activities are not isolated events. For people with ambulatory problems or vision or hearing impairment, the open plan is most convenient and functional.

But open plans also have certain disadvantages. For one thing, noisy activities may interfere with those requiring quiet, and the retiring soul finds little opportunity for solitude. Also, if not sensitively planned, the large space may seem barnlike. However, these drawbacks can be overcome in several ways. Incompatible functions can be segregated by shaping the space with partial walls, different floor levels, and furniture arrangement. L-shaped rooms, balconies, furniture set at right angles to the wall or placed away from the walls, and flexible screens or movable walls represent some of the major design possibilities. Noise can be controlled with surfaces that absorb sound waves. Some segregated areas can be provided—multipurpose or family rooms for active pursuits, seclusion rooms for quiet study, meditation, and relaxation.

The open plan owes much of its development to the inspiration of Frank Lloyd Wright with his prairie house designs and later to the innovations of Le Corbusier and Ludwig Mies van der Rohe. (See Chapter 19 for further discussion of these architects and illustrations of their open-plan designs.) The open plan reached its full flowering in one-story houses that spread out over the land and into the landscape by means of terraces and decks, at a time when acreage was relatively inexpensive, during the 1940s through the 1970s.

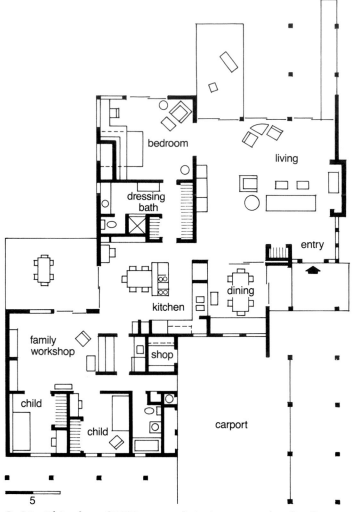

2–21 This plan of 2030 square feet gives a growing family plenty of elbow room but employs many devices for opening up space when needed and closing it off for more sheltered uses. Loch Crane, architect.

Today compact but open plans of 1½ and 2 stories capitalize on the natural potential for maximum air circulation to provide economical heating and cooling. Many solar home designs utilize multilevel open plans effectively for this purpose.

Horizontal and Vertical Plans

Plans can also be divided into one-or-more-storied types, with resultant advantages and disadvantages.

One-Story Plans

One-level plans are well suited to small houses, and to larger ones for which the cost of greater land, roof, and foundation area and of an extended perimeter will not be an excluding factor. Single-story plans avoid stairways, permit easy supervision of children, give ready access to the out-of-doors, and generally result in a horizontal silhouette that fits comfortably on level land. Until recently, indi-

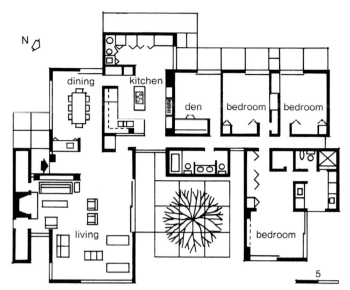

2–22 A *closed* plan that permits separating each activity in a different room offers a great deal of privacy, which the U-shape arrangement accentuates. Donald Gibbs and Hugh Gibbs, architects.

vidual apartment units have also been predominantly one-story even though contained in multistory apartment buildings.

Multilevel Plans

A major interest in the design professions today involves the manipulation of vertical spaces, of volumes. The sense of excitement produced by soaring interior spaces has found a ready acceptance among large segments of the public; even speculative builders resort to high ceilings with mezzanine or balcony projections. This trend indicates a radical departure from the Uniform Building Code minimum 8-foot ceiling that has been standard since World War II. Coincidental with the growing taste for verticality has been the pressing economic need to conserve square footage. The hollowed-out effect of tall interior volumes tends to counteract our awareness of shrinking floor areas and to eliminate a feeling of constriction. Whatever the reasons, the results often have been dramatic.

Multiple-story plans offer several advantages. Given two homes of equal square footage, the double-story version is less expensive to build than the single because of its smaller foundation and roof. Heating and cooling are also less expensive. Moreover, vertically separated rooms simplify the problem of zoning spaces for different activities. As the cost of land rises, multiple-story houses seem more practical, fitting onto awkward hillsides, tight city lots, or modest suburban sites, thereby freeing more land for outdoor enterprises. Sometimes multistory plans rise to catch desirable breezes or an otherwise hidden view. And the large steep roofs that can be a natural, effective part of the design have proved ideal for solar heating panels if the house is suitably oriented.

The 1½-story plan, often called the Cape Cod house, provides a smaller upper floor beneath a high-pitched roof. About half the area of the attic floor is useful (space with less than 5 feet of head room is usable only for storage), and dormer windows penetrating the roof to admit light are characteristic. Although the upper rooms are small, this is a very inexpensive way to add living space with minimal effect on construction cost and exterior design. Even more square footage

2–23 The *multilevel* floor plan of the house in Figure 2–24 easily and naturally divides group and private spaces, a concept enhanced by the way rooms cluster around the space-saving circulation core.

2–24 Tantalizing glimpses of different levels and areas bring an exhilarating sense of the spaces beyond. In this house, each activity has its own separate but not isolated room. Charles Moore and Rurik Ekstrom, architects. *(Photograph: Maris/Semel)*

second floor

first floor

5

2–25 The plan of this house is a square, which encompasses the most space with the least foundation, exterior walls, and roof. A two-story square plan further reduces exterior maintenance and keeps heating costs low. John Black Lee and Harrison DeSilver, architects.

of living space results from the full two- or even three-story plan without increasing the overall ground area occupied.

The only real disadvantage of the multiple-story house is the necessity of always climbing and descending stairs, an especially hazardous activity for the very young, the elderly, and the infirm. Increased interest in these groups of people has brought with it research into different stairway designs. Spiral staircases occupy the least space, but this economy may be offset by the difficulty of moving furniture up and down, as well as the increased danger of accidents on the narrow treads near the center support. A flight of stairs broken at some point by a landing provides the easiest way for the climber to bridge the space between two floors.

The multilevel floor plan has reestablished itself in popularity after a period of disfavor caused by the aggressive onslaught of the one-floor ranch house. The split-level plan first reignited interest in multilevel living, since it offered the opportunity for three well-separated zones of activity over a relatively small ground area. Originally an adaptation to hillside lots, it pushes the basement halfway out of the ground for light and ventilation while still benefiting from the earth's insulation. At a time when acreage is scarce and expensive, we can no doubt anticipate a greater concentration on vertical building to exploit each plot of land more fully.

Multifamily Housing

The Romans built thousands of apartment houses, some of them seven and eight stories high, during the second century. Their presumed reasons were the same as those that motivate multifamily housing today: commerce and industry concentrated in specific large cities require a parallel concentration of people; also, land in such focal areas tends to be scarce and expensive, so it is more efficient to expand vertically than horizontally. The plans of the individual units are much the same as those for single-family housing except that most of the windows may face in only one or two directions along the facade of the building. A major disadvantage then is often an absence of cross ventilation for summer cooling, rendered unnecessary perhaps by air conditioning but once again becoming an important energy-saving device. Other disadvantages of such plans are the relative lack of privacy and the absence of outdoor living areas. Many newer multifamily dwellings overcome the latter problem with terraces or outdoor decks and balconies.

Attached Housing

Called row houses, townhouses, or garden apartments, attached dwellings have once again become a major solution to the problem of accommodating a large number of families on a small area of land. They represent one of the fastest growing segments of the current housing market. Rising two to four or five stories in height, row houses by definition have their side walls abutting those of adjacent houses. They combine the psychological privacy of a completely integral structure with the economy of limited ground area and shared walls to shelter a household of people.

A major disadvantage of the row-house plan is the necessity of placing all windows on the two short walls at front and back. In older buildings, space tended to be broken up into many small rooms, with the result that internal spaces were completely deprived of daylight and fresh air. Traffic patterns also tended to be poor, with rooms arranged along a long corridor of wasted space, or else traffic was routed through activity areas. However, the present wave of interest in building or renovating townhouses has fostered new ideas for opening up the long, narrow space. The remodeled Samton house (Fig. 2-26) answers admirably the problems of light, ventilation, and articulation of space. Two main structural changes were made: as many internal walls as possible were removed to create a free-flowing space, and window walls were added at back on two floors to flood the interior with natural light.

Duplexes offer many of the advantages of the single-family detached house with only a single shared wall or floor between two otherwise distinct units.

A recent innovation in multifamily plans is the living environment shared by two individuals or two groups of people. The plan provides two large bedroom suites with baths and sitting areas for complete privacy when desired. The living, dining, and kitchen areas are shared. However, such a plan can be designed with nooks and crannies for semi-private intimacy so that independent adults don't feel that too much togetherness is being forced upon them. The advantage is that both parties save on utility bills, mortgage payments, and maintenance. This type of cooperative, shared lifestyle probably began as a necessity but may well become a popular solution to rising housing costs.[6]

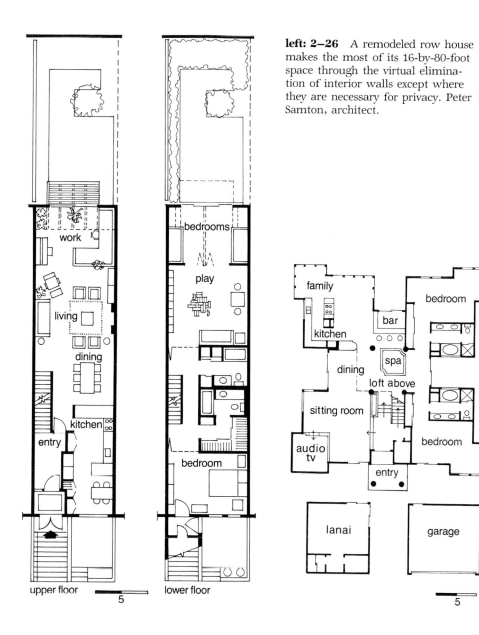

left: 2–26 A remodeled row house makes the most of its 16-by-80-foot space through the virtual elimination of interior walls except where they are necessary for privacy. Peter Samton, architect.

family

kitchen

bar

spa

dining

loft above

sitting room

audio tv

bedroom

bedroom

entry

lanai

garage

5

2–27 Illustrating the privacy and amenities essential to viable shared housing, this design provides two widely separated master suites—self-contained apartments that include bed, bath, dressing room, sitting alcove/media center, and compact laundry facilities. The balance of the interior is one grand room, with functions defined by changing levels rather than walls. Barry A. Berkus, AIA, Berkus Group Architects.

Selecting and Evaluating an Existing Plan

It is all very well to talk about various planning possibilities and requirements, but sooner or later everyone must select a place to live. In order to effect the transition from abstract to concrete, this section presents a series of questions designed to bring out the pertinent factors to consider in choosing a lifespace.

Is the total amount of enclosed space, plus the usable outdoor space, suited to the needs of the occupants? To arrive at a per-person space quota, simply take the entire gross area of the house plan and divide it by the number of occupants. While the 200-square-feet-per-person minimum suggests a convenient rule of thumb, many factors (including, of course, finances) will influence the actual

2–28 Within an enclosed area of only 1000 square feet this plan compacts most of the amenities that result in comfortable family living while still allowing both physical and psychic expansion of space. Bruce Walker, architect.

amount of space available to each member of the household. For one thing, as the size of the group increases, the amount of space required by each individual generally diminishes. Households composed of people who are heterogeneous in age and interests, as well as those who are gregarious and extroverted, generally need more space per person than those whose members are homogeneous and relatively quiet. The home with flexible and multiuse space—enhanced by good zoning, convenient relationships among rooms, minimum traffic through rooms, thoughtful furniture arrangements, and livable outdoor areas—may be satisfactory with considerably less space per person. The measure should not be limited to square feet alone, but should also incorporate shapes of floor areas, number of rooms and sleeping areas, number of occupants, their ages, sex, relationships, and how their leisure time is spent. Multiuse space becomes more and more the solution to shrinking square footage.

In addition, the mood or atmosphere of the home should be appropriate to the needs of the family. Image too can play a role in selection. An impressive entry or one that projects friendliness may be important to some while one that is less open might provide the security and privacy desired by others. Many of us think we want as much space as possible until we see a large old house for sale or rent. Then we begin to wonder about cleaning, maintaining, and heating it, and how we and our furnishings would fit into rooms planned for another way of life. This suggests that the largest affordable space may not be ideal, even though there is no substitute for adequate square footage. On the other hand, people are beginning to realize that the ample space provided by some old houses and apartments can be recycled to fit the kinds of lifestyles we practice today.

Is the space appropriately allocated? The proportion of space devoted to living, sleeping, and working can vary markedly even in homes of the same size. The most significant relationship probably will be that between group and private

2–29 In a low-income housing project, a plan (left) reworked in response to a user survey not only resulted in an apartment more in keeping with the probable life style of the occupants (right) but also opened up the spaces to make the most of available square footage.

spaces. One plan may offer a condensed living space so that bedrooms and baths can be larger and more numerous for individuals who like privacy; another could limit the bedrooms to mere cubicles, thus allowing for large or multiple group spaces. The importance of the personal zone may be further indicated by the seclusion given bedrooms and baths by a private hallway, movable partitions, or the potential of a separate space for individual pursuits.

Work areas normally occupy proportionately larger sections of the overall plan in bigger homes, because, as noted earlier, when space is limited the service functions are the first to be compressed. However, families to whom the kitchen is very important may want to devote a greater proportion of the space to that room even in a small home. The specific requirements of the activities carried out in each space must be considered.

Is the enclosed space well zoned and adjacent to related outdoor areas?
The basic consideration in zoning involves segregating quiet areas from noisy areas. Plans can be checked quickly for this factor by coloring noisy spaces red, quiet ones green, and transitional or buffer areas yellow, then studying the resulting pattern. One of the most common zoning errors in one-story houses appears in the indoor-outdoor relationship: separating the kitchen from the garage (thereby precluding a convenient service entrance and yard) or facing the living room toward the street (which makes it difficult to unite the major group space with a protected terrace or lawn).

Is the pattern of circulation satisfactory? Short routes from point to point simplify housekeeping and make home life more pleasant, but they can be hard to achieve. Trace traffic paths on the floor plan to aid in analyzing the distance of frequently traveled routes and the privacy needed for the job being done, keeping in mind the points raised in the section on circulation.

Table 2–2 Typical Square Footages for Certain Portions of the House

Room	Small	Medium	Large
entrance	25–30	35–40	45 +
living space	150–200	220–280	300 +
dining area	100–130	150–180	200 +
dining space in kitchen	25–40	50–70	80 +
kitchen	75–90	100–140	160 +
bedroom	80–130	140–190	200 +
bathroom	33–35	40–45	50 +
utility room	12–15	18–25	30 +

Are the rooms of suitable size? Beyond the *actual* square footage of a room, we must consider its *usable* and *apparent* size. These factors are affected by shape, location, and size of openings; relation to other rooms and to the landscape; treatment of walls, floors, and ceiling; kind, amount, and arrangement of furniture. Some families prefer many small rooms, others a few large spaces. Table 2–2 lists typical square footages. An open plan with wide expanses of window to unite indoors and out and with built-ins or minimal furnishings can visually provide more space in the small home.

Will the rooms take the required furniture gracefully and efficiently? The primary consideration here is naturally adequate floor space for both furniture and traffic. But in planning a home we must also consider the question of suitable wall space—especially for such large items as beds and sofas—and the problem of arranging the furniture into satisfactory groupings. Doors, windows, heating and cooling vents, electrical switches and outlets, closets, and built-ins all take wall space and require access. (Furniture arrangement will be considered in detail in the next several chapters.)

Is there adequate storage space? A phenomenon almost everyone faces sooner or later is that storable items expand to fill and overflow the space allocated to them, regardless of how commodious that space might be. Ample built-in storage reduces the amount of furniture needed and thus provides more living space. Often-used items should be stored where used; seasonal or infrequently used articles can be stored in more out-of-the-way locations. Storage demands are usually heaviest during the expanding family years and also later years when a lifetime's accumulation of possessions (and often children's possessions) must be dealt with. For houses without basements or attics, rental storage is often necessary. Specific storage requirements are discussed in succeeding chapters.

Is the plan effectively oriented on the site? Skillful orientation for maximum climate control is treated in Chapter 6. But other factors that affect the livability of a plan also deserve consideration: the presence or absence of pleasant views, the degree of privacy needed in each room, and the amount of light—particularly sunlight—desirable in various parts of the house at different times of the day. All these are very personal decisions and must be dealt with on an individual basis. Even so, several typical situations present themselves:

- Major group spaces deserve the best view, the privacy needed for living behind large windows, and the winter sun. South to southeast is generally preferred.
- Kitchens merit a pleasant vista outdoors and ample daylight, preferably with morning sun. This suggests northeast orientation.

- Bedrooms demand privacy; if the occupants enjoy the morning sun, these rooms could be focused generally toward the east.
- Bathrooms have no great need for outlook or sunlight, although both are pleasant.
- Utility rooms can be anywhere, since they need few if any windows.
- Garages and carports must only be convenient to the street and house entrances. They may be placed on the least desirable side of the house to buffer noise, block wind, shade the walls of living spaces, or protect privacy.

All of these factors represent ideals. Most people, in choosing a preexisting plan, find they have to compromise on a few essential qualities. Perhaps the overriding factors in site orientation will be knowing the house is not so dark that electric lights must burn all day, so much subject to relentless summer sun that it can never be comfortable, or so lacking in privacy that its occupants feel continually exposed to neighbors and passersby.

Is the plan economical? Both initial and continuing costs must be evaluated to determine whether the plan is affordable. Use costs can be minimized if plumbing and other utilities are located in close proximity, low maintenance materials are used both inside and out, windows are located to capture natural ventilation, and flexible spaces allow changing uses as needs vary over time. Location may also influence initial cost independent of the merits of the plan itself. A good location increases the home's value while a poor location decreases it.

Does the home lend itself to desirable or necessary change? It is impossible to predict just what the future will bring, but knowing that life and change go together suggests planning for flexibility. Family patterns change as children are born, develop, and leave home (and sometimes return again), or parents or grandparents move in. The typically limited funds of young people may necessitate beginning with minimum quarters, but as financial stability increases the question of upgrading or enlarging the lifespace—or moving to a new one—arises. Business opportunities, health, or simply the desire for something new can result in selling or renting a home. New lifestyles are continually evolving, and tastes inevitably change and develop over the years. Demands upon the lifespace will vary with these changes.

Remodeling

The changing needs of today's households are reflected in the fact that 71 percent of owner-occupied homes are altered or repaired each year.[7] Most of our existing housing supply was built when the nuclear-family household and the industrial society were the norm. Today we are moving to become a technological society and a wide variety of household forms exist. Older homes are being expanded, opened up, retrofitted, rehabilitated, renovated, restored, subdivided, refurbished, and updated in every conceivable way to make them more livable. And, with housing in short supply, industrial buildings and farm buildings are being converted to living spaces to help satisfy the need. The adaptive reuse of these structures also preserves some of our architectural heritage.

Structurally, floor space can be expanded by removing interior or exterior walls. When *load-bearing* walls are involved, the structure must be supported by some alternative method such as steel beams or columns. Exterior walls are usually removed to allow the addition of square footage to the home, while interior walls are removed to open up inside spaces without adding square feet.

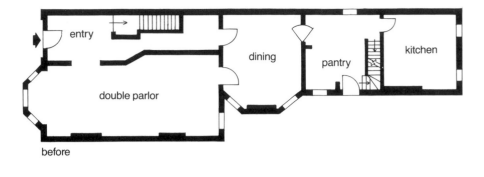

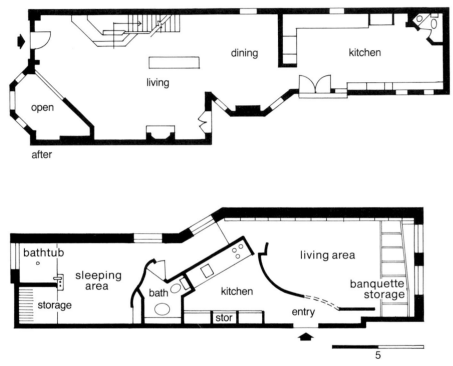

top: 2–30 The before and after plans of this renovated row house illustrate how much space can be expanded with the removal of interior partitioning walls. Sanford Bond, AIA, architect.

bottom: 2–31 To make a New York apartment look larger, designer Michael Kalil removed all original walls and put up new partitions using diagonals and curves that extend sight lines.

Space can be added physically and/or visually by building on new rooms, perhaps a greenhouse or a remodeled garage, even just a bay window, dormer windows, or possibly skylights. By finishing the attic space, a one-story house can be expanded to 1½ stories. Or a full second story can be added, although this requires major reconstruction. To give the feeling of spaciousness in a small living area with a standard 8-foot ceiling, the ceiling can often be removed and extended up to the rafters. Skylights can be added and beams can span the open space, or a soffit can be left around the perimeter to support the roof. Lighting installed in the soffit will dramatize the heightened space at night.

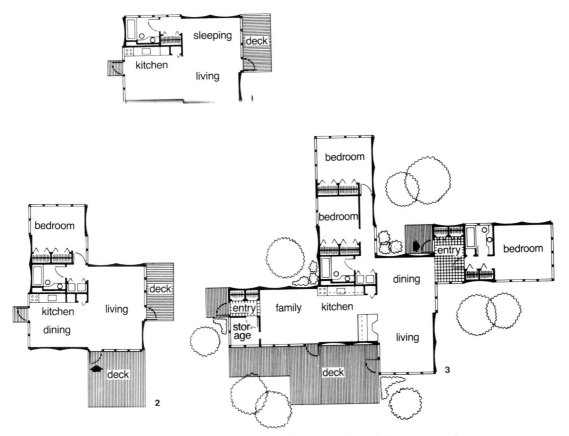

2-32 An interesting aspect of some industrialized houses is their ability to expand, with minimum disruption, as family needs change. This version begins as a compact 507-square-foot unit; grows to 845 square feet with the addition of a bedroom wing; and fills out to 1521 square feet as a master bedroom, family room, new living room, and deck are attached. Several other arrangements are possible. Mark Hildebrand, designer.

When the problem is too much space, walls and partial walls can be added to enclose and separate activities and provide greater privacy. If differentiation of the space is desired without actually closing off sections of it with walls, vertical distinctions can be made. A platform can be constructed to raise one activity area above another. Or, sometimes, part of a group space can be lowered to ground level if the house has a raised foundation with an above-ground crawl space. This requires pouring a concrete slab for the new floor surface.

If the existing rooms have high ceilings, a false or lowered ceiling can create greater intimacy for some areas. Very high ceilings also permit the construction of loft spaces that can be used for sleeping, play, or work.

Outdoor living space can be found even in crowded areas with balconies and bay-, box-, sunroom-, and greenhouse-style bump-out windows added to the exterior of the home. They admit light and visually (as well as physically) extend space by linking indoors and outdoors. In these ways, space built for another time, for other occupants, can be altered to suit the needs of the present day.

2–33 A housing rehabilitation project in Boston increased the size of two small apartments by combining them into a single unit with some rearrangement of walls and doors. *(The West Broadway Team: a Joint Venture of Lane, Franchman and Associates, Inc. and Goody, Clancy and Associates, Inc., Boston)*

There is no ideal home plan. As with every other aspect of housing design discussed in this book, the plan best suited for a particular household will emerge from the needs, desires, personalities, and lifestyles of its members. When all these elements have been analyzed and understood, the plan that begins as a graphic outline on paper can begin to take shape as truly personal lifespace.

Notes to the Text

1. Ernest R. Weidhaas, *Architectural Drafting and Design*, 4th ed. (Boston: Allyn and Bacon, 1981), p. 156.
2. Marjorie Branin Keiser, *Housing: An Environment for Living* (New York: Macmillan, 1978), pp. 134–135.
3. Richard Rush, "Body Insults from Buildings," *Progressive Architecture*, July 1981, p. 124.
4. Ibid., p. 124.
5. Walter B. Kleeman, Jr., *The Challenge of Interior Design* (Boston: CBI Publishing Co., 1981), p. 21.
6. Constance Roe, "Shared Design: A New Concept for Contemporary Needs," *Designers West*, June 1982, pp. 158–163.
7. Suzanne Lindamood and Sherman D. Hanna, *Housing, Society, and Consumers: An Introduction* (St. Paul, MN: West Publishing Company, 1979), p. 94.

References for Further Reading

American National Standard Specifications for Making Buildings and Facilities Accessible to and Usable by Physically Handicapped People, ANSI A117.1-1980. New York: American National Standards Institute, 1980.

Casto, Marilyn Dee and Savannah S. Day. "Guidelines for Adaptive Housing for the Elderly and Handicapped," *Housing Educators Journal*, V.4, n.2 (May 1977).

Family Housing Handbook. Ames: Iowa State University, Midwest Plan Service, 1971.

Friedmann, Arnold, John F. Pile, and Forrest Wilson. *Interior Design: An Introduction to Architectural Interiors*, 3rd ed. New York: Elsevier, 1982. Pp. 105–112, 157–164.

Hartwigsen, Gail Lynn. *Design Concepts: A Basic Guidebook*. Boston: Allyn and Bacon, Inc., 1980. Chaps. 4, 5, 6, 9.

Ittelson, William H., Harold M. Proshansky, Leanne G. Rivlin, and Gary H. Winkel. *An*

Introduction to Environmental Psychology. New York: Holt, Rinehart and Winston, Inc., 1974. Pp. 200–201, 352–353, 356.

Keiser, Marjorie Branin. *Housing: An Environment for Living*. New York: Macmillan, 1978. Chaps. 7, 8, 12.

Kleeman, Walter B., Jr. *The Challenge of Interior Design*. Boston: CBI Publishing Company, 1981. Chaps. 2, 8, 10.

Lindamood, Suzanne and Sherman D. Hanna. *Housing, Society, and Consumers: An Introduction*. St. Paul, MN: West Publishing Company, 1979. Chap. 5.

Meeks, Carol B. *Housing*. Englewood Cliffs, NJ: Prentice-Hall, 1980. Chap. 9.

Minimum Guidelines and Requirements for Accessible Design. Washington, DC: U.S. Architectural and Transportation Barriers Compliance Board, 1982.

One- and Two-Family Dwelling Code, 1983 ed. Whittier, CA: International Conference of Building Officials.

Packard, Robert T. (ed.). *Ramsey/Sleeper Architectural Graphic Standards*, 7th ed. New York: Wiley, 1981.

Panero, Julius and Martin Zelnick. *Human Dimension and Interior Space: A Source Book of Design Reference Standards*. New York: Whitney Library of Design, 1979.

Rush, Richard. "The Age of the Aging," *Progressive Architecture*, August 1981, pp. 59–63.

Rush, Richard. "Body Insults from Buildings," *Progressive Architecture*, July 1981, pp. 122–129.

Slesin, Suzanne. "For Elderly, The Triumph of Having a Place to Call Their Own," *The New York Times*, August 13, 1981.

Spence, William P. *Architecture: Design, Engineering, Drawing*, 3rd ed. Bloomington, IL: McKnight Publishing Company, 1979. Chap. 4.

St.Marie, Satenig S. *Homes Are for People*. New York: Wiley, 1973. Pp. 13–201.

Thompson, Marie McGuire. *Housing and Handicapped People*. Washington, DC: The President's Committee on Employment of the Handicapped, 1976.

Uniform Building Code, 1982 ed. Whittier, CA: International Conference of Building Officials.

Weidhaas, Ernest R. *Reading Architectural Plans for Residential and Commercial Construction*, 2nd ed. Boston: Allyn and Bacon, 1981.

3 Social Spaces

The social spaces in any home are the areas where members of the household gather and where friends are entertained. They provide a congenial atmosphere for such activities as general conversation, games, parties, listening to or making music, eating, and children's play. Most homes throughout history have included such communal gathering places in which the entire household could assemble for recreation, companionship, and often warmth. In medieval England the "great hall" of a castle or house functioned as a group space and was perhaps the only room that was adequately heated. American families of the seventeenth and eighteenth centuries typically congregated in the kitchen, drawn by the triple sensory pleasures of warmth, delicious aromas, and freshly cooked food—all conducive to easy companionship. For the same reasons, the kitchen in many a home today serves as a magnet for the entire family. Comparatively recently, however, new kinds of activities have become important in family life—reading, watching television, listening to music, pursuing home crafts, hobbies, and even work. All of these, plus our increased leisure time (thanks to labor-saving devices), make different demands on the living spaces in today's home, demands that architectural design is only beginning to satisfy. The social area is the one most intensely used by the inhabitants, as well as guests, in the home.

The emphasis given each social activity varies from individual to individual and from household to household. Furthermore, our priorities inevitably change as we grow older and experience changes in family life and economic status. The group space that, for example, makes ample provision for children's play will assume a different character when those children are grown. Because none but the very wealthy can accommodate all kinds of activities equally well, today most of us must decide carefully which social pursuits are most important, then plan accordingly. A logical first step is to consider specific group activities, as well as the environment and equipment desirable for each, and then to design the living space so that it will best meet these requirements. Time spent in leisure refreshes the mind and body; the social core of the home should be pleasant and stimulating to attract people to it and, once there, encourage interaction with others or with the environment itself.

Activities and Spaces

Greeting Guests

Greeting and welcoming guests as they enter the public sector of the house is an important social activity. Although perhaps taken for granted by household members, the entry foyer creates the visitors' first strong impression of the home and sets the stage for their ensuing introduction to the lifestyle of its inhabitants. The entry also serves the critical function of efficiently directing and controlling traffic into and throughout the home. The physical requirements are:

- **Space** sufficient to open the inward-swinging front door and stand aside for visitors to pass, and to assist them with coats. A space of 3 by 5 feet allows the host to open the door, stepping out of the way, while a 5-by-7-foot entry provides space to remove coats and hang them in a closet.
- **Closet** in or near the entrance with an interior at least 2½ feet wide and 2 feet deep for coats. A 27- to 30-inch depth is better for accommodating bulky garments.
- **Lighting** both indoors and out for safety, security, and mood. Visitors should be able to see to enter without being blinded by excessive brightness; soft foyer lighting helps direct traffic to the brighter living area.
- **Window(s)** or a peephole device to determine who is there before opening the door.

3-1 The view from the entry establishes the character of an adobe house and draws guests into the living area. Maurice J. Nespor & Associates, architects; Diana Cunningham, interior designer. (*Photograph: Hyde Flippo*)

65

- **Surfaces** on which to place packages, gloves, keys, or other objects while waiting or removing coats. A table or chest, a wall-hung console, or a shelf in a small foyer will serve this purpose and help add character.
- **Seating** for donning or removing boots or just waiting. A bench can provide both seating and a surface on which to put things down.
- **Mirror** for checking appearance.
- **Flooring** that is durable and easily cleaned.

The entrance provides the transition from outdoors to indoors and should be compatible with both, architecturally and decoratively. It establishes the character and mood for the rest of the home and for the reception of guests. It can be friendly and inviting, indicating a warm open hospitality, or fortresslike, perhaps reflecting a desire for privacy on the part of the occupants. Either way, the first impression is often lasting.

If at all possible, full sight of the living/dining quarters should be shielded from immediate view at the entry. In larger homes this can easily be accomplished by a separate, centrally located entrance foyer that routes visitors to the major social areas located adjacent to it or off the central hall. However, since it doesn't contribute to the living space, a separate area is not often included in lower-cost, smaller homes. In this case a divider—storage wall, bookcase, planter, or screen—can help segregate activities, provide some privacy, and create a sense of the larger living space drawing one toward it.

Conversation

The most pervasive social activity is conversation, an exchange so much a part of life that we tend to take it for granted. Conversation may be seen as an amalgam of both verbal and nonverbal forms of communication—a pleasant exchange among family and friends. Obviously, we can and do talk together in any part of the home. But the most natural settings for group interaction are those group spaces where people congregate—the living and dining areas. The elements conducive to easy conversation are:

- **Space** sufficient for the usual number of people who are present. A person in an easy chair, for example, needs a space nearly 3 feet wide by 4 feet deep, but with legs extended, a tall person may need a space over 5 feet deep. Aisle space for easy movement is also needed. Table 3–1 gives some standard furniture sizes and necessary clearances.
- **Comfortable seats** for each participant; a minimum of one good seat for each permanent member of the household and additional ones to accommodate guests. Stable seating, not too low and with arm supports, is advisable for the elderly or disabled. The choice of individual or multiple seating pieces may be a reflection of the size of household members' personal space bubbles, discussed in Chapter 1.

3-2 A comfortable conversation group may consist of both sofas and occasional chairs, allowing flexibility and choice for household members and guests. Ginne Kelsey Hilsinger, ASID, designer. *(Photograph: Kenneth D. Rice)*

66

Table 3–1 Furniture Sizes and Clearance Spaces

Living Room	Small			Large	
	Depth	*Width*		*Depth*	*Width*
sofa	2'6"	x 6'	to	3' x	9'
love seat	2'6"	x 4'	to	3' x	5'
easy chair	2'6"	x 2'4"	to	3'4" x	3'3"
pull-up chair	1'6"	x 1'6"	to	2' x	2'
coffee table, oblong	1'6"	x 3'	to	3' x	5'
coffee table, round	2' diam.		to	4' diam.	
coffee table, square	2'	x 2'	to	4' x	4'
occasional table	1'6"	x 10"	to	3' x	1'8"
card table	2'6"	x 2'6"	to	3' x	3'
flattop desk	1'6"	x 2'8"	to	3' x	6'
secretary	1'6"	x 2'8"	to	2' x	3'6"
upright piano	2'	x 4'9"	to	2'2" x	5'10"
grand piano	5'10"	x 4'10"	to	9' x	5'2"
bookcase	9"	x 2'6"	to	1' x	—

Clearances

traffic path, major	4' to 6'	
traffic path, minor	1'4" to 4'	
foot room between seating units and edge of top of coffee table	1'	
floor space in front of chair or sofa for feet and legs	1'6" to 2'6"	
chair or bench space in front of desk or piano	3'	

Dining Area	Small			Large	
	Depth	*Width*		*Depth*	*Width*
table, square, 4–8 people	2'6"	x 2'6"	to	5' x	5'
table, rectangle, 6–12 people	3'	x 5'	to	4' x	8'
table, round, 4–10 people	2'7" diam.		to	6'4" diam.	
straight chairs	1'4"	x 1'4"	to	1'8" x	1'8"
arm chairs	1'10"	x 1'10"	to	2' x	2'
buffet	1'8"	x 4'	to	2' x	6'
serving table	1'6"	x 3'	to	2' x	4'
china cabinet	1'6"	x 3'	to	1'8" x	4'

Clearances

space for occupied chairs	1'6" to 1'10"
space to get into chairs	1'10" to 3'
traffic path around table and occupied chairs for serving	1'6" to 2'

- **Arrangement of seats and tables** in a generally circular or elliptical pattern so that each person can look at others easily and talk without shouting and so that a dead end is formed, averting traffic intended for other destinations that might disrupt conversation. This primary arrangement should be ready for group conversation without moving furniture. A diameter of 8 to 10 feet across the seating area has proved the most desirable in typical situations. Research has shown that people prefer to sit across from one another to talk. However, if the distance across the conversation space is greater than the distance between two people seated side by side, most people will choose to sit side by side. Also, there is some evidence that as room size increases, conversation seating distance decreases. (Conversation distance in the home is much longer than in larger-scale public places because of the smaller scale and more intimate atmosphere.) Increasing noise level and distraction also draws people closer together.[1]

- **Light** of moderate intensity with highlights at strategic points. Soft, subtle general illumination helps create an intimate atmosphere while bright lighting is very arousing.
- **Surfaces** (tables, shelves, and the like) on which to place accessories.
- **Privacy** from the entry and from traffic to other parts of the home.

Conversation thrives in a warm, friendly atmosphere if the architecture, furnishings, and accessories are spirited but not overpowering, if distractions are minimized, and if sounds are softened (Plate 5, p. 73). Segregation from noise and traffic, and good ventilation (particularly if some members of the household smoke) help create pleasantly intimate and relaxed surroundings conducive to social interaction. Flexible seating arrangements that allow easy eye contact yet sufficient personal space for everyone are generally more successful than rigid built-in seating units, furniture lining the walls of the room, or too many large couches. The very formal parlor (from the French *parler*, "to talk") or sitting room of past eras, used only on special occasions when someone came "to call," is not suited to most current lifestyles, activity patterns, or budgets.

A large space may accommodate a secondary seating group or activity center for one to four people. Usually smaller than the primary grouping, the additional furnishings may consist of two easy chairs with a table and reading lamp, a window seat, a game table and chairs, a writing desk, and/or a comfortable reading chair with good lighting, or a piano. Figures 3-3 through 3-6 illustrate spatial requirements for both primary and secondary seating arrangements. Each unit will be held together visually by a compact arrangement and by the use of architectural or decorative features that make it cohesive. A fireplace or pleasant view, for example, creates a strong natural focal point while an area rug delineates a specific space. The arrangement should invite use while discouraging the cross-traffic of nonparticipants, as shown in Figure 3-7.

Group conversation is also the normal accompaniment of meals because the furniture and its arrangements afford ideal conditions for an hour or so. Terraces and patios are natural conversation centers as well when they offer good seating, privacy, and some degree of shelter.

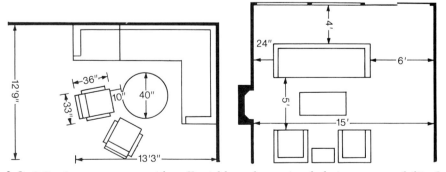

left: 3-3 A corner group with coffee table and occasional chairs, one possibility for arranging furniture in the major group space, with dimensions noted.
right: 3-4 A sofa facing two easy chairs and set at right angles to a fireplace creates a strong unit for the primary conversation center.

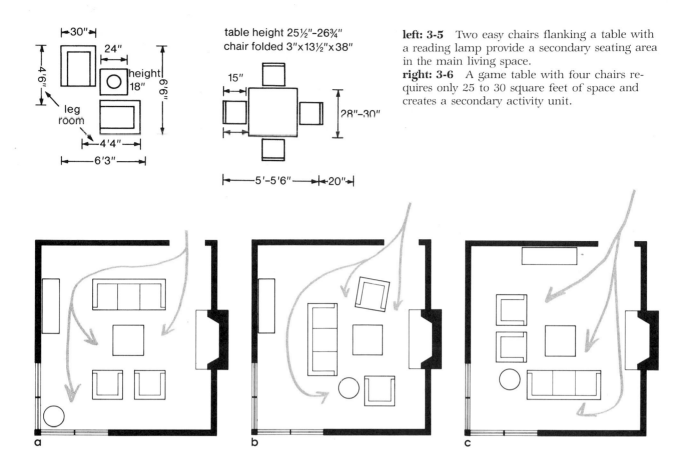

table height 25½"–26¾"
chair folded 3"×13½"×38"

height 18"

leg room

left: 3-5 Two easy chairs flanking a table with a reading lamp provide a secondary seating area in the main living space.
right: 3-6 A game table with four chairs requires only 25 to 30 square feet of space and creates a secondary activity unit.

Reading

Some fortunate people can read with total concentration even in the most trying circumstances—noise, people talking, movement back and forth around them—by screening out all distraction. But most of us, when we settle down for a quiet hour or an evening with a book, prefer a more tranquil environment. The essentials are:

- **Seating** that is resilient but not soporific, giving adequate support to the back (and to the neck and arms as well) for maximum comfort.
- **Light** coming over one shoulder, either moderately strong daylight or artificial light that illuminates the room and concentrates fairly intense but diffused light on the reading material. The entire room does not need to be flooded with uniformly strong light, but neither should it be left in darkness with only a pool of light on the reading material. (More specific lighting information is provided in Chapter 16.)
- **Security** from distracting sights, sounds, and household traffic. Soft music without lyrics can provide a soothing method of muffling other household sounds without distracting attention from reading material.

Beyond these minimum amenities, we might add nearby tables or other surfaces, accessible shelves to hold books and magazines, and enough space to stretch the eyes occasionally. Such conditions, which are adequate for more or less casual reading, can be achieved easily in the typical living room. If, however, one or more

above: 3-7 Furniture placement creates traffic patterns within a room. The arrangement in **a** is cumbersome. The sofa blocks the main view into the room. Although privacy is afforded for conversation, moving around would be difficult. In **b** the sofa is better placed, allowing room for circulation. A living room should welcome people into the conversation area; the best arrangement is shown in **c.**

left: 3-8 The quiet balcony provides a perfect spot for a variety of activities with its natural light, beautiful view, and card table and chairs all set up for a game. Nelson Denny, designer-builder. *(Photograph: © Karen Bussolini)* **above right: 3-9** Unlike most chairs of this type, the Kirkpatrick folding chair is handsome both open and in profile—and comfortable as well. *(Courtesy C. I. Designs)*

members of the family often do serious or technical reading, they may require greater seclusion, and a study or other private place should be planned appropriately.

Quiet Games

Cards, checkers, and chess require concentration. A well-illuminated table about 27 inches high plus moderately high straight chairs, all arranged in a spot free from distractions, will provide the most relaxing situation for the players. Folding card tables or the new lower dining tables and dining chairs set up in the living, dining, or family space will suffice for most households. However, serious gamesters may want a table and chairs permanently and suitably placed, a neutral background for fewer distractions, lighting over the table, and storage for games and accessories nearby.

Audio-Visual Entertainment

Bringing the theater, cinema, concert hall, sports field, and even the classroom, office, and arcade into the home has markedly altered patterns of both leisure and home life. Stereo and television especially, but also movies, slides, and home computers have become important sources of home entertainment and require special planning if they are to become integrated into the total home design.

Music

For many Americans today, music is an integral part of life, as natural as eating or sleeping. Its source may be simply a small radio or television, but more and more in recent years music in the home has become centered on a complex arrangement of stereo components that require considerable space. Further, the space must be kept flexible because the number and shape of the components change as new designs become available and as the listeners' sophistication increases.

At the same time, greater numbers of people enjoy creating their own music. Small instruments such as guitars pose few problems, but the placement of a piano is a major design consideration. A piano can be flat against a wall or at a right angle, in the latter case helping to demarcate a partially segregated area. Diagonal placement is not recommended for spatial efficiency or architectural harmony. A concert grand piano requires 50 square feet of space (a baby grand occupies just over 20 square feet, a parlor grand 30 square feet) and should be placed with curved side facing listeners so that when the top is raised, it will project sound toward them. Because fluctuations in temperature and humidity can affect sound quality, a piano should not be placed near a window or heating/cooling vent.

Serious musicians may want a separate music center in a corner, an alcove, or even a whole room, where everything can be kept together and out of the way of other activities. Such an arrangement would be especially necessary when several instruments are involved or when they are connected to amplifiers—a combination that occupies quite a bit of space, produces a staggering volume of sound, and may require sound insulation or barriers from the rest of the house, such as acoustical paints, wallboard, and ceiling; sound traps in ducts; and insulated pipes. During initial planning and construction, hallways, stairs, closets, built-in cabinets, and bookshelves can be located to help provide sound barriers (further explained in Chapter 6).

Optimum acoustic conditions for listening to music depend on what the particular listeners want. For many people, conditions similar to those recommended for group conversation or quiet reading will suffice—comfortable seating, moderate illumination, and a minimum of distraction. But committed musicians who have an intense concern for the quality of sound will demand further refinements. Although the quality can be no better than that produced by the instruments and performers or by the stereo equipment, several factors (notably the arrangement, composition, and shape of a room) can enhance or detract from the production of ultimate quality.

- **Seating** should be arranged so that the listeners hear a balanced projection from the instruments or from multiple speakers.
- **Space** can be shaped to enhance the sound. Experts have long known that musical sounds have a finer quality in rooms whose opposite surfaces are not parallel to each other or in which the space is broken up in some way.
- **Materials** often are chosen and placed for their acoustical qualities. In acoustical terms, materials are classified as sound-reflecting or "live" if they bounce the sound (as does plaster or glass) and as sound-absorbing or "dead" if they soak up sound (as do heavy draperies, upholstered furniture, carpet, books, cork, or other so-called acoustical materials). An excess of live materials gives strident amplification and reverberation; the converse, having too many dead surfaces, robs music of its brilliance. Studies have also demonstrated that, for best results, live surfaces should be opposite dead surfaces.

Many of the devices that improve acoustical quality have been incorporated in the living room planned by interior designer Eve Frankl, whose husband Michael Pollen is a pianist and conductor (Fig. 3-11). Placed before a storage wall at the inner end of a long living area, the piano is protected from sudden temperature changes that might affect the strings and hammers. An overhanging balcony at this end of the room and a slanting wood surface above a glass wall at the opposite end answer the requirement for contradictory opposing surfaces breaking up the space for good sound quality. Rugs, deep upholstered seating and pillows, and a bookshelf-storage wall balance sound-absorbing materials against the live surfaces of plaster and glass walls. As the plan shows (Fig. 3-12), sufficient seating is

below: **3-10** A wall storage system provides ready access and convenient visibility for stereo components, albums, and tapes. *(Courtesy Interlübke)*

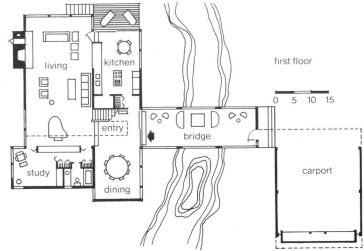

left: **3-11** A living room designed for live musical performances should meet as many of the criteria for good acoustics as possible: a combination of live surfaces to bounce sound and dense ones to absorb reverberations, both properly placed for their sound-enhancing qualities. Eve Frankl, interior designer; George Van Geldern, architect. *(Photograph: © Ezra Stoller/ESTO)*

above right: 3-12 The plan shows the flexibility of space for accommodating large or small audiences.

bottom left: 3-13 This stereo component system has movable speakers mounted at a proper level for good listening. *(Courtesy AKAI AMERICA, LTD.)*

bottom right: 3-14 The stereo speakers and seating are positioned for optimum sound quality in this plan. *(Adapted from Larry Klein)*

provided for a small group of listeners, but plenty of open area leaves the potential for a larger audience who could sit on the floor or on specially set-up chairs. Good lighting is suspended above the piano for reading music, and enough space has been left for other instrumentalists to participate in an evening of live music.

Stereo Speakers

The placement of stereo speaker systems within a room can have a significant influence, for better or worse, on the way they sound. Some experimentation is always necessary to achieve best results. In general, speakers should be installed as the manufacturer recommends: systems intended for shelf mounting should not be placed on the floor, nor should they be installed too high above the ear level of

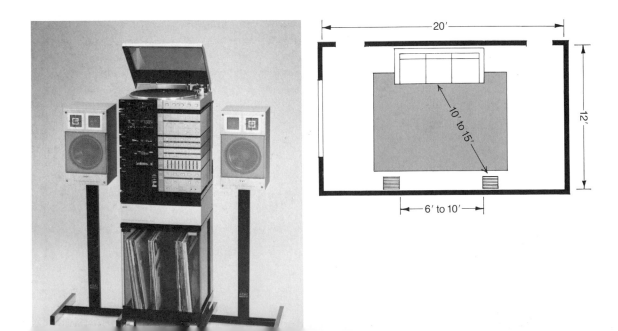

above: Plate 5 Traffic may be routed around rather than through a conversation area by placing the sofa a few feet away from the wall to divert anyone passing through behind it. *(Photograph: Tim Street-Porter)*

right: Plate 6 In a renovated 1906 Long Island carriage house, architect Robert A. M. Stern used traditional elements such as classical columns and moldings to ornament and enrich the open space with references to the past. The dining room is adjacent to the entrance foyer. *(Photograph: Tim Street-Porter)*

above: Plate 7 In most households today, dining space must fulfill more than one role. When not in use for meals, this handsome room doubles as a library-study. George Hartman and Ann Hartman, designers. *(Photograph: Robert C. Lautman)*

left: Plate 8 A sensitive demarcation of different areas—created by varying levels, structural members, and furniture placement—can prevent a large, open group space from seeming barnlike, even in a converted barn. James McNair, designer. *(Photograph: John T. Hill)*

a seated listener. Unless the design requires it, speakers meant for floor mounting should not be placed in, or too close to, a corner. A more "open" sound quality is often achieved when, decor permitting, speakers are spaced 2 or 3 feet away from the rear wall. Avoid installing speakers behind draperies or large pieces of upholstered furniture that will acoustically absorb their high-frequency sound output.

Speakers usually have the most balanced sound when they are located on the long wall of a room, spaced 6 to 10 feet apart, equidistant from the room corners. The preferred listening position is in the area opposite the speakers and roughly centered between them. In general, the speakers-to-listening area distance should be a little less than one and a half times the distance between the speakers. For a spacing between the speakers of, say, 7 feet, this would mean a listening distance of roughly 10 feet. This rule depends very much upon the specific acoustic characteristics of the speakers and of the room. A thick rug or carpet between the speakers and listening area will do much to control excessive acoustic reflections.

If the stereo image is too narrow, the speakers are too close together for the listening area. If, on the other hand, there appears to be an acoustic "hole" between the speakers, they are spaced too far apart. The distance between the speakers—and between the speakers and the listening area—should be adjusted by trial and error to achieve the most natural spread of sound. This natural quality is referred to by audio professionals as "stereo imaging."

Television, Movies, and Slides

Major considerations for home projection activities are good seating, control of light and sound, and insulation for those who do not care to participate.

- **Seating** requirements are much like those for conversation, except that the seating should be arranged within a 60-degree angle of the center of the screen to avoid distortion. Easily moved or swivel chairs offer flexibility; backrests or cushions on the floor increase a room's seating capacity, while long lounges accommodate viewers in a variety of positions.
- **Height of screen** should be as near eye level as possible. Eye level for a seated adult is 38 to 42 inches above the floor.
- **Lighting** of low intensity is necessary especially for watching television, but the light should shine neither on the screen nor in the viewers' eyes.
- **Acoustical** control is similar to that for music.

Although still cumbersome, especially in depth, television receivers can be put in many places, depending upon the lifestyle of the household and its members. Living rooms and family rooms are perhaps the most typical locations, but television sets, possibly small second ones, also appear in bedrooms and kitchens. If they are mounted in walls, television receivers can be treated as part of the wall design or hidden behind doors. Where feasible, they can be positioned to face more than one room. Mounted on a portable stand, a television set can be pushed from place to place as it is needed, although this precludes permanent hookup with an outside antenna or cable. A swivel base permits turning the set toward viewers.

With the introduction of giant-screen projection television, a specially designed space for audio-visual entertainment—the media center or even a media

3-15 With the television placed at correct height, comfortable seating, and good lighting, this room provides excellent viewing conditions. Hank Bruce, architect. *(Photograph: Philip L. Molten)*

3-16 Plenty of cushions atop a well-padded seating platform provide comfort for those watching big-screen television. Joe D'Urso, designer. *(Photograph: © Peter Aaron/ESTO)*

room—is becoming popular in today's homes. The projection television set provides a movie-size picture many times larger than even a 25-inch TV screen for conventional TV programs, movies, video games, or home movies filmed with the family's own color video camera. With the advent of cable television networks, home satellite receivers (microwave dishes), and videocassette recorders, the home entertainment center offers a wide choice of viewing subjects. Even the sound can be enhanced by connecting the projection set to an audio system also located (often built into the walls) in the media room. Videodisk players can be connected to the projector and the home stereo system.

The components of big-screen television may be either a one-piece unit that folds up in a cabinet about the size of a regular TV console when not in use or two pieces—a projection cabinet (receiver) that can be used as a table, built-in or suspended from the ceiling, and a separate screen ranging in dimensions from 3'4" × 2'6" to 5'8" × 4'6". The specific requirements are:

- **Space** for comfortable viewing. The largest projections require a minimum of 12 feet from screen to the viewers; smaller projections can be viewed from shorter distances. The depth of the viewing area should be greater than its width, but room size will probably be more directly related to the number of viewers to be accommodated and other desired uses for the room (a guest room, for example). Or, a separate room may not be necessary: an alcove or corner of another living/social space may be used.
- **Seating** that is comfortable and within the critical viewing angle for a bright picture. This varies with different screens and systems; a deeply curved screen provides a narrower viewing angle, and those sitting to the side will see a dimmer picture. Generally, the better systems have a less critical viewing angle. The equipment selected should have a viewing angle that fits the proportions of the area in which it is to be installed.
- **Lighting** placed outside the viewing angle so that it doesn't reflect on the screen. Lighting can be of low to moderate level as long as it doesn't distract. If placed so that windows are not within the viewing angle, projection television can be used in daylight.

Screens for movies or slides fold easily for storage when not in use. However, when home projection is an important activity, a permanently mounted screen that disappears behind a cornice or other fixture near the ceiling should be considered.

Video Games

Electronic games are a new phenomenon that has yet to become integrated into our social lives. Unlike stereo and television, which are usually a group diversion, these games are essentially a one- or two-person pastime. They range from small handheld units through a great variety of components that can be plugged into computers or into the television set itself. Being small and movable, they can usually fit into any available space, from hand to table to floor, but the noise they may generate can quickly become disruptive. Placement in a space remote from general living may be indicated—a separate family or media room or a bedroom.

The home computer, however, is more than just an entertainment medium. It is becoming increasingly important as a tool for work in the home, the processing of data, business transactions, and even shopping. Its place in the total pattern of home life is only now being explored. See Chapter 5 for further discussion of the home office.

Active Indoor Entertainment

Dancing, table tennis, billiards, and other such vigorous games require plenty of space, noise control, light, storage, a durable floor, and furniture that can be pushed out of the way. So do a stationary bicycle or other exercise equipment. Space may be the primary consideration and a precluding factor for activities such as table tennis, which requires 5 feet of clearance on each side and 7 feet at each end of the 5- by 9-foot table, or pool, with the table measuring approximately 5 by 10 feet and 5 feet of clearance needed all around. A family room, recreation room, or similar space accessible to family members and visitors in the social zone—and, increasingly, community group spaces—can offer an ideal location.

Outdoor Entertainment

Most of us feel the urge to get a little closer to nature. Even in the cities, more and more apartments boast outdoor terraces, which may be quite small but give a semblance of expansion into the out-of-doors. For those fortunate enough to live in more spacious quarters, outdoor areas—decks, terraces, patios, porches, or lawns—are a logical extension of the indoor group space. Well conceived, outdoor living areas can augment the usable entertainment area. For maximum use, these spaces should be located adjacent to living rooms, family rooms, and/or dining rooms and

above: 3-19 A wooden deck has been cut away around existing trees to preserve a natural source of shade, moisture, and beauty—and sturdy hammock supports. Liebhart, Weston, & Goldman, architects. *(Photograph: George Lyons, courtesy California Redwood Association)*

oriented for sun (or shade), breeze, and privacy. Outdoor furniture should be lightweight, durable, and easily cleaned to cope with sun, rain, dust, and casual treatment. Many times furnishings can be used indoors in a solarium, greenhouse, or recreation room during winter months.

The frequency with which outdoor space is enjoyed depends on the durability and dryness of the underfoot surfaces, the protection from weather, the privacy given by fences or hedges, the safety for young children, and the comfort with which some can rest while others play energetically.

Children's Activities

The needs of children range from boisterous play to quiet reflection; from eagerness to join others of their own age to desire for solitude; from wanting to be with the family to carefully avoiding it. Basic elements of a child's play area are:

- **Space** adequate for the discharge of abundant energy
- **Convenience** to a toilet and to the outdoors, as well as to the kitchen or informal eating area, and perhaps the home office for adult supervision
- **Surfaces** and **fixtures** (walls, floors, and furniture) that can take punishment gracefully and lend themselves to change
- **Light, warmth,** and **fresh air** conducive to healthy young bodies

Ideally, all this should be segregated from what (it is hoped) will be the quieter portions of the house.

A living room is clearly unsuitable for a permanent play space, and the dining area is only slightly better. A kitchen has the requisite durability, but even without children's play it is usually the most intensively used room in the house and moreover contains the household's greatest assembly of potential hazards. In older houses attics and basements served as playrooms for children, but these were often cold, dark, damp, and far from any supervising eye. Garages and carports have obvious disadvantages. This leaves two major solutions.

A family room, particularly if it is located off the kitchen or outside the children's bedrooms, can be an ideal play space during the day, transformed into a general group leisure area in the evening. A truly multipurpose space, the family room can provide for changing needs as children grow. Furnishings in a family room are generally less "formal" and more durable than those in the living room and may be dual-purpose for greater flexibility. Too, such rooms often serve for storage of games and sporting gear and frequently house the television set and other audio-visual equipment.

The children's bedrooms themselves or an adjacent area may make excellent play spaces since they already are (or should be) planned for the children to make into their own territories. A widened bedroom hallway can be both economical and efficient; the bedrooms might open into a multipurpose room or combine with each other to provide a space large enough for a playroom, library, museum, and hobby center as well as a study and retreat for teens who need privacy and sound control.

Although it is desirable to have a children's play space within the home, many small houses and apartments cannot offer even a modest area that meets the above criteria. This limitation is one of the reasons for the inclusion of community leisure facilities in large-scale housing developments, a feature that is becoming ever more popular. Such public entertainment spaces very often serve adults as well as children.

Dining

Eating is a lively part of group living, for meals are often one of the few daily events that bring an entire household together with a single purpose. Entertainment of friends almost always involves the consumption of food, ranging from snacks to multicourse dinners. Nearly every society recognizes the offering of food as the standard token of hospitality to guests.

The traditional multipurpose house with single-purpose rooms, common in the United States through the early part of this century, generally set aside one enclosed space called *dining room* in which all meals with the possible exception of breakfast were taken. Frequently, this room had no purpose other than dining. Even today many families enjoy the specialness of a separate dining room that creates a particular atmosphere for meals. However, with increasing interest in flexible space, fewer and fewer households are willing to set aside for eating a completely isolated space that will be used for only about three hours or less a day.

Just how open or closed the dining space should be depends in large part on the amount of room available and on the lifestyle of the household. In many homes, instead of one totally separated dining room, there are two or more dining spaces that merge into other areas and that can be used as circumstances indicate (Plate 6, p. 73). Common examples include the living-dining area in an open-plan home and eating space provided in kitchens or family rooms.

Dining Needs

When planning dining situations, we need to consider the requirements for eating in general, the specific needs for meals of different types, and finally the individual living patterns of the household. The essentials are:

- **Access** from the kitchen for ease in serving and clearing, and on the same floor level as the kitchen for convenience and safety. Easy access from other social spaces is also advantageous for both guests and family members.
- **Surfaces** on which to put food and utensils, usually 27 to 30 inches high, but lower when indicated or desired. The age and physical condition of various group members are important here: limber young people can be happy at low tables that would be uncomfortable for many older people; small children are safer and more content at child-size tables. Each place setting requires a space 2 feet wide and 16 inches deep.
- **Seats** giving comfortable, usually upright support, such as chairs, stools, built-in or movable benches (banquettes), scaled to the height of the table. Chairs with arms can assist the elderly or disabled in sitting and rising from the table.

above left: 3-20 In a housing complex geared toward families with young children, rugged outdoor play areas and equipment are a necessity. A play sculpture of heavy wooden beams at various heights and set in a sand base allows young imaginations free rein and is virtually indestructible. Fisher-Friedman Associates, architects. *(Photograph: Joshua Freiwald)*

above right: 3-21 A community "playspace" for adults complements that intended for children. Here the swimming pool is adjacent to a clubhouse. Fisher-Friedman Associates, architects. *(Photograph: Joshua Freiwald)*

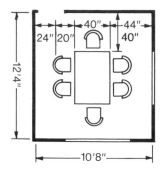

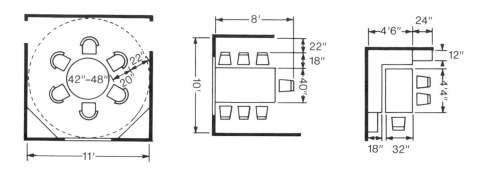

far left: 3-22 A rectangular table in the center of the room requires space for access and circulation all around.

second from left: 3-23 A round table in the center of the room requires less space than the rectangle seating the same number of people.

second from right: 3-24 A rectangular table with one short side placed against a wall can seat an additional person in still less total area.

far right: 3-25 A table placed for built-in seating along two sides seats six in the least amount of space but limits accessibility.

- **Light,** natural and artificial, that illumines food, table, and people without glare. Too strong light in a downward direction on diners' faces is very unflattering; softer light in an upward direction such as candlelight is more becoming.
- **Ventilation** free of drafts.

To these essentials we must quickly add that *convenience to kitchen and dish storage* saves energy, *freedom from excessive noise* calms nerves and helps digestion, and *pleasant surroundings and table settings* raise spirits.

Many dining areas allow little choice in arranging furnishings. The table is usually placed in the center with a cabinet or buffet for storage against the longest wall. A storage wall between kitchen and dining area, accessible to both, is very efficient. Corner cupboards provide storage and display space in small rooms. Where space is limited, a round or oval table will free more floor space and seat people more easily than a rectangular table of the same outside dimensions. Chairs that are wider in front than in back often unnecessarily take up too much space around the table. Figures 3-22 through 3-25 illustrate the amount of space required for six people in various dining arrangements. A wall-hung shelf or counter can suffice for serving or eating in cramped quarters (Fig. 3-26).

Remember that people need space too: 24 inches by 16 inches when seated at the table, with 20 inches of leg room under the table. Figure 3-27 shows the access space that people need for serving and dining. Figures 3-28 and 3-29 show standard sizes of rectangular and round tables, indicating the number of people they can accommodate.

left: 3-26 A counter eating space is usually limited to informal, quick dining. Drawing by Robert L. Keiser. *(Adapted with permission of the Macmillan Company from* Housing: An Environment for Living, *p. 175. © 1978 by Marjorie Branin Keiser)*

right: 3-27 Space required to access a dining table. *(Keiser,* Housing, *p. 171)*

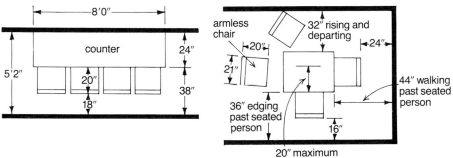

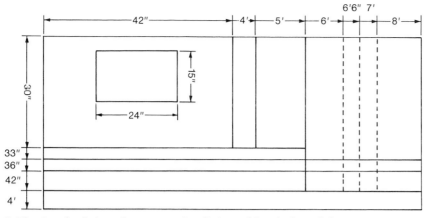

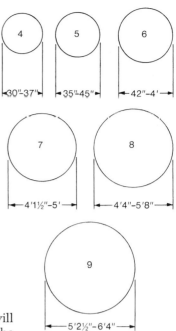

3-28 Standard sizes for rectangular dining tables. (*Adapted from* Nomadic Furniture)

3-29 Standard sizes for round dining tables. The figure in the center shows the number of people who can be accommodated comfortably by each. (*Adapted from* Nomadic Furniture)

Dining Patterns

In many homes a variety of eating patterns prevail, but usually one will predominate, sometimes at different times of the day: a short breakfast at the kitchen counter as members start the day one by one; snacks during the day, often in front of the television set; and perhaps a leisurely sit-down dinner where the day's events are discussed.

Sit-Down Meals Because they traditionally represent the ideal norm, family sit-down meals deserve first attention. For these there should be one adequately large, relatively permanent space planned so that the table can be prepared, the seating arranged, the meal served and eaten, and the table cleared with minimum interference to and from other activities (Plate 6, p. 73). The dining area may answer these criteria and yet remain integrated with the rest of the group space, flowing easily into kitchen and/or living space with only partial seclusion from other activi-

3-30 In a renovated schoolhouse apartment, the dining area can easily expand into the open space under the stairway when the number of guests increases. Siris/Coombs, architects. (*Photograph:* © *Karen Bussolini*)

81

below left: 3-31 A separate dining room provides a fresh and pleasant area specifically designed for serving and eating meals. In this room built-in cupboards hold tableware and linen and act as serving counters. A small breakfast for one or two would be delightful in the bay window. Judith Chaffee, architect; Christina A. Bloom, interior designer. *(Photograph: © Ezra Stoller/ ESTO)*

below right: 3-32 The serving cupboards pivot 90 degrees to open the dining area to the living room.

ties. The household that entertains frequently with rather formal dinners may want a completely separate dining space that can be screened from living-room view during setting and clearing and is protected from kitchen odors and noises.

Important events involving the extended family may occur infrequently, and the necessary space can rarely be reserved for them alone. This suggests a dining area with at least one side opening to another part of the house or to the out-of-doors, permitting the celebration area to extend as the number of participants increases.

Buffet Meals Buffet meals simplify the labor of serving food and make it possible to use the entire group space for eating, all of which can lead to a lively informality. If buffet meals are to be handled often and successfully, cafeteria procedures suggest a number of guidelines: good carrying trays, not-too-precious dishes and glassware, service counters near the kitchen, traffic paths that avoid collisions between tray-laden people, convenient places to sit and to rest the food. The dining space in Figures 3-31 and 3-32 would serve well for buffet meals, since it opens to both the outside deck and the living room. Built-in buffet cupboards on one side of the dining area pivot 90 degrees to merge the living and dining spaces.

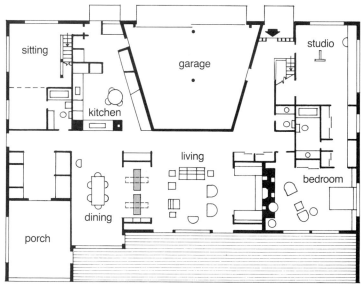

below: 3-33 A dining space can perform several functions. In this house it is used for circulation, but the placement of the table off to one side and linked to a built-in bench would also encourage its emergence as a secondary group-gathering spot. Huygens and DiMella, Inc., architects. *(Photograph: Lisanti, Inc.)*

5

Snacks and Quick Meals Some families rarely eat "meals" at all but rather maintain a lifestyle that calls for a series of snacks or fast foods, for one or a few people, at frequent intervals throughout the day. When members of the household function on different time schedules, mealtimes will inevitably vary. The primary goals in planning space for eating, then, will be speed and economy of effort, but a minimum of interference with other activities is also important. Counters and stools adjacent to the cooking area of the kitchen often work well. A small dining table and chairs near a supplementary quick-meal preparation unit such as a microwave oven can be most helpful in reducing congestion in the kitchen proper. Small, collapsible TV tables can be useful elsewhere in the house.

Small Children's Meals A central part of family life, the meals consumed by small children represent an educational situation that is often poorly handled. We might as well acknowledge that eating is both an adventure and a problem for small children. They will play and experiment as well as eat. Common sense suggests providing a place—preferably in the kitchen, playroom, or family room—with durable, easy-to-clean surfaces where spilled or scattered food does not precipitate a crisis. But at an early age children want to eat with adults and quite rightly object to conditions midway between those for grownups and those for household pets. Again, the design of the house, as well as the way it is finished and furnished, strongly affects the way this problem can be handled.

Because dining space functions for only short periods during the day, many newer houses are designed in such a way that the dining area has a dual role. For example, in a small remodeled house in Georgetown (Plate 7, p. 74), the dining space is also a library, with a bookcase wall and a table serving for reading or study when it is not needed for meals. In a New Hampshire vacation house (Fig. 3-33) dining space has been created in what is essentially a widened hallway connecting the living room and the kitchen. Between meals it would be a likely spot for games or just sitting and talking on the comfortable built-in banquette.

Planning Social Spaces

After considering the character and demands of specific social activities, it is obvious that many social activities occur in more than one part of the home and result in different levels of noise and movement. Planning for the social spaces demands that everyone's needs and desires be considered and realized insofar as possible. If the spaces are designed to elicit positive emotional reactions, what environmental psychologist Albert Mehrabian calls *approach behavior*, rather than the negative

3-34 A living room filled with personal mementos and art objects projects a warm invitation to enter and explore. Peter Stamberg, architect. *(Photograph: © Paul Warchol/ESTO)*

83

avoidance behavior, they will draw people to them, enhance interaction, and can even improve the performance of tasks. Living areas will also be used more often if they provide a pleasurably stimulating atmosphere that allows the household members to feel in control, according to Mehrabian.[2] The steps suggested in Chapter 1 for creating a lifespace are applicable.

Location

Basically, two options present themselves in designing the living space for a home. It can be one large open area, suitable to a variety of purposes and used intensively

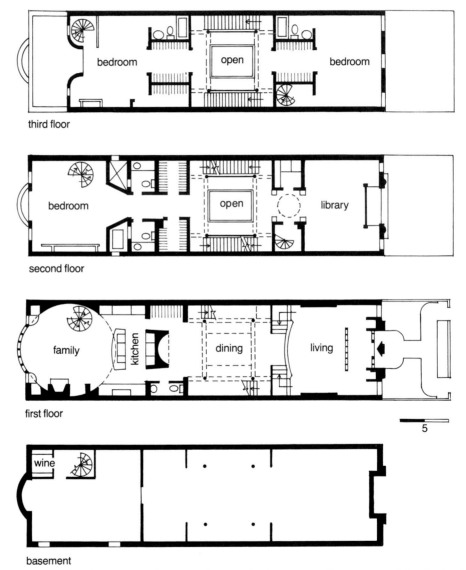

third floor

second floor

first floor

5

basement

3-35 A family room on the same floor as the living room but separated by the kitchen and dining area allows for interaction or separation as desired. Booth/Hansen & Associates, architects.

by all members of the household, or the total space may be subdivided into a series of smaller spaces, each suitable for a particular range of activities.

The converted barn illustrated in Plate 8 (p. 74) obviously chooses the former point of view. Spacious, airy, and open, this group space functions as sitting room, entertainment center, music room, and game room; it flows easily up onto the balcony studio and into the library. Nevertheless, the space has been shaped imaginatively to partially segregate various activities. Exposed wood beams serve visually to break up the space and demarcate certain areas; the placement and orientation of furniture cause it to fall into several natural groupings; and positioning the studio on a balcony isolates it from the rest of the space both physically and psychologically to allow for a great measure of privacy.

For many homes today, two separate group spaces seem the only way to meet the needs of differing age or activity groups and maintain a degree of civilization. The first, of course, is what for the last century has been called the living room—a portion of the home intended as the main social area. But in the second half of the century the need of a second discrete social space came to the fore. Originally considered as a device to keep the living room neat and clean, such areas (called family rooms, playrooms, recreation rooms, media rooms, or multipurpose rooms) have increasingly become alternative spaces for group living. As a rule they are informal and easily maintained. They can be partially visible extensions of the main group space but work best when they have the potential for total segregation. Typically, such rooms provide for children's or adults' play and possibly for hobbies. They are ideal locations for television, radios, games, and both live and recorded music. Family rooms often adjoin the kitchen for ease in serving informal meals or snacks, or they may be near children's bedrooms to provide overflow space for their play. Easy access to the outdoors is highly desirable.

Room Shapes and Sizes

Engineer Ernest Weidhaas advises that "there is no such thing as an average, or standard, or even ideal, size or shape for a room. Design a size and shape that will best meet the requirements of function, aesthetics, and economy."[3] Architects and designers begin with minimum or average room sizes and a knowledge of good proportion, then plan spaces according to how and by whom and for what they will be used.

Most rooms are rectangular with width and length approximating a ratio of 2:3. (Proportion is discussed in Chapter 9.) Another shape based on the rectangle is the popular L, often used for combined activity areas such as living-dining. Square shapes are difficult to arrange furniture in, as are long narrow rooms that may seem like corridors. However, much can be done to alter apparent size and shape through furnishing, light, and color. Arrangement of space can be more important than amount; well-planned multipurpose spaces can functionally surpass the individual rooms often found in the larger homes of years past; open plans contribute to an illusion of space by combining activity areas, while large window areas and outdoor living spaces appear to expand space to the outdoors. More specific information regarding perceptual space can be found in Part II, Design. From the beginning it is important to realize that perceptual space consists not only of physical space but also of visual and acoustical space that may contribute as much to psychological well-being as actual square footage.[4]

The size of social spaces may be strongly affected by family values in the areas of aesthetics, leisure, and social prestige. Many people want the living room to be the largest and best-furnished room in their home. Generally, the more occupants to the household, the more space devoted to personal and/or leisure activities. This rule of thumb directly increases the relative size of social and private zones while the service areas remain fairly constant in size.[5] Reduced workweeks and household labor-saving devices also increase leisure space needs. Federal agencies such as the Public Housing Authority and the U.S. Department of Housing and Urban Development recommend minimum sizes for some rooms, but average sizes are usually considerably larger. The figures in Table 2-2 are only a starting point. Each room should be planned with its specific purpose in mind; size is interdependent with function and psychological space needs.

The many details discussed in this chapter are important, but they should not obscure major goals, which focus on basic human values. The social quarters of any home should give each person who lives in it a sense of belonging in the household group and encourage each to play a supportive but unconstrained role in the family pattern. Each individual deserves the opportunity to express personal aptitudes, feelings, and desires. In short, a successful group space should promote the security, self-realization, and socialization of each member of the family.

Notes to the Text

1. Robert Sommer, *Personal Space: The Behavioral Basis of Design* (Englewood Cliffs, NJ: Prentice-Hall, 1969), pp. 66–67.
2. Albert Mehrabian, *Public Places and Private Spaces: The Psychology of Work, Play, and Living Environments* (New York: Basic Books, 1976), pp. 5–7, chaps. 2 and 3.
3. Ernest R. Weidhaas, *Architectural Drafting and Design*, 4th ed. (Boston: Allyn and Bacon, 1981), p. 139.
4. Gail Lynn Hartwigsen, *Design Concepts: A Basic Guidebook* (Boston: Allyn and Bacon, 1980), p. 25.
5. Marjorie Branin Keiser, *Housing: An Environment for Living* (New York: Macmillan, 1978), p. 123.

References for Further Reading

Family Housing Handbook. Ames: Iowa State University, Midwest Plan Service, 1971.

Keiser, Marjorie Branin. *Housing: An Environment for Living*. New York: Macmillan, 1978. Chap. 11, pp. 199–204.

Packard, Robert T. (ed.). *Ramsey/Sleeper Architectural Graphic Standards*, 7th ed. New York: Wiley, 1981.

Panero, Julius and Martin Zelnik. *Human Dimensions and Interior Space: A Source Book of Design Reference Standards*. New York: Whitney Library of Design, 1979.

Spence, William P. *Architecture: Design, Engineering, Drawing*, 3rd ed. Bloomington, IL: McKnight Publishing Company, 1979. Pp. 30–37, 68–71.

Weidhaas, Ernest R. *Architectural Drafting and Design*, 4th ed. Boston: Allyn and Bacon, 1981. Chap. 19.

Work Spaces

4

Those areas of a home responsible for the maintenance of daily living—for the stocking and preparation of food, the care and perhaps fabrication of clothing, the physical upkeep of the home, the storage of equipment—can be termed *support spaces* in the sense that they nurture the individuals and the lifestyle that takes place within the home. Group spaces and private spaces would exist in a vacuum if they were not supported by the work areas of the home. The kitchen—the major work center—provides bodily sustenance, and often emotional sustenance as well when it serves as the principal gathering point for family members. Depending upon the requirements of the household, work spaces may also include facilities for laundry, sewing, record-keeping and paying bills, potting plants, and different types of shopwork or hobbies as well as various storage needs. Taken together, these areas constitute the foundation on which life in the home rests. Both the tasks and the people who perform them need to be considered when the work space is designed.

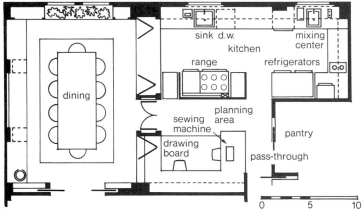

above: 4-1 An extravagant kitchen designed to the last detail according to the specifications of two master cooks provides the most efficient working spaces possible for preparation of all manner of foods. It incorporates a sewing area and office and also serves as the major entertainment center for the household. Donald Mallow, architect. *(Photograph: © Norman McGrath)*

left: 4-2 The plan shows how various work centers have been arranged to allow for a smooth progression of activities.

Kitchens

The kitchen is usually the control center for the household. In addition to providing a place for food preparation, eating, planning, and sometimes laundry, the kitchen is often the most lived-in room in the home and a room that can sell a house. It is initially the most expensive room to complete and is the most remodeled room as well. Remodeling the kitchen is often a good investment because it increases the value of an older home while money spent to remodel other rooms may not. A rule

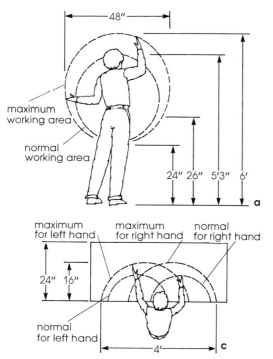

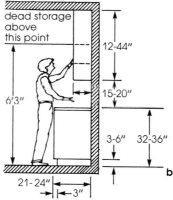

4-3 Kitchen dimensions should be based on the height and reach of the person who will use the room most. The dimensions given in these drawings are for the average individual.

of thumb suggests spending approximately 10 percent of the value of the home or the price of a new car when remodeling a kitchen.[1]

Few areas of the home have received such intensive study as the kitchen. Manufacturers continually redesign standard appliances and equipment to make them more efficient, more attractive, and thus more desirable to potential buyers. Research conducted by home economists, Cornell University, the University of Illinois, and the U.S. Department of Agriculture, among others, has provided designers with many facts, figures, and formulas that offer assistance in organizing the physical layout of work areas.[2] Studies have focused on the use and efficiency of facilities, performance of tasks, the design and placement of work centers, and the relationship of work centers to each other as well as to changing lifestyles. Three concepts of functional planning have emerged from the research:

- The **physical limitations** of the principal cook or cooks should be a major determinant in achieving an energy-saving, comfortable working environment.
- The kitchen is best organized around **work centers** that incorporate appropriate appliances with sufficient storage and work surfaces and that are arranged in logical sequences.
- The principle of **first use** —of storing items where they are needed rather than by category— fosters efficiency.

These findings say little about how a kitchen should look, but deal only in efficiency and comfort. Coupled with standard appliance and cabinet sizes (Table 4–1), they can serve as a foundation for planning the work areas of the room. The emphasis here is on *work*: physical exertion. People will work in the kitchen; the kitchen must work for *them*. Design efficiency is particularly important for busy working people. We must bear in mind, however, that functionalism and aesthetics need not be incompatible. The most efficient kitchen can also be beautiful.

Table 4–1 Standard Kitchen Appliance and Cabinet Sizes*

	Small				Large		
	Height	*Depth*	*Width*		*Height*	*Depth*	*Width*
cooktop (built-in)		21" x	26"	to		21" x	36"
range (cooktop at 36")	43" x	24" x	20"	to	66" x	25" x	40"
oven (built-in)**	27" x	21" x	22½"	to	42" x	21" x	24"
microwave oven	9" x	12½" x	18½"	to	15½" x	21" x	24"
refrigerator	52" x	24" x	20"	to	66" x	29" x	30"
refrigerator-freezer	65" x	29" x	31"	to	66" x	29" x	60"
freezer	33" x	25" x	42"	to	66" x	29" x	33"
dishwasher (built-in)					35" x	24" x	24"
dishwasher (portable)					38" x	28" x	24"
clothes washer	42" x	25" x	25"	to	45" x	28" x	29"
clothes dryer	42" x	25" x	27"	to	45" x	28" x	31"
ironing board	30" x	44" x	11"	to	36" x	54" x	14"
trash compactor					36" x	24" x	15"
sink	(single)	20" x	24"	to	(double)	22" x	33"
cabinets, base	30" x	25" x	15"	to	36" x	25" x	30"
cabinets, wall	12" x	6" x	15"	to	30" x	13" x	30"

*Larger sizes are available for special installations. Dimensions do not include an allowance of 3 to 5 inches
 clearance behind large motored appliances and ranges.
**Cut-out space needed for single and double units.

Physical Limitations

4-4 This kitchen system is engineered specifically to address the needs of the disabled. For full access from a wheelchair, the counter top is 28 or 32 inches high rather than the standard 36 inches and upper cabinets are limited to a single reachable tier. *(Courtesy Dwyer Products)*

In general, physical limitations vary with a person's height; to conserve human energy, we should consider normal work curves when planning the dimensions of counters and cupboards or the placement of storage and appliances within reach at each work center. Of critical importance in work comfort is the distance between elbow and work surface. Most tasks can be performed easily on a counter that is 3 inches below the level of the elbow (with the upper arm vertical and the forearm horizontal to the floor). But when a particular chore—like beating or chopping—requires force, a work surface 6 or 7 inches below elbow height serves better. This suggests that not all counters in the kitchen should be at the same level. Kitchens are usually designed for the average person; it is up to the designer to adapt or refit standard cabinets and appliances to the individual user when desirable or necessary.

Plate 9 A kitchen can be an exciting and stimulating place to work, bright with color, as is this kitchen-dining area designed by architect Alfredo De Vido. *(Photograph: © Peter Aaron/ESTO)*

Plate 10 The striking blue wall on one side of this kitchen picks up the unusual blue color of the sink. Claude Stoller, architect. *(Photograph: © Ezra Stoller/ESTO)*

above: Plate 11 A cheerful, comfortable bedroom follows an Early American theme with its exposed cedar beams, antique furniture, and collection of handmade patchwork quilts. (*Courtesy* American Home Magazine)

left: Plate 12 A variety of textures prevents monotony in a monochromatic design. Careful placement of color areas keeps them from becoming overwhelming. Michael Sands, architect; Cindi Sands, designer. (*Photograph: Philip L. Molten*)

The Work Centers

The design of work centers and the sequence in which they are arranged determines how smoothly a kitchen functions and how much energy will be expended in everyday tasks. Each work center should have adjacent counter and cabinet space. The centers may be classified by the major appliance around which activities center or by the type of activities performed, whether in conjunction with a large major appliance or smaller, less basic ones. There are three primary centers, each containing a necessary major appliance; two supplementary work centers encompassing mix and serve activities, which are often combined with the primary areas; and several specialty centers that are found in some but not all kitchens for planning, quick-cooking, eating, storing additional food and equipment, or doing laundry. Work should progress continually forward from task to task, center to center, without backtracking, to save time and energy.

The **refrigerator/storage center** is placed either first or last in the work sequence—near the outside entrance and the sink for easy storage of food, or near the serving center and dining area for convenience of serving refrigerated items. In addition to the **refrigerator,** it should have:

- A **counter** at least 18 inches wide and about 36 inches high on the latch side of the refrigerator door for holding supplies. This often can be integrated with the counter space of adjacent centers.
- **Wall cabinets** to hold serving dishes for cold food and storage containers for foods going into the refrigerator. File space for trays often fits well here.
- A **base cabinet** with drawers for bottle openers, refrigerator and freezer supplies, and bottle storage.

The refrigerator itself should not be placed within 15 inches of a corner, beside a wall, or next to a line of cabinets because the door usually needs to be free if it is to open more than 90 degrees for removal of shelves and crispers. So that it doesn't interrupt the flow of counter work space, the refrigerator is often placed at the open end of a line of cabinets, always opening on the side toward the counter.

The refrigerator center often incorporates a **freezer,** although a larger freezer can be placed in a storage or utility room, basement, or garage. With a side-by-side refrigerator/freezer, 18 inches of counter space beside the freezer is also desirable when possible. A pantry, which is often considered a specialty storage center, may also be included in this work center.

The **sink/clean-up center** is indeed multipurpose, serving to wash fruits and vegetables, dishes, and children's hands, and providing water for mixing, cooking, freezing, and drinking. The sink center is often located between the cook-

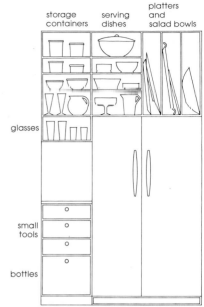

storage containers   serving dishes   platters and salad bowls

glasses

small tools

bottles

4-5 The refrigerator and adjacent counter and storage space make up one of the major kitchen work centers.

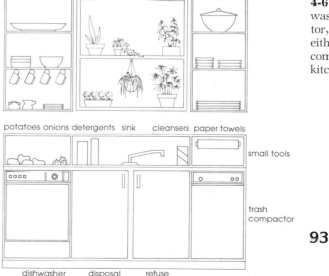

potatoes onions detergents   sink   cleansers paper towels

small tools

dishwasher   disposal   refuse

trash compactor

4-6 The sink(s), dishwasher, and trash compactor, as well as counters on either side and cabinets, comprise the most-used kitchen work center.

93

ing and the mixing centers, since its proximity to both is desirable and it is involved in both the beginning and the end of kitchen activities. Since 40 to 47 percent of all kitchen activities take place here, the sink center is often the first center to be positioned to ensure its central convenience.[3] This center needs:

- A **sink** or **sinks,** probably the most important piece of equipment in the kitchen by virtue of frequency and variety of use. Double sinks facilitate hand dishwashing, but they may be too small for large cooking pans. With a dishwasher, a single large sink often suffices. Two separated sinks are especially convenient when more than one person uses the kitchen. For comfort, the sink should be about 3 inches below elbow height and not more than 3 inches back from the front edge of the counter.
- **Counters** on both sides—at least 30 inches wide on the left for draining or stacking clean dishes, 36 inches wide on the right for stacking dirty dishes, and usually 36 inches high—with at least one of them a waterproof drainboard. The left and right side measurements may be reversed according to direction of work flow.
- A **dishwasher,** which will generally be easier to use if it is placed to the left of the sink for right-handed users and to the right for left-handed users. However, the location of dish storage must also be considered. The 24-inch counter width above a front-opening dishwasher is adequate for stacking dishes. Do not position the dishwasher at an immediate right angle to the sink; 18 to 24 inches is needed from the corner for standing space when the door is opened.
- **Cabinet space** for those items generally used at the sink—utensils for cleaning, cutting, and straining food; dish cloths and towels, soaps and detergents. Many people find it convenient to store near this center the foods that need peeling or washing or require water in their preparation, a miscellany ranging from potatoes and onions to coffee and dried fruits.
- **Provision for garbage and trash,** with a food waste disposer and possibly a **trash compactor.**
- A **stool** and **knee space,** which lessen the labor of cleaning vegetables and dishes, especially when conservation of human energy is a factor.
- **Light** directly over the sink.

A **hot-water heater** and **water softener** may also be considered clean-up-center appliances. A water heater may be installed beneath the sink to supply near-boiling tap water for the preparation of instant foods and drinks.

The **cook center** becomes the busiest area of the kitchen during the half hour or so before meals, accounting for approximately 22 to 29 percent of all kitchen activities.[4] A location near the sink, mixing, and serving centers and convenient to the eating space is most desirable. The cook center should include:

4-7 Cooking units, ovens, ventilation systems, counter tops, and storage cabinets form the cook center.

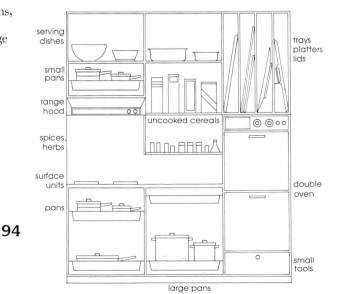

serving dishes

trays platters lids

small pans

range hood

uncooked cereals

spices, herbs

surface units

double oven

pans

small tools

large pans

- Gas, electric, or magnetic reactance (induction) **surface units** incorporated into a range or installed in a heat-resistant counter. Range tops are almost uniformly 36 inches high, but surface components can be installed on counters of whatever height the cook prefers. Usually, this would mean 3 inches below elbow height, but if the typical cuisine demands much stirring of sauces or use of a portable mixer, 6 or 7 inches below elbow height is more comfortable. The cooking unit should be at least 12 inches from a window and 9 inches from an adjacent corner cabinet for safety.

- A **heat-resistant counter** 24 inches wide and usually 36 inches high on at least one side of the surface units and built-in wall ovens. For safety, counter surfaces on both sides of the range are best with 12 inches the minimum for the second side. A 15-inch counter or cabinet should separate the range from a kitchen doorway or traffic path.

- An **oven** or **ovens,** either as part of the range or separate from the cooking surface. **Single ovens** below the surface units make a compact cook center, but access requires bending over. Many ranges incorporate a **built-in second oven** above the surface units, and this can be a desirable feature provided it presents no hazard to head and eyes. This arrangement, however, does not leave sufficient space for such oversize vessels as canning kettles and large soup pots and may position the oven racks above convenient view and reach. **Built-in wall ovens** should not interrupt the flow of counter space, although they need an adjacent counter area; they are best positioned so that the opened door is between 1 and 7 inches below elbow height for safety and convenience. A **microwave oven** for quick cooking of certain foods may be located in the cooking center or elsewhere, perhaps in the mix center, serve center, or quick-cook specialty center. Oven doors should not open into traffic at the end of a line of cabinets or into a corner.

- **Wall cabinets** nearby for cooking utensils, small appliances, and seasonings. A 24- to 30-inch open vertical space is required between the range top and the bottom of any wall cabinet above it.

- **Ventilation** provided by a quiet exhaust fan over or within the cook surface.

- **Light** directly over the cook surface.

In many homes, the availability of new equipment has caused the cook center to explode into two or more smaller components. A kitchen might have, for example, a **quick-cook center** in addition to the major cooking area. Quick-cook apparatus could include a microwave or convection oven, an electric broiler-oven, electric skillet, gas or electric barbecue, and a whole array of other small plug-in appliances. With the addition of a small sink and two or more surface units, even an undercounter refrigerator, this unit becomes totally self-contained. If it is properly arranged, a person working in this center would not interfere in the least with the activities of another cook in the major cooking area.

The **supplemental mix center** handles all kinds of mixing, from breads and pastries to salads and casseroles. It might be located between the sink and the refrigerator (which holds many mix-first items) or next to the cook center. The mix center should include:

- A **counter** at least 36 inches wide; if combined with another center a width of 48 to 54 inches is needed. If considerable time is spent in mixing, knee space and a stool could be provided, and a counter top at a height comfortable for the principal cook. Often this will be 30 to 32 inches high (in contrast to the standard 36-inch height), although a pull-out cutting/rolling board at this height may suffice.

- Sufficient **electrical outlets** for small appliances—mixers, blenders, and food processors.

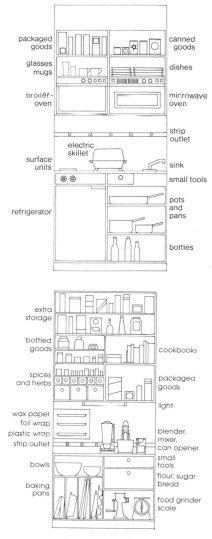

top: **4-8** Small or portable appliances compactly arranged can form a secondary quick-cook center. bottom: **4-9** The mix center, often located between two of the major work centers, contains counter space and storage cabinets.

4-10 The mix center of the kitchen shown in Figures 4-1 and 4-2 has special bins for dry ingredients and a marble top slightly lower than the adjacent counter for rolling pastry. *(Photograph: © Norman McGrath)*

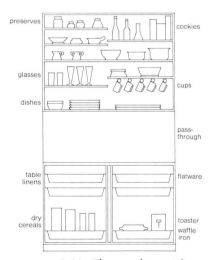

4-11 The supplemental serve center is primarily a storage area with some counter space for collecting dishes and mealtime accessories.

- **Wall cabinets** to store condiments, packaged foods, and cookbooks.
- **Base cabinets** with drawers for small tools and either drawers or sliding shelves for bowls, pans, and heavy items used in mixing.
- **Light** directly over the work surface.

The oven is often located within or next to the mix center for baking convenience. Specially designed storage spaces for flour, sugar, and bread as well as for small appliances such as mixers and food processors will often be included in the wall or base cabinets of this center. Some 11 to 15 percent of kitchen activities take place in the mix center.

The **serve center** holds those items that go directly from storage to table—dishes and flatware, linens and accessories, possibly toasters and waffle irons, and such condiments as sugar and catsup. Often integrated with either the cook or the refrigerator center, it should be near the eating area and should have:

- A durable **counter** at least 24 inches wide and from 30 to 36 inches high, perhaps with a pass-through to facilitate serving. When combined with another center, the widest counter should be used, with 12 inches added to it.
- Ample **cabinet space** designed for the items to be stored. If the serve center is located between the kitchen and the dining area, cabinet space might well be accessible from either side. This space usually must be supplemented by cupboard space in the dining area or by a pantry.

Besides these centers, a **storage wall** or **pantry** serves to accommodate extra supplies and is especially necessary if wall-cabinet space over counters is lost to windows and ovens. It should be near the refrigerator/storage center. **Cleaning equipment** and **supplies** need a well-planned closet either in the kitchen or in the laundry. A **planning center** may include a place to sit down to make shopping lists, and for cookbook storage and a telephone. A minimum of 30 inches in width

is needed, located outside the work areas. A **kitchen eating area** may consist of counter space (29 inches high for chairs, 40 inches high for stools, a minimum of 24 inches wide by 15 inches deep per person) or a table with built-in seating or chairs. The table should be located conveniently for serving but at least 48 inches from a base cabinet front and 60 inches from a major appliance front.

Storage Space in the Work Centers

The principle of first use assumes primary importance in organizing storage space for the work centers. The cook will conserve time and energy if items are stored where they will be needed, rather than putting all similar things—bowls or sharp knives, for example—in one place.

The *amount* of storage space in the work centers is a critical factor in their design. Research in this field indicates that the sizes given for counter space in each of the five work centers will ensure enough storage space for the average kitchen if wall and base cabinets are placed above and below the counters. When windows, range, or corners cut into these figures, compensating space should be provided elsewhere. If the work centers are placed alongside one another, all counters between appliances can be eliminated *except the largest counter, which then should be made 1 foot wider than usual.* According to these formulas, the counter space provided by the work centers totals at least 10 lineal feet. Accessible frontage for base and wall cabinets is lessened by installation of appliances and hard-to-reach locations (in corners and above 72 inches). Recommended standards from The Small Homes Council at the University of Illinois are 6 feet minimum and 15 feet maximum total counter frontage to prevent either too cramped to too excessive distances between centers.[5] Each set of dinnerware for twelve demands an extra 4 feet of wall cabinet space beyond the 6-foot minimum for service for four.

Equally important, the *quality* of the storage space deserves careful consideration of when and how objects will be used and who will use them:

- **Visibility** suggests storing items (except for such identical articles as tumblers) only one row deep. Ideally, canned goods and condiments should be shelved in this manner to facilitate finding a particular item.
- **Accessibility** indicates putting the most frequently used items at the most convenient height, heavy objects below, and those seldom used above. Drawers in base cabinets are more accessible than fixed shelves; pull-out shelves are intermediate in convenience. Space located above the maximum reach of a given person can be considered dead storage since a stool or ladder would be required to reach articles kept there. For accessibility of often-used items, the top shelf should be within 72 inches of the floor.
- **Flexibility** will be enhanced by adjustable shelves and drawers with removable dividers, which can adapt to changing family needs and design of kitchen tools.
- **Maintenance** generally recommends enclosed storage, but items that are used daily may be kept on open shelves.

Placement of the Work Centers

The cardinal principle of work-center organization is appropriateness to the desires and work habits of those using the kitchen most intensively. For most situations, four general planning principles are basic.

Location of the work centers usually starts with placing the sink, since it is used most, in the most desirable location (perhaps under a window) with the other centers located around it according to the busiest paths between them (the work triangle discussed below). Work should progress from storing to preparing to serving food in a constantly forward-moving direction with as little backtracking as possible. The normal sequence of work is counterclockwise from refrigerator to sink to range for a right-handed person but it can be reversed. Traffic in and around the work centers should be limited to that connected with preparing meals, with miscellaneous traffic diverted elsewhere.

Distances between counters or walls and appliances that face each other should be a minimum of 40 inches for one worker (48 inches for two, or a more liberal 60 inches), and between counter and breakfast table at least 48 inches. Distances between work centers are best kept short and the routes as direct as possible while still allowing for the necessary counters and storage.

The **traffic routes** between the three primary work-center appliances form the efficiency experts' *work triangle*, the perimeter of which should not exceed 22 feet nor be less than 13 feet. Each segment or leg should be at least 4 feet in length to avoid crowding and insufficient storage space. The shortest of the three legs is the most traveled path, from sink to range; it should not exceed 6 feet. The maximum distance from refrigerator to sink is 7 feet, and from refrigerator to range, the least traveled route, the maximum is 9 feet.

The **standard arrangements** for work centers fall into four categories: *one wall (Pullman, or strip)*, *corridor (or galley)*, **L**-*shape*, and **U**-*shape*. The efficient **L**- and **U**-shaped kitchen plans began with home economists who analyzed the steps necessary in meal preparation and the backtracking required, then applied time-motion studies from industry to work out the best way to eliminate unnecessary steps and wasted energy. At times, an island is added to shield the work space from view or to supplement it, or a peninsula may be used to divide an open kitchen from the adjoining space. Although most kitchens relate basically to one of these four types, those designed to meet individual needs may differ markedly from standard practice.

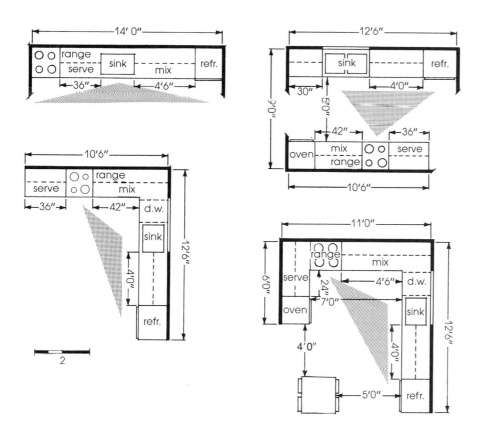

Designing the Kitchen

In planning the physical layout of the kitchen, the *subtraction method* is useful. The width of each cabinet or appliance used is subtracted from the total space available until all space is used to best advantage. The size or placement of appliances is adjusted so standard sized cabinets can be used with no more than a single 3-inch filler in any given space. Costs can be held down by using stock dimensions for cabinets and appliances. The sink/clean-up center is placed first, then corner cabinets, the range, and the base and wall cabinets between. The refrigerator is located at the end of a run of cabinets (or the broom closet at the end, next to the refrigerator) with base and then wall cabinets filled in back to the sink.[6]

Some kitchens are planned for maximum efficiency, others with children foremost in mind, some for two-cook (or more) families, others for households that do almost no cooking. At one end of the spectrum we might find the enormous, professionally equipped kitchen in which domestic employees do most of the work, at the other the modular unit that makes an instant kitchen wherever it is placed. In every case the lifestyle of the particular family will determine the major factors in kitchen planning. However, to be functional, kitchen planning must take into consideration location within the home, size, shape, placement of doors and windows, lighting, and maintenance in addition to the previously discussed arrangement of equipment and work centers.

Location

A kitchen placed at the shortest feasible distance from indoor and outdoor eating and entertainment areas, as well as from the garage and service areas, will save steps. Further, the kitchen should be convenient to the main entrance and to

top left: 4-14 One-wall kitchens can be fitted into alcoves and concealed with folding doors when not in use. They are available in complete prefabricated units and concentrate plumbing and wiring economically. However, if they contain standard-size appliances (rather than scaled-down "kitchenette" units) they require a great deal of walking.

top right: 4-15 Corridor arrangements decrease distances between work centers but invite unwelcome traffic when often-used doors are located at both ends.

bottom left: 4-16 L-shape plans also have somewhat less distance between centers than one-wall kitchens. They leave room for eating and laundry and divert miscellaneous traffic a little.

bottom right: 4-17 U-shape kitchens generally are the most compact and efficient. They have the further grace of almost eliminating bothersome intrusion.

below: 4-18 This minimal kitchen unit contains a sink, two cooking burners, an under-counter refrigerator-freezer, above and below storage cabinets, and a microwave oven on a full-width open shelf. It measures only 48 inches wide by 26 inches deep by 87 inches high. *(Courtesy Dwyer Products)*

any service entrance, and if possible not far from a lavatory. (The last of these often follows naturally, since many homes centralize plumbing to save expense.) It should be accessible to and from all parts of the home without being a thoroughfare. Access and traffic should be limited and kept in one part of the space to prevent interruption of the work flow. As long as these requirements are taken into account, there can be great freedom in placement, especially in a one-family home.

A pleasant view from kitchen windows is desirable, although in a multifamily or high-rise construction the economics of building often suggest interior placement in a service core that concentrates utilities.

Size

Size is determined not only by the number of persons using the kitchen and the amount of food prepared for family or guests but also by the kind and number of other activities that take place in the kitchen area. The space needed in a small home for food preparation alone should be at least 80 to 100 square feet, in larger homes it should not exceed 150 to 160 square feet. The addition of laundry or eating space and family, hobby, or relaxation areas may be necessary to maintain efficiency if the kitchen is oversized. Too large an area results in too great a distance between work centers; too small an area creates cramped spaces difficult to work in, particularly for more than one person. Open spaces with kitchens visible from living areas do not isolate the cook during meal preparation, an ideal time for the family and/or friends to interact.

4-19 This kitchen allows interaction between cook and guests or family members yet keeps observers out of the work area with a counter and places to sit. Robert A.M. Stern, architect. *(Photograph: © Peter Aaron/ESTO)*

Shape

Although typically rectangular, kitchens lend themselves to many other configurations. Experts generally agree, however, that a small food-preparation area requires fewer steps if its shape falls between that of a square and a rectangle with proportions of about 2:3.

Windows and Doors

Doors in kitchens are necessary evils—necessary as entrances and exits, evils because they take space, determine location of work centers, and invite miscellaneous traffic. The best solution is to keep doors to a minimum (no more than 2 or 3), set them as close together as possible, and locate no major work center between them. Of course, the overall design of a plan may make this ideal impossible.

Windows make kitchens light and pleasant as well as provide ventilation, but they do take space. Many people are more comfortable working in a kitchen that has some natural daylighting, perhaps a window over the sink that admits light and also gives an outlook. HUD/FHA minimum property standards specify a minimum window area totaling 10 percent of the floor area; a good kitchen has 15 percent, 20 to 30 percent is even better.[7] Two windows are desirable whenever possible for cross-ventilation and more balanced light.

Lighting

Architects have invented many ingenious ways of lighting kitchens. Sometimes small windows between counters and wall cabinets or high windows over

4-20 The entire ceiling in this kitchen is a glass skylight, bringing the outdoors inside. Plants add to this effect. David Shaw, architect. *(Photograph: Gordon H. Schenck, Jr.)*

101

the cabinets bring light in unexpected ways. Skylights illumine many interior kitchens without reducing wall cabinet space, and some rooms open over a counter wall to a windowed dining area. Among the most pleasant kitchens are those that lead directly to a garden or deck. However, care must be taken so the sun does not shine directly into the individual's eyes while he or she works. This problem can be prevented through initial planning and orientation, the addition of a roof overhang, plants, fences, or louvers to the exterior, or with interior window treatments.

Artificial lighting must also be planned in the design of kitchens. More light is required here than in any other room in the house. Both general lighting and task lighting over the work surfaces and the cooking and sink/clean-up centers must be provided in generous amounts. (Lighting is discussed in detail in Chapter 16.)

Maintenance

Kitchens require the most maintenance of any room in the house. They are noisy and the center of all housework. These factors suggest choosing shapes and materials for floors, counters, cupboards, walls, and ceilings with an eye to *resistance to wear*, *heat*, *dirt*, and *grease*; *ease of cleaning*, *sound control*, and *pleasantness* to sight and touch. Part III, Materials for Interiors, provides more information to aid in the selection of appropriate materials.

New lifestyles, new concepts of planning, and technological advances all play a role in transforming kitchens from necessary but dull and sterile work areas to cheerful, colorful centers for group living (Plates 9 and 10, p. 91). Whether brand-new and ultramodern or old and full of mellowed charm, a kitchen can happily reflect the tastes and character of its owners.

4-21 This kitchen provides pleasant space for a variety of activities, including typing. John F. Saladino, Inc., architects and interior designers. *(Photograph: © Peter Aaron/ ESTO)*

Utility Spaces

Undeniably, the kitchen is the most important service area in the home, and in some smaller houses and apartments it may serve as the *only* work space. But larger homes often delegate supplementary areas according to the particular needs of a given family. These may include provisions for laundry, sewing, shopwork, flower arranging or potting, and storage.

Laundry Facilities

Every week millions of pounds of clothing and household linens are washed in American homes. Three factors have altered the nature of this chore: the development of automatic washers and dryers; the trend toward bringing laundry equipment up from dark, inconvenient basements; and the evolution of fabrics that require minimum care. Provisions for home laundering range from a sink or washbasin in which small things can be rinsed out to a fully equipped separate laundry. Laundry planning will be affected by the size and age distribution of the household, the size of the home, and the attitude toward sending out laundry. If, for example, economy of time is more pressing than economy of money, a family may prefer to have the laundry dealt with by commercial services.

Laundry activities fall into four categories:

- **Receiving, sorting,** and **preparing,** steps that may require a 6-foot counter, a cart, sorting bins, or simply the top of the washer plus a sink or tub for presoaking
- **Washing,** which necessitates laundry tubs and/or an automatic washer as well as storage for supplies
- **Drying** in an automatic dryer or convenient drying yard, with some provision for drip-drying indoors
- **Finishing** and **ironing,** which require a 3- by 5-foot folding counter, an iron and ironing board or ironer, plus space to put finished laundry and, ideally, space and equipment for mending

In small houses and apartments, laundry space may be reduced to a minimum and compacted into the kitchen or a closet. Utility rooms, however, segregate the clutter and noise of laundry processing. Rooms that have laundry tubs or deep sinks, even a shower, and are near the family entrance can serve as mud rooms— good places to clean up after work or play. In basementless houses, the utility room will also house heating and cooling equipment, a water heater, and perhaps a freezer. It is desirable that the washer be as near the water heater as possible, while the dryer needs to be near an outside wall for venting. The maximum venting distance is 30 feet less 5 feet for each elbow (2 elbows maximum).[8] The washer and dryer should not be placed beside the freezer; heat forces the freezer to be less energy-efficient.

Although space may be saved by incorporating a laundry in the kitchen, it should be kept separate from food preparation counters for sanitation, and the inevitable noise of the machinery is bothersome. Basements and garages are practical alternatives, chiefly because they offer plenty of space and give sound insulation, although stairs present a tiresome hazard. Washers and dryers can be placed side by side or stacked on a frame in a closet in the bedroom area, usually in a space adjoining or within a bathroom for plumbing economy keeping in mind the minimum space needs given in Table 4–2. Since most laundry originates in and returns to bedrooms or bathrooms, and since laundering is seldom done at night when noise might disturb those trying to sleep, this location deserves considera-

above: 4-22 The bathroom is an excellent location for a space-saving 5-square-foot washer/dryer unit because this room is a natural accumulation point for laundry. With plumbing connections right at hand, installation is simplified. *(Courtesy The Maytag Company)*

below: 4-23 When not in use, this compact sewing area can be stowed away completely. Both it and the laundry facilities can readily fit into a family room alcove. *(Courtesy The Maytag Company)*

tion. Many apartment houses provide laundry facilities on each floor for tenants, or there may be one large common laundry room somewhere in the building.

Like the kitchen, the laundry should be easy to keep clean, with washable walls and durable stain-resistant countertops. Smooth surfaces will help prevent dust and lint accumulation. (Woven wood blinds, so often selected for utility rooms and kitchens, collect dust, lint, and grease.) Good general lighting is necessary plus task lighting for preparing, mending, and ironing.

Sewing Areas

In recent years the popularity of home sewing has increased remarkably. Factors influencing this trend include the rising cost of clothing and household textile goods, greater sophistication of home sewing equipment, an amazingly wide variety of yard goods available, and the development of quick, simplified construction techniques.

The household in which one or more members do considerable sewing almost mandates a permanent, isolatable sewing area, perhaps even a whole room. Extensive sewing not only requires a vast array of small tools and supplies but also generates a fair amount of debris in the form of fabric scraps and threads. A well-designed sewing center helps to organize all this paraphernalia and allows the work-in-progress to be left out. It should include:

- A **sewing machine,** either built into a 2- by 5-foot cabinet or placed on a smooth surface, and so arranged that fabrics will not drape on the floor.
- An upright **chair** of a height that will permit the sewer to work comfortably without excessive bending (anthropometric research suggests a secretarial chair). A minimum of 3 feet is needed in front of the machine for the chair and access.
- A **cutting surface** at least 3 feet wide and 6 feet long for laying out patterns.
- Adequate **storage** for fabrics and remnants as well as for tools and supplies. Pegboards are useful for holding and keeping at hand the many small pieces of equipment needed.
- A **steam iron** and **ironing board,** possibly including a sleeve board. An area approximately 4½ feet wide and 6 feet long is needed for ironing.
- Good **lighting** directly over the sewing machine and illuminating the general area to facilitate hand work.

Optional equipment includes a dress form, three-way mirror, skirt-hemming guide, and comfortable chair for hand sewing. There should also be provision for a library of sewing books and patterns and for hanging garments.

As with kitchens and other work spaces, strict efficiency need not preclude charm and attractiveness. Bright colors, attractive furnishings, and perhaps a sunny window will help to make even the most utilitarian sewing more enjoyable.

Table 4–2 Minimum Space Needs in the Laundry to Permit Freedom of Action*

Space in front of the washer or dryer alone	3'8" x 3'6"
Space in front of the washer and dryer	5'6" x 3'6"
Space between opposing washer and dryer (or if the space between is a traffic path)	4'
Space for ironing (ironing board, chair, laundry cart)	5'10" x 4'3"
Working space beside a clothes rack	2'4"

*From a University of Illinois study of home laundry operations. These measurements are in addition to space for the appliances.[9]

Workshops and Garden Rooms

For many individuals woodworking and the many chores associated with home maintenance represent more than a hobby or a necessary evil. The serious cabinetmaker deserves a suitably equipped workshop, as does the person much involved in furniture refinishing and similar pursuits. Specific needs will vary widely according to the nature of the work, but most such activities require:

- A **location** reasonably isolated from the rest of the household so that the debris, odors, and noise created will not contaminate living spaces. Often this means a garage or basement, but a large-scale operation may suggest a separate outbuilding. Some large housing projects provide special facilities.
- **Storage** for tools and supplies.
- Sufficient **electrical outlets** of the proper voltage for power equipment.
- If possible, a **sink** for cleaning hands and tools.
- **Lighting,** both general and for tasks.

The dedicated gardener can, if space permits, indulge in a special potting or flower-arranging room either within or adjacent to the house. An ideal space would offer:

- Durable and easily cleaned **surfaces,** perhaps even a floor that could be hosed down
- **Storage** for vases, pots, soil, fertilizers, and tools
- **Plant lights** for starting seeds
- A **sink** for watering and for cleaning hands.

4-24 A greenhouse addition to a home can have space for garden work as well as a growing/display area. *(Photograph: © Peter Aaron/ESTO)*

General Storage

It is a lamentable fact that many small houses and apartments dismiss the problem of storage outside the kitchen with a few small closets. This ignores the reality that *people*, by and large, have *belongings*. The kinds of storage that each household needs will depend, of course, on what kinds of possessions its members own, so we can give only general guidelines and show how some families have met their storage requirements. One planning guide is to allow 10 percent of the total square footage of the home for storage. This includes the space occupied by kitchen cabinets as well as closets and all other available spaces. (Storage needs for private spaces are presented in Chapter 5.) Other guidelines include storing articles according to frequency of use, where they are used, together if they are used together, at convenient heights (heavy items lower, lighter ones higher), and for ease in seeing, reaching, and replacing if they are used often.

A storage wall with built-in shelves, drawers, and cupboards holds many diverse objects and can be decorative. Some units of this type are set at right angles to the wall and function as space dividers. More individual needs, however, require specific planning. For example, the family that enjoys games and puzzles might consider a bank of very shallow drawers or closely spaced shelves. At the other extreme, a large collection of bulky sports equipment warrants generous space and perhaps special hanging racks. Closed storage will best protect some possessions while others may safely be stored in an open display. Good storage is not only planned, but also flexible. Children grow and needs and hobbies change, suggesting adjustable fixtures rather than elaborate, permanent facilities.

When either designing a house or renting an apartment, one must consider the availability of some empty, lockable, storage space for such limited-use items as suitcases and tents, bicycles and lawnmowers, summer furniture and winter sports equipment, out-of-season clothing and bedding, and furniture and other items not presently in use but not yet ready for discard.

The design of standard household fixtures and appliances has changed markedly over the past two decades as manufacturers have understood and demonstrated that function and beauty are not mutually exclusive. There is no reason, after all, why something that works hard at some mundane chore needs to advertise that fact by its drab appearance. With skillful planning, the work spaces in a home can be supportive not only of its daily maintenance but of its overall character as well.

4-25 Hand-crafted wood cabinets designed by Al Garvey create an attractive storage wall for any room in the house. *(Photograph: Norman Peterson & Associates)*

Notes to the Text

1. Cecile Shapiro, David Ulrich, and Neal DeLeo, *Better Kitchens* (Passaic, NJ: Creative Homeowner Press, 1980), p. 8.
2. Glenn H. Beyer (ed.), *The Cornell Kitchen: Product Design Through Research* (Ithaca, NY: Cornell University, College of Human Ecology, 1952), Rose E. Steidl, *Functional Kitchens*, Cornell Extension Bulletin 1166 (Ithaca, NY: Cornell University, College of Human Ecology, 1969); *Beltsville Energy-Saving Kitchen, Design No. 2*, U.S. Department of Agriculture Bulletin No. 463 (Washington, DC: U.S. Government Printing Office, 1961).
3. Robert Wanslow, *Kitchen Planning Guide* (Urbana: University of Illinois, 1965), p. 14.
4. Ibid., p. 14.
5. Hugh S. Donlan and Jeremy Robinson (eds.), *The House and Home Kitchen Planning Guide* (New York: The Housing Press/McGraw Hill Book Company, 1978), p. 83.
6. Ibid., pp. 174–175.
7. Ibid., p. 88.
8. Ibid., p. 122.
9. Ibid., pp. 120–121.

References for Further Reading

Brett, James. *The Kitchen: 100 Solutions to Design Problems*. New York: Whitney Library of Design, 1977.

Danlan, Hugh S. and Jeremy Robinson (eds.). *The House and Home Kitchen Planning Guide*. New York: The Housing Press, 1978.

Faulkner, Sarah. *Planning A Home*. New York: Holt, Rinehart and Winston, 1979. Chap. 14.

Galvin, Patrick J. *Kitchen Planning Guide for Builders and Architects*. Farmington, MI: Structures Publishing Co., 1972.

Keiser, Marjorie Branin. *Housing: An Environment for Living*. New York: Macmillan, 1978. Chap. 10.

Kleeman, Walter B., Jr. *The Challenge of Interior Design*. Boston: CBI Publishing Company, 1981. Chap. 10.

Klein, Stephan Marc. "Images of Housework," *Residential Interiors*, May/June, 1980, pp. 92–93.

Lindamood, Suzanne and Sherman D. Hanna. *Housing, Society and Consumers: An Introduction*. St. Paul, MN: West Publishing Company, 1979. Pp. 119–129.

Midwest Plan Service. *Family Housing Handbook*. Ames: Iowa State University, 1971.

Panero, Julius and Martin Zelnick. *Human Dimension and Interior Space: A Sourcebook of Design Reference Standards*. New York: Whitney Library of Design, 1979. Pp. 37–45, 157–162.

Shapiro, Cecile, David Ulrich, and Neal DeLeo. *Better Kitchens*. Passaic, NJ: Creative Homeowner Press, 1980.

Small Homes Council-Building Research Council. *Kitchen Planning Principles, Equipment, Appliances*. Champaign: University of Illinois, 1975.

St.Marie, Satenig S. *Homes Are for People*. New York: Wiley, 1973. Pp. 115–145.

Wanslow, Robert. *Kitchen Planning Guide*. Urbana: University of Illinois, 1965.

5

Private Spaces

Privacy is both a necessity and a luxury today. At the same time that every human being needs privacy for psychological well-being, increasing numbers of people concentrated in increasingly smaller areas make that necessity progressively less attainable. In an environment of rapidly growing population, privacy may be, in the words of Professor Alexander Kira, "one of the last luxuries left."

Privacy can be attained in many ways, ranging from total physical seclusion to the ability to concentrate so intensely that the rest of the world is screened out. Individuals require different degrees of privacy—both physically (for sleeping, dressing, bathing, and the like) and psychologically (for development and renewal).

Most families today cannot afford to provide individual rooms or suites to satisfy each member's privacy quota. The huge, rambling houses of a few generations ago—built when materials, labor, and fuel were cheap—have ceased to be practical. Intelligent planning is therefore crucial to provide each person a private space in which to retreat for rest and spiritual regeneration. Typically that space is in the private sector of the house containing bedrooms and bathrooms, grouped for privacy of sight and sound, and separated from the social and work spaces of the house.

Sleeping and Dressing

One of the basic human needs is sleep—the blessed time that "knits up the ravell'd sleave of care" while physically refreshing the body. Historically, this need has been met in increasingly refined style. Primitive peoples slept on the ground on piles of leaves or straw (or fur hides if they were fortunate) in a spot sheltered from the elements. They simply made bed-room. With civilization came the building of shelters and the reservation of a specific place for sleeping. However, the evolution of a separate room for sleeping came slowly, and with it the idea that beds should be elevated from the floor. Gradually people, particularly the wealthy, began to regard the bed as more than utilitarian, seeking comfort, warmth, and even privacy with pillows, mattresses, quilts, curtains, and canopies. Today many traditional ideas such as tents, alcoves, and curtains are retained at the same time newer innovations, like the water bed, are being adopted. Most bedrooms now are planned to accommodate only one or two people, and considerable attention is devoted to making the time spent in those rooms as pleasant, relaxing, and comforting as possible, adding space for reading, relaxing, exercising, or working in addition to sleeping.

Comfort, warmth, and privacy can now be precisely and scientifically controlled to provide an optimum sleeping environment. Some research has indicated that effective sleeping time can be reduced by about two hours under such ideal conditions. However, the scientifically optimum requirements for sleep may not be the most psychologically gratifying. Too small a space, accommodating only a bed and other minimally necessary furnishings, may produce claustrophobic fear. Too much space or too "busy" a space may cause feelings of insecurity or provide too much stimulation, preventing relaxation and sleep, particularly for children.

5-1 The canopy bed in the Colonel Stephen Ford house, built in 1720 in Durham, Connecticut, recaptures the refined elegance of the 18th century. Restored by the 18th Century Company. *(Photograph: © Karen Bussolini)*

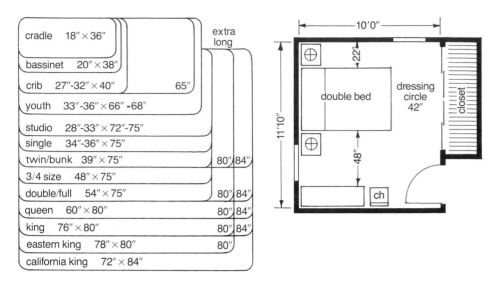

left: 5-2 Mattresses are available in a wide range of sizes to accommodate people from infancy to adulthood. (*Adapted from* Nomadic Furniture)

right: 5-3 A bedroom should have sufficient space in front of the closet and chest of drawers for dressing, and space on either side of the bed for making it up and cleaning beneath it. (*Adapted from* the Family Housing Handbook *MWPS-16, 1/e, 1971.* © *Midwest Plan Service, Ames, Iowa*)

cradle	18″ × 36″		extra long
bassinet	20″ × 38″		
crib	27″-32″ × 40″	65″	
youth	33″-36″ × 66″ -68″		
studio	28″-33″ × 72″-75″		
single	34″-36″ × 75″		
twin/bunk	39″ × 75″		80″ 84″
3/4 size	48″ × 75″		
double/full	54″ × 75″		80″ 84″
queen	60″ × 80″		80″ 84″
king	76″ × 80″		80″ 84″
eastern king	78″ × 80″		80″
california king	72″ × 84″		

Since we spend almost one-third of our lives in bed, provisions for sleep are the first consideration in planning a bedroom. The requisites for sleeping are:

- A **bed** or **beds** long enough and wide enough for one or two people. Figure 5-2 illustrates standard mattress sizes.
- A **bedside table** or built-in **storage** unit to hold necessary items within convenient reach.
- A **light source** next to or over the bed for reading and emergencies.
- **Control of natural light** by draperies, blinds, or shades.
- **Ventilation** from windows or other air sources. The best solution calls for cross-ventilation with windows on opposite walls, next best on adjacent walls but away from corners, minimum on only one wall with an open door to draw air from another part of the house. High strip windows allow the escape of hot air to reduce summer heat in many climates. Mechanical heating and cooling vents should be located to avoid causing a draft near the bed.
- **Quietness,** achieved by locating bedrooms away from (or insulating them against) noisier parts of the house and by using sound buffers such as closets, halls, and absorptive materials.

Nevertheless, in our culture a bedroom is usually more than just a "bed room." It also doubles as a dressing room and sometimes as a study, den, play area, or work room. These various roles, and the activities related to them, will affect the design of the space. Dressing activities involve a variety of requirements, many of them quite different from those best for sleeping:

- **Space** sufficient to stand, stretch, turn around, and bend over. An area with a diameter of 42 inches is considered sufficient for these dressing motions. Space is also needed in front of closets and drawers to retrieve clothing (see Table 5–1).
- **Seating** for donning shoes and stockings.
- **Storage** for all types of clothing; a minimum of 5 lineal feet of hanging space per person, plus shelf and/or drawer space.
- **Counter space** with a well-lighted mirror, combined with storage for shaving and hair-care equipment and for cosmetics.

Table 5-1 Bedroom Furniture Sizes and Clearances

Bedroom	Small			Large	
	Depth	Width		Depth	Width
twin bed, head and footboard	6'6"	x 3'3"	to	7'6"	x 3'8"
full bed, head and footboard	6'6"	x 4'6"	to	7'6"	x 6'
cot	5'9"	x 3'			
crib	2'	x 4'	to	2'6"	x 4'6"
night stand	1'	x 1'3"	to	2'	x 2'
chest of drawers	1'6"	x 2'6"	to	1'9"	x 5'
wardrobe or closet	1'7"	x 3'1"	to	2'	x —
easy chair	2'4"	x 2'4"	to	2'8"	x 2'8"
pull-up chair	1'3"	x 1'6"	to	1'6"	x 1'9"
Clearances					
space for making bed	1'6" to 2'				
space between twin beds	1'6" to 2'4"				
space for cleaning under bed	4' (on one side)				
space fronting chest of drawers	3'				
space fronting closet	2'9"				
space for dressing	3' to 4' (in both directions)				

- A **full-length mirror** for the overall view, if possible.
- **Lighting,** artificial and/or natural, that enables us to find things and evaluate the effect.

Ideally, a separate dressing area exists between the sleeping space and the bath, but too often it is sandwiched into whatever space the bed and other furniture leaves in the bedroom. Such conditions will be less frustrating if a "dressing center" is planned with the clearances given in Table 5-1. Certainly, each person deserves an adequate closet, incorporating or near a chest of drawers.

In designing a bedroom, several factors come into consideration: the number of people who will occupy the room and their ages (children, teenagers, and adults will have quite different priorities), the various roles the room will have to play, and the amount of space that can be utilized. Particularly when space is very limited, the amount of room available may be a major determining factor in planning a private area.

5-4 A large free-standing unit gives ample closet, cupboard, and drawer storage for two people's wardrobes. On one side the storage unit serves as a headboard, on the other it creates a dressing area. Robert A. M. Stern and John Hagman, architects. *(Photograph: Maris/Semel)*

5-5 This bedroom functions as a work space, study, and private retreat for watching television, a truly multipurpose use of space in a New York apartment. William Cohen, architect. *(Photograph: © Norman McGrath)*

Size of Sleeping Area

Sleeping spaces can range in size from the berths found in inexpensive accommodations on trains and ships—barely large enough to contain a human body—through extravagant quarters that include areas for reading, relaxing, working at a desk or sewing table, and keeping fit. In between we find an entire spectrum of variations. A tiny bedroom of 90 square feet allows only a single bed and little space for other furniture or activity. A primary bedroom with adequate space for a double bed and other necessary furniture contains approximately 120 square feet. Adult bedrooms are usually larger than children's bedrooms; master bedrooms must be approximately 145 square feet to accommodate a king-size bed.

Generally speaking, as housing construction costs rise, bedroom size decreases. Expanding the size of bedrooms can indeed add to the cost of a house if the space is added just for more elbow room. Or it can reduce the overall cost of a house if the extra space eliminates the need for additional play, study, sewing, work, or exercise areas. The bedroom should thus be considered a possible source of bonus living/working space. Since we spend two-thirds or our lives awake, we must concern ourselves with the function of the bedroom during those hours as well. A well-designed bedroom is more than just a place in which to sleep or dress; it affords a quiet retreat at any time of the day as a haven for rest and relaxation, peace and comfort, solitude and intimacy (Plates 11 and 12, p. 92). For these reasons, a bedroom ideally should be a moderate-size, multipurpose, segregated space. Among the many methods of maximizing usable space in the bedroom are built-in storage, work, and play areas.

Number, Location, and Layout of Bedrooms

The **number** of sleeping areas in a home is conditioned by the size of the household, its economic status and lifestyle, and often by the stage of family life that prevails. Generally, the number rises with the number of people in the household and with income. The maximum number of people per bedroom is considered to be two, with three bedrooms per family accepted as standard.[1] The one- or two-bedroom home, however, is often the preferred choice at either end of the family life scale—by the childless person or couple setting up separate living quarters or retiring from overlarge accommodations.

In **location,** bedrooms demand accessibility from a hallway rather than another room, physical separation from social and work spaces, and easy but out of view accessibility to baths. When these basic needs are met, more sophisticated wants such as segregation of adults from children, greater acoustic seclusion, and visual privacy can be considered. Families often feel opposing needs of supervision and emancipation as children grow. The amount of surveillance children require must be balanced against a desire for the quiet and independence that separated private spaces will give to different age levels. Buffering the bedroom wing of the house from both indoor and outdoor noise and view requires careful orientation of the entire plan (see Chapter 2).

Careful, efficient, well-planned **placement of doors** and **windows** contributes substantially to a bedroom's effectiveness. Doors should open into the room against the wall and, if more than one, should be as close together as is compatible without interfering with each other. Since we change clothes more often than we go to bed, the traffic path to closet and chest of drawers should be short and direct. If the door is not directly in line with the bed or dressing area, there will be some measure of privacy even when the door is open.

The U.S. Department of Housing and Urban Development (HUD) specifies a minimum of 10 percent **window area** in relation to bedroom floor area with a

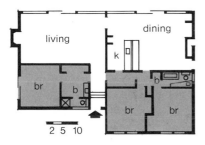

5-6—5-8 Careful placement of bedrooms and bathrooms within the home contributes to their effectiveness as private spaces.

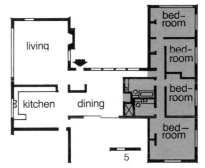

first level

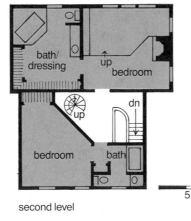

second level

top left: 5-6 Bedrooms and bathrooms normally are grouped together in the quietest part of the house. Moreover, both parents and children may find greater peace if their bedrooms and baths are separated. Dreyfuss and Blackford, architects.

above: 5-7 In more complex plan shapes, bedrooms and baths can be in a segregated wing remote from household noises. Richard Pollman, architect.

bottom left: 5-8 In two-story houses, the bedrooms and baths are usually upstairs, as in this house designed by Suzanne Kasler, ASID, IBD.

ventable portion of at least 5 percent.[2] Ten percent is barely adequate by most standards; 20 percent is much better. High strip windows 5 feet above the floor increase privacy, but at least one window should be both large enough and low enough (36 inches to the sill) to be used as a fire escape. It may also be desirable to have one window low enough (sill within 24 inches of the floor) to allow an outdoor view from a reclining position on the bed.

Windows grouped on one wall can make the room seem larger and result in more usable wall space, although the need for ventilation dictates placement of windows in two or more walls. Sunlight is desirable psychologically and aesthetically, and also as a home heating source with the best orientation generally being southerly. Architectural methods such as skylights can also be utilized to gain natural light, ventilation, and warmth when a south orientation is not possible.

Storage

The demand for convenient **storage** in bedrooms is exceeded only by the same need in kitchens. Basic principles suggest designing storage space specifically for whatever it is to hold. Minimum closet dimensions are 2 feet in depth and 5 lineal feet of hanging space per person. For children under twelve, the hanging rod should be 48 inches high, adjusting to a standard 64 inches with growth. The wardrobe closet takes up more wall space than the walk-in but requires less depth. The deeper the walk-in area, the more wasted space for a traffic path. Closets located near the bedroom door are most convenient. All closets should be equipped with artificial light for visibility of contents. Closets, shelves, and surface areas are needed elsewhere in the room to store and display books, hobbies, toys, sound equipment, and television sets as well as clothing.

Special Needs

Bedrooms are perhaps the most appropriate places in the home for members of the household to indulge their individuality. Dramatic color, lighting, and materials may be chosen to suit individual taste.

5-9 This very personal bedroom reveals the occupant's individual taste in furnishings and accessories. Peter Stamberg, architect. *(Photograph: © Paul Warchol/ESTO)*

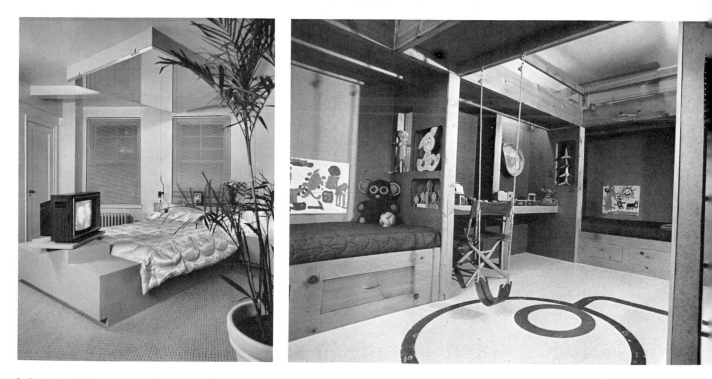

left: 5-10 This bedroom has a simple sculptural character and reflects the occupant's enjoyment in television viewing. Peter Wilson, architect. *(Photograph: © Norman McGrath)*

right: 5-11 Intelligent planning created this sleeping-play-work space for two children. All materials are sturdy and easy to clean, so they will weather the onslaughts of very young children, yet the room is sufficiently adaptable to "grow" with its occupants. Sheltered bunks give a measure of privacy for sleeping. Douglas White, designer. *(Photograph: © Robert Perron)*

Children delight in having space to play without having to be careful of expensive furnishings or wary of getting into things that don't belong to them. They may select their own color scheme, enjoy a fantasy environment or flexible space that permits changing at will. Needs for play and study space will change as children grow older. Durability is the prime consideration in selection of materials for the child's room, along with easy-access storage that encourages putting belongings away. For older children, a room designed for day use will satisfy a desire for privacy, provide a place for friends and study, and insulate the rest of the family from music and other noisy activity.

5-12 Antique furniture, handmade quilts, and simple accessories create a cozy, personal retreat, perhaps for a young girl. Mary Emmerling, designer. *(Photograph: © Robert Perron)*

When two people share a bedroom, a different situation arises, for the room should suit and express both. One or both may want a bedroom that doubles as a private study, which would affect the character of the space and the furnishings selected. When different tastes demand individual expression, separate areas, particularly "his" and "her" dressing areas, may meet the need if space permits. Thoughtful choices can satisfy both partners aesthetically and functionally.

In addition, sexual privacy should be provided in the master bedroom. A door latch, soundproofing, and direct access to hygienic facilities help insure seclusion. Comfortable, beautiful surroundings enhance intimacy which is an integral part of life.

Finally, lighting should be given special consideration in bedrooms. Lighting can help create a climate for relaxation with different intensities in different areas—brighter in the dressing area, lower in intensity for the central ceiling luminaire, more direct for reading in bed. Intensities can also be varied by the simple device of a dimmer switch to create desired moods or add brightness when needed (see Chapter 16).

Hygiene

The bathroom is used every day by every person within the household. This once utilitarian necessity has become a major selling point for new homes and often an ultimate expression of self-indulgence and luxury. Indeed, features at one time considered an extravagance are now quite common—the partitioned bathroom, dual lavatories, sunken tub, and bidet. Quick heat, abundant light, rapid and effective ventilation ensure comfort and convenience. Today people want more, larger, and brighter bathrooms with plenty of space. In both number and size, bathrooms are equated with status.

Cost alone checks the desire to multiply bathrooms. The minimum acceptable standard for a three-bedroom home is one full bath with tub and shower and one lavatory (half bath), or one bath or lavatory per floor. Ideally, a home for three or more people will have at least two bathrooms, as will one with sleeping quarters on two floors. As the household expands, so should the plumbing. The number of bathrooms can be decreased, however, if the tub or shower and the toilet are in separate compartments so they can be used by more than one person at the same time, or if dressing areas incorporate washbasins.

Ergonomic research into the design of bathrooms, primarily by Alexander

Kira at Cornell University, has led to the reshaping of standard fixtures for greater ease of use and safety. Nonskid surfaces and grab bars as well as seating spaces are often built into one-piece bathing facilities; controls are located within reach and should be designed for ease of operation. Water closets can be wall-hung for ease of maintenance, and acrylic, fiberglass, and prefabricated steel make all fixtures easy to install, clean, and maintain because they are seamless and mold-resistant.

However, many of Kira's findings have yet to be incorporated in standard fixture design and installation. For example, both the washbasin and water closet are poorly designed, according to Kira, due in part to improper height for function or comfort. (For the average of the total adult population, a comfortable working height for the hands is 38 inches, with a water source at approximately 42 inches and the height of the washbasin rim at 36 to 38 inches. Present standards set the rim at approximately 30 inches and the water source at 29 inches, forcing a working height for the hands of 26 inches, about one foot lower than desirable. Water closets are currently designed to provide maximum comfort in sitting and rising rather than to facilitate elimination of waste, which would indicate both shape and height more akin to a squatting position.)[3]

Designers now recognize that bathing and grooming can be pleasurable as well as hygienic activities. Related to the new interest in bathing as a therapeutic pastime are the spa and sauna (Plate 13, p. 125). Many Americans bathe primarily in the shower. Relaxation is often the basic reason for taking baths, with the result that soaking tubs (hot tubs, whirlpool baths, and spas) for shoulder-deep water have gained considerable popularity. Of Scandinavian origin, the invigorating sauna, with its hot, dry atmosphere, is often a cubicle adjacent to the bathroom in the American home, while the spa or hot tub, often with whirlpool jets, may be located in the bathroom or master bedroom, or outdoors.

As interest in and awareness of the importance of physical fitness rises, a home gym is being combined with the master bath or bedroom area with increasing frequency. We steam, tan, exercise, and bathe our bodies in bathrooms that can be a personal paradise (Plate 14, p. 125).

below left: 5-14 The addition of a spa changes an ordinary bathroom into a luxurious retreat for relaxation and contemplation. Marsden Moran and Andrew Robinson, architects. *(Photograph: © Karen Bussolini)*

below right: 5-15 Kohler's "Habitat," placed on a loft over the bathroom proper, is a controlled environmental enclosure that envelopes the user(s) in effects similar to sun, steam, wind, and rain at the desired temperatures. *(Photograph: © Karen Bussolini)*

Location and Layout

Location of bathrooms is primarily a matter of convenience, privacy, and cost. A bath should be accessible from all bedrooms without visibility from group spaces. On the other hand, at least a lavatory with washbasin and water closet should be as near the kitchen and major group space as feasible. Bathrooms located between two bedrooms with a door to each, although often convenient, can also cause problems with "leaks" of both noise and light under the doors, and forgotten locked doors preventing use from one of the bedrooms. For soundproofing, fixtures backed against closet walls are most efficient and economical. However, pipes in shared walls can be insulated to help deaden sound.

Because of its restricted area and need for light, heat, ventilation, and humidity control, the design of the bathroom, its layout and finishes, takes careful thought. Layout is usually predetermined, but the following criteria can be of help in evaluating a room and in remodeling.

- **Minimum size** is 5 by 7 feet for a full bath, but these dimensions preclude use by more than one person at a time and seriously limit storage space. A few more square feet usually justify their cost. A 2-foot-wide traffic path is necessary; other clearances are listed in Table 5–2, page 120. For wheelchair access, a bath should be approximately 6½ by 10½ feet.
- The **door** should be located so that, when opened, it will swing into the bathroom without hitting anyone using any appliance, and can be left partially open for ventilation without giving full view of the room, and most particularly of the water closet. It should be equipped with a device on the outside to permit emergency entry or, for use by someone in a wheelchair, it should swing outward and provide a minimum clear opening 32 inches wide to allow passage. Sliding or folding doors may also be used, although they provide a less soundproof closure.
- Critical factors in **window design** include light, ventilation, easy operation, and privacy. The bathroom requires the most heat and best ventilation of any room in the house. Windows should not be located over the tub or toilet

left: 5-16 A skylight may be the solution to bringing natural light into the bathroom while at the same time maintaining privacy. James Caldwell, architect. *(Photograph: Philip L. Molten)*

right: 5-17 A skylight in a slanted roof and an arched window at treetop level, a transparent shower curtain over a sunken tub, turn a bathroom into a personal retreat. Nelson Denny, designer. *(Photograph: © Karen Bussolini)*

because of the danger of uncomfortable drafts, moisture deterioration of window frames and treatments, and difficulty of operation and cleaning. For privacy, windows should be at least 48 inches above the floor. High windows, skylights, and vented fans can illuminate and/or ventilate inside bathrooms while exterior-wall bathrooms can have entire window walls with private gardens or balconies.

- **Heat** can be provided quickly and efficiently by electric heaters, infrared lights, or quartz heaters, while skylights make use of solar heat. (Unshaded skylights are not recommended in hot climates.)
- Typical **arrangements of fixtures** are illustrated in Figures 5-18 through 5-22. Compartmentalized bathrooms increase utility considerably for relatively small expense. To simplify plumbing and reduce costs, the appliances should be located so all plumbing can utilize one wall.
- **Storage** at point of first use is a cardinal principle, as always. This indicates the need not only for medicine cabinets (with locks for security) but also spacious cupboards and drawers for the miscellany of supplies and equipment associated with hygiene and grooming. Professor Kira recommends at least 1 square foot of storage per user near the washbasin.
- **Finishes for walls** permit almost total freedom of choice. Nearly every material can be made to withstand moisture and mildew.

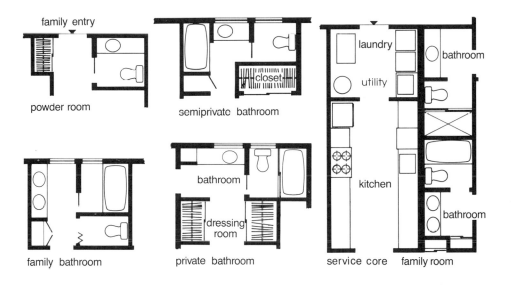

5-18—5-22 Various types of bathrooms can fulfill different functions.

top left: 5-18 A powder room near the main entrance to a house is often useful for quick cleanups, especially in a two-story home.

bottom left: 5-19 A family bathroom should be large and centrally located, but out of sight of the social spaces. Since all family members use this room, dividing the space to increase simultaneous use is often a good idea.

top middle: 5-20 A semiprivate bathroom, planned for two or three members of the family should be near bedrooms but entered from the hall.

bottom middle: 5-21 A private bathroom for one or two persons is entered from a bedroom. A second entrance is useful if guests use the room as well. Dividing a private bathroom gives even more privacy.

far right: 5-22 A service core concentrates all plumbing—for bathrooms, kitchen, and laundry—and centralizes the inevitable noise. Construction costs are also lowered.

- **Flooring materials** range from practically impervious tile through the more resilient vinyls to the warmth of synthetic carpeting. Nonskid flooring is recommended.
- **Color** is important both for its visual impact and for its reflectance, which can change skin tones. Oranges and pinks make one look healthy; blues, yellows and greens may cast a sallow tinge. Light values with high reflectancy factors assist in distributing light throughout the bathroom. Lower-value colors require more attention to both quantity and location of light.
- **Lighting,** both natural and artificial, is critical to provide good illumination for shaving and cosmetic application. In type and placement, lighting must avoid glare and harsh shadows. Light fixtures should be located in front of the person using the mirror and placed to provide light evenly on all sides of the face, including under the chin. This can be accomplished with small luminaires surrounding the mirror, light sources on both sides of the mirror, or a strip of lights above the mirror combined with a light-color countertop to reflect the light back up onto the lower part of the face. Light sources must not reflect directly in the mirror, but if located near the mirror they provide reflected indirect light for the entire room. Incandescent sources are most flattering to skin tones. If fluorescent sources are used, deluxe warm white and natural white are the most complimentary. If the bathing facility is located so it does not receive sufficient general room illumination, supplementary lighting is necessary. Also, for safety, night lighting is desirable. All electrical outlets and switches should be at least 3 feet from the tub or shower.
- **Shape and size of fixtures** become critical factors in space planning. Typical dimensions and necessary clearances are listed in Table 5–2, but luxury fixtures can be much larger and of irregular shapes. A word of caution: although elegant, the sunken tub is both hazardous and difficult to clean.

Aesthetically, the bathroom need no longer look like a laboratory. Its functionalism can be made delightful to the senses with appliances, finishes, and accessories in a wide range of colors, textures, and designs. The bathroom is a relatively small space in which a limited amount of time is spent. This allows boldness in decor which would not be attempted in other areas. Theatrical lighting adds drama, perhaps framing the mirror on two, three, or four sides with thin chrome or brass

---

Table 5–2   Standard Bathroom Fixture Sizes and Clearances*

Fixture	Small		Large	
	Depth	*Width*	*Depth*	*Width*
bathtub	30″	x 48″	42″	x 66″
soaking tub	40″	x 40″		
washbasin	15″	x 18″	24″	x 30″
toilet	24″	x 22″	30″	x 24″
bidet	25″	x 14″	28″	x 16″
shower	30″	x 30″	42″	x 60″
bathinette	21″	x 35″	24″	x 36″
vanity cabinet	30″	x 24″	32″	x 26″
Clearances				
space between front of tub and opposite wall	30″	— 42″		
space in front of toilet	18″	— 24″		
space at sides of toilet	12″	— 18″		
space between fronts of fixtures	24″	— 36″		

*Luxury fixtures are available in larger sizes.

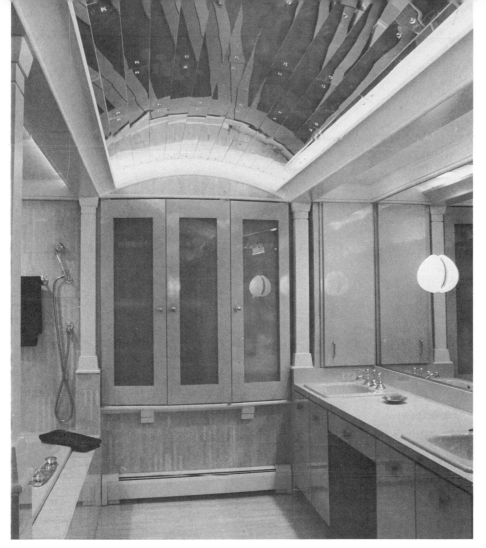

strips studded with small lamps (if they do not produce too much heat). The strong task light recommended for the bathroom allows the use of darker colors; pastels are not mandatory for light reflectance, although they do help distribute light more evenly than dark surfaces. Mirrors are visual spacemakers, as are luminous ceilings and windows. The bath can be humanized and individualized with plants for a soothing private garden atmosphere. This aura of relaxation can be further enhanced with paintings, graphics, and other personal accessories.

Guest Accommodations

Until only a few decades ago, entertainment of overnight guests represented a major form of recreation, a welcome change of pace from everyday living. The combination of great distances separating friends and relatives and somewhat larger houses, often with domestic help, made hospitality a simple pleasure. Guests could be accommodated for long periods of time without seriously disrupting the household, and the visitor who arrived for dinner and stayed for a week was not cause for dismay.

Today, houses are smaller and live-in servants almost unknown; even one unoccupied bedroom seems a luxury. Nevertheless, with careful planning most houses can accommodate overnight guests in a comfortable manner, particularly if their lifestyles correspond to those of their hosts.

For those who travel lightly, perhaps even with their own sleeping bags, comfortable surfaces on which to place them may be all that is necessary. Many vacation houses provide this minimum in bunk rooms.

Going one step beyond this, we should consider that houseguests deserve the same elements of private space as do members of the family: a secluded area in which to sleep and dress, storage space for clothing, bathroom facilities, and the possibility of getting outside the social circle occasionally. The ultimate would be a separate **guest house,** with its own kitchenette and eating counter. Other possibilities include:

- A **bedroom-sitting room** with private bath, separated from family areas and always in readiness because it serves no other purpose
- A **secluded room** or study that doubles as a guest room—a sensible solution because a room well planned for seclusion has most of the qualities of a good guest room
- A **quiet alcove** or small room off the group space that can readily be made private by folding or sliding doors, curtains, or screens
- An **extra bed** in one or more of the bedrooms—perhaps a bunk or a studio couch
- A living room **sofabed**

5-24 A one-room guest cottage becomes a separate apartment for four, enabling hosts and guests to maintain their own rhythms of living. It has been fitted with kitchen equipment for an early breakfast or late snack, plus a library for browsing. Easy access to the outdoors permits guests to move about without disturbing the household. Richard and Sue Rogers with Norman and Wendy Foster, architects. *(Photograph: © Ezra Stoller/ ESTO)*

above: 5-25 A built-in banquette in the music alcove of a renovated 1950s apartment doubles as a sleeping accommodation for overnight guests. Joan Halperin, interior designer. *(Photograph: Robert Levin)*

left: 5-26 Vacation homes are often expandable to accommodate overnight guests. In a minimally divided bunkroom, recycled lumber makes sturdy double-decker beds, while coat hooks take the place of closets for short-term use. Donald MacDonald, architect. (*Courtesy* American Home Magazine)

Home Business Activities, Individual Work, and Hobbies

Home business activities, individual work, and hobbies (ranging from paying bills and computer shopping to writing and painting) may take place in several areas within the home or be concentrated in a single area. Since segregation from noisy activities is generally desirable, full discussion of these work centers and the requirements for the business of running a home and personal record-keeping is included here rather than with exploration of social or work spaces.

The Home Office

Every household has family documents, medical and tax records, legal papers, bills, receipts, addresses, household inventories, recipes, and so forth that must be organized, filed, or simply kept in some manner and in some place. It is convenient if much of this information is stored in a single location for easy reference. Such a home business center might be located in the kitchen, family room, or bedroom, or it might be a separate study, office, or library. In addition to storage facilities, it should contain communication devices and materials—a telephone, typewriter and/or writing supplies, and increasingly a home computer. Basic needs include:

- **Work surfaces** for writing and paying bills, for a typewriter, and for computer components (keyboard and video display terminal). A standard desk of 29- or 30-inch height is suitable for writing; a typewriter return is normally 3 inches

left: 5-27 More and more people are working from home today. The home office may occupy a converted bedroom or a room over the garage such as this workroom for a copywriter. Bumpzoid, architect. *(Photograph: © Karen Bussolini)*

above: 5-28 An efficient office can be fitted into a small area through the judicious use of built-in desk, bookcases, and wall cabinets. *(Photograph: © Peter Aaron/ESTO)*

above: Plate 13 The spa bath reflects an interest in well-being with emphasis on soothing relaxation. *(Photograph: © Karen Bussolini)*

right: Plate 14 Unusual custom-designed fixtures, including a contoured platform for "sunbathing," help give this bathroom its look of luxury. Charles Gwathmey, architect. *(Photograph: © Ezra Stoller/ ESTO)*

right: Plate 15 Warm colors may help create a psychological "climate" of warmth, encouraging interaction, and counteracting cold outdoor temperatures. Mark Simon AIA, of Centerbrook, PC, architect. *(Photograph: © Norman McGrath)*

below: Plate 16 Cool colors in rooms such as this tend to make people feel cool and calm and can be quite refreshing on a warm day. Mark Simon, AIA, of Centerbrook, PC, architect. *(Photograph: © Norman McGrath)*

126

shorter. A computer keyboard can utilize approximately the same 26- to 27-inch-high surface while the display screen should be closer to eye level, requiring a surface height of 33 to 36 inches. Modular furniture can allow flexible keyboard height, screen height, and viewing distance for the comfort of all users. Drawing tables, easels, and other special work surfaces may be appropriate for different types of work.

- **Seating** for one or more, with one adjustable office chair to avoid backaches and stress while working at the computer or typewriter. Other seating may consist of side chairs that can be pulled up to the desk or used for comfortable reading.

- **Storage** for writing supplies, computer disks, books, and files. Built-in units do not take up precious floor space but are expensive to construct and perhaps less flexible than freestanding units. As more transactions are conducted by computer, less storage space for printed materials will be required; all the information will be stored in the computer memory bank or in a master computer. There will nevertheless still be a need for storage of computer software.

- **Lighting,** with no shadows or glare in the work area. Windows, shiny work surfaces and keyboards, and bright lighting or incorrectly placed lighting can all cause glare. Some computer screens have nonreflective glass and some can tilt and swivel to reflect glare away. Green, yellow, and orange lettering on the screen has been found to be easier to view for long periods than black and white. (Lighting for task performance is discussed further in Chapter 16.)

The computer is capable of streamlining many home business transactions—from electronic banking to ordering products from the comfort of home. It can even be hooked up to a master computer to provide fire, burglar, and medical alert devices that call for help automatically if the computer senses anything wrong.

If the home office is used for professional business pursuits (which might involve visits from clients), it may need a separate outside entrance and increased privacy from family activities. This would require a location in the plan that is farther removed from the noisy areas of the house, or at least good acoustic control to provide quiet, uninterrupted working conditions.

5-29 The home computer can reduce the amount of space needed for the conventional storage of many paper records and files, allowing plenty of room for other furnishings in a study/guest room. Judith Green, interior designer. *(Photograph: Kenneth D. Rice)*

Arts and Crafts in the Home

Knitting and crocheting can be done wherever one can read, but mending, sewing, needlework, weaving, and other crafts—either as profession or hobby—are not so easily handled. The collection of needles, scissors, and "findings" seems to invite disorder and the fingers of small children, to which they are a definite hazard. Adding a sewing machine and space for a cutting table, or a loom, brings further complications. In descending order of desirability would be: a sewing room or studio (these days a luxury); space in one of the bedrooms; or a spot in the family room, the already crowded kitchen or laundry.

Pursuits such as woodworking, photography, or painting also deserve appropriate space and equipment. Important as these may be to individuals, however, such enterprises can quickly endanger the composure of other household members unless they are isolated in a separate room or household studio.

above: 5-30 This room contains a modern version of the Murphy bed, a unique solution to the problem of multiuse space. When the bed is folded into the storage cabinet at right, the room becomes a spacious studio for an artist. Joan Regenbogen, designer. *(Photograph: © Norman McGrath)*

right: 5-31 The bed takes up a good part of the room when opened. Joan Regenbogen, designer. *(Photograph: © Norman McGrath)*

128

Solitude

For people who live in groups and for parents raising children—as well as the children being raised—occasional solitude is a rare and precious gift. Too often the bathroom provides the only haven in the home, the only area in which one feels reasonably secure from being disturbed—and this leads to certain difficulties. Much stress is laid upon the two-week vacation to "get away from it all," but travel cannot substitute for the half-hour vacations most individuals need every day. This returns us to the question of privacy. In the quest for solitude some families and individuals have planned tranquil "meditation rooms," in the home or in a separate building; most find it in a bedroom or study. The opportunity to find total seclusion, free from interruption, can not only sustain emotional well-being but also enrich contacts with other people when the private space is left behind.

Notes to the Text

1. Suzanne Lindamood and Sherman D. Hanna, *Housing, Society and Consumers: An Introduction* (St. Paul, MN: West Publishing Company, 1979), p. 83.
2. Marjorie Branin Keiser, *Housing: An Environment for Living* (New York: Macmillan, 1978), p. 138.
3. Alexander Kira, *The Bathroom: Criteria for Design*, Research Report No. 7 (Ithaca, NY: Center for Housing and Environmental Studies, Cornell University), pp. 15–16, 64–65.

References for Further Reading

American National Standard Specifications for Making Buildings and Facilities Accessible to and Usable by Physically Handicapped People. ANSI A117.1-1980. New York: American National Standards Institute, 1980.

Family Housing Handbook. Ames: Iowa State University, Midwest Plan Service, 1971. Pp. 21–30.

Hartwigsen, Gail Lynn. *Design Concepts: A Basic Guidebook*. Boston: Allyn and Bacon, 1980. Chaps. 3 and 4.

Keiser, Marjorie Branin. *Housing: An Environment for Living*. New York: Macmillan, 1978. Chaps. 9 and 12.

Kira, Alexander. *The Bathroom: Criteria for Design*. Research Report No. 7. Ithaca, NY: Center for Housing and Environmental Studies, Cornell University, 1966.

Lindamood, Suzanne and Sherman D. Hanna. *Housing, Society and Consumers: An Introduction*. St. Paul, MN: West Publishing Company, 1979. Chaps. 4 and 5.

Packard, Robert T. (ed.). *Ramsey/Sleeper Architectural Graphic Standards*, 7th ed. New York: Wiley, 1981.

Panero, Julius and Martin Zelnick. *Human Dimension and Interior Space: A Sourcebook of Design Reference Standards*. New York: Whitney Library of Design, 1979.

Small Homes Council–Building Research Council. *Bathroom Planning Standards*. Champaign: University of Illinois, 1978/1979.

6

Environmental Control

The home itself is actually a kind of environment, one we create for ourselves and can control far more easily than we can our surroundings as a whole. James Marston Fitch speaks of architecture as the "third environment" formed by building an interface between the *micro*environment of the human body and the *macro*environment of nature.[1] This interface provides a selective filter capable of either excluding or admitting specific elemental forces. The *meso*environment of architecture has as one of its primary functions the shielding of people from excessive energy in nature—severe cold, intense heat, driving wind and rain. But all too often such protection requires an excessive expenditure of energy. Certain office buildings and other public structures built during the late 1960s stand as the worst examples of this approach. Windowless, or fitted with windows that cannot be opened, they rely utterly upon artificial lighting, heating, cooling, and ventilation. Even noise control is dealt with artificially, when unpleasant sounds are masked by the hum of the air conditioner or by canned music. Given a power or fuel shortage, these buildings are useless.

If modern technology can devise artificial support systems, it can also teach us to refine natural systems of environmental control. Egyptians and Romans,

6-1 A house designed to exploit the natural elements of Hawaii also achieves distinctive cultural and structural expression. A series of louvered doors around the second floor can be completely rolled aside to catch sea breezes, partially closed to control the sun, or shut altogether to protect from the almost daily rain showers. Oda McCarty, architect. *(Photograph: Julius Shulman)*

Eskimos and South Sea Islanders adapted their homes to their climates with an efficacy that should put many architects to shame. Fortunately, not all contemporary builders ignore the most obvious devices for living in equilibrium with nature. A house designed to temper the impact of natural forces in its surroundings not only represents an economy for its owners and for the environment as a whole but simply makes good sense.

We in the United States have increasingly become a people who live the greater part of our lives indoors. We even travel about in a kind of mesoenvironment—the car—to a larger extent than any other nation. Nevertheless, we cling to our desire for union with nature, as evidenced by the widespread use of glass in houses, the popularity of a second home in the country. This apparent contradiction can be resolved only when we cease trying to bend nature to our will and learn the lesson that every other surviving species on earth has mastered: the technique

6-2 On the hot, arid, windswept coast of the Gulf of California, insulation from the elements is of preeminent concern. Thick, projecting walls shelter both interior and exterior spaces of a house designed to moderate the climate. James Flynn, architect. *(Photograph: Koppes)*

of adapting ourselves to our environment. And one of the most pressing factors in that adaptation right now involves the rational use of energy. People are again thinking in terms of warmth from the sun, cooling from the wind, and an intelligent use of natural resources and modern technology. Our goal should be to maintain a reasonable level of comfort and convenience while simultaneously preserving environmental harmony.

Temperature Control

In order to maintain comfort, the human body demands a relatively stable, quite narrow range of temperature variation in its near environment. Traditionally, thermostats were set at 75°F. in winter and 72°F. in summer to maintain maximum bodily comfort. If the air surrounding the body is too cool, the body's natural heat is lost too rapidly, causing one to feel chilled; if the surrounding air is too warm, too slow a heat loss results in feeling hot.

Energy Consumption

About one fifth of the energy consumed in the United States is used in the home.[2] Rising fuel prices for home heating, air conditioning, water heating, cooking, and lighting affect the costs of housing for everyone. In fact, energy use may be one of the most important factors in the total cost of housing. Most of the energy consumed in homes is used for space heating.

Energy Sources

Energy for home heating and cooling has historically been obtained from renewable resources, fossil fuels, and hydroelectric power. More recently, nuclear energy has been harnessed, and we are once again making use of the primary source of energy—the sun.

Wood, the oldest source of heat, is considered a *renewable resource*: its rate of production exceeds its rate of consumption. Readily available and replenishable, wood has regained popularity for home heating in recent years and fireplaces and wood-burning stoves have been redesigned for increased efficiency.

Fossil fuels, created within the earth over a period of millions of years, include coal, natural gas, and fuel oil. These precious energy sources are *finite resources*; they cannot be replenished as fast as they are being consumed even though we continue to search for and discover new reserves of natural gas and petroleum. A renewed interest in coal resources has been a result of our dependence upon OPEC (the Organization of Petroleum Exporting Countries) crude oil and its fluctuating price. Over half of U. S. homes are heated with natural gas, which was relatively cheap until 1974 and is still less expensive than most fuels. Newer oil and gas furnaces have about 75 percent combustion efficiency.[3]

Electricity heats about 15 percent of all homes in the United States.[4] **Hydroelectric power** initially produced most of the electricity, with falling water turning the generators. Only a small percentage of the total energy produced in the United States comes from hydroelectric power, however, with an almost equal amount from nuclear generators. **Nuclear energy** was introduced in the 1940s, first with nuclear fission reactors producing power, then with fusion reactors,[5] but concern for nuclear safety has perhaps slowed its development. Some electricity is also produced today by coal-fired generators. Electric heat is efficient, but electricity has remained costly for home heating.

Solar energy is used so differently that it will be considered separately later in the chapter. Although not fully utilized at present, solar energy has the potential to meet a major portion of the energy needs in a home.

Conventional Heating and Cooling Systems

Heating systems are mechanically complicated. It is difficult to know which system would be best for a given house, and only experts should be trusted with the planning. However, the designer and householder will benefit from knowing a few basic facts and principles.

Artificial Heat   Warmth for homes can be produced by:

- Heating air in a warm-air furnace, fireplace, or wood-burning stove
- Heating water in a boiler
- Sending electricity through a resistant conductor, as in toasters
- Extracting heat energy by means of a heat pump

Heat is brought to the living spaces through:

- Registers, which are small openings in floors or walls emitting warmed air
- Baseboard heaters—comparatively long high-temperature units along baseboards or sometimes ceilings
- Radiant panels with large low-temperature surfaces
- Infrared heat lamps that provide quick, concentrated heat

6-3   In an unusual combination of functions, a brick fireplace column provides the structural support for a spiral stair, doubling the use of the space. Ford, Carson, and Powell, architects. *(Photograph: Julius Shulman)*

6-4 An ornate old iron stove and a plain modern log holder have been related to the wall behind by the imaginative use of paint. Don Metz, architect. *(Photograph: John T. Hill)*

Heat, then, affects us and our homes by *conduction* through solid matter, either continuous or in close contact, as when our feet are warmed by a warm floor; by *convection*, or moving currents of air, as when the warm air blown from a register decreases the heat loss of our bodies and when warm air rises naturally; and by *radiation*, when heat jumps from one solid to another without making the air uncomfortably hot and stuffy, as in infrared heating lamps. The general characteristics of different systems can best be understood if they are grouped in terms of the way heat is brought into rooms.

Registers convect air warmed in a furnace, give quick heat, and are moderately low in initial cost. The moving air, which can be cleaned and humidified or dehumidified, dispels stuffiness and tempers moisture content. Since the same ducts and registers can serve also for cooling, the additional cost of air conditioning is lowered. The registers, though, may interfere with furniture arrangement. Except in the best installations, temperatures may fluctuate noticeably, and the air may seem uncomfortably hot at times. Fireplaces and wood-burning stoves can be equipped with conducting pipes or air ducts that convect hot air, naturally or with the assistance of a fan, even into adjacent rooms.

Baseboard heaters circulate hot water or steam, or the heat generated by electric resistance coils, to provide relatively uniform temperatures through natural convection and radiation, although rooms cannot be heated or cooled so quickly as with registers. Usually more expensive to install, they give no control of the air other than temperature.

Radiant panels, most often installed in ceilings but occasionally in floors or walls, are transformed into large warmed surfaces by means of water or air heated in a furnace or by wires that convert electricity to heat. The heat radiates to the opposite surface without affecting the air. Thus they keep us, our furnishings, and the architectural shell pleasantly and uniformly warm while the air stays relatively cool and without drafts. No intrusive registers or radiators mar the design of the room. However, this system has a slow heating response since it must heat the ceiling, wall, or floor before it can heat the room. Radiant panels require good insulation. They are rather expensive to install, and operating costs can be very high because of the expense of converting primary fuel into electricity.

Infrared heat lamps can give quick heat in bathrooms or in any other place where instant but not continuous heat is needed. They are inexpensive to purchase but fairly expensive to operate.

The specialized needs of each interior should be assessed in order to provide optimum heating. Small units, individually heated by gas or electricity and usually placed in walls, may be quite adequate in mild climates. On the other hand, a house located in the far North might benefit from a combination of two or more heating systems.

Air Conditioning   In many parts of the United States home air conditioning has come to be regarded as essential. Excessively high temperatures and humidity enervate us so that we cannot function at full capacity for either work or play.

Operating on the same principle as mechanical refrigerators, most air conditioners remove heat and moisture from the air, keep clean air in motion, and reduce housecleaning. Evaporative coolers, which extract cool air from the evaporation of water, humidify the air. Central cooling systems (often combined with heating apparatus) are generally much more efficient and cheaper to operate than individual room units, although the cost of installation is higher. Most air conditioning systems rely on electrical energy, so operating costs may be high.

In years to come the demonstrable advantages of air conditioning will have to be weighed against the potential dangers of excessive fuel consumption and detriment to the environment. One example demonstrates how an overdependence on artificial climate regulation can spiral out of control. The weather in New York City has actually changed over the last quarter century, partly because of the great amount of moisture released into the atmosphere by air conditioners. Night breezes can no longer move in to cool the paved streets and heat-retaining surfaces of the buildings. Instead, heat builds on heat, so that yet more air conditioners must be called into service. If such chains are not broken the results could be disastrous.

Solar Systems

The primary source of energy in this solar system is our star, Sun. Conventional sources of energy—fossil fuels, wind, and hydropower—all began with the sun giving life to photosynthesis, heating air masses and producing the cycle of evaporation and rainfall.

Now we are capturing the sun's thermal radiation to heat our homes. There are many alternative methods of using the sun's energy, but all can be categorized as basically active or passive, or a hybrid combination of the two.

6-5 Architect Sam Davis' design for a northern California condominium project incorporates active and passive solar features.

1 Water type solar collectors
2 Solar storage tanks
3 Domestic hot water tank
4 Deciduous trees provide summer shade
5 Recessed south facing windows
6 Clerestory windows for light and ventilation
7 Wingwalls provide wind protection
8 12" grey roof gravel insulation equalizes heat transfer
9 Skylights
10 All double-glazed windows
11 6" wall insulation
12 White stucco reflects heat gain
13 Protected south entrance
14 Trellis provides east-west shading
15 Minimal north windows

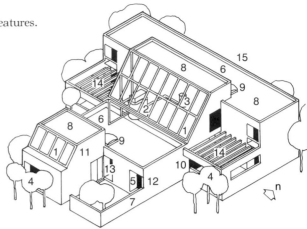

Active Solar Systems If mechanical devices—pumps and fans and controls—are required to help transfer heat from one place to another, the system is active. Active systems consist of **collectors,** usually panels, that use water or air to transport the heat to **storage,** usually a large container of either water or rock, so that it is available for **distribution,** usually through forced-air registers or radiant floor or ceiling systems, as needed.

Collectors are most often mounted on the roof, where they are easily angled for maximum sun exposure, but they may be attached to the vertical side of the house or placed on the ground. When incorporated into new housing design, they are less noticeable than when added to existing homes, giving the appearance of dark skylights or windows on the south-facing facade. The heat-storage component enables the system to retain the heat for use at night and on cloudy days. In addition to water and rock, phase-change chemicals, most often salt hydrates, are being used for heat storage. They undergo a change in state from solid to liquid at a melting point readily obtained from solar collectors, and release heat for the home as they "cool" to a solid state again. The advantage of salt systems is that they require a much smaller area for heat storage than either water or rock.[6]

Automatic controls activate the movement of heat from collectors to storage when heat is being gained and stop the circulation system when the temperature in storage is higher than that at the collectors, preventing heat loss on cloudy days and at night. The distribution of heat to the interior spaces is also regulated by mechanical controls, the same as conventional heating systems. The heat supply registers must be carefully located within the home to provide a slow and even air flow unfelt by occupants because the heat supply is lower in temperature than the warm air from conventional furnaces and may feel cold by comparison. Radiant floor or ceiling systems provide uniform, "draft-free" heat but are less responsive to immediate needs.

Although the fuel is free, active solar heating systems can be quite expensive to install, with their complex of controls, ducts, and fans. And a back-up conventional heating system is required as well, although it may be smaller than would have been necessary without the solar system. Over the long run, as the price of fossil fuels continues to rise and as supplies diminish, the initial expense of installation can probably be justified. Combined solar heating and air-conditioning could use the same equipment year-round for greater economy.

Today solar energy is widely used to provide domestic hot water. It requires little specialized machinery and is used year-round, so it is very economical. (A conventional back-up system is also required for heating water.)

6-6 The north side of this contemporary saltbox house is protected from winter winds by the long sloping roof and small windows, while the taller south side, nearly all glass, captures the low angle of the winter sun to heat the interior. Alfredo De Vido, architect. *(Photograph: Hans Namuth)*

Passive Solar Systems Simple solar heating methods that utilize the house itself to absorb, store, and distribute the sun's heat to the interior without mechanical aids are called passive and have been utilized for centuries. Selection and use of building materials and orientation to sun and wind reveal a deference to environment in vernacular architecture throughout the world. Nearly every existing home can take advantage of the sun to gain some direct and immediate heat through windows oriented to the winter sun and the use of dark-colored surfaces to absorb heat. However, to make maximum use of the solar energy available, homes must be designed and built with that purpose in mind.

Properly oriented **windows** provide direct heat gain without adding too much to construction cost since some windows are needed anyway for light, ventilation, and view. In the Northern Hemisphere, south-facing windows gain heat in winter and can easily be shaded by a roof overhang to prevent overheating in summer. North-facing windows lose heat, so they are undesirable. Windows that face east and west also gain heat in winter, but the overheating problem in summer is not so easily solved because the sun from these directions is much lower in the sky. Mature deciduous trees can provide the ideal solution, with needed shade in summer and not in winter. Though less effective than exterior solutions, interior window treatments can be helpful in insulating against overheating, but they block light and ventilation. To maximize window orientation, the house should be rectangular, positioned on an east-west axis. Generally, rooms used during the day are located on the south side of the house. Rooms having morning use warm up more quickly with exposure to the rising sun.

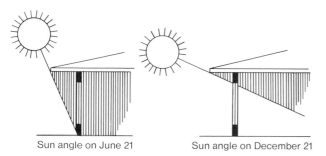

Sun angle on June 21 Sun angle on December 21

6-7 Properly designed roof overhangs admit desirable winter sun through south-facing windows but keep hot summer sun off the glass; they also reduce glare and soften the light.

6-8 The greenhouse addition to this New Jersey home provides a sunny space for dining and for plants. French doors and window coverings provide temperature regulation. *(Photograph: © Peter Aaron/ESTO)*

A **greenhouse** attached to the home provides even more solar heat gain than a vertical window while adding living and indoor gardening space at less cost than a fully insulated extra room. By opening the greenhouse to the rest of the house during the day, warm air can be drawn to other rooms by natural convection or assisted with fans. If heat is not removed from the greenhouse during the day, it may become too hot to use as living space. Also, building materials, fabrics, and furnishings must be carefully chosen to withstand sun fading and drying, or mildew if many plants share the space. To prevent heat loss at night, the greenhouse can either be closed off from the rest of the house or the glass can be insulated. During summer months, it must be shaded and ventilated to prevent overheating. In addition to free heat, the greenhouse provides humidity and fresh air.

Roof monitors (cupolas, skylights, or clerestory windows) normally designed for light and ventilation can also be used to help evenly heat interior spaces that would otherwise gain little or no direct solar heat. In addition, they allow natural cooling ventilation in summer in many climates.

To ensure availability of heat during the night, passive solar systems also need some method of **heat storage.** Materials used in house construction become the heat storage mass or "heat sink". Masonry, adobe, concrete, and stone are used for walls and floors because they absorb the sun's direct heat and store it until the air in the room cools sufficiently to draw the heat from them. Water can also be

above: 6-9 The tile floor functions as a heat-absorbing thermal mass in Con Edison's Conservation House in Briarcliff, New York, Alfredo De Vido, architect. *(Photograph: © Norman McGrath)*

left: 6-10 An earth-colored masonry trombe wall collects heat in the major living-entertainment space of a home designed by architects Kelbaugh & Lee. Windows puncture the trombe wall for light and view. *(Photograph: © Robert Perron)*

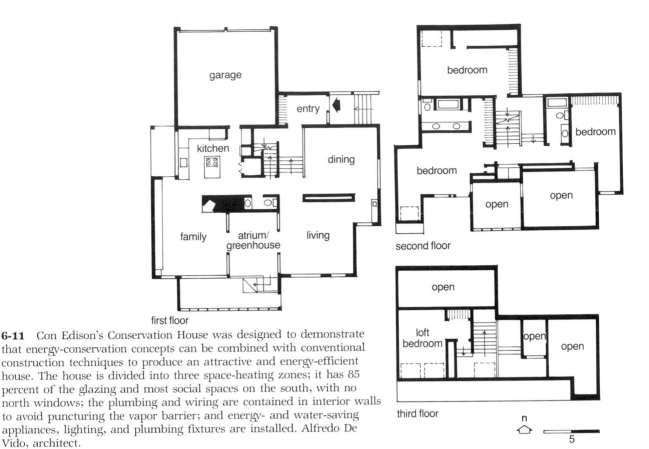

6-11 Con Edison's Conservation House was designed to demonstrate that energy-conservation concepts can be combined with conventional construction techniques to produce an attractive and energy-efficient house. The house is divided into three space-heating zones; it has 85 percent of the glazing and most social spaces on the south, with no north windows; the plumbing and wiring are contained in interior walls to avoid puncturing the vapor barrier; and energy- and water-saving appliances, lighting, and plumbing fixtures are installed. Alfredo De Vido, architect.

used in drums, columns, roof ponds, or building panels. These high-thermal-capacity materials also help control overheating because of the time lag between absorption of heat on one side of the wall, conduction through it, and radiation of heat from the opposite side. Heat thus absorbed during the hottest part of the day is not released until nighttime. Wall composition and thickness can be designed to control the time lag of the day's heating effect into the interior at night as in a house with *trombe walls* (double walls) that collect the day's heat in the empty space between the inner and outer layers.

Passive solar design represents a high level of energy consciousness attainable at little additional cost in new housing construction. Taking advantage of site, windows, and heat-absorptive materials are simple requirements that can at least reduce the energy consumption of mechanical systems.

With presently available technology, 80 percent of the power requirements in a typical house can be met by utilizing solar systems. The long-range advantages are obvious. While conventional fuel reserves are rapidly being depleted, solar energy is theoretically unlimited. It does not pollute the environment in any way. Until the last decade the cost of solar equipment had been high in relation to the savings in utility bills. Now solar homes are being built and sold in competition with conventionally fueled homes. The operating costs are competitive with those we are accustomed to paying for conventional fuels.

Alternative Energy Sources
Many other ways of producing energy are now being investigated: windmills

on land and ocean, geothermal energy from the heat of the earth's interior, hydroelectric power from tides that in some places form huge waves, solar photovoltaic cells for electric conversion, nuclear fission and fusion, even biological methods that utilize bacteria to change organic materials such as algae and sewage into gas and oil.

Supplies of oil, gas, and coal are finite; we cannot continue tapping them at an ever-increasing rate. In order to cope with the problem of energy for the present and for future generations, we must undertake a two-faceted program: curtailment of waste in currently available energy resources and development of new methods to produce energy for the years to come.

Energy Conservation

Energy in the home can be conserved both by reduction of initial intake—consumption—and by prevention of unnecessary loss. There are several methods by which each can be accomplished in either new or existing homes. Some require human behavioral adaptation, others can be achieved with more energy-conscious planning in the design of the structure itself.

Although people are generally slow to change habits, the last few years have witnessed a definite modification in standards for comfortable temperature ranges. Thermostat settings have dropped in winter (to approximately 68°F.) and risen in summer (to 78°F.) at the urging of power companies and as a result of government regulation in public places. Heating and cooling bills can thus be reduced. People adjust by wearing warmer or cooler clothing.

An alternative to reducing temperatures throughout the house is to close off parts of it that are not in use at various times of the day or night, heating only major activity areas. Sleeping spaces need not be heated during the day, for example; any activities that would have taken place there may be relocated to warmer parts of the home. In summer, naturally cooler parts of the house may be used more, with activities "migrating" according to seasonal temperature fluctuations as much as possible. Surface materials, textures, and colors may also be chosen to heighten feelings of warmth or coolness in rooms used predominantly in one season or the other, or they may be changed each season (Plates 15 and 16, p. 126). During summer, pilot lights for natural-gas furnaces should be turned off for further energy savings.

Many appliances are high energy users. Although people may not be willing to forego the time-saving convenience of clothes dryers, self-cleaning ovens, and dishwashers, many have learned to use them more prudently. And newer appliances, such as convection and microwave ovens and redesigned refrigerators and dishwashers, have energy-conserving features and devices.

In housing design, many steps can be taken to conserve energy. All-year comfort is a matter of house orientation and design, of materials and construction, as well as of mechanical equipment and energy consumption. First, overall shape and size, discussed in Chapter 2 as it affects construction costs, also affects heating/cooling costs. Again, the more square the shape, the more enclosed space in relation to the amount of perimeter. (Technically, circular shapes, exemplified by the geodesic dome, are the most efficient but they create unconventional interior spaces that have not gained wide acceptance.) Interior spaces maintain constant temperatures with less heat loss or gain potential than exterior exposures. Multi-family housing structures such as row housing expose even less exterior surface to climatic extremes. Also, the more space covered with the least roof area (as in multistory homes), the more efficient in terms of both energy intake and energy loss. However, open vertical spaces make it difficult to maintain comfortable temperatures at both levels; open stairways and high ceilings draw warm air to the upper spaces, leaving lower levels cool. The warm air can be returned to lower levels by a system of ducts and/or fans. Compact plans of smaller size present fewer cubic feet to heat and cool.

Internally, homes can be zoned for energy savings as well as for activities. Day-use rooms can be grouped in the most desirable location for natural heat and light, with provision for closing them off from other sections. Night-use spaces, also clustered, can have smaller and fewer windows, and sleeping areas can have lower thermostat settings. Access through vestibules or air chambers with double doors prevents the entry of cold (or hot) air from outside and the escape of temperature-controlled air from inside. Enclosed stairways help maintain desired temperatures on each level and internal chimneys radiate heat to internal spaces rather than the outdoors.

Siting and orientation in relation to sun exposure also reduces heating/cooling costs, as explained in the discussion of passive solar heating. All homes can benefit from a reduction in the total amount of window area, with necessary

upper level

entry level

5

left: 6-12 A compact 2000-square-foot two-story house plan utilizes an air-lock entry and positions utility and night-use spaces with few windows on the north side to conserve energy. Douglas Gidvan, chief designer, and Mark Kelley, energy systems engineer, Acorn Structures, Inc.; with Gordon Tully, Tudor Ingersoll, and Stewart Roberts, Massdesign Architects and Planners.

below: 6-13 The south side of a house in Connecticut orients living spaces to maximize direct solar heat gain while other exterior exposures have reduced window areas to minimize heat loss. *(Courtesy Acorn Structures, Inc.)*

windows oriented to gain natural solar heat as much as possible. If more than 15 percent of the wall area in a room is devoted to windows, they should be used for solar gain. Heat loss can be reduced by sheltering exterior walls from cold winds— again, through siting and orientation as well as landscaping and design.

Where excessive heat is a problem, high-pitched roofs collect less heat and permit easy attic ventilation. Light-colored roofs also reflect the sun's heat and help keep attic temperatures lower. Exterior walls and windows can be shaded with roof overhangs, verandas, trees, or shrubs. Grassy areas around the house do not reflect heat as do paved areas. Reflecting glass can be used on windows to further reduce solar heat gain if necessary and, of course, various interior (and exterior) window treatments help control heat gain. Glass areas facing the hot sun may need to be reduced in size. Natural ventilation is aided by carefully locating windows and selecting the best types of windows to capture breezes. (For a fuller discussion of windows, see Chapter 15.) Ceiling fans help circulate air throughout rooms. Venting hot air that accumulates under the roof as well as careful orientation of rooms and windows is the most economical means of cooling; when it is not sufficient, it must be supplemented with mechanical air conditioning.

Heat conduction through exterior walls, windows, and roof accounts for most of the energy loss from the average home. Insulation provides resistance to this heat loss. The two basic elements in insulation are the materials in the house shell and the way they are put together. Generally speaking, dense and uniform materials, such as metal and glass, conduct heat and cold readily, while such porous substances as wood or lightweight-aggregate concrete blocks are poor conductors: good insulators. Most houses, regardless of construction material, need further applied insulation.

Standard housing insulation comes in three basic forms:

- **Porous substances**—cellulose fibers, rock wool, fiberglass, and vermiculite granules—which imprison air in the small spaces between particles. Such materials are available either loose, for blowing into walls, or in batts to be stapled between studs and joists.
- **Rigid panels** of plastic materials or glass fiber that are installed above roof decking but under finished roofing, between wall studs, or against masonry walls.
- **Sprayed** polyurethane **foam.**

6-14 Standard greenhouse blinds across the top and down the side of a solarium-dining room create fascinating patterns of light and aid in temperature control. Robert Stern and John Hagman, architects. (Photograph: © Robert Perron)

143

above: 6-15 The triple-glazed window has an air space between all three panes to provide a thermal barrier against air leakage and heat loss or gain. *(Courtesy Pella/Rolscreen Company)*

below: 6-16 This double-glazed window contains a narrow-slat blind between the two panes that allows privacy and control of light. Specially coated blinds are available that reflect radiant heat, helping keep inside heat in and outside heat out. *(Courtesy Pella/Rolscreen Company)*

right: 6-17 The sunroom is an ideal use for windows with blinds incorporated between panes, which can help control heat gain and loss. *(Courtesy Pella/Rolscreen Company)*

Materials are rated by their R value, or thermal resistance (the higher the R value, the greater the insulating properties). The use of recommended amounts of insulation for walls, ceilings, and floors can retard heat loss substantially more than ordinary building materials. Because heat rises, higher R values are needed in ceilings.

Insulation installed for heating efficiency also helps keep the house cool in summer. Water pipes and heating/cooling conduits can be wrapped with insulation too. Both initial building costs and operating costs can be reduced by insulating since smaller heating and cooling units will be needed for the space. It has been estimated that a properly insulated house uses only 50 percent of the energy required to heat a noninsulated one, and appreciable savings will also be realized in air-conditioning costs.

Windows can be a source of much heat loss and gain because of the high conduction qualities of glass and air leakage around the frame and between parts. Single-pane glass transmits up to thirty-five times as much of the sun's radiant heat in summer and ten times as much in winter as insulated walls. Double- or triple-glazed construction or storm windows, plus weather-stripping and caulking, reduce heat loss and gain by more than half. Insulating interior window treatments are very effective in retaining heat inside. Exterior treatments prevent heat gain most effectively. Methods of automatically insulating window areas, such as the Beadwall system in which Styrofoam beads are blown between the two layers of glass at night, are continually being developed, especially in conjunction with solar heating technology.[7]

Doors also need to be tight-fitting, weatherstripped, and caulked to prevent drafts. Solid-core doors are better than hollow doors for the exterior, and storm doors or air-lock entries are desirable.

6-18 Insulating window shades, installed in tracks along the window perimeter, help save energy year-round by maintaining more stable interior temperatures. (*Courtesy Appropriate Technology Corporation.*)

The earth is an excellent temperature moderator. This has led to the development of *earth-sheltered* housing in which underground portions are warmed by direct contact with the earth which, at 8 to 12 feet down, remains close to the average annual temperature at the surface for any given location.[8] Savings of up to 75 percent in energy consumption can be realized—the deeper the earth cover, the greater the energy savings.[9] Earth-sheltered housing can be built entirely underground, with only window openings, light shafts, or atriums penetrating the ground or mostly above ground, with earth berms on one or more sides. The "elevational" type, with one side exposed and the other three buried, is ideal for combination with solar systems.

6-19 An earth berm house has no windows on the sides buried in the ground. This kitchen has an interior rubble wall along the berm side and a window wall along the south side. Steve Badanes, architect. (*Photograph:* © Peter Aaron/ESTO)

Existing homes can be *retrofitted* with materials and devices to reduce energy consumption and loss. Newer, more efficient heating/cooling systems can be installed if long-range savings justify their expense or older oil and gas systems may be tuned up for increased efficiency and measures can be taken to recover some heat loss. Active solar heating systems can quite easily be retrofitted for water heating. They may also be used for space heating but require considerable adaptation of the typical hydronic radiator or forced-air register distribution system found in most homes. Passive solar techniques might involve major remodeling. However, sun-capturing windows, skylights, or even greenhouses may be enlarged or added without too much expense. Energy loss may be prevented with added insulation, storm windows, weather stripping, caulking, wind buffers, and exterior shading, if needed. Tax credits have provided an incentive for homeowners to retrofit their homes for energy savings.

Energy conservation has gained widespread attention, both because of concern for the environment and high costs. There may be some trade-off of convenience, luxury, and conventional form in housing for affordable energy. But, as human expectations and values change, new technology continually offers exciting solutions for the future.

Designing for climate control varies from one section of the country to another; it can even pose different problems on sites only a few hundred feet apart because of changes in elevation, the presence of trees, or adjacent bodies of water. In some areas of the United States summer cooling is the overriding consideration,

6-20 An unused second-floor bedroom in this house was removed to create a high central space with a greenhouse wall in the living room area. Charles A. Farrell of Short and Ford, architect. *(Photograph: © Tom Bernard)*

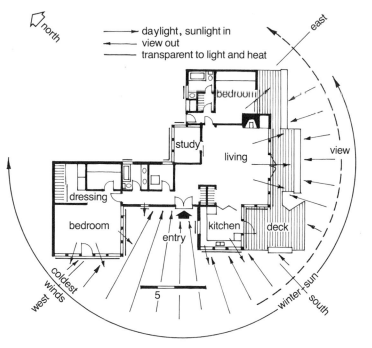

north

→ daylight, sunlight in
← view out
— transparent to light and heat

east

bedroom

study

living

view

dressing

bedroom

entry

kitchen

deck

coldest winds

west winds

5

winter sun

south

6-21 James Marsten Fitch designed and oriented his own house to take full advantage of the site and to moderate the climate in as many natural ways as possible. (From American Building 2: The Environmental Forces That Shape It)

in others it is winter heating. Sometimes both factors must be dealt with, while a few areas experience neither extreme cold nor extreme heat. There are some fairly safe rules of thumb—such as keeping large areas of glass directed toward the south—but the wise architect studies the general and local climate carefully. Perhaps architects should give even more thought to environmental factors than to the family who will live in the house, because the house is less likely to move than the people.

The plan shown in Figure 6-21 represents a house in Stony Point, New York, that was designed with several environmental considerations in mind: sun, prevailing winds, slope of site, and view from the windows. Nearly all glass faces toward the south, the southeast, and the southwest, while the opposite side of the house is sheltered with opaque and insulated materials. Because the northwest portion of the building is partially submerged in a hillside, it acquires further protection from both cold winds and the hot summer sun of late afternoon.

Air Quality Control

In addition to temperature control, providing a pleasant indoor climate includes regulating air movement and moisture content and removing odors, pollen, dust, and smoke. Balancing air temperature, humidity, and circulation creates the most comfortable environment and can even help moderate heating and cooling costs. Humidity affects comfort by retarding or enhancing the loss of body heat. High moisture levels in the air slow evaporation of skin moisture, keeping the body warm, while low humidity increases skin moisture vaporization, cooling the body. Moisture added to the normally dry warm air emitted from heat registers in the winter can increase human comfort in spite of lower thermostat settings. A relative humidity of 40 to 60 percent is recommended. In summer, low relative humidity increases comfort.

Proper humidity levels prolong the life of wood, metal, and painted surfaces. Too much moisture causes wood to warp and mildew, condensation and rust to form, with accompanying musty odors and peeling paint and wallpaper. Not enough moisture dries woods, leather, and adhesives, causing splitting and separation and also causes human discomfort by parching delicate respiratory membranes, aggravating allergies, and contributing to the build-up of static electricity.

Excess humidity and too little humidity can both be controlled. Mechanical humidifiers and dehumidifiers can be included as part of a year-round central heating/cooling system or installed separately. Exhaust fans in baths, laundries, and kitchens help remove high humidity during use. Ventilators in basements, crawl spaces, and attics also remove water vapor before damage occurs.

Good ventilation removes hot, stale air from the tops of rooms, brings in fresh air, keeps the air in gentle motion, and accomplishes all this without uncomfortable drafts. The major devices involved are doors and windows that can be opened, ventilating grilles, exhaust fans, warm-air furnaces with blowers, air-conditioning units, and fans.

Hot air rises, so it is best removed by windows, grilles, or exhaust fans placed high in the room or house. Ventilating skylights also release stale air. A forced-draft warm-air furnace, with the heat on or off, circulates air, as does most cooling equipment or a ceiling fan. Without one or more of these, a layer of practically motionless air will stay near the ceiling or in the attic. When this dead air is taken out, fresh air will enter to replace it. Usually fresh air comes through windows or doors, but ventilators strategically placed in the walls sometimes work better. These generally have horizontal louvers on the outside to ward off rain or snow, fixed insect screens, and hinged or sliding panels on the inside to control the flow of air. The good points of ventilators are numerous: being unobtrusive, they can

6-22 A ceiling fan recirculates air throughout this house. Centerbrook PC, architects. *(Photograph: © Norman McGrath)*

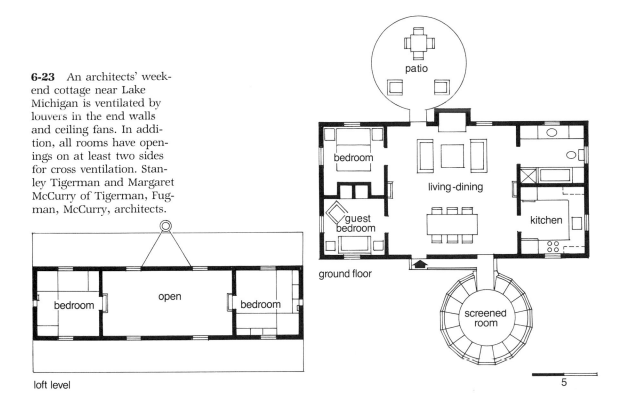

6-23 An architects' weekend cottage near Lake Michigan is ventilated by louvers in the end walls and ceiling fans. In addition, all rooms have openings on at least two sides for cross ventilation. Stanley Tigerman and Margaret McCurry of Tigerman, Fugman, McCurry, architects.

loft level

ground floor

patio

bedroom

living-dining

guest bedroom

kitchen

screened room

5

vary more in size, shape, and location than can windows; since they do not interfere with privacy, they can be placed where windows are unsuitable; and their permanently fixed and inconspicuous screens lessen the need for visually distracting insect barriers at windows.

Of all rooms, kitchens require the best ventilation; most kitchens have exhaust fans, which can be used only as necessary, to supplement windows and doors. Bathrooms come next but seldom fare as well. Windows or grilles high in the wall help to remove stale air; controllable ceiling ventilators furnish both privacy and fresh air. Living and dining spaces also need good air circulation, but the fact that they are typically large and have windows on two or more sides often takes care of the problem automatically. In contemporary planning, air flows through group spaces and to the outside as easily as people do. A good solution includes doors and windows plus grilles, some high and others low, located on different walls. Bedrooms benefit from fresh air without drafts. Again, high windows or ventilators on two walls, supplemented by other windows and doors, allow flexible control. Pollutants such as pollen, dust, and smoke are partially removed from the air by filters on most forced-air heating systems or more completely eliminated by electronic air cleaners added to the central air system.

Sanitary Control

Minimum standards for health and safety are established by federal, state, and local housing policies. Building codes specify, among other regulations, the installation of plumbing to assure sanitary conditions for both water supply to the home and disposal of sewage waste from it.

Water is necessary to bodily functions, to life itself. In the home, it is also needed for cooking, laundry, and cleaning. Health officials set standards for the safety of the water supplied to the home while building codes stipulate the materials and methods through which it is delivered. Pipes should not corrode, rust, leak, or in any way affect the taste or color of the water. Neither should they make noise or reduce water pressure. Hot-water pipes should be kept as short as possible to conserve energy; if longer than 15 feet, they need insulation. The water heater should be centrally located in relation to fixtures supplied by it, or, if fixtures are widely separated, more than one water heater should be considered.

If the water supply contains undesirable though not harmful minerals, softeners and/or purifiers can be installed in the home to remove them. Minerals can affect the taste of the water, cause laundry problems, and accumulate as deposits in pipes and on fixtures.

Soil and waste pipes remove solid and liquid refuse from the house without contaminating the fresh-water supply. Sanitary conditions for the disposal of sewage are necessary to prevent the spread of contagious diseases. Materials and methods involved are regulated by government agencies and building codes. Sewage systems depend upon gravity so soil pipes are large and must avoid sharp turns and long horizontal runs to prevent clogging. Traps and vent pipes are required to prevent seepage of sewer-gas odors into the house.

Sound Control

A pleasant living environment, offering comfort and privacy, requires sound control. Noise levels in general (measured in *decibels* on a scale of 0 to 130, with 30 decibels a general noise level to which people can adapt) are on the rise. The reverberation characteristics (amount of sound absorption) of interior spaces are of proven importance in reducing stress, irritability, nervousness, and sleeplessness and in promoting a restful environment conducive to psychological composure, physical comfort, and physiological well-being.

Homes are zoned, to some extent, according to the noise levels of various kinds of activities, with the work zone being the noisiest, the private zone the quietest, and the social zone somewhere between. A good floor plan incorporates structural sound buffers between zones: walls, closets, hallways, staggered doorways, and windows placed so as not to reflect sound back to the interior.

Exterior noise from the street can be controlled somewhat by the insulating materials and devices used to conserve energy (double-glazed windows, storm doors, insulated walls and ceilings), trees and shrubs, fences or walls, and earth berms. For maximum buffer from street noise, the noisiest areas within the home should face the street, the street side should have as few windows and doors as possible, and the house should be placed as far from the street as possible.

Special construction techniques can further reduce the transmission of noise from one space to another. Walls can be built with staggered studs so the two wall faces do not connect directly, for example, and floors can be similarly constructed. Suspended ceilings of sound-deadening materials also deter noise conduction. Conduits and pipes can be insulated to prevent sound from traveling through them; heating ducts can contain sound traps. Quiet mechanical equipment and appliances can be selected; they can be placed away from walls and mounted on sound-absorbing rubber, vinyl, or cork pads to reduce vibration. Stair landings that change direction and hallways that turn help diffuse sound, while stairwells and courtyards with one open side eliminate reverberation of noise.[10]

Finally, acoustical materials that absorb sound can be used in the interior spaces. Floors can be covered with carpet, vinyl, or cork; walls and ceilings can be

6-24 A whole wall of books emphasizes the unusual shape of this room, adds a decorative texture to the wall, and provides sound insulation. George Cody, designer. *(Photograph: © Morley Baer)*

covered with acoustical panels or paints or fabric. Bookcases, cabinets, upholstered furniture, draperies, and curtains also absorb sound. Acoustical materials can cut decibel levels in half, making work, conversation, and rest more enjoyable. Quiet background music can also contribute to a pleasant environment, masking other noise and setting the mood for rest, concentration, or social activity. (Acoustical control for music in the home was discussed in Chapter 3.)

Light Control

Marjorie Branin Keiser states in her book *Housing: An Environment for Living*, "Maximum physical comfort and safety, and optimum emotional, aesthetic, and social satisfaction depend on light."[11] Daylight is a determining factor in the design of homes, while artificial illumination allows us to extend our activities into the night and to control our waking environment creatively. Light is a form of energy to which we react immediately, although often subconsciously. Our responses to light rely upon a complex of physical and psychological phenomena. Much of our information about the world we live in comes to us through vision, but without light there can be no vision. Light is discussed as an element of design in Chapter 8. More technical aspects of lighting are presented in Chapter 16, where lighting is considered as a component of the total finished interior.

Control of temperature, air quality, sanitation, sound, and light makes our homes physically comfortable. Except for light, most have little to do with the beauty or character of the completed home, but they do seriously affect human health and happiness. The most attractively designed lifespace cannot be considered successful if it is too hot, too cold, too damp, too noisy, too dark, airless, or unsanitary. Planning for environmental control should begin at the very outset and continue through every aspect of home design. Because the structure of the home must often accommodate environmental controls unobtrusively, they have been considered here primarily as a part of the initial planning and design process rather than later as interior components.

6-25 The enormous window in this living room provides enough natural light for reading so that artificial light is not needed during the day. The brightness also sets the mood for the room. Plants thrive in the sunlight, and pale colors emphasize the feeling of airiness. Dan Solomon, designer. *(Photograph: Joshua Freiwald)*

Notes to the Text

1. James Marston Fitch, *American Building 2: The Environmental Forces That Shape It* (Boston: Houghton Mifflin, 1972).

2. S. David Freeman, *Energy: The New Era* (New York: Vintage Books, 1974).

3. Mildred Deyo Roske, *Housing in Transition* (New York: Holt, Rinehart and Winston, 1983), p. 317.

4. U. S. Bureau of the Census, *Statistical Abstracts of the U. S.*, 100th ed. (Washington, DC: U. S. Government Printing Office, 1979), p. 788.

5. Suzanne Lindamood and Sherman D. Hanna, *Housing, Society and Consumers: An Introduction* (St. Paul, MN: West Publishing Company, 1979), p. 149.

6. Donald Watson, *Designing and Building a Solar House: Your Place in the Sun* (Charlotte, VT: Garden Way Publishing, 1977), pp. 76–77.

7. Ibid., pp. 27–28.

8. Ibid., pp. 15–16.

9. David Martindale, *Earth Shelters* (New York: Dutton, 1981), pp. 38–42.

10. Marjorie Branin Keiser, *Housing: An Environment for Living* (New York: Macmillan, 1978), p. 260.

11. Ibid., p. 244.

References for Further Reading

Fitch, James Marston. *American Building 2: The Environmental Forces That Shape It*. Boston: Houghton Mifflin, 1972.

The Housing Press, Donlon, Hugh S. and Jeremy Robinson (eds.). *The House and Home Kitchen Planning Guide*. New York: McGraw-Hill, 1978. Pp. 88, 132–136.

Keiser, Marjorie Branin. *Housing: An Environment for Living*. New York: Macmillan, 1978. Chap. 13.

Lindamood, Suzanne and Sherman D. Hanna. *Housing, Society and Consumers: An Introduction*. St. Paul, MN: West Publishing Company, 1979. Chap. 6.

Makela, Carole J., LaRae B. Chatelain, Don A. Dillman, Joye J. Dillman, and Patricia A. Tripple. *Energy Directions for the United States: A Western Perspective*. Western Rural Development Center (WRDC) Publication No. 13. Corvallis: Oregon State University, August 1982.

Martindale, David. *Earth Shelters*. New York: Dutton, 1981.

Roske, Mildred Deyo. *Housing in Transition*. New York: Holt, Rinehart and Winston, 1983. Chap. 14.

Spence, William P. *Architecture: Design, Engineering, Drawing*. Bloomington, IL: McKnight, 1979. Chaps. 12 and 13.

Watson, Donald. *Designing and Building a Solar House: Your Place in the Sun*. Charlotte, VT: Garden Way Publishing, 1977.

Weale, Mary Jo, James W. Croake, and W. Bruce Weale. *Environmental Interiors*. New York: Macmillan, 1982. Chap. 10.

Weber, Margaret J. and Jacquelyn W. McCray. *Perceptions of Earth Sheltered and Passive Solar Housing by Consumers and Housing Intermediaries*. Division of Agriculture, Research Report P-849. Stillwater: Oklahoma State University, July 1984.

II

Design

"Futura"—a fabric designed by Jack Lenor
Larsen. *(Courtesy Jack Lenor Larsen, Inc.)*

7 Design Elements

Design is the selection and organization of materials and forms to fulfill a particular function. It has been with us since the first primitive hunter shaped a stone or twig to make a more effective weapon. In its simplest form this process of tool-making embodies all the basic concepts that still apply to the design of very complicated objects today: the hunter saw a need, sought the material that would best answer that need, considered how to shape and adapt the material, and worked out the process of forming to achieve a particular goal. Carrying this idea one step further, we should point out that the *second* hunter who saw the first's design and admired and imitated it was not designing but in fact merely copying—unless the second weapon incorporated an improvement of the first.

No more can the beaver's dam, the spider's web, or the bird's nest be considered the products of design, for these creatures are following instincts and learned patterns of behavior. Design as we understand it today is an intrinsically *conscious* process, the deliberate act of forming materials to fit a certain utilitarian or aesthetic function. Still, the marvelous structures built by animals do refer to one of our most fundamental ideas of design—the so-called grand design of nature. From the tiniest unique snowflake to the mightiest mountain range, we find our world beautiful, satisfying, appropriate: in short, well-designed. But beyond these isolated elements, it is the interrelationship of all the various earth's components that we call nature's design. Every living thing has its place in the food chain because of what it eats if it is an animal, what it absorbs if it is a plant, what it is eaten by or what it gives off to enable others to live. A rock is a rock, but at the same time it may be part of a mountain that catches rain clouds and helps dump the water out of them onto the thirsty land. A rock eventually breaks down into sand to form a totally different landscape with a different function. One of the most serious concerns of our time revolves around the ways in which human beings, in the name of progress, have interfered with this natural design, perhaps paving the way for a total breakdown in its harmony.

In recent years we have become increasingly aware that manufactured things, as well as natural ones, have a part in this overall design. A chair is a chair, but it is also a former tree or hide or chunk of metal or collection of chemicals. When it has ceased to function as a chair, it must go somewhere—up in smoke, into some other product, or simply to the top of an ever-more-immense pile at the dump. Design becomes a very serious business indeed when we realize that its application to any object—from the largest building to the tiniest electronic component—is bound to affect other objects and structures, the people who use them, and possibly the environment as a whole. A chair made of wood demands that a tree be cut down; one upholstered in leather or fur exacts the life of an animal. Whether the tree will be replaced by planned reforestation, whether the animal's species will remain stable are factors the designer should keep in mind, even though they are largely beyond the individual's control. On the other hand, a chair with plastic components may be ultimately responsible for causing health problems in workers at the plastics factory.

As far as disposal is concerned, it may be difficult for the designer involved in creating something beautiful to anticipate its eventual destruction. But most objects wear out sooner or later, and the combined refuse of more than 200 million people in the United States alone makes for a staggering problem. Intelligent design takes into account the entire spectrum—the source of materials, the shaping of materials, and the return of materials to the environment.

Influences on Design

Several factors inevitably influence design: the *function* an object is to serve, the *material* or materials from which it will be made, the *technology* or method of production to be employed, and changing ideas of *style* and appropriateness.

Function

We might consider the "purest" form of design the creation of something that has never existed before, so that we have no preconceived ideas about how it should look. However, relatively few designers ever have the opportunity to create something totally new. Most design is actually *re*design, or improvement of designs that already exist. If a manufacturer presents a new line of tables and advertises them as a radically new design, this is true only up to a point, because tables have been with us for many thousands of years and serve the same basic purposes they did centuries ago. Furthermore, it is hoped that a new design means improved function, for we place very high value on things that work efficiently. The company that makes kitchen appliances may change their appearance every year, altering them physically if not functionally, to conform with prevailing tastes. But in advertising a new product, they will take pains to point out its improved features—additional jobs it can perform, ease of cleaning, quietness, speed, and so on.

7-1 Deliberate, methodical planning went into the design of this kitchen work area published by Catherine Beecher and Harriet Beecher Stowe in *The American Woman's Home* (1869). It provides space for all the staple foodstuffs and working surfaces a cook of that era would need, while keeping an array of tools and cooking implements close at hand.

Only since the Industrial Revolution have designers systematically investigated the role of function in planning objects and whole systems. Production of thousands or even millions of identical objects gives both the opportunity and the incentive to evaluate their effectiveness. Deliberate, scientific investigations of function have played a major role in shaping the contemporary home, and, as mentioned in Chapter 4, no part of the home has been more thoroughly researched than the kitchen. Time-motion studies, studies of work patterns and the flow of activities all relate function to design. Today's researchers utilize highly sophisticated methods, but the concept of ergonomic planning for the home is by no means new.

In the mid-nineteenth century the thoroughgoing inefficiency of most American homes spurred Catherine Beecher, with her sister Harriet Beecher Stowe, to undertake a personal study of the ways in which function could be related to design. Although certainly not an advocate of women's liberation as we know it today, Catherine Beecher was concerned with the idea of liberating women within the home in terms of economy of labor, money, health, and comfort. Her designs stressed function—in the kitchen, for example, cabinets and surfaces built for specific purposes and storage near the point of use. Beecher designed a movable storage screen that could be placed in a large room to subdivide it for different activities at different times: a true multipurpose space. Surprisingly for that era, she gave serious attention to the quality of air inside the home. The Franklin stove, which was efficient in providing heat, had come into popular use, replacing the much less effective open fireplaces that gulped large quantities of air to keep the fires going. But the Franklin stove creates less turnover of air in the room, keeping it warmer but also keeping stale air inside. To counteract this, Beecher designed house plans that provided good circulation. She also advocated the inclusion of more bathrooms in the home and compartmentalized them for flexible use. All in all, Beecher's designs were predicated on function rather than style and emphasized a trend toward specific applications.

If we compare Catherine Beecher's ideal kitchen work area (Fig. 7-1) with the

left: **Plate 17** In a Washington, D.C., apartment a hallway is enlivened by the interplay of rectangular shapes, from slender to square and even poised on corners in the rug. George Hartman and Ann Hartman, designers. *(Photograph: John T. Hill)*

below: **Plate 18** A few gentle curves soften the basic rectangularity of an antebellum interior in Savannah, Georgia. *(Photograph: Elliott Erwitt/ Magnum Photos)*

right: Plate 19 A New Haven home combines striking modern architecture with mellow antique furnishings. White walls act as a perfect foil to the curves and vivid upholstery of the sofas. Caswell Cooke, architect. *(Photograph: John T. Hill)*

below: Plate 20 Architect Robert Graves juxtaposes straight and curved geometric forms in unexpected ways in a townhouse library. *(Photograph © Peter Aaron/ ESTO)*

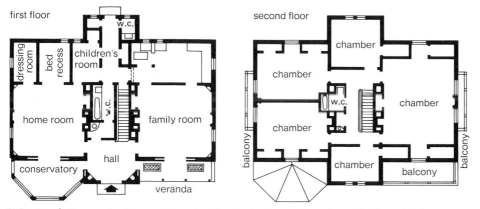

7-2 Revolutionary in its provision for closets, bathrooms, and ventilation, this house plan, also from the Beechers' *The American Woman's Home* (1869), has the multiroom comfort and graciousness we associate with the 19th century.

contemporary mix center shown in Figure 4-10, we find many similarities. That the two kitchens, separated by more than a century, have so many points in common should not surprise us, for basic food-preparation techniques have changed little. What should surprise us is the fact that so few kitchens incorporate planning of this nature. The task of the designer is to formulate ideas that answer the needs of function; the task of the consumer is to demand them.

Much has been made of the credo *form follows function*, announced in the nineteenth century by American sculptor Horatio Greenough and first applied to architecture and interior design by Louis Sullivan. This means simply that the form of an object or space should be a straightforward reflection of its intended use, that it should *look* like what it *does*. Yet function can never be an absolute determinant of form, since any given end use might be satisfied perfectly well by two or four or a dozen different forms. Leafing through the pages of this book alone we might easily find twenty or thirty different chairs that fulfill the function of offering comfortable seating, but their forms seem to have little in common.

Materials

Possibly the single most important influence on interiors and their furnishings for the last two decades has been that of Italian designers. Their contributions have been twofold: the bold, imaginative use of new synthetics, both hard and soft; and the investigation of totally innovative forms that are flexible in use, made possible by these plastics. Chairs and sofas exist not as discrete objects but as parts of modular seating arrangements capable of being assembled, combined, rearranged, repositioned, even reshaped as needs and whims dictate. The familiar seat, back, and four legs of a chair may disappear entirely into an amorphous or geometric shape that assumes contours only when someone sits in it.

Italian designers have exploited the universe of plastics in two directions. Rigid plastic chairs and tables may be light in scale and weight, assuming shapes not possible with the more conventional wood, but they are remarkably strong. On the other hand, soft plastics, such as polyurethane foam, have brought back the bulky look in furniture, because it is now possible to have solidity without weight. The success of Italian designs rests on the fact that their creators had the insight to go beyond traditional forms, techniques, and conventions to explore the possibilities for design in materials that had never before existed.

7-3 "Monte Carlo," modular seating units designed by S. Parravicini, can be assembled to fit a particular situation. *(Courtesy The Pace Collection Inc.)*

Materials can both limit and inspire the designer—limit because no material should be forced into shapes contrary to its nature, inspire because an understanding of the particular qualities inherent in a material can free the designer to innovate. *Integrity* in the use of materials is an important aspect of good design. It means an honest use and true expression of the intrinsic qualities of the substances used. Plastics, so effectively used by the Italians, have been used too often in imitation of other materials with totally different qualities. Vinyls and melamines simulate textiles, leather, clay, marble, and wood for use as wall and floor coverings, upholstery, and counter tops. Although such simulations may offer greater durability and ease of maintenance, they lack the warmth, feel, and smell of the real thing and designers may be missing the opportunity to explore and develop the unique qualities of plastics (see Chapter 11). The two chairs shown in Figures 7-4 and 7-5 illustrate this point. Both are simple, armless units essentially **Z**-shape in outline; both depend on cantilever construction, and both are surprisingly com-

left: 7-4 Verner Panton's 32½″ high side chair, designed in 1968, is molded in one piece of plastic. Its contours are specifically engineered to accept the seated human form. *(Collection Museum of Modern Art, New York [Gift of the manufacturer, Herman Miller A.G. Switzerland])*

right: 7-5 This replica of a 28⅞″ high side chair designed by Gerrit Rietveld in 1934 shows the natural grain and the joinings typical of wood. *(Collection Museum of Modern Art, New York [Gift of Mrs. Phyllis B. Lambert])*

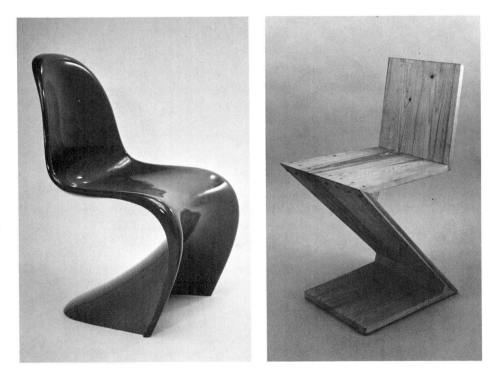

fortable. However, the first, a 1968 design by Verner Panton, is a smooth, sinuous expression of the flowing qualities of plastic. It has no joints, nor does it require them, for the molded plastic, shaped imaginatively for balance, is sufficiently strong to hold the sitter's weight. Gerrit Rietveld's side chair, designed in 1934, is an angular assembly of flat wood boards, joined in three places and reinforced at the joints. With appropriate construction, wood possesses adequate tensile strength to resist breaking, yet this chair actually is somewhat resilient.

While Rietveld's chair would seem to be an unusually honest and straightforward use of wood, designers of the twentieth century have not restricted themselves to the board and plank forms we often associate with the material. By laminating together many small pieces of cherry wood, Wendell Castle created a chopping block that suggests the form of a live tree (Fig. 7-6). Its celebration of grain patterns and whorls highlights the most attractive quality of wood. The classic example of curvilinear design in wood is the bentwood chair, developed in response to new methods of steaming wood that were introduced in the late nineteenth century (see Chapter 19). In its rocker form, the bentwood chair with caned back and seat has enjoyed enormous popularity (Fig. 7-7). This in turn has inspired contemporary designers to reinterpret the form in metal—a material also capable of assuming thin, curving lines (Fig. 7-8). Along with plastic, metal is very much a material of the present; although many people still prefer furniture of wood or other organic substances, metal and plastics seem particularly in touch with the industrial age and could be considered a prevailing trend.

7-6 The laminated wood furniture of Wendell Castle, with its sinuous organic forms, refers back to the natural growths from which the material originated. *(Photograph: John Griebsch)*

***below left:* 7-7** A process for steaming and bending wood, developed by Michael Thonet in the 19th century, made possible the creation of the bentwood rocker, whose function seems appropriately mirrored in its medley of swirling curves. *(Courtesy Thonet Industries, Inc.)*

below right: 7-8 A modern adaptation of the bentwood rocker replaces the wood frame with metal, the cane seat and back with vinyl upholstery. *(Courtesy The Door Store. Photograph: Bruce C. Jones)*

Technology

When a weaver sits down at the loom to create a tapestry, there is almost no limit to the design possibilities. A contemporary art fabric might be two- or three-dimensional, have many colors and textures, and involve an array of yarns. But if the same weaver were to design an upholstery textile for commercial production, very different rules would apply. No doubt there would be a restriction on the number of yarns and colors used, and the complexity of pattern would depend on the sophistication of the looms involved. Whether a designer is limited or challenged by such restrictions will depend on his or her imagination.

Taking the example given above, the field of textiles, a number of contemporary designers have met the challenge brilliantly. Jack Lenor Larsen was among the first to refuse inhibition, demanding that the designs come first and the technology be developed to cope with those designs. The result was a series of unique, sumptuous textiles that dispel the image of boring mass design.

Often the best of modern design results from a combination of machine and hand processes, as is true for the steel-wire furniture created by Warren Platner (Fig. 7-10). A specially tailored mold system that involves some hand work in shaping the wires allows the Platner furniture to be made as one piece, with frame and supports an integral unit. The smooth flow of these weblike forms contrasts with older furniture styles, in which separate parts had to be joined with nails, pegs, bolts, and glue. Thus, the design and the method of construction are practically inseparable.

The designer who creates a single object may not be so concerned about its method of production, for if one system doesn't work, there is always time to find another. But the vast majority of objects designed today are intended for mass production, and this raises all sorts of new questions. It was only in the mid-eighteenth century, when it became feasible to manufacture many identical objects, that people began to analyze the nature, goals, and principles of design.

The Industrial Revolution had an enormous impact on the methods by which things were produced, but it also profoundly affected the design of objects. Machinery made it possible for the first time to turn out large quantities of goods at

7-9 "Swazilace," designed by Jack Lenor Larsen and handspun and handwoven by Coral Stephens in Swaziland, is composed of only two fibers—mohair and linen. By varying size, twist, and regularity of yarns, and by the way they are put together, Larsen has created a textile of infinite interest. *(Courtesy Jack Lenor Larsen, Inc.)*

7-10 A complicated mold system had to be devised to permit the mass production of Warren Platner's steel-wire furniture. The one-piece frame construction results in an unusually graceful curving shape. *(Courtesy Knoll International)*

relatively low cost. In so doing, however, it dramatically changed the relationship of designer to the object, consumer to the object, and eventually the whole precarious balance among producer, consumer, object, and environment.

Before machines took over the business of manufacture, most articles—from spoons to houses—were designed and made either by the people who wanted them or by craftsmen in the community who were thoroughly familiar with the available raw materials and how they could be fashioned, how the objects would be used, and often how successful they proved to be in meeting the original needs. If a particular item did not serve in the way it was intended, it could be taken directly back to the maker, who might then be inspired to alter the design. Industrialization changed this situation drastically.

If in preindustrial society design responded to felt needs—the lack of something inspiring its creation—the reverse situation prevails today. Large manufacturers competing with one another produce vast quantities of items for which they must then generate a desire among consumers, and preferably a "need." The typical household did not "need" an electric can opener until it became aware that electric can openers existed. Particularly active in this field are makers of large appliances, which usually have a working life of from ten to twenty years. To encourage the consumer to discard an appliance before it ceases to operate, manufacturers annually introduce "improvements"—some of them truly useful, some at best whimsical. More often than not, design asks "What will the public buy?" rather than "What does the public need?"

Fortunately for the course of mass design, there always have been those who sought to maintain high standards within the framework of machine technology. The most organized and deliberate movement of this type occurred in the Bauhaus, a school of design active in Germany during the 1920s and early 1930s (see Chapter 19). The Bauhaus had as its guiding principle the establishment of standards of excellence in design and workmanship that would be compatible with mass production. Many of the designs formulated under its auspices, such as the side chair created by Marcel Breuer (Fig. 7-11), have remained modern classics and are still in production today.

7-11 A chrome-plated steel tube, wood, and cane side chair designed by Marcel Breuer in 1928 demonstrates the strength of steel even in very thin tubes. *(Collection Museum of Modern Art, New York [purchase]. Gebruder Thonet A.C. Germany)*

7-12 A high-Victorian bedroom from the Leland Stanford house in San Francisco was furnished for comfort, solidity, and richness in 1878. *(Photograph: Eadweard Muybridge; print made from a negative in the Stanford University Archives)*

Style

It is extremely difficult to separate materials and technology from style because they are so interdependent. If the technological processes necessary for working with metals and plastics did not exist, there could be no style for metal and plastic objects. With this in mind, we can say generally that styles and tastes and preferences do fluctuate periodically. For example, the fashion in Europe and the United States during the nineteenth century was for opulence, profusion of ornament, and a kind of heavy solidity in design. In the twentieth century most people have come to prefer cleaner lines, less applied decoration, and an overall impression of lightness. To see these principles operating, we need only compare the bedroom from the 1870s with a bedroom from the 1980s (Figs. 7-12 and 7-13).

The Victorian bedroom was the product of a society that held in high esteem the possession of material goods. The home existed as an expression of self-importance and self-worth. Therefore, the reasoning went, the more objects it contained, and the more heavily decorated those objects were, the higher would be the owners' apparent position in the social scale. A contributing factor to this value system was the new availability of consumer goods made possible by the advancing machine age. Upward mobility and possession of objects became synonymous. Thus, the Victorian bedroom contains heavy, ponderous furniture with pseudo-classical decorations and other enrichment over virtually every square inch.

To a certain extent, many of us still use our homes as the visible yardstick of material wealth and social status, but if this is true, then our criteria have changed. The bedroom in Figure 7-13 is all light and air and space compared to the rather dark and cramped Victorian version. Clean-lined, built-in furniture blends imperceptibly into the architecture and provides an ample amount of concealed storage whose unobtrusive character would have been out of place in a Victorian home. The twentieth century does not place a high premium on clutter, so a different lifestyle demands different expression in designs.

We could give numerous other examples to show how tastes and styles have

changed over the centuries and how design in architecture, furnishings, and all kinds of objects have followed those trends. It is important to remember, however, that style is a cumulative process. It would not be impossible to find a room generally in the character of the Victorian bedchamber today, but the bedroom shown in Figure 7-13 could not have existed in the 1870s. This fact depends partly on the absence of built-in furniture, plastics, and metal structures in the nineteenth century, but it also relates to questions of taste, for the contemporary room would have seemed eccentric or even shocking a hundred years ago.

7-13 A bedroom in a renovated 1910 cottage has small-paned windows whose rectangularity and simplicity are echoed in the furnishings. Robert A. M. Stern, architect. *(Photograph: Robert C. Lautman)*

We have come a very long way from the shaping of a primitive tool to the design of whole environments or even, what is not far in the future, of extraterrestrial structures. In traveling this distance, we have begun to understand the implications of design. The hunter making a new tool seemed to affect only himself. Today we know that the creation of any object may have repercussions throughout the design continuum. The responsibility is enormous, and it remains to be seen how designers of the future will meet that challenge.

Elements of Design

Writers use words, mathematicians numbers, and musicians sounds to express their verbal, mathematical, and musical ideas. Literature is, of course, a refined coalescence of language preserved in durable form; but mathematics and music each have their own "languages" composed of symbols, words, and concepts that are as readily comprehensible to initiates as the letters of the alphabet would be to the layman.

In design, expression is achieved through organizing the elements of *space*, *form and shape*, *line*, *texture*, *light*, and *color*. The last two of these, being highly specialized, form the subject of a separate chapter.

Space

Space is one of the most essential elements in home design. Simply by erecting walls we have enclosed a space, defined it, and articulated it. Painters often experience a kind of "block" when confronted with a pristine canvas, writers when facing a pure white sheet of paper in the typewriter. The first mark on canvas, the first letter struck represents an enormous commitment and the establishment of all sorts of relationships. So it is with space, but to an infinitely greater degree. We deal with the mechanism of articulating space thousands of times during the day without realizing it. In placing an object on a surface, we are not filling a void but carving out sections of space around the object. Before a structure is built, the space it will occupy exists as a continuous, diffuse entity; the construction of walls and a roof isolates two segments of space—that inside the structure and that outside.

Space suggests the possibility of change, of freedom to move physically, visually, or psychologically until we collide with or are diverted by a barrier. The element of *time* also plays an important role in our perception of interior space, for unless the space is very small, we cannot perceive it all at once, but must move through bit by bit, gradually accumulating impressions, until a sense of the whole has been assembled. Walking through a sensitively designed space, we participate in its expansion and contraction as naturally as we breathe. Space becomes a space-time continuum, because it changes constantly as we move.

As we move through space our eyes, our bodies, and our spirits explore its constantly changing contours—that which is open and that which is closed. Everyone recognizes the sense of exhilaration felt upon emerging from a forest into a meadow or walking across an open plaza in a city. Architects and city planners always have understood the drama implicit in passing from a constricted space to an expansive one. Entrance to the great urban plazas—the Piazza San Marco in Venice, the Zocalo in Mexico City, St. Peter's Square in Rome—typically is gained through narrow, congested streets, thus magnifying the element of surprise and delight upon reaching the square.

Splendid as these open spaces are, most people feel a psychological need to return periodically to sheltered spaces that enclose and protect. We respond to the spaces that envelop and include us, and we adapt to them. In doing so, we share their triumphs or failures. The merging of open and closed spaces represents one of the hallmarks of modern architecture. Instead of sequences of boxed rooms, cut off from view of one another, we find spaces that flow together, expanding and contracting as the need arises, providing physical, visual, and auditory variety.

The two most obvious and common space problems in homes are a lack of space and an excess of it. Both conditions tend to indicate an unwise *use* of the available space rather than an unmanageable number of cubic feet. The knowledgeable designer modulates spaces, using the other elements of design—line, form, light, color, and texture—to achieve a sense of spaciousness or intimacy. It is this impression of *apparent* space that affects us so dynamically and that turns spatial problems into "ideal" living environments. There are many ways to articulate space, physically, visually, and even audibly.

To increase apparent spaciousness:

- Allow the eye (and the body if possible) to travel freely beyond the immediate space through uncluttered openings into other spaces or outdoors.
- Place large pieces of furniture near walls so that they do not interrupt the open space, dividing it into even smaller segments.
- Use small-scale furniture, textures, and patterns.
- Keep furnishings and accessories few in number.
- Leave some empty, silent space in the room—between furniture or on walls.
- Expose as much floor area as possible by choosing furniture that sits up off the floor (on legs or hung from walls) rather than furniture with bases that sit directly on the floor and by using transparent glass or plastic pieces.
- Use mirrors and *trompe-l'oeil* (three-dimensional "deceive the eye") effects to create the illusion of depth.
- Unify the space as much as possible, using wall-to-wall floor coverings, floor-to-ceiling window treatments, and colors, textures, and patterns that blend rather than contrast.
- Select light, cool colors that seem to expand space.
- Light the perimeter of the room, the ceiling, and/or possibly the under side of heavy pieces of furniture such as beds or sofas to make them appear to float above the floor.

When space lacks definition, seeming to have neither beginning nor end, it may be made to appear more secure and intimate. To create this spatial perception:

- Subdivide the space physically and visually, placing furnishings perpendicular to walls to act as room dividers.
- Choose furnishings of varied height to obstruct extended views.
- Group furniture in clearly defined areas of activity.
- Select large-scale furniture and perhaps more pieces that sit on solid or skirted bases, obscuring floor area.

lower level

upper level

deck

living

dining

kitchen

hall

up

entry

den

deck

bedroom

open

open

bridge

dn

bedroom

deck

5

right: 7-16 A plan illustrates the way in which just a few irregularities in outline contribute to the flexible space within. John Sampieri, architect.

below: 7-17 Inside this prefabricated modular house, diagonal sight lines have been used to counteract the essentially square format. John Sampieri, architect. *(Photograph: Maris/Semel, and* House Beautiful)

above: 7-18 Furniture arrangement and style define space and produce a feeling of enclosure in a living room designed by John F. Saladino, Inc., architects and interior designers. (*Photograph: © Peter Aaron/ESTO*)

left: 7-19 A dining area in a large open space has been partially defined by the placement of two simple columns. Joan Krevlin of Paul Segal & Assoc., designer. (*Photograph: Robert Levin*)

- Break up the expansive area of walls and floors with contrasting colors, textures, and patterns.
- Contract space or improve its proportions with warm, dark colors.
- Create distinct, cohesive spatial units with controlled natural lighting and sensitive placement of artificial lighting.
- Use soft, rough textures to absorb sound and further feelings of privacy and intimacy.

Space is among the most important elements of home design. Unless it is thoughtfully planned, nothing else will ever seem quite right. Yet almost any space, if sensitively handled, can be made effective, livable, even dramatic.

7-20 This classic visual device reverses constantly, depending upon how we focus our eyes. At one glance it is a white vase on a black background; at another it shows two profiles facing each other. Such tools help broaden our concepts of the relationship between space and form. *Cups 4 Picasso*, 1972 lithograph by Jasper Johns. *(Courtesy Leo Castelli Gallery, New York)*

Form and Shape

Form is the counterpart of space, its three-dimensional structure, a limiting of infinity into human scale. Except for purposes of analysis, the two are inseparable, because form gives space whatever dimension it has, and space reveals, even determines form. Usually form seems more constant and permanent than space, which implies the possibility of change and the infinity of space-time.

Form and *shape* are two terms often used interchangeably, both as nouns and as verbs: indeed, we have so used them in this book. But in the purest descriptive sense, subtle differences do distinguish them. *Shape*, the simpler of the two, refers to the measurable, identifiable contours of an object, generally expressed in relation to its outlines. We speak of a square shape, a round shape, a triangular shape. *Area* refers to the two-dimensional extent of a shape, such as the floor area of a house or the wall area of a room. A much more inclusive term, *form* takes account of shape but may also encompass substance (solid or liquid form), three-dimensional volume or mass, internal structure, and even the idea implicit in shape.

In our discussion of interior design, we might do well to consider shape and form on two different levels. Shape is best understood in relation to space, as the classic positive-negative reversal silhouette (Fig. 7-20) illustrates. Looking at the drawing one way, we see the positive shape of a stemmed goblet with negative space on either side; when we allow the drawing to reverse, we see the shapes of two human profiles with space between them. If we permit our perceptions to expand, we can apply the same kinds of interrelationships to the home. The act of putting a chair into an empty room affects both the form and the space. When a second chair is added to the room, *both* forms and the space will be affected. The objects with which we fill our homes are not isolated, self-contained items but forms that relate to each other and to the spaces they articulate.

Well-designed objects for the home also relate to *human* form. Ergonomics (see Chapter 1) has had a positive impact on the design of both furnishings and spaces, particularly for work activities. Objects and spaces that accommodate the human form most readily produce the most comfort and satisfaction in use.

Additional aspects of form may be illustrated with three chairs (Figs. 7-21 through 7-23). In the first, we perceive form as *mass*, which fills space solidly. In the second group of chairs, it is *shape* that catches the eye, a wondrous assortment of contours that are reminiscent of earlier designs. The third chair calls attention to its form by concentrating on *structure*, the continuous swirl of the supporting frame. Contemporary architecture and furnishings are often characterized by their frank expression of structural design, exposing materials and methods of construction as inseparable from design. Good structural design relies on simplicity, function, integrity, and good proportion.

above left: 7-21 An easy chair designed by Mario Bellini illustrates the use of *mass* to achieve a desired effect, in this case comfort. *(Courtesy Atelier International, Ltd.)*
above right: 7-22 The cutout shapes of these Robert Venturi chairs capture the essence of Chippendale, Queen Anne, Empire, Art Deco, and other historical styles. *(Courtesy Knoll International)*
left: 7-23 The 'Penelope" chair exploits the strength of steel for its thin-lined sculptural design. *(Courtesy Castelli Furniture, Inc.)*

Despite the infinite diversity of shapes and forms in our world, all can basically be categorized as *rectilinear*, *angled*, or *curved*. In their purest expression, these shapes become the geometric figures of square, triangle, and circle or in solid form cube, pyramid, and sphere. The circle often occurs in nature, the triangle occasionally, the square or rectangle rarely. Yet so perfect are these shapes, so satisfying in their completeness, that they serve as the basis for every kind of design, from massive buildings and the layout of whole cities down through the smallest implement. Today designers are applying geometric shapes and forms to domestic architecture in new ways. Dramatic angles, unexpected planes, sculptured space, and architectural cutouts characterize some of the most innovative designs for interiors (Fig. 7-24). Where previously the circle, the triangle, and the square represented stability and repose, today's geometry provides an exciting freedom and a whole new concept for shaping internal space.

7-24 Architectural elements from an imaginary villa provide a postmodern reference to history in this redesigned city apartment by architect Wayne Berg. *(Photograph: Gene Maggio/ NYT Pictures)*

Not every shape, of course, is identifiable as a pure circle, square, or triangle; but every shape contains one or more of these elements, so we can discuss objects in terms of the predominant shapes and investigate the ways in which these shapes can be combined.

Rectilinear Forms

That **rectangularity** is typical of the larger spaces and forms in today's homes is evident in all but a few of the illustrations in this book. It prevails not only in entire houses and rooms but in such furniture as beds, tables, storage units, and television sets, plus many sofas, chairs, and benches, even putting in an appearance in smaller artifacts and textiles. Among the reasons for this widespread acceptance we might note that rectangles:

- Are easily handled on designers' drafting boards, by carpenters and masons on the site, and by machines in factories.
- Fit snugly together—an important factor when multitudinous elements coming from many sources are assembled on the job and when space is becoming increasingly expensive.
- Have a sturdy, secure relationship of exactly 90 degrees, which gives a sense of definiteness and certainty.
- Establish an apparent unity and rhythm when repeated (Plate 17, p. 159).

7-25 Architect Wendell H. Lovett calls attention to the composition of geometric shapes in this house by outlining them in decisive colors. The window in the far wall illustrates the excitement generated by poising such a simple shape as a square on one corner, and then further emphasizing it by supergraphics. (*Photograph: Christian Staub*)

The qualities of clarity, stability, and certainty that combine to make rectilinear forms popular can also bring a harsh, boxlike monotony that many people deplore. When handled imaginatively, however, the right angle has a pure, strong, absolute character—its own quality of beauty. When the rectangle or square is placed on the diagonal, it ceases to be restful and becomes a dynamic element. In sum, then, rectilinear shapes can create very different effects and call forth a variety of emotional responses from the people who see them, depending upon size, placement, color, and orientation.

Angular Forms

Triangles and **pyramids** differ from rectangles in their pointed, dynamic character. Among the most common angular elements in contemporary homes are the sloping rooflines that introduce a note of variety and surprise to the basic room cube. The living room in Figure 7-27 has a sharply angled ceiling, its form echoed in the triangular fireplace and hearth jutting into the space. While remaining stable and welcoming, this room takes on life and spirit with the inclusion of dramatic angles.

From a structural point of view, triangles are among the most stable forms known, since their shape cannot be altered without breaking or bending one or more sides. Still, they express greater flexibility than rectangles, because the angles can be varied to suit the need. For example, the triangles formed by the legs of

7-26 Rectangles can be lively. "Landis II," a fabric designed by Richard Landis. (*Courtesy Jack Lenor Larsen, Inc.*)

Design Elements **175**

7-27 In a home set into a natural woodland, a triangular theme echoes some of the shapes apparent in the branching tree trunks but brings an unmistakable human order. The sizing of triangular shapes—from the sheltering roof through the unusual fireplace configuration down to the pattern in the Oriental rug—makes a satisfying design progression. Thompson and Peterson, architects. *(Photograph: © Morley Baer)*

7-28 "Horsetail," a fabric designed by Jack Lenor Larsen, illustrates the liveliness of triangles. Crystal Palace Collection. *(Courtesy Jack Lenor Larsen, Inc.)*

standard folding chairs can, with a flick of the wrist, be transformed from stable support to space-saving linearity. Used with discretion and in large size, as in the ceiling or gable end of a pitched-roof house, triangles are secure yet dynamic. Small repeated triangles or diamond shapes in textiles, tiles, or wallpaper add briskness to interiors, while a three-sided table between two chairs sets up a congenial relationship. Diagonals generally increase apparent size; because angular forms imply motion and are relatively uncommon, they usually attract and hold attention beyond what their actual dimensions would otherwise suggest.

7-29 A living room by Paolo Ciusti employs dramatic diagonals and a mirrored end wall to create an effect of great space. *(Photograph: Kenneth D. Rice)*

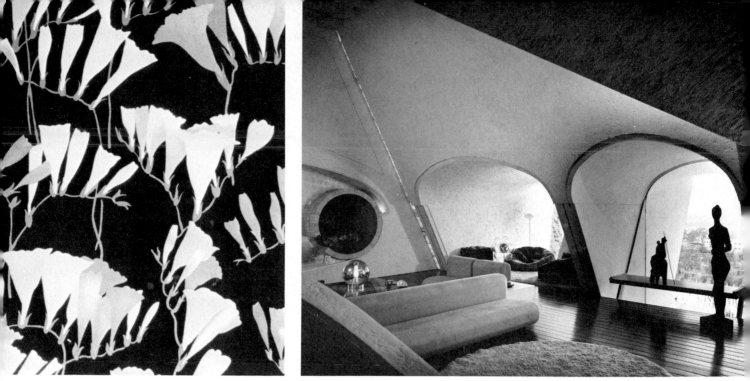

left: 7-30 "Freesias," a fabric design by Jason Polland and Larsen Design Studio, employs gently curving lines and shapes that remind us of flowers in a breeze. *(Courtesy Jack Lenor Larsen, Inc.)*

right: 7-31 A fascinating mixture of straight and curved, geometric and amorphous shapes makes this house in Mexico a constant but ever-changing sequence of delights. G. E. Arenas, architect. *(Photograph: Julius Shulman)*

Curved Forms

Curves bring together the lively combination of continuity and constant change. They remind us sympathetically of flowers, trees, clouds, and our own bodies. Until recently, large curvilinear elements, such as circular rooms, domed or vaulted ceilings, and curved stairways, have been rare in contemporary houses, but there is increasing interest in their possibilities.

The house illustrated in Figure 7-31 owes its great rounded spaces and sinuous curves to the owner's fascination with seashells. This is design inspired by nature, but abstracted to a high degree so that forms are compatible with architectural integrity. The roofline and walls are steeply angled; we would be hard pressed to find a simple rectangle anywhere in the house, so plastic and sculptural is its quality. Nevertheless we sense a stability, because in spirit as well as in shape this delightful home recalls its source: just as the tiny sea animal is protected by its shell, so would the inhabitants of this embracing home feel secure.

Circles and **spheres** have a unique complex of qualities:

- They are nature's most conservative and economical forms, since they not only enclose the greatest area or volume with the least amount of surface but also strongly resist breakage and other damage.
- Although as rigidly defined geometrically as squares or cubes, they do not seem so static, probably because we cannot forget that balls and wheels roll easily.
- They have an unequaled unity, for every point on the edge or surface is equidistant from the center—a natural focal point, especially when accented.

Inside our homes, circles and spheres are most noticeable in plates, bowls and vases, lampshades and pillows, and in a few tables, chairs, and stools. They also form the basic motif in many textiles, wallpapers, and floor coverings. Curvilinear forms seem particularly appropriate for fabrics, especially those meant to be hung, for the sinuous curves only enhance the quality of draping (Fig. 7-32).

Cones and **cylinders,** too, are curvilinear forms, but they entail a definite, directional movement not found in circles or spheres. While cones and cylinders resemble each other, there is an important difference. Cones, like pyramids, reach toward a climactic terminal peak, whereas cylinders, like rectangles, could continue forever. This makes cones more emphatic and directs attention to a focal point. Both forms please us, because they relate to our own arms and legs. They frequently serve as the vertical supports of furniture, as lamp bases and shades, candle-holders, and vases. Furniture legs of wood or metal often take the form of truncated cones, tapering toward the top or bottom for visual lightness and grace.

Only rarely do we find a home composed entirely of rectangles, triangles, or circles. Instead, most interiors reveal a combination of forms chosen to balance and counterpoint one another. The essence of combining forms lies not in seeing how many one can include but in making them work together to present a pleasing juxtaposition for overall unity (Plates 18, 19, and 20, pp. 159, 160).

above: 7-32 When choosing fabrics, consider how a pattern will look when draped. The stylized flower pattern "Allegro," by Gloria Vanderbilt, is shown hung in folds and stretched flat. *(Courtesy James Seeman Studios, Inc.)*

below: 7-33 An unusual house plan for a hillside site combines straight segments focusing on a circular pool and the broad view beyond. John M. Fuller, architect. (See photograph 7-34, facing page.)

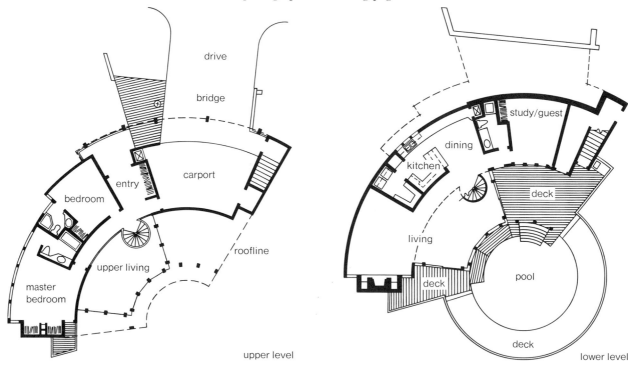

7-34 The curved outthrust of the pool deck is counterpoised against the strong rectangular mass of the hillside house. (*Photograph: Don Henderson*)

Line

Theoretically, line has only one dimension, since by definition it is the extension of a point, but in practice lines can be thick or thin. In interior design, the word *line* is frequently used to describe the outlines of a shape or space, or the dominant direction, as when the "lines" of furniture or houses are said to be pleasing. But line has a more concrete meaning when it serves to ornament or accentuate a form.

Textiles make a natural exponent of line, since the warp and filling yarns are themselves lines. When closely woven, textiles absorb the lines, but an openwork fabric such as the one illustrated in Figure 7-35 gives ample evidence of its linear structure.

Among the most expressive qualities of line is its direction. In studying the ways in which direction affects our feelings and our movements, psychologists and artists have come to such generalizations as the following:

- **Vertical lines** imply a stabilized resistance to gravity and seem to lend dignity and formality to spaces. If high enough, they evoke feelings of aspiration and ascendancy.
- **Horizontals** tend to be restful, relaxing, and informal, especially when long. Short and interrupted horizontals become a series of dashes.
- **Diagonals** are comparatively more active in that they suggest movement and dynamism. Long diagonals extend space.
- **Big upward curves** are uplifting and inspiring.
- **Horizontal curves** connote gentleness and relaxed movement.

7-35 In "Gossamer," a leno-weave fabric of long silky wool fibers, the lines produced by the yarns between the woven areas form a major design element. (*Courtesy Jack Lenor Larsen, Inc.*)

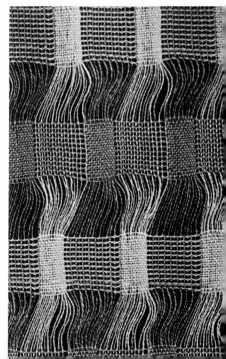

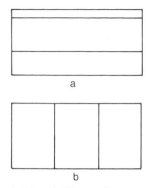

7-36 Dividing a shape into segments and reinforcing parallel contours in first the horizontal direction (a), then the vertical (b), can result in quite different effects.

- **Large downward curves,** seldom seen in homes, express a range of feelings, including seriousness and sadness. They may, however, bring a welcome sense of solidity and attachment to the earth.
- **Small curves** suggest playfulness and humor.

Lines can act either to emphasize or to deemphasize shapes, thereby changing the apparent proportions of objects and rooms. Figure 7-36 depicts two rectangles of equal dimensions, one divided with vertical lines, the other with horizontal lines. The horizontal lines reinforce the horizontal direction of the rectangle, seeming to further extend its length, while the perpendicular lines counteract it, producing a more vertical effect.

As interpreted for home design, these generalizations recommend that verticals be emphasized—high ceilings, tall doors and windows, upright furniture—for a feeling of loftiness and cool assurance; horizontals—low ceilings, broad openings, stretched-out furniture—for an impression of informal comfort; diagonals—sloping ceilings, oblique walls or furniture—for an active environment. Usually, several or all of these lines are brought together at varying levels of dominance and subordination so that the total effect seems varied and complete.

Texture, Ornament, and Pattern

Referring to the surface qualities of materials, **texture** describes how they feel when we touch them. **Ornament,** a somewhat broader term, relates to the decorative qualities visible on the surface of things. As a kind of ornament, **pattern** generally refers to the decoration applied to two-dimensional surfaces, such as fabrics. The three are closely related, because texture can serve as a kind of ornament, and ornament and pattern usually provide some texture. Every surface has a texture that affects us physically and aesthetically, but only when texture is consciously manipulated to beautify an object do we call it ornament or pattern.

Texture

A distinction is often made between *actual* or *tactile* textures, in which the actual three-dimensional surface qualities can be felt, as in bricks and woolen tweeds or hammered metal, and *visual* textures (sometimes called illusionary or simulated), in which a material reveals a textural pattern under a smooth surface.

left: 7-37 The spontaneous flowering of a sky-blue crystalline glaze on a cream background resulted in a somewhat rough *visual* but actually quite smooth *tactile* texture on a covered jar by Jack H. Feltman. *(The Fine Arts Museums of San Francisco, gift of the artist)*
right: 7-38 "Pythagory," a knotted linen "jar" by Patti Lechman has a *tactile* ribbed texture that produces a strong pattern of light and dark. *(Courtesy International Linen Promotion Commission)*

The texture results from a translation of one sensory experience—touch—into another—vision—by means of variations in dark and light that are perceived as highlights and shadows created by hills and valleys on a surface.

The effectiveness of a texture is a matter of relationships among forms, colors, and the textures themselves. A decidedly tactile texture will be more obvious when contrasted against a uniform surface than it will against a rough one. In home design texture plays an extremely important role in creating interest and variety as well as providing needed sensory stimulation.

Texture affects us in a number of ways. First, it brings a physical impression of everything we touch. Upholstery fabrics, for example, if coarse and harsh, can be actually irritating. If too sleek, they look and feel slippery and cold. The most popular fabrics tend to be neither excessively rough nor smooth. Second, texture influences light reflection and thus the appearance of color. Very smooth materials—polished metal, glass, or satin—reflect light brilliantly, attracting attention and making their colors look clear and strong. Moderately rough surfaces absorb light unevenly, hence their colors look less bright. Very rough surfaces set up vigorous patterns of light and dark, as can be seen especially in plants. Texture can be further emphasized or minimized by the light that falls on it. Strong light falling at an angle dramatizes natural highlights and shadows; uniform "wall-washing" light minimizes texture; diffuse light tempers harshness. (See Chapter 16 for further explanation of the effects of light.) Third, texture affects sound quality. Hard, smooth surfaces reverberate and magnify sound while soft, porous textures absorb it. Fourth, texture is a factor in household maintenance. The shiny surfaces of brightly polished metal or glass are easy to clean but show everything foreign; rougher surfaces, such as bricks or rugs with high pile, call less attention to foreign matter but are harder to clean; and smooth surfaces with visual textures combine most of the good qualities of both. Finally, texture is a source of both beauty and character. When organized and used repetitively in home design, texture becomes an ornamental as well as a structural pattern.

Ornament and Pattern

Many people distinguish two major types of ornament: inherent and applied. *Inherent* ornament comes from the intrinsic character of the materials, the way in which they are fabricated, or the sensitivity with which the object and each of its parts is shaped. It encompasses such sources as the natural beauty of wood grain or the qualities of silk or linen; textures and patterns originating in the weaving process or in the laying of a brick floor; the deliberate design and shaping of objects beyond utilitarian or structural demands so that they provide visual and tactile pleasure. Structural ornament is the texture of the material intrinsic to the object it enriches; it seems natural and fundamental. Usually it is less subject to physical deterioration, and is less likely to go out of fashion than is applied ornament.

Applied ornament refers to that added to an object after it is structurally complete, such as patterns printed on fabric or wallcovering, carved moldings on walls, or designs etched on glass. Patterns consist of repeated designs called *motifs* that can generally be categorized as **naturalistic** or realistic reproductions of natural subjects; **stylized** or conventional representations that simplify the subject to emphasize its basic qualities; **abstract** designs, which may be based on familiar motifs but are generally used in such a way as to be unrecognizable and include nonrepresentational **geometric** designs, using stripes, plaids, or geometric shapes.

In order to develop a pattern, the design units or motifs may be organized and repeated in a variety of ways, several of which are described in Chapter 9 as methods of achieving rhythm. Motifs may be repeated regularly, matching straight across the surface, or dropped so the figure matches midway in the design, or alternated in size, color, position, or subject, to name just a few of the variations.

top left: 7-39 Naturalistic floral designs are common in such glazed chintz fabrics as "Savannah." *(Courtesy Brunschwig & Fils, Inc.)*

top right: 7-40 "Pictograph" is a fine Egyptian cotton fabric with a stylized flower repeat. Graphics Collection. *(Courtesy Jack Lenor Larsen, Inc.)*

bottom left: 7-41 This hand-printed silk fabric has an abstract pattern which may be reminiscent of rippling water. *(Courtesy Jack Lenor Larsen, Inc.)*

bottom right: 7-42 "Radiance," a Jacquard Wilton wool carpet designed by Jack Lenor Larsen, has a geometric design with a three-dimensional appearance. *(Courtesy Jack Lenor Larsen, Inc.)*

The effect created when the pattern covers a flat surface may be quite different from the same pattern seen draped or folded as illustrated in Figure 7-32. Also, when viewed from a distance, the contrast of light and dark colors used in patterns are interpreted as visual textures, adding yet another variation to their effect.

Pattern applied to either an object or the surface of a room (floor, walls, or ceiling) will modify the apparent size of the object or space enclosed. The larger the pattern, the larger it makes the object appear while the smaller it makes the space seem. This is explained by the expectation that nearer objects and surfaces should seem larger than those that are farther away. A large pattern covering the walls of a small room will seem to diminish the size of the room more than its actual dimensions. Pattern as applied to furnishings and surfaces or as achieved through the simple repetition of materials is a major influence in many interiors.

Only two factors limit the range of applied ornament: the nature of the materials and the imagination and taste of the designer. Ornament can be admirably suited to an object's use, form, and materials—or it can be distressingly inappropriate. The most satisfying ornament fits the functions, form, size, and material of which it is a part, being, moreover, worthwhile in itself. Specifically, ornament should be:

- Pleasant to feel, especially if it is touched frequently. Resting one's arms or back against sharp carving on a chair or handling angular silverware can be physically uncomfortable.
- Supportive of the form it enriches. Ornament generally is at its best when it accentuates the particular quality of the object of which it is a part.

- Related to the size, scale, and character of the form. Generally, ornament and pattern should be similar to the object they adorn in both scale and character; small areas are best covered with small patterns that are less dominant than the form of the object itself and that reinforce its character.
- Appropriate to the material. Fine, linear decoration can be effective on smooth, light-reflecting metal or glass, whereas on wood it might look merely scratchy.
- Vital in itself. Spirit and character are as crucial in ornament as in the design of form and space.

The stemware in Figure 7-43 embodies all these criteria. Taking the form of a delicate, perfect flower poised on a striated stem, these glasses contrast the pure, unadorned transparency of crystal against the overlapping pattern that is possible with molten glass. Beyond its decorative capacities, the textured pattern in the stem actually enhances function, since it provides a better grip. The ornament, while rich, has a light, linear quality in keeping with the size and fragility of the glasses, and it leads the eye upward to the expanding volume of the bowl.

Attitudes toward ornament, especially toward applied ornament, vary from one period to another. In contemporary design two seemingly contradictory viewpoints are evident: on the one hand a distaste for any kind of applied ornament, with emphasis on keeping design clean and "minimal"; on the other a great delight in ornament, especially as provided by old furnishings and handcrafted objects. The quality that will be stressed in each home depends upon the tastes, personalities, and lifestyle of the occupants.

Our discussion of space, form, shape, line, texture, and ornament has necessarily been rather abstract, isolating one quality at a time for analysis. In practice, however, these elements plus light and color, considered in the next chapter, are so closely interwoven in the fabric of design that each reacts upon the others. This synthesis will be analyzed in Chapter 9 when the principles of design, such as balance, rhythm, and emphasis, are examined to explain how the elements and principles together contribute to the total effect.

7-43 Ornament growing naturally out of the material, form, and function enhances these crystal goblets. Pavel Hlava, designer. *(Courtesy © Rosenthal Bilderdienst)*

7-44 In a restored 18th-century mill in Pennsylvania, French and Italian antiques with restrained ornament seem perfectly at home. Lilias Barger and Raymond Barger, designers. *(Photograph: John T. Hill)*

References for Further Reading

Allen, Phyllis Sloan. *Beginnings of Interior Environment*. 5th ed. Minneapolis, MN: Burgess, 1985. Part 4, pp. 67–77.

Bevlin, Marjorie Elliott. *Design Through Discovery*, brief ed. New York: Holt, Rinehart and Winston, 1984. Chaps. 1–7.

Cheatham, Frank R., Jane Hart Cheatham, and Sheryl A. Haler. *Design Concepts and Applications*. Englewood Cliffs, NJ: Prentice-Hall, 1983.

Faulkner, Sarah. *Planning a Home*. New York: Holt, Rinehart and Winston, 1979. Chap. 3, pp. 53–74.

Friedmann, Arnold, John F. Pile, and Forrest Wilson. *Interior Design: An Introduction to Architectural Interiors*, 3rd ed. New York: Elsevier Science Publishing Co., 1982. Parts I and II, pp. 1–100.

Kleeman, Walter B., Jr. *The Challenge of Interior Design*. Boston: CBI Publishing Company, 1981. Chaps. 3 and 7, pp. 202–371.

Ocvirk, Otto G., Robert O. Bone, Robert E. Stinson, and Philip R. Wigg. *Art Fundamentals: Theory and Practice*, 4th ed. Dubuque, IA: William C. Brown, 1981.

Richardson, John Adkins, Floyd W. Coleman, and Michael J. Smith. *Basic Design: Systems, Elements, Applications*. Englewood Cliffs, NJ: Prentice-Hall, 1984.

Russell, Stella Pandell. *Art in the World*, 2nd ed. New York: Holt, Rinehart and Winston, 1984.

St.Marie, Satenig S. *Homes Are for People*. New York: Wiley, 1973. Pp. 202–371.

Stepat-Devan, Dorothy, Darlene M. Kness, Kathryn Camp Logan, and Laura Szekely. *Introduction to Interior Design*. New York: Macmillan, 1980. Chaps. 3, 6, 7, 8, pp. 49–60, 98–133.

Thiel, Philip. *Visual Awareness and Design*. Seattle: University of Washington Press, 1981.

Zelanski, Paul and Mary Pat Fisher. *Design: Principles and Problems*. New York: Holt, Rinehart and Winston, 1984.

8

Light and Color

Although color has long been considered a fundamental of home design, only recently have we become fully aware of its potentialities beyond mere pleasantness or unpleasantness. That it can be influential, for better or for worse, has been proved countless times. Such phrases as *functional color* and *color conditioning* describe its use in business for increased efficiency. And psychologists have reported studies that seem to show that young children tested in brightly painted rooms the children themselves thought of as "beautiful" earned higher IQ scores than those tested in rooms of "ugly" (black, brown, and white) colors. In the theater the emotional and symbolic effects of color have long been exploited. Color can work similar magic in homes, by cheering us or relaxing us. With receding colors or appropriate contrasts, the apparent size of a room can be markedly increased. Ceilings can be made to seem higher or lower with a coat of paint. Where there is no sunlight, its effects can be simulated with yellow walls, and excessive brightness or glare can be reduced with cool, darkish surfaces. Some or all furnishings can be brought into prominence or allied with their use of color. In short, color can significantly alter the appearance of form and space, change our moods, and perhaps even affect our performance abilities.

Color, however, and the other elements of design discussed in the preceding chapter, depend upon **light** to make them visible. Most of our perceptions are

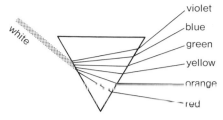

8-1 When light passes through a prism, the component colors are separated into clearly distinguishable bands.

based upon the sense of sight. Light is the most vital element of design, for without it there is no sight. Light is electromagnetic energy from the sun or other celestial bodies, from fire, or from artificial (electric) sources traveling in *wavelengths* that range in size from too long (infrared) to too short (ultraviolet) for us to see. Between the infrared and ultraviolet sections of the spectrum lies a short visible band of light energy that makes vision possible. This *visible spectrum* can be broken into equal bands of colored light (red, orange, yellow, green, blue, and violet) with a prism, each color having a different wavelength. When recombined in equal amounts, these colors of light create the seemingly "white" or colorless light that we regard as normal and ideal.

The color of an object that we see results from two factors: the way in which the object absorbs and reflects light and the kind of light that makes the object visible. When light strikes an opaque object, some of the colors of light rays (or wavelengths) are absorbed and others reflected. Those wavelengths that are reflected give the object its color quality. Lemons and yellow paint, for instance, absorb almost all colors of light except yellow. White objects reflect almost all the colors in light, while black objects absorb most of them. We say *almost* because pure colors are very seldom found. The true color quality of anything is revealed when it is seen in white light. Usually, however, light itself is not completely colorless.

The color of light depends on its source and whatever it passes through before coming to our eyes. Light from the noon sun contains all the spectrum's hues balanced and blended so that the effect is white or colorless. Light from the moon is bluish, while that from open fires, candles, and the typical incandescent lamp is yellowish. Incandescent and fluorescent lights, however, come in many colors, and we can choose those that are most effective, even changing them for special occasions or blending colors by means of colored spot- or floodlights. We can also alter the color of artificial light with translucent shades that are not white. Daylight can be changed by sheer, colored curtains or by tinted glass. In general, warm light intensifies red, yellow, and orange and neutralizes blue and violet. Light that is cool and bluish does the opposite. (Lighting, as a component of interior design, is considered in greater detail in Chapter 16.)

Working with color is a science as well as an art. As a designer, one must consider more than just the visual effects of color; it is vitally important to people's physical and psychological responses to their environment as well, and may even affect health. The designer must know what result is desired, how to achieve it, and how to predict its effects.

Color Theory

Organizing facts and observations on color into a systematic theory is the first step in understanding color relationships and effects. Three different kinds of theories have been developed: physicists base theirs on light, psychologists on sensation, and artists on pigments and dyes. Our interest is chiefly with the last, because anyone who works with paint or fibers—from the interior designer to the do-it-yourself home painter, from a fabric manufacturer to a handweaver—necessarily works with pigments and dyes. There are a number of accepted color theories, but basically all are predicated on the fact that to describe a color with reasonable precision at least three terms are needed that correspond to the three dimensions or attributes of color: **hue,** the name of a color; **value,** the lightness or darkness of a color; and **intensity** or chroma, its degree of purity or strength.

Hue

The simplest and most familiar color theory is based on the concept that there are three primary hues—red, blue, and yellow—that cannot be produced by mixing any other hues; however, mixtures of them will result in nearly every other hue. If the visible spectrum of color is bent into a circle and intermediate hues placed between red, orange, yellow, green, blue, and violet, it can be diagrammatically visualized as a twelve-hue *color wheel* (Plate 21, p. 193). The twelve hues divide into three categories:

- **Primary hues,** labeled *1* on the color wheel, are red, blue, and yellow. Theoretically, the three primary hues cannot be created by mixing any other hues together.
- **Secondary** or **binary hues,** labeled *2*, are green, violet, and orange. Each stands midway between two primary hues of which it is the product, as green is equidistant from blue and yellow.
- **Tertiary** or **intermediary hues,** labeled *3*, are yellow-green, blue-green, blue-violet, red-violet, red-orange, and yellow-orange. These stand midway between a primary and a secondary hue of which they are the product. For instance, yellow-green is between the primary hue yellow and the secondary hue green.

Hues are *actually* changed, or new ones produced, by combining neighboring hues as indicated above. Red, for example, becomes red-violet when combined with violet. If more violet were added, the hue would be changed again. The twelve hues on the color wheel are only a beginning because there can be an almost infinite number of hues. The effects of light and background also lead to *apparent* changes. Cool light will make any blue-based hue seem bluer and any yellow- or red-based hue seem gray, while warm light enhances the yellow and red hues, graying blue. Backgrounds are equally important: red placed against cool blue or green seems warmer and brighter than when seen against orange or red-violet. Texture, reflectance, and the size of the color areas also affect an individual's color perceptions, as will be explained later.

In the retailing industry, colors are given fanciful names. But these are imprecise and could easily bring different visual images to different people. To identify colors accurately, it is better to name their standard hues, as affected by value and intensity—such as light, grayed green.

Interaction of Hues

When placed next to each other, hues produce effects ranging from unity to decisive contrast. Some combinations, such as blue, blue-green, and green, give a unified, restful sequence. But if blue is put next to orange, there is excitement and contrast. Two adjectives describe these relationships:

- **Analogous hues** are near each other on the color wheel, as are yellow, yellow-green, and green.
- **Complementary hues** lie directly opposite each other, as do yellow and violet.

Hues can be combined to produce any degree of harmony or contrast. If only one hue is used in a room, a strong *monochromatic* unity results. When *analogous* hues are placed next to each other, the effect is one of harmonious sequence. By intermingling small areas of color as in small-scale patterns, the original hues may appear to combine to form in-between colors.

Complementary hues, when placed next to each other, contrast vividly; each color seems to gain intensity if the area of each hue is large enough to be perceived as a separate color. This effect is known as **simultaneous contrast.** But if the areas of two complementary hues are very small, as in a textile woven of fine red and green yarns, the effect at normal distances is lively but more neutralized, a result of visually blending the two hues. And if opposites are actually mixed together, a brownish gray is likely to be the result.

Another phenomenon associated with complementary colors is **afterimage,** an effect created by concentrated exposure to a bright hue. The complementary hue is "seen" when the eyes shift away as a relief from the visual fatigue experienced from the first hue. The designer needs to be aware that such an effect can occur and affect surrounding colors if areas of strong hue are used where the eyes may focus for any length of time. Afterimage can be a particular problem for the individual who works at a home computer, looking at the video display terminal for an extended period of time.

Warmth and Coolness of Hues

Each hue has its own "temperature" that affects us and our homes in several ways. Red, orange, and yellow seem warm and active; they tend to bring together whatever is seen against them. Warm hues are called **advancing** hues because they seem nearer to us than they actually are, which leads to two seemingly paradoxical results. Upholstering a piece of furniture in intense red increases its apparent size, but painting the walls of a room red decreases the room's apparent spaciousness because the walls seem closer to us. The *area* of color usage determines the effect: a piece of furniture is a *segregated* color area while the walls are a *surrounding* color area.

Blue, green, and violet tend to seem cool and restful. Because they appear to be farther away than they actually are, they are referred to as **receding** hues. They reduce the apparent size of objects, but when used on walls they seem to increase a room's dimensions.

Value

Value is defined as relative lightness or darkness. It is perhaps easiest to understand in neutrals, where it indicates degree of lightness or darkness between pure white (full light) and pure black (the absence of any light). But value gradations apply equally to colors and are also determined by the amount of light the colors reflect.

There can be any number of value steps between white and black, but the seven shown in the gray scale (Fig. 8-2) make a convenient number. Even without considering color for the moment, we can see how value levels affect the character of a home. A room composed of nearly all light values seems bright, airy, and cheerful; its effect is distinctly "uplift." But if not handled with care an environment of all light values can seem cold and laboratorylike. A room consisting of nearly all dark values, handled skillfully, can bring a sense of security and solidity. But unless careful, it can be very gloomy and claustrophobic. Sharp contrasts of light and dark in a room are dramatic and stimulating, emphasizing the shapes of furnishings. A few middle values are usually needed, to provide a transition and avoid harshness. Close values blend together (even when the hues are strongly

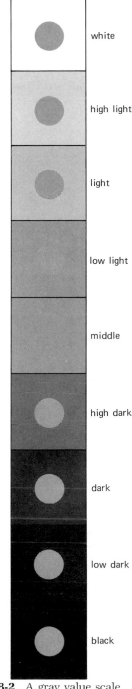

white

high light

light

low light

middle

high dark

dark

low dark

black

8-2 A gray value scale shows seven gradations between black and white. The dots are all of identical (middle) value, but appear lighter against a dark background and darker against a light one.

8-3 "Black Magic," a rug designed by Eileen Gray (1923) in four shades of gray, black, ivory, and white—value gradations that give it dramatic impact. *(Courtesy Furniture of the Twentieth Century, Inc., New York)*

contrasting, if viewed from any distance or under a low level of illumination) and may be calm and serene or both monotonous and a safety hazard. Even apparent size is affected by value; light values seem to increase size because they reflect light while dark values reduce size because they absorb light.

Value gradations become very important in a monochromatic color scheme or in a design based primarily on neutrals. Plate 22 (p. 193) illustrates a masterfully subtle treatment of the latter. A bedroom of unusual tranquility and dignity, this room has been planned almost entirely around grays and beiges, with four slight transitions of value. The walls, an off-white, mark the lightest value, followed by the light beige macrame window curtain, the darker gray on the beds and stools, and the yet darker carpet. Even the last of these, however, could only be placed at middle value on the gray scale. A bowl of fresh flowers and the books (or whatever other artifacts might be brought into the room) offer the only accents.

The seven intervals in the gray scale also correspond to the **normal value** of the pure hues in the sequence of the color wheel. We know from subjective experience that yellow is a light color and violet a dark color. But if we were to place the hues of the color wheel side by side with the gray scale, they would appear to have equal value in the following order:

Hue	Value Step	Hue
yellow	8, high light	yellow
yellow-orange	7, light	yellow-green
orange	6, low light	green
red-orange	5, middle	blue-green
red	4, high dark	blue
red-violet	3, dark	blue-violet
violet	2, low dark	violet

Every hue can range in value from light to dark, but we tend to think of hues at their normal values. Yellow, for example, comes to mind as the color of a lemon or dandelion rather than of a cream-colored carpet. **Tints** are values lighter than normal; **shades** are values darker than normal. Pink is a tint of red, maroon is a shade of the same hue. Sky blue is a tint, navy blue a shade. Plate 23 (p. 194) illustrates value scales for three hues.

Combinations of hues appear at their best when normal value relationships are maintained, particularly when used in large areas. **Discord** results when normal values are reversed. Discord may be very effective as an accent but is regarded as unbearable in large quantity. Imagine a room with pale lavender walls and a deep rust carpet!

Values are changed by making colors reflect more or less light. With paints, *actual* changes are made by adding black, gray, or white, by adding a color lighter or darker than the original, perhaps by adding the complement of the basic color. *Apparent* changes can be made by reducing or raising the amount of natural or artificial light reaching the color surface which provides corresponding effects (less light, darker-appearing color; more light, lighter-appearing color), or by placing the color against backgrounds of differing degrees of light or dark. Values affect one another much as hues do—contrasts accentuate differences (simultaneous contrast). The same gray looks much darker when seen against a light surface than when seen against black. The same holds true for values of any hue.

Value contrasts are vital in distinguishing form, judging depth, and discerning a change in plane, particularly for the very young or old or anyone with poor vision. Value is the single most important characteristic of color where perception is concerned.

Intensity

Any hue can vary in its purity or strength—in other words, in the degree to which it differs from gray. Pink, for example, is always red in hue and light in value, but it can be *vivid*, almost pure pink, or it can be *neutralized*, grayed pink (Plate 24a, p. 194). This is called intensity. A *pure* hue is at its fullest intensity, as on the color wheel. **Tone** is often used to describe intensity; a *jewel* tone is a brilliant color while a *muted* tone denotes a grayed color.

Scales of intensity can have many or few steps. Full intensities, which are possible only at the normal value of each hue, are often described as *high* or *strong*, the more neutralized as *low* or *weak*.

Intensities can be *actually heightened* by adding more of the dominant hue. They can also be *apparently raised* by illuminating the object with bright light of that hue or by throwing it into contrast with its complementary hue, a grayed tone of the hue, or a completely neutral color. For example, a wall of grayed yellow can be intensified by repainting it with a purer yellow, by casting a yellowish spotlight on it, or by placing chairs in front of it that are upholstered in violet, a less intense yellow, or gray.

Actual and *apparent* intensities can also be *decreased* in several ways. First, the designer can lessen the amount of the dominant hue by adding varying amounts of its complementary hue; yellow is grayed by adding violet, violet by adding yellow, blue by adding orange, and so on. A similar effect is produced by mixing a color with gray, black, or white. A second method calls for illuminating an object with less or more diffuse light, or light of the complementary hue. A blue wall, for example, would be grayed during the day by light filtering through sheer, orange-tinted glass curtains and at night by translucent lampshades of the same hue, by a lower level of light, and by the warm-colored light from incandescent lamps. A third device is to introduce something—a painting, a wall hanging, a chair, a sofa—that is noticeably more intense in color than is the wall. This apparent change is most pronounced if the object and the wall are of the same or similar hues; a bright blue chair against a gray-blue wall. Even placing a hue beside an analogous hue makes it appear less intense compared to placing it beside its complement (Plate 24b, p. 194).

Changing any one dimension of a color almost inevitably changes the other two, at least slightly. Available pigments are almost never absolutely pure: grays, blacks, and whites tend to be either warm or cool and thus alter the hue with which they are mixed. It is possible to change intensity without altering value if a gray or complementary hue that absolutely matches the color's value is used, but this is seldom achieved. One of the dimensions can be modified much more than the other two, but it is difficult to change one and hold the others constant.

Large areas of color tend to be more pleasing in effect if they are of less than pure intensity. Bright color can be very tiring and confusing if overused. Nature uses large areas of lower intensity enlivened with small quantities of pure color, the basis for the **law of chromatic distribution** used by artists and designers. Bright colors weigh heavily in their power to attract attention and can balance much larger areas of grayed color.

A great deal can be learned about the qualities of hue, value, and intensity by analyzing the color organizations seen in rooms, furniture and textiles, and gardens. Trying a few simple experiments will give firsthand information. Mixing different hues will show how they change. Colors can be neutralized by adding complementary hues or by black, white, or gray. They can also be diluted with a suitable colorless thinner. Construction paper or textile samples can show what happens to the apparent hue, value, and intensity of any color when it is placed against various backgrounds. A lighting box with white-painted cubicles containing different types and colors of lamps will demonstrate the effects of light on colors. Small fabric swatches and paint chips can be placed in each cubicle to compare their appearance under different lights.

Effects of Hue, Value, and Intensity

Generalizations about color relationships and their effects are well worth knowing, although we should be aware that none of them always holds true.

How do colors affect our feelings and activity? Warm hues, values lighter than the middle range, and high intensities tend to raise our spirits and stimulate us to be active. Pronounced contrasts of any sort, such as blue-green and red-orange or deep brown and white have similar energizing effects. Intermediate hues, values around the middle range, and moderate intensities are relaxing and visually

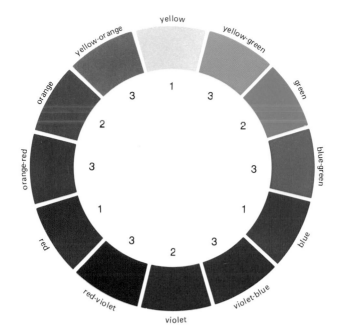

above: Plate 21 A color wheel shows a sequence of hues, divided into primary (1), secondary (2), and tertiary (3) hues. Complementary colors appear opposite each other.

right: Plate 22 The neutral color harmony that dominates this bedroom takes on interest because of changes in value. A large macrame hanging behind the bed hides an unattractive outdoor view. Paul Rudolph, architect. *(Photograph: © Ezra Stoller/ESTO)*

193

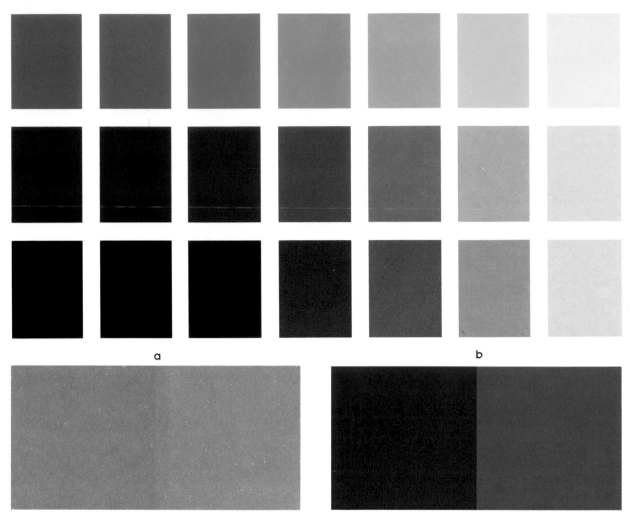

a

b

top: Plate 23 Value scales for green, orange, and violet, showing tints, shades, and normal values.

bottom: Plate 24a The two examples of pink have the same value but different intensities.

Plate 24b If a hue is placed next to an analogous color, it will appear to have a lower intensity than when it is placed next to its complement.

Plate 25 Cool blues and muted grays visually enlarge a living room designed by architects Margaret McCurry and Stanley Tigerman. *(Photograph: © Howard N. Kaplan)*

above: Plate 26
Sometimes the colors in a room are coordinated with part of the architecture. This red-brick fireplace wall serves as a background for the warm, subdued earth colors of the furniture and carpets that complement it. Roger Larson, architect. *(Photograph: © Morley Baer)*

right: Plate 27 A modern painting and an Oriental rug serve as the color keynotes in this room. The soft blue sofa picks up the blue of the painting while color accents and accessories—even the warm yellow-brown of the wood furniture—also refer back to the painting's hues. Dark blue-black slate on the floor is a harmonizing base. The clear Lucite sculpture reassembles to become a dining table. Francis Mah, architect. *(Photograph: John T. Hill)*

undemanding. Cool hues, values below the middle range, and low intensities usually seem quiet and subdued. There are, of course, innumerable other ways of selecting and organizing varied hues, values, and intensities to achieve the effect that is desired.

What colors and combinations attract our attention? Any degree of dominance or subordination can be produced by skillful handling of color. We are immediately attracted by colors that are striking and bold, and these may be indicated where dominance is wanted. Extreme values and strong intensities also tend to attract attention, but no more so than emphatic contrasts or unexpected, out-of-the-ordinary color relationships. Colors that are grayed and moderate in value as well as familiar color combinations are unemphatic and seldom noticed, which makes them passive backgrounds unless they are interestingly textured or otherwise patterned. Thus, with color alone attention can be directed toward that which is important and away from that which is less consequential.

How do colors affect apparent size and distance? The degree to which color can seem to alter the apparent size of any object is often dramatic, but this, too, is a matter of complex relationships. In general, warm hues, values above the middle range, and strong intensities make an object look large. Cool hues, darker values, and lower intensities reduce its apparent size. Decisive contrasts, textures, and ornamentation may or may not increase apparent size, depending on exactly how they are handled.

Apparent distance, or spaciousness, is increased by cool hues, the lighter values, and the lower intensities. This is the effect of **aerial perspective** taken from observation of the natural landscape in which colors appear cooler, lighter, and grayer on the far horizon than they do in the immediate proximity of the viewer. These color characteristics can be used to make a small room seem larger, give the appearance of a higher ceiling, or alter and improve the apparent proportions of a square-shaped room. The latter is accomplished by using a cool, light, dull color on one wall or two opposite walls and possibly the ceiling. On the other hand, warm, dark, bright colors can be used to make a large room seem smaller and more intimate, make a ceiling appear lower, or visually widen a long, narrow space (by placing the advancing color on one or both end walls). Although some contrast is needed as a yardstick, strong contrasts usually make objects seem nearer than they actually are (diminishing apparent space), while low contrast can increase the sense of spaciousness. Similar colors carried from one room to another also increase visual space.

Putting all of this to work is fascinating but complex. Rooms with white or very light, cool walls seem more spacious than those with darker, warmer surfaces. Houses painted white seem bigger than those of red brick or natural wood. *But* the value relation between any object and its background is important because strong value contrasts make objects stand out, which tends to increase their apparent size. Thus against a white background a sofa with light upholstery might look much less conspicuous than it would set in a room of predominantly dark and middle values (Figs. 8-4 and 8-5).

How can colors be used to accentuate or deemphasize the outlines or contours of objects? Differences in hues, intensities, and especially values make us conscious of an object's shape and contours. White against black makes the strongest contrast, and as the values become closer to each other, forms tend to unify and merge with their surroundings. The shape of a white lamp is much more emphatic when seen against dark gray or black than when seen against a light value of any hue. Diametrically opposite hues attract attention to outlines, but if the values of

above: 8-4 The light value of this sofa blends with the light value of the background, making it seem smaller and increasing the apparent spaciousness of the room. Deborah Rae Sanchez, ASID Associate, interior designer. *(Photograph: Kenneth D. Rice)*

right: 8-5 A light sofa stands out in marked contrast to its setting of predominantly dark values—a scheme that increases the apparent size of the sofa. *(Courtesy Ege Rya, Inc.)*

Table 8–1   Summary of Effects of Hue, Value, and Intensity

	Hue	Value	Intensity
feelings	warm hues are stimulating, cool hues quieting	light values are cheering; dark values range from restful to depressing; contrasts are alerting	high intensities are heartening; strong, low intensities are peaceful
attention	warm hues attract more attention than cool hues	extreme values tend to attract the eye; but contrasts or surprises are even more effective	high intensities attract attention
size	warm hues increase apparent size of objects; used on walls, they decrease apparent size of room	light values increase apparent size of objects; but strong contrast with background is equally effective	high intensities increase apparent size of objects; used on walls, they decrease apparent size of room
distance	warm hues bring objects forward; cool hues make them recede	light values recede, dark values advance; sharp contrasts in values also bring objects forward	high intensities decrease apparent distances
outline, or contour	warm hues soften outlines slightly more than cool hues; contrasting hues make outlines clearer than related hues	value contrasts are a potent way of emphasizing contours	intensity contrasts emphasize outlines

the two hues are similar, the edges seem fuzzy rather than distinct, a visually disturbing phenomenon known as **vibration,** in which the boundary between the two colors appears to move when viewed at close range and to blend into neutral color at a distance. Varying the values of the two complements, usually with the cool hue darker, will restore a more pleasing effect. Related hues also soften contours, and warm hues make the edges of anything seem less sharp than do those that are cool. We could summarize the effects of hue, value, and intensity, as in Table 8–1, bearing in mind that all generalizations about any one of these three factors assume that the other two dimensions of color, the background, and the lighting, are held constant. For example, artillery red is normally more stimulating than mint green—both are of middle value and full intensity. *But* mint green is likely to attract more attention than cocoa brown, a color that is red in hue but low dark in value and tending toward neutral in intensity.

Color Systems: Munsell and Ostwald

Although similar to the color system discussed above (in that the hues are arranged in a circle, which becomes a three-dimensional form when fully developed) the systems formulated by Albert Munsell and Wilhelm Ostwald deviate from it in two basic ways. First, the primary hues are not the same, and second, both have intricate, standardized methods of notation with which innumerable colors can be precisely labeled and identified by referring to the appropriate color charts. These

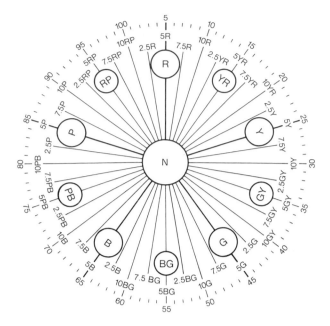

8-6 The Munsell system divides the spectrum into five principal and five intermediate hues, indicated by letters on the color wheel. Each of the ten hues can be subdivided into ten more, creating the hundred hues indicated by the outer circle of numbers.

are of inestimable value in science, commerce, and industry where universal specifications of color are necessary; they are also useful to professional designers for precise communication.

The **Munsell system**[1] of color notation has *five principal hues*—red, yellow, green, blue, and purple—and five intermediate hues—yellow-red, green-yellow, blue-green, purple-blue, and red-purple (Fig. 8-6). Each of these hue families has been subdivided into four parts, indicated by the numerals, 2.5, 5, 7.5, and 10, which when combined with the initial of a hue designates the exact hue. The number 5R, for example, refers to "pure" red, 7.5R is toward yellow-red, and 2.5R toward red-purple. Further refinement divides each hue into ten steps, as indicated on the outermost circle of Figure 8-6.

8-7 The relationship of hue, value, and chroma appears in a three-dimensional diagram. The circular band indicates the hues, as in Figure 8–6. The central vertical axis shows nine value gradations from near black to almost white. Chroma, indicated on the radial spokes, goes from neutral in the center to full chroma at the periphery. (*Munsell Color Company*)

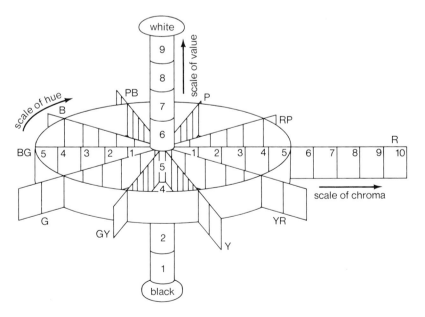

Table 8–2   Relationship between Munsell Value and Reflectance*

Munsell Value	Reflectance
9/	79%
8.5/	68%
8/	50%
7/	43%
6/	30%
5/	20%
4/	12%
3/	7%
2/	3%

*For standard source C as specified by the International Commission on Illumination, approximating daylight at 6500 K. (Reprinted with permission from Design Criteria for Lighting Interior Spaces, Publication #RP-11, Illuminating Engineering Society of North America.)

Figure 8-7 shows the nine *value* steps going from 1/, the darkest, to 9/ as the lightest, with 0/ and 10/ as theoretically pure black and pure white. The relationship between Munsell value and reflectance of light is shown in Table 8–2. This information is used by designers when calculating the quantity of light needed in a room.

The term *chroma* is used instead of intensity. The chroma scale begins with /0 for complete neutrality at the central axis and extends out to /10, or farther for very vivid colors (Fig. 8-7). The number of chroma steps is determined by the varying saturation strengths of each hue. Notice in the diagram that red, a very strong hue, extends to /10, but the weaker blue-green reaches only to /5.

The complete Munsell notation for any color is written as hue value/chroma. Hue is indicated by the letter and numeral that defines that particular hue on the color wheel. This is followed by a fraction in which the numerator designates value and the denominator specifies chroma. Thus 5R 5/10 indicates "pure" red at middle value and maximum chroma. Blue that is light in value and low in chroma is written 5B 9/1.

The **Ostwald system**[2] is derived from three pairs of complementary color sensations—red and green, blue and yellow, and black and white. The color wheel begins by placing yellow, red, blue, and green equidistant from one another. Placing five intermediates between each pair of hues makes a circle of twenty-four hues (plus six additional hues that are needed to complete the color range). These are indicated by the numbers around the equator of the color solid (Fig. 8-8).

No sharp distinction is made between value and intensity: the hues are lightened or darkened or neutralized by adding appropriate amounts of white and black. This expands the color wheel into a color solid composed of a number of triangular wedges packed together as in Figure 8-8. In each wedge there are eight steps from top to bottom and eight from center to periphery.

Colors are designated by a formula, which consists of a number and two letters (8 pa for example). The number indicates the hue. The first letter indicates the proportion of white in any color, and the second letter designates the proportion of black. The scale goes from a, which is almost pure white, through c, e, g, i, l, n, to p, which is almost pure black. Thus these two letters tell how light or dark a color is as well as the degree of saturation. In each triangle there are twenty-eight colors, which multiplied by the twenty-four hues gives 672 chromatic colors. Adding the eight neutral steps brings the total to 680. Pure red has the symbol of 8 pa: the number indicates "pure" red, and the letters indicate that no black or white has been added. Intense orange-red has the symbol 5 pa, grayed orange-red has the symbol 5 lg, and dark orange-red has the symbol 5 pn.

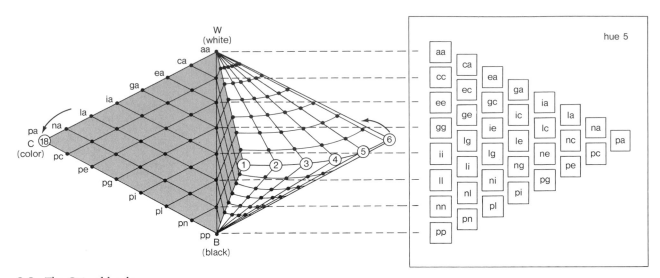

8-8 The Ostwald color system is illustrated by a solid double cone, partially cut away here to show relationships inside. Colors are most saturated at the equator and become increasingly neutralized as they approach the central axis of gray values. Colors become lighter toward the top, darker toward the bottom. At the right, a triangle illustrates 28 variations of one hue with lightest at the top and darkest at the bottom, proceeding from neutral at the black-white axis to saturation at the periphery.

Planning Color Harmonies

Planning the colors to be used in a room or a series of rooms can be a delightful part of furnishing a home. Color that is satisfying and exhilarating costs no more than hues that are depressing and without character. But colors are not used alone. We need to know what happens when colors are combined (as explained in the preceding pages) to be able to produce the effect that is wanted. The systematic relating of colors has resulted, over the years, in easily recognizable color harmonies or schemes. These do not dictate colors but they do give us an orderly way of discussing and predicting what will happen when various hues are combined.

In theory, countless color harmonies are suited to homes. Practically speaking, however, only a few can be classified, probably because these types just about exhaust the possibilities of orderly selection from the color wheel. In color, as in design, an underlying sense of order is satisfying but stereotyped, commonplace organization is tedious. The standard color harmonies are nothing more than time-tested basic recipes; actual color schemes may not fit perfectly into any of the categories. They can be varied and individualized, be simply points of departure, or be disregarded entirely.

Typical color harmonies fall into two major categories, **related** and **contrasting.** Related color schemes, which are composed of one or several neighboring hues, lead toward an unmistakable harmony and unity. Contrasting schemes, based on hues that are far apart on the color wheel, offer greater variety as well as a balance of warm and cool hues. The two types are basically different, but neither is inherently better than the other. Depending on the hues chosen and the dominant pattern of intensities, any of them can be vividly brilliant or comparatively quiet. Beyond this, we can subdivide color harmonies into seven categories, of which the first two are considered related, the other five contrasting. Most color plans utilize no more than three hues for backgrounds and major furnishings, varying values, intensities, and amounts. In all schemes, one hue should predominate. Equal quantities of the colors chosen would lack interest in rhythm, emphasis, and balance.

Monochromatic and Achromatic

Monochromatic (literally, "one hue") color harmonies (Fig. 8-9) evolve from a single hue, which can be varied from high light to low dark and from full saturation to almost neutral. White, grays, black, and small amounts of other hues add variety and accent, as do applied and natural textures and decorative patterns. Thus, even with only one basic hue, the possibilities are legion.

The advantages of monochromatic color schemes are that some degree of success is almost assured, because unity and harmony are firmly established. Usually, spaciousness and continuity are emphasized, and the effect is quiet and peaceful (Plate 25, p. 195) except in those dramatic cases in which saturated colors predominate or extreme contrasts are utilized. A major danger—monotony—can be avoided by diversified values and intensities and by differences in form, texture, and spatial relationship.

Achromatic or **neutral** color schemes utilize only value variations, without intensity. Neutral harmonies usually need an accent color in accessories or a few furnishings. Although black, white, and gray are the only true neutrals, the very low intensities of the warm colors (ranging from ivory to dark brown) are neutral in effect when used for the majority of surfaces and furnishings. Basic hue identity is important in these subtle colors to ensure harmony. Off-white colors or wood tones may be cool or warm in hue, for example, a factor to consider when coordinating any scheme.

The room shown in Plate 22 (p. 193) is achromatic, since it contains only the neutral grays and beiges; while it seems reserved, it could scarcely be described as dull. We might imagine this same room done in a hue—blue or green or red—with the same value gradations from light to middle.

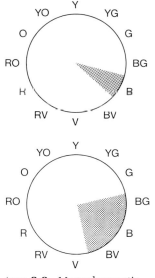

top: 8-9 Monochromatic harmony.
bottom: 8-10 Analogous harmony.

Analogous

Strictly speaking, analogous color harmonies are based on two or more hues each of which contains some degree of a common hue (Fig. 8-10). In other words, the hues fall within a segment of the color wheel that is no more than halfway around it. Thus, if the common hue is blue, the colors could be as closely related as blue-green, blue, and blue-violet, or as separated as yellow-green, blue, and red-violet. Analogous color schemes have more variety and interest than do monochromatic color schemes (Plate 26, p. 196). The effect is usually automatically unified because of the shared color, and analogous schemes are often used throughout an entire home, carrying the common thread of color from room to room.

Complementary

Built on any two hues directly opposite each other on the color wheel, complementary harmonies (Fig. 8-11) are exemplified by orange and blue, or yellow-orange and blue-violet (Plate 27, p. 196). They offer a great range of possibilities. Yellow and violet, for example, can be as startling as gold and aubergine, as moderate as ivory and amethyst, or as somber as olive drab and gunmetal. Complementary schemes provide the balance of opposites (which, when mixed, form neutral) and of warm and cool hues. They tend to be livelier than related harmonies but their success depends upon careful handling of value and intensity.

Double Complementary

A development of the complementary scheme, double complementaries (Fig. 8-12) are simply two sets of complements. Orange and red-orange with their respective

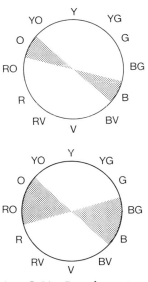

top: 8-11 Complementary harmony.
bottom: 8-12 Double-complementary harmony.

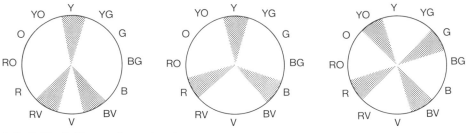

left: 8-13 Split-complementary harmony.
middle: 8-14 Triad harmony.
right: 8-15 Tetrad harmony.

complements, blue and blue-green, are an example. Worth noticing in this case is the fact that orange and red-orange, as well as their complements, are near each other on the color wheel. This is usually the case, because if the hues are widely separated, it is difficult to see the order on which this harmony is based.

Split Complementary

Another variation on the complementary theme, the split complementary (Fig. 8-13) is composed of any hue and the two hues *at each side of* its complement, as in yellow with blue-violet and red-violet. Violet, the complement of yellow, is split into red-violet and blue-violet. This makes the contrast less violent than in the simple complementary type and adds interest and variety.

Triad

Red, blue, and yellow; green, orange, and violet; blue-green, red-violet, and yellow-orange—any three hues equidistant from one another on the color wheel—are known as triad color harmonies (Fig. 8-14). In case such combinations sound shocking, remember that full-intensity hues are seldom used in homes. Red, blue, and yellow might be translated as mahogany, French gray, and vanilla. Green, orange, and violet could be sage green, cocoa brown, and dove gray. Thus, although triad harmonies can be vigorous, they can also be subdued. In any case, the effect is one of well-rounded balance with variety held in check by a readily apparent, systematic unity.

Tetrad

Any four hues that are equidistant from one another on the color wheel produce a tetrad color harmony (Fig. 8-15). Yellow-orange, green, blue-violet, and red are an example. Such combinations lead to rich, varied yet unified, fully balanced compositions.

Factors to Consider in Selecting Colors

People

Color preferences and responses of different cultures, ages, sexes, and mental states have been researched extensively. However, consensus of findings is elusive, apparently because so many variables are involved. Reaction to color is highly subjective and emotional. Therefore, the designer must spend the time to learn the preferences and responses of individuals in the household before making color decisions.

Many times one or more household members will have collected clippings of color combinations they particularly like, perhaps started a scrapbook, may even have had their own color profiles worked up to help in deciding what color of clothing to buy that will best fit their skin, eye, and hair tones, as well as the colors they respond to. A verbal or written inventory of color preferences and responses to paintings, flowers, model homes and designer showcase houses, and color illustrations in books and magazines will provide additional information from which to gather inspiration. These sources will present valuable clues for the designer, whether in-house or professional, when a project is started.

To help in deciding on specific colors, swatches of fabric and carpet and wallpaper samples as large as possible will enable the designer and homeowner to visualize the finished effect. Color chips from paint stores are a starting point for deciding on the hues for walls and ceilings. It may save money in the long run to get a large piece of wallboard and paint it the color under consideration. These can then be studied at different times of day or night since their appearance will change with the kind of light. Large samples are important because increasing an area of color changes its apparent hue, value, and intensity as a result of **amplification,** a phenomenon in which light reflected from one wall to the next gains intensity and increases the strength of the color we see. Reflection from the floor and other furnishings also alters color perception, as does the amount of light available in the room. Paint will also appear several times darker when seen on a large area such as a wall, in part because vertical surfaces receive less direct illumination than horizontal surfaces. Textures of materials and finishes will have an effect as well. Color appears brighter on a smooth, shiny surface than on a matte or rough surface that neutralizes intensity. Where strong light strikes a very shiny surface, color may disappear entirely from specular reflection, the mirrorlike reflection of the actual light source on the surface. Color combinations, whether solid or patterned, in small scale only hint at the full-scale effect.

Other factors, more specific and easier to categorize than the people who will be using the home, also will influence choices of colors: household possessions, specific rooms and their orientation, as well as the whole house and the environment.

Possessions

The furniture and accessories now owned, as well as planned purchases, both limit and suggest possible color schemes.

- A collection of antique furniture, good paintings, or individualized accessories might determine colors.
- Miscellaneous furnishings can often be pulled together by a related scheme.
- When starting from nothing, a favorite color or combination of colors might be the guide in selecting furnishings.
- Existing furniture or architectural backgrounds may be the basis for other color selections (Plate 26, p. 196).

The living room in Plate 27 (p. 196) can be analyzed in terms of the colors in one dramatic painting and a beautiful Oriental rug. Dark slate floors with a bluish cast form a harmonious background for both; the sofa has been upholstered in a blue similar to one rectangle in the painting and in the rug's motif; accents of orange and red throughout the room pick up other colors from the painting. Even the warm tones of wood furniture and paneled ceiling seem to blend with the orange-and-blue color scheme for a totally unified effect.

Rooms

The walls of a room—including the windows and their treatment, the doors, and fireplaces—are the largest color areas. Floors and ceilings come next in size, then furniture and, finally, accessories. In the past, typical color relationships broke down as follows:

- Floors moderately dark in value and low in intensity to give a firm, unobtrusive base and to simplify upkeep
- Walls usually lighter in value than floors in order to provide a transition between them and the ceilings, and typically quite neutral in intensity to keep them as backgrounds
- Ceilings very light in value and very low in intensity for a sense of spaciousness and for efficient reflection of light

Although this standard approach can give a satisfying up-and-down equilibrium, there are many reasons for deviating from it. Light floors, for example, make a room seem luminous and spacious, and maintenance is less of a problem with new materials and textures. Dark walls give comforting enclosure, and they unify miscellaneous dark objects (Fig. 8-16). Intense colors for floors, walls, or furniture are a welcome relief from all-too-prevalent drabness. A survey of the color illustrations in this book will disclose many of the devices that can be used successfully to personalize and individualize color harmonies.

8-16 Walls painted chocolate brown create a sense of warm enclosure and make a coherent mass of books and miscellaneous objects arranged on shelves across an end wall of the room. *(Courtesy Karastan)*

Room size, shape, and character seem to change with different color treatments, a factor often underestimated. In planning a new house, color should be considered along with the other aspects of design. Older houses are most easily remodeled by an "architectural" use of color. A few generalizations bear repetition:

- Cool hues, light values, and low intensities make small rooms seem larger.
- Rooms too long and narrow can be visually shortened and widened by having one end wall warmer, darker, and more intense than the side walls.
- Rooms that are too square and boxlike seem less awkward if one or two walls are treated differently from the others or if one wall and the ceiling or the floor are similar in color.
- Vigorous color implies noisy, social areas.
- Sleeping areas and spaces for quiet work benefit from subdued colors or may express personal preferences.
- Communal spaces usually employ favorite colors or at least avoid colors disliked by any of the individuals in the family or household.
- Colors that flatter complexions are most desirable in bathrooms and grooming areas. If cool colors are used, lighting may be chosen to enhance skin tones.

Windows and their orientation affect the character of rooms and have a bearing on color schemes:

- In rooms well lighted by large windows or good artificial illumination, colors will not be distorted. In rooms with less light, colors seem darker and duller.
- Rooms facing south and west get more heat and more light (of a yellowish hue) than those facing east or north. These differences can be minimized by using cool colors in south and west rooms, warm colors in east and north rooms.

Regarding the rooms of a home separately, especially those of the group living spaces, has dangers because a home is a unit, not a collection of rooms. Unified color schemes recognize this and bring harmony and continuity; they increase visual spaciousness and make it possible to shift furnishings from one room to another without disturbing color harmonies.

Economies with Color

Color can more than earn its cost; it can actually save money if wisely used:

- A coat of paint on one or more walls of a room will change the atmosphere less expensively than any other single device.
- Old, battered, nondescript furniture takes on renewed vitality with new paint.
- Bands of color painted around windows are inexpensive substitutes for draperies; floors painted in suitable colors, possibly textured or patterned, lessen the need for rugs; painted graphics on walls cost less than wallpaper.
- A preponderance of light-value colors can cut electric bills and probably improve vision.
- Warm colors in the home help make people comfortable at lower, probably more healthful temperatures.
- Cheering colors may lessen the need for vitamins and tonics.
- Colors that do not fade or that fade gracefully minimize replacement.
- Nature's colors, especially if patterned, not only reduce daily and weekly maintenance but remain passably good-looking longer than do most clear, sharp colors.
- A unified color scheme throughout the house makes for economical interchangeability of furniture, draperies, and rugs.

Notes to the Text

1. The Munsell system of color notation is accepted by the United States of America Standards Institute for color identification.
2. The Ostwald system of color notation is used as the basis for the *Color Harmony Manual* and *Descriptive Color Names Dictionary*, published by the Container Corporation of America (Chicago, 1948).

References for Further Reading

Albers, Joseph. *Interaction of Color*, revised pocket ed. New Haven: Yale University Press, 1975.

Beebe, Tina. "An Expert's Guide to Color," *House and Garden*, September 1981, pp. 146–150.

Birren, Faber. *Color and Human Response*. New York: Van Nostrand Reinhold, 1978.

Birren, Faber (ed.). *Color Primer: A Basic Treatise on the Color System of Wilhelm Ostwald*. New York: Van Nostrand Reinhold, 1969.

Birren, Faber (ed.). *A Grammar of Color: A Basic Treatise on the Color System of Albert H. Munsell*. New York: Van Nostrand Reinhold, 1969.

Birren, Faber. *Light, Color and Environment*. New York: Van Nostrand Reinhold, 1969.

Birren, Faber. *Principles of Color: A Review of Past Traditions and Modern Theories*. New York: Van Nostrand Reinhold, 1977.

Blake, Jill. *Color and Pattern in the Home*. New York: Quick Fox, 1978.

Buckley, Mary and David Baum (eds.). *Color Theory* (Arts and Architecture Information Guide Series, Vol. 2). Detroit, MI: Gale, 1975.

Design Criteria for Lighting Interior Living Spaces. New York: Illuminating Engineering Society of North America, 1980.

Drimer, Margaret. "Structuring and Detailing with Color," *Residential Interiors*, January–February 1980, pp. 74–77.

Ellinger, Richard G. *Color Structure and Design*. New York: Van Nostrand Reinhold, 1963.

Faulkner, Sarah. *Planning a Home*. New York: Holt, Rinehart and Winston, 1979. Chap. 6, pp. 130–148.

Halse, Albert O. *The Use of Color in Interiors*, 2nd ed. New York: McGraw-Hill, 1978.

Horn, Richard. "Connecting with Color," *Residential Interiors*, January–February 1980, pp. 78–81.

Itten, Johannes. *The Art of Color*. New York: Van Nostrand Reinhold, 1961; reprint 1974.

Kuppers, Harald. *Color: Origin, Systems, Uses*. New York: Van Nostrand Reinhold, 1973.

Libby, William Charles. *Color and the Structural Sense*. Englewood Cliffs, NJ: Prentice-Hall, 1974.

Light and Color. Cleveland, OH: General Electric Company, 1974.

Marshall Editions Limited (ed.). *Color*. Los Angeles: Knapp Press, 1980.

Munsell Color Company, Inc., Baltimore. *Munsell Book of Color: Defining, Explaining, and Illustrating the Fundamental Characteristics of Color*. Baltimore: Munsell Color Company, Inc., 1929.

Sharpe, Deborah T. *The Psychology of Color and Design*. Chicago: Nelson-Hall, 1974.

Smith, Charles N. *Student Handbook of Color*. New York: Van Nostrand Reinhold, 1965.

Vincent, Helen Diane. "Color in Design," Perspective, *Restaurant Design*, Fall 1981, pp. 48–57.

Wagner, Carlton. "The Language of Color," Viewpoint, *Designers West*, September 1982, pp. 140–148.

Wilson, Jose and Arthur Leaman. *Color in Decoration*. New York: Van Nostrand Reinhold, 1971.

Design Principles

In the search for ways to create functional and pleasing objects, certain principles are observable in both nature and art. Balance, rhythm, and emphasis—a simple but inclusive trio—explain why some combinations of space and form, of line and texture seem to work better and to look better than others. To these we add the concepts of scale, proportion, and harmony. No one can set absolute rules for the creation of effective design. Indeed, some of the most striking designs seem deliberately to violate theory, but they are the exception rather than the rule. If the elements of design described in Chapters 7 and 8 are the raw ingredients of design, the principles outlined here can be considered the organized fashion in which those ingredients should be combined. They are concepts that have evolved to explain how and why certain combinations and relationships of elements are pleasing. A working knowledge of these guidelines gives us a means of communication to evaluate the success of design in achieving its objectives. (The objectives of good design—utility, economy, beauty, and character—were presented in Chapter 1.)

Balance

Defined as *equilibrium*, balance is a major precept in all phases of living, from furniture arrangements to bank accounts. Through balance we gain a sense of equipoise, but this may range from static permanence to repose and from suspended animation to actual motion. Balance results when interacting forces, attractions, or weights tend toward resolution.

Nature provides many examples of divergent kinds of balance. The Rock of Gibraltar typifies static permanence, with changes too slight to be noticed. Sand dunes are continuously shifting, but without loss of equilibrium. Trees, too, are always changing equilibrium, because their shapes vary as they grow and because winds and the seasons affect them. Thus balance can be an ever-changing resolution of forces as well as an equalization of dead weights. It is also evident from nature that balance exists in four dimensions—time as well as length, breadth, and width.

In balancing an interior, we deal with the **visual weights** of architecture and furnishings. The visual weight of anything is determined by the psychological impact it makes on us and the attention it demands. Although there are no rigid formulas that always hold true, some general characteristics apply:

- Large objects and spaces appear heavier than small ones, but a grouping of small objects can counterbalance a large mass.
- Physically heavy materials such as stone have greater visual weight than lighter materials.
- Opaque materials look heavier than transparent materials.
- Bright, warm, dark colors seem heavy when compared to dull, cool, light colors.
- Active textures and patterns hold attention longer than smooth, plain surfaces.
- Unique, irregular shapes and objects have importance beyond their size, while the expected and typical usually settle into the background.
- Strong contrasts of texture, pattern, and color have greater impact than close harmonies.
- Objects placed above eye level appear heavier than those placed below.
- Brightly lighted areas attract more attention than dim ones.

For example, a small spot of bright color can balance a large grayed area; visually, a significant painting may be as "heavy" as many square feet of plain wall. Well-balanced interiors hold this interplay of forces in poise.

Balance in a home is as ever-changing as nature's equilibrium is, but in different ways. People are the first factor, for a room is never complete except when being used. As people walk about, they not only see a home from different angles but actually change the equilibrium by their movement and by the clothes they wear. The second factor is light. Natural illumination is altering every minute of the day and changes markedly with sky conditions and the seasons. Only within small limits can its effects be controlled, yet it affects our homes drastically. For example, subtle nuances of color and very fine detail can be readily appreciated in moderately bright light, but they are all but obscured in very strong sunlight or at dusk. Artificial light can be precisely controlled but has to be flexible to meet a number of needs, and flexibility brings variance. The third factor is the composite of all the little things that happen in the course of a day (the reading material and other portable paraphernalia brought in and left) as well as the modifications that come with the months and years (the scarcely noticed fading of textiles and mellowing of wood, to say nothing of the replacement of worn-out or unwanted objects). What does all this mean? Simply that in view of these inevitable changes, many of them beyond our strict control, the fundamental pattern of equilibrium should be strong enough to take these onslaughts in stride, to gain from, rather than be destroyed by them.

It is customary to differentiate three types of balance: **symmetrical, asymmetrical,** and **radial.**

Symmetrical Balance

Also known as *formal* or *passive* balance, symmetrical balance is achieved when one side of something is the exact reverse (mirror image) of the other half. Our clothes, furniture, and household equipment are nearly all symmetrical to fit our symmetrical bodies. Such balance is easy to appreciate, because we can see quickly that, since one side is the reversed replica of the other, the two must be in equilibrium. The effect is typically quiet and restful, perhaps because it demands little effort from the observer. Its overtones of stateliness and dignity are exemplified by

9-1 An almost perfectly symmetrical balance gives serenity to a sitting room, with furniture, paintings, and lamps reversing around an imaginary axis at the center. The occasional chair and stool to one side, plus the T'ang horse on the coffee table, prevent the composition from being totally static. *(Photograph: John T. Hill)*

classical architecture and traditional interiors. Also, people stand or sit as symmetrically as they comfortably can when they wish to appear dignified and in control. Symmetrical balance tends to stress the center, creating a logical focal point for something one wishes to emphasize. But the resultant division into two equal parts usually reduces apparent size.

Although these observations are generally true of symmetrical balance as used in homes, we should note that totally different effects are possible. Violent rhythms or swirling curves, regardless of symmetrical arrangement, will not seem stable or reposed. Shapes or colors that lead the eyes away from the middle weaken the focal point at the center.

Basically, symmetrical balance is as simple as *aba*, the quantitative formula or pattern from which it is derived, and this simplicity contributes to its popularity. While very easy to handle at an elementary level, it can be imaginative, subtle, and complex. Few entire homes or even single rooms are completely symmetrical (utility and the need for variety rule this out) but many have such symmetrical parts as centered fireplaces or identical sofas or chairs facing each other. Often, however, symmetry is imposed arbitrarily or comes out of habit or laziness when it is not appropriate. Then it can lead to inconvenience or dullness. For example, doors in the centers of walls are seldom logical because they leave two equal areas that may be difficult to furnish unless the room is very large and they generally contribute to poor traffic patterns. Too much sameness can lead to predictable monotony, although in small areas or objects symmetry is familiar and comfortable. Minor variations within the major theme of symmetry help maintain interest.

Symmetry is indicated *but not dictated* when:

- Formal, traditional, or tranquil effects are desirable
- The designer wishes to focus attention on something important
- Use suggests symmetry—such as a table with chairs positioned so that diners face one another for easy conversation
- Contrast with natural surroundings is a desirable factor since the natural landscape, as seen through large expanses of window, is seldom symmetrical

Asymmetrical Balance

Also referred to as *informal*, *active*, or *occult* balance, asymmetry results when visual weights are equivalent but not identical. This is the principle of the lever or seesaw: weight multiplied by distance from center. Both physical and visual weights follow similar laws in that heavy weights near the center counterbalance lighter ones farther away. Asymmetrical balance is often found in buildings or gardens designed to harmonize with their natural surroundings and to use space most efficiently, as well as in furniture arrangements planned for convenience. It is seen in some historical periods—Rococo and Art Nouveau, for example—and in much Oriental and contemporary design.

The effects of asymmetrical balance differ markedly from those of symmetry. Asymmetry stirs us more quickly and vigorously, and it suggests movement, spontaneity, and informality. Being less obvious than formal balance, it arouses our curiosity to see how equilibrium was found and, in so doing, it provokes thought and is therefore more lasting in appeal. Subject to no formula, asymmetry allows freedom and flexibility in arrangements for utility as well as for beauty and individuality but requires imagination and individual *qualitative* judgments regarding weight and placement factors.

A specific aspect of asymmetry is seen in the **vertical balance** of wall elevations that positions heaviest items at the bottom and succeedingly lighter objects toward the top to counteract the expected pull of gravity. The same object "weighs" more as its distance above eye level increases. A kind of *perpendicular*

left: **9-2** Although the fireplace is symmetrically placed in the center of the far wall in this living room, most of the other elements are asymmetrically disposed. The heavy sofa balances a light, open chair before the window wall; the square-cut window at top left plays against a much smaller but round lamp at head level, the latter bouncing the eye down toward the fireplace tools to the left of the hearth. George Nemeny, architect. *(Photograph: John T. Hill)*

below: **9-3** A daring use of asymmetry in a coffee table of marble and glass. We know that the top must be firmly anchored on the base, but the bowl of anthuriums reinforces its equilibrium. J. Wade Beam, designer. *(Courtesy Brueton Industries)*

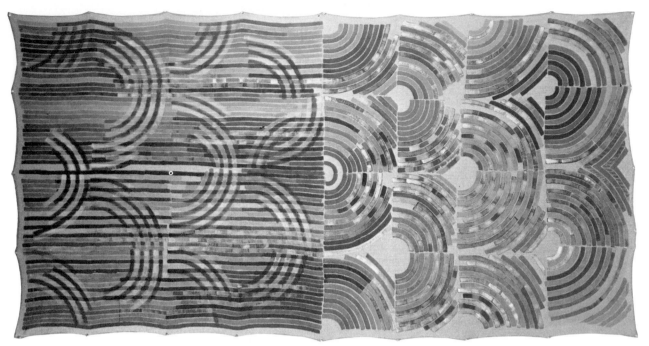

9-4 In "Breaking," artist Mary Anne Rose uses a motif of concentric circles that provides radial balance in her acrylic–on–unprimed-linen composition. *(Photograph: Suzanne Kaufman, courtesy International Linen Promotion Commission)*

balance can also be achieved by playing horizontal configurations against vertical with distance from the point of junction increasing apparent weight.

Asymmetrical balance is indicated when:

- Informality and flexibility are desirable
- The designer seeks an effect of spaciousness
- Use suggests asymmetry
- Harmony with nature is a goal

Radial Balance

When all parts of a composition are balanced and repeated around the center—as in the petals of a daisy or the widening ripples from a pebble thrown into a pond—the result is called radial balance. Its chief characteristic is a circular movement out from, toward, or around a focal point. In homes it is found chiefly in such circular objects as plates and bowls, lighting fixtures, flower arrangements, and textile patterns. It may be static and formal, focusing on the pivotal center point, as in a table with a floral centerpiece, or active and swirling about a less emphasized central focus, as in a spiral staircase. Although of lesser importance than the two preceding types, radial balance makes its own distinctive contribution in many small objects and provides a refreshing counterpoint to rectangularity.

Balance lends stability to a composition. In the design of a room a balanced distribution of high and low, large and small objects and spaces is needed. In Plate 28 (p. 229) the quiet composition of smaller objects counterbalances the large four-poster bed, giving the room a dignified equilibrium.

9-5 Radially balanced, an exposed spiral staircase adds dynamic movement to any room. Allen/Buie Partnership, architects. *(Photograph: Greg Hursley)*

Rhythm

Defined as *continuity*, *recurrence*, or *organized movement*, rhythm is a second major design principle and one through which an underlying unity and evolving variety can be gained. It is exemplified in time by the repetition of our heartbeats, the alternation of day and night, and the progression of one season into another. In form and space it appears in the more or less repetitive character of the leaves on a tree, the alternating light and dark stripes of a zebra, and the sequences and transitions in a river of curves that lead our eyes along its path.

Rhythm contributes to the beauty of homes in several ways. Unity and harmony are consequences of rhythmic repetition and progression. Character and individuality are in part determined by the fundamental rhythms—festive and light, dynamic and rugged, precise and serene. Homes gain a quality of "aliveness" through the implied movement and direction that rhythm induces. This, however, is fully achieved only when a congruent pattern of rhythms prevails—a pattern of which we may be consciously or only subliminally aware. **Repetition, progression,** and **contrast** are the three primary methods of developing rhythm.

Repetition

Repetition is as simple as repeated rectangles or curves, colors, textures, or patterns; but it can be given more intriguing complexity in *alternation* of shapes, colors, or textures, or in *continuous related movement* seen in the natural textures and patterns of the earth, plants, water, and all living, changing things. Even the most commonplace home is full of repetition—evidence of its universal appeal and also of the fact that merely repeating anything anywhere is not very stimulating. Some useful guides are:

- Repeat consistently the forms and colors that underline the basic character.
- Avoid repeating that which is ordinary or commonplace.
- Too much repetition, unrelieved by contrast of some sort, leads to monotony.
- Too little repetition lacks unity and leads to confusion.

9-6 A series of gossamer strips with curvilinear designs, hung in two parallel lines, changes in response to the slightest air movement. This art fabric by Gerhardt Knodel could act as a room divider or window treatment, yet it remains a creative work in its own right. *(Courtesy Cranbrook Academy of Art, Bloomfield, Michigan)*

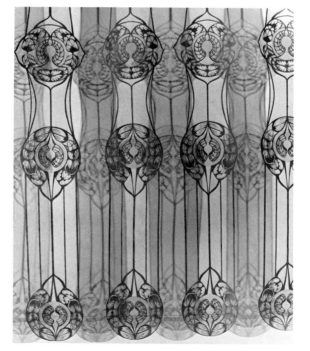

216

left: **9-7** A unique corner cupboard designed by Charles Moore depicts stepped progression in its design. *(Photograph: Hedrich-Blessing, courtesy Formica Corporation)*

9-8 The rectangular shapes and line configurations in a rug designed by Loja Saarinen develop a rhythm that is picked up in the chair fabric, desk, and wood wall paneling. Cranbrook Academy of Art Museum. *(Courtesy Cranbrook Archives)*

Progression

A sequence or transition produced by increasing or decreasing one or more qualities, progression is ordered, systematic change. Because it suggests onward motion by successive changes toward a goal, progression can be more dynamic than simple reiteration.

Progression is easiest to see in small things—in patterns on china and in textiles or furniture. Charles Moore, for example, has designed a corner cupboard (Fig. 9-7) composed of intriguing sequences of steps leading the eye across and up, in and out to the final piling up of blocks in precarious equilibrium at the top. But while it will necessarily be more subtle, progression is just as valid in design for the whole home, even in exterior design. The facade of a wood-sheathed house (Fig. 9-9) is broken by rectangles of different shapes and sizes, beginning with a small square at upper right, progressing through stacked vertical rectangles in the entry and at far right, and culminating in large horizontal rectangles in the center and at far left. This exterior also illustrates the principle of asymmetrical balance, for the visual weights of the windows on either side of an imaginary central axis (supplied here by the single leafless tree) offset each other to create equilibrium. In the interior, progression may be seen in the ways in which a single pattern is used, or in the building up of a group of furniture, or in the sequence of spaces, shapes, or colors within a room.

above: 9-9 The basic rectangular forms of this house are enlivened by a series of progressions in forms, placement, weights, and materials. George Nemeny, architect. *(Photograph: John T. Hill)*

right: 9-10 Designer Juan Montoya used a progressive sequence of heights to lead the eye from the sunken conversation area with its low seating to the raised platform, sculpture, taller chair backs, lamps, curtains, and finally to the high curved ceiling. *(Photograph: Mark Golderman)*

9-11 Contemporary furniture and architecture are contrasted with Renaissance and medieval antiques in this eclectic living room renovated by architect Paul Rudolph. *(Photograph: Robert Levin)*

Contrast

Contrast is the deliberate placing of forms or colors to create *opposition* by abrupt transition instead of gradual—round next to square, red beside green. It is a favorite device to awaken response. The rhythm produced is exciting (Plate 29, p. 229). If the manner in which the forms or colors adjust to one another is bolstered by similar juxtaposition of opposing forces elsewhere, it provides the continuity upon which rhythm is established.

Contrasting rhythm has become an increasingly popular theme in home design, although it has always been used to some extent. Ornate objects are complemented by quiet backgrounds, old is played against new. This can be an exciting and challenging design concept but is one that must be used knowledgeably and with some restraint so as not to disrupt the overall continuity.

The key to rhythm, in a dance, a fabric, or a room, is *continuity*—the organized movement of recurring or developing patterns into a connected whole. Consistency of rhythm—through repetition, progression, or contrast—establishes a solid foundation upon which composition rests.

Emphasis

A third design principle, emphasis, is often considered in terms of *dominance* and *subordination*. Emphasis suggests giving proper significance to each part and to the whole, calling more attention to the important parts than to those of lesser consequence, and introducing variety that will not become chaotic. It has to do with focal points, "rest areas," and progressive degrees of interest in between. Without emphasis, homes would be as monotonous as the ticking of a clock, and without subordination as clamorous and competitive as a traffic jam.

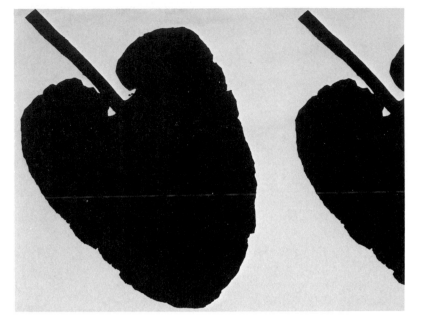

Many homes suffer from a lack of appropriate dominance and subordination. Such homes may have rooms in which almost everything has about the same dead level of nonimportance or, at the opposite extreme, rooms in which too many assertive elements compete for simultaneous attention. Those rooms in which attention is directed toward a few important elements are usually more livable—a substantial fireplace or a distinguished piece of furniture, a painting, or a window with an outlook, shown to advantage by quieter areas. Rooms of this kind result in neither boredom nor overstimulation. Attention is held and relaxed at many levels, providing balance and rhythm throughout.

Two steps are involved in creating a pattern of emphasis: deciding how important each unit is or should be and then giving it the appropriate degree of visual importance. This is not so simple as the superficial concept of "centers of interest and backgrounds," because here we are dealing with a scale of degrees of significance, not with two categories. A start can be made by thinking in terms of four levels of emphasis, such as emphatic, dominant, subdominant, and subordinate (although this, too, is an oversimplification, because there can be innumerable levels). For example, the room shown in Plate 30 (p. 230) might break down in the following way:

- *Emphatic*—view of the outdoors through a window wall
- *Dominant*—fireplace, one important painting
- *Subdominant*—major furniture group, ceiling treatment, other paintings and sculptures
- *Subordinate*—floor, walls, accessories

If we analyze this room, it becomes clear that certain elements have been consciously manipulated to assume levels of importance they might not otherwise possess. Because the house sits on a rocky bluff overlooking a quarry, full access to the dramatic view was important to the owners. Three large window walls in the living room thus make the outdoor panorama the most emphatic feature in the composition. At the next level, the fireplace—dark and isolated in a light-colored wall—stands out and assumes major significance, a not surprising treatment in

the harsh climate of upper New York state. And, since the painting by Nicholas Krushenick on the wall at left has virtually the only color in a room full of neutrals (its hue echoed in a few sofa cushions), it too becomes dominant. Ordinarily, a large multisection seating unit would be a dominant element in any room, but here the sofa components have been upholstered in dark chocolate brown to blend with the carpet, so they take a secondary or subdominant role to the fireplace and painting. Conversely, a ceiling, if flat and painted white, recedes into a subordinate role, but here the exposed wood beams and dark color against light walls bring it up one level to subdominant status. The Louise Nevelson sculpture over the fireplace blends with the wall it occupies; it takes on full significance only under close scrutiny, so in the overall view of the room it acts as a subdominant. The floor and walls, as neutral, two-dimensional planes, are subordinate elements.

Other conditions and desires would lead to different solutions. Many people do not have an impressive fireplace, an extensive view, a distinctive collection of paintings and sculpture, or a dramatic architectural feature. Fortunately, there are many ways of creating interest in a dull room. One approach is to concentrate spending on a single important piece of furniture, to locate it prominently, and to key it up with accessories, a painting, lighting, or a mirror. Funds permitting, one or two other distinctive pieces or an area rug, less emphatic than the major unit, might be secured and made the centers of secondary groups. A strongly patterned wallpaper or a large painting or graphic on one wall would also be effective. Very low in cost is an out-of-the-ordinary color scheme achieved by painting walls, ceiling, furniture, and perhaps even floor so that the color harmonies and contrasts become noteworthy. At little expense, a room can be given exciting emphasis.

In general, the focal point in any room should be supported by other elements so that it is not the only area of interest. It should bear some relationship to the other furnishings that rhythmically lead the eye to the dominant area. No single feature in a room should demand constant attention, else the whole will lack balance.

above left: 9-13 The low-ceilinged perimeter emphasizes the soaring height of the central living room area in a remodeled cottage. A large painting over the fireplace provides a focal point from both levels. Charles A. Farrell of Short and Ford, architect. *(Photograph: © Tom Bernard)*

above right: 9-14 A "before" view of the renovated cottage shows how bland the original room was. *(Photograph: Charles A. Farrell)*

Scale and Proportion

Two closely associated terms, scale and proportion, relate to both the size and the shape of things. They deal with questions of magnitude, quantity, or degree. In architecture or interior design, **proportion** is relative, describing the ratio of one part to another part or to the whole, or of one object to another, such as 2:1. **Scale** deals with the absolute size or character of an object or space compared to other objects or spaces, such as 20 feet to 10 feet. In these definitions, the proportion is the same but the scale may have varied substantially. The fine shade of meaning between these two may seem elusive until we offer some examples.

In the most simplistic terms, proportions usually are said to be satisfactory or unsatisfactory, scale to be large or small, "in" scale or "out of" scale. For instance, the design on an object should have a satisfactory relationship to the size, shape, and heaviness of the object. If the design were very large, it would appear awkward and overwhelm the form; if very small, it would become lost and seem like an afterthought. Similarly, large, massive, and bulky—almost monumental—furniture in a small, low-ceilinged room would appear ludicrous, almost like standard-size furniture filling a doll's house. But in a towering, oversized space, it would be in perfect scale.

No foolproof system of proportioning that holds good in all cases has been devised. The so-called *golden rectangle* and *golden section* of ancient Greek origin, which often give safe, pleasing results, come nearest. According to Greek design, a square is the least pleasing proportion for an enclosure while a rectangle with its sides in a ratio of 2:3 is the most pleasing. Square rooms do, in fact, present many design problems. Among them is an awkward relationship of typically rectangular furniture forms to the square enclosure itself. The golden section is the division of a line or form so that the smaller portion has the same ratio to the larger as the larger has to the whole. The progression 2, 3, 5, 8, 13, 21 . . . , in which each number is the sum of the two preceding ones, approximates this relationship. For those in need of formulas, these are as good as any. They may aid in deciding on the proportions for a room, of many architectural features such as window shapes and molding placement, or the proportional size, shape, and placement of furnishings within a room. Skillful use of color, texture, pattern, and furniture arrangement can alter and improve *apparent* proportions of spaces as well. But the application of formulas may be limited. Specific pieces of furniture may not be able to follow such rigid guidelines and still fulfill needs adequately.

Scale, as we said, is generally described as large or small, but by this we mean large or small compared to something else. The sofa shown in Figure 9-15

9-15 Robert Venturi's overstuffed traditional sofa seems even larger because of the scale of the pattern that covers it. *(Courtesy Knoll International, Inc. Photograph: Mikio Sekita).*

has large, heavy contours compared to the furniture we normally see, and the upholstery fabric is an unusually large floral pattern. Both elements, then, could be spoken of as large-scale and the pattern is in scale with the sofa. Large textures and patterns and bold colors that attract attention can make an object or area *look* larger than small-scale textures and patterns and subdued colors.

A phrase one often hears is *grand scale*, and this certainly describes the house in Figure 9-16. Everything here is oversized, from the massive masonry wall, through the thick boards that form the uprights and immense wood beams, to the generous-size furnishings. A house as expansive and monumental as this needs very careful use of scale, for otherwise people would feel lost and intimidated.

A vital consideration in the home is **human scale.** Physically, typical people are between 5 and 6 feet tall and weigh between 100 and 200 pounds. These figures are a yardstick for sizes of rooms, furniture, and equipment. Suitably scaled homes make us look and feel like normal human beings, not like midgets or

9-16 The massive scale of a vacation house on Long Island is carried out in every detail, but the informal and bulky yet soft seating helps humanize the effect. Norman Jaffe, architect. (*Photograph: Maris/ Semel*)

9-17 Designer Stanley Barrows solves the problem of a small room with a skillful use of scale and proportion. Tall objects are used around the perimeter of the room with low furnishings in the center of the space, directing the eye to the elements above and behind the seating area. *(Photograph: Gene Maggio/ NYT Pictures)*

giants. Yet within this framework there is ample room for variation. A room for a child or children may be deliberately *scaled down* to small-human size. Furnishings that are low and shallow and relatively narrow spaces between pieces would make a child feel comfortable and at home. Size may be diminished or scaled down while proportion remains constant, as in a scale model or drawing.

The success with which scale is used depends on some consistency. It is not simply a matter of size—of placing small furniture in a small room—but of harmonious relationships. Scale relationships in the home cover the entire range of design: of furnishings to space and to each other; of texture, pattern, and ornament to surfaces and furnishings; and of accessories to larger pieces. The standard of measurement relating objects to each other, to us, and to the spaces they occupy may well be one of the most important principles in interior design.

Harmony

Even within the schema of different levels of emphasis, it is important to maintain an overall harmony, so that various elements do not seem to be thrown together arbitrarily or to be competing with one another. Defined as *consonance*, *concord*, or *agreement among parts*, harmony suggests carrying through a single unifying theme that consistently relates the varied components of an interior, whether a single room or an entire house.

In essence, harmony results when its two aspects—**unity** and **variety**—are combined. Unity unrelieved by variety would be monotonous and unimaginative; variety without some unifying factor, such as color, shape, pattern, or theme, would be overstimulating, unorganized and discordant.

224 Design

9-18 Robert Venturi's sofa (see Fig. 9-15) even in a plain fabric would still seem out of scale in the room in Fig. 9-17 because of its bulk. *(Courtesy Knoll International, Inc. Photograph: Mikio Sekita)*

Unity

Generally, unity is achieved by repetition, similarity, or congruence of parts in a composition. Architecture usually establishes the basic character of a space, both inside and out. Furnishings that echo the structural lines of the interior architecture may be chosen. Or color, texture, or patterns may be matched or coordinated to provide continuity. Major components should express a consistent basic character with subordinate elements complementing the dominant feature. There have been periods in history when furniture was designed to blend with architecture as part of a total unit, as in Figure 9-19. In more recent times, "built-in" furniture

9-19 A Gothic Revival room in the Museo Sartorio in Trieste, Italy, was created during the 1850s, when the city belonged to Austria. *(Photograph: Giornalfoto)*

left: 9-20 A single structure forms sofa frames and end tables, creating a unified conversation area in front of the fireplace in this weekend house in Michigan. Stanley Tigerman and Margaret McCurry of Tigerman, Fugman, McCurry, architects. *(Photograph: Karant and Associates, Inc.)*

below: 9-21 Rounded corners on cabinet frames, doors, and handles are an important safety feature in the kitchen and provide a harmonious overall effect. Kitchen cabinets are carefully fitted to give a unified design. *(Courtesy Poggenpohl USA)*

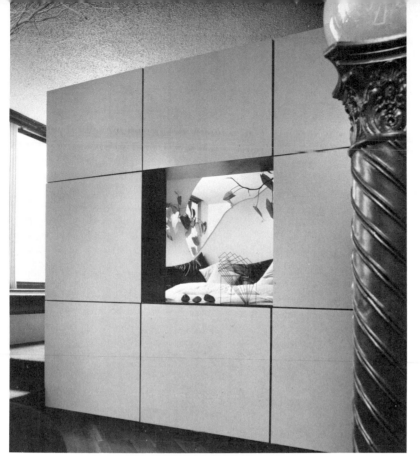

9-22 Storage units may be designed to perform double duty as free-standing space dividers with individual compartments concealed behind a unified facade. Variety is provided here by the open cubicle in the center and by contrast of the simple contemporary storage unit with the ornate historic column. Charles Damga, designer. *(Photograph: © Wolfgang Hoyt/ESTO)*

accomplishes a similar goal (Fig. 9-20). Our kitchens today are a prime example of unity in the home, with components built in, both to appear uncluttered and for ease of maintenance. Occasionally, too much unity can lead to visual discomfort if complicated design elements are too often repeated. The Gothic Revival interior might have too much carving (even if related) for comfort.

Variety

Variety brings vitality, diversity, and stimulation to design. It may be subtle, as in slight differences in color and texture or form and space that are easily assimilated, or it may be a surprising contrast such as the juxtaposition of old and new (Plate 31, p. 230). Excessive diversity without any apparent underlying scheme can appear chaotic, cluttered, and confusing. A profusion of patterns, colors, textures, and forms seen against one another, as exemplified by Victorian design, may lack visual clarity. With such complexity, the relief of some empty "rest" space is needed to provide the contrast necessary for full appreciation of intricate design.

The window treatment shown in Figure 9-23 makes splendid use of variety and unity to create a fascinating assemblage from mundane objects. Composed entirely of functional items found in the kitchen—spoons, rolling pin, wire whisk, meat pounders, and so on—the composition has overall unity in the similar shapes and materials involved. Variety comes from the ways in which different objects are hung, their orientation toward each other, and discrepancies in size and spacing.

As should be clear from the foregoing discussion, variety and unity achieve a happy merger when most of the design elements—space, form, line, texture, light, and color—are held fairly constant and only one or two are changed. Harmony is

9-23 A mobile of kitchen utensils becomes a window treatment, the variety of shapes carefully placed to make a unified composition. (*Courtesy* Better Homes and Gardens 100s of Ideas. © *Meredith Corporation, 1973. All rights reserved*)

the result of able use of the other guidelines to design—balance, rhythm, emphasis, scale, and proportion.

The elements and principles of design can seldom be applied self-consciously. Indeed, it is folly to imagine that by injecting suitable doses of balance, rhythm, emphasis, harmony, scale, and proportion into a home we will inevitably arrive at the perfect design. More often, such principles come to our attention only when we have violated them, perhaps when two chairs placed together are obviously in horrible proportion to each other. However, once we have come to understand the factors involved, we can more easily grasp what is wrong and how we can correct it. The purpose of studying this language of design is not to memorize rules but, first, to recognize the basic elements we are working with and, second, to discover what principles have proved successful in other designs. By studying home designs that have worked for different situations, we will gradually develop a sense of how elements can be combined. And this is one of the most important ingredients of a personal lifespace.

References for Further Reading

Bevlin, Marjorie Elliott. *Design Through Discovery*, brief ed. New York: Holt, Rinehart and Winston, 1984. Chaps. 8–10.

Cheatham, Frank R., Jane Hart Cheatham, and Sheryl A. Haler. *Design Concepts and Applications*. Englewood Cliffs, NJ: Prentice-Hall, 1983.

left: Plate 28 Castle Howard, an 18th-century Baroque palace in England, has been renovated and refurnished in a style befitting its history but comfortable for today's tastes illustrating rhythmic continuity. John Vanbrugh, architect. *(Photograph: Derry Moore)*

below: Plate 29 Except for the mellow brown of the wood floor, pure saturated red is the only real hue used in this room, the color contrasted stunningly against the neutrals of black and white. One large green plant provides the opposition of a complementary color. Robert Whitton, architect. *(Photograph: © Ezra Stoller/ ESTO)*

above: Plate 30 This living room was planned in such a way that the view through large window walls to the rocky hillside outdoors became the dominant element. Works of art and the fireplace attract our attention next, while the furnishings, flooring, and ceiling are subdued. Keith Kroeger and Leonard Perfido, architects. *(Photograph: Maris/Semel)*

right: Plate 31 Variety is introduced through an eclectic mixture of old and new in both furnishings and architecture in many homes being designed today. Val Glitsch, architect. *(Photograph: Paul Hester)*

230

Faulkner, Sarah. *Planning a Home*. New York: Holt, Rinehart and Winston, 1979. Chap. 3, pp. 53–74.

Friedmann, Arnold, John F. Pile, and Forrest Wilson. *Interior Design: An Introduction to Architectural Interiors*, 3rd ed. New York: Elsevier Science Publishing Co., 1982. Parts I and II, pp. 1–100.

Kleeman, Walter B., Jr. *The Challenge of Interior Design*. Boston: CBI Publishing Company, 1981. Chaps. 3 and 7, pp. 202–371.

Ocvirk, Otto G., Robert O. Bone, Robert E. Stinson, and Philip R. Wigg. *Art Fundamentals: Theory and Practice*, 4th ed. Dubuque, IA: William C. Brown, 1981.

Richardson, John Adkins, Floyd W. Coleman, and Michael J. Smith. *Basic Design: Systems, Elements, Applications*. Englewood Cliffs, NJ: Prentice-Hall, 1984.

Russell, Stella Pandell. *Art in the World*, 2nd ed. New York: Holt, Rinehart and Winston, 1984.

Thiel, Philip. *Visual Awareness and Design*. Seattle: University of Washington Press, 1981.

Zelanski, Paul, and Mary Pat Fisher. *Design: Principles and Problems*. New York: Holt, Rinehart and Winston, 1984.

III

Materials for Interiors

Wood and masonry in a remodeled New York apartment. Michael Kalil, designer. *(Photograph: Michael Datoli)*

10 Wood and Masonry

Wood
    Form in Wood
    Ornament in Wood
    Wood Finishes

Masonry
    Form and Ornament in Masonry
    References for Further Reading

Wood and masonry have served human beings as building materials ever since the earliest civilizations were inspired to improve upon animal skins and existing caves for their shelters. Abundant in nature, wood and the raw materials for masonry offer the advantages of strength and relative permanence, yet they can be shaped with a measure of ease. In addition to its role in structural building, wood has functioned as a basic material for furniture and other artifacts in the home at least since the days of ancient Egypt. Today, despite the incursion of plastics, many people still think automatically of wood in terms of furnishings, particularly for such items as tables, chairs, and chests.

Both wood and masonry possess special warm qualities that cause them to retain their popularity even though other newer materials may prove superior for practical considerations (Plate 32, p. 247). In the case of wood, there is perhaps a subtle awareness of its once having been part of a living tree, and thus being more responsive to us as living creatures. Masonry, on the other hand, has as its major component the substance of the earth itself; a timeless, enduring quality in masonry makes us feel safe and protected.

10-1 These unique wood doors exploit both the structural qualities of wood as a traditional building material and its beauty in a functional yet highly decorative manner. Al Garvey, designer. (*Photograph: Norman Petersen & Associates*)

Wood

As a material, wood has many useful and aesthetic qualities inherent in its very nature. One is the remarkable strength of wood in relation to its size and shape. Notable in this respect is its *tensile strength*: it resists breakage when subjected to bending or pulling forces, as anyone who has handled a bamboo fishpole knows. Its tensile strength permits wood to be used for spanning gaps, such as those above windows and in the wide stretches of ceilings, and in table tops. Tensile strength also suits wood to *cantilever* construction, in which a horizontal member projects beyond a support, as in a table top that extends beyond the table legs.

Wood, further, has considerable strength in *compression*: it retains its shape under pressure. This feature makes wood practical for such upright forms as posts, columns, and chair legs. In addition, wood is slightly *resilient*, so it is appropriate for floors and furniture; a good *insulator*, it does not get so hot or cold as masonry and metal, nor does it readily transmit heat or cold.

Wood is comparatively expensive in original cost, but it can be maintained economically. Such woods as cedar, cypress, and redwood survive exposure to weather with little upkeep, making them suitable for exterior walls and outdoor furniture. The original cost of wood walls for interiors exceeds that for plaster walls, but wood requires less maintenance. At the end of ten years the total cost of wood and plaster is about the same; from then on wood costs less in time, energy, and money. Hardwood furniture requires relatively little care beyond keeping it from drying out by timely waxing and polishing.

We would enjoy wood for its beauty and character even were it not for its utility and economy. Wood grain and color show a perfect union of variety and unity; no two pieces of wood are identical and yet a powerful, organic unity marks each piece and relates many pieces (Plate 33, p. 248). The rhythms are as subtle and inevitable as those in waves or clouds, ranging from almost parallel linearity to a complexity of curves. Some wood grains are emphatic, others quietly subordinate. Finally, wood is as pleasant to touch and to smell as it is to look at.

Wood has several major limitations: it scratches, burns, rots, and decays; insects attack it; and it may swell, shrink, or warp with changes in humidity. Also, as a natural resource, it is finite in quantity. These factors, however, can be minimized to a great extent. Research has disclosed many processes for eliminating the less desirable qualities of wood. Impregnation with plastics, for example, will harden and stabilize wood. And of the greatest importance is the judicious farming and management of our forests to ensure a continuing stock, coupled with the consideration of other materials, such as masonry, metal, and plastics, where their qualities can serve to advantage.

Form in Wood

Wood normally grows in tapering, pole-shape trunks and branches. Stripped of bark and cut into usable lengths, these poles have served in most parts of the world as the framework for tents covered with bark or skins, or for huts sheathed in bark or bunches of grass. Refined in shape, such poles are found in homes as posts and pillars, as legs of tables, chairs, or cabinets, and as lamp bases. Clearly the pole is the basic wood shape, but further refinement is necessary to make the material truly versatile.

10-2 Furniture designed by Richard Meier expresses clarity of form using the basic linear quality of wood. *(Photograph: Richard Meier & Partners, Architects)*

Trunks and branches can be squared to make heavy or light beams, or they can be sawed into planks or boards for furniture, floors, ceilings, and wall paneling. Rectangularity facilitates fastening the pieces together.

Wood structure is a complex organization of cellulosic fibers and pores. Concentric *annual rings* increase the tree's girth; *vertical fibers* and *pores* run parallel to the trunk; and *medullary rays* radiate from the center at right angles to the vertical fibers and pores. When wood is cut, this structure becomes apparent and is called *grain* and *figure*. The method of cutting will therefore produce notably different results, often a structural ornament of great beauty.

Beyond cutting and sawing, several other possibilities exist for handling wood. Small pieces can be glued or *laminated* together to create forms that would be impossible in straight-sawed lumber. Another method consists of literally "unwrapping" the log by peeling it into very thin continuous sheets for *veneers* and *plywood*. Wood can also be subjected to heat and bent into curved shapes often seen in chairs. Finally, wood can be ground or split into small pieces, then the fragments pressed together for wallboard and similar applications, and many synthetic fibers depend upon dissolved wood as one component of the mixture.

In selecting wood, designers keep in mind that every piece does not have to be top quality in all respects. Of course, wood must be strong enough to do its job, but for some purposes relatively weak wood suffices. Wood is usually classified as *hard* if it comes from broad-leafed, deciduous trees that drop their leaves in winter, such as maple, oak, and walnut; as *soft* if it comes from those trees with needlelike leaves retained throughout the year, such as pine, cedar, and redwood. In general, the hardwoods are in fact harder, as well as finer in grain, more attractively figured, and more expensive. The less costly softwoods shape more easily with typical tools, but they do not take fine finishes and intricate shapes as well. Considerable overlapping, however, occurs between the two types.

Hardness offers an advantage when the wood is subject to wear, but may be unnecessary otherwise. Capacity to take a high finish, desirable for the surface of furniture, is not needed for the hidden framework. And beautiful grain and figure provide a rewarding type of indoor ornament that would be wasted outdoors. Table 10–1 lists the significant characteristics of woods often used in homes.

Other factors that enter into the choice of wood for specific uses center on whether it is solid or layered; each type has its advantages and possibilities.

above left: 10-3 Quarter-sliced lumber is cut at approximately right angles to the growth rings, producing a series of longitudinal stripes—straight in some woods, varied in others. It shrinks less in width and also twists less than does plain-sliced lumber. *(Courtesy Fine Hardwoods Association)*

above middle: 10-4 Plain-sliced lumber, cut parallel to a line through the center of the log, is usually cheaper than quarter-sliced lumber. The grain pattern generally is variegated parabolas. *(Courtesy Fine Hardwoods Association)*

above right: 10-5 Rotary-cut wood is peeled off the log into thin, continuous sheets by holding a cutter against the log while it is turning on a lathe—something like taking paper towels off a roll. It often produces complex wavy or ripple patterns. Rotary-cut veneers can be exceptionally wide. *(Courtesy Fine Hardwoods Association)*

Table 10–1 Qualities of Selected Woods

Name	Source	Color and Grain	Character	Uses
alder (red)	one of few native hardwoods in Pacific Northwest	pleasant light colors from white to pale pinks, browns; close, uniform grain	lightweight, not very strong; resists denting, abrasion; shrinks little; stains well	chairs, other furniture
ash (white)	central and eastern United States; Europe	creamy white to light brown; prominent grain resembling oak; emphatic elliptical figures in plain-sawed or rotary cut	hard, strong; wears well; intermediate to difficult to work; intermediate in warping	furniture frames requiring strength; exposed parts of moderate-priced furniture; cheaper than most durable hardwoods
bamboo	tropical Asia	yellowish tan; treelike grass with smooth, lustrous woody stem up to 6″ in diameter	knobby joints, tubular	furniture and many decorative purposes
beech	central and eastern North America; Europe	white or slightly reddish; inconspicuous figure and uniform texture, similar to maple	strong, dense, hard; bends well; warps, shrinks, subject to dry rot; relatively hard to work, but good for turning; polishes well	middle-quality, country-style furniture; good for curved parts, rocker runners, interior parts requiring strength; also floors, utensil handles, woodenware food containers
birch	temperate zones; many species; yellow birch most important	sapwood, white; heartwood, light to dark reddish brown; irregular grain, not obtrusive; uniform surface texture; undulating grain	usually hard, heavy, strong; little shrinking, warping; moderately easy to work; beautiful natural finish; stains, enamels well	plywoods; structural, exposed parts of furniture, usually naturally finished (esp. Scandinavian); can be stained to imitate mahogany, walnut
cedar	north Pacific coast and mountains of North America	reddish brown to white; close-grained	rather soft, weak, lightweight; easily worked; little shrinkage; resists decay; holds paint; red cedar repels moths	shingles, siding, porch and trellis columns, vertical grain plywood, cabinetwork, interior paneling
cherry	United States, Europe, Asia	light to dark reddish brown; close-grained	strong, durable, moderately hard; carves and polishes well	associated with Early American and Colonial furniture; now often used as a veneer
cypress (southern)	southeastern coast of United States; southern Mississippi Valley	slightly reddish, yellowish brown, or almost black; weathers silvery gray if exposed	moderately strong, light; resists decay; holds paint well	doors, sash, siding, shingles, porch materials; occasionally outdoor furniture
ebony	Africa, Sri Lanka, India	heartwood black or coffee brown with black streaks, sometimes red or green; close or indistinct grain	dense, hard, heavy; smooth texture takes a high polish	furniture and inlay

Table 10–1   Qualities of Selected Woods *(continued)*

Name	Source	Color and Grain	Character	Uses
elm	Europe and United States	light grayish brown tinged with red to dark chocolate brown; white sapwood; porous, open, oak-like grain; delicate wavy figure	hard, heavy; difficult to work; shrinks; swells; bends well	somewhat sparingly in furniture; curved parts of provincial types; extensively used now for decorative veneers
fir (Douglas)	Pacific coast of United States	yellow to red to brownish; coarse-grained, irregular wavy patterns, especially in rotary-cut plywood; "busy"	rather soft, quite strong, heavy; tends to check, split; does not sand or paint well	plywood for exterior, interior walls, doors; cabinetwork; interior, exterior trim, large timbers, flooring; low-cost furniture, especially interior parts
gum (red or sweet)	eastern United States to Guatemala	reddish brown; often irregular pigment streaks make striking matched patterns; figure much like Circassian walnut	moderately hard, heavy, strong; tends to shrink, swell, warp; susceptible to decay; easy to work; finishes well	most-used wood for structural parts, with or imitating mahogany, walnut; also exposed as gumwood
mahogany	Central and South America, Africa	heartwood pale to deep reddish brown; darkens with exposure to light; adjacent parts of surface reflect light differently, giving many effects; small-scale, interlocked, or woven grain; distinctive figures	medium hard, strong; easy to work, carve; shrinks little; beautiful texture; takes high polish; always expensive	most favored wood for fine furniture in 18th century; much used in 19th century; used today in expensive furniture finished naturally, bleached, or stained dark
maple (sugar and black, both called hard)	central and eastern United States	almost white to light brown; small, fine, dense pores; straight-grained or figures (bird's-eye, curly, wavy)	hard, heavy, strong; little shrinking, swelling if well seasoned; hard to work; has luster; takes good polish	Early American furniture; now used as solid wood for sturdy, durable, moderate-priced furniture and hardwood floors
oak (many varieties; two groups: white and red)	all temperate zones	white oaks: pale grayish brown, sometimes tinged red; red oaks: more reddish; both have quite large conspicuous open grains; fancy figures rare	hard, strong; workable, carves well; adaptable to many kinds of finishes	standard wood in Gothic period, Early Renaissance in northern Europe, continuously used in U.S.; suitable for floors, panels, plywood; furniture, solid and veneer
pecan	southern United States, east of Mississippi	sapwood creamy white; heartwood reddish brown often accented with dark streaks; very little figure with small pores, close grain	strong, dense, heavy, durable, hard; easily stained and finished	furniture and veneer
Philippine mahogany (actually red, white Lauan, and Tanguile)	Philippines	straw to deep reddish brown according to species; pales when exposed to light; interlocking grain gives ribbon figure	about as strong as mahogany, less easy to work; greater shrinking, swelling, warping; less durable, harder to polish	extensively used for furniture in past few decades; also plywood wall panels, which should be fireproofed

Table 10–1 Qualities of Selected Woods *(continued)*

Name	Source	Color and Grain	Character	Uses
pine (many varieties similar in character)	all temperate zones	almost white to yellow, red, brown; close-grained	usually soft, light, relatively weak; easy to work; shrinks, swells, warps little; decays in contact with earth; takes oil finish especially well, also paint; knotty pine originally covered with paint	used throughout world for provincial, rustic furniture; in Early Georgian furniture for ease of carving, also paneled walls; often is painted or has decorative patterns; used for inexpensive cabinetwork, doors, window-sash frames, structural members, furniture
poplar	eastern United States	white to yellowish brown; close-grained, relatively uniform texture	moderately soft, weak, lightweight; easy to work; finishes smoothly; stains and paints well	siding; interior, exterior trim; inexpensive furniture, cabinetwork, especially when painted or enameled
rattan	Philippines and Indonesian jungles (dwarf variety from Hong Kong)	light yellowish tan; vine rather than wood, rarely over 2″ in diameter	can be bent into curved forms	wicker furniture; peel-cane, naked pole-reed
redwood	Pacific coast of United States	reddish brown; lightens in strong sun; weathers to gray or blackish; parallel grain in better cuts, contorted in others; decorative burls	moderately strong in large timbers, but soft and splinters easily; resists rot and decay	exterior siding, garden walls, outdoor furniture; some use for interior walls, cabinetwork
rosewood (several species, grouped because of fragrance)	India, Brazil	great variation from light to deep reddish brown; irregular black, brown streaks in fanciful curves	hard, durable; takes high polish	extensively used in fine 18th-century furniture, chiefly veneers, inlays; 19th-century solid wood; increasing use in furniture today
teak	Asia (India, Burma, Siam, and so on)	straw yellow to tobacco brown; striped or mottled in pattern	heavy, durable, oily; works and carves well; takes oil finish beautifully	widely used in Far East, both plain and for ornately carved furniture; now often used by Scandinavians for sculptural qualities
Tupelo gum	southeastern United States	pale brownish-gray heartwood merges gradually with white sapwood; lack of luster makes interlocking grain inconspicuous	hard, heavy, strong; good stability; moderately easy to work; tendency to warp	same purposes as red gum, although it is somewhat weaker, softer
walnut (American or black)	central and eastern United States	light to dark chocolate brown, sometimes dark irregular streaks; distinctive, unobtrusive figures of stripes, irregular curves; or also intricate figures	hard, heavy, strong; warps little; moderately easy to work, carve; natural luster; takes good finish	in America from earliest times for good furniture, but especially in 19th century; now in high-grade furniture, paneling

Table 10–1 Qualities of Selected Woods (continued)

Name	Source	Color and Grain	Character	Uses
walnut (Circassian); (also called English, Italian, European, Russian, and so on)	Balkans to Asia Minor, Burma, China, Japan; planted in Europe for wood and nuts	fawn-colored; many conspicuous irregular dark streaks give elaborate figures; butts, burls, crotches add to variety	strong, hard, durable; works, carves well; shrinks, warps little; takes fine polish	a leading furniture wood since ancient times; used in Italian, French, Spanish Renaissance; in England, during Queen Anne period, 1660–1720, called age of walnut; imported for American furniture
yew	Europe, especially England	deep red-brown; close-grained, fine and compact	hard, resilient; resists dents	cabinetwork

Solid Wood

Solid wood is the same throughout and is sometimes called "genuine." Its advantages include:

- The satisfaction that comes from knowing all the wood is the same as the surface.
- The edges of table tops, chair seats, and other pieces do not expose the layer-cake construction of plywood (although these are usually concealed by another strip of plywood covering the edge).
- The wood can be turned or carved.
- The surface can be planed in case of damage, or thoroughly sanded for refinishing, without fear of going through to another wood.
- The surface cannot loosen or peel off (as it may in improperly constructed veneers).

Major disadvantages are high cost and a tendency to warp, shrink, or swell.

10-6 Tage Poulsen's settee exposes its solid white oak frame and slats as an attractive design feature. (*Courtesy C. I. Designs*)

Layered Wood

Veneers, plywood, and **laminated wood** are layered constructions consisting of one or more sheets of thin wood, thicker boards, or even paper.

Veneers Thin sheets of wood produced by slicing with a knife, by sawing, or by rotary cutting, veneers can be glued to the top of thicker lumber to make what is referred to as "veneered wood," glued to paper for wall coverings, or glued to other veneers, as in plywood and laminates. Often, though, the term is used to refer specifically to the exterior surfaces that are usually of wood more expensive than that underneath.

Plywood *Lumber-core plywood* is composed of a number of veneers glued to either side of a thicker center core of solid wood with the grain of adjacent sheets at right angles to each other; it is suitable for table tops and cabinet doors. *Particle-board plywood* is similar, but with a thick center core of particle-board or hard-board (a composite of small pieces of wood held together with resin binders) and is common in table or desk tops. *Veneer-core plywood*, used for paneling or curved shapes, has a center core of veneer and all layers of approximately the same thickness. All plywoods usually contain an odd number of veneers glued together.

Laminated Wood A type of plywood in which the grain of successive layers goes in the same direction, laminated wood is frequently used for those parts of furniture that are bent and in which the major stresses and strains are in one direction.

The popular notion that veneers and plywood are cheap substitutes for the real thing is a misconception. To be sure, they are usually less expensive than solid wood, especially the better grades of hardwood, because the expensive wood goes much further when used as a veneer. But they also have other advantages:

- They are available in much larger pieces than solid wood. Plywood wall paneling, for example, is commonly available in $4' \times 8'$ sheets.
- Typically they are stronger than solid wood of the same thickness and weight.
- They are less likely than solid wood to shrink, check, or warp.
- They are not as liable as solid wood to splitting by nails or puncturing by sharp objects.

10-7 The laminated bent-wood frame of this sofa illustrates the pliability of wood when used in several thin layers. Warren Platner, designer. *(Courtesy C. I. Designs)*

- Almost identical grain on several pieces can be matched to produce symmetrical figures.
- They permit the use of fragile, highly figured wood that, if solid, might split apart or shrink irregularly.
- They lend themselves readily to curved and irregular forms.
- They permit flush surfaces of large size that are dimensionally stable.
- They allow rare and costly woods to be used more extensively.

The disadvantages of veneers and plywood include limited refinishing capability, possible separation and peeling of the layers if improperly constructed or poorly cared for, and occasional visibility of the sandwichlike edge. Some people may also object to not knowing what is underneath the surface finish, thereby not knowing what they are "paying for."

The characteristics of layered wood open many new design possibilities, such as factory-built wall paneling that speeds the construction of housing and results in a prefinished surface that is attractive in itself. Many pieces of furniture, especially chairs, make optimum use of molded plywood or laminated wood, with compound curves of remarkable strength. And veneers are popular because they enable designers to match grain and figure effects.

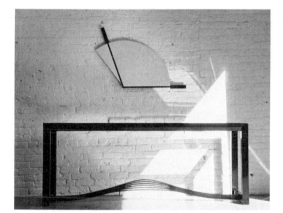

left: 10-8 The individual layers of laminated wood are separated to ornament the center stretcher of this table designed by Tom Bouschard. *(Courtesy Norman Petersen & Associates)*

below: 10-9 A stacking chair of molded plywood is an example of wood's versatility. The wood can be finished or varnished to suit any interior. The base of chromium-plated steel lightly supports the seat and back, which are shaped for comfort. Poul Pedersen, designer. *(Courtesy Cado/Royal System, Inc.)*

Ornament in Wood

Wood possesses a great diversity of inherent or structural ornament in its grain, figure, texture, and color. Not only does each species of wood have its own general type of pattern, but different aspects of these patterns can be brought to light by the ways in which the wood is cut, as we have seen. In addition to the beauty of typical grains, some woods show amazingly intricate deviations of figures, which have long been cherished by furniture designers. *Stripes* and *broken stripes*, *mottles* and *blisters* of irregular, wavy shapes, and *fiddleback*, *raindrop*, *curly*, and *bird's-eye* figures are but a few, to which must be added the figures found in stump or butt wood: *crotches*, *burls*, and *knots*.

Texture

Actual surface texture makes a kind of ornament and largely determines the effectiveness of a grain. *Roughly sawn* wood has an uneven, light-diffusing texture that minimizes grain and is not pleasant to touch, so wood designers normally reserve it for exterior work or for pieces that exhibit a rustic character. *Resawn* wood is considerably smoother, with a soft texture not unlike that of a short-pile fabric; it reveals but does not emphasize the grain. *Smoothly finished* wood reflects light, emphasizes the figure, and is pleasant to touch.

Color

Different woods naturally display an enormous variety of colors, from whitest birch to darkest ebony. A room entirely paneled in redwood, for example, has a warm, mellow quality; knotty pine paneling is also warm but actively patterned. Furniture made of birch has a light, airy character quite different from the usually more formal rosewood. Designers often exploit the contrast of different wood colors in such techniques as inlay and parquetry.

Joints

Beyond the need for structural stability, the ways in which different pieces of wood are brought together can create structural design of considerable importance. Beveled edges on wall paneling result in a rhythmic pattern of subtle light and shadow around a room; the joining of horizontal to vertical members in a piece of furniture can be emphasized as design features by the way they are joined. (Types of joining are illustrated in Chapter 17.)

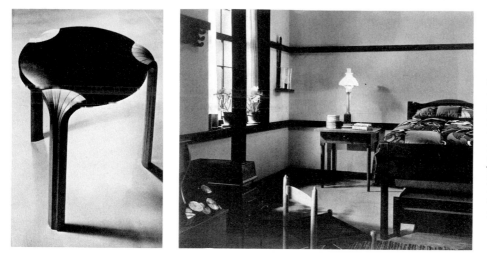

Moldings

Applied, narrow strips of wood that project from the surface of walls or ceilings are called moldings. Their popularity declined in modern interiors with emphasis on simplicity and clean lines, but they are used in all period rooms and have regained favor in post-modern design. In practical terms, wall moldings can help maintain the home, since they prevent furniture from rubbing against the wall proper. They can also emphasize direction or set up a pattern of their own that must be acknowledged when placing furniture, wall ornaments, or fixtures. Often they frame such elements as paintings to separate them from their background and form transitions between planes, as in elaborate crown moldings that relate walls to ceilings.

10-14 Wooden moldings around the windows retained during the remodeling of a kitchen recall an earlier era. Peter Stamberg, architect. *(Photograph: © Paul Warchol/ESTO)*

245

10-15 An exuberantly turned bed frame contrasts vividly with the simplicity of a rocking chair in this eclectic bedroom. CBT/Childs Bertman Tseckares & Cassendino, Inc., architects. *(Photograph: © Nick Wheeler)*

Carving and Turning

The nature of wood has suggested **carving** from earliest days in all parts of the world, and the great periods of furniture are known as much for their carving as for their more basic qualities of design. Gothic carving in oak, Renaissance carving in walnut, and eighteenth-century carving in mahogany effectively enhanced form. **Turning** is also an old art, and ever since the lathe was invented we have enjoyed the many diverse ways in which a rapidly rotating piece of wood can be shaped for furniture parts, balusters, columns, and utensils. Designers of almost every period produced turnings with distinctive profiles, such as the sixteenth-century melon bulbs, the seventeenth-century balls or sausages, and the spool, the bead and ball, the knob, the vase, and composite types that were popular in many countries at various times.

Elaborate turning and carving of high quality are rare but not unknown in contemporary design. They require much time and skill to produce and can increase household maintenance noticeably. But beautifully carved elements offer wonderful decorative accents for otherwise clean-lined designs.

Plate 32 A wall of concrete blocks finished with etched plaster functions as a heat-retaining mass and contrasts with the ceiling and balcony of dark wood paneling. Jefferson B. Riley of Centerbrook, PC, architect. *(Photograph: © Norman McGrath)*

above: Plate 33 Many different woods are combined to create a warm, personal living space. The flowing curves of a Victorian sofa and bentwood chairs serve as a counterpoint to flat areas of wood in the paneling and curved inner wall, as well as to the angles of the ceiling beams. Alfredo De Vido, architect. *(Photograph: © Norman McGrath)*

right: Plate 34 An old mill in Bucks County, Pennsylvania, has a rubble masonry wall and rough-hewn beams that contrast with a rather formal tile floor and traditional furnishings. The whole achieves a gracious "country" look. *(Photograph: John T. Hill)*

248

Pieced Design in Wood

Inlay, intarsia, marquetry, and parquetry are techniques that combine different woods—or sometimes metals, ivory, shell, and other materials—in such a way that the contrasting colors and textures make patterns in a plane surface.

- **Inlay** is a general term that has come to encompass all the various methods of excising shapes and inserting, flush with the surface, different materials for ornamentation.
- **Intarsia** refers to that type of incised work employed in the Italian Renaissance in which the pieces are inlaid in solid wood, somewhat like a mosaic using shell, bone, and ivory insets.
- **Marquetry** applies to intricate designs inlaid in hardwood veneers like puzzle pieces and then glued to a solid backing.
- **Parquetry** indicates strips of wood laid in geometric patterns and glued to a solid ground, especially in floors and tables.

Contemporary taste has moved away from the harsh austerity often associated with "modern" design, but there is still very little complex applied wood ornamentation of good quality. Design in wood today covers a wide range, from the simple contrast of putting old, ornate furniture in a contemporary setting to the exploration of concentrated enrichment suited to our own age. Many designers are working with sculptural form in wood that is pleasing when seen from any angle and that combines comfort and convenience with sensuous delight and lyricism.

below top right: 10-16 Inlay of different colored woods creates a trompe l'oeil effect on this desk designed by Edward Gottesman. *(Courtesy Norman Petersen & Associates)*

below left: 10-17 A French secretary of about 1780 features inlays of various woods and restrained mountings of gilt bronze. *(The Fine Arts Museums of San Francisco [Roscoe and Margaret Oakes Collection])*

below bottom right: 10-18 A solid wood burl scooped out for a seat is a sculptural fantasy exploiting its origin in the forest. Designed by John Makepeace. *(Courtesy French Company)*

10-20 A rolltop desk, handcrafted of walnut by Espenet, is an example of 20th-century "art" furniture that exploits the beauty of wood.

10-19 The beauty of the wood figure in Carpathian elm is emphasized by gold-plated brass and lacquer in Wendell Castle's handcrafted jewelry box (1982). *(Photograph: Steven Sloman)*

10-21 Often the same piece of furniture is available in a number of finishes, some revealing the natural wood grain, others covering it. Each gives a different quality to the piece. The Richard Meier Collection, Richard Meier & Partners, architects.

Wood Finishes

Anything done to a freshly sanded piece of wood takes away some of its pristine satiny beauty—but that beauty will soon disappear if no finish whatever is put on it. All but a few woods used in certain ways need some protective finish to keep the surface from absorbing dirt and stains; to give an easy-to-clean smoothness; to minimize excessive or sudden changes in moisture content; to protect the wood from rot, decay, and insects; and to prevent wood from drying out by replacing lost oils. An appropriate finish might enhance the grain with oil, change the color with stain, or hide an unattractive color and grain with opaque paint. Table 10–2 lists the typical wood finishes and their characteristics.

Finishes can penetrate or stay on the surface; be transparent and colorless, transparent but colored, semiopaque or opaque; and they can vary from a dull matte to a high gloss. To say that any one of these finishes is better than the others, except for a specific purpose, would be pointless. Many people like to see wood changed as little as is compatible with its use and therefore prefer transparent, colorless, satin finishes. On the other hand, extremely durable, opaque finishes are becoming popular for certain applications. The following general principles may serve as guidelines in choosing the best finish for a particular wood and purpose:

- **Opaque** finishes hide the wood character, give a smooth uniformity, and offer great possibilities for color.
- **Transparent** finishes reveal the character of the wood and absorb minor damage that comes with use.
- **Penetrating** finishes, such as linseed oil, produce a soft surface that may absorb stains but will not chip or crack.
- **Plastic-impregnated** finishes harden wood, give it greater density and strength, and can make it almost totally impervious to damage although the natural texture and aroma of the wood are lost.
- **Glossy** finishes reflect more light than **matte** ones, are more durable because of their hard, dense surface, and facilitate cleaning, but they also show blemishes more readily. Gloss can be reduced by adding thinner to the paint or by rubbing with sandpaper, steel wool, or pumice. The shine also dulls with age and use.

Table 10-2 Wood Finishes

Name	Composition	Application	Result	Use
bleach	various acids, chlorine compounds	brushed on	lightens wood, neutralizes color, usually makes grain less conspicuous; not dependably permanent; wood loses some luster	to make furniture and wood paneling pale, blond, also used on outdoor furniture to give a weathered look
enamel	varnish mixed with pigments to give color, opaqueness	brushed or sprayed over undercoat since it has less body and covering power than most paints	generally hard, durable coat, like varnish; usually glossy, may be dull; wide range of colors	chiefly on furniture, cabinets, walls getting hard use and washing; also on floors
lacquer	cellulose derivatives, consisting of resins, one or more gums, volatile solvents, a softener, and a pigment (if colored)	regular lacquer best applied with spray since it dries rapidly (15 min.); brushing lacquers dry slowly, make brush application feasible	hard, tough, durable; resistant to heat, acids; not suitable for outdoor wood because of expansion, contraction; glossy, satiny, or dull	transparent lacquers much used on furniture, walls; opaque on furniture
oil	boiled linseed oil or various other oils; usually thinned with turpentine	brushed or wiped on, excess wiped off, allowed to dry, sanded or rubbed; between five and thirty coats—more the better; hot oil sinks into wood, brings out grain	penetrating, very durable finish with soft luster; darkens and yellows wood somewhat at first, considerably in time; protective, not conspicuous; must be renewed	oil, often mixed with beeswax, used in Europe from early times to 17th century; now used on indoor and outdoor furniture
paint	pigments suspended in linseed oil or, more commonly now, in various synthetics and water; usually contain a drier to hasten hardening	brushed, rolled, or sprayed on	opaque coating, varies from hard, durable gloss to softer dull finishes; hides character of wood; new types dry quickly with little odor, are easy to apply and have good covering power	protects and embellishes; painted furniture popular in ancient Egypt, the Orient, Europe since Middle Ages; much Colonial furniture was painted; widely used now on walls and furniture
shellac	resinous secretion of an insect of southern Asia, dissolved in alcohol	brushed, rubbed, or sprayed on; dries rapidly; many thin coats, each rubbed, gives best finish	changes character and color of wood very little; soft satiny to high gloss finish; fragile; wears poorly; affected by heat, moisture; water spots	primarily as an easily applied, quick-drying undercoat
stain	dye or pigment dissolved or suspended in oil or water	brushed, sprayed, or rubbed on	changes color of wood without covering grain (often emphasizes grain or changes surface noticeably); usually darkens wood to make look richer	frequently used to alter color of furniture woods thought unattractive, or in imitation of expensive woods; outdoors compensates for weathering
synthetics	wide range of polyester, polyurethane, polyamide, vinyl; liquid or film; newest type finish; continuing new developments	usually factory-applied; *liquid* impregnates wood; *sprays* form a coating; *film,* typically colored, is bonded to wood with laminating adhesive	durable, long-lasting finish; resistant to abrasion, mars, chemicals, water, or burns; clear or colored, mat to glossy surface; film type difficult to repair	walls, floors, furniture; very good wherever abrasion, moisture, or weathering is a problem

Table 10–2 Wood Finishes *(continued)*

Name	Composition	Application	Result	Use
varnish	various gums, resins dissolved in drying oils (linseed, tung, or synthetic), usually combined with other driers; dye or pigment makes varnish-stain	brushed or sprayed on; many thin coats best; dries slowly or quickly, depending on kind, amount of thinner used	thin, durable, brownish skin coating, little penetration; darkens wood, emphasizes grain; dull mat to high gloss; best when not thick, gummy	known by ancients; not used again until mid-18th century; widely used today on furniture, floors, walls
wax	fatty acids from animal, vegetable, mineral sources combined with alcohols; usually paste or liquid; varies greatly in hardness, durability	brushed, sprayed, or rubbed on, usually several coats; often used over oil, shellac, varnish, but may be used alone	penetrates raw wood; darkens, enriches, emphasizes grain; soft to high luster; must be renewed often; may show water spots and make floor slippery; other finishes cannot be used	very old way of finishing wood; generally used today as easily renewed surface over more durable undercoats; some liquid waxes used alone on walls, floors, furniture

- **Distressed** finishes are artificially aged by gouging and denting with chains or spraying to imitate wormholes and flyspecks.
- **Antiqued** finishes are also artificially aged with paint or stain applied in layers with the surface rubbed off to produce an effect of aged *patina* (a soft sheen, color, and texture produced by age, use, and care).
- Many coats of any finish, sanded or rubbed between coats, give a more durable, attractive result than one or two coats applied thickly.

More than any other material, wood ties the interior together structurally and visually. It remains one of our most useful, beautiful resources and has more than held its own in spite of the great advances in plastics, glass, and metal. In fact, the newer materials, having relieved wood of some applications to which it was never completely suited, have allowed us to see more clearly how wonderful wood really is. Much as we admire other materials, few of them arouse the deep responses that wood generates. Metal and plastic, for example, can never replace the warmth, texture, and aroma of wood although they have other appealing attributes.

Masonry

Strictly speaking, masonry is defined as anything constructed of such materials as stone, brick, or tiles that are put together, usually with mortar, by a mason. Today, however, the term also includes plastering and concrete construction. The materials of masonry derive from inorganic mineral compounds in the earth's surface. They are of crystalline structure and typically hard, dense, and heavy.

Masonry materials offer numerous advantages. They do not support combustion, rot, or decay, nor do they invite insects or rodents. Most of them are long-lasting, require little maintenance, and retain their shape under great pressure. Their colors and textures range from smooth white plaster, through an almost limitless range of colors and patterns in tile, to abrasive black lava rock. They can be shaped with rectangular solidity or curved buoyancy; some are left plain and simple, others laid in complex patterns. Above all, a timeless quality—the seeming imperviousness to destruction—makes us feel secure.

These properties explain why most historic architecture still in existence is of masonry. Best known are the large religious or public buildings, but throughout the world thousands of unpretentious houses of stone and brick still stand. The essence of historic masonry construction (with the exception of Roman work in concrete) was the piling of blocks on top of one another and usually joining them with mortar. Because such walls must be very thick and rest on solid foundations, they are expensive. They do not allow large unobstructed openings (unless these are arches), and they offer no space for the pipes and wires now so essential. Thus, solid masonry construction is seldom used today for an entire structure, but often serves for one or more walls of a home, usually a fireplace wall. Tile is used extensively as a wall, floor, or counter finish surface, and many houses, and even high-rise apartment buildings, have concrete floors that are then covered with wood or vinyl flooring or wall-to-wall carpeting.

In the nineteenth and twentieth centuries, many new methods and materials have been developed. These include masonry reinforced with steel to decrease weight and bulk while adding tensile strength, hollow blocks of brick or concrete, and thin-shelled concrete structures. In the latter part of the twentieth century, a new use of masonry has appeared, brought about by the interest in solar energy. Rocks, concrete, brick, and tile absorb heat slowly and release it slowly. Thus a rock wall or a concrete floor can be designed to act as a passive heat trap during the day and a passive radiant heater at night (see Chapter 6).

10-22 Rough-hewn rubble masonry used for a partial wall relates a house to its mountainous site near Taxco, Mexico. Anshen and Allen, architects.

Masonry has its limitations, including high original cost for some types. Although comparatively permanent, plaster and stucco crack, as does tile; concrete blocks chip, and the softer stones disintegrate more rapidly than might be expected. All are difficult to repair. In comparison with wood or metal, masonry is not very strong in tension. Further, most masonry offers fairly poor insulation against cold and dampness, and most types reflect rather than absorb noise.

Form and Ornament in Masonry

Masonry can be divided into two major categories: **block** and **moldable materials.** These categories largely determine the finished forms.

Block Materials

Stone, bricks and tiles, concrete or glass blocks—block materials—are delivered to a building site in their finished form and assembled on the job with mortar. Block masonry further subdivides into three basic types:

- **Rubble masonry,** rugged and informal, has untrimmed or only slightly trimmed stones laid irregularly (Plate 34, p. 248). It is generally the least costly and least formal kind of stonework.
- **Random ashlar masonry** is more disciplined but still rustic. The stones will be more or less rectangular but will vary in size. Usually it gives a decided feeling of horizontality, even though the joints are not continuous.

10-23 Random ashlar masonry makes a striking, massive fireplace wall in this Minnesota house. John H. Howe, architect.

- **Ashlar masonry** calls for precisely cut rectangular stones or bricks laid with continuous horizontal joints. It tends to have a more formal quality and is the most expensive type of stonework.

Stone Stone has so many desirable qualities that it would undoubtedly be used more widely if it were not so expensive. Because of its resistance to fire, stone seems naturally associated with walls and fireplaces. Belonging to the earth, it has a natural application in floors that are subject to hard use. Absorbing heat and releasing it slowly makes it ideal as a solar heating mass. Its permanence gives walls a uniquely reassuring character. Wherever stone is used, its crystalline structure, varied colors and textures, and differing degrees of opaqueness and translucency provide a very special visual and tactile appeal.

Although innumerable kinds of stone could be adapted to homes, four are commonly seen today.

10-24 A massive pillar in the center of a house was built of brick laid in an ashlar pattern but made less formal and more rustic by reusing old bricks. Alfredo de Vido, architect. *(Photograph: Louis Reens)*

10-25 The random pattern of a slate floor lends a garden atmosphere to a sunny room filled with plants. Hank Bruce, architect. *(Photograph: Philip L. Molten)*

- **Granite,** an igneous rock composed of feldspar, quartz, and various minerals, is dense, hard, and fine- to coarse-grained. Available in light to dark grays, pinks, greens, and yellows, it can take a high polish and be precision-cut for use in furniture pieces (usually tables), but in house design granite is most often used in its natural state for walls and fireplaces and as a solar heat mass.
- **Limestone,** which includes various sedimentary rocks, is relatively soft and easy to cut. Colors range from almost white to dark grays and tans. Its most common use is in fireplace walls and, as travertine, in table tops.
- **Marble,** a compact crystalline limestone, takes a beautiful polish, is often variegated, and comes in white, grays, pinks and reds, greens, and black. Contemporary designers, searching for structurally ornamented materials, have found it a handsome substance for fireplaces, table tops, and counter tops.
- **Slate,** a sedimentary rock that splits easily into thin sheets with smooth surfaces, makes good flooring or table tops. In addition to the typical bluish-gray, slate is available in green, red, or black.

Brick Among the oldest of artificial building materials, brick is still much in favor because, in addition to having the assets of masonry, it can be made by hand or machine from clays found almost everywhere. Brick weighs less than stone, an important factor in shipping and laying. Because of their relatively small size, bricks can be laid up around a hollow core or simply as a facing on one side of a wall, which leaves room for pipes and wiring and still forms a reasonably thin wall. Bricks come in many sizes, shapes, colors, and textures, and they can be laid in a number of patterns. Being fireproof, weather-resistant, and easy to maintain, they have long been a popular material for fireplaces and their surrounding walls

10-26 Brick floors with individual bricks "locked" in place by fine grains of sand sprinkled between them rather than mortar, adobe walls, and Indian pottery relate this home in Nevada to its southwestern heritage. Maurice J. Nespor & Associates, architects; Diana Cunningham, interior designer. *(Photograph: Hyde Flippo)*

and hearths. They are also increasingly used as flooring in solar rooms where an informal or country look is desired. No matter where they appear, bricks introduce an orderly rhythmic pattern of a scale suitable for homes. They are particularly effective in large, comparatively simple masses. Their chief drawback is cost.

Typical **clay bricks** are blocks of clay hardened by heat in a kiln. A standard size is 2¼ by 4 by 8¼ inches, but the dimensions can vary considerably. Although *brick red* is a common designation, colors range from almost white, pale yellow and pink, through oranges and reds to browns and purples. Their somewhat rough, uneven texture hides dirt and stains, but at the same time they can be difficult to clean when such soil is apparent. On the basis of texture, as well as resistance to breakage, moisture, and fire, clay bricks are conventionally divided into several types:

- **Common** or **sand-struck bricks,** made in a mold coated with dry sand, have slightly rounded edges and are used for exposed side walls or as a base for better-quality bricks.
- **Face bricks,** generally formed by forcing clay through a rectangular die and cutting it with wire, have sharp edges and corners; they are more uniform in color and texture, as well as more resistant to weather than common bricks.
- **Paving** or **flooring bricks** are still harder, because they have been fired at higher temperatures to withstand abrasion and to lessen absorption of moisture.
- **Firebricks** are most often yellow. They make an ideal material for places subject to great heat, such as the lining of fireplaces.
- **Glazed bricks,** with one surface finished with a hard ceramic glaze, are more impervious to stains and are available in a wide range of colors.

Wood and Masonry **257**

- **Adobe brick** differs from clay brick in that the clay is generally combined with a cement or asphalt stabilizer and dried in the sun. Builders in the warm, dry parts of the world have employed adobe brick for centuries, and the material has come back in favor in the southwestern United States.

Tile   Like clay and adobe bricks, ceramic tiles consist of heat-hardened clay, but they are thinner than bricks and more often glazed. They are used essentially as a surface finish rather than a structural material.

- **Mosaic tiles,** usually 1 inch square, come in innumerable colors, often mounted on a mesh or paper backing for ease of installation. They can, however, be hand-laid in creative designs of any complexity on walls, counters, or floors.
- **Wall** or **floor tiles** are somewhat larger in size (often 4 inches square), usually heavily glazed to withstand hard use, and come in a rainbow of colors, either plain or patterned. These tiles are often used on counter tops as well as walls and floors.
- **Quarry tiles,** made of clay that is heat-hardened as it comes from the ground, have a smaller range of natural colors in unglazed versions, but can also be glazed in almost any color. In size they range from 4- to 9-inch squares to interlocking shapes that create quiet patterns on the floor.

10-27   A modern kitchen is given an old-time country flavor with ceramic mosaic 2-by-2-inch tiles on floors and counter tops. The "Little Piggy" figure and geometric border illustrate the versatility of design motifs possible with mosaics. Kevin Cordes, designer. *(Courtesy American Olean Tile)*

Ceramic tiles have long been a favorite way of introducing into the home color and pattern combined with durability. Glazed-tile kitchen and bathroom counters and walls are practically impervious to water and are easily cleaned. Floor tiles in various configurations and patterns are also easily swept and mopped. The chief disadvantage of tile floors, which they share with all masonry floors, is that they may seem hard and cold, but they can act as a mass dispenser of heat once they have been warmed.

Concrete Blocks   Concrete blocks, today usually lightweight aggregate blocks made with such porous materials as cinders, pumice, or volcanic ash, are larger than bricks, typical sizes being 8 by 8 by 16 inches and 4 by 8 by 16 inches. Consequently they can be laid quite rapidly. Their porosity and hollow cores provide some insulation against heat and cold and also absorb noise. Moreover, the hollow cores provide a natural space through which utilities can be threaded. They are available in a narrow range of colors, tending toward very light pinks, greens, yellows, and grays, and need no treatment other than waterproofing, although they can be painted, plastered, or stuccoed.

Glass Blocks   Hollow blocks of glass that can be set together in mortar come in many sizes and shapes. Different types vary in the amount of light and heat they transmit. Some, for example, reflect the high summer sunlight but allow the win-

10-28 Mexican quarry tiles link indoors and out and function as a heat-storage mass in this sunspace. Gus Dudley, designer. *(Photograph: © Karen Bussolini)*

259

10-29 A dining room wall made of glass building blocks gives the space an open feeling. Light enters the room but privacy is maintained. Pucci and Benedict, Bumpzoid, architects. *(Photograph: © Robert Perron)*

ter sun's low rays to penetrate to warm a home's interior. Glass blocks are one of the few materials that admit light but give a degree of privacy, provide reasonable insulation against heat and cold, and make a supporting wall of any strength. Further, the manner in which they diffuse light and create changing abstract patterns from objects seen through them can be highly decorative. Although a rectilinear medium, glass blocks have the potential for a certain "softness" when laid in a curvilinear form.

Moldable Materials

Those masonry materials that are shaped at the building site from a semiliquid state include **concrete, plaster,** and **stucco.** They are hardened in forms or molds, or in a thin layer on a wall, extruded through dies in plain or fanciful shapes, and even carved after hardening.

Concrete Concrete is a mixture of cement with sand and gravel or other aggregates. It begins its existence as a thick slush, takes the form of any mold into which it is poured, and hardens to a heavy, durable mass. The bland, rather institutional color and texture has tended to limit poured concrete to such basic but unemphasized parts of the home as foundations, floors, walls, and terraces. However, the inclusion of aggregates other than sand and gravel improves the color and texture of concrete, as well as its insulating properties. The surface can be varied by adding colored pigments or other materials, troweling it smoothly, or giving it any number of textures and by exposing the gravel. **Terrazzo** refers to a concrete made with stone chips and polished to reveal an irregular mosaiclike pattern; **broom-finished** describes a pebble-surfaced concrete made with round pebbles from which the surface coating of concrete has been brushed off. Plaster or stucco can be applied as a surface coating and paints and dyes change the color. Paints are thick enough to smooth the surface; dyes are transparent and penetrating.

Plaster and Stucco Plaster and stucco have been popular building materials for centuries in many parts of the world because of their special qualities. **Plaster** is a thick, pasty mixture of treated gypsum and water, combined with such materials as sand and lime. (Plaster walls and moldings are discussed in Chapter 13.) **Stucco** refers to weather-resistant plaster most often used on exteriors. Both plaster and stucco generally are applied on a *lath*, a term now used for a lattice of thin strips of wood, metal sheets with grillelike perforations, or special types of hardboard. They can also be applied to any masonry surface that is rough enough to hold them, such as concrete blocks.

10-31 Robert Adam, the arbiter of English neoclassic taste, designed the dining room of Saltram House, Devonshire (England), in about 1768. A delicate play of straight and curved lines governs the entire room from the ornate plaster relief designs on the ceiling and matching carpet pattern to architectural moldings and oval-back Hepplewhite chairs. *(Photograph: A. F. Kersting)*

Like concrete, plaster and stucco will hold any shape given them before they harden. They can smoothly cover simple or complex surfaces with no visible joints. Both accept texturing, coloring, or painting, and plaster can be covered with paper or fabrics for embellishment and protection. Many older homes show how well suited these materials are to varied kinds of sculptural enrichment. A further advantage is their moderate original cost. The current interest in renovating and restoring older homes has resulted in a revival of such craft skills, and even in their use in new construction.

Under some conditions both plaster and stucco create maintenance problems. Cracks or chips are common unless precautions are taken. On smooth, light-colored walls these may be conspicuous, as are fingerprints, soot, and scratches. Although not expensive, the original cost of plaster is higher than that of many of the hardboards, which provide better insulation against heat, cold, and noise.

Over the centuries, much masonry has been recycled, linking the past with the present. For example, archeologists often find only foundations when they search

10-32 A wood-floored conversation area appears suspended midway between sky and earth, solidly anchored by a fireplace wall of large stones and surrounded by open space and a glass wall. John M. Johansen, architect. *(Photograph: Pedro E. Guerrero)*

for evidences of earlier civilizations; the stones or bricks from the old walls provided the raw material to build new structures. In our own time, many people prefer "used brick" to new for its more mellow look, and stone barns are recycled into homes or give up their stonework for new fireplaces. It is evident that masonry has its own very special appeal of enduring and substantial security. Particularly of this century is the way the weight and density of masonry is contrasted with the comparative lightness of wood and the transparency of large areas of glass.

References for Further Reading

Brodatz, Philip. *Wood and Wood Grains: A Photographic Album for Artists and Designers*. New York: Dover, 1972.

Constantine, Albert. *Know Your Woods*. New York: Scribner, 1972.

Dieter, A. "Waste Knot, Want Knot—Boise Cascade's Wood Products Mix," *Boise Cascade Quarterly*, November 1979, pp. 2–5.

Hayward, Charles. *Complete Book of Woodwork*. New York: Drake, 1972.

Pinzler, Arlene. "Guide to Grasses: How to Buy Wicker, Rattan and Bamboo," *American Home*, November 1976, p. 58.

Raffel, Deanne. "A Lumberyard Primer: What You Should Know to Choose the Right Building Materials," *House and Garden*, April 1980, pp. 56–58.

Thomsson, Arne. "Wood Veneer," *ASID Industry Foundation Bulletin* (reprinted from *Interior Design*, October 1974).

Willcox, Donald. *New Design in Wood*. New York: Van Nostrand Reinhold, 1970.

11

Ceramics, Glass, Metal, and Plastics

As materials, ceramics, glass, metal, and plastics share important characteristics. Since all are shaped while in a plastic, liquid, or malleable state, they lend themselves to a tremendous diversity of shapes. All are subjected to heat and/or pressure in processing. Except for some plastics, all are inert; that is, they will not burn, rot, decay, or appeal to insects and vermin. Each of these materials nonetheless has its own special potentialities and limitations that challenge designers and bring liveliness to our homes. In this chapter we will see how the specific qualities of each material have led to forms characteristic of its unique nature.

Ceramics

Long before early civilizations began to write, they fashioned useful and symbolic objects from clay. Since then, this material has been of continuing and conspicuous importance in homes. All of us are aware of the dishes used for eating, of figurines, vases, and lamp bases. But this inventory also includes many sculptural pieces, as

264

well as bricks and tiles, chimney flues, and drain pipes. All of these are *ceramics*, which is a short way of saying objects made of clay hardened by heat. Essential steps in the forming process are:

- Combining clays to make a suitable *body*
- Moistening the clay sufficiently to make it workable
- Shaping the clay by hand, on the potter's wheel, or in a mold
- Allowing the pieces to dry
- Firing the pieces to harden them permanently

The process may also involve decorating the object with carving, painting, or other techniques; and perhaps *glazing*—that is, applying a glasslike coating to the surface, and then firing the piece once again.

Clay Bodies

The clays used for a ceramic body naturally affect the characteristics of the finished product, and clays differ in many properties. Colors range from white through the most common reds, tans, grays, and browns to black. Textures vary from coarse, irregular, and open to fine, even, and dense. Clays also have different *maturation points*, or firing temperatures at which they will attain their maximum hardness but not yet begin to melt and deform. Generally, those clays that hold their shapes at high temperatures make the stronger objects, because the separate clay particles fuse together, or *vitrify*, into a homogeneous and waterproof mass. Almost never does a single clay offer all the qualities desirable for working and design; consequently the ceramist will mix two or more clays in varying proportions to produce the desired combination. The result is a clay *body*. For convenience, ceramic bodies can be grouped into four major types, although each has a wide range of characteristics that may overlap those of the other types.

Earthenware

Coarse clays fired at comparatively low temperatures produce earthenware, a typically thick, porous, fragile, and opaque ware. Most often red or brown, earthenware is the material of bricks, tiles, and most folk pottery. Unglazed, it lends itself particularly well to flowerpots and planters, since the clay body "sweats" and allows the soil to breathe. Another common application is in special baking dishes for meat and fowl that permit food to cook in its natural juices. The

11-1 These earthenware bowls have a sturdy quality characteristic of their coarse clay body. Stephen Pearce, potter. *(Photograph: © Karen Bussolini)*

glazes suitable for earthenware tend to be soft and may have very bright, glossy colors. In recent years many artists have begun to explore the possibilities of earthenware for sculptural form.

Stoneware

Finer clays—generally gray or light brown—fired at medium temperatures result in stoneware, a relatively strong, waterproof, and durable ware. Most common in medium-price dinnerware, to which such imprecise designations as *ironstone* may be attached, stoneware is also the predominant material of sculptural ceramics. Typical glazes have a matte finish, more subtle colors, and a much wider range of effects than are possible with earthenware.

China

A somewhat general term, china describes a white, vitrified ware that is translucent if thin. Originally the term was coined for European ceramics that imitated fine Chinese porcelains. In common usage, china differs from porcelain only in its slightly lower firing temperature, but some manufacturers produce a ware called *fine china* that is indistinguishable from porcelain. *English china* or *bone china* has a white, translucent body and a soft but brilliant glaze; it actually contains a certain percentage of animal bone. *American vitreous china* offers unusual resistance to breakage and chipping of the body, and to scratching in the glazes and decorations.

Porcelain

High-grade, expensive dinnerware and ornamental ware represent the major products of fine porcelain. A brilliant white, translucent ware fired at extremely high temperatures, porcelain is a vitrified combination of white kaolin clay and the mineral feldspar. The body resists breakage, and the glazes are very hard.

The purist would say that earthenware suggests simple, vigorous shapes and ornamentation and that increasing precision and refinement should be expected as one goes from stoneware to china and porcelain. Not always, however, does this formula apply, for other factors affect ceramic design.

11-2 An unglazed porcelain bowl reveals the strength of this fine ware in its thin undulating walls. Marsha Berentson, designer. *(Exhibited at the Elaine Potter Gallery, San Francisco)*

Form in Ceramics

The possibilities and limitations of form in any material are determined by its physical properties, the methods by which it is formed, the intended use of the end product, and the skill and sensitivity of the designer.

The physical properties of clay differ markedly before and after firing. In its unfired state clay consists of small powderlike or granular particles. When a small amount of water is added to the dry clay, the result is a malleable, plastic mass; the addition of more water produces a creamy liquid called *slip*. After firing, clay is hard and brittle, with little tensile strength. Ceramic objects therefore break quite easily when struck or dropped, and thin edges or protrusions including raised surface designs are vulnerable.

The forming methods for clay divide into two general categories: hand techniques and mass-production techniques. In hand construction, the clay can be *thrown* on the potter's wheel, rolled into sheets or *slabs* (which may then be assembled in different ways), or carved and molded sculpturally. Mass-produced ceramic ware is shaped by pouring slip into molds, by pressing plastic clay in molds, or by *jiggering*, a process in which plastic clay on a revolving mold is formed by a template. Almost any shape is possible in clay, as the history of ceramics proves, but most dishes, vases, and similar household objects are round and relatively compact, because round forms come naturally from the wheel and the jigger. Rounded shapes are easy to hold, and they provide a pleasant relief from the basic rectangularity of our homes. Important, too, is the fact that they have a minimum of edges to chip. In sum, rounded forms with compact outlines seem especially appropriate to many ceramic objects.

However, the practical aspect of round forms for certain purposes does not rule out other possibilities. Angular shapes are basic in bricks and tiles, which receive wear only on their flat surfaces; in household ceramics they can occasionally be useful as well as welcome surprises. Some extending forms, such as spouts on teapots or handles on cups, are worth the hazard of breakage. Then, fortunately, there is the creative urge to explore and experiment, to find forms that will reawaken our senses.

Ceramic Glazes

Glazes are coatings compounded from glasslike materials fused at high temperatures to the body of ceramic ware. In purely utilitarian terms, they increase efficiency by making the ware waterproof and easy to clean. Most important, though, as an example of structural ornament, the textures and colors of glazes are primary sources of beauty.

Glazes differ in the degree to which they join with and "fit" the clay body. A broken piece of glazed earthenware will show that the glaze forms a distinct layer on the porous body, but on most porcelains the glazes are so completely wedded with the clay that no sharp division can be perceived. Both clay and glazes shrink in firing. If the glaze and the body do not have the same rate of shrinkage, the glaze may develop a network of cracks. Some potters plan such effects deliberately for their ornamental value, but on dishes meant to hold food the cracks are more likely to be the result of poor workmanship.

Ornament in Ceramics

Often the basic form of a clay piece, with the addition of a glaze or glazes, is sufficient unto itself, making applied ornamentation unnecessary. However, because of the ever-present urge to enrich a plain surface, ceramic objects are often decorated. The medium seems to invite modeling, carving, and painting.

Modeling and **carving,** which give a three-dimensional play of light and shade, range from scarcely noticeable incised designs to vigorous shaping and cutting. Sometimes stamps are used to impress designs on the clay while it is still plastic. *Sgraffito* (literally, "scratched") decoration results from coating a piece with slip—different in color from that of the base—and then scratching through to reveal the color underneath.

Colored pigments can be applied with a brush or through a stencil, transferred from decalcomanias or printed mechanically. This decoration might be either under or over the glaze, and it offers endless design possibilities. *Underglaze* designs are applied before the final glazing (which is transparent), so they are protected from scratches and wear. *Overglaze* patterns are applied to the surface of glazed ware and fused with it at a low firing temperature. An overglaze design represents the cheapest and most common type of ceramic enrichment and when well done can be moderately durable. Gold and silver trim on dinnerware are applied as overglazes which explains why they soften in dishwashing if the water temperature is high.

With so many possibilities, it is easy to see why ceramic design has always fascinated artists and industrial producers alike. Clay is, first and foremost, a sensuous material. A lump of it in the hands invites manipulation. Fascinated perhaps by this direct urge transmitted by the material and by the variety of modeled forms it would take, ceramists have made clay one of the most versatile media known.

11-3 Humble earthenware drain tiles imaginatively shelter a passageway from extreme natural elements while still allowing in some light and breeze. Anshen and Allen, architects. *(Photograph: Maynard L. Parker)*

268

Ceramics in the Home

Bricks and tiles, glazed or unglazed and cemented together with mortar, play a very important design role in many homes. That tiles can be a significant component of domestic architecture is shown by the wide variety of patterns available in floor and decorative wall tiles. (More information on brick and tile and their use in the home appeared in Chapter 10.)

An interesting and unique application of ceramics in the home marks a contemporary Mexican house (Fig. 11-3) in which ordinary clay drain pipes, banked in even rows, have been used to make a whole wall, filling the gaps between stone piers. They not only create an ever-changing pattern of light and shade but give protection against rain, sun, and wind as well.

Finally, of course, there remains the potential for "spot" enrichment in the home with individual ceramic pieces. Their design importance and character can range from a large, dramatic pot that is a major focus of attention to the simple, classic lamp base. Either one represents a modern interpretation of a continuing tradition for clay objects in the home that is almost as old as civilization.

Glass

The evolution of glass from a semiprecious substance available only in small quantities (for making such things as beads and amulets) to a commonplace material that can be bought anywhere and installed in large sheets has altered our homes as much as any single factor. Its history is fascinating. Glassmaking appears to have developed from ceramic glazes, some of which were made at least six thousand years ago; but the oldest known glass objects are about four thousand years old. The Romans fabricated glass objects of such beauty that the best were valued higher than vessels of gold. Sheets of glass for windows were also known in the Roman Empire, but window glass was not common in small homes until the end of the eighteenth century. Today glass is an everyday, extraordinarily versatile material found in everything from cooking utensils to house walls.

Glass is made by melting and fusing at very high temperatures the basic ingredients—silicates, alkalis, and lime—plus various other materials that give certain qualities. Crystal, the finest glass, contains lead. Color traditionally comes from minerals: red from gold and copper, blue from copper and cobalt, yellow from cadmium and uranium. Many of these minerals are too costly or have other more critical uses today, which explains why old glassware has risen in value. Special effects such as opacity, bubbles, or crystallization and special forms, including glass fibers and insulation, result from chemicals or from the way in which glass is treated. *Obsidian*, a natural glass that is usually black, is created by volcanic heat.

The general characteristics of glass are:

- Transparency unrivaled until recently by any other common material
- Capacity to refract light in a gemlike way
- Wide range of colors, degrees of transparency, and textures
- Plasticity, malleability, and ductility that permit a great variety of shapes, from threadlike fibers to large thin sheets
- Imperviousness to water and most alkalis and acids
- Resistance to burning (but will melt at very high temperatures)
- Moderately high resistance to scratching
- Low resistance to breakage through impact, twisting or bending, and sudden temperature changes (except with special types)

In sheet form, glass serves as the standard material for mirrors and windows, and sometimes for sliding doors and table tops. For her Lunario tables, Italian designer Cini Boeri cantilevers severely plain round or oval glass shapes from bases of polished steel in a daring display of the transparency and relative tensile strength of glass (Fig. 11-6).

Unless it is kept polished, glass—especially colorless and transparent glass—loses most of its beauty. Finger and water marks or specks of dust are more conspicuous on clear, shiny glass than on most other materials. Under some circumstances the transparency of glass can make it a hazard to the unwary, especially in poorly designed window walls or sliding doors.

Form in Glass

What was said about form in ceramics might almost be repeated for glass; because, in both, an amorphous substance takes form while it is plastic or liquid; the final product is hard, usually brittle, and breakable; and process, material, and use lead naturally (although not exclusively) to rounded forms. Glass, however, adds a second major form category in flat sheets for house furnishings and architectural elements.

Two other distinctive qualities of glass should be mentioned. The first is that glass, technically speaking, always remains a liquid. Therefore, even when rigid, as it is at ordinary temperatures, it is actually a "supercooled liquid." Second, an almost perfect union of form and space can be achieved with glass. We look less *at* a transparent glass bowl or tumbler than *through* it to the space enclosed and the space beyond. Large windows give a similar effect. Contemporary designers and architects interested in the relation of form to space have a special feeling toward this material so closely uniting the two.

Hand-blown Glass

Just as the bowl is a natural shape for ceramics formed on the potter's wheel, the bubble is the natural form for hand-blown glass. In blowing glass by hand, the craftsman dips a hollow metal rod into molten material, blows it into a bubble,

above: 11-6 In the "Lunario" table, the transparency of glass reveals and accentuates the off-center poise of the table top on an ellipsoid base. Cini Boeri, designer. *(Courtesy Knoll International, Inc.)*

left: 11-7 A free-blown clear-glass vase—an assemblage of three bubbles topping a hollow tube—strongly evokes the act of blowing glass. Willem Heesen, designer. *(Courtesy Glasvormcentrum Leerdam)*

and then forms the hot, soft mass into the desired configuration by rolling, twisting, or shaping with tools while it is still hot and plastic. But because hand-blowing is a time-consuming, expensive technique, most household glass derives from procedures more suited to quantity production.

Molded and Pressed Glass

In a mass-production situation, molten glass is blown or pressed by machinery into cast-iron or wooden molds. The molds can be simple or intricate in shape and leave a plain or patterned surface on the glass.

Drawn or Rolled Glass

Two processes apply to the manufacture of sheet glass. *Drawing* (the method by which inexpensive window glass is made) calls for molten glass to be drawn from furnaces in never-ending sheets, flattened between rollers, and cut into usable sizes. Although satisfactory for most purposes, drawn glass tends to be weaker, thinner, and more subject to flaws than plate glass. In *rolling*, the method for making plate glass, molten glass is poured onto an iron casting table, distributed and smoothed by rollers, then ground and polished. Today, sheets of plate glass more than 50 feet long are possible, and manufacturers can incorporate special qualities to make the glass shatterproof or to give sound, heat, cold, and glare control as well as reflective properties.

Ornament in Glass

It is not easy to draw a sharp line between form and ornament in glass. Structural ornament can be added before glass is shaped by incorporating in the material substances that give color, make the glass translucent or cloudy, or produce such visual textures as bubbles or opaque streaks. Sometimes form becomes so complex that it serves as its own decoration. An entire glass piece can be fluted, ribbed, or ringed with swirling patterns. The glassblower can also "drop on" globs of molten glass to produce almost liquid ornament on the one hand or practical appendages such as handles on the other. Molded or pressed glass takes its texture, as well as its form, from the mold in which it is processed. Beyond this, several other types of applied enrichment are possible.

Cut Glass

Although glass was beautifully cut by the Romans, the technique experienced a renaissance about A.D. 1600, when a court jeweler in Prague applied gem-cutting

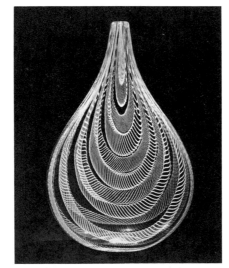

11-8 A *latticinio* pattern of white and amethyst threads of glass embedded in clear glass accentuates the teardrop shape of a bottle designed by Archimede Seguso of Italy. *(Corning Museum of Glass, Corning, New York)*

techniques to glass. Rich effects come when the design is cut through an outer coating of colored glass to reveal colorless glass underneath. In colorless crystal, cutting gives many facets to catch and break up light.

Engraved Glass

As with cut glass, engraving is done with wheels and abrasives, but engraving produces a shallow intaglio that by optical illusion often seems to be in relief. Finer pictorial and decorative designs are engraved rather than cut. Firmness of form, sharpness of edge, and easy-flowing curves distinguish engraved glass from that which is pressed, cut, or etched.

Etched Glass

Either hydrofluoric acid or sandblasting will etch glass. The frosty etched surface can be left in that state or polished to smooth transparency. Etching is often used to imitate engraving, but the designs are not so sharp or so subtly modeled. Usually shallow and delicate, etching can be 2 inches deep, as it is in some heavy French pieces.

Enameled and Gilded Glass

In the past some very beautiful glass was made by burning colored enamels (opaque, vitreous materials) or gold and silver into the surface.

Leaded, Stained, and Beveled Glass

Composed of small pieces of glass set in a pattern and held in place by strips of lead or copper foil, leaded and stained glass have undergone a revival because of their capabilities as enrichment (Plate 35, p. 281). Leaded glass usually refers to transparent glass, colored or clear, often used as a window. Stained glass— enameled, painted, or colored by pigments baked onto its surface or by metallic oxides fused into it—can serve in windows, lampshades, or wherever its translucency can be highlighted by a strong light source. Some modern techniques laminate or bond colored glass to a sheet of glass or plastic instead of piecing it together by means of lead or foil. Beveled glass has a narrow band near the edges cut at an angle and can be used for leaded glass windows, ordinary windows, mirrors, or glass panels in furniture pieces.

11-9 An etched glass panel by Sandy Moore shows the renewed interest in glass etching as an art form. *(Photograph: © Karen Bussolini)*

below: 11-10 Louis Comfort Tiffany (1848–1933) revived stained glass as an art form and made lamps, vases, and windows, often using sinuous plant forms in the Art Nouveau style. *(Metropolitan Museum of Art, Gift of Hugh Grant, 1974)*
right: 11-11 A handsome old doorway with a clear leaded-glass fanlight and stained-glass side panels awaits recycling by an imaginative builder. *(Photograph: Thomas B. Hollyman/ Photo Researchers)*

11-12 Only the introduction of glass with glareproof, reflective, and insulating properties made possible a house set in the woods of upstate New York in which walls almost entirely of glass wrap around the living core. Robert E. Fitzpatrick, architect. *(Photograph: Joseph W. Molitor)*

Architectural Glass

Although glass for buildings is generally thought of as transparent, colorless, smooth, and flat, it can be frosted or pebbly, ribbed or corrugated, and colored to control light, heat, even vision. Glass bricks bring in light but allow privacy, also creating a subtle rhythm because of their shapes. Glass can also be curved to fit specific installations. Some architectural glass is tempered for safety; other types have a core of metal mesh that reduces the hazard of breakage in addition to being decorative. In the past, homeowners had to choose between opaque walls and transparent windows and then frequently cover the windows with curtains or blinds for visual protection. Now there is a glass that allows people to see out but blocks the inward view. And insulating glass, which has double or even triple panes welded together with a special dry gas between, makes possible large areas of glass even in cold climates. Architects have made use of these new capabilities to produce houses with walls almost totally of glass but still private and secure inside.

Glass Mirrors

In the past mirrors were almost exclusively utilitarian in bedrooms and bathrooms, but they, too, have come into their own as a source of visual pleasure. Many metals can be given reflecting finishes, but mirrors as we usually think of them consist of glass with a metallic backing that provides distortion-free reflections of whatever is in front of them. They can be invaluable in visually expanding the size of a small room. Mirrors also spread light throughout a room and bring sparkle into dark corners. Although most often given a plain silvery backing, they can be of other colors or of smoked glass; their usual flat surface can be curved to give interesting distortions or broken up by facets to create dazzling interplays of light and color.

Fiberglass

The great versatility of glass is indicated by the fact that its ingredients can also be spun into fibers for insulation, fabrics, or rigid forms. Spun glass was used for centuries in a purely decorative way, but not until about 1893 were its utilitarian values appreciated. Then neckties and dresses of spun glass and silk were exhibited as curiosities: they were heavy, scratchy, and too stiff to fold. (As discussed in Chapter 12, glass textiles have come a long way since 1893.) Today glass fibers provide insulation against extreme temperatures and sound. Another development is foam glass, made by introducing a gas-producing agent into molten glass. Filled with so many tiny air bubbles that it will float on water, it has excellent insulating properties. And we are all familiar with the many types of fiberglass panels that can make lightweight, translucent fencing and roofing materials. Fiberglass also appears in molded integral bath fixtures and walls and furniture that is so durable it can be used for public seating as well as less demanding home furnishings.

Metals

Although metal was first reduced from ore about 5000 B.C., its application to domestic architecture was unimportant until recently. Today the typical "wood house" uses more than four tons of metal, but only a small portion is visible.

Metal—like masonry, ceramics, and glass—is inorganic and therefore does not burn, rot, or decay. But metal differs from these other inorganic substances in some important respects: most metals rust or corrode when exposed to moisture and air, and they have great tensile strength. Metal's capacity to transmit heat, cold, and electricity stands unequaled. The surface is usually shiny and nonabsorbent.

above: 11-13 Faceted in mirrors, a circular guest room shimmers with reflected light. Paul Rudolph, architect. *(Photograph: Robert Levin)*
below: 11-14 Fiberglass reinforced plastic can be formed into light stacking chairs. *(Courtesy Stendig)*

Table 11—1   Metals

Metal	Color and Finish	Special Characteristics	Uses
aluminum	whitish, oxidizes to a soft gray; highly polished or brushed to silvery gray; anodizing gives satiny surface in bright metallic hues	lightweight; easily worked; does not deteriorate; impervious to water; nontarnishable	cooking utensils, pitchers, and trays; screens, sliding doors; maintenance-free indoor-outdoor furniture
brass	copper alloyed with zinc; bright yellow color; takes a high polish; must be polished frequently to stay bright	soft but durable; easily shaped; can be incised or inlaid with other materials; tarnishes easily; often protected by a coat of lacquer	musical instruments, lighting fixtures, decorative door hardware, faucets, fireplace accessories
bronze	copper alloyed with tin; rich brownish-red; develops mellow, subtly colored patina over time	hard, long-lasting, durable; does not deteriorate	bells, cast sculptures, desk accessories, commemorative medals and plaques
chromium	blue-white; takes and keeps high polish; can be given brushed finish	hard; resists corrosion; cold, glittery unless brushed; often used as thin plating; durable; finger and water marks	faucets; toasters and other small appliances; lighting fixtures; maintenance-free furniture
copper	orange color quickly oxidizes to dull greenish brown or lively blue-green; must be kept polished to retain orange hue and lustrous surface	soft, easily shaped, but durable; good conductor of heat, electricity; impervious to water; tarnishes but does not rust; considered everlasting	water pipes; electrical wiring; eave troughs and roofs (expensive); cooking utensils, often displayed for beauty of finish; can be alloyed with tin or zinc to make bronze or brass
iron	grayish, galvanized with zinc coating, painted to resist rust	strong; worked easily by hand or machine	cookware, railings, decorative hardware
pewter	tin alloyed with antimony, copper and lead; mellow warm gray; polishes to a satin finish	easily worked; resistant to tarnish and hard usage	pitchers, trays, tableware, lighting fixtures, decorative accessories
steel	iron alloyed with carbon, also needs painting except for special types	harder than iron but still easily formed by machine	cookware, window and door frames, painted or enameled furniture
stainless steel	addition of chromium makes pleasant blue-gray color	resistant to rust and staining; hard, durable; nontarnishable	cooking utensils, flatware, counter tops, sinks, and cooktops
silver	whitest of metals; takes beautiful polish; reflects light; can be plated over alloy base	soft until hardened with copper (sterling silver); ductile, malleable; tarnishes, but easily cleaned and polished; frequently plated over an alloy base	flat and hollow tableware, decorative accessories
tin	dull silver color	very soft; easily worked; resistant to tarnish; nonrusting	lighting fixtures, ornamental frames, small accessories

With the possible exception of plastics, no other material can be shaped in so many ways. Metal can be melted and cast in simple or intricate molds; in the solid state it can be rolled, pressed, or turned on a lathe as well as hammered, bent, drilled, or cut with saws and torches; separate pieces can be welded together or joined with bolts and rivets.

This unique complex of qualities—tensile strength, meltability, ductility, malleability, conductivity, resistance to fire and decay, and potential beauty of color and surface—makes a house built today without metals hard to imagine. A partial list would include such inconspicuous but essential elements as structural members and reinforcing in masonry; conductors of water, heat, and electricity; weatherproofing and foil insulation; and nails and screws. Metals are thinly concealed by protective coatings of enamel in stoves, refrigerators, and other appliances. They become noticeable in hinges, handles, and doorknobs; in faucets, radiators, or warm-air vents; and in windows and door frames. Finally, metals are treasured for their visual attractiveness in tableware, furniture, cooking utensils, and lighting fixtures. The metals that are most often used in the home, their qualities and applications are given in Table 11–1. Metal used in furniture design is explored in Chapter 17.

Form in Metal

Were it not for the fact that metal is heavy and expensive, we might say that almost any form imaginable lends itself to metal design. Metal will take and hold any shape that can be given to wood, masonry, ceramics, or glass. Its most distinctive quality, though, is its great tensile strength, which makes possible, as well as durable, quite slender shapes. Sharp edges, as on knives, are more durable in metal than in any other material. When used expressively, metal contributes a precise thinness that distinguishes it from the comparatively heavy solidity of wood, masonry, and ceramics.

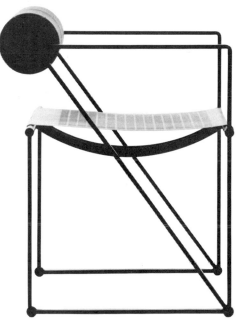

left: 11-15 The slender structure of a table designed by Giacometti, made possible by the inherent strength of metal, gives it the appearance of being light in weight. *(Photograph: © Peter Aaron/ESTO)*

above: 11-16 The strict geometry of the "Secondo" armchair with its pencil-thin lines is a forthright expression of the metal from which it is constructed. Mario Botto, designer. *(Courtesy ICF Inc. Photograph: Peter Paige)*

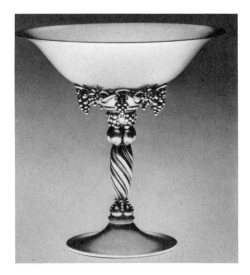

top: 11-17   The brilliance of highly polished silver has been emphasized by areas of satin finish in these "flower vases" designed by Lino Sabattini for Argenteria Sabattini, Italy. *(Courtesy Sabattini. Photograph: Foto Ciceri)*

middle: 11-18   When it is polished, pewter, an alloy usually of tin with various other metals, takes a soft, natural luster that is responsive to the amount of light reaching it. *(Gorham, courtesy Bloomingdale's)*

bottom right: 11-19   A footed bowl created for Georg Jensen in 1918 is still being reproduced because its contrast of form and ornament is unusually harmonious. *(Courtesy Georg Jensen, Inc.)*

Ornament in Metal

The surface treatment of metal, which can give varied light-and-dark patterns and reflections, acts as a basic kind of ornament. Highly polished metal gives mirrorlike reflections, interestingly distorted when on rounded forms. By contrast, softly polished pewter produces more mellow and diffuse patterns. Three-dimensional textures, such as those on stamped sheet metals can lead to myriad juxtapositions of highlights and shadows.

As with form, there are almost no physical limitations for ornament. If we wish to exploit each material's individuality, we will emphasize its most distinctive qualities. This leads to several suggestions. First, the strength of metal permits boldly projecting ornamental parts; second, the very fine grain and smoothness make delicate embellishment effective; third, the hardness of metal reconciles linear or angular decoration with the material; fourth, the long life and cost of most metals may suggest relatively formal, controlled, and precise enrichment but does not preclude other approaches.

Plastics

The phenomenal development of plastics in the past few decades has affected our homes markedly and will continue to do so. Today's scientists transform wood, coal, milk, petroleum, natural gas, and many other substances into new compounds tailor-made for specific purposes, while designers and engineers invent efficient methods of shaping these materials. Thus we can now produce on an enormous scale materials that in many instances are better suited to contemporary needs than the substances nature provides.

At first, plastics were considered cheap substitutes for more costly materials and a rash of plastic pseudo-wood, plastic pseudo-marble, and plastic pseudo-metal objects flooded the market. We have since learned to appreciate the material for what it is, to exploit plastic-as-plastic. Not only can plastics assume shapes and perform tasks that no other material could, but the pure beauty of well-designed plastic form delights the eye. Plastic dishes are lightweight and resist chipping. Chairs and other furniture can be molded from transparent, translucent, or opaque plastics or shaped from foamed plastics whose density can be controlled to vary from rigid framework to soft cushioning. Wall, floor, and ceiling panels and coverings come in great variety of plastic forms and counter-top materials are available in a wide array of colors. Even houses in which plastics act as the major construction material, although still largely experimental, are slowly becoming available.

11-20 The development of foamed plastics has had a strong influence on furniture design. "Le Bambola" seating by Mario Bellini is constructed of polyurethane in varying densities embedded in a tubular steel frame, making it bulky but lightweight, extremely resilient but form-retaining. *(Courtesy B & B America/Stendig International)*

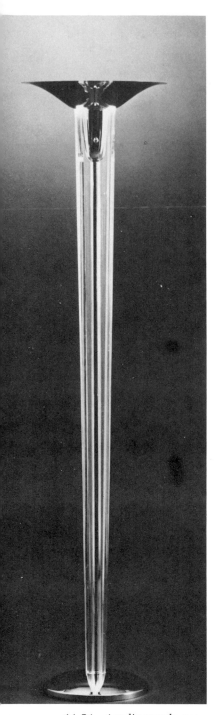

11-21 Acrylic panels surround the stem of the classic "City of Paris" torchère, creating a reflective column of light down its length. *(Courtesy Boyd Lighting Company)*

Plastic resins, principally carbon compounds in long molecular chains, come to forming machines as powders, granules, compressed tablets, or liquids, which under heat and/or pressure can be shaped as designers wish. Many techniques exist for forming plastics; the materials can be compressed in molds; extruded through dies to form continuous sheets, rods, filaments, or tubes; injected into cavities of complex outline; drawn into molds by the vacuum method; blown full of gas or air to make rigid, semirigid, or flexible foams; or sprayed over forms.

Film and sheeting for shower curtains, upholstery, or laminates are made by spreading plastic solutions on wheels up to 25 feet in diameter, by extruding the compound through a wide die, or by *calendering*—that is, by passing the compound between several rollers to get the desired thickness and surface texture. Rollers also aid in giving other materials a plastic coating. In laminating such materials as Formica or Micarta, layers of cloth, paper, wood, or glass fibers are impregnated with uncured resin or alternated with uncured plastic film, then pressed into a single sheet.

Families of Plastics

Although innumerable plastics exist, some of those most used in homes derive from the types of resins discussed in Table 11–2. Each name refers to a family of plastics with basic shared characteristics but with considerable diversity in form and application. And more and more resins are being cross-bred to produce plastics that demonstrate specific unique traits. Four terms associated with plastics explain some of their distinctions:

- The terms **plastic** and **synthetic** can be applied to the same basic material: molded nylon is called a plastic; nylon thread a synthetic. In this chapter we shall consider only the plastics; Chapter 12 deals with synthetic fibers.
- **Thermoplastic** substances can be softened and resoftened by heat and pressure, short of the point of decomposition. Vinyl and urethane are examples.
- **Thermosetting** plastics cannot be modified after the initial chemical change during the curing process. Melamine is a thermoset plastic.

Certain qualities taken together differentiate plastics—despite their variability—from other materials. The range of color and texture, actual or simulated, seems limitless, and plastics exhibit all degrees of transparency and opacity. They feel warm and pleasant. Truly "plastic," they can be formed into almost any rigid or flexible seamless shape. Typically, plastics are tough and durable in relation to weight and thickness. Absorbing little or no moisture, they neither rot nor mildew. Their resistance to chemicals varies but is generally good. However, their strength and dimensions are with a few exceptions noticeably affected by extreme temperatures. Plastics cover a broad range of prices.

Three environmental problems have become apparent within the last decade in connection with the tremendous proliferation of plastics. In each case, research is being conducted to find answers, but the consumer should be aware of these concerns and press for solutions.

Flammability

While many plastics are rated as slow-burning or self-extinguishing, a few types—including some acrylics, polyurethane foams, and polystyrenes—have been found not only to burn and/or melt or break down molecularly under certain conditions but to give off lethal and possibly explosive gases in the process. The plastics industry is attempting to overcome these hazards with new flame retardants, new chemical formulas, and the issuance of consumer information about the

Plate 35 Stained glass, popular in Victorian houses in the late 19th century, has returned to favor in contemporary homes. Peter Green designed this front entry of leaded, imported pastel glass for a home in Connecticut. Victor Chris-Janer, architect. *(Photograph: © Karen Bussolini)*

above: Plate 36 Color-Core, a plastic laminate, can be used for counter-top and cupboard surfacings that are colorful as well as extremely practical. Available in 72 shades with the color going all the way through the material. *(Courtesy Formica Corporation)*

below: Plate 37 Sheila O'Hara's 1983 woven wall piece, "Only My Palmreader Knows for Sure," creates a striking illusion of depth. *(Courtesy Modern Masters Tapestries, Inc. Photograph: Gary Sinick)*

282

Table 11–2 Families of Plastics

Name	Characteristics	Uses
ABS (Acrylonitrile, butadiene, styrene)	tough, hard, great tensile strength; resistant to scratching, chemicals, weather; moldable; lightweight	"fitting" ability leads to everything from plumbing systems to modular furniture that can be assembled in various configurations
ASA (Acrylonitrile, styrene, acrylic)	good integral color; cross-bred for specific applications and for plating, alloying with other plastics	
acrylics Plexiglas Lucite Perspex (also acrylic yarns)	strong, rigid, light in weight, excellent color; exceptional clarity, ability to pipe light; resistant to weathering, temperature changes and extremes; may scratch but can be buffed; molded into rigid shapes, then carved	domes and skylights, furniture, tableware, sculpture, paint (much used by artists)
FRP (fiberglass-reinforced plastics, often polyester)	stiff to flexible, hard to soft; good color range; resistant to chemicals, weather; strong	patio covers, luminous ceilings, light-transmitting panels, walls, skylights, molded and laminated furniture, sculpture
melamines Formica Micarta Melmac	hard, durable, transparent to opaque; resistant to scratching, chipping, water, food stains, heat, fading; thin layer used in laminates shows material underneath; thicker molded, opaque; extensive color range; high-gloss, satiny or matte surface	high-pressure laminates for counter tops, table tops, and as wood substitute for case goods; dinnerware
nylon generic term for group of plastics; also trade name and nylon yarn	thin layer transparent, thicker opaque; relatively rigid, high tensile strength; resistant to many chemicals, but not to food stains, coffee, tea; to abrasion but not to scratches or weathering; good color range; can be frozen, boiled; not recommended for continuous outdoor exposure	tumblers, dinnerware, kitchenware; especially useful for long-wearing gears, bearings, rollers; furniture
polyethylenes	flexible to rigid, often waxy surface; semitransparent to opaque, lightweight; resistant to breakage, chemicals, freezing, boiling water, but cannot be boiled; good color range	kitchen bowls, dishpans, squeeze bottles; more rigid form used for molded, nonupholstered chair shells
polystyrenes	hard, rigid, but will break under bending, impact; resistant to household chemicals, foods (except citrus fruits, cleaning fluids), but not to abrasion; transparent types pipe light; range of translucent, opaque colors; lustrous surface warm, pleasant to touch	kitchenware to modular furniture
urethanes cellular plastics so called because of structure, ability to foam (also as nonwoven fabric)	can be given any density, degree of hardness, from resilient to rigid; hard can be worked, finished, repaired like wood; can be foamed in place, bonded to any surface; good insulating properties, lightweight; foams are combustible and must be covered with fire-rated material	cushioning material, covering fabric, to furniture itself; insulation
vinyls (also as nonwoven fabric)	rigid, nonrigid, foam or cellular types; transparent, translucent, opaque; tough, strong, lightweight; resistant to foods, chemicals, normal use; cuts readily, may stiffen in cold; cellular form a wood substitute; can be embossed, printed in wide range of colors and textures	upholstery, wall coverings, lamp shades, luminous ceilings, counter surface; vinyl floor coverings combine most wanted characteristics in single material

properties and appropriate uses of the materials. But the buyer of a mattress, for example, should seek a guarantee that it is indeed fireproof.

Biodegradability

The possibility of a plastic being reabsorbed into the environment is also a matter of public awareness and demand for accountability. Plastics that can be melted down presumably could be reformed. In one experiment, plastics have been ground into chips and then combined with sand to make concrete. Other such uses could be found. Chemists continue to work on formulas for plastics that would eventually break down into harmless particles and decompose in landfills.

Noxious Fumes

The chemicals contained in the many plastics used throughout the home release vapors. With the emphasis put upon energy conservation and the resulting nearly air-tight enclosures modern technology has made possible, these fumes can easily become a health hazard. Adequate ventilation prevents a noxious buildup of fumes.

Form and Ornament in Plastics

Plastics differ from natural materials in that their basic qualities are chemically and physically determined by humans. Thus, instead of designing to suit a material, manufacturers can actually create a material to meet a specific need, real or imagined. This brings new challenges and problems. For one thing, such absolute flexibility indicates the need for close, steady cooperation among chemist, manufacturer, and designer. The designer is not only confronted with a characterless substance to mold, but has no age-old craft tradition in which to seek accumulated knowledge or inspiration. On the other hand, this absence of guidelines frees the designer from the stereotypes of past forms.

Design in plastics can be a completely liberated merger of designer, material, and machine. No longer hampered by preconceived notions of what is proper for any particular material, the imagination can soar in many directions, starting with the composition of the plastic itself and ending with new shapes and even new functions. This does not mean that shapes *must* be invented simply because the potential exists. The contours of plastic dishes and tumblers closely resemble those of clay or glass because these have been found serviceable and pleasant. But in some fields, major breakthroughs have been achieved. Furniture designers have been investigating whole new vocabularies of shape and function allowed by the properties of the new materials, while architects continue to explore the possibilities of free-form structures of intriguing shapes. And some of the simplest forms assume a completely new quality when translated into pristine plastic.

Successful ornament in plastics remains largely structural, where the inherent possibilities for varied colors, different degrees of transparency, translucency, or opacity, embedded materials, and molded form and surface texture seem to be in the nature of the materials and in the processes used to form them. The traditional materials also have these possibilities, but a plastic can combine some of these characteristics in a different way or may add other qualities that are desirable, usually that of durability and/or ease of maintenance.

Because the conventional types of applied ornament are so closely allied with the natural materials they were originally designed to enhance, they are likely to appear weak, imitative, and inappropriate when used on plastics. Perhaps this is so because, as yet, little applied ornament has been developed for plastic that intensifies its unique quality, as, for example, etching or cutting heightens the sparkle of glass or intricate ornament throws into relief the luster of polished silver.

left: 11-22 An Art Deco table has a glass top cantilevered from a sculptured acrylic base like an abstract ice carving. Michael Berkowicz, designer. *(Courtesy Plexability. Photograph: Paul Aresu)*
above: 11-23 On Rory McCarthy's sideboard/secretary, plastic laminate is used in a contemporary dimensional version of the traditional marquetry patterns usually seen on wood furniture. *(Courtesy The Workbench. Photograph: Si Chi Ko)*

The history of plastics is very short, and the development of any new vocabulary takes a long time. Many consumers and manufacturers conservatively prefer that which is at least partially familiar to something wholly new. At the other extreme, the lack of restrictions imposed by the material has resulted in much poor design or in some cases an overexuberance of design. However, increasingly effective design in plastics continually becomes available as their nature is more fully understood.

The introduction of plastics has had enormous impact on today's homes. Plastic surfaces on furniture, counters, walls, and floors lighten housekeeping and reduce noise. Plastic furniture is light in weight, easy to move around the house and from house to house; plastic houses of the future may change many of our concepts of home planning and furnishing. Even now, many of the familiar components in the traditional house may be of plastic, from the plumbing to insulation to wall panels. Designers have accepted it as an exciting new medium, and many are busy exploring its potentialities (Plate 36, p. 282).

References for Further Reading

Almeida, Oscar. *Metalworking*. New York: Drake, 1971.
Bevlin, Marjorie Elliott. *Design Through Discovery*, 4th ed. New York: Holt, Rinehart and Winston, 1984. Pp. 177–180.
Burton, John. *Glass: Handblown, Sculptured, Colored: Philosophy and Methods*. Philadelphia: Chilton, 1968.

Carron, Shirley. *Modern Pewter: Design and Technique*. New York: Van Nostrand Reinhold, 1973.

Charleston, Robert J. *World Ceramics*. New York: McGraw-Hill, 1968.

Hardner, Paul V. and James S. Plant. *Steuben: Seventy Years of American Glass Blowing*. New York: Praeger, 1975.

Hughes, Graham. *Modern Silver Throughout the World: 1880–1967*. New York: Viking, 1967.

Labino, Dominick. *Visual Art in Glass*. Dubuque, IA: William C. Brown, 1968.

McKearin, George and Helen S. McKearin. *200 Years of American Blown Glass*, rev. ed. New York: Crown, 1966.

Nelson, Glenn C. *Ceramics: A Potter's Handbook*, 5th ed. New York: Holt, Rinehart and Winston, 1984.

Newman, Thelma R. *Plastics as an Art Form*. Radnor, PA: Chilton, 1964.

Newman, Thelma R. *Plastics as Sculpture*. Radnor, PA: Chilton, 1974.

Roukes, Nicholas. *Sculpture in Plastics*. New York: Watson-Guptill, 1978.

Savage, George. *Glass*. New York: Putnam, 1965.

Textile Fibers and Fabrics

More than anything in a house except the people, fabrics humanize our homes because of their pliant responsiveness to our needs. Fabrics make us more comfortable, control light coming through windows and give privacy without solid walls, insulate against extreme heat and cold, and absorb noise. They provide easily removable and cleanable coverings for tables and beds, as well as pleasant-to-touch upholstery for chairs and sofas. Beyond these service functions, fabrics bring beauty and individuality unlike that of any other material. Several distinctive characteristics of fabrics are worth noting:

- No other materials come in such width and length and can be readily used in those dimensions.
- Uniquely pliable and easily manipulated, fabrics can be folded, draped, pleated, or stretched; and they can be cut, sewed, or glued together.
- Of all the materials in the home, fabrics are most frequently and easily replaced.
- They are noticed because they appear in quantity throughout the home, look and feel softer than other materials, and are often brightly colored or patterned.

287

- Fabrics link together people, furniture, and architecture in a way unequaled by anything else. Carpets and other fabrics attached to floors and walls adhere strictly to the "architecture" of the home. Upholstery and table linens adapt themselves to the seating or to the tables on which they are used and at the same time relate those pieces to our clothing. Curtains and draperies can partake of the architectural quality of windows as well as relate openings to the enclosing structure and to the furniture in the room. Fabrics can even become the total interior environment.

Beyond their everyday usefulness, fabrics have two important functions: first, they make their own visual and tactile contributions to the home; second, they can be strong unifying elements within a room and between rooms. Traditionally, fabrics were used primarily for their functional qualities or to improve the appearance of functional items. Today fabrics are increasingly used strictly for their aesthetic appeal. In addition, the use of fibers and fabric has emerged as a legitimate art form (Plate 37, p. 282).

The creation of a textile product, whether commercially or by hand, involves several stages of development: from fiber to yarn to fabric construction and the application of finishes, color, and pattern. The performance and appearance of a finished fabric depend upon the decision made at each step in the process.

12-1 Weaver Aleksandra Kasuba, with the aid of designer Vytautas Kasuba, constructed an architectural fabric interior that would be a totally new experience for most of us—a world of enveloping softness, muted sounds, expanding and contracting vistas. *(Courtesy Allied Chemical Corporation)*

Fibers

Fibers are the raw materials, the basic units that form the building blocks of fabrics. They may occur naturally or be man-made. Nature provides four major fibers that have been used for centuries: cotton, flax, wool, and silk. However, the majority of fibers used today in this country are products of modern technology and the scientist's laboratory due to the availability and the expense of processing natural fibers.

The natural fibers, with the exception of silk, are **staple** fibers, available only in short lengths measured in centimeters or inches or fractions thereof. They must be combed and carded to straighten and align them before spinning to form yarn. Man-made fibers and silk are **filaments:** long continuous fibers measured in yards or meters or even miles. They have a higher luster, are smoother, more even, and require considerably less processing than staple fibers to form yarns. Filament fibers may be cut into shorter lengths to use as staple fibers to blend with natural fibers, to imitate natural fibers, or to produce fabrics with greater insulating properties, higher bulk, or fuzzier surfaces less susceptible to snagging.

Fibers may also be characterized as **thermoplastic** if they become soft or moldable when heat is applied and can thus be heat-set to stabilize dimensions, give a permanent-press finish, or emboss designs upon their surface. All *synthetic* fibers (those man-made fibers such as nylon that are synthesized from chemical substances in the laboratory) are thermoplastic. Most synthetic fibers such as glass are **hydrophobic** or nonabsorbent, while the *natural* fibers such as cotton, linen, and wool are **hydrophilic** or absorbent, which makes them comfortable and more easily dyed. *Crimp* denotes the waviness of the fiber and affects its resilience; wool has a natural crimp, man-made fibers can be given a crimp. *Loft*, the springiness of a fiber, can also affect resiliency.

Fibers differ from one another in many ways: strength and elasticity; resistance to abrasion, stains, sun, moisture, mildew, and fire; appearance qualities; and maintenance. Each fiber has its strong and weak points. Although some are more versatile than others, none is ideally suited to every purpose. Moreover, important developments occur all the time—new man-made fibers are created, familiar ones are modified, and processing and finishing techniques are improved. Table 12–1 gives basic facts about the performance characteristics of the more important fibers.

Natural Fibers

The sources of natural fibers are plants, animals, and, to a lesser degree, minerals. The major textile fiber-producing plants and animals have long since been domesticated and may be considered renewable sources although some "harvests" may be cyclical rather than continuous.

Cellulosic Fibers

Plant stems, stalks, leaves, seed hairs, and even barks that consist mostly of cellulose and need only be changed in physical form make up the natural vegetable fibers. The two most common are cotton and flax. **Cotton** is one of the most versatile and durable fibers; it may be used in fabrics that range from sheer to heavyweight, from inexpensive to expensive, and from window coverings and linens to upholstery and floor coverings. Cotton is absorbent, dyes easily, retains color, reflects heat, is flexible and easily laundered. It can be processed and finished to overcome most of its disadvantages (wrinkling, shrinking, soiling, and burning) and it is often used in combination with other fibers to produce blends that capitalize upon the best characteristics of each.

Table 12–1 Performance Characteristics of Common Textile Fibers

Fiber, Fiber Substance, Trade Names*	Appearance	Resistances	
		Poor	**Good**
acetate (cellulose diacetate) *Acele* *Avisco* *Celanese* *Chromspun* *Estron*	drapes well; good color range	abrasion, aging, heat, sunlight, wrinkling	felting, fire (Acele), insects, pilling, shrinking, static electricity, stretching
acrylic (acrylonitrite and other monomers) *Acrilan* *Creslan* *Orlon* *Zefran*	warm, bulky, woollike touch; good color range in some types	pilling, static electricity unless treated	abrasion, felting, fire, shrinking, stretching, sunlight, wrinkling
cotton (cellulose)	pleasant, soft, dull surface; fair drape; excellent color range	felting, fire, mildew, shrinking, wrinkling	abrasion, aging, fading, insects, stretching, sunlight
glass (silica sand, limestone, aluminum, and borax) *Beta* *Fiberglas* *Uniglass* *Pittsburgh PPG*	lustrous, silky; good drape; fair color range in dyes, printed many hues	abrasion, flexing (nonelastic) but new processes increase flexibility	
linen (cellulose, from flax)	clean, fresh, lintless; fair drape; good color range	fire, shrinking, wrinkling unless treated or blended	abrasion, mildew, pilling, stretching, sunlight
modacrylic (modified acrylics) *Dynel* *Verel*	warm, bulky, heavy, dense	heat, shrinking unless stabilized by heat-setting, sunlight (*Dynel*)	abrasion, pilling, static electricity, wrinkling
nylon (polyamide) *6, 6.6, 501* *Antron* *Caprolan* *Cumuloft*	natural luster; good drape; good color range	pilling, static electricity unless treated, sunlight	fire
olefin (ethylene, propylene, or other olefin units) *Herculon* *Vectra*	woollike hand; fair color range	heat, shrinking, static electricity	abrasion, felting, fire, stretching, sunlight, wrinkling

Excellent	Special Characteristics and Processes	Maintenance	End Uses
	newer processes have color as integral part of fiber, increasing resistances to sunlight, cleaning	fair soil resistance; dry-clean or wash; dries quickly; iron with *cool* iron	bedspreads, curtains, draperies, rugs, upholstery
aging, insects, mildew, sunlight	warmth without weight; retains heat-set pleats and creases	slow to soil; easy to spot-clean; dry-clean or wash; dries quickly; little ironing, under 325°	blankets, curtains, rugs, upholstery
pilling, static electricity; all resistances greatly improved by special treatments and blends	mercerizing increases luster, softness, strength, dye absorption; wash-and-wear, spot- and wrinkle-resistant finishes	soils, stains, wrinkles easily unless treated; dry-clean or wash; irons easily	bed and table linen, bedspreads, draperies, rugs, towels, upholstery
aging, chemicals, felting, fire, insects, mildew, shrinking, stretching, sunlight	*Beta* yarn one-half size of any other fiber; can be woven into very sheer fabric; fireproof, impervious to moisture and salt air; shed fibers can cause skin rash	slow to soil; easy spot removal; hand-wash, hang with no ironing; dries quickly	bedspreads, curtains, draperies, wallpaper
aging, insects, static electricity	stronger when wet; *Sanforized* to reduce shrinking; can be made wrinkle-resistant	soils and wrinkles easily; washes and irons well	curtains, draperies, household linens, rugs, upholstery
aging, felting, fire, insects, mildew, sunlight (*Verel*)	self-extinguishing; special processes result in dense, furlike pile, textured, three-dimensional effects	similar to acrylics, but highly resistant to chemical stains; iron setting varies	blankets, draperies, rugs, upholstery
abrasion, aging, felting, insects, mildew, shrinking, stretching, wrinkling	outstanding elasticity, strength, and lightness; can be heat-set to keep permanent shape; sometimes damaged by acids; may pick up color and soil during washing	slow to soil; easy spot removal; dry-clean or wash, dries quickly; little ironing at low heat	bedspreads, rugs, upholstery
insects, mildew, pilling, aging	lightest fiber made; excellent insulator; transmits humidity well; is very cohesive (can be made into nonwoven carpets); low cost	slow to soil; spot-clean or wash; little ironing, at *very* low heat	blankets, rugs, upholstery, webbing

Fiber, Fiber Substance, Trade Names*	Appearance	Resistances	
		Poor	Good
polyester (dihydric alcohol and terephthalic acid) *Dacron Fortrel Kodel*	crisp or soft, pleasant touch; good drape; fair color range	dust, soil, pilling because very electrostatic	abrasion, fire, sunlight
rayon (regenerated cellulose) *Avril Cupioni Enka Fortisan*	bright or dull luster; drapes well; excellent color range	felting, fire, mildew, shrinking, wrinkling	abrasion, aging, insects, stretching (poor when wet), sunlight
silk (protein from silkworm cocoon)	lustrous, smooth, unique crunchy softness; drapes well; excellent color range	fire (but self-extinguishing), static electricity, sunlight	abrasion, aging, felting, insects, mildew, shrinking, stretching, wrinkling
triacetate *Arnel*	pleasant luster; drapes well; excellent color range		abrasion, insects, pilling, static electricity, stretching
wool (protein from sheep or goat and camel families)	soft or hard finish; dry, warm touch; drapes well; good color range	insects, felting, shrinking unless treated	abrasion, aging, fire, mildew, pilling, stretching, static electricity, sunlight

*Only partial listing of trade names

Linen, made from flax fibers, is the oldest fiber used in the Western world. It is crisper and more lustrous than cotton but may also range in use from sheer and smooth to coarse. Linen is strong and wears well with good resistance to deterioration from age and, to a lesser degree, sunlight.

Other plant fibers include jute, ramie, hemp, kapok, and sisal. Still other plants woven into mats or used as wall coverings include various palm, grass, and straw fibers. Even bark may be pounded into a kind of cloth.

All cellulosic fibers have low static electricity but they burn easily, a characteristic that must be taken into consideration by the designer where safety is important. It should be noted that fabrics burn more quickly in an upright position such as when used for draperies and curtains than when used in a flat or horizontal position.

Excellent	Special Characteristics and Processes	Maintenance	End Uses
felting, insects, mildew, shrinking, stretching, wrinkling	lightweight; ranges from sheer, silklike to bulky, woollike; as strong wet as dry; retains heat-set pleats and creases; picks up colors in washing	soils easily; dry-clean or wash, dries quickly; very little ironing, moderate heat	bedding, curtains, draperies, upholstery
pilling, static electricity; all resistances greatly improved by blending, finishes	most versatile fiber—can resemble cotton, silk, wool; absorbs moisture and swells when wet unless specially processed; reduces static electricity in blends; low cost; wash-and-wear and spot- and wrinkle-resistant finishes	fair soil resistance; dry-clean or wash; iron like cotton or silk, depending on type, finish	blankets, curtains, draperies, rugs, table "linens," upholstery
	most desirable combination of properties of any fiber; smoothness, luster, resiliency, toughness for its weight, adaptability to temperature changes	good soil resistance; dry-clean or hand-wash; irons easily, moderate heat	draperies, rugs, upholstery
aging, felting, fire, mildew, shrinking, wrinkling, sunlight	excellent retention of heat-set pleats and creases; ability to withstand washing, ironing	slow to soil; dry-clean or wash; dries quickly; little ironing, higher setting than diacetates	draperies
wrinkling; new processes make it even more resistant to soil, stains, water, wrinkling	notable for warmth, absorbency (without feeling wet), resiliency, durability; wool-synthetic blends reduce shrinkage but have tendency to pill	good soil resistance; spot-clean, dry-clean, or wash in cold water; press over damp cloth at low heat	blankets, draperies, rugs, upholstery

Protein Fibers

Most of the protein fibers are obtained from the hair of animals, some from animal secretions. Hair fibers include the fleece of sheep, goat's hair (mohair and cashmere), camel's hair (including alpaca, llama, and vicuña), horsehair, and the fur of animals such as mink, rabbit, or beaver. Fibrous secretions are obtained primarily from the silkworm.

Wool, although considered a weak fiber, is very durable because of its exceptional resiliency and good elasticity and elongation properties. It makes an excellent carpet and upholstery fabric. Wool dyes readily and retains color, in part because it is highly absorbent. Yet it also resists soil. Wool fibers tend to yellow with age and exposure to sunlight, to shrink and felt, and to be susceptible to insect damage (from moths and carpet beetles).

Other animal-hair fibers, also identified as wool, are considered specialty fibers because they are less readily available and are usually desired for their special luxurious characteristics. Animal skins (leathers) may also be considered specialty fabrics although they are not fibrous or typically constructed as most fabrics are.

Silk has long been considered a luxury fiber, in part perhaps because of the romantic legends concerning its history. It is produced by the larva of the silkworm in spinning its cocoon, which is then unreeled by man to use in yarn manufacture. Silk filaments are very long, smooth, strong, and quite lustrous. Wild silk is more coarse, uneven, and less lustrous than cultivated silk. Spun silk is made of short fiber lengths from the outermost layer of the cocoon. A wide variety of yarn and fabric structures is possible with excellent color and durability. However, silk is quickly damaged by sunlight.

All the protein fibers share the properties of moisture absorbency, which helps make them easy to dye; resiliency and elastic recovery, which helps with wrinkle resistance/recovery; low heat conductivity, which enhances insulating capabilities; static electricity buildup; and poor resistance to alkalies.

Mineral Fibers

Asbestos, a fireproof mineral fiber, is not used to any extent in fabrics due to its carcinogenic nature.

Man-Made Fibers

Man-made fibers are not all synthetic; some are extruded from natural solutions that have been chemically altered or regenerated. True synthetics are synthesized primarily from petrochemicals. The man-made fibers have several characteristics in common: they are produced in either monofilament or multifilament form and may not require additional processes to form yarns; they resist damage from moths and insects; they are generally nonallergenic; many repel, rather than absorb, moisture and soil, making them easy to care for. Production can be controlled for uniform quality, and it is continuous, keeping costs fairly stabilized. Also, man-made fibers can be designed and created for particular purposes.

Cellulosic Fibers

These man-made fibers originate as plant fibers, primarily from soft woods, but are regenerated and modified to produce rayon, acetate, and triacetate fibers.

Noncellulosic (Synthetic) Fibers

The generic families, each chemically distinct, which belong in this group of fibers include nylon, polyester, acrylic, modacrylic, olefin, and saran.

Elastomeric Fibers

These fibers are elastic, rubberlike substances such as rubber (either natural or synthetic) and spandex. They are used with other fibers to give improved form-fitting qualities.

Mineral Fibers

Man-made fibers of mineral source include glass fiber and metallic fibers. Because none of these materials are fibrous in their natural state, they are considered man-made fibers. Glass fibers may produce allergic reactions in some people, perhaps due to irritation from the fiber ends. Fiberglass has low abrasion resistance, a factor to consider in selecting a fiber suitable for a window treatment.

Metallic fibers may be composed of metal, plastic-coated metal, metal-coated plastic, or a core covered by metal. The metals most often used are gold, silver, aluminum, and stainless steel, which is often incorporated into carpets to reduce static buildup.

Fiber Blends

A textile may consist of only one fiber or may combine two or more to maximize favorable qualities and minimize disadvantages. Different fibers can be extruded as a single filament, spun together into one yarn, or yarns spun from different fibers can be combined in a single fabric. These combinations of fibers have yielded some of the most successful changes in fabric characteristics. We are all familiar with the advantages of adding polyester fibers to cotton, in varying proportions, to produce textiles that are almost wrinkle-free and remarkably dirt-resistant. Nylon increases the strength of wool, and stretch nylon combined with cotton makes slipcovers that are form-fitting and pleasant to touch. The permutations are almost endless; they permit the manufacture of fabrics that can embody the best attributes of various fibers. But the fiber blends also present problems, for consumers must try to keep up with the advantages and disadvantages of all the new fibers and fabrics that keep appearing. Considerable progress has been made in consumer protection by requiring that fabrics be labeled with their fiber content and method of care. However, consumers will need to keep educating themselves on the characteristics of fibers so that their probable performance *in use* can be to some extent predetermined. For practical purposes, a textile blend of less than 5 to 10 percent of a fiber benefits very little from the characteristics of that fiber. In this sense, blends are only as strong as the weakest fiber contained therein.

Yarns

Yarn results when fibers are twisted together to make a strand long enough and sufficiently strong for weaving or other fabric-construction processes. With natural fibers, yarn-making includes cleaning the fibers, drawing them out so they are more or less even and parallel, then spinning or twisting them into yarn. Man-made fibers are clean, continuous, and parallel as soon as they have been extruded as filaments, so the process is simply one of twisting them together. Yarns vary in the kinds of fibers used either alone or in combination, in the type and tightness of twist, in the *ply* (the number of strands in the yarn), and in the size of the finished product.

below left: 12-2 A textile woven of only one fiber can have decided structural interest because of the yarn composition. In "Ticino" the yarn consists of a number of strands, almost casually laid and loosely twisted. *(Courtesy Stow/Davis Furniture Company)*

below right: 12-3 Marianne Strengell's hand-woven off-white casement fabric of linen, fiberglass, rayon, and goat hair contrasts thick and thin, tightly and loosely spun yarns in a seemingly spontaneous construction. *(Photograph: Ferdinand Boesch)*

12-4 Complex yarns give this knitted cotton drapery-weight fabric its interesting nubby texture. *(Courtesy E.I. duPont de Nemours & Co.)*

Filament fibers form **filament yarns** while staple fibers are combined to create **spun yarns.** Twisting fibers tightly or loosely is one possible variation in yarn construction. Filament yarns and yarns twisted firmly (but not so tightly as to curl back on themselves) tend to be noticeably stronger and more durable than loosely twisted and spun yarns. Increased twist adds elasticity.

Fiber strands can form **single yarns, ply yarns,** or **cord yarns.** In *single* yarns individual fiber strands are twisted together. *Ply* yarns are made by combining two or more single yarns twisted together; *cord* yarns consist of two or more ply yarns. Yarn sizes range from spider-web single filaments to silk yarns of two hundred strands or ropelike cords. Many textiles contain only one size of yarn, but others combine several or many sizes, depending upon the desired effect.

Simple yarns are relatively smooth, even in size, and have a uniform number of twists per inch. They produce plain, smooth, flat-surface, relatively hard-finish fabrics that are usually easy to maintain and durable although fiber content, fabric construction, coloring methods, and finishing procedures also affect use and care. Fabric pattern is achieved through woven-in or printed-on decorative finishes.

Complex or **novelty yarns** are irregular in size, twist, and effect. They are used primarily for appearance and include slub yarns found in fabrics such as shantung and some linens, flock yarns found in tweeds, bouclé yarns, and chenille yarns. Fabrics constructed of complex yarns are relatively highly textured and tend to be more vulnerable to wear than fabrics made with simple yarns; they derive their decorative quality from the appearance of the yarn more than from fabric construction or finishing processes.

Fabric Construction

Although there are endless ways of making fabrics, all of them fall generally into one of three basic categories. Each of these methods has its own special advantages and each lends itself to certain effects and end uses.

Weaving

Weaving is the interlacing of warp and filling yarns, usually at right angles, to make textiles. **Warp** yarns run lengthwise on the loom and in the fabric. **Filling** yarns (also called *weft* or *woof*) run crosswise to fill and hold together the warp. The apparently enormous complexity of weaves can be reduced to three general categories: plain, twill, and satin.

Plain weave is simply one filling yarn carried over one warp yarn and under one. When plain weaves utilize warp and filling yarns of identical size, a smooth surface fabric such as organdy or percale results. The variations include *rep*, which has a definite ribbed texture produced by interweaving relatively heavy yarns with thinner ones and *basket weaves*, a construction of two or more filling yarns crossing two or more warp yarns to produce a noticeable pattern, as in monk's cloth. Other patterns such as chambray, checks, and plaids are created by varying the colors of the yarns.

Twill weaves show a definite diagonal line or *wale* on the surface of the fabric, caused by having the filling yarns "float" across a number of warp yarns in a regular pattern. Typical fabrics include serge, gabardine, and denim. Herringbone patterns result from reversing the direction of the twill weave. Twill weaves resist soil and wrinkle less severely than do plain weaves of similar quality. They also tend to be the most durable fabric constructions.

12-5 The regular over-and-under pattern of a plain-weave textile becomes pronounced with the introduction of decided color variations. *(Courtesy Boris Kroll Fabrics, Inc.)*

above left: 12-6 Alternating squares of plain weave and basket weave result in a distinctive structural design in Jack Lenor Larsen's wool fabric, "Spellbound." *(Courtesy Jack Lenor Larsen, Inc.)*

above right: 12-7 The diagonal line characteristic of a twill weave can be emphasized to produce a visually exciting kinetic effect by varying the angle and color of the pattern. *(Courtesy Stow/Davis Furniture Company)*

Satin weaves differ from twill weaves in that the warp yarns make longer floats over the filling yarns, or the filling may float over the warp less regularly. These floats minimize the over-and-under texture. If the yarns are fine and lustrous, the fabric surface will be smooth and will shine with reflected light. Satin, sateen, damask, and chino are examples of this weave category. Satin weaves are the most vulnerable to wear of the basic fabric constructions.

Within the three basic classes of weaves, there are special variations particularly relevant to home furnishings that should be mentioned. **Leno weaves** result when the warp yarns (or occasionally the filling yarns) are crossed or twisted at certain points to create an open, gauzelike effect. The most popular leno weave fabrics are marquisette and grenadine. Usually, the open weave has such a small scale that the design is hardly noticed, but coarser versions produce handsome patterns. Leno weaves appear frequently in curtain fabrics.

below: 12-9 "Leno Sheer," designed by Hugo Dreyfuss, has a linen warp with hemp and rayon filling crossed and locked in the typical figure-8 leno weave. Its fragile appearance masks its actual strength. *(Courtesy Kagan-Dreyfuss)*

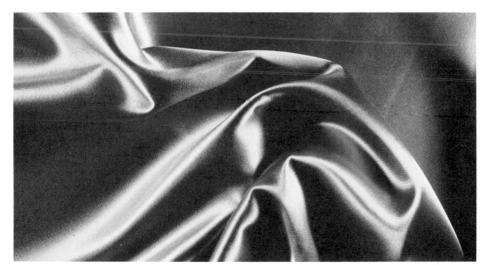

above: 12-8 A satin weave, with its long floating yarns on the surface, produces a shimmering, glossy fabric.

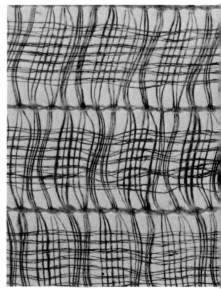

12-10 The possibilities for creating patterns by varying the length, cut, and color of pile weaves have inspired many fine rug designers. This Jacquard Wilton carpet was designed by Jack Lenor Larsen. *(Courtesy Jack Lenor Larsen, Inc.)*

Pile weaves add a third element to the basic warp and filling: a set of yarns that protrude from the background to make a three-dimensional fabric. In commercial production, the pile generally is added with a single continuous yarn that leaves loops on one side of the fabric. When the loops are left uncut, such textiles as terry cloth and frieze result. Cutting the loops produces velvet, plush, and the like. Patterns can be formed by cutting some loops and leaving the remainder uncut, as in corduroy; by having some portions of the pile higher than others; or by employing different colored yarns. Chenille fabrics have a pile that results from the use of chenille yarns with their soft fiber ends fluffed up like caterpillars. Certain fine carpets—including rya and Oriental rugs—are created by hand-tying individual strands of yarn onto the warp between rows of filler. This gives maximum flexibility in design. A variation on pile fabrics, *tufting* involves inserting pile yarns through previously constructed backing, which may or may not be woven. The hand version of this technique is more often called *hooking*. (See Chapter 14 for more information on carpet construction.)

Jacquard weaves are pattern weaves produced on a highly complex machine—the Jacquard loom—that operates like a computer. They include flat *dam-*

left: 12-11 "Carnevale," a hand-tufted rug, has a unique abstract pattern. *(Courtesy Saxony Carpet Company, Inc.)*
right: 12-12 The Jacquard loom is capable of weaving complex figured patterns similar to hand-made tapestries. This textured design is called "Kaleidoscope." *(Courtesy Stroheim & Romann)*

298

12-13 "Brookville," a soft knit drapery fabric, derives its interest from the uneven yarn and the complexity of the fabric structure. The reverse has a plain surface. (Courtesy Robert Tait Fabrics)

asks, raised *brocades*, complex *tapestries*, and some kinds of carpets. A Jacquard pattern can be almost anything, from a simple geometric motif to a complex, irregular design.

Knitting

Knitting is a process by which blunt rods or needles are used to interlock a single continuous yarn into a series of interlocking loops. Patterns result from a combination of plain, rib, and purl stitches, plus many variations. Because machine knitting can be two to five times as fast as machine weaving, and therefore less expensive, its possibilities have been reassessed in recent years. New fibers and techniques have produced dimensionally stable knit fabrics that have gained wide acceptance because of their stretch recovery, wrinkle resistance, and form-fitting characteristics.

Weft knits, also known as **filling** or **circular knits,** have horizontal or circular loops, resemble hand knitting in appearance, and include jersey, rib knit, double knit, and imitation fur fabrics. Horizontal stripe patterns are easily created in weft knits, and a Jacquard attachment makes a variety of patterns possible. **Warp** or **flat knits** have vertical loops and are flat. They include tricot and patterned open-structure raschel knits, laces, and drapery fabrics as well as some upholstery fabrics for foam furniture. Warp knits are usually more expensive than weft knits and do not have as much stretch.

Other Constructions

Although most fabrics are produced by weaving or knitting, there are many other methods of fabrication, old and new. They may be grouped as fabric webs, knotted and twisted constructions, multicomponent fabrics, and films.

Fabric Webs

Felt, bark cloth, and the more recent nonwoven fabrics are constructed by bonding together a web of fibers, with the aid of pressure, heat, moisture, and/or chemicals. Probably the earliest method of constructing fabrics, and one of the latest to be updated by new methods, felting is simply the matting together of fibers to form a web. **Tapa cloth** results from pounding together the fibers of the bark of the paper mulberry tree, often with leaves or other decorative materials added. Traditional **felts** are of wool, hair, or fur fibers matted by a combination of moisture, pressure, and heat, a process that induces shrinkage and increases density. The result is a continuous dense cloth—firm, slightly fuzzy, with comparatively low tensile strength, used mostly as a nonscratch protective padding or as insulation.

Needle felts or **needle-punched fabrics,** constructed by a newer technique, depend upon machines pushing barbed needles through a mat of fibers to entangle them without the intervention of heat or pressure. According to the characteristics and arrangements of the fibers and needles, products with low or high strength can be produced. Padding for furniture, floors, and home insulation, indoor/outdoor carpet, and blankets are the products of needle-punched fabrics.

Nonwoven fabrics consist of layers of fibers **bonded** together by a binding agent that is set by wet or dry heat or by chemical action. **Spun-bonded fabrics** take the fibers directly from the spinnerette to the fabric without costly intermediate processes. Backings for carpet, wall covering, and vinyls are made from various spun-bonded fabrics.

Knotting and Twisting

The processes by which **nets, macrame,** and **laces** are made, twisting calls for the intertwining and sometimes knotting of yarns that run in two or more directions. Although lace had long been out of favor for household use, fresh and imaginative designs are opening the way for its reintroduction.

12-14 Quilted fabrics for interiors have regained favor for their insulative qualities. Here, a quilt by Delci Lev provides color and pattern on a plain sofa. *(Photograph: © Karen Bussolini)*

12-15 Two 19th-century quilts hang in the living room of a renovated barn on Long Island, warming it physically and visually. Owners Anne and George Crawford wanted to preserve the character of the barn, so the natural materials of brick and stone remain exposed. *(Photograph: Edward Hausner/NYT Pictures)*

Multicomponent Fabrics

Quilted fabrics, **bonded, laminated,** or **foam-backed** fabrics have in common the fact that they are all comprised of at least two layers of material that are joined together with stitching, adhesive, or heat. Many upholstery fabrics use the bonding technique to provide a stable backing for loosely constructed surface fabrics while drapery fabrics utilize it for insulative lining. This cuts the cost of producing a separate lining for these fabrics. Both tricot knits and foams are used as backings. Quilts utilize three layers and are traditionally hand-stitched but today may also be machine-stitched or "heat-stitched."

Films

Films result from forming processes that—by means of extrusion, casting, or calendering—produce sheets instead of filaments. Originally appearing as thin plastic sheeting or film, the new plastic fabrics come in varied thicknesses, from the thin films suitable for shower curtains to heavier weights for wall coverings. Upholstery grades are usually fused onto a knit or woven backing. Wall coverings may or may not be supported by a backing; they can also be laminated onto a layer of foam, which adds to the insulating and sound-absorbing properties of the fabric. Textures range from leatherlike smoothness through suedelike softness to deeply molded, three-dimensional patterns. Vinyl fabrics can also be printed, embossed, or flocked with a soft fuzz. Not surprisingly, many of the designs imitate leather or textiles, but a few exploit the unique possibilities of these products.

The newest techniques in fabric construction eliminate the costly cut-and-sew operations necessary to make a fabric fit a particular form. *Vacuum-formable fabrics* can be shaped into a single piece of upholstery to cover a chair in as little as two minutes. Liquid vinyl flows onto polyurethane foam and becomes bonded to it, resulting in a no-seams, perfect-fit, durable surface. Another method utilizes short-cut fibers that are electromagnetically *flocked* to the surface of a chair or sofa to become the upholstery.

Finishing the Fabric

Most fabrics, when they come from machine or loom, are far from ready to be passed on to the consumer. Various kinds of finishing give them their ultimate appearance and qualities. We can divide these finishes into three types according to how they affect the function, the color, or the decorative qualities of the fabric.

Functional Finishes

Finishes that affect the basic appearance or performance of a fabric include the following:

- **Beetling,** or pounding with steel and wood hammers, gives luster to linens and linenlike fabrics.
- **Calendering** is a process by which fabrics are pressed between rollers to give smooth finishes and to tighten the weaves. It can also polish fabrics to a highly glazed sheen or emboss them with moiré, crepe, or other patterns.
- **Crabbing** tightens and sets the weave in wool.
- **Fulling** shrinks, compacts, and softens a wool weave.
- **Gigging** and **napping** produce such textures as are found in flannel and suede cloth.
- **Heat setting** produces dimensional stability and aids in pleat retention.
- **Mercerization,** as applied to cellulosic fibers such as cotton, involves treatment with a solution of sodium hydroxide. If mercerized under tension, the fabric will be stronger, more lustrous, and more receptive to dyes; without tension (slack), mercerization causes the fibers and yarns to swell and contract, increasing the crimp of the yarn as well as its stretchability.
- **Shearing** and **singeing** remove surface fibers, fuzz, and lint, and prevent pilling.
- **Shrinking** lessens the tendency of most fibers to contract when exposed to moisture.
- **Weighting** compensates for gum lost by silk in the cleaning process.

By such means, lifeless, sleazy textiles are transformed into usable, attractive materials. In addition, there are some special treatments that notably change the behavior of fibers and fabrics. Textiles can be made:

- **Antistatic** to prevent the buildup of static charges and reduce soiling.
- **Bacteria-, mildew-,** and **moth-resistant** in varying degrees of permanence.
- **Fire-** and **flame-resistant** through chemical treatments. A worthwhile safety precaution, these processes can be durable but sometimes need to be renewed. They may make textiles heavier and stiffer but may also increase resistance to weathering and sometimes to insects and mildew. Specific controls have been set by federal laws (the Flammable Fabrics Act) for carpets, mattresses, and mattress covers. A *flame-resistant* or *flame-retardant* finish reduces flammability. However, fabrics thus treated will burn, albeit slowly, in the direct path of flame. They self-extinguish when the source of flame is removed and do not propagate the fire. A *fireproof* fabric will not burn at all. Asbestos is about the only fireproof fiber. Flame-inhibiting finishes should be durable to satisfy flammability regulations. However, consumers should be aware that the care given these fabrics often determines finish durability.
- **Fume-fading resistant** through solution dyeing of man-made fabrics or the application of finishes to reduce damage from smog and atmospheric gases.
- **Soil-resistant** or **soil-releasing** by coating or impregnating fibers or fabrics with chemicals to make them less absorbent.
- **Water-repellent** by coating or impregnating the fibers with wax, metals, or resins. Such treatment makes fabrics hold their shape better as well as helps to keep dirt on the surface.
- **Heat-reflectant** with metallic substances, usually aluminum, adhered to one side.
- **Insulating** through the application of a thin or foamed coating on the back, which keeps out the heat rays of the sun and keeps in winter warmth.
- **Crease-resistant** ("wash and wear," "easy care," "permanent press," and so on) by impregnating the fibers with resins or with agents that either cross-link cellulose molecules or build a "memory" into the fiber, causing it to return to its original shape. Crease-resistance gives textiles more firmness and sometimes better draping qualities; but it may also weaken fibers, reduce abrasion resistance, and wash out. Dyes become more permanent with this treatment, and shrinkage of spun rayons, light cottons and linens, and velvets diminishes. Bonding to a form or tricot backing also enhances wrinkle-resistance.
- **Elastic** by including spandex fiber in the blend or by inserting stretch properties through special construction techniques, such as the twisting or crimping of yarns, slack mercerization of fabrics, or heat setting.
- **Stable,** chiefly through carefully controlled shrinking tendencies. In some processes, chemicals supplement moisture, heat, pressure, and tension.
- **Glossy** with resins that provide a more or less permanent smooth, lustrous surface. Glazed fabrics resist soil and have improved draping qualities. Glazing is usually limited to textiles meant for curtains, draperies, and slipcovers.

Color Application

Dyes can be introduced at several stages of the fabric-construction process. As the need demands, manufacturers dye unspun fibers, spun yarns, or woven textiles. In some synthetics and plastics, the dye is mixed with the liquid from which the fiber or film is made. Although generalizations about dyes cannot be absolute, the synthetic substances in which dye forms part of the fiber or film seem to be the most thoroughly colorfast. Next come the fibers and yarns dyed before fabric construction, and last the piece-dyed textiles. Today, however, less difference separates the latter two than was true in the past, thanks to new processes.

The kind of dye and its hue affect colorfastness, but almost all colors will fade in varying degrees when exposed to sun or polluted air, washed, or dry-cleaned. Unless we want to protect fabrics from sun and use at the possible cost of relaxed living, we should think about getting the most nearly fadeproof textiles available. Since all textiles change with time, it would seem sensible to select those that will mellow gracefully rather than those that will look tired and worn out when they fade. The following characteristics mitigate the results of fading:

- **Colors** most common in nature—grays, greens, browns, soft yellows and oranges—retain their appearance longer than do colors of higher intensity. Mixtures, such as in tweeds, do not become as listless as faded solid colors. Dark colors may lose richness and depth with even a little fading.
- **Textures,** with their play of light and shade, compensate for loss of color.
- **Patterns** that are intricate or diffused lose less of their character than those whose interest lies chiefly in brilliant contrasts, precision, or clarity.

It is worthwhile to consider whether a little fading or wear need be so deplorable. Fabrics that have mellowed and that show evidence of having been lived with give some people a comfortable feeling of continuity and coziness. The softening of colors, textures, and patterns can result in a harmonious richness. We have only to compare, even mentally, an antique Persian rug with a modern equivalent to realize that this is so.

Nevertheless, it should again be emphasized that one of the simplest ways to introduce color into the home is through fabrics. Textiles contribute the brilliance and stridence of primary hues, the richness and depth of purples or chocolate browns, the subtlety of pastels. Large or small areas of solid colors or of decisive patterns can be achieved easily and inexpensively, and just as easily and inexpensively changed.

Decorative Finishes and Enrichment

Printing

The easiest, least expensive way to add design to fabrics is by printing, a process known for at least four thousand years. Pigments mixed to the consistency of thick paste are applied to the finished fabric (or occasionally to the yarns before weaving) by one of the following methods:

- **Roller printing,** by far the most common technique, involves the application of pigments from copper rollers engraved with the design. One roller is made for each color, but an effect of more colors than rollers can be achieved by engraving different parts of a roller to different depths or by printing one color over another. Sometimes the warp yarns are printed before weaving, which gives a soft, diffuse quality.
- **Block printing** is most often done by hand, although semimechanized methods now exist. Wood blocks that may be surfaced with metal or linoleum transfer color to the fabric. Block-printed textiles have the slight irregularities characteristic of handcrafted designs and are expensive.
- **Screen printing,** often called *silk screen*, is a type of stencil printing especially suitable for patterns produced in relatively small quantities. The initial cost is less than that of roller printing, but stencils do not last as long as do the copper rollers. Screen printing involves forcing a thick dye through a mesh that has been coated with moisture repellant in some portions. Color passes through

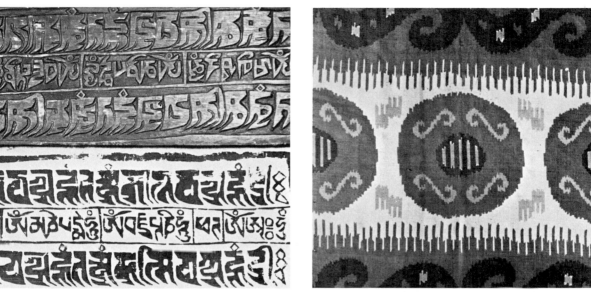

only the untreated areas. A number of screens may be used to add to or vary the colors. Automatic screen printing methods have greatly speeded up the process and lessened the number of workers needed, while still retaining many of the advantages of the medium.

- **Resist printing** is a technique in which parts of the fabric are protected from the dye during each application. In **batik,** a dye-resisting wax or paste applied to sections of the cloth prevents dye from being absorbed in those areas. After each dye bath the wax is removed and perhaps reapplied to other parts of the fabric; the process can be repeated to form a design of more than one color. Still a much-admired handcraft, the technique is also being adapted to machine processes. **Tie-dyeing,** another resist method, requires an arrangement of pleats, knots, and ties, causing portions of the fabric to resist the dye bath into which it is immersed. The resulting pattern is usually diffuse, since the dye advances and recedes around the bound areas.
- **Discharge printing,** the reverse of resist dyeing, results when parts of the fabric are treated with a chemical to remove color.

- **Photographic printing** uses a process very similar to that for developing photographs. Either black-and-white or full-color prints can be made.
- **Transfer printing,** similar to ironing on a decal, transfers patterns from paper to fabric by applying heat and pressure. Although slower than roller or screen printing, transfer printing is less expensive because all colors are printed at once.

Stitchery

The general trend toward increased enrichment in design has brought renewed interest in embroidery, appliqué, quilting, and other types of needlework. These may be done by machine in the factory, by hand in small workshops, or individually at home. Many people enjoy adding some sketchy crewel embroidery to a pillow cover, or they may actually reconstruct the face of a fabric by needlepoint for a seat cover. Patchwork—old and new, real and simulated—exemplifies the tendency for rich, complex designs.

The explosion of interest in handcrafts as personally rewarding experiences has led many people to the creation of fabrics through weaving, knitting, or macramé. Others make rugs by braiding fabrics, hooking yarns, or even tying yarns on a loom or frame, as in the rya technique. The satisfactions that come from designing and making things by hand can be very real, and handwork of this type adds a dimension to the home that is sometimes amateurish but personalizing, and often surprisingly professional and spirited. (Handcrafts as accessories are discussed in Chapter 18.)

Decisions made at every step of the textile production process are very important to the final appearance and end-use appropriateness of a fabric. Although the selection of the fiber and the fabric construction are often considered the most important aspects, all of the selections are important factors in the performance of the finished product. For example, a fabric constructed of nylon fibers in the twill weave should be very strong and durable for a heavy-use upholstery fabric since both of these choices are considered the strongest possible. But, if a complex yarn is used, the durability of the final product is greatly diminished. In addition, a noncolorfast dye and the lack of a stain-resistant finish can in effect negate the positive effects of the strong fiber and fabric construction.

12-21 Crewel embroidery is a relatively fast method of applying surface ornament to fabrics by stitchery. It lends itself to informal, meandering designs. Here the wing chairs, hand-embroidered in six weeks, seem quite at home in a comfortable wood-paneled room. *(Photograph: Bill Aller/NYT Pictures)*

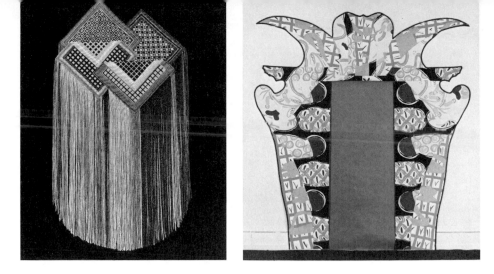

left: 12-22 Diane Itter has used knotted linen in her work "Bandana Quartet," an example of the creative use of fiber as art medium. *(Courtesy International Linen Promotion Commission)*
right: 12-23 A silkscreen design on cotton canvas and satin, "Turandot Doorway" by Betty Woodman, expands the textile medium as art statement. Created at The Fabric Workshop, Philadelphia. *(Photograph: Will Brown)*

Fiber as Art Form

Beyond fabrics-used-as-fabrics there are the fabric constructions that can be considered in the same category with other art media. In recent years fiber has begun to be accepted as a viable material for "fine art," as stone, metal, and oil paints always have been. Fiber artists are among the most innovative designers of recent years. If we try to imagine their works in any other medium, we realize that the artist's choice of yarns opens up totally new dimensions in aesthetic expression.

List of Fabrics

Table 12–2 lists some of the fabrics most frequently used in the home. They have been divided into four categories, based primarily on weight, which is an important factor in determining their applications. However, there is quite a range within each category and some overlapping between categories. Most of the fabrics can be woven from a number of different fibers, but a few are made from only one. Fabric names constitute a strange miscellany, being based on the fiber, such as *linen*, which has come to mean a special kind of linen textile; the weave, such as *satin*; the early use, such as *monk's cloth*; or a trade name, such as *Indian Head*.

Sheer, almost transparent fabrics are suitable for glass curtains and for summer bedspreads, table skirts, and table coverings. They can be made from cotton, silk, synthetics, or even wool.

Lightweight, translucent fabrics are suitable for glass curtains or for draperies. They have sufficient body to be used alone and give a measure of privacy, although not at night. They are suitable for draperies, bedspreads, table skirts, pillows, screens, wall coverings, table coverings, and slipcovers. In the heavier grades they sometimes serve for upholstery. Many are made of cotton, silk, wool, or synthetics. They come in a wide color range and can be washed.

Medium weight fabrics are suitable for heavy draperies and upholstery, as well as for wall coverings and pillows. Some also adapt to slipcovers, bedspreads, screens, and table coverings. Made of heavier fibers of cotton, flax, hemp, jute, linen, silk, synthetics, or wool, they are available in a wide color range; some are washable.

Heavy fabrics are perfect for upholstery because of their weight and durability; in lighter grades they make draperies, pillows, bedspreads, slipcovers, wall coverings, even table coverings. Most are available in a variety of fibers and a wide color range. Few are washable.

Textile Fibers and Fabrics **307**

Table 12–2   List of Fabrics

Sheer

bobbinet   A fine and sheer to coarse open plain net with hexagonal meshes. Soft yet with character; most effective when very full; coarser types best for straight folds; sheer types well suited to tiebacks and ruffles. White, cream, ecru, pale colors.

cheesecloth   Cotton in loose, plain weaves, very low thread count. Very inexpensive; short-lived; informal. Usually off-white.

dimity   Fine, tightly twisted, usually combed cotton; plain weave with thin cord making vertical stripe or plaid. Often mercerized. Fine, sheer, crisp; suited to straight folds or tiebacks. White, tints, or printed patterns.

filet   Square-mesh lace knotted at intersecting corners. Fine to coarse but usually giving a bold, heavy effect. White, cream, ecru, and plain colors.

marquisette   Leno weave in many fibers. Sheer and open; soft or crisp; fine to coarse. Serviceable; launders well. White, cream, or pale colors; sometimes printed or woven patterns.

net   Any lace with a uniform mesh, such as bobbinet or filet; fine to coarse, sheer to open; made of almost any fiber.

ninon   Plain voilelike or novelty weaves. Very thin; smooth, silky, pleasant sheen. Best in straight folds. Plain colors; self-colored stripes or shadowy figures; sometimes embroidered.

organdy   Cotton in plain weave; like sheer, crisp muslin, but crispness washes out unless specially treated. Folds keep their place. Often used without draperies; frequently tied back. Many plain colors; also printed or embroidered designs.

point d'esprit   Variation of bobbinet with dots that give it more body. White, cream, and pale colors.

swiss muslin (dotted swiss)   Cotton in plain weaves; usually embroidered or patterned in dots or figures. Fine, sheer, slightly crisp. Can be used alone, usually draped; effect generally informal. White and plain colors, usually light; figures may be colored.

theatrical gauze   Linen or cotton in a loose, open, crisp weave with a shimmering texture. Often used without draperies for colorful, informal effect. Wide range of plain colors, often two-toned.

voile   Open, plain weave, sheer and smooth. Drapes softly; gives more privacy than marquisette. Various textures; many colors; usually pale; sometimes woven patterns.

Lightweight

antique satin   Variation of smooth satin, with a dull, uneven texture. Variety of weights but usually heavier than satin. Widely used for upholstery and drapery materials.

batiste   Delicate and fine, plain weave, usually cotton or polyester, often with printed or embroidered designs. Needs fullness to be effective; when embroidered, has considerable body. Light and dainty. White or pastel colors.

broadcloth   Cotton, synthetic, or silk in plain or twill weaves; spun rayon or wool in twill weaves. Varies greatly in terms of fiber and weave. Cotton and synthetic types used for draperies, bedspreads, tablecloths.

calico   Cotton in a plain weave, printed with small-figured pattern. Inexpensive and informal.

casement cloth   Almost every known fiber in plain or figured weaves. Flat and lustrous. Often ecru, but can be other colors. Frequently used alone as draw curtains.

challis   Wool, synthetic, or cotton in a soft, plain, firm weave. Usually printed with small floral designs but sometimes a plain color.

Table 12–2 *(continued)*

chambray   Cotton or linen in a smooth, close, plain weave. White-frosted appearance on wide range of colors.

chintz   Cotton in a close, plain weave, usually with a printed design and often glazed. Washing removes glaze in many types.

12-24   The firm, smooth surface of glazed chintz supports the delicate but colorful pattern of "Kowloon." *(Courtesy Stroheim & Romann)*

drill   Cotton in diagonal twill weave. Firm, heavy, very durable textile. Typical color is gray, but other colors available.

faille   Plain weave with decided flat, crosswise ribs. Difficult to launder, but wears well if handled carefully. Varies from soft yet firm to quite stiff.

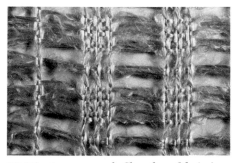

12-25   An openwork fiberglass fabric is ideal for window curtains, since it is not only attractive and translucent but also easy to care for. *(Courtesy Owens/Corning Fiberglas)*

fiberglass   Glass fibers in varied weaves and weights, from sheer marquisette to heavy drapery fabrics. Translucent to opaque; can be washed and hung immediately without shrinking or stretching. Good range of colors; plain or printed.

films (plastic)   Smooth or textured, plain or printed, thin or thick. Used for shower curtains, table coverings, upholstery, or wall coverings. Waterproof; wipes clean.

gingham   Cotton or synthetic in light to medium weight, plain weave; woven from colored yarns. Strong; launders well. Checked, striped, and plaid patterns.

homespun   Irregular yarns woven in loose, plain weave. Texture somewhat rough and irregular; informal character. Plain colors, dyed, or woven of mixed yarns.

India print   Printed cotton cloth from India or Persia with characteristic intricate design in clear or dull colors. Inexpensive and durable. Fades, but pleasantly.

Indian Head   Plain weave, firm and smooth. Trade name for a permanent-finish cotton, vat-dyed, colorfast, shrink-resistant. Inexpensive and durable.

insulating   Fabrics coated on one side with metallic flakes to reflect heat or with foam plastic to trap heat.

Jaspé cloth   Plain weave; varied yarns give unobtrusive, irregular, blended stripes. Generally firm, hard, and durable. Can be in any color, but usually fairly neutral, medium dark, and monochromatic.

linen   Flax in a plain, firm weave. Cool to the touch, good body, launders well; wrinkles easily unless specially treated. Often has hand-blocked designs.

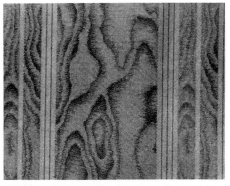

12-26   The irregular pattern of moiré is pleasingly contrasted with stripes in a fabric designed by Jack Lenor Larsen. The Graphics Collection. *(Courtesy Jack Lenor Larsen, Inc.)*

Table 12—2   List of Fabrics *(continued)*

moiré   Ribbed, plain weave with a watermarked appearance. Most moiré finishes can be steamed or washed out—more permanent on synthetic fibers.

muslin   Cotton in a soft, plain weave; light to heavy qualities. Bleached or unbleached; also dyed and printed. Inexpensive, durable, informal; often used alone at windows.

Osnaburg   Cotton yarns, coarse and uneven, in an open, plain weave; similar to crash. Usually medium-weight, natural color, but can be light or heavy-weight, any color, printed patterns. Strong and long-lasting; rough-textured; informal.

oxford cloth   Plain basket or twill weave, light to rather heavy weights. Durable and launders well.

piqué   Plain weave with narrow raised cords running in one direction or at right angles to each other (waffle piqué). Durable; interesting texture.

pongee   Wild silk in plain weave with broken crossbar texture caused by irregular yarns; also imitated in cotton and synthetics. Fairly heavy; often used without draperies. Shrinks unless treated. Usually pale or dark ecru, but can be dyed. Also called Tussah, antique taffeta, and doupioné (douppioni).

poplin   Plain weave with fine crosswise ribs. Firm and durable.

rep   Plain weave with prominent rounded ribs running crosswise or lengthwise.

sateen   Cotton, usually mercerized, in a satin weave; flat and glossy, with a dull back. Durable, substantial, but with a tendency to roughen. Often used for lining curtains.

satin   Satin weave, smooth, delicate fabric with a very high sheen. Somewhat slippery.

seersucker   Plain weave with woven, crinkly stripes. Durable, needs no ironing.

shantung   Plain weave with elongated irregularities. A heavy grade of pongee, but with wider color range.

sheeting (cotton)   Smooth, plain weave, light to medium weight. Inexpensive and informal. White, colors, or printed.

silk gauze   Plain weave with a slight irregularity in threads, making an interesting texture. Hangs well; is never slick. Wide range of colors.

stretch   Knit or woven of cotton, rayon, or other synthetic with special stretch properties or of spandex. Smooth to rough textures. Valuable for slipcovers and contoured shapes.

taffeta   Close, plain weave, slightly crossribbed. Crisp; sometimes weighted with chemical salts; cracks in strong sunlight. Antique taffeta has unevenly spun threads.

Medium Weight

bark cloth   Cotton in a firm, plain weave with irregular texture due to uneven yarns. Plain or printed. Durable.

brocade   Woven on a Jacquard loom; raised designs are produced by floating some

of the filling yarns. Usually has a multicolored floral or conventional pattern.

brocatelle   A Jacquard weave similar to brocade but with a heavier design. Used mostly as upholstery on large sofas and chairs.

burlap   Loose basket weave. Heavy and coarse; interesting texture. Often fades quickly.

canvas   Cotton in a plain, diagonal weave. Heavy, firm, and durable. Strong solid colors, as well as stripes or printed designs. Often used for awnings, outdoor curtains, and upholstery.

crash   Plain weave with a rough texture caused by uneven yarns. Often handblocked or printed.

12-27 A cotton brocade, "Harmony" has a conventionalized overall flower design formed by yarns floating over the plain-weave background. *(Courtesy Boris Kroll Fabrics, Inc.)*

310

Table 12–2 *(continued)*

cretonne Cotton in a firm, plain, rep, or twill weave. Fairly heavy texture and bold design. Similar to chintz but heavier, never glazed. Patterns are usually more vigorous.

damask Any combination of two of the three basic weaves; flat Jacquard patterns. Firm, lustrous, reversible. Similar to brocade but design is not in relief. May be referred to as figured satin. One or two colors used.

12-28 An intricate design of wildflowers is woven into the fabric of "Santee Flowers," a damask. *(Courtesy Greeff Fabrics, Inc.)*

denim Cotton in a heavy, close twill weave. Warp and filling often in contrasting colors; can have a small woven pattern. Inexpensive; washable; Sanforizing prevents shrinking; reasonably sunfast.

duck Cotton in a close, plain, or ribbed weave. Durable; often given protective finishes against fire, water, mildew. Similar to canvas.

hopsacking Loose, plain weave. Coarse and heavy. Inexpensive and durable.

laminated Any fabric bonded to a lightweight foam backing, or two fabrics bonded together. Wrinkle-resistant; good for upholstery, slipcovers, insulating draperies.

mohair Hair of Angora goats (now often a mixture of cotton and wool) in a plain, twill, or pile weave or with a woven or printed design. Resilient and durable. Novelty weaves, sheer to very heavy.

monk's cloth Jute, hemp, flax, usually mixed with cotton or all cotton in a loose plain or basket weave. Coarse and heavy; friar's cloth and druid's cloth similar but coarser. Not easy to sew, tendency to sag. Usually comes in natural color.

sailcloth Plain weave. Heavy and strong. Similar to canvas or duck. Often used on summer furniture.

serge Twill weave with a pronounced diagonal rib on both face and back. Has a clear, hard finish.

terry cloth Cotton or linen in a loose, uncut-pile weave; loops on one or both sides. Very absorbent; not always colorfast; may sag. Not suitable for upholstery but useful for draperies and bedspreads.

ticking Cotton or linen in a satin or twill weave. Strong, closely woven, durable. Best known in white with colored stripes, but may have simple designs. Not always colorfast, but washable.

Heavy

bouclé Plain or twill weave. Flat, irregular surface, woven or knitted from specially twisted bouclé yarns; small spaced loops on surface.

corduroy Cotton or a synthetic in a pile weave, raised in cords of various sizes giving pronounced lines. Durable, washable, inexpensive.

expanded vinyl Plastic upholstery fabric with an elastic knit fabric back. Stretches for contour fit.

felt Nonwoven fabric of wool, rayon and wool, or synthetics. Nonraveling edges need no hemming. Available in intense colors; used for table coverings, pillows, even for draperies.

frieze Also called *frizé*; a heavy-pile weave. Loops uncut or cut to form a pattern; sometimes yarns of different colors or with irregularities used. Usually has a heavy rib. Extremely durable.

311

Table 12–2   List of Fabrics *(continued)*

leather   Treated animal hide used as a fabric. Top grain is most desirable. Very durable. Used for upholstery, wall covering, even floor covering.

matelassé   Double-woven fabric with quilted or puckered surface effect, caused by interweaving to form the pattern. Needs care in cleaning, but otherwise durable.

needlepoint   Originally handmade in a variety of patterns, colors, and degrees of fineness. Now imitated on Jacquard loom. At best, has pronounced character, from delicate (*petit point*) to robust (*gros point*); at worst, looks like weak imitation.

plastic   Wide variety of textures from smooth to embossed; used for upholstering and wall covering. Resists soil, wipes clean. Not for use over deep springs unless fabric-backed, which is more pliable, easier to fit, less likely to split.

plush   Cut-pile weave. Similar to velvet but with a longer pile. Sometimes pressed and brushed to give surface variations; sculptured by having design clipped or burned out of pile, leaving motif in relief. Also made to imitate animal fur.

tapestry   Weaves with two sets of warps and weft; woven on a Jacquard loom. Heavier and rougher than damask or brocade. Patterns usually pictorial and large.

tweed   Soft, irregularly textured, plain weave. Yarns dyed before weaving; often several or many colors combined.

velour   Short, heavy, stiff cut-pile weave. Slight luster and indistinct horizontal lines. Durable.

velvet   Pile weave with loops cut or uncut. Luxurious but often shows wear quickly. Lustrous or dull; light to heavy grades; plain, striped, or patterned.

velveteen   Cotton or a synthetic woven with a short, close, sheared pile. Strong, durable, launders well.

webbing   Cotton, jute, or plastic in narrow strips (1 to 4 inches) of very firm, plain weave. Plain, striped, or plaid design. Jute used to support springs; cotton or plastic interlaced for webbed seats and backs.

12-30   Webbing, used for chair backs and seats, offers resiliency without bulk or weight. Alfredo De Vido, architect. *(Photograph: © Peter Aaron/ESTO)*

References for Further Reading

American Fabrics Magazine. *Encyclopedia of Textiles*, 2nd ed. Englewood Cliffs, NJ: Prentice-Hall, 1972.

Constantine, Mildred and Jack Lenor Larsen. *Beyond Craft: The Art Fabric*. New York: Van Nostrand Reinhold, 1972.

Frings, Virginia S. *Fashion: From Concept to Consumer*. Englewood Cliffs, NJ: Prentice-Hall, 1982. Chap. 5.

Gaines, Patricia Ellisor. *The Fabric Decoration Book*. New York: Morrow, 1975.

Held, Shirley E. *Weaving: A Handbook for Fiber Craftsmen*, 2nd ed. New York: Holt, Rinehart and Winston, 1978.

Hicks, David. *David Hicks on Decoration—with Fabrics*. London: World, 1971.

Jackman, Dianne R. and Mary K. Dixon. *The Guide to Textiles for Interior Designers*. Winnipeg: Peguis Publishers, 1984.

Joseph, Marjory L. *Essentials of Textiles*, 3rd ed. New York: Holt, Rinehart and Winston, 1984.

Joseph, Marjory L. *Introductory Textile Science*, 4th ed. New York: Holt, Rinehart and Winston, 1981.

Klapper, Marvin. *Fabric Almanac II*, 2nd ed. New York: Fairchild, 1971.

Larsen, Jack Lenor and Jeanne Weeks. *Fabrics for Interiors: A Guide for Architects, Designers, and Consumers*. New York: Van Nostrand Reinhold, 1975.

Murphy, Dennis Grant. *The Materials of Interior Design*. Burbank, CA: Stratford House Publishing Company, 1978.

Scobey, Jean. *Rugs and Wall Hangings*. New York: Dial, 1974.

Textile Handbook, 4th ed. Washington, DC: American Home Economics Association, 1970.

Tortora, Phyllis G. *Understanding Textiles*, 2nd ed. New York: Macmillan, 1982.

Wingate, Isabel B. *Textile Fabrics and Their Selection*, 7th ed. Englewood Cliffs, NJ: Prentice-Hall, 1976.

IV

Interior Components and Treatments

Floor, walls, and ceiling in a house on the Connecticut River. William H. Grover of Centerbrook, PC, architect. *(Photograph: © Norman McGrath)*

Walls, Fireplaces, and Ceilings

Three architectural elements—walls, fireplaces, and ceilings—have increasingly come to assume major design roles in the home. Walls are virtually essential for a dwelling; they give protection and privacy, affect light, heat, and sound. At the same time, though, they demarcate areas and control our movements and vistas. If only because they constitute such a large area of square footage, walls and their treatment can largely determine the character of a home.

Fireplaces rarely function as the only source of heat in today's homes, but the fact that we have not abandoned them offers testimony to their psychological importance. A fireplace becomes the focus of any room; it is there people gather, even in summertime—partly, to be sure, because furniture is typically grouped around a hearth. Obviously, the focal point of a room, and of the principal group space, merits serious consideration in its design.

Both architects and homeowners have shown renewed interest in the positive effects of ceilings. All of us are aware of how we instinctively duck when we go through a lower-than-usual doorway, how we tend to look up when we come into a space with a soaring ceiling. These almost unconscious physical reactions have psychological overtones that can be usefully employed in the design of space for different moods and activities.

316

Walls

Walls govern the shape, size, and character of rooms or spaces; they become the enclosure against or with which we live. Increasingly, walls are being "used" as windows and doors, for built-in storage, and as supports for attached furnishings. That walls can be far more than innocuous backdrops can be demonstrated by the contemporary interest in geometrics, cutouts, overlapping, and interpenetration. While cutout walls maintain their function of separating areas, they allow intriguing glimpses and half-views into the areas beyond to give the space a fascinating molded quality.

Well-proportioned walls are a continuing source of satisfaction. Appropriate colors, textures, and materials relate architecture to people and to furniture in a positive manner. Seen and used in relation to the windows, doors, stairs, and fireplaces that are parts of them; to floors and ceilings that complete the architectural enclosure; and to furniture, accessories, and people, walls should be considered integral parts of a whole. Whether we are conscious of it or not, walls constitute a stage setting. The mood they establish is vital in its influence on everyday living.

In the living room of a house designed by architect Eliot Noyes for a rocky site overlooking a valley, the walls establish the character and carry the theme of the architect's vision (Fig. 13-1). Three different types of walls appear in progression: the massive masonry bastion that provides anchorage for the cantilevered room; smooth plaster side walls, less bulky and more passive but still enclosing; and finally glass walls, framed in wood, light and open, exposing the view over the countryside. During the day this progression leads outside to the balcony, protected only by a low railing, and to an almost unlimited expansion of space. At night, possibly with the curtains pulled, the progression is reversed, drawing attention back to the stone wall with its promise of protection and shelter.

13-1 Massive masonry walls physically and visually support a country house designed by architect Eliot Noyes. Stepping into the living room is a liberating experience, for the walls become progressively brighter and lighter in weight. *(Photograph: Joseph W. Molitor)*

13-2 In a Vermont condominium, the walls themselves provide design interest while still fulfilling their function of shielding vistas and shaping space. Peter Gluck, architect. (*Courtesy* American Home Magazine)

The design of the living room furnishings integrates the differing elements of the room. Sturdy and comfortable, the sofas and chairs complement the immensity of the stone wall and yet also have the crisp, square lines of the ordered glass wall. Placed opposite each other, the sofas invite focus on whichever scene, view of fire or panorama of changing seasons, is most rewarding at the time. The rectangularity of the seating arrangement reinforces the shape of the room and creates a setting conducive to conversation. Overall, the character of the room is one of a natural, relaxed poise established by the materials.

How different are the walls in the vacation condominium shown in Figure 13-2! Neutral walls of smooth plaster are a lively mixture of flat planes, curves, angles, and cutouts. The walls of the staircase have been dramatized by its changing forms, the dark wood railing that emphasizes those forms, and the painted design on the underside of the upper stairs. Low walls on the balcony level partially segregate the dining and kitchen areas but leave them open to the major group space. Walls serve as open shelving in the dining area; as closed, dropped cupboards in the kitchen; and as a snug backing for the sofas in the living room. They create an animated, useful environment for vacation living.

Design

Contemporary architects and designers enjoy a freedom to use a vocabulary far more extensive than in the past, when walls were almost always fixed, thick, opaque, and supportive of the roof. Although many walls today have these characteristics, the following types are also common:

- Nonstructural curtain walls that hold up nothing other than themselves, acting only as space dividers and backgrounds
- Thin, transparent, or translucent window walls of glass or plastic
- Walls that are integrated with ceilings
- Movable walls of all kinds that slide into pockets, fold like accordions, or are storage units on casters
- Storage walls that unite the enclosing functions of walls with many kinds of storage space
- Partial walls of less than ceiling height to give visual privacy without tight, boxlike enclosure
- Spur or freestanding walls (or fireplaces) that stop short of joining the adjacent walls at one or both ends
- Walls that become furniture, with built-in seating or counter space
- Walls with cutouts and open spaces giving views to adjacent rooms

Of the specific qualities that can be combined to invest walls with the desired quality, some pertain primarily to utility, others to economy, beauty, or character. Taken together, they determine the expressive and functional properties of walls.

Degree of Formality or Informality
The living room of the Noyes house (Fig. 13-1) is more formal than that of the condominium (Fig. 13-2). Formality results when a room gives the feeling of a strict, firmly established, unchanging order, which the condominium certainly does not attempt to do. Symmetrical balance and pronounced regularity in the placement of doors and windows are the fundamental means to achieve this, but formality usually increases when the forms seem stable and precise, when surfaces are smooth, and when proportions are mainly vertical. But the Noyes living room, like many today, is semiformal. The walls are not symmetrically balanced throughout the room but achieve equilibrium through our unconscious awareness that the weight of the fireplace wall counterbalances the cantilevered section of the room with its appropriately lighter walls. In general, rougher textures, active patterns, and open plans with their easy flow of space characterize informal rooms.

Degree of Activity or Passivity
Walls become active when their design and materials arouse visual interest, especially if they suggest movement. Patterned wallpaper or tiles, wood grain, or the design formed by the way in which wood is used can attract attention with their lively rhythms. Activity can also derive from built-in furniture, fireplaces, displays of collections, or the use of a wall for storage space. Typical smoothly

plastered, uniformly painted walls remain passive backgrounds for furnishings unless their color is vigorous.

Degree of Smoothness or Roughness

Wall textures range from glassy smoothness to stony roughness, with countless intermediate steps provided by plaster and gypsum board, tile and brick, wood and plastics. Smoothness is often associated with formality, roughness with informality. A basic pattern of companionable surface textures gives a sense of coherence, but variety and contrast are needed to awaken it.

13-5 A variety of wall surfacings—smooth plaster, thin wood strips laid horizontally, wider wood planks climbing the sloping wall to the roof, and glimpses of wood shingles—enliven an upstairs hall bounded by walls of varying heights, angles, and distances. Neil Goodwin, designer. (*Courtesy* American Home Magazine)

Largeness or Smallness of Scale

Of tremendous importance is the scale of the walls in relation to the size of the space, the character of furnishings, and the personalities of the people using the room. The stone and concrete wall in the Noyes living room (Fig. 13-1) is bold and impressive but not overpowering, because the room and its furnishings are large in scale. In the living room shown in Plate 38 (p. 331) the smaller scale of the walls with the dentil molding and quiet paneling relates to the more intimate character of the room.

The scale of walls can establish the scale of the room as a whole. High walls seem to expand space, as do long, unbroken expanses of wall. Too long a wall can

13-6 A head-height working divider wall demarcates group and support spaces in a large glass-walled pavilion. Throughout the house white walls intensify the feeling of spaciousness; the divider walls seem less bulky because of the dark-painted cutouts for bookshelves, cupboards, stereo equipment, and fireplace. Donald E. Olsen, architect. *(Photograph: Ronald Partridge)*

be broken by a spur wall perpendicular to it or by variations in surface treatment that direct attention to one part at a time. Walls that are too high can also be broken into segments with a chair rail or picture molding, with a dado treatment, or with the ceiling treatment carried down onto the wall, perhaps to the picture molding.

Degree of Permanence or Mobility

In a mobile society, walls that can be moved to create the spaces current occupants need make a lot of sense. Movable walls that are at the same time storage walls can be doubly efficient. The owner or tenant of a large open space, such as a loft or barn, may be reluctant to break it up into smaller cubbyholes. In place of permanent interior walls, various kinds of dividers ranging from free-standing screens to folding sections to hanging fabrics can create "rooms" within and between them with some visual privacy, yet they do not interfere with the

left: 13-7 Two angled partitions contain large paintings that slide out to divide a large space into separate living areas. When retracted, the paintings barely jut out from the partitions. Osborn/Woods, architects. *(Photograph: Joshua Freiwald)*
right: 13-8 In the opposite view, one painting has been extended to create a private place. Osborn/Woods, architects. *(Photograph: Joshua Freiwald)*

sense of flowing space. More substantial but still movable wall partitions can be mounted in tracks in the ceiling and on the floor, in the manner of Japanese shoji screens. Depending upon their thickness, they may provide acoustical as well as visual control.

Of course, movable walls give less actual and psychological privacy than permanent ones. Some people feel insecure in the absence of permanent, fixed, floor-to-ceiling walls. On the other hand, permanent walls are often removed or opened up to enlarge space in the remodeling of older homes that typically had small, totally enclosed rooms. Whether the goal should be stability or fluidity will depend on many factors, including the composition of the household, the lifestyle of its inhabitants, and the particular dispositions of individuals.

Degree of Enclosure or Openness

Enclosure results from such things as opaque, substantial-looking walls, warm dark colors, and noticeable textures. Small, separated, framed doors and windows with small panes and heavy draperies also contribute to a feeling of protection.

Openness comes with a maximum of transparent, translucent, or apparently thin unobtrusive walls, with wide windows and doorways without frames, and with a minimum of partitions that block view or movement. Receding colors and inconspicuous textures also contribute to openness. Of great importance is a continuity of materials, form, and colors—not only inside a room but with the space in adjacent rooms and with the outdoors.

Degree of Light Absorption or Reflection

Color value is the most critical factor in light absorption and reflection. White reflects up to 89 percent of the light striking it, black as little as 2 percent. But surface texture must be considered also, because the smoother the surface, the more light is reflected. In the past, when windows were small and artificial illumination poor, very light walls were frequently needed to make rooms bright. Today, with large windows and improved artificial lighting, many people find that darker, textured walls create a complementary enclosure for themselves and their furnishings. Nevertheless, light-colored walls are refreshing, increase apparent size, make rooms easier to illumine (an energy-saving consideration), and serve as an effective background for anything placed against them.

Durability and Maintenance

The amount of time and money needed to maintain walls affects the satisfaction they give. Some materials (masonry, tile, wood, and vinyl plastics) are durable and easy to maintain. Others, including fragile but colorfast wallpapers, will endure with little care on walls that do not get hard use. The basic questions in selection are: What kind of use will the wall get? How easily is the material damaged? How easily can it be cleaned or repaired?

Degree of Sound Absorption or Reflection

Smaller houses and open plans, greater freedom for children, music systems and television, labor-saving but noisy appliances, and the trend away from heavy upholstery and draperies all make many contemporary homes noisy. It is possible to control this effect to a large extent, however, by means of wall construction or finishes. "Hard" surfaces bounce and reflect sound; if they predominate in a room, noise is bound to be magnified and distorted. Conversely, "soft" porous materials absorb sounds and can noticeably lower the decibel level in a room. In terms of wall construction and surfaces, the hardest materials are metal, plastic, masonry, and glass; wood, plaster, and wallboard are somewhat less sound-reflective; and the most sound-absorbing materials include cork, fabric, vinyl, and the various "acoustical" substances. To keep noise from leaking through walls, staggered stud construction, insulation (including double-glazed windows and wrapped pipes), sound traps in ducts, and the positioning of closets, stairways, and storage walls, as explained in Chapter 6, can all be utilized during planning and construction. Rooms that require good quality of sound within, such as music rooms, need a planned mix of sound-absorbing and sound-reflecting walls for balanced sound (see Chapter 3).

We can imagine two extremes of noise and silence contrived by manipulating the structure and furnishings of a room. The noisiest possible environment might consist of a precisely rectangular space with walls, floor, and ceiling of smooth metal or glass, furnished with a few rectangular, smooth metal or plastic pieces set parallel to the walls. The quietest room could have broken walls and a projecting or recessed fireplace and storage cabinets; a ceiling plane interrupted by beams; walls surfaced with cork or fabric, a carpeted floor (the shaggier the better), and plaster or acoustical-tile ceiling; heavy upholstered furniture, thick draperies, large plants, and many books on open shelves. As noted, these two examples are extremes. The former would probably be so nerve-shattering as to drive us out of the house, but the latter could be so eerily silent that it became equally unsettling. Depending on the purpose of the room and the needs of the household, the best solution lies somewhere in between.

Degree of Heat-Cold Insulation

In the interests of both comfort and conservation of energy, the construction of walls with a high degree of heat and cold insulation is of the utmost importance and a determining factor. (Chapter 6 deals with these matters.) Undoubtedly, more materials will become available to remedy poorly insulated walls.

The designer may supplement the insulating qualities of walls with surface treatments of vinyl, fabric, carpet, cork, and the like. Possibilities for windows are described in Chapter 15.

Construction

Although we often take walls for granted, the building of efficient, protective enclosures was a notable achievement for early peoples. Recently, there have been tremendous technological advances, especially in factory-made wall units. The technology of wall construction is beyond the scope of this book, but some knowledge of how walls are constructed and how materials affect their characteristics can help in deciding on the walls most appropriate for homes.

Walls that are fixed, opaque, and of one material are easiest to understand. Examples include houses built of heavy timbers—such as log cabins and chalets—and structures of solid stone or adobe brick. These are rare today, being expensive and comparatively poor insulators. Moreover, they leave no concealed space for pipes, ducts, wiring, and insulation, and are not amenable to the broad, unobstructed openings now in favor. Walls entirely of masonry have great appeal, however, with their comforting sense of permanence as well as their color and texture. Steel reinforcing increases their stability, and space can be left for insulation and utilities. The possibilities of concrete as a distinctive material have received relatively little attention in residential architecture, but its use in multiple-family dwellings has increased enormously.

Today, most walls consist of more than one material, or of the same material used in different ways. Wood-frame walls are most common in single-family homes, since they are familiar to builders and not expensive. In addition to resilient stability, they allow space for insulation and utilities. Usually, but not necessarily, they support the roof. Surface treatment, inside and out, can be varied. Although wood-frame walls may have five or more layers, they can be thought of as three-layer sandwiches:

- **Structural frame** of wood studs (closely spaced two-by-fours or more widely spaced heavier posts) from floor to ceiling. Studs typically are set 16 inches on center—a useful thing to know when hanging things.
- **Exterior layers** of diagonal wood sheathing and insulation or sheets of strong insulating composition board, covered with weather-resistant surfaces of wood, plastic, or metal sidings, shingles, or sheets; with lath and stucco; or with a veneer of brick or stone.
- **Interior layers** of lath and plaster, plywood, gypsum board, or wood paneling.

Increasingly, metal and plastic structural framing systems take the place of wood, because of their labor- and cost-saving potentials. And the need for efficient insulation becomes apparent to decrease our dependence on energy resources for heating and cooling.

Although walls of this type are still the most familiar for single-family homes, manufacturers have made great strides in the prefabrication of walls. Panels of wood, metal, or plastics—comprising in one component the layers of materials mentioned above—can be made in factories, which results in lowered construction costs without loss of individuality. Hundreds of different designs are available.

Materials and Surfacings

Table 13–1, a comparative list of wall materials, enables us to evaluate the many differences in structures and surfacings. We should also be aware that:

- All exterior materials can be used for inside walls, a possibility highly regarded by contemporary architects and designers because it accentuates indoor-outdoor relationships and by householders because it often reduces maintenance on interior surfaces.
- Some materials usually thought of as flooring—such as cork, vinyl, or carpeting—bring to walls the same serviceability they give floors.
- Many new materials expand the range of possibilities.

None of this need concern those who are happy with plaster or gypsum board painted white or low-intensity colors, which become passive backgrounds. But the sampling of old and new products may provide inspiration for those who want more distinctive walls.

Plaster

Used for centuries to surface and enrich walls, plaster is applied over lath (a lattice of thin strips of wood or metal grilles), special types of wallboard, or concrete block. It may be given a variety of finish textures ranging from smooth to stuccoed, or it may be cast to form intricate and beautiful moldings as seen in some old homes that have been preserved or restored. In renovation and adaptive reuse projects, designers are likely to have to repair or replace plaster. Unfortunately, there are few contemporary craftsmen who can match the skill of their ancestors. However, rag-paper moldings that imitate plaster are available at reasonable prices.

The advantages of plaster include the facts that it can cover simple or complex surfaces without visible joints, it can be textured, colored, painted, covered with wallpaper, fabrics, or tile, and it is moderate in cost. Its disadvantages include cracking, chipping, and easy soiling (see Chapter 10). Plaster is also more

Table 13—1   Wall Materials

Material	Character	Use	Exterior and Interior Finishes	Advantages	Disadvantages
brick (adobe) cost: varies greatly from one locality to another	earthy solidity combined with handcraft informality; large in scale; noticeable pattern of blocks and joints unless smoothly plastered	interior-exterior walls, chiefly in mild climates; heat storage mass	stucco, special paints, or transparent waterproofing	unique character; resists fire and insects; newer types stronger, weather-resistant; traps heat and releases it slowly	older types damaged by water; walls must be thick or reinforced; sturdy foundations required; comparatively poor insulation for weight and thickness
brick (fired clay) cost: high but less than stone	substantial and solid; small-scale regularity; many sizes, shapes, and colors; can be laid in varied patterns	interior-exterior walls, exterior surfacing or garden walls; around fireplaces; heat storage mass	none unless waterproofing necessary; interior walls can be waxed	satisfying texture and pattern; durable, easily maintained; fireproof; traps heat and releases it slowly	none other than heat-cold conduction and noise reflection
concrete cost: moderately high	typically smooth and solid-looking, but can be highly decorative	interior-exterior walls in mild climates; heat storage mass	exterior painted or stuccoed if desired; interior painted, plastered, or surfaced with any material	permanent, durable, low maintenance; can be cast in varied shapes and surface patterned; traps heat and releases it slowly	comparatively poor insulator; requires sturdy foundations and costly forms
concrete blocks (lightweight aggregate) cost: moderate	typically regular in shape, moderately textured, and bold in scale, many variations	interior-exterior walls in mild climates; exterior and garden walls anywhere	exterior waterproofing necessary; no interior finish needed but can be painted, plastered	durable, easily maintained; fireproof; fair insulator	none of any consequence, except perhaps lack of domestic character
glass (clear, tinted, and patterned, blocks) cost: moderately high	open and airy; patterned glass and blocks transmit diffused light	interior-exterior window walls; blocks or patterned glass for translucency; tinted for privacy, glare; double or triple panes or blocks for insulating qualities	none (except for curtaining for privacy and control of light, heat, and cold)	clear glass creates indoor-outdoor relationships; blocks, patterned, and tinted glass combine light and varying degrees of privacy	breakable; very poor heat-cold insulation unless double or triple pane; needs frequent cleaning; blocks more durable, easily cleaned, insulating
metal (panels, siding, shingles, and tiles) cost: moderate	varies greatly depending on size, shape, and finish; often regarded as unhomelike	sometimes used in kitchens and bathrooms; exterior house and garden walls; mobile homes	aluminum and steel available with long-lasting factory finishes in many colors	lightweight in relation to strength; resistant to fire; enameled and aluminum panels need minimum upkeep	although very durable, metal surfaces are difficult to repair if damaged
plaster and stucco cost: moderately low	typically smooth and precise but can be varied in texture; only surfacing material that shows no joints, breaks; quiet background	plaster in any room; stucco usually for garden or exterior house walls	special weather-resistant paints; paint, paper, or fabric for interiors	moderately durable if properly finished; suited to many easy-to-change treatments; fireproof; special types absorb sound	often cracks or chips

Table 13–1 Wall Materials (continued)

Material	Character	Use	Exterior and Interior Finishes	Advantages	Disadvantages
plastic (panels, siding, glazing; often reinforced with glass fibers) cost: moderate	opaque or translucent, often textured and colorful; thin and flat or corrugated; thicker with cores of varied materials	interior walls where durability, upkeep are important; partitions; interior-exterior walls; exterior siding	factory finished	similar to patterned glass except breaks less easily, lighter in weight; can be sawed and nailed	not thoroughly tested for longevity
stone cost: high	substantial, solid; impressive; natural colors and textures	around fireplaces; interior-exterior walls	none unless waterproofing is necessary	beauty and individuality; durability, ease of maintenance; fireproof; ages gracefully; traps heat and releases it slowly	reflects sound; not amenable to change
wood (boards, plywood, shingles, and thin veneers) cost: moderate to high	natural beauty and individuality of grain and color	interior and exterior walls	needs protective finish to seal it against water, stains, dirt	fairly durable, easily maintained; good insulator; adaptable; ages well inside	few kinds are weather-resistant unless treated; burns; attacked by termites

			Interior Only		
cork cost: moderately high	sympathetic natural color and texture	any room; only plastic-impregnated types suitable for baths and kitchens	none needed but can be waxed	durable, easily maintained if properly sealed; sound-absorbent; good insulator	harmed by moisture, stains, and so on, unless specially treated
paint (water-base, oil-base) cost: moderately low	flat to gloss, smooth to textured; endless color range	any wall; select for specific use	none needed	inexpensive, versatile, colorful	must be chosen and applied properly
plastic (thin, rigid tiles) cost: relatively low	similar to clay tile except variety is sharply limited	kitchen and bathroom walls	no finish needed	easy to keep and apparently durable; simple to install; lightweight	similar to clay tile
plastic (resilient tiles or sheets) cost: moderately high	great variety of colors, patterns, textures	where durable, resilient walls are wanted, such as in play space or above kitchen counters	some need waxing; many now do not	very durable and resistant to cuts and stains; easy maintenance; can extend into counter tops	can be scratched

Table 13–1   Wall Materials (*continued*)

Material	Character	Use	Interior Only Finishes	Advantages	Disadvantages
tile (clay) cost: moderately high	repeated regularity sets up pattern; great variety in size, shape, ornamentation	kitchens, bathrooms, and around fireplace; heat storage mass	no finish needed	great beauty, individuality; very durable, easily maintained; resists water, stains, fire; traps heat, releases it slowly	hard and cold to touch; reflects noise; can crack or break
wallboard (gypsum, sheetrock) cost: moderately low	noncommittal; joints show unless very well taped and painted	any room	paint, wallpaper, or fabric	not easily cracked; fire-resistant; can be finished in many ways	visually uninteresting in itself; needs protective surface
wallboard (plastic laminates) cost: high	shiny, matte, or textured surface; varied colors and patterns	kitchens, bathrooms, or any hard-use wall	none needed	very durable, unusually resistant to moisture, stains, dirt; cleaned with damp cloth	although wear-resistant, it can be irremediably scratched or chipped; reflects noise
wallboard (pressed wood) cost: moderate	smooth, matte surface with slight visual texture; also great variety of patterns	hard-wear rooms	needs no finish but can be stained, waxed, painted	tough surface is hard to damage	none of any importance
wall covering (plastic) cost: moderately high	many patterns; pleasing textures; matte or glossy surfaces	good for hard use walls	none needed	very durable; resists moisture, dirt, stains; cleans with damp cloth	none of importance
wallpaper and textiles cost: moderately low	tremendous variety of color and pattern	any wall	usually none but can be protected with lacquer	inexpensive to costly; can give decided character; some kinds very durable and easy to keep	must be chosen and used carefully

13-9 This room from Kirtlington Park in Oxford-shire, England, was completed in 1748. Rococo swags of fruit and foliage, as well as C-shaped scrolls and ribbons, appear in the marble fireplace, wood-carved door and console table, a bronze chandelier, and especially in the delicate plasterwork of the walls and ceiling. The furniture of the period includes a pair of fine Chippendale chairs. (*Metropolitan Museum of Art, New York [Fletcher Fund]*)

expensive than many types of wallboard available today that provide better insulation against heat, cold, and noise.

Wallboard

Many interior walls today are of dry-wall construction, consisting of one of the various types of wallboards: gypsum plasterboard (sheetrock), pressed wood, or plastic laminate. Most of them are relatively inexpensive and easy to install. They come in 4-by-8-foot sheets that are attached directly to the stud walls. The joints and indentations from nail heads in sheetrock must be taped, spackled, and sanded carefully so they do not show. Wallboard takes readily to many different finishes (which help conceal imperfections) and can be refinished. If paper or vinyl wall coverings are planned, wallboard should be sealed prior to their application to facilitate removal at a later date.

The plastic laminate panels and some of the pressed woods are totally prefabricated, with finishes ranging from solid colors to wood grains, fabric textures, and a variety of patterns produced by a photographic process. They are very durable.

Wallboard will not bear much weight, being light and not very dense. To hang anything of any size or weight on the wall, the underlying studs must be located or special screws (such as molly bolts) that pierce through the panel and clamp on the inner side must be used.

Wood

As boards, shingles, or panels, wood is available in an immense variety of grains, colors, and styles. The patterns produced by shingles or by boards laid horizontally or vertically—the joints beveled, shiplapped (overlapped), or covered by battens (thin narrow strips of wood)—make up part of the architectural vocabulary that can set the character of the wall. A quite different effect results when plywood sheathes the wall. Another variable is the way in which the wood is finished, whether smooth or rough-sawn, treated with vinyl or other substances to preserve attractiveness and reduce maintenance. (The qualities of various woods and wood finishes were described in Chapter 10.)

13-10 Wood is available in numerous colors and grains. Shown here are different woods for interior use. *(Photographs courtesy American Plywood Association; Bangkok Industries; Expanko Cork Co., Inc.; Potlatch Corp; and U.S. Plywood)*

13-11 The wood-shingled walls of a garden room seem a natural foil for plants, as well as being a practical solution to the problem of rather high humidity. *(Photograph: Bill Engdahl/Hedrich-Blessing, courtesy Red Cedar Shingle & Handsplit Shake Bureau)*

Wood has been popular throughout history for its warmth and richness. Distinctive wood trim—baseboards and moldings, door and window frames, mantels, and cabinets—helps to establish the character of historical periods and styles.

Solid wood with good grain is expensive but is available in a wide range of colors and patterns. Boards are usually joined with butt, tongue-and-groove, or beveled joints. Paneled walls will pay for themselves in ten years. A less expensive alternative is a plywood veneer or pressed-wood wallboard with a photo-process wood-grain pattern. Very thin veneers are also available, some so thin they are flexible and can be applied to walls like wallpaper.

Shingles, normally thought of as exterior sheathing, make a casual interior wall surface especially useful in rooms subject to much dampness—such as garden rooms, bathrooms, and saunas—because they absorb moisture. Cork, which is actually the thick, elastic outer bark of the cork oak, gives both sound and temperature insulation, in addition to serving (in children's spaces particularly) as tack boards.

Wood is a good insulator and can be finished in a variety of ways. It can also be refinished. However, it will fade and is flammable unless treated to make it fire-resistant.

left: Plate 38 Paneled walls, a simple fireplace, and crown molding retain a touch of the past in a remodeled house. Abi Babcock, interior designer. *(Photograph: © Karen Bussolini)*

below: Plate 39 A festive table setting takes its key from the warm pink color scheme in a Mexico City dining room. Luis Baragan, designer. *(Photograph: Hans Namuth/Photo Researchers)*

right: Plate 40 A fireplace set into a fanciful arabesque-sculptured chimney breast is an eye-catching focal point. Jefferson B. Riley of Centerbrook, architect. *(Photograph: © Norman McGrath)*

below: Plate 41 A metal stove with elaborate stamped and wrought designs is delightfully at home in an upper New York State farmhouse. *(Photograph: John T. Hill)*

Masonry

Various types of masonry walls were discussed in Chapter 10. They include concrete block, exposed brick and stone, ceramic tile, and stuccoed brick.

Masonry walls in solar homes function as heat-storage devices, absorbing direct heat from the sun and heat from the air itself, to radiate it slowly during the night hours. The exposed masonry surfaces may be brick, concrete, clay tile, or adobe. Such surfaces also help moderate the overheating effect if constructed with sufficient mass to heat through slowly.

Concrete-block structural walls are used in moderate climates, multiple housing units, and basements. They absorb sound as a result of their construction. Drawbacks include an institutional look when painted and the difficulty concrete-block walls present to anyone trying to hang something on them.

Ceramic-tiled bathrooms have come a long way since the days of stark white uniform tiles bordered in a row of black. Custom ceramic walls come in a wide variety of patterns and colors, from the "natural," earthlike effect to uniquely individual designs. Tiles can be hand-set but they also come in mesh-backed sheets that can be set in place with adhesive instead of grout. Some larger tiles have a peel-and-stick backing, making them popular with do-it-yourselfers. Tile offers easy maintenance since it is impervious to water, but it is noisy, hard, and cold to the touch, and can crack or chip.

Stone and brick are typically associated with fireplace walls and exterior walls but need not be limited to these locations. Thin sections of stone available in panels or tiles offer the rugged durability of the material without the bulk and weight. Marble veneer can contribute elegance to a formal interior. Stone and brick have been used since ancient times but are well suited to contemporary as well as period styles. Their texture is warm and casual but they are noisy, hard, and often cold to the touch, like most other masonry surfaces. Pictures and other wall-hung accessories are difficult to mount. All masonry materials are fireproof.

above left: 13-12 An informal, irregular pattern of glass blocks set in a stuccoed concrete-block wall actually lets in small amounts of light while figuratively lightening the large expanse of wall. Joseph Amisano, architect. *(Photograph: Gordon H. Schenck, Jr.)*

above right: 13-13 The possibilities for design with ceramic tile have a long history. In this bathroom a stylized "weeping willow" pattern of small glazed and unglazed mosaic tiles of different colors brightens the stall shower while providing an almost impervious surface. *(Courtesy American Olean Tile Company)*

right: 13-14 A solid wall of mirrors not only seems to double the space in this small dining room but also reflects the glow from the chandelier and the shimmer of glassware and silver in the cupboard. Schule-McCarville, designers. *(Photograph: John T. Hill)*
below: 13-15 A remodeled kitchen makes use of glass block to admit light while obscuring the view. *(Photograph: © Peter Aaron/ESTO)*

Glass

Broad areas of glass represent a fairly new development in home design, but for the most part this innovation has been confined to window glass. In a sense we might see this as an expansion, rather than a change, with windows growing larger and larger until they take over whole walls, flooding rooms with light (or glare) and heat (or cold), and expanding space into the outdoors. Windows influence color schemes, present problems in insulation and appropriate treatment, and often determine possible furniture arrangements. Other problems and possible solutions are presented in Table 15–2. (Chapter 15 discusses windows and their treatment in more detail.)

Another common use for glass on walls, more popular now than ever before (perhaps because our rooms are shrinking in size), is in the form of mirrors, which expand the apparent size of a room and create brilliant patterns of reflected light. Mirrors come in sheets or tile, and may be antiqued, gold- or silver-veined, tinted or clear glass, with etched designs and beveled edges. They can mask structural details at the same time that they add drama to the interior decor.

Glass blocks, either patterned or plain, have returned to use. They permit light to pass through but obstruct clear vision and may be used for interior or exterior walls, set in concrete block or by themselves, in curved or straight lines.

13-16 A tin wall and ceiling, reminiscent of Colorado's gold-rush era, adds character and keeps in the heat from the wood-burning stove in architect William Lipsey's house near Aspen. *(Photograph: Gordon H. Schenck, Jr.)*

Metal

Metal does not often appear on interior walls, being primarily confined to outside sheathing. But metal tiles of copper, stainless steel, or aluminum, used with taste and imagination, can provide a striking wall surface. The extreme sound- and light-reflective qualities of polished metal must be handled carefully, but brushed finishes and natural patinas have a soft, burnished quality.

A unique idea is to cover a metal-sheathed interior wall with fabric, using it for an easily changed and rearranged picture wall. The pictures are hung with magnets.

Plastics

Rigid plastics are used on walls with increasing frequency. They masquerade as other materials or stand on their own to make superior wall surfacings for special installations, such as bathrooms, or any place where their imperviousness to water and soil as well as their ease of maintenance is an advantage. They are available in sheets or tiles. Formed plastic is also used for bath and shower enclosures.

Resilient tiles and sheets of plastic add sound- and temperature-insulating qualities to the other advantages of plastic, as well as a softer look. Their peel-and-stick backing makes them ideal for the do-it-yourself remodeler.

All plastics are difficult to repair or refinish if damaged.

Paint

Paints today are made from a broad range of natural and synthetic materials selected for their special attributes, and new types and combinations continue to appear. Their properties are impressive. Some can be applied to wood, masonry, stucco, metal, or gypsum board; many resist sun, fading, and blistering; and most dry in a short time. Others are sound-absorbing, fire-resistant, or rust-inhibiting. The newer synthetic resin paints are easier to apply than older varieties; they usually go on with a roller, have little paint odor, dry quickly, and can be touched up. When dry, they offer matte (flat), semigloss, or high-gloss surfaces. Water-base paints are extremely easy to handle, because paint spots can be wiped up with a damp cloth and brushes cleaned with soap and water. After a short period of curing, they become impervious to water. Solvent-base paints may be more durable, but the application and clean-up are somewhat more tedious.

A flat finish is normally used on walls and ceilings, except for woodwork and in bathrooms and kitchens, which benefit from the more durable scrubbable semigloss and gloss finishes. Darker colors reflect more light if semigloss paint is used. Pastel colors reflect more light in gloss paints as well but may become washed out in appearance and lose too much color. Pale colors are usually better in flat finishes. The number of different colors available has been vastly increased by the automatic mixing machines most paint dealers have, and colors from other materials can be closely matched in paint. Since the color will appear darker and more intense when applied to walls, paint colors slightly lighter and less saturated should be selected.

Being the easiest of all finishes to apply, paint leads many people into doing their own wall finishing. Nothing so quickly and inexpensively changes the character of a room. Paint finds its place in the smallest apartment and the most elaborate mansion, in good part because it is an excellent, unobtrusive background for furnishings, art objects, and people. In itself paint has little beauty or individuality, but these goals can be attained by choosing exactly the right color or a distinctive combination of colors that seem eminently suited to the walls they cover and to the people who live with them. Figures 13-17 and 13-18 and Plate 39 show three quite different effects that can be achieved with ordinary paint.

13-17 The transformation of a room by paint is one of the delights of interior design. Here the white boxiness of a living room has become an apparently sculptured flow of space through the judicious use of a supergraphic that carries through the group spaces. Donald MacDonald, architect-designer. *(Photograph: © Morley Baer)*

The dining space in Plate 39 (p. 331) has painted walls of different colors. A deep plum color on the right calls attention to that wall while making us aware of the other colors in the room. The pinks and reds of the table setting, chair cushions, and rug, the warm wood tones of the furniture, and the heavy darkness of the beams overhead are all brought to life by the one unusual color.

An essentially boxy room (Fig. 13-17) assumes trompe-l'oeil curves from the painted stripes on walls and ceiling. Taking his cue from the fireplace, which juts out slightly into the room at bottom, the owner carried the pattern of light against dark out across the ceiling in an expanding swath that makes the ceiling appear to slope upward. A dark stripe to the left of the fireplace curves out into the entry hall to unite the two spaces, thus also helping to enlarge the room visually. In a period when odd-shape rooms are popular but most of us retain the basic cube, an ingenious use of paint can almost miraculously transform a static space into a dynamic one.

Paint can also be used to add pattern to a wall, as in Figure 13-18. Stenciling (painting a design through a stencil) was used to enliven the walls of a living room with floral motifs in keeping with the eclectic character of the space and furnishings. The owners and their friends spent long hours doing the stenciling with designs that are varied in size and scale, resulting in a much freer and personal expression than wallpaper could have achieved.

Next in importance to color is paint's ability to give a smooth uniform surface to whatever it covers. Sometimes smooth paint will not cover all blemishes, and occasionally smoothness is not wanted. In such cases, paint can be *stippled* with a stiff brush to obliterate brush marks and to provide a soft, matte finish; or it can be *spattered* with one or more colors to give some vibrancy and minimize spots or scratches. More pronounced textures are produced with special paints which produce a sandy surface, by applying the paint with special rollers, or by going over the wet paint with a sponge or a whisk broom. These are easy and inexpensive

13-18 Stenciling, an old craft, was revived for a renovated living room to add color and pattern to the walls. Robert Venturi and Denise Scott Brown, architects. *(Photograph: © Paul Warchol)*

13-19 A trio of patterns in Mary McFadden's "Mosaic Dreams" collection of wallcoverings and fabrics demonstrate the variety of innovative designs available. Their ability to set the style and tone for furniture, lighting, and flooring makes wallcoverings and fabrics an important element in interior design. *(Courtesy Kirk-Brummel Assoc., Inc.)*

ways to cover plaster cracks or gypsum board joints, and they create unique surfaces.

Measuring and Estimating To determine the amount of paint needed, measure the perimeter of the room and multiply by the height of the room. This yields the total square footage to be covered. A gallon of paint will normally cover from 400 to 500 square feet of surface (one coat of paint on the walls and ceiling of a 9-by-12-foot room with an 8-foot ceiling), depending on the surface material, its condition, and previous color. Porous materials, rough surfaces, and dark colors may require more paint to cover adequately. Paint coverage per gallon is usually noted on the container label and may vary with type of paint being used.

Wallpaper

Long known in the Orient, wallpaper has been used in Europe for about five centuries and in the United States since the Colonial period. "Poor man's tapestry" was a good name for it, because wallpaper came into use in humble homes as an imitation of the expensive textiles used by the wealthy. Wallpaper's advantages are many:

- It can be used in any room in the home.
- It can be tested for its effect in advance by borrowing large samples.
- It is available in many colors, patterns, and textures, and in varying degrees of durability.
- It is a quick and easy way to remodel with prepasted or self-adhesive (peel-and-stick) types.
- It has the most positive character of any wall surfacing in its price class and can establish the feeling of a period in history.
- It makes a room seem to shrink or expand, gain height or intimacy, become more active or subdued, more formal or less formal.
- It minimizes architectural awkwardnesses by illusion or camouflage.
- It hides disfigured walls.
- It makes rooms with little furniture seem furnished.
- It distracts attention from miscellaneous or commonplace furniture.

So virtually infinite are the patterns, colors, and designs available in wallpaper that we can barely suggest the range of effects possible. In Figure 13-20 the structural awkwardness of an under-the-eaves bedroom was turned to positive advantage by a brown-and-white graph-paper print on the wall surfaces. The bedspreads carry out the theme but are not identical in pattern; in one, the colors reverse to give a progression of emphasis to the dark bolster coverings.

Wallpaper seems natural for many traditional or restored rooms. The Early American bedroom in Figure 13-21 is an assemblage of authentic antique toys and furnishings. The small-scaled pattern and light color of the wallpaper join with dormer windows and exposed beams to provide a background for the mellowed furnishings and hand-stitched patchwork quilts.

Wallpaper has a few inherent disadvantages. Some people may not like its "papery" look, and it may not be very durable or easily maintained in high-use areas. However, it is possible to find papers appropriate to almost any way of living, any kind of furnishings, any exposure or special factor.

Wallpapers are produced by roller printing, screen printing, or block printing. They range from solid colors through textured effects, from small to large patterns, from abstract to naturalistic mural or scenic designs which may create an illusion of depth and enlarged space. Most have a matte finish that may or may not be washable, but some are glossy and may be vinyl-coated for washability,

13-20 For a bedroom in a remodeled horse barn, the strong linear pattern established by exposed posts and beams is emphasized by the wallpaper design; the bedspreads repeat the diagonal of the sloping walls. George Washington Orton, 3d, designer. *(Photograph: Hans Namuth/ Photo Researchers)*

13-21 An attic can be the ideal place for a cozy room for children. Here the wallpaper reflects the traditional pattern of a handmade quilt. Snezana Grosfeld of Litchfield-Grosfeld, architect. *(Photograph: © Norman McGrath)*

durability, and soil resistance. Flock papers with their raised, fuzzy nap look like textiles. Marbleized papers hint at the gloss and depth of marble, and metallic papers add luster. Available in a wide range of prices, wallpaper is quick and relatively easy to apply. Coordinating wallpapers and fabrics provide easy harmony for any interior.

Selecting a pattern and color is not easy. Wall-length samples of several patterns can be fastened up and observed at different times of day and night. Wallpaper is a kind of applied ornament that may noticeably affect the apparent size, shape, and character of rooms. Strong designs set the character of a room and other furnishings must be keyed to them. A bold pattern may make it difficult to coordinate other accessories, especially wall-hung ones which may require large, plain mountings. Consider wallpaper in the light of the criteria for ornament discussed in Chapter 7, making these more specific by keeping in mind that the wall and paper are flat and continuous, like fabrics, and that in most instances the pattern will cover very large areas. In addition:

- Plain colors look much like paint but come in varied textures.
- Textural patterns are more active, more pronounced in character, and more effective in concealing minor damage than are plain colors. Metallic foils, on the other hand, emphasize wall blemishes. Flocked papers should be avoided in kitchens and utility areas where grease and lint may cling to them.
- Abstract patterns do not go out of fashion quickly and seem especially suitable to walls.

13-22 An overscale pattern by painter Roy Lichtenstein on silver Mylar dramatizes the stair wall in a house remodeled for his own use by architect Robert A. M. Stern. Its pattern repeats the rectangular wall paneling but shocks it into life with bold diagonals and circular motifs. *(Photograph: John T. Hill)*

13-23 "Greenwich," a wall covering of Vymura, produces a strong architectural quality in both its subject matter and the overall pattern. *(Courtesy ICI America, Inc.)*

- Scenic wallpapers are somewhat like murals, and may seem to broaden the space when they contain a predominance of horizontal lines or deepen the space with perspective.
- Repetitive, bold, conspicuous patterns may reduce the visual importance of the space, furniture, and people, but a supergraphic can provide a focal point.
- Conspicuous, isolated motifs often make walls look spotty.

Measuring and Estimating Wallpaper is priced by the single roll although it is produced in double or triple, sometimes quadruple, roll bolts which result in less waste. A single roll contains about 30 usable square feet, allowing as much as 6 square feet for waste in cutting and matching patterns. To determine the quantity of paper needed, measure the total square feet of wall space to be covered (length times height of each wall, then add) and divide by 30, rounding fractions up to the nearest whole number. This formula will tell you the number of single rolls needed with perhaps a little excess for walls that are not "plumb" or truly square and straight. Subtract one roll for every two normal openings (doors and windows) or subtract the area of such openings. Some large patterned papers may require as much as 20 percent extra in order to align the pattern properly on the walls. However, many patterns are produced in modular-sized repeats that space evenly from floor to ceiling in standard-height rooms. Pattern repeats of 2, 3, 4, 8, and 12 inches, for example, divide evenly into a 96-inch wall height.

Vinyl Wall Coverings

Nearly all the things that were said about wallpaper apply equally to vinyl wall coverings. However, certain qualities are easier to achieve. Application requires less delicate handling because the vinyl film, often backed by a fabric, doesn't stretch or tear as easily as paper. Removal is made quicker and less tedious than paper as well; many can easily be stripped from a wall in large sheets and even reused. Because vinyl presents fewer problems in application than does wallpaper—and is thus easier to match at the seams—it lends itself well to supergraphics and large-pattern repeats. Vinyls for commercial use are available in 52-inch widths which might be used in kitchens, baths, and utility rooms where fewer seams are desirable. Textured, three-dimensional effects and metallic shine are particular strong points of vinyl coverings. They can very realistically simulate anything.

In terms of maintenance and long life, of course, vinyl wall coverings tend to be superior to wallpaper, but the initial cost may be higher. Vinyl is *scrubbable* with soap and a soft brush while paper is usually only *washable* with a damp sponge if it is vinyl-coated. With proper application, heavyweight, tough vinyls can hide serious wall defects, even hold cracked plaster in position. Some vinyls come with special backings for sound insulation, and a number of them perform well as upholstery, thus allowing for harmony between two elements of the interior.

Wall Fabrics and Fibers

Just about every fabric known has at one time or another been draped over, stretched on, or pasted to walls. Centuries ago the walls of nomadic tents were constructed of fabric and poles. In other, more northerly regions, heavy tapestries were hung over cold stone walls for beauty and warmth. Today, such effects still fall into two main categories: wall fabrics that surface a wall and cover at least one section completely, and those that are simply hung on walls as enrichment.

Almost any fabric can be made into a wall covering by tacking it directly to the wall (if that is allowed) or to a wooden frame, or by using double-faced carpet tape or vinyl adhesive. Fabric can also be hung in soft folds by gathering it at top and bottom, or walls can be padded and upholstered, both of which increase

13-24 A metallic wallcovering reflects light and adds shine to surfaces that ordinarily have a matte or diffuse reflective finish. *(Courtesy Diversi Tech General)*

13-25 A media room makes use of upholstered walls for increased sound-proofing. Linen fabrics for walls and sofa also provide harmony between the two. Jane Victor, designer. *(Courtesy International Linen Promotion Commission)*

sound-absorbing and cold-insulating qualities. Fabrics can be vinyl-coated and paper-backed and hung like wallpaper as well.

The various kinds of grass cloth, longtime favorites for adding texture to a wall, are also easy to apply, because they are glued to a tough paper backing and then handled much as wallpaper. They come in textures from comparatively smooth to bold and in many colors, although we tend to think of them as being most appropriate in their natural colors. Other natural fibers and materials, such as wool, flax, leather, and cork are also used in this manner.

Carpets have also begun to climb the walls, providing sound and cold insulation, a soft, sensuous texture in an unexpected place, and continuity between floor covering and wall. This technique can be especially successful when it serves to tie built-in seating into the structure of the room. It is very durable in hard-use areas. However, carpet designed for flooring may not meet flammability standards when used on walls. Carpet designed especially for walls is available in a limited range of colors and textures.

Wall hangings of many types can add enrichment wherever desired. Heavier woven or stitchery panels—even rugs—open up many new possibilities for walls, to replace the standard paintings or prints. A textile can act as a partial wall or space divider, separating but not shutting off one part of the room from another. All told, textile fabrics give variety and mobility, often with little time or effort.

Chapter 12 provides more detailed information on the soil resistance characteristics of the various fibers and finishes. Generally, rough textures catch more dust but show less soil than smooth textures. Removable fabrics can easily be washed or dry cleaned and rehung. A soil-repellant can be applied before or after hanging to reduce soiling and make cleaning easier.

13-26 For a surface that is natural in texture and material with a clean, soft look, wall coverings made of grasscloth, string, and textiles provide the solution. *(Courtesy Shibui Wall-coverings)*

13-27 A fabric panel, set at right angles, breaks up a long wall without closing off space. Joy Wulke, designer. *(Photograph: © Robert Perron)*

Walls, Fireplaces, and Ceilings **343**

Fireplaces

Conventional fireplaces are extravagant. A fireplace may cost as much to construct as a bathroom. Further, storing fuel takes dry space, getting it into the firebox requires labor, and the later cleanup is a chore. Many fireplaces are actually used for fires less than 1 percent of the time. When lit, they provide some physical and psychological warmth, perhaps heat for cooking, and some light and ventilation—but all of a hard-to-control sort, and at high cost.

Still, open fires are beautiful, and fireplaces even without fires can be substantial centers of interest (Plate 40, p. 332). A fire's warm, constantly changing, beautifully shaped and colored flames and embers produce a kind of lighting equaled only by sunrises and sunsets. Open fires are also probably associated with deeply buried feelings about the importance of fire to humankind. Nothing lifts the spirits on a cold, cheerless day or night like a fire. Then, too, every fire has its own character. Thus, even though conventional fireplaces are hopelessly out of date in terms of utility and economy, open fires are not outdated in terms of human satisfaction. And they do serve some useful purposes.

Heat from a fireplace on a cold day seems worth its cost, even though it creates drafts on the floor, draws warm room air up the flue, and may throw thermostatically controlled furnaces off balance. Heat output can be increased and controlled by designing the firebox to throw heat into the room, by keeping the damper open just enough so smoke doesn't enter the room, and by using a projecting or suspended hood to radiate heat. Glass doors also decrease draft and heat loss, and special grates consisting of metal pipes which draw in cool air from the room, circulate it around and over the fire to warm it, then allow it to re-enter the room improve the efficiency of conventional fireplaces markedly. Prefabricated fireplaces with vents, like small warm-air furnaces, circulate heated air effectively. For example, an energy-efficient heat exchanger can be built into a fireplace to push more heat into the room and possibly even into other rooms with additional ducts and fans. Or wood-burning stoves can provide the sight and smell of a fire with much greater efficiency and economy than a conventional fireplace.

Light is an aesthetic contribution of fireplaces, because the illumination they provide is unique. It is restfully soft and warm enough in color to make even pallid complexions look sun-tanned. The concentrated, flickering light can be hypnotically relaxing and draw people together like a magnet.

Ventilation is hardly a major function of fireplaces, but they do air rooms—violently with a good fire, moderately when they are cold and the damper is open.

The *symbolism* of "hearth and home" continues to be important. The experience of gathering around a fire for stories, popcorn, or whatever unites people of all ages and interests and can make a group feel relaxed and secure.

Design

Certainly the most important functional aspect of a fireplace is how well it draws, because one that does not draw well enough to allow a fire to start or keep it going—or one that sends smoke into the room—negates its original purpose. This matter should be left to experts. Equally important is safety; the several hazards can be reduced by fireproof roofs and chimney tops that retard sparks; by screens or glass to keep sparks out of the room; by andirons or baskets to keep fuel in place; and by hearths high enough to keep babies and toddlers at a safe distance. Then comes fireplace maintenance, which can be lessened if both indoor and outdoor wood storage is nearby. The most efficient fireplace has a wood bin that can be refilled from the outside, an ash pit to permit outside ash removal, and a fire pit lowered a few inches below the hearth to restrain the ashes.

Location

When fireplaces were used for heating, nearly every room had one. Today, few houses have more than a single fireplace, and this generally is located in the living, dining, or family social space. Occasionally, one or more additional fireplaces will be put in rooms in the private zone. Because of its traditional association with food preparation, the fireplace located in a family kitchen seems natural though it is rarely used for cooking.

Fireplaces most often are large, more-or-less dominant elements. They demand considerable maintenance when a fire is burning and therefore should be accessible. Fireplaces make natural centers for furniture arrangement and usually attract as many people as space around them permits.

A typical location is the center of a long wall. While such an arrangement allows maximum visibility for large groups, it also suggests an evenly spaced furniture placement, which can lead toward static symmetry and tends to shorten the room visually. A fireplace in the center of one of the short walls is also familiar but somewhat less common. Another stable situation, this location can make the room seem longer and may inspire one furniture grouping near the fireplace and another at the opposite end.

A fireplace may also be in a spur wall that acts as a room divider; it might be a freestanding structure that delineates continuous space into areas for different activities; or it may serve as the focus for a recess specifically designed as an intimate area away from the main group space. Locating a fireplace in the corner of a room emphasizes that room's longest dimension and limits furniture grouping to a quarter circle.

13-28 The fireplace provides a focal point for the family-room conversation area and backs up against the open kitchen while appearing to anchor and support the balcony above in a unique home designed by architect Alfredo De Vido. *(Photograph: Jeremiah Bragstad)*

345

13-29 A fireplace projecting slightly from the wall and capped by a mantelpiece gains an unobtrusive prominence that sets the character of this quiet, comfortable room. Thomas A. Gray and William L. Gray, designers. *(Photograph: Bill Aller/NYT Pictures)*

Appearance

Although consistency with the whole house is a major consideration, fireplaces can have their own special beauty and individuality. Of all elements in the home, fireplaces lend themselves best to overscaling without seeming unpleasantly obtrusive. But very small fireplaces can have a certain refreshing charm. It is easy to increase the importance and apparent size of fireplaces by enriching them with bands of contrasting materials, by integrating them with bookshelves, or architectural niches (Plate 38, p. 331), or built-in furniture, or by making them an integral part of large areas of masonry. Also, fireplaces seem larger on small walls than on big ones.

Relationship to walls, floors, and ceilings profoundly affects the character of fireplaces. They can be simply holes, perhaps framed unobtrusively, in an unbroken wall—the least noticeable treatment. Some project from the wall a few inches or several feet, which increases their impact. The fireplace outlined by a mantle and possibly a molding remains classic in modern as well as traditional homes. When the fireplace leaves the wall entirely, as an independent unit, it becomes still more conspicuous.

13-30 A wood-burning stove partially separates kitchen from living space with its sunken conversation area oriented toward the warmth of the crackling fire in this home designed by Les Walker. *(Photograph: © Peter Aaron/ESTO)*

346

left: 13-31 A traditional sculptured adobe fireplace fits snugly into the corner of a bedroom with a small built-in seating space adjacent. Maurice J. Nespor & Associates, architects; Diana Cunningham, interior designer. *(Photograph: Hyde Flippo)*

below: 13-32 A monumental fireplace mantel and solid-slab construction make a strong design statement in a contemporary living room. Juan Montoya, designer. *(Photograph: Mark Golderman)*

The fireplace unit may extend to the ceiling, which accentuates its verticality. If it terminates a little or well below the ceiling, it can create a horizontal or blocky effect. The bottom of the fire pit may be either at floor level or at seat height; in the latter case, the hearth usually is extended to give sitting space. Or the fire pit and surrounding area may be depressed below the main floor, with space large enough for furniture around it. This arrangement tends to draw people into a convivial huddle and subdivides a room without partitions.

Materials turn our thoughts at once to masonry and metal, since neither is damaged by fire. Brick and stone look substantial and permanent, tile can be plain or decorated, and metal not only lends itself to shaping in many ways but also transmits heat, thus using all of the fire's energy potential. These materials come in many colors and textures: smooth tile and polished marble, shining copper and dull iron, brick and stone in all gradations of roughness.

The present concern with energy conservation and with fuel shortages has led many families to consider returning to wood as a partial or emergency source of warmth. Homes have begun to sprout old-fashioned wood-burning stoves partially inset within a fireplace or free-standing with only a heavy-duty pipe outlet through the ceiling or wall. The farmhouse living room in Plate 41 (p. 332) boasts such a piece—a splendid example of ironcraft enriched with touches of brass. It is set on a brick pad a safe distance from a brick wall, in accordance with fire codes. Given the superior efficiency of free-standing metal stoves, this unit could keep such a small room comfortable on all but the coldest nights. But even if it could not, it earns its place in the room by the charm of its design and embellishment. A feeling of safety and stability emanates from its squat, sturdy contours as surely as from the glowing embers within. Unfortunately, some localities are finding that too many such wood-burning stoves are resulting in a serious smog problem because of all the smoke, an environmental concern that affects everyone.

Ceilings

Although they are rarely *used* in the same sense that other major elements of the house can be, ceilings do have several important functions. They not only protect us but affect illumination, acoustics, heating, cooling, and character in a room as well, yet they are often neglected. Typical ceilings are the same size and shape as the floors they parallel, are surfaced with plaster or gypsum board, and are painted white or some very pale hue. There are several reasons for this stereotype. A flat, neutral ceiling literally designs itself and is inexpensive to build and maintain; it gives unobtrusive spaciousness; and it reflects light well. In most cases we barely notice ceilings and do little about them. Perhaps it is just as well in a busy world to retain one large undecorated surface in every room for visual respite. Nevertheless, ceilings play an important role in the architectural background of a room and need not be so plain, as we shall see in discussing their height, shape, direction, materials, and general design.

Design

Ceilings during the time of the Renaissance were coordinated with wall designs and were executed in molded or carved plaster. These backgrounds set the mood of the room, stating its character and even dictating furnishings and accessories. Decorative treatment of ceilings continued into the eighteenth century, when plain ceilings came into vogue. In the second half of the twentieth century, however, there has been a renewed interest in ceilings, especially high ones. In some cases, the overhead plane has been elevated so high as to be practically unnoticeable. Rather than the ceiling itself, it is the dramatic open space that dominates.

Height

Ceiling heights are determined by reconciling our needs for head room, air, and economy with our desire for space pleasantly proportioned and in character with our life style. Minimum human heights are 7 feet for basements, 8 feet for the main level and for upper stories. Heights beyond these may well be justified for aesthetic reasons, and lowered ceilings, especially in part of a room, may seem cozy and sheltering.

There are notable differences in the effects of low and high ceilings. Space seems to expand under high ceilings while low spaces are more intimate. The *appearance* of increased or decreased ceiling height can also affect the character of the room. To make a ceiling seem higher, use a light color on it, light it or place a skylight in it, run the wall color onto the ceiling a short distance, or use vertical lines on the walls to lead the eye up. To create the appearance of a lower ceiling, use a dark color (but not a glossy finish), a pattern, or horizontal beams on the ceiling, drop the ceiling color onto the wall (where it can end with a picture molding), or use horizontal lines on the wall to lead the eye along its length rather than its height.

Ceilings of different heights can energize space and differentiate one area from another. For example, dining rooms can be set apart by lowering the ceiling or raising the floor, and quiet conversation spaces can be demarcated by ceilings appropriately lower than those in the rest of the group space.

In remodeling older buildings, which often have high ceilings, the designer can make use of that verticality to provide more floor area and the contrast of varied ceiling heights with balconies and lofts.

One other aspect of high and low ceilings should concern us now, at a time when the energy required to heat and cool our homes has become an important consideration. Low ceilings reduce winter heating costs but make rooms warmer in summer, because the rising hot air has nowhere to go. High ceilings bring in cooler air at floor level, so they are more comfortable in summer, but they require much more energy to keep them warm in winter. The warm air that rises, however, can be directed downward by means of fans, or recaptured and recirculated at floor level.

Shape and Direction

While it is often suitable to have ceilings that are nothing more than uninterrupted horizontal planes, some other possibilities offer more interest.

Dropped ceilings can enliven the overhead plane even on the first floor of a two-story house, where horizontal ceilings are almost mandatory. They can demarcate certain areas and provide a handy recess for indirect lighting that will softly illuminate a room. A dropped ceiling over a hallway will emphasize the

below left: 13-33 A sleeping loft greatly expands usable space in small but high-ceilinged apartments. *(Photograph: Michael Boys)*
below right: 13-34 A change in ceiling height dramatizes the curved shape of this entry hall while providing space for recessed lighting around its perimeter. David Estreich, architect. *(Photograph: Robert Levin)*

sudden, exhilarating elevation of ceiling over the larger living space. The effect of transition is magnified.

Integrated ceilings combine lighting and ceiling as a total, unified system. Lighting is discussed further in Chapter 16.

Coved ceilings, in which walls and ceiling are joined with curved surfaces rather than right angles, make space seem more plastic and flexible. A variation provides a recessed space for cove lighting around the perimeter of the room, washing the ceiling with light from an unseen source.

If carried to their logical conclusion, coved ceilings become **domed** or **vaulted ceilings.** Contrasting materials add visual as well as actual weight to enhance the sense of enclosure in a room.

Coffered ceilings are generally wood-paneled with ornamental sunken panels between closely spaced beams running at right angles to each other. Height is necessary to prevent such a ceiling from seeming oppressive.

Shed, lean-to, or **single-slope ceilings** provide excellent acoustics and call attention to the highest part of the room, often in a quite dramatic manner.

Gabled or **double-pitched** or **cathedral ceilings** encourage one to look up, and they activate and increase the apparent volume of a space. If the beams are exposed, the eye tends to follow their direction. For example, a gently sloping ceiling with beams running longitudinally from one end of the room to the other will accentuate the room's length and lower the ceiling's apparent height. When large beams follow the direction of steeply pitched ceilings, they emphasize the room's height dramatically. Ceiling planes can also slope in four directions when under a hip or mansard roof. A-frame houses have double-pitched ceilings that come down almost to floor level for an unusually strong architectural statement.

13-35 A steeply sloping site provided the incentive for distinctive architecture in this Vermont house. The sharp angle of the ceiling over the group space and hall brings a dramatic and constant reminder of the slope. Peter L. Gluck, architect. *(Photograph: © Norman McGrath)*

13-36 In this house of curves and planes, heavy wood beams and steel reinforcement flaunt their structural role and transform utility into a thing of beauty. The striking radial pattern of the ceiling, cut by a large triangular window, becomes the focal point of the room. *(Photograph: © Ezra Stoller/ ESTO)*

Sculptured ceilings defy classification because they are uniquely themselves. The ceiling shown in Figure 13-36 exposes structural members to create a striking radial pattern that is interrupted by the curving fireplace and the plane of the adjacent space cutting across it. This ceiling is clearly not a neutral backdrop but the focus of the whole room.

Materials

Plaster and wallboard are today the most common ceiling materials, since they are inexpensive and easy to apply. But these conventions by no means exhaust the possibilities for ceiling embellishment.

Plaster provides an uninterrupted surface that can meet plastered walls without joints, thereby passively unifying the sides and top of a room. It can be smooth or textured, plain, painted, or papered. In the days of more leisurely craftsmanship, plaster often was embellished with designs, a refinement preserved with care in many remodeled homes. Acoustical plaster is sprayed on, resulting in a rough texture. Low in cost, it is quite popular.

Gypsum board resembles plaster, except that it leaves joints that must be concealed with tape or with wood battens. The latter provide lines of emphasis.

Ceiling tiles and panels come in many sizes and patterns; they can contribute a ready-made texture. Some are easy to apply by the householder to cover a less-than-attractive surface; many are acoustical and offer the very obvious advantage of reducing noise at its source. There are also tiles with foil backing that cut down on air-conditioning costs. The framework for ceiling panels establishes a repetitive grid pattern. Translucent panels can be integrated with lighting behind them. Such panels can be used to drop a ceiling.

above left: 13-37 An intricate plaster molding highlights this formal turn-of-the-century Brooklyn living room. *(Photograph: John T. Hill)*

above right: 13-38 Small saplings called *latias* span the spaces between large supporting logs called *vigas*, traditional in Spanish pueblo-style architecture, creating an unusually emphatic ceiling in an adobe house. The saplings, peeled but left unfinished, are also used to front a wall of closets in the master bedroom. Maurice J. Nespor & Associates, architects; Diana Cunningham, interior designer. *(Photograph: Hyde Flippo)*

Wood—in the form of strips, planks, or panels—is both handsome and homelike. It can be left in its natural state (in which case it will need minimum care over the years), stained, or perhaps painted to brighten the room. Wood is not often used for the entire ceiling today but beams, as part of the structure, are exposed to give character (Plate 39, p. 331).

Transparent, translucent, or reflective materials like plastics and glass admit natural daylight, or artificial light from fixtures concealed above them, to provide all-over illumination to the room and allow glimpses of the sky. **Mirrored** ceilings reflect light and give an illusion of height.

Fabrics are rarely used on ceilings, but they can add warmth and softness to a room in unexpected ways. In addition to lending its drapability, fabric also diffuses and softens light.

Besides the surface materials that finish a ceiling, of the utmost importance are insulating materials placed between ceiling and roof or, in a multistory building, under the floor of the level above.

Color and Texture

Heaviness overhead is usually unpleasant unless the weight is clearly supported from above and balanced from below. This fact, together with the advantage of having ceilings that reflect and spread light, explains the frequency of light colors and fine textures on overhead surfaces. Certainly this characterizes most apartments, in which ceilings tend to be low and daylight comes in through windows on one exterior wall.

It should be remembered that ceilings, especially at night if much light is directed toward them, bathe everything below with their reflected color. A yellow ceiling, for example, would enliven yellows, oranges, or yellow-greens beneath it but would gray any blues or violets. Special effects of considerable impact, however, can be achieved with ceilings painted in strong colors or made of a dark wood. Glossy color should generally be avoided on ceilings (because of glare), and additional lighting will be needed to compensate for the lack of reflected light from above.

Although often neglected, ceilings play an important role in the architectural background of a room. They are often the largest plain space and thus serve the subtle function of a visual rest space in addition to influencing the mood, temperature, and quality of light and sound in a room. That ceilings can also be a strong design statement can be seen in Fig. 13-38.

Of the three elements discussed in this chapter, only two could be considered essential: the walls and ceilings that surround and cover our enclosures. Yet just as walls and ceilings give protection and privacy, fireplaces contribute both actual and psychological warmth. When handled with taste and imagination, each of the three elements can bring its own design integrity into the home.

References for Further Reading

Baillie, Sheila and Mabel R. Skjelver. *Graphics for Interior Space*. Lincoln: University of Nebraska Press, 1979. Pp. 162–164.

Faulkner, Sarah. *Planning a Home*. New York: Holt, Rinehart and Winston, 1979. Chap. 7, pp. 167–172; chap. 8, pp. 174–189.

Friedmann, Arnold, John F. Pile, and Forrest Wilson. *Interior Design: An Introduction to Architectural Interiors*, 3rd ed. New York: Elsevier Science Publishing Co., 1982. Unit VI, chaps. 1 and 2, pp. 357–408.

Hornbostel, Caleb and William J. Hornung. *Materials and Methods for Contemporary Construction*, 2nd ed. Englewood Cliffs, NJ: Prentice-Hall, 1982.

Whiton, Sherrill. *Interior Design and Decoration*, 4th ed. Philadelphia: Lippincott Company, 1974. Chap. 12, pp. 419–436; chap. 16, pp. 505–521.

14

Floors and Stairways

Floors
    Finish Flooring Materials
    Selection

Stairways
    Design and Construction
      References for Further Reading

Interest in vertical space has traditionally had a profound effect on the design of floors and stairways. For many years these elements were considered relatively innocuous blank surfaces serving utilitarian purposes only, but some homes now treat them as strong architectural members with decisive influence on the character of the space. Instead of a flat, horizontal plane covered with the ubiquitous gray-beige tile or a neutral beige-gray wall-to-wall carpeting, floors now often bridge many levels: a few steps up or down to define different areas of the main group space; balconies overlooking other parts of the house; even two or three stories flowing into one another. At the same time, interest in floor coverings has revived. We see greater variety in hard-surface flooring, more conspicuous colors and textures in carpeting. Area rugs once again function as strong accents in the interior design vocabulary.

    Stairs, of course, permit us to move from one level of an enclosure to another. By their nature—as an efficient system for changing levels in minimum space—stairs usually cut a diagonal line or sometimes spiral upward. This feature introduces a diversion from the predominantly rectilinear quality of most homes. Unless they are completely buried behind walls, stairs attract (and deserve) much attention.

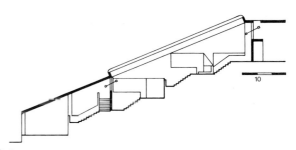

In a house built on a hillside bordering a lake (Figs. 14-1 and 14-2), the stepped-down configuration of the plan takes on vivid definition because of the treatment of floors and ceilings. Entering at the top of the hill, one is immediately aware of the ceiling that swoops down over the living room. The dark slate floor balances the visual weight of the ceiling and heightens the effect of protective white walls alongside the stairs. The floor also halts, at intervals, the downward plunge of the stairway.

The living room's area rug has an abstract pattern reminiscent of the rectangular floor tiles. This defines the generous conversation group of sofas and chairs, which assumes warmth and intimacy because it is under the lowest part of the ceiling in the living room and because the hard floor has been softened by a deep pile rug. Beyond the living-room windows, a terrace on the roof of the next lower level counters any tendency to fear of heights. Floors and ceilings have been used in opposition to each other to state the theme of the steep site yet anchor the house firmly on its foundations in the hillside.

Floors and stairways, together with walls, ceilings, doors, and windows, define the space we live in, keep us warm, dry, and safe, and depending on their design and materials, establish the character of our enclosures.

Floors

Floors are flat, horizontal surfaces meant to be walked on—less often to be run, jumped, or danced on—and sometimes to be sat on. They take a limited amount of wheel traffic such as vacuum cleaners, service carts, children's toys, and occasionally wheelchairs. They support us and our furniture and provide insulation against the earth's cold dampness. As we all know but sometimes forget, floors get the greatest wear and the most dirt of any part of the house. But floor design and materials are not so completely mundane as these factors imply. In fully developed interior design, they contribute to the expressive character of the whole house. They can define and separate areas without benefit of walls, can suggest traffic patterns, and can be as dominant or subordinate as desired.

14-3 The wood screeds in this concrete floor allow for expansion and thus eliminate the danger of cracking; they also take part in the rhythmic motif of rectangularity on which the design of the interior is based. The owner designed and built most of the inside fixtures and finishes over a period of several years. Bob Batchelder and Dick Whittaker, architects. *(Photograph: Philip L. Molten)*

In houses with basements, the floors are typically of two sorts. Basement floors are concrete slabs poured directly on the earthen subgrade or on a foundation of crushed rock. Those above grade (on the main story and second or third floor, if any) usually consist of supporting floor joists, a subfloor layer of inexpensive wood or plywood for strength, and perhaps an insulating membrane to retard the passage of air and moisture. All this will be topped by a finish flooring of hardwood, masonry, tiles, sheet vinyl, or carpeting.

The growing popularity of ground-hugging, basementless houses on the one hand and precast concrete slab high-rise apartments on the other has changed the situation. In both types of construction, all floors may be concrete slabs basically like those in basements but with important differences: they are reinforced with metal to minimize cracking; intermediate floors may have much thinner slabs, with the space between them and the ceilings underneath used for sound and temperature insulation; and the upper and lower surfaces can be integrally colored or patterned through the use of various materials in the concrete mix or with wood or metal screeds, which also allow for expansion. By heating concrete floors or covering them with resilient floor coverings, the householder can lessen one unfortunate side effect—cold, tired feet. It appears that combined coldness and hardness, rather than hardness alone, results in fatigue. In summer, however, with the heat turned off, the coolness of concrete floors is welcome.

Finish Flooring Materials

The rock ledges of caves and earth beaten down by use were probably the first hard-surface floors. Stones smoothed and set into place represented an improvement, constructed floors of brick, tile, and wood yet a further refinement. Until a century or so ago these were the only possibilities for permanent flooring. Today, many new materials supplement the standard ones. Table 14–1 summarizes briefly the characteristics of finish flooring materials commonly found in contemporary homes. Compared with carpeting, almost all are durable, cool, either hard or moderately resilient, more or less stain-resistant, and easy to clean with water. But these general similarities should not obscure the equally important differences in appearance and behavior among them.

Hard Floors

Hard-surface flooring materials are remarkably durable and ageless in their versatility; high initial cost and lack of resilience are their chief drawbacks. Hard floors of masonry materials or wood are used throughout today's homes.

Masonry Stone, brick, and ceramic tile have a high original cost but last for generations, indoors or outdoors. Stone floors of slate, marble, or other composition can produce almost any effect, from the very rugged to the coolly formal, depending upon how the stones are cut, set, and finished. Irregularly cut and unpolished stones placed in random patterns tend to be more casual than identical polished stones set close together in an even configuration. Unglazed red bricks seem especially suited to kitchens and bathrooms, because of their natural, domestic quality. However, unless sealed, they will absorb grease and stains that are difficult to remove.

The popularity of ceramic tiles for flooring has persisted through many centuries and remains high today, despite the introduction of newer materials. In fact, many types of vinyl tile and sheet vinyl imitate clay-tile flooring as well as stone and brick. The classic terra-cotta red quarry tiles nearly always create a warm earthy effect. Their durability permits the same tiles to surface and unite indoor and outdoor spaces. On the other hand, small glazed tiles can be as elegant as the most sumptuous marble floors. Ceramic tiles come in many sizes and shapes— square, oblong, hexagonal, octagonal, round, and fluted, for use alone or in combination. Glazing provides an impervious finish that resists stains, but also makes dust and soil more noticeable.

below: 14-5 Large clay tiles set in a brick pattern contribute to the casual country style of a kitchen and dining room. Hank Bruce, architect. (Photograph: Philip L. Molten)

above: 14-4 Slate may be broken irregularly or cut precisely into shapes, left unfinished or given a sheen for floors with distinctly different characters. In this International-Style home by architect Richard Meier, slate tiles complement the glass, concrete, and brick structure. Fox-Nahem Design, interior designers. (Photograph: Gene Maggio/NYT Pictures)

Table 14–1 Finish Flooring Materials

Material	Source or Composition	Use	Size and Shape	Patterns
Hard				
concrete cost: least expensive flooring; can be both base and finish flooring	cement, sand, aggregates, and water; can be integrally colored	can be left bare; a base for clay, tile, brick, and stone; coverable with wood, resilient flooring, carpets; heat-storage mass	usually poured in slabs but tiles available; at times marked off in rectangles by screeds	exposing aggregates gives surface interest; terrazzo has mosaiclike patterns from marble chips
stone cost: very expensive	slate, flagstone, marble, and so on	chiefly entrances and near fireplaces, but can be used in any room; heat-storage mass	usually not more than 2′ square; rectangular or irregular	natural veining, shapes of stones, and patterns in which they are laid
tile and brick (clay) cost: expensive	heat-hardened clay; tile is usually glazed	areas getting hard wear, moisture, and dirt; entrances, hallways, bathrooms, or any place where effect is wanted; heat-storage mass	tiles are ½″ to 12″ square or rectangular, hexagonal, and so on; standard bricks are 2″ × 4″ × 8″	tile has varied designs; typical brick patterns come from the way in which the bricks are laid
wood (hard) cost: moderately expensive	oak, birch, beech, maple, pecan, teak, walnut; sealable with liquid plastics, finished with synthetics	any room; often covered by carpets	strips 1½″ to 3½″ wide; planks 2″ to 8″ wide; parquet blocks 9″ × 9″ and so on	color and grain of wood; usually laid in parallel strips; also blocks of varied parquetry patterns
Resilient				
asphalt tiles cost: least expensive composition flooring	asbestos or cotton fibers, plasticizers, pigments, and resin binders	recommended for laying over concrete directly on ground, especially in much-used areas	standard is 12″ × 12″ but others available	tiles are plain or marbleized; laying creates typical tile patterns
cork tiles cost: moderately expensive	cork shavings, granules compressed and baked to liquefy natural resins	floors not subject to hard wear, water, grease, stains, or dirt	squares 9″ × 9″ or 12″ × 12″; also rectangles	chunks of cork of different colors give fine to coarse textural patterns
rubber tiles cost: moderately expensive	pure or synthetic rubber and pigments vulcanized under pressure	can be laid directly over on-grade concrete floors	9″ × 9″ to 18″ × 36″	usually plain or marbleized
vinyl-asbestos tiles cost: inexpensive	similar to asphalt but with vinyl plastic resins	any indoor floor including on-grade and below-grade concrete floors	12″ × 12″ tiles are typical	wide range of patterns, printed or embossed
vinyl-cork tiles cost: moderately expensive	same as cork but with vinyl added as a protective sealer	any floor where heavy-duty durability is not important	same as cork	same as cork
vinyl sheets and tiles cost: moderately expensive	vinyl resins, plasticizers, pigments, perhaps cheaper-grade fillers, heat-formed under pressure; sheet vinyl laid on alkali-resistant backing	any indoor floor; special types available for basement floors; also counter tops, wall covering; foam backed for greater resiliency	usually 12″ × 12″ tiles; also by the roll, 6′ to 15′ wide; new types poured on floor for completely seamless installation	great variety, new designs frequent; marbled, flecked, mosaic, sculptured, embossed, veined, and striated
Soft				
carpeting and rugs cost: wide range	almost all natural and manufactured fibers	recommended over any flooring that is moisture-proof	almost unlimited	plain to ornate, structural to applied

Table 14–1 Finish Flooring Materials (*continued*)

Colors	Durability	Maintenance	Comments
Hard			
concrete limited range of low-intensity colors, but can be painted, color-waxed, and so on	very high except that it often cracks and can be chipped; serious damage difficult to repair	markedly easy if sealed against stains and grease; waxing deepens color and gives lustrous surface but is not necessary	hard and noisy; cold (welcome in summer) unless radiantly heated; absorbs and releases heat slowly
stone usually black, grays, and tans; variation in each piece and from one piece to another; marble in wide range of colors	very high but chipping and cracking difficult to repair	easy—minimum sweeping and mopping	solid, permanent, earthy in appearance; usually bold in scale; hard and noisy; cold if floor is not heated; absorbs and releases heat slowly
tile and brick (clay) glazed tiles in all colors; bricks usually red	generally high but depends on hardness of body, glaze; may chip or crack, fairly easy to replace	easy—dusting and washing; unglazed types can be waxed; porous types absorb grease and stains	satisfyingly permanent and architectural in appearance; can relate indoor to outdoor areas; noisy and cold; absorbs and releases heat slowly
wood (hard) light red, yellow, tan, or brown; can be painted any color	high but shows wear; irradiated types very durable	medium high—must be sealed, then usually waxed and polished; irradiated need minimum care	natural beauty, warmth; moderately permanent; easy to refinish; but fairly hard, noisy
Resilient			
asphalt tiles full range of hues, but colors are neutralized; becoming available in lighter, clearer colors	excellent but can be cracked by impact and dented by furniture; some types not grease-proof	moderately easy—mopping and waxing with water-emulsion wax	eight times as hard as rubber tile; noisy; slippery when waxed
cork tiles light to dark brown	moderately high; dented by furniture	not easy; porous surface absorbs dirt, which is hard to dislodge, sweep, wash, and wax	luxurious in appearance; resilient and quiet
rubber tiles unlimited range; often brighter and clearer than in asphalt	moderately high, resistant to denting; some types damaged by grease	average—washing, wax or rubber polish	similar to asphalt, but more resilient
vinyl-asbestos tiles almost unlimited	high general durability, resistant to grease, alkali, and moisture; can be dented by furniture	among the easiest; resilient underlay retards imbedding of dirt	somewhat hard and noisy but more easily kept than asphalt
vinyl-cork tiles same as cork	same as cork, but more resistant to denting, dirt, grease	very easy—sweep, wash, and wax as needed	vinyl makes colors richer; less resilient and not so quiet as cork
vinyl sheets and tiles wide range including light, bright colors; in some, translucency gives depth in color similar to marble	excellent; cuts tend to be self-sealing; resists almost everything including household acids, alkalies, or grease, denting, chipping, and so on	very easy; built-in luster lasts long; foreign matter stays on surface; can be waxed but not always necessary, especially for some types; dirt collects in depressions of embossed types	pleasant satiny surface; quiet and resilient, some types have cushioned inner core; patterns developed from material itself seem better than those imitating other materials
Soft			
carpeting and rugs infinite range of hues, tints, shades alone or in rich designs	depends on fiber (see Table 12–1); surface texture and density	daily spot cleaning, weekly vacuuming, sweeping for Orientals; occasional deep cleaning	appreciated for possible beauty, as well as insulation, comfort, safety, ease of care

above left: 14-6 The varied shapes possible with clay tiles, the many patterns they can assume, help to explain their long and continued history. *(Courtesy Country Floors, Inc.)*

above right: 14-7 When exposed to the sun, dark masonry floors absorb heat that is released slowly to the interior. John Saladino, Inc., architects and interior designers. *(Photograph: © Peter Aaron/ESTO)*

14-8 Wood floors add warmth in color, texture, and pattern to any room. Here different patterns demarcate spaces. David Estreich, architect. *(Photograph: Robert Levin)*

Concrete, as mentioned previously, is usually used as a subflooring material, to be covered with a finish flooring that will provide resilience, sound insulation, warmth, and greater aesthetic appeal. But concrete may take on a completely different quality when colored or textured aggregates are added to the mix.

In spite of the warm or cool appearance of color and texture, all masonry floors are hard and cold unless radiantly heated. In warmer climates, this quality can be an advantage, keeping the house cool even in uncomfortable outdoor temperatures. Masonry materials that are dark and unglazed for maximum heat absorbency use a reverse heat lag to advantage in passive solar homes.

Wood The most popular of the hard flooring materials, wood varies in cost with the type and method of placement. It requires a good deal of day-to-day maintenance but is fairly easy to repair and refinish. Some wood floors must be waxed,

but if the wood has been irradiated or impregnated with polyurethane or similar plastic, it can be cleaned with a damp mop. This type of flooring is high in initial cost but low in maintenance. Less expensive alternatives include surface applications of paint, stain, or clear urethane. Above all, wood has a homelike, enduring character that appeals to many people.

Wood floors generally take one of three forms: narrow, regularly spaced strips of similar-grained wood joined with tongue-and-groove or butt joints; random-width, rough-finished planks typical of barns and country houses; and inlaid squares of alternating grain known as parquet. Most often highly polished, parquet floors follow many different designs and configurations.

Resilient Flooring

Once confined to work spaces and baths, resilient flooring is now seen throughout the home, offering a wide range of visual effects and flexibility underfoot.

Sheet Flooring and Tiles An endless variety of resilient flooring materials, most synthetic but some of natural composition, are now available. Cork and rubber are much more resilient than asphalt, and some of the newer cushioned vinyls have an inner core of foam or foam backing to increase springiness and warmth.

Sheet vinyl comes in rolls 6 to 15 feet wide. It has fewer dirt-catching seams than do tiles of the same material, but usually requires professional installation and is more expensive than tile. The design layer (color and pattern) in sheet vinyl is either printed in a rotogravure process or "inlaid" with tiny chips of vinyl fused together, both of which make the design one of the actual layers comprising the sheet of vinyl. However, the inlaid design is more durable.

Tiles can be installed with less waste if the floor is irregular in outline. They also permit replacement of an area that is subjected to unusual wear. The self-sticking versions enable any handy person to change the character of a floor with little effort. However, the pattern is printed on the surface with ink in one of the final stages of production, limiting some design possibilities.

Resilient flooring offers many choices. Cushioned vinyls are easy on the feet and legs, but they can dent under heavy loads and often have an embossed surface

14-9 Parquet floors with their rich patterns are once again in favor, now that they are available in block form for easy installation. This design is called "Saxony." *(Courtesy Harris Manufacturing Company)*

14-10 "Acclaim," a one-sheet vinyl flooring, requires no adhesive and can be installed by do-it-yourself enthusiasts. *(Courtesy Mannington Mills, Inc.)*

14-11 Vinyl tile can set the stage for bold contrasts or subtle harmonies, traditional patterns or modern graphics in a room. Traditional checkerboard design is at home in this country kitchen. *(Courtesy Azrock Floor Products)*

that can require extra scrubbing to remove soil from the depressed areas. Most vinyls are available with a no-wax surface and a high-gloss or matte finish. Even a no-wax finish will dull in high-traffic areas, however, and requires regular application of a protective dressing. Scratches and stains will show more on a high-gloss finish than on a duller matte finish.

A smooth, level, clean subfloor is necessary beneath vinyl flooring because the finish surface will reveal any bumps, cracks, or holes. A moisture barrier may also be needed to prevent mildew if installed in basements or places where moisture is a problem. If the flooring is laid over an older existing flooring material, it must also be smooth, level, clean, and securely attached.

Superior-quality vinyl is moderately expensive, highly diversified in color and pattern, and probably the nearest approach to the ideal of an attractive, easily maintained, smooth-surface flooring material for high-use areas now available.

Soft Floor Coverings

Soft floor coverings add warmth, texture, resilience, quietness, and visual appeal to floors. As with wallpaper, soft floor coverings give rooms a more intimate, "furnished" look, even with little furniture. Floor textiles explicitly relate the floor to the softness of upholstered furniture, curtained windows, and clothed occupants. With their color, texture, and pattern, they contribute markedly to the character of homes, and, like harder materials, they can alter the apparent size and shape of rooms. Technical advances, together with changing tastes and concepts, have added new possibilities for individual expression.

Types A few definitions will help classify the broad range of soft floor coverings. **Rugs** are made in or cut to standard sizes, have finished or bound edges, and are seldom fastened to the floor. **Carpet** comes by the yard from a roll of carpeting 27

inches to 18 feet or more wide, must be cut (and pieced if necessary) to cover all the floor, and is fastened down. *Broadloom* refers to floor textiles woven on looms more than 36 inches wide. The term does not describe the weave, fiber, color, pattern, or any quality other than width. Rugs, carpets, or a combination of both can be appropriate for different situations. For purposes of this discussion, the word *carpeting* is applied to all soft-surface floor coverings.

Size   Wall-to-wall carpets are one of the best means of unifying a room or of relating several adjacent spaces. Because they do not define special areas within a room, they simplify arranging furniture. If the pattern is quiet and the color muted, they lend an aura of spaciousness. Because they fit a room exactly and are fastened to the floor, carpets give a sense of security and permanency as well as warmth and comfort. Covering a larger area than a typical rug, a carpet is more expensive (except for handwoven rugs), but it is a finished floor covering, eliminating the need for expensive flooring underneath. Maintenance costs and bacterial counts are lower than for resilient flooring that needs constant washing and waxing; but wall-to-wall carpeting must be vacuumed regularly and thoroughly cleaned about once a year to remove embedded soil and stains, which can harm fibers. Carpet cannot be moved to another room or house or turned to equalize wear. Once thought appropriate only for the more formal areas of the home, carpet now appears in all rooms, even the kitchen and bathroom, because of the variety of materials and qualities available. An antimicrobial treatment is even obtainable for carpeting used in areas where the growth of microorganisms can be a problem.

Rugs can be purchased in many sizes and shapes. If they cover the entire floor or most of it, the effect is similar to that of a carpet except that most rugs have a definite pattern that makes them more emphatic. **Area rugs** cover only part of the floor and can hold together a grouping of furniture, defining the space

14-12   In painter Frank Stella's huge living loft wall-to-wall carpeting unifies the space, moving up to cover a central seating platform. Oriental rugs create internal spaces to break up the expanse. *(Photograph: John T. Hill)*

Floors and Stairways   **363**

14-13 A large Oriental rug defines an open area at one end of the open living space in photographer Morley Baer's home. Its handsome, decided design can thus be fully appreciated, much as if it were hanging on a wall. Wurster, Bernardi, and Emmons, architects. *(Photograph: © Morley Baer)*

without enclosing walls in homes with open plans. Rugs can also be small accents calling attention to a special part of the home or protecting sections of the floor subject to hard use and soiling. Small rugs are often called **scatter** or **throw rugs.**

Rugs can be used on top of hard, resilient, or soft flooring materials. Their mobility and cleanability make them particularly useful; they can easily be moved from one room or even one home to another since they are not attached to the floor, and they can be adjusted to spread wear and soil. They are usually (though not necessarily) striking in color, pattern, or texture. Oriental, Indian, Scandinavian, rya, hooked, or braided (Plates 42 and 43, p. 365), and an infinite variety of handwoven rugs add particular character to a room and play a more prominent role in the total room design than a plain floor material.

left: Plate 42 Comforta
ble old-fashioned furnishings, including an Indian
dhurrie rug, offer a striking counterbalance to the
modern interior of a
Greenwich Village pent-
house. Shelton, Stortz,
Mindel & Associates, ar-
chitects. *(Photograph: Bo
Parker)*

below: Plate 43 A huge
braided rug with concen-
tric bands of color provides
the classic floor covering
for this Colonial-style bedroom. The canopy bed and
other antique furnishings,
soft old wallpaper, exposed
beams, and rough-hewn
wood paneling are all in
character. Mr. and Mrs.
James Tyson, designers.
(Photograph: John T. Hill)

left: Plate 44 The treatment of the stairway and dumbwaiter, a major design feature, is echoed in the ceiling supports of a house in Los Angeles. Frank O. Gehry & Associates, architects. *(Photograph: Tim Street-Porter)*

below: Plate 45 In a remodeled 19th-century townhouse in Chicago, a bridge carries the floor across an open stairwell and a flying stair rises up to another level. Chrysalis Corp., architects. *(Photograph: © Karant & Associates, Inc., Barbara Karant)*

A more recent innovation in floor coverings takes the form of **carpet tiles** or **modules,** which have a self-stick backing and can be laid just like their vinyl-surfaced counterparts. They function best as wall-to-wall carpeting, since the edges are not bound, and the tiles are easy to cut to follow the contours of a room. Carpet tiles can be uniform in color and texture; if the pile is sufficiently long, the seams will not show. On the other hand, the 9-inch-square or foot-square tiles readily lend themselves to combination for making patterns. Tiles can be replaced individually when worn or soiled. Seams may separate and lose some adhesive capability if too much water is used in cleaning.

Methods of Construction   Typical carpet-construction processes fall into several categories:

- **Tufting** now accounts for 90 percent of soft floor coverings. In this process, pile yarns are attached to a preconstructed backing by multineedled machines.
- **Weaving** and **knitting** interlock the surface yarns and backing simultaneously. Machine-woven rugs are sometimes subdivided into *Axminster, velvet,* and *Wilton,* according to the type of loom on which they are made. Most Oriental and Indian rugs are woven, usually by hand, as are Navajo and similar tapestry (free-woven) designs and floor cloths.
- **Needlepunched** or **needlebonded** carpetings have a dense web of short fibers punched into a backing, resulting in a feltlike surface. Originally confined to kitchen and indoor-outdoor use—because the polypropylene fibers used resisted liquids and did not dye well—needlepunched carpets, with newer dye and printing techniques, have moved into every part of the house.
- **Flocked** carpeting is made of short, chopped fibers electrostatically embedded in an upright position on a backing fabric to make a very dense plush surface.
- **Hooking,** a hand process related to tufting and needlepunching, calls for pile yarns to be forced through a woven backing. Hooked rugs generally exploit their potential for free use of color and intricate, nonrepetitive designs.
- **Braiding,** too, originated as a hand process. In Colonial times it provided a second life for used garments, sewing remnants, and other fabric scraps, which were braided together (like hair) in strips and the strips sewn together. Today, commercial braided rugs are available; they give a particular warm, homey quality to traditional rooms (Plate 43, p. 365).

Carpet backings, as distinguished from separate padding or cushions, are also important in the life of a carpet and can affect the way it lies on the floor. In many processes, the backing (which is the foundation on which the carpet is constructed) is coated with latex or a similar product to hold the surface yarns securely; other methods will add an extra layer of backing of jute, polypropylene, or latex for greater strength and shape retention. Both techniques help in keeping the carpet flat, prevent it from skidding, and aid in noise control.

Pattern   The pattern in a carpet can result from structure (the size and type of yarn, method of construction, and resulting texture) or from the colors of the fibers and the way they are fabricated, ranging from a tiny, almost imperceptible figure to a striking one-of-a-kind design. Commercially manufactured carpets most often have repetitive designs, because of the exigencies of industrial looming; but this very uniformity can serve as an asset in the room where the floor covering functions as a subdominant feature. Almost invariably a vivid handwoven rug calls attention to itself, becoming the focus of a room.

above: **14-14** Native handwoven rugs often have vivid, spirited designs. In the sitting alcove of this Tacoma, Washington, condominium, an area rug with a dominant but simplified key pattern unifies the major furniture grouping. Moore-Turnbull, architects. (*Photograph: © Morley Baer*)

right: **14-15** Many rugs handwoven by native Americans are highly prized works of art; wall mounting displays them to advantage. David Sellers, architect. (*Photograph: © Robert Perron*)

One special characteristic of rich patterned rugs deserves mention here: their tendency to migrate to the walls. Rya rugs, for example, which are universally marketed as floor coverings in the United States, would never have been used for this purpose in the Scandinavian countries of their origin. So ornate are the patterns—and so intricate the process of weaving them—that the rugs earned a place of honor on the wall. Such is also the case with some beautiful old Navajo rugs.

In recent years great innovations have been made in dyeing and texturizing techniques, so that pattern has become easier to create in industrial carpets. Printing, similar to fabric printing or rotary news printing, is now possible over pile textures with deep penetration of colors. Programmed processes drip and jet dyes onto the face of carpeting to give a brindled effect or draw washes of color. Fibers themselves can be constructed with multiple sides to reflect a shimmering light. Combinations of colors, as many as twenty per carpet—in high or low pile, cut or uncut—result in distinctive patterns. Pattern, whether textured or printed, helps the carpet hide soil, adds interest, and contributes to the character of a room.

Texture   Carpeting can generally be classified in texture as either **cut pile** or uncut **loop pile,** although great variety in effect is achieved by the length of pile as well. Most carpeting made today has some type of pile (the visible surface fibers), from the very low plush of flocking, through uncut loops of varying heights, to the cut pile loops of velvets and the high pile of shags. The size of the yarn and spacing between yarns or *density* of the pile also affects texture. There are several basic carpet textures.

- **Plush** or **velvet** carpet has a dense pile with cut loops of uniform, relatively low height (less than 1 inch). It has a luxurious, smooth surface appropriate for more formal rooms and wears well in moderate traffic areas.
- **Saxony** also has a uniform-height cut loop pile but it is deeper and less dense, often with thicker yarns that have been twisted for extra body. The appearance is nubbier than velvet pile with yarns that seem to flow to the touch.
- **Frieze** is a rough, grainy textured carpet resulting from tightly twisted yarns in a cut pile. It is very good for heavy traffic areas because the tight twist makes the pile very resilient.
- **Splush** has a cut loop pile of a height between plush and shag with a density lower than saxony. It has a more highly textured appearance and is less formal than either velvet or saxony since the yarns tend to lay down more under traffic.
- **Shag** carpet has a cut loop or sometimes a twisted loop pile with a height of more than 1 inch and low density. It is designed to bear the weight of traffic on the sides of the fibers rather than the ends. The longer pile gives shag carpeting a feel similar to plush but it is "shaggy" and very informal in appearance.
- **Tip-sheared** carpet is similar to plush, but not all the loops are cut, creating a subtle pattern of color and texture. Also called *cut and uncut loop* or *random sheared.*
- **Level loop** carpeting has a low uncut loop pile that can stand the heavy wear of a kitchen, bathroom, or activity area. Foam backing gives added resilience and comfort. Level loop construction combined with high density produces the highest grade of commercial carpeting.
- **Multilevel loop** or **sculptured** carpets are produced by combining varied heights of looped pile in a seemingly random or controlled pattern. Some sculptured carpets are tip sheared in addition to having different lengths of pile.
- **Tweed** is both a texture and a pattern. It is similar to level loop but with larger loops and lower density, making it generally less expensive and less resilient.

Tweed carpeting is normally cross-dyed, resulting in tufts of different colors or a "tweed" pattern.

Deep pile carpets offer the potential for complete self-indulgence as few other materials in the home do. They also contribute a feeling of warmth and informality. Flat-surface carpeting generally is confined to the needle-punched indoor-outdoor types or to braided and other handcrafted rugs. Whatever the texture, it strongly affects light reflection, sound absorption, and both visual and tactile sensations of comfort and luxury.

Fibers Many changes have taken place in the manufacture of carpeting during the past two decades. Above all, there has been a great increase in the use of man-made fibers. Fibers affect the cost, cleaning time, and appearance of carpet; many of the synthetic fiber carpets are durable, dirt-resistant, and easy to clean. Moreover, they are less expensive than natural fibers and come in almost any color or texture.

- **Wool** is the traditional carpeting fiber and retains its popularity today because it has so many good qualities and because it appeals to our love of natural materials. It is extremely resilient and long-lasting, takes dyes beautifully, and is resistant to burns (whereas many synthetics will melt if touched by a flame and retain a permanent scar). A blend of 70 percent wool and 30 percent nylon is often used in areas such as hotels with very hard, continuous wear. Wool needs mothproofing and some people are allergic to it, but it remains the standard by which all man-made fibers are judged for appearance and hand. Wool is the only natural fiber used to any extent in mass-produced carpeting. Costs vary tremendously but all are quite expensive. Many handmade rugs use wool as well. Antique Oriental rugs are regarded as art objects and financial investments.
- **Nylon** accounts for over 80 percent of carpet sales and is the most popular synthetic fiber for its endurance, easy maintenance, and resistance to insects. It is resilient and nonallergenic. New treatments counteract its tendency to pilling and static electricity. Common brand names are Antron, Cumuloft, 501, Anso, or often just Nylon.
- **Polyester** is second to nylon in popularity and is less expensive and softer. It has a wool-like hand, wears very well, cleans easily and resists soiling, dyes well, and is *naturally* almost static-free. However, polyester is resilient only when the pile is dense. Appearance may not be as good after cleaning, and it stains. Labels range from Dacron, Fortrel, and Kodel to various generic names.
- **Acrylic** is the most wool-like of the man-made fibers, is nonallergenic and easily spot-cleaned. It wears well, dyes well (takes brighter, truer color than wool), and is very resilient. Yarns must meet flammability standards, particularly for commercial use. Trade names include Orlon, Zefran, and Acrilan.
- **Olefin** (polyethylene and polypropylene) is growing in popularity because of its low cost and near-indestructibility. It wears and cleans exceptionally well, does not fade, has low static-electricity build-up, and will not absorb moisture. It has little resilience but is often found in indoor-outdoor types of needle-punched carpet and tiles as well as in indoor pile carpeting. Herculon is a common brand name, but the fibers may be offered as generic names.
- **Cellulosic fibers** sometimes used as floor coverings include **jute, sisal, hemp,** and **various grasses.** Available in both pile and woven designs, they make cool and inexpensive floor coverings well suited to today's natural look. They usually have an unobtrusive pattern resulting from the weave and the way the sections are assembled, although they can be quite fanciful in design. They are

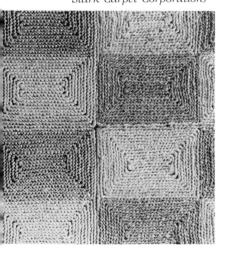

14-16 Although stitched together, carpet tiles are individually constructed so that they may be cut apart, replaced, and generally treated like tile. This maize floor covering has a dark-and-light checkerboard pattern. *(Courtesy Stark Carpet Corporation)*

flammable and can harbor insects, and they are not very durable. However, in some parts of the world, particularly tropical regions, grassy materials are basic for floor coverings. *Tatami* or grass mats take the place of carpets in traditional Japanese homes, for example.

- **Cotton** and **linen** frequently appear in flat-woven rugs. While not as durable as wool, these natural materials can contribute special qualities, such as intense color and a soft, hand-loomed effect. Cotton or linen carpeting is also less expensive than wool and easier to clean. Cotton carpeting has little resilience and sheds (lints) excessively, however. Cotton dhurries from India, rag rugs, and floor cloths with handpainted designs are popular area rugs.

New fibers and combinations of fibers, techniques, and finishes are constantly appearing, so it is important to find out as much as possible about a carpet's specific fiber and processing before deciding on a purchase.

Installation   Carpet may be professionally installed by one of two methods. Either it is stretched between pretacked strips that have been attached at the perimeter of the room, or it is glued directly to the floor. In the first method, a pad or cushion is also installed beneath the carpeting for comfort, 50 percent or more longer carpet life, and insulation. Carpet padding is made from natural fibers such as jute and hair felted together or from foam or sponge rubber. Natural fibers will mildew and mat down while rubber will disintegrate in time, but rubber is initially more resilient and resists moisture better. The pad can be too thick, causing installation problems, breakdown of the carpet backing, and track marks and fatigue from the trampoline effect of walking on it. Generally, rubber pads should not exceed ½ inch in thickness and, if the pad is dense, ¼ inch may suffice. If measured by ounces per square yard, a 40-ounce pad is recommended for most residential use. Twice the padding may be needed on stair treads because of the tremendous wear on the edges. For glue-down installations, foam-backed carpeting provides some cushion.

Measuring and Estimating   Measuring the floor to determine the amount of any finish flooring material needed is a job for a professional. However, a rough estimate can be obtained by figuring the area of the space, dividing by 9 to convert square feet to square yards, and adding up to 10 percent if carpet must be pieced or patterns must be matched. This method will result in more waste when a plain design or a very small pattern is chosen than when a larger pattern is used but will allow for the excess needed to piece with carpet nap all flowing in the same direction. A more accurate method involves using graph paper to plot the exact location of all seams and pattern repeats.

Selection

The matter of choosing suitable floor materials deserves careful planning, especially in view of the size of the areas involved, the probable cost, the long-term consequences, and the numerous possibilities hardly dreamed of a generation ago. Some of the important factors to consider are these:

- **Durability** is of primary importance, because floors take severe punishment from the abrasion of feet and the weight and possible movement of furniture. Durable floors have a surface sufficiently tough to prevent wearing through to another material. They do not crack, splinter, or disintegrate, nor do they become permanently indented or otherwise make noticeable the hard use they get. In pile carpets, density of pile is of primary importance: the more tufts per square inch, the longer the life of the rug. Length of pile is also important, because carpets with high pile last longer than those with short pile. The backing should be strong and flexible, tightly woven, and capable of holding the tufts securely. In flat-woven rugs, the fibers and thickness plus tightness of yarn and weave prolong usefulness.

- **Economy of upkeep** allows us to enjoy the atttractiveness of flooring materials. Upkeep is lessened when floor materials resist stains and bleaches, do not absorb liquids or dirt. Camouflage patterns and neutralized colors near middle value reduce labor, regardless of the material or surface texture. Floor areas without jogs or crevices are easier to sweep, vacuum, or mop than those of complicated shape. And, somewhat surprisingly, tests indicate that carpeted floors take less labor to maintain than those with hard surfaces.
- **Resilience** cushions impact, thereby reducing foot fatigue, breakage, and the noise produced when we move around.
- **Warmth,** actual and apparent, is welcome in all but excessively hot climates. There are three ways to make floors *actually* warm: putting the heating elements in the floor, having the heat in the ceiling so that the floor will be warmed by radiation, and insulating the floor. There are also three characteristics that make floors *look* warm: warm hues, middle to dark values, and soft textures.

above: 14-17 Truly an art form, "Le Soleil Couchant," a rug designed by Charles Gwathmey for V'Soske, is available in a limited edition, signed by the artist. The bold abstract design was inspired by an aerial view of the American landscape.

right: 14-18 Persian, Indian, and Oriental rugs, handmade for centuries in traditional patterns, may be valued as collector's items or selected for their coloration. *(Courtesy Doris Leslie Blau, Inc.)*

- **Light reflection** is generally associated with ceilings and walls, but much light hits floors both day and night. The more light floors reflect, the brighter the home will be and the lower the utility bills. Part of the reason a room seems bright and open may be the degree of light reflectance from the flooring.
- **Sound absorption,** as differentiated from the noise reduction that comes from resilience, relates to muffling of sounds at the point of origin. Especially in large apartment buildings, the use of sufficient sound-insulating material between the floor of one apartment and the ceiling of the next beneath is desired. Within each home, flooring of soft, porous materials helps to absorb the sound of footsteps and of things being moved across the floor. Carpeting, the thicker the better, makes the most efficient kind of sound insulator. In some instances, this has led to the use of carpeting on walls, to further reduce the almost constant noises of the city or perhaps of neighbors and the household itself.
- **Appearance** depends on appropriateness to specific situations and on the individual tastes of the household. Many people overlook the strategic potential of floors as sources of personalized aesthetic expression and satisfaction. Floors can be keyed up or subordinated; can alter drastically the apparent size, shape, and character of a room; can suggest division of space without walls, unifying or demarcating various sections of the home.

Obviously, these are broad generalizations to which we could point out many exceptions. For example, durability and economy of upkeep are vastly more critical in a kitchen or a family room than in a study, where appearance might be more significant. These factors also set up conflicts, for there is as yet no one flooring material that is perfect in every respect. Thus, once again, it is only sensible to decide what is most important and to make such compromises as are necessary.

The design of floors and floor coverings can seem very complicated, since there are so many variations available. It is easy to see from the examples reproduced in this chapter and elsewhere in the book how important a role floor treatment plays in establishing the character of a home.

Stairways

If we think of stairs as physical entities, they are a series of steadily rising small pieces of flooring. Visually, stairs belong to walls; they become part of the wall if set against it, or act as dividers—a wall function—if they are free-standing. The basic stair consists of a straight set of risers (vertical increments), attached to a wall on one side and supported by another wall opposite; the latter may go all the way to the ceiling or end in a simple railing or balustrade for protection. But architects always have been fascinated by the inherent sculptural possibilities of stairs (Plates 44 and 45, p. 366).

Some of the delight possible in a free-standing staircase is apparent in Figure 14-19. Here a wood stairway, reduced to its simple elements—treads, risers, supports, and protective railing—curves down in a dramatic spiral from the upper floor.

The balustrade on the staircase in Plate 44, p. 366, states the design theme of the house. Sturdy and refreshing, the upright banisters echo the exposed studs overhead, and carry on as a protective wall around the living area. The dumb-waiter in one corner fuses the two functions of floors and stairs by bringing the floor up and down to carry heavy parcels to and from the street level.

14-19 The "snail" stair-case in a town house restored by Henry Smith-Miller provides the perfect setting for a pair of high-backed chairs. *(Photograph: © Norman McGrath)*

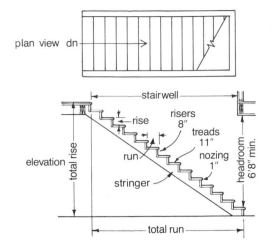

14-20 The sizes of risers and treads are important in planning safe and comfortable stairs.

Design and Construction

Stairs cannot be considered only from the point of view of visual impact. The physical dimensions and their comparative proportions are of the utmost importance for the comfort and safety of those negotiating the stairs (Fig. 14-20). These points should be considered in appraising stairs for use. In general:

- A **tread** deep enough to take the entire sole of the shoe feels most secure. Eleven inches is suggested.
- A **rise** (the vertical measurement between each tread) of no more than 8 inches seems easiest for most people. Some authorities recommend that the sum of the tread and rise be between 17 and 17½ inches.
- Bare treads can be slippery; carpeting provides firmer footage.
- A landing offers a welcome breathing space on long stairs.
- Ample headroom (6 feet 8 inches, minimum) at the top of the staircase is a self-evident safety precaution.
- Variation in the size or spacing of steps (except for well-defined landings) can be a trip hazard.
- Winding stairs may be perilous, especially if the inner edge of the tread is too narrow to accept a firm footstep. A minimum diameter of 48 inches is needed for a spiral stair.
- Some kind of handrail running the length of the stairs is essential for safety. When the household includes a person whose limited eyesight or other physical condition makes stair-climbing precarious, there should be an easily gripped rail on *both* sides of the stairway. Codes require a handrail 32 to 34 inches above the floor (24 inches for children) on at least one side where there are three or more risers. The handrail should be 1¼ to 1½ inches in diameter with a 1½ inch clearance between the wall surface and handrail. In an open railing, the upright supports can be no more than 9 inches apart.

This list of utilitarian considerations may seem confining, but it need not be considered binding for every flight of stairs. When planning a secondary staircase or one that leads to a hideaway area of the house—not to the essential rooms—imagination can have freer rein. In Figure 14-22 the spiral stair rising up to the owner's studio brings a delightful, romantic accent, its curves echoed in the old stained glass window and the bentwood rocker.

In one-story dwellings stairs usually are not a consideration, except for an occasional one- or two-step drop or rise in floor level to define different areas of a

above: 14-21 A twisting stairway of marble and stucco invites immediate exploration in the Palazzo Carignano, built in Turin between 1679 and 1692. Guarino Guarini, Italian architect. *(Photograph: Aschieri)*

right: 14-22 Oak treads and a steel railing spiraling upward to a secluded studio loft bring a playful, delightful contrast to the basic rectangularity of this architectural setting. Fisher-Friedman Associates, architects. *(Photograph: © Morley Baer)*

14-23 A wood stairway follows the curve of a bay window down to a lower floor, making an event of the passage. Dick Whittaker, architect. *(Photograph: Philip L. Molten)*

larger space. Nevertheless, consideration must be given to making these steps both evident and safe for the unwary. Clear definition by furniture arrangement, a low wall or railing, or the placement of large plants and other accents can prevent a twisted ankle or even a broken leg.

Among the most telling aspects of interior design are the treatment of floors, floor coverings, and stairways. Together with walls and ceilings, they give a room or an entire dwelling its basic character and, once established, begin to channel decisions about other steps in home planning. A sympathetic integration of these elements constitutes a major step in creating a personal lifespace.

References for Further Reading

Con, J. M. *Carpets from the Orient.* New York: Universe, 1966.

Eiland, Murray L. *Oriental Rugs: A Comprehensive Study.* Greenwich, CT: New York Graphic Society, 1973.

Faulkner, Sarah. *Planning a Home.* New York: Holt, Rinehart and Winston, 1979. Chap. 7, pp. 149–167.

Formenton, Fabio. *Oriental Rugs and Carpets.* New York: McGraw-Hill, 1972.

Hollister, Uriah S. *The Navajo and His Blanket.* Glorieta, NM: Rio Grande, 1974 reprint.

James, George Wharton. *Indian Blankets and Their Makers.* New York: Dover, 1974 reprint.

Kahlenberg, Mary Hunt and Anthony Berlant. *Navajo Blanket*. New York: Praeger, 1972.

Keough, James G. "Carpeting: The Soft Touch," *Home*, December 1983, pp. 68–74.

Keough, James G. "The Easy Care Option: Vinyl," *Home*, November 1983, pp. 40–45.

Minimum Guidelines and Requirements for Accessible Design. Washington, DC: U.S. Architectural and Transportation Barriers Compliance Board, 1982.

Morgan, Jim. "Building Stone Endures," *Residential Interiors*, July-August 1980, pp. 68–69.

Scobey, Jean. *Rugs and Wall Hangings*. New York: Dial, 1974.

Whiton, Sherrill. *Interior Design and Decoration*, 4th ed. Philadelphia: Lippincott, 1974. Chap. 15.

15

Windows, Window Treatments, and Doors

Windows and doors relate spaces to one another both visually and physically. The "wind's eye" of old was a narrow opening to let out some of the fire's smoke and let in a little fresh air, to help light the room, and to permit peephole glimpses of what was going on outside. Today we think less in terms of one self-contained "inside" standing firm against the forces of nature than of different kinds of spaces, carved by walls, penetrated by windows and doors. The types of window treatments we adopt—curtains, draperies, shutters, shades, blinds, plant screens, or nothing whatever—govern the amount of interrelationship two adjacent spaces will have.

Windows

Of the three functions performed by windows—*ventilation*, *light admission*, and *visual communication*—only the last is unique. Ventilation often can be handled through louvered and shuttered openings, air conditioning, exhaust fans, and other mechanical devices. Electric light is sometimes more convenient and is capable of

more precise control than natural light. But only through transparent windows, doors, and walls can we enjoy a view of the outdoors from protected enclosures. When windows expand to fill large areas of a wall, interior and exterior spaces become closely united. In the house shown in Figure 15-1 a window wall at one end of the huge living room serves as a natural magnet for an intimate seating group. Overlooking a pond and gently rolling hills, the window affords a peaceful view to the outside, the pleasure of which is enhanced by soft textures and muted colors. At night, shutters close off the window and turn the focus inward.

Types

Despite immense variation in the appearance of windows, all can be classified in one of two general categories: **fixed** windows meant essentially for light and views, and **movable** windows that are additionally useful for ventilation. In this century movable windows have predominated, although the popularity of air conditioning and modern concepts in solar architecture have also caused a dramatic rise in the use of fixed glass.

15-1 A bay-window wall in furniture designer Warren Platner's house makes an elegant composition of wall and window elements. The projection of the bay into the landscape gives the visual pleasure of the outdoors, the bodily comforts of the protected interior. *(Photograph: © Ezra Stoller/ESTO)*

15-2 A view of the Connecticut River and an adjacent stand of trees prompted architects Alfredo De Vido Associates to design a high sloped-ceiling living space with a progression of fixed and movable glass openings. *(Photograph: Otto Baitz, Inc.)*

15-3 The parts of a double-hung window.

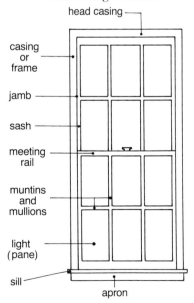

Rather than a strict reliance on either form of window, a combination of movable and fixed glass windows—and of various types of glass—often provides the best solution to climate control in the home from both an aesthetic and an environmental point of view. Fixed and movable windows come in standard sizes and in systems of prefabricated units, which have lowered the cost of acquisition and installation.

Wood and metal are the materials typically used to hold the panes of glass in windows and walls. Metal is stronger (which makes thinner strips possible), does not shrink or swell noticeably, and has a uniform texture harmonious with glass. With the exception of aluminum and stainless steel, metals in windows must be protected by paint; and because all metals conduct heat and cold readily, moisture may condense on the inside of metal sashes in cold weather. Better-quality aluminum windows now utilize a vinyl heat-loss block in the aluminum frame, but steel frames still do not use such a thermal break. Wood shrinks, swells, and requires a protective finish, but it does not encourage condensation. The use of plastic as a material for framing windows is also rising because of the relative stability of many plastics, their imperviousness to heat and cold, and their integral finishes.

The various types of windows are illustrated in Table 15–1. Each type has certain advantages and disadvantages that influence its location, treatment, and also the furniture arrangement nearby.

Table 15-1 Types of Windows

	Advantages	Disadvantages
double hung single hung vertical sliding	sashes slide up and down so they can be opened top and/or bottom for ventilation; weatherproofing is effective; do not get in way of people or curtains; usually taller than wide; seldom warp or sag	only half can be opened at one time; little protection from rain; difficult to clean from inside, unless sash can be removed or pivoted; inconvenient to operate with furniture under them; horizontal meeting rail may interfere with view
horizontal sliding	advantages and disadvantages similar to above, except for horizontal slide; vertical divisions interfere less with view than horizontal often combined with fixed glass to give broader horizontal proportions; furniture can be placed under fixed portion	
casement	panels hinged at one side, swing in or out; whole area can be opened; panels direct breezes, reduce drafts; crank-operated hardware easy to use over furniture	usually fairly small panels, larger may warp; in-swinging interfere with furniture; out-swinging hazardous if at ground level; little protection from rain
awning projected	similar to casement but hinged at top and occasionally at bottom; give precise, draft-free ventilation, block rain or snow	similar to casement, but collect dust when open; look institutional; normally direct air flow above occupied area of room; horizontal divisions interfere with view; hopper (bottom hinged, inward swinging) must be placed low in wall for effective ventilation but interferes with window treatment, furniture, and traffic; inward swinging top hinged window must be placed high in wall
jalousie	similar to awning type but with narrow, unframed slats of glass, plastic, even wood that operate in unison; take little space, and can be made to fit odd shapes; excellent, precise control of ventilation	many small panes difficult to clean and weatherproof; may interfere somewhat with view
fixed glass	free design from constraints of standardized shapes and sizes; need no screens or hardware; easy to wash if accessible; furniture usually stands away from wall, lessening usable space, increasing visual space; unified with wall	hard to control light and heat, and to clean inaccessible areas; attention must be called to glass in some way to prevent collisions

Table 15–1 Types of Windows *(continued)*

	Advantages	Disadvantages
skylight and clerestory	bring light and air into center of house; balance light and remove air efficiently; introduce light from unexpected source to give new dimensions to form and space	difficult to control light and heat; difficult to clean; special hardware needed if operable

Design and Location

Heat and cold, light and ventilation, views and privacy, and furniture arrangement are among the major factors determining window design and placement. Accessibility for cleaning follows closely. Interwoven with these is the larger concern of architectural composition—the relationship of windows to the mass and space of the whole structure and its site.

Heat and Cold

Most colorless, transparent materials are poor insulators. Hence, extreme temperatures will be important factors in window design and placement. By reducing costs for heating and air conditioning, special types of glass, such as double and triple insulating glass and glass that reflects excess solar heat, usually pay for themselves in a few years. Orientation of windows, however, is more important in achieving equable temperatures indoors at the least cost (see Chapter 6).

- Glass facing south brings welcome winter sun but with a properly designed overhang excludes summer sun because then the sun is high in the sky.
- Glass facing east admits the morning sun, cheering in winter and seldom too hot in summer.
- Glass on the west side lets hot afternoon heat deep into the house.
- Glass on the north brings in winter cold.

Undesirably oriented windows necessitate relying on insulating window treatments or on something outside, such as nearby shade trees, vine-covered arbors, very wide overhanging roofs, or awnings. Generally speaking, in terms of heat and cold—and in most parts of the United States—glass on the south is best, followed by that on the east.

Light

Natural light is cheerful; for eyes and spirit, no room can have too much daylight. But it is unfortunately easy to design rooms that seem unpleasantly bright because strong contrasts of light and dark lead to glare. Oddly enough, glare generally comes not from too much light but from *too little light* in the *wrong places*. More light means less glare if the windows are well planned. Until recently, most windows were holes cut out of the wall, and the first thoughts were of getting curtains to "soften" the light. In the best contemporary design, however, large areas of glass seldom cause excessive brightness. Major factors in planning include:

- Light coming from more than one direction minimizes heavy shadows and makes one feel enveloped by light, rather than being caught in a spotlight.

15-4 A huge skylight angling across the raftered ceiling creates a dramatic architectural statement as well as a light source in the living room of architect Ivan Poutiatine's house. The redwood paneling was salvaged from a 70-year-old aqueduct. *(Photograph: Joshua Freiwald)*

- Light entering near the top of a room illumines the ceiling and spreads through the room more than does light penetrating the lower levels.
- Overhangs projecting beyond windows reduce the glare of the sky and mellow light entering a room.
- Windows to the floor will admit less glare if the surfacing material outside does not reflect light unduly. Light-absorbing materials or the shade from trees or trellises help solve this problem.
- In extreme situations it may be necessary to use nonglare glass, which can be clear, smoked, or gold-colored. Some types are also sound- and heatproof, even reflecting.

The lightest elements of a room by day, windows are very dark—almost ominous at night unless they are lighted or curtained, or unless the immediate view outside is illuminated.

Ventilation

The most comfortable ventilation inconspicuously lets stale air out from near the room's top and draftless fresh air in from the floor level. High windows, openable skylights, exhaust fans, or louvered openings above windows accomplish the first, while low windows or ventilators do the second. There are times, though, when we want to feel a breeze sweeping through the house from wide-open doors and windows. Rooms are most quickly aired if the openings are on opposite sides, one of which faces the prevailing winds. Cross ventilation reduces the need for air conditioning, an important energy conservation measure.

Views and Privacy

Large windows often face the best outlook: a view out over a city, into a private garden, or toward a body of water. When such a vista does not occur naturally, perhaps when a solar orientation takes precedence, it is possible to create one with landscaping or interior courtyards or atriums.

Windows facing the street or nearby neighbors offer less privacy both day and night and often are smaller, higher in the wall, or of more opaque materials than those with more desirable views. Otherwise privacy can be achieved by building fences or planting hedges outdoors, by creating an indoor greenhouse window area, and as a last resort by closing off the window with view-blocking fabrics, grilles, or shutters. Nighttime privacy can also be increased somewhat with outdoor lighting, which lessens the contrast between indoors and out, making forms and shadows less noticeable.

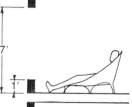

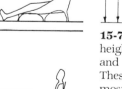

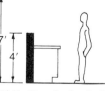

above: 15-5 In remodeling a 19th-century Boston stable the owners were restricted by local ordinances that prohibited altering the facade. The solution came from opening up the interior with sliding glass windows around a private interior courtyard. CBT/Childs Bertman Tseckares and Cassendino, Inc., architects.
top right: 15-6 Greenhouse-style windows admit more light than ordinary windows confined to the vertical plane of a wall. The additional light is conducive to an indoor garden of flowers and greenery which, in turn, provide privacy for residents. Acorn Structures, Inc., architects. (*Photograph: © Robert Perron*)

15-7 Practical windowsill heights vary with room use and furniture arrangement. These three heights meet most needs.

Furniture Arrangement

The location and design of windows and doors largely determines how furniture can be arranged. The more openings the walls have, the harder it is to place furniture. This situation is aggravated if the openings are separated from one another or if windows come below the ordinary table height of 27 to 30 inches. Windows grouped in bands high enough to allow the placement of tables, desks, or sofas beneath them facilitate furniture arrangement that leaves a maximum of usable space open in the center of the room. Of course, skylights and clerestories (windows located very high on the wall) present no problems. In larger rooms or open spaces, the tendency is to group furnishings away from the walls, thus minimizing the influence of windows except when they provide a view. Windows that extend to the floor make indoor and outdoor space seem continuous, but they lose most of their value if heavy furniture must be put beside them. In other words, window walls increase *visual* space but may reduce *usable* space.

Cleaning

All glass needs cleaning occasionally, especially in dusty or sooty locations or where it can be reached by small children and pets. It is easiest to clean when the panes are large, when they can be reached without excessive stooping or climbing, and when they are accessible from outside as well as inside. Clerestories and skylights bring special cleaning problems, often lessened with translucent glass. Indoor access to windows is often controlled by furniture arrangement.

Architectural Composition

So far we have discussed windows in terms of what they can do to make home life more comfortable; however, the architect and designer cannot stop here. Openings today, as in the past, are a vital factor in architectural design, but no single aspect of home planning shows greater change. The general aims and principles of window design still prevail, but the specific patterns are notably different from anything known heretofore. Contemporary trends can be summarized as follows:

- *Fenestration*, the arrangement and design of windows and doors, is considered an integral part of the architectural shell.
- Windows typically are grouped in bands, usually horizontal but with a recent tendency toward vertical strips. When feasible, windows and doors are combined in harmonious units.

15-8 A window wall divided by heavy supports forms a strong geometric composition of simple rectangular shapes. Venturi, Rauch, and Scott Brown, architects. *(Photograph: © Tom Bernard)*

- Architects place large areas of glass where they serve best; small windows are strategically located for balanced lighting and ventilation, with privacy.
- Unity and simplicity of effect result from using as few shapes, sizes, and types as possible, with the tops of windows and doors aligned.
- A less formalized attitude toward the design and placement of windows is also evident, with odd-shaped windows sometimes being set in unusual locations for a forceful design impact.

From an architectural point of view, the design of openings is at least as important as the design of opaque portions of the home. Windows are conspicuous day and night, inside and outside. Their thin, smooth, light-transmitting material contrasts strikingly with what is around it. Beyond these physical characteristics, the fact that enclosed and unenclosed spaces interpenetrate one another through windows and doors endows them with a unique psychological importance.

Window Walls

The act of audaciously opening the home to its surroundings is, in some respects, as significant as the age-old struggle to secure dwellings against the environment (Plate 46, p. 399). Box-tight enclosure has never been completely satisfying, and the urge to combine the paradoxical goals of security and openness has a long, varied history. Walled gardens allowed the early Egyptians, Greeks, and Romans to open part of their homes to the outdoors. In the medieval period, areas of glass large enough to be called "window walls" were introduced. Many houses built fifty or more years ago had sizable "picture windows." Though seemingly revolutionary, window walls represent an evolutionary step toward broader expanses of glass.

Window walls are now standard features even in some tract houses, but many designers and builders fail to understand them completely. A window wall should be thought of not as merely a bigger window but as a different way of planning the house and garden. The dining space in Figure 15-10 gives the illusion

15-9 Many styles of windows are used, sometimes in combination, in postmodern architecture. Pappageorge Haymes Ltd., architects.

15-10 A window-walled bay ensures privacy for diners by setting them up among the treetops for an ever-changing panorama of the seasons. Edward A. Killingsworth, architect; John Hallock, interior designer. *(Photograph: Chuck Crandall)*

Table 15—2 Special Considerations for Window Walls

Problem	Solution
loss of privacy	Choose window wall facing toward private part of property or above sight lines. Build fences or plant hedges. Use curtains and draperies, and potted plants indoors and out.
glare of light	Light should be balanced with windows in other walls or with skylights. Overhanging roof or trellis will help. Plant suitable shade trees nearby. Use glass curtains and hanging plants.
excessive heat or cold	Look for orientation toward south or southeast, insulating glass, overhead protection or trees. Use insulating draperies that can be drawn when necessary.
more glass to clean	No easy solution; use professional window-washer's techniques.
greater quantity of curtaining	Look for window wall placed so that curtains are not essential.
furniture arrangement	Plan room so that major furniture group is related both to window wall and another dominant unit, such as a fireplace.
color schemes	Take account of relationship between colors inside and those seen through the glass.
danger of being mistaken for an open door	Use proper design—a raised sill, obvious supports, or colorful stick-on designs—to indicate physical presence of a window wall. Arrange furniture and/or floor materials indoors and out to steer traffic to a door, not a window.
fading of colors	Choose colors that do not fade or that fade pleasantly. Exclude sun with projecting roof, planting, or curtains.
black and cold at night	Illumine window with lighting trough above it. Light terrace, balcony, or garden outside. Use draperies or reflective glass.
design and maintenance of landscape	Plan at least the immediate landscape architecturally to harmonize with interior; use paving, fixed outdoor furniture, sculpture, and plants that will remain attractive all year with little care.

of being in a treehouse, because the projecting room it occupies is completely walled in glass. Indoors and outdoors are thoroughly integrated, yet the diners remain protected from heat, cold, and insects.

At best, window walls flood rooms with light; at worst they admit glare, heat, or cold. By visually uniting house and landscape, they affect furniture arrangements and color schemes as well as the design of the exterior. It should be remembered that curtains generally make unsatisfactory solutions to the problems offered by window walls, since they defeat the primary purpose by limiting the feeling of openness. Table 15—2 lists several of the difficulties created by window walls and suggests ways of dealing with them.

There are innumerable ways of designing window walls. When they fill an entire wall from floor to ceiling, a minimum break remains between indoors and outdoors. Greenhouse or sun-room windows may constitute both walls and ceiling; they are relatively easy to install and are often included in or added to homes for their solar capabilities. If windows begin above the floor, they leave room for furniture. Window walls may have few divisions or a strong pattern of verticals or horizontals. They can join a room with an extensive view or focus attention on a small enclosed court. Although typically associated with living or dining areas, glass walls can make kitchens or halls expansive. If well planned they are quite feasible in bedrooms—even bathrooms—in almost any part of the United States.

Large windows add to the cost of a home. Glass is expensive to buy and replace, difficult to make weathertight around the edges. It must be cleaned often and is likely to increase heating and cooling bills. Movable glass needs screens and window hardware. Many windows bring the added expense of curtains, draperies, or blinds. But sensibly large, well-placed windows are worth their cost in aesthetic delight and energy savings.

15-11 In a solar home in New Jersey, the large expanse of angled glass forms both wall and ceiling in an emphatic diagonal line. Alfredo De Vido Associates, architects. (*Photograph: © Peter Aaron/ESTO*)

Window Treatments

It is tempting to say that perfectly planned windows need no "treatment," but we would then ignore the great changes in outdoor light and heat and the varying needs of the people inside. Thus, for the sake of *utility*, we often need curtains, draperies, blinds, or shades inside to control the privacy of the home, the amount and kind of light that enters it, and the transmission of heat and cold. From the point of view of *economy*, efficient window treatment can reduce heating and cooling bills, although the fewer accessories used at windows, the more money will be available for other purposes. Whatever is put on the window should be durable; resistant to the ravages of sun, moisture, and moths; and easily maintained.

Beauty comes from the inherent attractiveness of the materials chosen and from the way in which they relate the windows to the whole room. *Character*, here as elsewhere, is less a matter of being "different" than of solving problems well. The architectural design of windows can be changed by remodeling; window replacements are one of the most popular home improvements. But often we use what is there and modify it by way of window treatments that act as *controls* on windows.

Exterior

Too often overlooked, exterior window treatments have one overriding advantage: they provide the most effective climate control without interfering with furniture or taking wall space within the room.

Awnings

Awnings made of weather-resistant fabrics can be adjusted as the weather varies to protect windows from sun, rain, and dirt while casting a soft, pleasant light inside and outside. They come in many designs and colors. Unfortunately, fabric awnings have a relatively short life, since they are subject to fading, soiling, and wind damage. However, they can reduce solar heat gain as much as 65 to 75 percent. Metal awnings, usually aluminum, can either be stationary or roll up. They are higher in initial cost than fabric types but pay for themselves over the years. The major design problem with awnings is making them look like integral parts of the structure rather than afterthoughts.

Shutters

Increasing in popularity today, true shutters temper light, heat, and cold. They also serve to secure houses against marauders or windows against violent storms. More common are the dummy shutters employed to make small windows look larger on pseudo-Colonial houses.

Cutouts and Projecting Elements

Overhanging roofs and trellises are popular exterior shading devices. In addition, they can shelter outdoor living areas and visually relate a house to its site. But they can also control the quantity and quality of light entering the windows. Cutouts are semiopen spaces, missing a wall or two or perhaps a roof, that nevertheless seem an integral part of the structure.

Grilles and Fences

Masonry, wood, plastic, or metal grilles and fences—placed close to windows or some feet away—control privacy, sun, and wind in any degree desired, depending on their design and location. They also add security against invaders when attached to window frames.

Louvers

Ventilating panels of wood, metal, or plastic can be especially effective as sunshades and for weather protection. Normally used over windows, they can take the place of glass completely in very temperate climates.

Interior

Besides the traditional curtains and draperies, interior window treatments include other kinds of controls such as shades, blinds, panels, and shutters. These elements can move sideways or up and down, the latter having the definite advantage of being completely out of the way when not wanted. They are more rigid and archi-

15-12 Adjustable wooden louvers shield the three-story window walls of a Florida house to permit flexible control of the semitropical climatic conditions of bright sun tempered by daily breezes, sometimes heavy rainfall, and high winds. Dwight E. Holmes, architect.

tectural by nature and may be better for certain situations than the traditional "soft" window treatments.

Hard Treatments

Shades **Roller** shades are inexpensive; they may cover part or all of the glass. Shades reduce light and give privacy in relationship to their thickness and translucency or opaqueness. The newer ones are easy to clean and come in many colors, textures, and patterns. A fabric used elsewhere in the room can be laminated onto a plain shade to give unity and individuality. **Gather** shades, while performing in the same manner as roller shades, have a different mechanism for raising and lowering them: **Roman** and **Austrian** shades are attached to tapes that pleat or shir the fabric horizontally when drawn by cords similar to those used on blinds. Roman shades pleat in definite horizontal lines as they are raised while Austrian shades fall in soft, scalloped folds of very lightweight, often sheer fabric.

Bamboo and **woven split-wood** shades function much like those made of fabric, either rolling or pleating as they are raised. They differ in that they usually let more light through, give a better view of the outside, and have pleasantly natural textures and colors.

Transparent or **semi-transparent** shades, made of a mesh material, filter sunlight while remaining visually unobtrusive. They are generally a very narrow

15-13 Roman shades are especially suited to angled windows and complement a crisp, clean look in contemporary design. *(Courtesy Interlübke)*

accordion-pleated shade and are excellent for tempering strong sunlight in greenhouses and sunrooms.

Thermal shades or **window quilts** constructed of multiple layers of insulating fabric, often surrounding a reflective Mylar sheet, are being used effectively to control heat loss or gain. They can also either roll or pleat, but require more space at the top of the window when opened because of their high bulk. Thermal shades are mounted in tracks or otherwise attached along the sides of the window frame to prevent air leakage. They can reduce heat loss/gain by up to nearly 80 percent. Even ordinary shades, if they are made of an impermeable material like vinyl-coated cloth, can cut heat loss through windows by 30 to 35 percent if mounted inside the window casings with a few adjustments to seal the top and bottom of the shade when drawn. Some shades offer a reflective backing that prevents excessive heat gain as well.

The drawbacks of most shades include the fact that, when pulled down, they cut out the light from the top of the window first—and that is the best light, offering the most privacy. Some shades roll from the bottom up, but these interfere with the operation of the window. Shades also block the breeze and may whip around noisily. They have neither the architectural quality of blinds nor the softness of draperies in many cases.

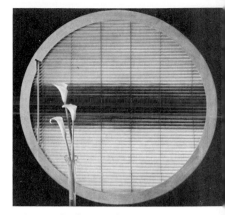

15-14 Blinds may have wood slats that not only lend visual warmth and beauty but also insulate against heat or cold. *(Courtesy Nanik Division of Wausau Metals Corp.)*

above: 15-15 A quilted shade, installed in tracks at either side, provides effective insulation for large glass exposures. Prevention of heat loss during the night is an important advantage. *(Courtesy Appropriate Technology Corporation)*
right: 15-16 Shades for skylights offer flexibility in controlling the amount of light entering the room. Pleated to look like miniblinds, these shades are made of an aluminum-backed Verosol fabric that also provides an effective thermal barrier against heat loss or gain. *(Courtesy Wasco Products Inc.)*

Blinds Colonial homes used Venetian blinds made of wood, but they are available now in metal and plastic as well. Their special advantages include almost complete light and air control—straight into the room, down toward the floor, or up toward the ceiling—as well as complete disappearance behind a valance or other fixture, if desired. Blinds are durable and not expensive. They create pleasing horizontal lines, and the newer **miniblinds** are constructed with very thin slats, causing minimal interference with the view. Blinds can have different colors on each side of the slats; some are available with a heat-reflective surface on one side. They do, however, collect dust and dirt and are somewhat difficult to clean.

Vertical blinds of metal, plastic, or fabric can be shaped easily to fit and unify odd-size openings and can be covered with fabrics or wallpapers to match other surfaces in the room. They control light from side to side, rather than from up or down, and emphasize the height instead of the breadth of windows and walls. Most vertical blinds afford a view directly in front of but not at the ends of a long window area. Newer materials are perforated for transparent effects. Of importance for household maintenance is the fact that the vertical surfaces collect less dust than do horizontal blinds. Vertical blinds may hang loosely from the top like a drapery or slide in tracks (and for long runs they may even be motorized).

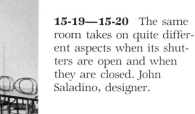

15-19—15-20 The same room takes on quite different aspects when its shutters are open and when they are closed. John Saladino, designer.

above: 15-19 The shutters fold out of sight into piers between the windows. A grouping of plants, by their placement and feathery foliage, softens the incoming light. *(Photograph: John T. Hill)*

right: 15-20 When the shutters are closed, they join the panels beneath to become an interesting wall composition as well as affording privacy and banishing the blackness of night. *(Photograph: John T. Hill)*

Grilles, Screens, and Panels Under certain circumstances—when windows are not well designed, when there is no view, or when privacy becomes necessary—grilles or screens of wood or other materials deserve consideration. With a translucent backing added, they are called *shoji* by the Japanese and they mask windows but allow diffused light to enter. Stained, etched, beveled, and leaded glass panels may also be hung in place of standard window glass or in front of it. They add color, sparkle, and varying degrees of privacy.

Shutters The old-fashioned indoor type of shutters have become popular again. They consist of fixed or movable wood slats or louvers on a framework hinged to the window frame or wall. An architectural window treatment, shutters serve as a unified part of a wall. Because they are usually in hinged sections, shutters open and close off the windows as desired, providing flexible amounts of privacy and light control. Shutters collect dust, but the wood is usually sealed against soil. Although their initial cost is rather high, they last almost indefinitely. For many people they have pleasant associations with the past.

Bare Windows When window design itself or the outward view is truly striking, any added "treatment" becomes superfluous and could even detract from the ef-

fect. Such is the case in Figure 15-21. Sometimes owners and designers make a conscious choice between privacy and openness and opt for the latter. Any curtaining would destroy the drama.

Plants Plants can serve as effective window treatments, filtering but not shutting out light and giving some degree of privacy. The ultimate would be a jungle of live plants in a greenhouse window with temperature and humidity controls that completely block visual communication in and out. Plants are more a soft than hard kind of window treatment but they have been considered here because they leave the glass itself essentially bare.

Soft Treatments: Curtains and Draperies

In addition to flexibly controlling privacy, light, and heat, curtains and draperies soak up noise in proportion to the area they cover, the thickness of the fabric, and the depth of the folds. They make rooms homelike and effectively cover up the bareness of those not completely furnished—a point worth remembering. With curtains and draperies one can change the apparent size, shape, and character of a room (Plates 47 and 48, pp. 399, 400) or conceal architectural awkwardnesses. Small rooms look larger if curtains and draperies blend with and extend the length of the walls; low rooms look higher if draperies go from ceiling to floor. Gloomy rooms seem brighter when gay colors or invigorating patterns are used on windows. Walls chopped up with windows or jogs can be unified by generous glass curtains and draperies, and some eyesores can be completely concealed.

Almost any degree of attention can be directed toward windows by the fabrics selected and the way they are hung. Unpatterned materials similar to the wall color, acting as inconspicuous transitions between opaque walls and clear glass, encourage us to look *through windows*. Moderate color contrasts and patterns direct attention *toward windows*. Bold or unusual colors and designs usually cause us to *look at the draperies* rather than the windows. A few definitions will help to clarify the terminology of "soft" treatment for windows.

- **Curtains** are usually of lightweight, unlined fabric that filters and diffuses light. Curtains are used either alone or under drapery, close to the window.
- **Glass curtains** are of thin, often sheer or semisheer fabrics and hang next to the glass.
- **Sash curtains** are a type of glass curtain hung on the window sash. They can be stretched taut between rods on the top and bottom of window sashes or hung in loose folds. They are often used on doors that contain windows.
- **Draw curtains,** usually of translucent or opaque fabrics, are mounted on traverse rods. In the past, they came between glass curtains and draperies; today they are more often used alone.
- **Casement curtains** are of open-weave fabric usually more opaque than a sheer or glass curtain. They are used in much the same manner as glass curtains.
- **Draperies** are any loosely hung (not stretched) fabric. Thus, the term really includes all curtains. Generally, though, draperies are thought of as heavy, opaque fabrics that can be drawn or that stand idly at the sides of windows purely for decoration. Most draperies should be lined if not used with sheers.
- **Cornices** are rigid horizontal bands several inches wide placed at the window top (or the ceiling) to conceal curtain tops and the rods from which they hang. They are somewhat architectural in feeling and relate window treatment to walls and ceiling. Cornices are often used as part of an energy-efficient window treatment because they are closed at the top, stopping the air flow over the top of the treatment.
- **Lambrequins** are similar to cornices but, in addition to the horizontal member across the window top, they have rigid vertical members on either side of the window. They are very effective in preventing heat loss around windows when used with draperies but they can also be used without curtains or draperies. Lambrequins accent the vertical dimension of the windows and may be covered with fabric or painted as can cornices. Lambrequins have the potential of unifying windows, sometimes altering apparent size, shape, and location when used in conjunction with draperies.
- **Valances** are fabric draped across or covering a rod or shaped form at the top of the window. They may appear similar to cornices but are allied more closely with the drapery than with the wall and are more decorative in nature.

15-23 In a Philadelphia house built in 1840, Empire-style swagged valances draw the eye upward and add a crowning touch. Jean-Patrice Courtaud, designer. *(Photograph: Robert Levin)*

Valances are open at the top and do not serve the energy conservation function of cornices. Different styles of valances may help establish the character of various historical periods during which they were popular.

Glass Curtains Softening and diffusing light, glass curtains temper the hard glitter of window panes and relate them to the rest of the room, as well as giving partial privacy. As a bonus, they also decrease the necessity of keeping windows spotless. Thin curtains come into play when the outlook is unattractive or when the household desires some privacy during the day. Any fabric that hangs well and withstands sun, washing, or cleaning is suitable. Lightweight, sheer fabrics are most often used.

Glass curtains make one somewhat unique visual contribution; they bring light into the room *through* color and pattern. *Color* is especially important, because the light filtering through glass curtains will take on their color, thus tinting the whole room. Also, glass curtains are conspicuous from the outside. Therefore, they are usually a neutral light color and, for exterior harmony, identical or very similar in all rooms. They can, however, be pink or yellow to warm a cool room or pale green, blue, or lavender to cool a hot one. Although customarily plain, suitable fabrics are available with woven or printed patterns, which are useful in rooms that need interest at the windows without adding draw curtains or draperies.

If combined with draperies, glass curtains usually hang inside the window frame, close to it and the glass. Used alone, they can be hung outside the frame and cover two or more grouped windows with a unifying film. Sometimes two or more sets of glass curtains are hung in the *café* or *tier* manner to emphasize horizontality or give privacy without always reducing light from the window tops.

Draw Curtains and Draperies *Flexible* control of light, temperature, and privacy are the primary functional purposes of curtains and draperies that slide on rods. Often they are used alone, and then they take over all the aesthetic functions of window treatment as well. Draw curtains and draperies differ from glass curtains in that they do not veil the view; they either block or expose it.

Fabrics used for draw curtains need sufficient strength, durability, and flexibility to withstand being pulled back and forth and to hang gracefully when stretched or pulled together. The choice of material is wide, ranging from bedding through dress and upholstery fabrics to bamboo and woven wood. (Fabrics to avoid in strong sunlight are described in Chapter 12.)

Appropriateness to the home and its occupants is the primary criterion for *color* and *pattern*. Draw curtains are least noticeable when related to the walls. They become more conspicuous if they repeat or echo the color and character of such large units as furniture or floor, make emphatic statements when they contrast strongly with the rest of the room. If a variety of colors and patterns are used throughout the house, all curtains and draperies should be lined with the same color to unify their appearance from the exterior. Linings also prevent fading, provide extra insulation, absorb dust coming through the windows, protect from sun deterioration, and add fullness and weight that contribute to the appearance. Insulated and reflective linings provide even greater temperature control.

Color, chiefly color value, is typically the most noticeable quality of curtains; very dark curtains against a light wall (or vice versa) stand out sharply. Scale and character come next: large-scale patterns with vivid contrasts or those that differ from other large areas in the room become dominant. It is a matter of deciding what degree of dominance or subordination, harmony or contrast, will be most appropriate.

15-24 A glazed cotton fabric with a sprightly naturalistic design has been used as wall covering, chair upholstery, bedspread, and bed and window draperies, turning a bedroom into a delightful bower. *(Courtesy Schumacher)*

above left: 15-25 Draw draperies accentuate the vertical dimension in a room, particularly when open. CBT/Childs Bertman Tseckares & Casendino Inc., architects.

above right: 15-26 A Patuxent Manor, Maryland (1744) Colonial Georgian bedroom/sitting room features an imposing bed with crewel embroidery draperies. *(Courtesy The Henry Francis du Pont Winterthur Museum)*

Draw or **traverse curtains** are almost invariably most effective and service-able when they hang in straight folds that at least cover all the window frame and begin and stop at sensible points. They fit their setting best when they begin either slightly above the top of the frame or at the ceiling and when they end at the sill, slightly below the bottom of the frame, or near the floor. Usually, the longer draw curtains are the better they work in the room, unless there is a good reason for stopping them short. Also, fuller curtains (from two to three times the width of the space they cover) hang more gracefully. When pulled open, curtains should stack at the side of the window, covering the frame and wall rather than the glass. French or box pleats or shirring takes care of fullness at the top and a generous bottom hem, often weighted for a proper hang, helps them drape well. Exposed decorative rods may be used if they contribute to the total design.

Draperies began their life in the heavy textiles that physically and visually warmed the cold walls of early homes and then migrated from the walls to beds and windows. Today they are still found at windows, and sometimes on four-poster beds or secluding a bed alcove. Occasionally they serve as wall hangings. Draperies differ from draw curtains only in that they tend to be heavier and do not necessarily pull across the opening they guard. They may have a valance, tailored or draped, and sometimes are tied back, evoking an earlier, more romantic era.

left: Plate 46 A window wall is given definition with a stepped placement of tiered panes and mullions. Steven David Ehrlich, architect. *(Photograph: Tim Street-Porter)*

below: Plate 47 Simply hung, translucent curtains veil the view but allow light to enter. Heavier draperies can shut out the blackness and cold of night. Robert Hobbs, interior designer. Ungers & Kiss, architects. *(Photograph: © Karen Bussolini)*

above: Plate 48 Heavy silk draperies amply clothe the wall of a renovated New York apartment, adding luxurious softness. Machado-Silvetti, architects. *(Photograph: © Norman McGrath)*

right: Plate 49 Irregular stone masonry creates a massive, rough-textured surface whose rich, natural colors come to life in sunlight. A Dutch door, painted white, makes a crisp contrast. Wurster, Bernardi, and Emmons, architects. *(Photograph: © Morley Baer)*

400

Measuring and Estimating To compute a rough estimate of the fabric yardage needed for soft window treatments, first measure the width of the window in inches, including any wall space to be covered. Multiply this figure by 2 or 3 to provide adequate fullness (the lighter-weight the fabric, the fuller it should be; unless very heavy, multiply by 3). Divide by the width of the fabric that is to be used and round the answer to the next larger whole number. (Common widths of drapery fabric are 45 and 50 inches.) The result is the number of panels needed.

Next measure the height of the window in inches, including the wall space above and below that will be covered. Add 16 inches to allow for generous hems (4 inches at the top and a double 5-inch hem for weight at the bottom).

The yardage required for the window is the product of the number of panels needed multiplied by the length needed. Divide by 36 to convert inches to yards.

If the fabric chosen is patterned, divide the total length by the vertical repeat dimension and round the answer to the next highest whole number if a fraction results. This yields the number of pattern repeats in a panel. Multiply the number of repeats by the size of one motif to obtain the total length for one panel. The correct number of repeats is more important than the exact yardage because repeats must be precisely matched across all panels of the drapery.

An important element of the architectural shell, windows have gone through many developmental phases, from a slit in the wall to becoming the wall itself. Each stage has brought with it the need for window "treatment," modifications that will make this hole in the wall comfortable as well as appealing. Many such modifications—shutters, curtains, and the like—can be dispensed with if the building has been well designed or if the location, size, shape, and type of windows make them unnecessary. The design factor has become even more important as we have entered an era where we can no longer depend entirely on artificial means of lighting, heating, and cooling our homes. Here we have another example of the great need to think about *all* factors in advance of construction and to solve as many problems as possible architecturally. An ecological approach may well change the aesthetics of architecture.

Doors

Doorways allow us and our vision (as well as light, sounds, smells, breezes, warmth, and cold) to travel in and out of the home and from one room to another. Doors control this travel in varying degrees depending on their location, design, and material. Contemporary doors run the gamut from stout, opaque barriers of wood or metal that shut everything in or out, through sheets of translucent glass or plastic, to transparent glass. Folding doors of wood, bamboo, plastic, or fabrics offer additional possibilities. Further, doors can be designed so that only part of them opens, such as Dutch or barn doors, in which the top can be open but the bottom closed (Plate 49, p. 400). The sliding *shoji* panels—at once walls and doors—of traditional Japanese houses allow a flexibility in design that has had a marked influence on contemporary American architecture.

In rented quarters or in a home already built, less can be done about doors than about windows, but the following are possibilities:

- Remove unneeded doors to create greater openness.
- Seal up or cover with a wall hanging doors that are unnecessary for traffic.
- Refinish doors and their frames so that they blend with the walls.
- Paint some or all doors in contrasting colors or decorate them so that they become dominant features.

Types

As with windows, doors can swing or slide and they can also fold.

Swinging Doors

By far the most common type, swinging doors are hinged at one side, like casement windows. They are widely used because they are easy to operate, have simple hardware, can be made to close automatically with closing devices, and lend themselves to effective weatherproofing, soundproofing, and burglarproofing. Their major disadvantage is that the arc through which they swing must be left free of furniture. *Dutch* doors are divided in half so that the top or bottom half can be opened independently; *French* doors are a pair of wood-framed doors with glass panels.

Sliding Doors

Sliding doors need not take otherwise usable room or wall space when opened and can disappear completely to give a great sense of openness. They do, of course, have to go someplace, often into a wall (*pocket* doors). Or they can slide in front of a wall, which is often done when door and wall are of glass. Although sliding doors can be suspended entirely from overhead tracks, they usually perform better if they also slide along tracks or grooves in the floor (which are hard-to-clean dirt-catchers). On the debit side, the movements required to open and close them are not so easy to make as for swinging doors, and there is no inexpensive way to make a sliding door, especially a screen door, close itself. Exterior sliding doors present problems in both security and insulation. Many sliding doors do not glide so quietly and smoothly as one would wish, and the backs cannot have narrow shelves or hooks, which are especially convenient on closet doors. The fact that they can be very much wider than swinging doors emphasizes horizontality and spaciousness.

15-27 A 13-foot-long sliding door installed on a ceiling-hung track offers flexibility in the use of living space for daytime entertaining or privacy for a den/guest room. Kevin Walz, designer. *(Photograph: Edward Hausner/ NYT Pictures)*

Folding Doors

Sliding along tracks, usually at the top, folding doors open and close like an accordion. They take little space when collapsed and come in diverse colors and textures. In general, they are not so soundproof as other types and sometimes tend to stick, but they are excellent for those situations in which one wants to be able to open or close a large opening inexpensively. Bifold doors are a popular choice for closets because, when opened, they allow full access to interior contents without taking up much floor space.

Functional Aspects

Because doors and windows have so many points in common, almost everything said about locating windows applies to doors, but there are two important differences. Doors govern traffic paths, and they are often opaque.

Traffic paths, like highways, are usually best when short and direct and when they disturb areas for work or quiet relaxation as little as possible. From this point of view a room should have as few doors as is feasible, with necessary ones kept close together if other factors permit, as outlined in Chapter 2.

Furniture arrangement is in part determined by the location of doors, because a traffic path should be left between each pair of doors, and space must be allowed for those that swing. Major furniture groupings should be located away from main entrances and exits but should have two or three access paths to them.

Privacy is controlled by door location and material. In a bedroom, for example, a well-placed door, even when open, should not bring the bed or dressing area into full view. Doors between cooking and dining areas function best when they do not direct attention toward the major kitchen work areas. Opaque materials are typically used where view is nonexistent and privacy always needed. At the entrance, an opaque door insures privacy and provides greater security. Installing a peephole allows occupants to see out without visitors seeing in. Translucent materials serve well where there is neither view nor the need for absolute privacy. Transparent materials allow two-way vision.

Light can come through doors as well as windows, and transparent doors are frequently combined with windows as a means to architectural unity. Glass doors give a special pleasure in that they permit one both to *look* out and to *go* out. Sidelights and transom windows are often used beside and above doors to admit light and permit vision even when the door itself is opaque.

Ventilation can be accomplished quickly by opening doors, especially in opposite walls. There is nothing like opening doors to "air out the house" but ordinary doors are not suited to gentle, controlled venting. In Mediterranean countries, a heavy fabric is hung outside the doorway as a sunscreen and the door is left open for ventilation. Screen doors allow the luxury of cool breezes without the nuisance of insects.

Heat or cold coming through light-transmitting doors has the same characteristics as that coming through windows, and thus the same comments apply. Opaque exterior doors stand somewhere between windows and walls: they do an adequate job of climate control if well weatherproofed and concentrated on the side away from winter winds. Storm doors and two sets of doors, as in the air-chamber entry, also help conserve heat.

Cleaning a glass door is like cleaning a window, except that finger marks are more frequent, and it is easier to get at both sides. Opaque doors, too, get their full share of finger marks, particularly around the knobs. Metal or plastic plates help a little and offer a logical place for ornament. Kick plates may also be used, particularly to protect swinging doors.

Curtaining for glass doors is usually accomplished with draw curtains that can cover or expose the entire area of glass. The best solution locates glass doors where they need never be curtained, but this is not always easy. In older houses, sash curtains are sometimes used on glass doors, especially French doors.

Design

The doors most characteristic of today's design concepts are those as visually simple as possible. This style includes plain wood doors in which plywood sheathes a strong but light core, as well as doors of metal, glass, or plastic framed unobtrusively with metal, plastic, or wood. Many units that are little more than sheets of glass function as both windows and doors, calling attention not to themselves but to what they reveal. However, large transparent doors should be made from safety glass and must be so designed or marked that a closed door is obvious from both sides. Folding doors of wood, bamboo slats, or fabric-covered frames can provide some visual interest with their textures and patterns.

Paralleling this taste for simplicity is the still-popular concept of doors as accents. Even without unusual shape, size, or scale a door can serve as a point of emphasis and visual enrichment in the home. French doors composed of fairly small rectangular panels of glass have returned to popularity. The classic wood-paneled door seems just as comfortable in many contemporary homes as it did in the nineteenth-century manor house, and salvage companies do a thriving business in selling old doors to be recycled for new applications.

above: 15-28 French doors, combined with matching windows on either side, create a bright, cheerful space for dining in a country garden atmosphere. Snezana Grosfeld of Litchfield-Grosfeld, architect. *(Photograph: © Norman McGrath)*

right: 15-29 A beautiful leaded-glass door, preserved when the house it occupies was remodeled, maintains a continuity with the past yet seems comfortable in its new setting. Don Konz, designer. *(Photograph: Hedrich Blessing)*

The location and design of windows and doors are fundamentals in home planning, and they deserve far more thought than they often get. In many historic houses these elements gave architects and craftsmen a unique opportunity to use their inventiveness in enriching interiors and exteriors. This principle still applies today.

References for Further Reading

Baillie, Sheila and Mabel R. Skjelver. *Graphics for Interior Space*. Lincoln: University of Nebraska Press, 1979. Pp. 164–165.

Bedell, Ben. "Wrapping Up Windows," *Interiors*, September 1979, pp. 107–108, 128.

Breskend, Jean Spiro. "New Windows and Doors Are Energy Savers," *House and Garden*, September 1981, pp. 74–78.

"Energy-Saving Shades," *Better Homes and Gardens*, November 1981, p. 104.

Helsel, Marjorie B. (ed.). *The Interior Designer's Drapery Sketchfile*. New York: Watson-Guptill, 1969.

Ingersoll, John H. (ed.). "Windows: Return to Romantic," *House Beautiful*, September 1982, pp. 51–73.

Marks, Charles and Jack Whedbee. *Drapery Manual, A Designer's Guide to Decorative Window Treatments*, 2nd ed. Augusta, GA: Carole Fabrics, 1978.

Nolan, William L. "Bump-Outs: Bonus Space for Less," *Better Homes and Gardens*, September 1982, pp. 68–71.

Oddo, Sandra. "Energy Answers: How to Save Energy with Window Insulation," *House and Garden*, February 1981, pp. 86–88.

Selecting Windows. University of Illinois at Urbana-Champaign: Small Homes Council–Building Research Council, Circular F11.1, rev. 1984.

Speaking of Windows, University of Illinois at Urbana-Champaign: Small Homes Council–Building Research Council, TN #16, 1984.

Viladas, Pilar. "Through a Glass, Brightly," *Progressive Architecture*, November 1981, pp. 138–143.

Whiton, Sherrill. *Interior Design and Decoration*, 4th ed. Philadelphia: Lippincott, 1974. Chap. 18, pp. 568–585.

Window Planning Principles. University of Illinois at Urbana-Champaign: Small Homes Council–Building Research Council, Circular F11.0, rev. 1984.

16

Lighting

The definition and character of objects and spaces is largely determined by the kind of lighting that makes them visible to us. Strong contrasts of light and dark result when an object is illuminated by small, sharp light sources, less contrast when the light source is broad and diffuse, and almost no contrast when an object is evenly lighted from all sides. When small beams light an object, it will cast hard, sharp, dark shadows; a broad and diffuse light source creates softer shadows; and light coming from more than one direction will cause an object's shadows to be multiple and overlapping. The shape and form of objects and spaces can be emphasized, subordinated, or changed completely in appearance according to the strength, placement, and direction of the light source.

Light is a vital element of design and building that affects not only our perception but also our response to the environment. Contrasts of brightness and darkness can create drama and emphasis but may cause eyestrain; uniform lighting is good for many kinds of work but may be monotonous if used throughout a room. Bright light can be stimulating, low levels of illumination quieting. Warm-colored light tends to be cheerful, cooler light more restful. Working with lighting, the interior designer can influence the mood and atmosphere as well as the aes-

406

thetics of a space while providing functional illumination for the activities that will take place there.

Control of the luminous environment divides into two categories: natural daylight and artificial illumination.

Natural Light

The sun is, of course, our primary source of natural light. It represents wakefulness and warmth and is vital to the health of the human organism, both as our principal source of vitamin D and of **full-spectrum light.** Sunlight contains all visible wavelengths of radiant energy plus invisible infrared (felt as heat) and ultraviolet wavelengths at either end of the band. Current research seems to indicate that a wide variety of health problems may result from lack of full-spectrum light and the absence of ultraviolet light in some artificial light sources.

Both energy costs and health concerns have led to renewed interest in natural lighting. The direct radiant energy of the sun, daylight, is a determining factor in the design of homes, especially when large wall areas have been devoted to glass to capture solar heat, light, or a view. Large window areas provide more even, glareless light distribution than small windows oriented toward bright sunlight. However, strong light emanating from a single side of a room creates harsh shadows if not balanced by light from other directions, and may blank out the faces of people, or the details of objects, facing into the room. To distribute light more evenly throughout the space, careful window design and placement are important. Although discussed in Chapter 15, some reiteration is warranted here. More light reflection throughout a room with less glare is gained from windows located high in the wall than from lower positions. At the same time, high windows do not sacrifice wall space or privacy. Natural light can be admitted to interior rooms and private spaces perhaps otherwise inaccessible when clerestory windows, skylights, and inner courtyards or atriums are planned. Room size and shape should be designed so that no floor area is more than one and one half times the ceiling height away from the window wall.[1] Glass partitions between inner spaces, light reflective colors (especially on walls opposite windows), and mirrors all increase the availability of natural lighting as well.

16-1—16-2 Before and after photographs of a 1930s shingled cottage transformed into a more high-style vacation home on the New England coast clearly illustrate the effect of window size and placement. Charles A. Farrell of Short and Ford, architect.
below left: 16-1 Originally the living room was dark and restricted, and the second floor contained undefined loft space. The single small window in the west-facing door was a source of glare. *(Photograph: Charles A. Farrell)*
below right: 16-2 The renovation extended the west wall of the living room into an existing porch and removed the second floor extending the space up to the existing roof structure. The new light-filled room has more even natural light with less glare. *(Photograph: © Sam Sweezy)*

In many cases, the designer's task is not to maximize the effects of natural lighting but to modify, regulate, and redirect or otherwise control it. Direct sunlight can produce discomfort: too much heat or glare because of excessive contrast with an otherwise dim interior. It can also cause fabrics to deteriorate and colors to fade. (Many ways to temper and diffuse natural light entering the home were examined in detail in Chapter 15.)

Natural light is a calendar of passing time; its qualities change throughout the day and are affected by the direction from which it is admitted into the home. *North light* is cool and steady, with few shifting shadows, making it desirable for artists' studios and workrooms. Its revealing harshness may be mellowed with warm colors. *East light* signals the first approach of a new day with light that is initially tinged with reddish orange like a pale sunrise. It then progresses from bright to neutral as the day continues. It may be cheery, warm, and desirable to early risers in the household, while others may want to block its admittance. *South light* seems warm and constantly shifts direction throughout the day. It may need to be tempered, especially during the summer months. Its flat brightness may be counteracted with cool colors, and deciduous trees help diffuse the light and reduce heat gain in summer. *West light* may be very warm and rich, particularly in the late afternoon, making control necessary, from the exterior (trees, shrubs, awnings, or trellises) or the interior (blinds, curtains, shades, or shutters), or the glass itself may be tinted to filter the light. Cool colors in the interior will help also.

Plate 50 (p. 417) shows one way in which natural light can be brought into a house without overwhelming it. Located near the beach, where glare can be a problem one day, fog the next, the house has been sited among trees that temper but do not obstruct the ample light coming through large windows and skylights. Another kind of natural light, that from burning logs, flickers in the fireplace.

For untold ages people depended on the flames of fireplaces, candles, or oil lamps to illuminate their homes at night. Today we seldom limit ourselves to flame light, except occasionally from candles and fireplaces indoors, barbecues and torches outdoors. Although inefficient, all give a warm, flickering, flattering light that seems hospitable, even festive.

16-3 Both natural and artificial light are provided by a skylight above the sapling-and-log ceiling in this dining room. Maurice J. Nespor & Associates, architects; Diana Cunningham, interior designer. (Photograph: Hyde Flippo)

Artificial Lighting

Well-planned artificial illumination enables us to see without strain and helps to prevent accidents. But above all, it makes a vital contribution to the attractiveness of our homes. At night, much of a room's character is determined by its illumination. Even more than color, varying light can make rooms seem to shrink or expand, become intimate or formal. Important objects can be spotlighted, those of lesser interest deemphasized. And with the equipment available today, all this can be changed instantly by flicking switches or turning dimmers. When it is planned in relation to architecture, furnishings, and people, lighting can do far more than merely enable us to see. It is one of the most versatile aspects of home planning and powerfully affects our feelings.

In lighting our homes, we can learn much from theaters, aquariums, museums, stores, factories, and restaurants. Theaters have long exploited lighting as a vital part of dramatic production. Houselights lower, footlights come on as the curtains part, and from then on lights of all colors, brightnesses, degrees of sharpness and diffusion focus attention where it is wanted and underscore the mood of the play. Aquariums concentrate light on the fish, leaving spectators just enough lighting to let them see around, a practice sometimes also followed in museums to

16-4—16-6 Varied levels of indoor lighting can change the mood of a room dramatically. Marlene Rothkin Vine and David Vine, designers. *(Photographs: David Vine)*
above right: 16-4 Natural daylight streams in through windows and a skylight for an overall cheerful effect.
below left: 16-5 General artificial illumination brightens every corner of the room to produce a mood suitable for group entertainment.
below right: 16-6 Subdued night lighting from lamps and the fireplace creates intimate "pockets" of light while leaving the corners in shadow.

rivet attention on a few things. At the opposite extreme are factories, laboratories, and offices flooded with bright illumination everywhere to benefit production. Restaurants range from floodlighted and spotlighted lunchrooms to dark caverns with a candle on each table and gypsy music to reassure or unnerve you, according to your mood.

Our source of energy for artificial illumination is electricity. Electrical energy must be changed into another form of energy, visible light. The rate of change is expressed as *wattage*, the amount of power delivered to an electric fixture or appliance as a result of *volts* (pressure or potential energy available) times *amps* (rate of flow of electric current). The standard voltage supplied for home lighting is 120 volts. Fuses and circuit breakers prevent excessive amounts of current from flowing through wires and possibly causing a fire. The total watts of power used by a group of appliances and/or light fixtures cannot exceed volts times amps without blowing a fuse or tripping a circuit breaker, stopping the flow of electricity as a safety measure.

Light Sources

Lamps (or light bulbs, as they are commonly called) come in a wide range of types, sizes, colors, and shapes designed for an equal variety of purposes and effects. Selection may be made based upon energy consumption, efficiency, length of life/hours of expected service, quantity of light produced, or its qualities—color, shape, brightness, and functional, decorative, or psychological effects. General characteristics, advantages, and disadvantages of each type will be discussed along with the method of producing the light itself.

Incandescent Sources

Incandescent light is produced by heating any material (but usually metal) to a temperature at which it glows. Typical incandescent lamps have a tungsten filament in a sealed glass bulb. These lamps are available in many varieties and offer several advantages over other sources:

- Fixtures and lamps cost less.
- There is no flicker or hum and less likelihood of interference with radio or television reception.
- Textures and forms are emphasized because the light comes from a relatively small "point" source.
- The light is warm in color and flattering to skin tones.
- Control over quantity is made easy by the great variety of wattages available and by the use of dimmer switches.

The **tungsten filament lamp** has been the most common source of light for residential interiors since it was first produced at the beginning of the twentieth century. However, it has several disadvantages:

- It has a low *efficacy* or efficiency in terms of producing light in relation to the amount of energy consumed. Efficacy also declines over the life of standard incandescent lamps. Low-wattage lamps are less efficient than those of higher wattages.
- A considerable amount of heat is generated at the same time light is produced.
- The warm-colored light grays cool colors.
- Lamps have a short life expectancy (750-1000 hours). "Long-life" lamps last up to 2500 hours but at the cost of much lower efficacy.
- Exposed lamps can be an uncomfortable source of glare.

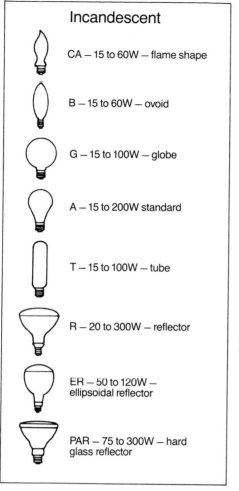

Incandescent

CA — 15 to 60W — flame shape

B — 15 to 60W — ovoid

G — 15 to 100W — globe

A — 15 to 200W standard

T — 15 to 100W — tube

R — 20 to 300W — reflector

ER — 50 to 120W — ellipsoidal reflector

PAR — 75 to 300W — hard glass reflector

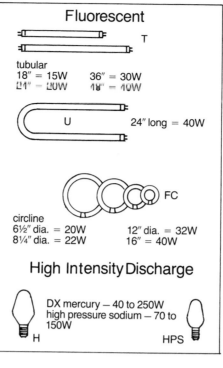

Fluorescent

T

tubular
18″ = 15W   36″ = 30W
24″ = 20W   48″ = 40W

U

24″ long = 40W

FC

circline
6½″ dia. = 20W   12″ dia. = 32W
8¼″ dia. = 22W   16″ = 40W

High Intensity Discharge

DX mercury — 40 to 250W
high pressure sodium — 70 to 150W

H

HPS

left: 16-7 Incandescent lamps are available in many sizes and shapes for a variety of uses. *(Adapted from American Home Lighting Institute)*
above: 16-8 Although available in less variety than incandescents, fluorescent and high intensity discharge lamps are more energy-efficient. *(Adapted from American Home Lighting Institute)*

There are many classes of incandescent lamps designed for specific uses and features. A few warrant mentioning. The **standard,** most-used are the A and PS shapes (arbitrary and pear-shape). There are also a variety of **decorative** shapes: G (globe), GT (globe-tubular or chimney), C (conical), T (tubular), and F (flame). These letters are used to identify and order lamps.

Reflector lamps have built-in reflectors and come in two types. The R (reflector) lamp is less expensive and lighter in weight than the PAR (parabolic aluminized reflector), which can be more accurately focused as a spotlight because of its lens. Either can supply floodlight.

Multiple-filament or three-way lamps have the built-in flexibility of three light intensities. They contain two filaments; either or both can be burned at one time for varied levels of light without the need for a dimmer. They are relatively expensive and, with the development of inexpensive dimmer switches, are becoming obsolete.

Low-voltage lamps are designed to operate at 6 to 75 volts rather than at the standard 120 V. The most popular ones operate on either 6 or 12 volts. They require a transformer to step down standard voltage. Low-voltage PAR lamps are very small and can project a brilliant, precise "pin spot" of light a great distance without "spilling" onto surrounding surfaces. They are excellent where space is limited and for highlighting special accessories. Low-voltage lamps also generate less heat than standard sources.

Tungsten-halogen lamps produce up to 20 percent more light than standard lamps because the halogen gases inside regenerate the filament and keep the lamp clean so the bulb is less blackened over time and the lamp has a longer life. They can also be quite small because the very hard, often quartz, glass used for the bulb will not crack when placed close to the hot filament.

Electric Discharge Sources

The family of electric or gaseous discharge lamps produce light by passing an electric current or arc through a gas vapor sealed inside a glass tube or bulb. They are filled with different gases, some kept at low pressure and others at high pressure. The spectral distribution of electric discharge lamps tends to be uneven or discontinuous, which affects their ability to produce certain reflected colors and may be detrimental to good health unless balanced with other full-spectrum light sources. All of these lamps require that a *ballast* be installed between the power line and the lamp to regulate the amount of electric current used in their operation and provide the proper starting voltage. The light produced is "cold" or *luminescent* (not produced by heat).

Low-Pressure Electric Discharge Lamps   **Fluorescent** lamps, introduced in 1939, are the most common luminescent light source used in homes. The glass tube is filled with vaporized mercury and argon under low pressure. When electric current activates the gases, invisible ultraviolet light rays are produced. The inside of the tube is coated with phosphors that "fluoresce" or transform the ultraviolet rays into visible light. Although fluorescent lamps vary less in size, shape, and wattage than do incandescent lamps, they have a considerable diversity. The most commonly used are the T12 lamps—tubular, approximately 1½ inches in diameter, ranging in length from 2 to 8 feet with the 2- and 4-foot lengths most used in homes. (The longer tubes are more efficient but difficult for homeowners to transport and install.) The advantages of fluorescent lighting are:

- Tubes last ten to fifteen times longer than incandescent lamps (three to six years) and produce about four times as much light per watt, conserving energy.
- Almost no heat is produced.
- The light source is considerably larger, which spreads the light more and produces less glare.

The deluxe colors (cool white deluxe and warm white deluxe) are more spectrally balanced than other colors. The color of the light is controlled by the chemical mix of the phosphors coating the tube. The deluxe colors are warmer in tone with warm white deluxe being closest to incandescent light. Although they have a lower efficacy than other fluorescent lamps, their better color rendition makes them desirable.

Fluorescent lamps are classified by one of three starting methods. *Preheat* lamps are the oldest types; they are the slowest to start. *Instant-start* lamps are the quickest; they start without any delay, but are slightly more expensive to operate. The most recently developed and the most widely used type is the *rapid-start* lamp. It is a compromise in starting speed but uses a smaller, more efficient ballast than a comparable instant-start lamp and is the only fluorescent lamp that can be electrically dimmed.

Disadvantages of fluorescent light include:

- Efficacy declines about 10 percent over the life of the lamp.
- Lamps may flicker and/or hum, particularly near the end of their lifespan.
- The cool colors are not complimentary to skin tones.
- The flat, diffuse light can be monotonous and tiring.
- The spectrally difficient lamps can cause health problems if they are the sole source of light.
- Ballasts are required and they generate heat.
- Dimmers are expensive and limited to one type of lamp.

Neon lights (an incorrect but popular name for **cold-cathode** lamps) are another kind of low-pressure electric discharge lamp. Neon itself, as the gas inside the tube, produces red light. Other colors often referred to as neon are actually produced by other gases within the tube and different phosphors used to coat the tube or even by painted or colored-glass tubing. Neon lamps are used primarily as decorative lighting and are often custom-designed (Plate 51, p. 418). The thin tubing is easily bent into interesting shapes and may be mounted on walls or ceilings. Neon lights have a very long life, are low energy consumers, and can be dimmed and flashed, but are quite fragile, require a large ballast, are expensive to replace, and often buzz.

High Intensity Discharge (HID) Lamps High-pressure electric discharge lamps are commonly available in three types, each with different characteristics, depending upon the gas vapor inside and the phosphor coating. In general, their advantages include:

- High efficacy (up to twice the output of fluorescents, ten times that of incandescents)
- Long life (15,000 to 24,000 hours)
- Lamp shape similar to incandescents (slightly larger)

HID lamps have been used primarily for industrial applications and outdoor lighting because of their poor color rendition (due to a discontinuous spectral composition), but new developments are improving them rapidly and they are now being used in interiors. Their traditional drawbacks have been:

- Lack of a well-balanced spectral distribution of light, resulting in both health and color-perception problems
- Noisier ballasts than fluorescent lamps
- Sensitivity to current variations (they shut down when the flow of electricity to them varies)
- Slow start-up time (up to 9 minutes) and dimming response
- Intense glare and uneven light patterns

One of the first HIDs developed was the **mercury vapor** lamp. Its blue-green color is vastly improved with a phosphor coating. It is inexpensive, has a high efficacy, and the longest life of any lamp. **Metal halide** lamps offer better color rendition, higher light output, and smaller size for more precise control compared to mercury vapor lamps. However, they also have a shorter life with more decrease in light output over their lifetime, and they produce a bluish-white light that varies in hue from lamp to lamp. The newest HID is the **high-pressure sodium** (HPS) lamp, which is very efficient and provides excellent optical control because it is very thin. Its drawbacks include a shorter life than other HIDs and a distorted salmon-colored light output. However, one new HPS lamp produces a feeling similar to incandescence. Other lamps, including a metal chloride source that produces a more even spectrum, are still experimental.

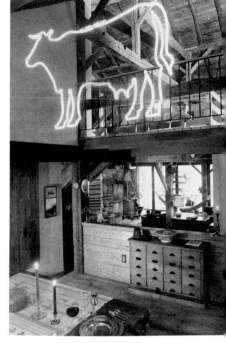

16-9 A large neon cow adds a whimsical note in a renovated barn. Neon: Joe Bucelli of Jo-Ran Neon; Centerbrook, PC, architects *(Photograph: © Robert Perron)*

16-10 Sections in the walls of this restored Connecticut farmhouse are illumined by cove lighting for an overall serene effect. Robert A.M. Stern and John Hagman, architects. *(Photograph: John T. Hill)*

Types and Uses of Light

In terms of purpose and effect, there are three major types of artificial lighting.

Ambient/General Lighting

Ambient lighting or general lighting illuminates a room more or less uniformly, as the sun illumines the earth. It lets us see every corner of a room in a safe, reassuring way and brings to equal attention the design and color of the whole space. At best, it minimizes the bulkiness of furniture, the darkness of shadows, and the often harsh contrasts of local lighting. General lighting very often emanates from ceiling fixtures or from lamps having reflector bowls and translucent shades. It is more truly general when lights concealed in coves evenly illuminate the ceiling or when troughs "wash" large wall areas or curtained windows with light. Finally, the entire ceiling or large sections of it can bring light through translucent plastics or glass. It is low-level background lighting, unobtrusive, restful, and often contributes to a sense of space.

General lighting can be either **direct** (with light shining downward full on objects to be illuminated) or **indirect** (when light is thrown against a surface, usually the ceiling, from which much of it is reflected into the room). For general illumination, indirect light usually produces a softer effect than direct light, but it costs more to install and operate and may overemphasize the reflecting ceilings or walls. Overall uniform lighting is shadowless and monotonous and seldom bright enough for reading or close work. For these reasons, it must be combined with local or task lighting.

Task/Local Lighting

The kind and amount of direct, functional illumination needed at specific places for specific activities, such as reading, cooking, sewing, eating, or grooming, is provided by task or local lighting. The light source can be high or low, but eye comfort suggests that it be shielded. Except in kitchens and bathrooms, local/task

lighting fixtures consist mainly of movable floor, desk, or table lamps, but fixtures attached to the wall, ceiling, or major pieces of furniture cause far less of a nuisance and are increasing in popularity (Plate 52, p. 418). Some furnishings even have lighting built in.

Local lighting also creates interesting pools of light that attract attention and draw people toward a circle of activity and warmth. It can be used to help direct traffic, set a mood, break up a large room into "islands," or make a small room appear to have several distinct areas, thus visually enlarging its space.

above left: 16-11 Individual fixtures on track lighting can be moved back and forth along the track and swiveled to direct light where wanted. Joe D'Urso, designer. *(Photograph: © Peter Aaron/ ESTO)*

above right: 16-12 Recessed ceiling fixtures provide direct general illumination. Hank Bruce, architect. *(Photograph: Philip L. Molten)*

16-13 Some degree of light contrast is both functional and aesthetically pleasing. The interesting architecture of this room has been enhanced by the placement of lighting within the structure. Lamps concealed at the top of the cement-block wall illuminate the timber roof, connecting it with other shapes in the room. The rug is lit by an internally silvered reflector floodlight mounted high and out of the picture to the right, and the floor lamp serves as a useful reading light. Peter Aldington, architect. *(Photograph: Richard Einzig)*

415

16-14 Christmas lights accent a hallway bridge daringly open on either side to the space below with only a handrail for support. Arthur Erickson, architect. *(Photograph: © Ezra Stoller/ESTO)*

opposite: Plate 50 Sky-lights extending a wall of glass bring the warmth and joy of sunlight deep into the living room of a house built on a wooded slope. Although the room faces south, the surrounding trees protect it from too much sun. Smith and Larsen, architects. *(Photograph: © Morley Baer)*

Accent/Decorative Lighting

The play of brilliants seen on Christmas trees or in fireworks, crystal chandeliers, and candelabra makes up the third type of lighting: accent or decorative lighting. It is produced by fixtures that break light into many small, bright spots or focus it onto art or other possessions. Typical sources include candles, fixtures with many small lamps, those in which light passes through many small openings, pin spots, framing projectors, even tiny Christmas lights and flexible strips of miniature lights that can be bent to conform to any shape. The special contribution made by accent lighting can be experienced immediately when one enters a room filled with sparkling light. It is stimulating, accentuates focal points, and provides the personal touch that highlights a room.

top: Plate 51 A neon sign from the American Southwest brings a touch of whimsy to a very personal East Coast house. Denise Scott Brown and Robert Venturi, architects. *(Photograph: © Paul Warchol)*

bottom: Plate 52 Track lighting, light poles, and a suspended ceiling fixture over a terrarium bring light where it is needed in a New York apartment. Hugh Hardy, designer. *(Photograph: © Norman McGrath)*

418

Table 16–1   Minimum Recommended Light for Certain Activities

	Footcandles
General Lighting	
most rooms	5–10
kitchen, laundry	10 20
passage areas	5–10
Local Lighting for Activities	
card playing	10–20
casual reading, easy sewing, makeup, easy musical scores	20–30
kitchen, laundry	30–50
prolonged reading, study, average and machine sewing, difficult musical scores, shaving, benchwork	40–70
fine sewing, any small detail work	100–200

Specific Factors in Lighting

Planned lighting demands attention to measures of quantity and quality, control of reflection, placement and size of light sources, direction of light, and color of light together with its effect on colors.

Measures of Light

There are four units of measure for light: **lumen, candela, footcandle,** and **footlambert.** The rate of light production by a source, the amount of light produced by a lamp, is measured in **lumens.** This is the measurement used on manufacturers' packages and in lamp catalogs. A lamp's *efficacy* is equal to the number of lumens of light produced per watt of electricity consumed. Fluorescent lamps produce much more light than incandescent lamps of the same wattage. The **candela** is a measure of the candlepower or luminous intensity of a light source in a specific direction; it aids in describing the directional kind of light produced by a PAR lamp, for example.

The amount of light that reaches a surface (incident illumination) is measured in **footcandles (fc).** The standard light meter can be used to measure this quantity of light. One footcandle is equal to the amount of light falling on one square foot of surface one foot away from a candle flame. Experiments have shown that people generally will select as most desirable the middle of almost any range of incident illumination. For example, if the range is from 10 to 30 footcandles, the typical subject will prefer 20. When, without the observer's knowledge, the range is stepped up from 30 to 100 footcandles, the middle will again be chosen. A great difference separates 20 and 65 footcandles, but over short periods of time our eyes do not tell us which is better. They automatically adjust to different levels of light like fantastic miniature cameras. (Perhaps their greatest defect is that they do not warn us quickly when they are being strained by ineffective light.) The Illuminating Engineering Society has prepared minimum recommended footcandles of illumination needed for many standard seeing tasks and activities and for the general illumination of rooms. Table 16–1 lists some of this information. More complete data are available in IES handbooks. The wattages necessary to obtain the desired footcandles of light will vary with the distance between light source and surface; the design of lighting equipment; the amount of reflection from ceiling, floors, and furnishings; and whether incandescent or fluorescent light is used. ·

Lighting technology is in the process of changing to the metric system, converting footcandles to *lux*, the amount of illuminance reaching a one square meter

Table 16–2 Seeing Zones and Luminance Ratios for Visual Tasks

Zone	Luminance (footlamberts)
2—Area adjacent to the visual task	
a) Desirable ratio	⅓ to equal to task[†]
b) Minimum acceptable ratio	⅕ to equal to task[†]
3—General surrounding	
a) Desirable ratio	⅕ to 5 times task[†]
b) Minimum acceptable ratio	¹⁄₁₀ to 10 times task[†]

[†]Typical task luminance range is 40 to 120 candelas per square meter [12 to 35 footlamberts] (seldom exceeds 200 candelas per square meter [60 footlamberts]).

Reprinted with permission from *Design Criteria for Lighting Interior Living Spaces,* Publication #RP-11 (New York: Illuminating Engineering Society of North America, 1980), p. 5.

surface one meter distant from the source. One lux is equal to 0.0929 footcandles. Footcandles can be changed to lux by multiplying by 10.76.

The light we see reflected or transmitted by a surface is called *luminance* and is measured in **footlamberts (fL).** The quantity of light leaving any surface is a product of the footcandles reaching it multiplied by the percentage of light reflected or transmitted by it (fL = fc × % reflectance or transmittance). *Brightness* is a subjective evaluation of differences in luminance. Impressions of brightness are dependent upon many variables including illuminance, surface textures, length of exposure, viewing angle, general surroundings, and even the viewer's acuity of vision and age.

Luminance ratios or brightness relationships in the visual field of a person performing a task are important for comfort, efficiency, and safety. The visual field consists of three zones: the first zone is the precise area in focus or the task itself, zone two is the area immediately surrounding the task (such as the counter top), and zone three is the general surrounding area (the walls and floor of the room). There are optimum contrast relationships between these three zones: for tasks requiring close vision, zone two should be no brighter than zone one (as a maximum) but no less than one-third of it (minimum); zone three should be no more than five times the luminance of zone one or less than one-fifth of it. The longer the task takes to complete, the more critical the brightness relationships of the three zones. In areas where critical visual tasks are never performed, higher luminance ratios are acceptable (see Table 16–2). The reflectance levels of major surfaces in a room are important in achieving desirable luminance ratios. Recommended reflectances are listed in Table 16–3.

Table 16–3 Recommended Reflectances for Residences

Surface	Reflectance (%)
ceiling	60 to 90
fabric treatment on large wall area	45 to 85
walls	*35 to 60
floor	*15 to 35

*In areas where lighting for specific visual tasks takes precedence over lighting for environment, minimum reflectances should be 40% for walls, 25% for floors.

Reprinted with permission from *Design Criteria for Lighting Interior Living Spaces,* Publication #RP-11 (New York: Illuminating Engineering Society of North America, 1980), p. 6.

Control of Light

When light strikes an object in its path, it may be reflected, absorbed, or transmitted, depending on the degree of transparency or opacity in the material and on its surface qualities. The eye responds to reflected light, which must be controlled for optimum visual conditions. Comfortable light has sufficient but not extreme contrasts for easy viewing without strain or fatigue.

When the intensity or brightness of light causes discomfort or interferes with vision, the effect is called **glare**. Glare from abrupt changes in light intensity is a particular problem for the elderly. *Veiling glare* results when excessive light is reflected from a shiny surface such as a glossy magazine page, creating extreme contrast on the task surface and preventing discernment of the task. *Specular reflection* is *reflected glare* or bright, sharp light reflected from a highly polished or mirrored surface. Reflected glare is not always disabling but is uncomfortable nonetheless. The angle of reflected light is equal to the angle of incident light so, if a painting hung at eye level is illuminated from above, at an angle of 30 degrees, the light reflected from its glass should not strike the viewer in the eyes. A wider angle of illumination may cause reflected glare from the surface of the painting, which would wash out the detail and be a source of glare to others in the room. The viewer may also come between the light source and painting, casting a shadow upon it. Dull or matte surfaces exhibit *diffuse reflection*; they appear equal in brightness from all viewing angles, without the "hot spots" associated with glare.

Light may pass through a material that is transparent or translucent. A translucent shielding material over a light source spreads the light distribution and softens its brightness. Some materials refract or bend the light rays as they pass through them. A lens has such an effect, either concentrating or scattering the light rays passing through it.

When no light is transmitted or reflected, it is absorbed by a material. Some materials absorb nearly all the light falling on them, resulting in a dark gray or black appearance; others selectively absorb some light rays while reflecting others, resulting in our perception of individual hues. The percentage of light reflected by certain colors is listed in Table 16–4. Lighter colors reflect more light, darker colors absorb more light. The relationship between Munsell value and reflectance (see Table 8–2, p. 201) is roughly that value is the square root of reflectance.

Blandness of light, with every part of a room equally bright, is also fatiguing—to both the muscles of the eyes and the spirits of the occupants. If we remember that natural light modifies constantly—from dawn through midday to moonlight, filtered by trees and clouds, varying with the time of year—we will realize that change is normal and even beneficial. Our aim should be moderation, in both quantity and contrast of light.

Selective switches allow people to turn on or off different fixtures at will. With rheostatic dimmers, brightness of light from most fixtures can be smoothly adjusted to any point between candlelike glow and full brightness. The small cost of these dimmers could, in many instances, be more than compensated by reducing the number of separate fixtures that would otherwise be needed to achieve varied levels of brightness.

Location and Direction of Light

Accustomed as we are to the sun being more or less overhead, lighting from above seems normal, that from other directions surprising. The following observations apply generally to location of potential light sources in the home:

- Location of both the light source and any surface from which light is reflected will be important in the total effect.
- Light high in a room is at the same time serene and revealing. It can be

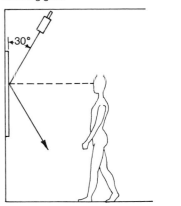

avoiding glare

angle of reflection=angle of illumination
angle should not exceed 30° from vertical

16-15 In lighting reflective vertical surfaces, to avoid glare the angle of incident light should not exceed 30 degrees from the vertical.

Table 16—4   Light Reflectance of Various Colors and Finishes

Color	Reflectance (%)
Dull or Flat White	75–90
Tints	
ivory	75
pink or yellow	75–80
light green, blue, orchid	70–75
beige or gray	70
Medium Tones	
tan, yellow-gold	55
gray	35–50
turquoise, blue	42–44
chartreuse	45
gold, pumpkin	34
rose	29
Deep Tones	
cocoa brown, mauve	24
green and blue	21
gray	20
olive green	12
navy, forest green	5–10
Wood	
birch	35–50
maple, oak	25–35
cherry	10–15
black walnut, mahogany	5–15

Adapted from *Planning Your Home Lighting,* House and Garden Bulletin 138 (Washington, D.C.: U.S.G.P.O., 1968), p. 4. Reprinted with permission of Macmillan Publishing Company from Marjorie Branin Keiser, *Housing: An Environment for Living* (New York: Macmillan, 1978), p. 245. Copyright © 1978 by Marjorie Branin Keiser.

16-16 Small ceiling fixtures placed to cast light where needed can also swivel as needs change. Joe D'Urso, designer. *(Photograph: © Peter Aaron/ ESTO)*

efficient to the point of boredom or a striking revelation of an architectural highpoint.

- Light below eye level seems friendly and draws groups together. It is also useful while watching television.
- Light coming from near the floor flatters people's appearance in the same manner as do theater footlights, and also contrasts pleasantly with more conventional lighting. Low light is a good safety device near steps and in halls.
- Light from a number of sources, or well-diffused light, makes a room seem luminous rather than merely lighted, tends to spread interest throughout the area, and is comfortably undemanding. However, entirely diffused light that casts no shadows is monotonous and perhaps unsafe because shadows are necessary to reveal form.
- Strongly directed light, for example that coming from one or two spotlights, may be dramatic, but it can seem harsh if not handled carefully. Our attention tends to follow its path—up, down, sideways, or at an angle—much as it does a solid form. Directional light casts highlights and shadows on surfaces which change with the position of the observer, adding interest and variety. *Downlights* over people create unflattering shadows under the eyes, nose, and chin.
- Light positioned near and parallel to a textured surface *grazes* the surface, highlighting its irregularities dramatically. However, grazing is an inefficient method of lighting a wall because the units must be placed as close as one foot from the wall and one foot apart and they do not provide light for anything hung on or sitting in front of the wall.
- Lights positioned 3 to 4 feet from the wall and the same distance apart *wash* the surface with an even, shadowless light.
- *Perimeter* lighting expands apparent space. A dark perimeter makes space seem to contract.
- Light for working should illumine the task without forming distracting shadows and should not shine in the worker's eyes. Task lighting should follow the recommended levels in the three visual zones to avoid glare and gloom contrasts.

Taking these many variables into consideration, lighting engineers have made some general recommendations about the placement of light fixtures and the wattage that will provide an adequate amount of light for both general illumination and concentrated light for reading, sewing, and other close work. Table 16–5 lists these recommendations.

Size and Shape of Light Source

Much depends on the size of a light source. To understand this, we need only compare the luminous vault of the sky by day with its myriad play of brilliants at night.

- Broad sources or "planes" of light—the sky, a skylight, an illuminated ceiling, a window wall—give flat, glareless, uneventful light excellent for general vision, health, and safety, because they minimize contrasts and shadows. In decorative terms, however, they can be monotonous.
- Smaller light sources that diffuse light broadly through lenses, translucent shades, or reflectors approximate this effect. Because of their resulting amorphous shape, these lights are sometimes referred to as "glob" sources.
- Very small light sources, especially bright ones, have high accent value, emphasize parts of rooms, and make silver and glass sparkle. But such lights must be used with care, for they can be visually fatiguing and may cause a spotty effect. These lights are called "point" sources.

16-17 A large suspended ceiling fixture can be useful when a spread of light is needed, as over a dining table. Robert Sonneman, designer. *(Courtesy George Kovacs Lighting, Inc.)*

Table 16–5 Recommended Placement and Wattage of Light Fixtures

Type	Placement	Range of Wattage
wall fixtures (incandescent)	at least 66″ above floor	60–100w every 8′ for general lighting
wall fixtures (fluorescent)	faceboards at least 6″ out from wall, and as high in inches as they are in feet from floor, to shield fluorescent tubes	general lighting—approximately 1′ of channel (10w) for each 15 sq. ft. of floor area special lighting—approximate width of area to be lighted
cornice	at edge of ceiling, sheds light down	
valance	at least 10″ down from ceiling, sheds light up, down, or both	
wall bracket	50–65″ above floor, sheds light up, down, or both	
ceiling fixtures		
shallow	centered, symmetrically placed, or placed to illumine special areas	120–200w in multiple bulbs; 60–80w in multiple tubes
recessed	as above	30–150w bulbs
pendant	as above; see below when used for reading	120–180w in multiple bulbs
floor lamps (for reading)	stem of lamp 10″ behind shoulder, near rear corner of chair; bottom of shade 45–48″ above floor	50/150w–100/300w bulb; 60–180w in multiple bulbs
table lamps (for reading)	base in line with shoulder, 20″ to left or right of book center; bottom of shade at eye level when seated, about 40″ above floor	as above
wall lamps (for reading)	42–48″ above floor, 15″ to left or right of book center	as above

- "Line" sources are typically fluorescent or neon lamps but they may also include strips of incandescent lamps, either exposed or concealed behind valances, brackets, cornices, or coves. They are usually general perimeter light sources, subdued and space-expanding except for neon lights, which are decorative and stimulating.

Color of Light

Artificial light seems to be most pleasing if it simulates natural light that varies by time of day and direction. Incandescent lighting has traditionally been favored for residential illumination because of its full-spectrum distribution of wavelengths. However, other types of light are also being developed with a more even spectral distribution and are gaining favor for the home.

16-18 A combination of high light sources gives excellent lighting and also emphasizes the interplay of ceiling planes in this striking kitchen. Fluorescent tubes are inset in the box beams, a strip of large clear bulbs follows the rise of the ceiling, and natural light pours in from a skylight set at the top level. Charles Moore and Rurik Ekstrom, architects. *(Photograph: John T. Hill)*

The color of light is determined by three factors: the light source, the diffusing or reflecting shade, and the room surfaces.

- White light shows colors as they are and has no pronounced emotional effect other than the important sense of normal well-being.
- Warm light flatters people, dispels the chill associated with darkness, and brightens warm colors but deadens blues and purples.
- Cool light makes rooms seem more spacious, separates objects one from another—and may make people look cadaverous.
- A combination of warm and cool light adds variety but needs to be planned with care.
- Light reflected from one colored surface to another is modified by each and affects each in turn due to the selective reflection and absorption of different wavelengths or "colors" of light. More of the effects of color on light were explored in Chapter 8.
- Colors look different under different lights, a phenomenon known as **metamerism.** The colors in a textile vary quite remarkably under incandescent, fluorescent, or natural light. That is why it is best to select and coordinate colors under the light conditions in which they will be used. Low levels of light render colors more grayed in intensity; higher levels, if not too harsh, tend to brighten colors.

Until recently, most people have been somewhat timid about using colored illumination in their homes. But the last few years have seen more experimentation with different colored lamps or lenses, even with patterns of colored light, either stationary or moving, thrown on walls.

Psychological Aspects of Light

Light is a psychological communicator of mood or atmosphere. The skilled designer can use it to establish the character of a space just as lighting designers for the theater use it to establish the mood of a play.

- **Bright light** is stimulating, calls forth energy, and makes us feel as though we should be up and about, but if overused it may ultimately be boring. Bright light casts strong shadows.
- **Subdued light** may seem relaxing, restful, and intimately romantic, or dingy, depressing, even frightening—depending upon the context. Soft light minimizes shadows and textural differences.
- **Too-brilliant light** often causes us to retreat in physical and emotional distress. A bright, focused light makes us feel the center of attention and may boost our ego or make us very uncomfortable. Small hard lights add brilliance and sparkle.
- **Moderately bright light** brings no pronounced feeling other than general well-being.
- **Flickering light,** as from a fireplace or candles, nearly always draws attention and physically draws people toward its warm, flattering light. As the primary light source, it is visually fatiguing.
- An appropriate **distribution of light quantities** results in an impression of balance and rhythm, of emphasis and moderation similar to that produced by nature.
- **Warm-colored light** seems cheerful and welcoming.
- **Cool light** is often more restful than warm light.

Lighting Fixtures

Ideal fixtures, called **luminaires,** give the kind and amount of light suitable to a particular purpose, thus fulfilling the principle of *utility*. They represent sound *economy* in balancing their original cost with the electricity they use, in the ease with which they are cleaned and the lamps are replaced, and in the space they take. They contribute to the *beauty* of our homes and they underline or create the distinctive *character* we seek. Almost inevitably lighting fixtures contrast with other furnishings, because they fill quite a different purpose. This suggests that *some* of them be deliberately chosen as accents. In general, though, sensible practice recommends having most fixtures appropriate in size, scale, and character to the rooms and other furnishings. Lighting devices can set up their own pattern of design running through the entire home, supplying a connective theme.

Architectural and Built-In Lighting

Architectural lighting is planned at the same time the structure is designed and wired during construction. Built-in lighting accounts for about half of all artificial lighting. It contributes to the total unity of a lifespace and can produce unique effects, usually reflecting off walls, ceilings, and furnishings. It can—and should—enhance the architectural outlines and forms of the space.

Ceiling Luminaires Fixtures attached to or mounted in the ceiling are available in many varieties:

- **Luminous panels** may cover all or most of the ceiling, illuminating large areas evenly and softly through diffusing materials.
- **Recessed** and **adjustable downlights** (highhats, eyeballs, and wall-washers) may direct a flood or a narrow beam of light downward or angle it toward an activity area or accessory, creating pools, scallops, or a wash of light.
- **Cornices** are mounted at the juncture of ceiling and wall. They wash the wall surface in light, providing reflected ambient light to the rest of the room.
- **Soffit lights** are most often used in the bathroom, laundry, or kitchen, over the sink. The underside of the soffit is covered with a diffusing panel with lamps above it. Soffit fixtures are effective task lights.
- **Flush-mounted** and **surface-mounted fixtures,** some dropped a few inches, are often centered in the ceiling to provide direct or direct/indirect ambient lighting. Some can reflect light from the ceiling, diffuse it through the bowl, and direct a pool of light downward, making them an inexpensive three-in-one way to light space for eating, hobbies, or homework. Others are similar to recessed luminaires except that they are surface-mounted (cans, eyeballs, and wall-washers). Although some of these fixtures may be removable (and not truly built-in), their wiring is permanent, making them architectural in nature.
- **Suspended luminaires** may be dropped well below the ceiling and may be adjustable in height and position for greater flexibility and ease of maintenance. A large suspended fixture may form a canopy overhead.
- **Track lighting** may be architectural if the wiring is concealed or the track is recessed into the ceiling. Tracks allow flexibility; many sizes and shapes of fixtures, even pendants, can be mounted on a single track to serve a multitude of purposes.

16-19 Surface-mounted track lights bring needed illumination to a room with no other fixtures and offer flexibility in placement and type which other architectural fixtures do not. Joan Halperin, designer. *(Photograph: Robert Levin)*

16-20 The "Luma" wall sconce, designed by Michael Berkowicz, is made of sandblasted acrylic that diffuses the light softly. Open at the top, it also emits less-diffused light, which is then reflected from the ceiling. *(Photograph: David Fishbein. Courtesy Plexability Ltd.)*

Wall Luminaires Wall fixtures are popular because they keep table and desk surfaces free for other things, they remain out of the way, and they provide direct light where it is needed or supply general overall illumination balanced throughout the room. However, they are attached to the wall and fixed in location, which may interfere with hanging pictures or changing furniture arrangements.

- **Valances** are located directly above windows. They supply both direct and indirect light, emphasizing the texture of window treatments and bouncing light off the ceiling into the rest of the room.
- **Brackets** are similar to valances but are not located over windows. They may be positioned high or low on the wall and used for ambient or ambient and task light, depending upon height and the shape of the face board. Brackets are often used over beds or to balance valance lighting on the opposite side of a room.
- **Coves** provide a trough to conceal lighting that is directed upward only, toward the ceiling. They may be used to add a feeling of height to a space or to emphasize a vaulted or cathedral ceiling.
- **Sconces** and luminaires mounted directly on the wall are available in many shapes and sizes, for use as direct and indirect lighting, or purely for decorative effects.
- **Luminous wall panels** are lighting panels placed in the wall surface. In confined spaces, luminous wall panels can create an ambience of natural light. The panels may be treated as windows with draperies, shutters, or milky diffusers.

above left: 16-21 Wall-mounted luminaires focus attention on the dining area in an open plan while providing light for art on the wall below. Peter Waldman, architect. *(Photograph: © Peter Aaron/ESTO)*

above right: 16-22 Built-in wall luminaires bring a soft glow to a narrow hall; a ceiling fixture illuminates the sculpture on the end wall. Michael Graves, architect. *(Photograph: © Peter Aaron/ESTO)*

Portable Lamps and Nonarchitectural Lighting

Floor and table lamps can be moved when and where they are needed. Moreover, they perform as lively decorative accessories. In some instances, lamps that are unornamented and inconspicuous seem best, but genuinely handsome, decorative lamps can greatly enrich a room at the same time that they provide light. A beautiful ceramic or glass piece or a richly modeled work of metal profits from light above or in it. Some lamps could be described as light-as-object. The light is captured in a sculptural form that in turn spreads the ambience of its glow in the immediate vicinity. Other types enclose the light source in an opaque base and emit light in one direction only. In still others, clear or frosted bulbs themselves become the fixture, while providing light. (Chapter 18 discusses the design and selection of portable lamps as enrichment for the home.)

Track lights and pinup fixtures of all kinds can also be nonarchitectural, with surface wiring and exposed cords, allowing them to be moved or removed at will.

Switches and Outlets

Every room in the house needs a light switch beside any access door. Besides providing instant illumination of the room, this will encourage the household to turn off superfluous lights. Stairs should have switches at top and bottom, halls at both ends. Ideally, the switches will be selective, controlling the different fixtures appropriate for different occasions. Dimmers also serve for adapting the level of light to a particular task or mood. Each wall space 3 or more feet wide that is separated from other walls by doors or floor-length windows requires an outlet for lamps and appliances. On very long walls, two or more outlets diminish the hazards of extension cords. The U.S. Department of Housing and Urban Development specifies outlets no more than 6 feet from any point along a wall. Outlets are usually mounted 12 inches above the floor, switches 50 inches high. These positions can, and perhaps should, be reevaluated and adjusted for easy access by the handicapped or elderly and for the safety of children.

- Switches controlling bed lamps should be within *easy* reach of a person lying on the bed.

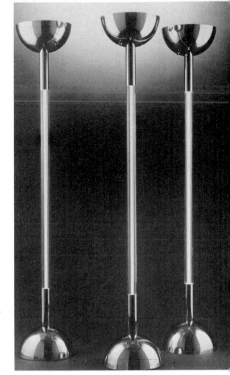

16-23 Brass shades and bases with light-transmitting acrylic stems between give these portable lamps unusual interest. Rudy Stern of Let There Be Neon, designer. *(Courtesy George Kovacs Lighting, Inc.)*

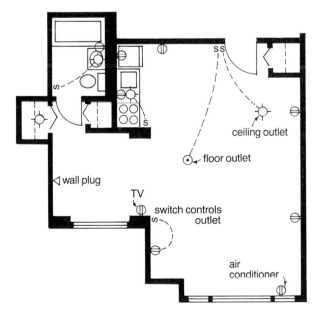

ceiling outlet

floor outlet

wall plug

TV

switch controls outlet

air conditioner

16-24 A wiring diagram reveals the location of switches and outlets and illustrates which switches control which lights or outlets. A reflected ceiling plan shows the position of light fixtures located on the ceiling and helps establish their correlation to furniture groupings.

- Switches for outdoor lighting are most convenient when they are inside the house.
- Outlets at table height present advantages in a number of situations: near ironing boards for electric irons; near dining tables for toasters, coffee pots, and so on; along the back of kitchen counter space for appliances used there; near sewing centers for sewing machines; and behind electric washers and dryers.
- Outlets in hallways provide a convenient power access for vacuum cleaners.
- Bathrooms require outlets for electric shavers, toothbrushes, and other small appliances.
- A workshop area should be equipped with heavy-duty outlets for power tools.
- Weatherproof outdoor outlets are desirable for electrically operated barbecues, portable lighting, or Christmas decorations.

An electrical plan showing the placement of switches and outlets and wiring is an essential tool for both the designer and electrician. Electrical symbols are illustrated in the Appendix of Designer Symbols on page 532.

Economic Aspects of Lighting

To conserve energy, windows should be planned and placed to admit as much natural light as possible during daylight hours. When artificial light is necessary, maximum control (allowing flexibility of use) will help reduce waste. This may mean adding a few more switches, installing dimmers, or changing lamps or luminaires. Multiple switches allow using as much or as little light as is needed. Dimmers lower the voltage needed by incandescent lamps and prolong their life up to three times longer when used. A higher-wattage lamp is more efficient than several lower-wattage lamps totaling the same number, and three-way lamps offer greater versatility of use than standard single-filament lamps. Reflector floodlights provide more light with less wattage than standard lamps. And low-voltage lamps have proved a highly successful method of dealing with state energy codes limiting the amount of electrical energy that can be used for lighting. These codes were established as part of a national effort to save energy.

Wherever possible, fluorescent, HID, and tungsten-halogen lamps can be used instead of incandescent lamps. Fluorescents consume less energy, produce more light, and have a longer lifespan than incandescents; HIDs have even higher efficacy and longer life than fluorescents. Longer fluorescent tubes are more efficient and HIDs are more efficient at higher wattages. Tungsten-halogen sources also produce more light with less decline over time, and have a longer life than incandescent lamps.

Finally, light-reflective colors used on ceilings, walls, floors, and furnishings will help maximize the effects of all light while dark surfaces will demand additional illumination. Refer to the reflectancy of various colors when planning an interior (Table 16–4, p. 422). Chapter 8 provided more information on the light reflectancy of color.

Lighting for Areas and Activities

In designing a home or revising the furnishings of a room, it pays to draw a plan with furniture arrangements. Once the furniture has been sketched in, lighting requirements can be assessed—where local illumination is needed, what kinds of general and accent lighting will best complement the character of the room, its colors, textures, and surfaces.

16-25 Good lighting at entrances and on stairs is important for safety as well as for providing a warm welcome. Callister and Payne, Henry Herold, architects. *(Photograph: Philip L. Molten)*

Entrance areas benefit from friendly, welcome illumination as a transition from the dark outside to the brightness of the interior. Guests and hosts see one another in a pleasant light, which provides a graceful introduction to the home. Diffused light from ceiling or wall fixtures, perhaps supplemented by more concentrated, sparkling light, creates a balanced effect.

Living rooms and **family rooms** need general illumination, preferably both direct and indirect, to bring walls and furniture, floors and ceilings into soft perspective. Flexibly controlled direct light is requisite where people read or sew, play games, or do homework. A touch of scintillating light adds interest. Dimmer switches provide versatility.

Conversation benefits from a moderate level of lighting, neither too stimulating nor too bland. Intimacy is encouraged by keeping the general background lighting low and by using fixtures placed low. High fixtures seem more conducive to formal exchanges. Warm-colored lighting draws people together at the same time that it flatters their complexions.

Television viewing requires well-balanced light with no sharp contrasts or glare reflected from the screen. A relatively low level of lighting may be sufficient since the television screen itself is a light source. Fixtures should be shielded or positioned to prevent reflection from the screen. Video display terminals for home computers require much the same kind of lighting conditions.

Reading of a casual nature can be done in moderate light, but more sustained reading or study needs direct light balanced by some general lighting to avoid glare. Placement of the lamp for light without shadows is illustrated in Figures 16-27 to 16-29. Other visual tasks, such as sewing, playing the piano, and personal grooming also have specific requirements for the best placement of fixtures.

16-26 A video room needs lighting that can be controlled for flexibility in the use of space. Xanadu Designs. *(Photograph: © Peter Aaron/ESTO)*

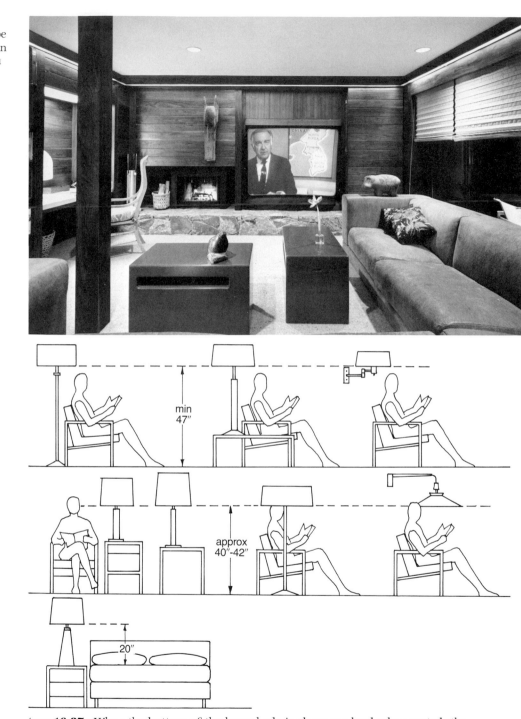

light behind

light at the side

min 47"

approx 40"-42"

20"

top: 16-27 When the bottom of the lampshade is above eye level when seated, the lamp stem should be about 10 inches behind the shoulder, near the rear corner of the chair. *(Adapted from American Home Lighting Institute)*
middle: 16-28 If the bottom of the lampshade is at eye level when seated, the lamp should be placed beside the chair, slightly in front of the shoulder. **bottom:** Lighting beside the bed should have bottom of shade 20" above mattress. *(Adapted from American Home Lighting Institute)*

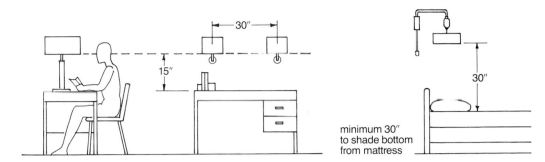

light in front
minimum 15"
to shade bottom

15"

30"

minimum 30"
to shade bottom
from mattress

30"

16-29 Desk lights should have the bottom of the lampshade at eye level and the shade should be of a fairly dense or opaque material in a light but not strong color. For reading in bed, a wall-mounted luminaire should be positioned high enough to ensure that the shadow of head and shoulders does not fall across the reading material. *(Adapted from American Home Lighting Institute)*

Active play, dancing, ping-pong, billiards, or other physical games usually benefit from high levels of general light. Table games need direct overhead light, positioned high enough to be out of the line of vision.

Dining spaces deserve primary emphasis on what is most important—the table and the people around it. Light directed downward makes silver, glass, and china sparkle, enhances the appetizing qualities of food and beverages, and, if carefully positioned, reflects back up onto diners' faces without casting harsh shadows under prominent features. However, some indirectly diffused light lessens glare and diminishes unbecoming shadows on the diners' faces. Pendant fixtures must be centered at least 22 to 30 inches above the table top so they do not interfere with conversation and visual contact between diners across the table from one another. Candles on the table should be either above or below eye level for the same reason, and should be supplemented with ambient light. Only the table itself needs a moderately high level of light; the remainder of the room can have lighting of a reduced level. A dimmer switch allows flexibility. Incandescent sources tend to render both food and faces more appealing than fluorescents do. Hanging fixtures are more practical if adjustable in height for multiple use in the dining area in today's smaller homes (for instance, for card-playing, studying, or sewing).

16-30 Downlights carefully positioned over a dining table highlight table appointments, establishing the focal point of the room. John F. Saladino, Inc., architects and interior designers. *(Photograph: © Peter Aaron/ESTO)*

16-31 Task illumination, devoid of shadows, is created with reflective surfaces and multiple light sources in a bathroom of Brazilian marble designed by architect Paul Rudolph. *(Photograph: Robert Levin)*

Kitchens absolutely demand good light, especially over the work centers. The eating table and the rest of the room should have a fairly high level of general illumination. Ceiling lights are almost indispensible, as are bands of task lighting placed at strategic points along work counters, especially under wall cabinets to dispel shadows on the work surface. The range, sink, and mix centers must have adequate shadow-free task lighting. The kitchen will frequently be the most thoroughly illuminated room in the house. Luminous ceilings are often used in kitchens and utility and hobby rooms. Much research has been devoted to kitchens, and we are likely to think in straightforward terms about this room.

Bathrooms require lights near the mirror to give shadowless illumination on the face. Bands of light on all sides of the mirror work best if heat can be kept to a minimum, lights on two sides or above and below almost as well. If placed above the mirror only, lighting causes shadows on the lower part of the face, making shaving and make-up application difficult unless a highly light-reflectant countertop is used. A bathroom also needs general illumination from a ceiling fixture or two, lighting over the tub and in the shower stall, and a night light.

Bedrooms should have lighting for dressing, reading in bed, and perhaps such activities as desk work, reading, or sewing. Direct-indirect lights over the beds, chairs, desks, and chests of drawers—as well as direct lights near mirrors—may be sufficient, but some general lighting, closet lighting, and a night light (particularly in children's rooms) is usually advisable. For reading, the light fixture should be 30 inches above the surface of the bed when located behind the bed, or 20 inches above when placed at the side, to provide sufficient illumination on the reading material. Switches near the bed allow control without maneuvering in the dark. Lighting should be comfortable, cheerful, restful, and glareless.

Halls need some overall lighting; its source might be ceiling or wall fixtures that send glare-free light downward, but lighting near the floor, as in theaters, not only focuses on the area we need most to see in hallways but offers a readymade opportunity for variety in lighting effects as well. Ornamental, colorful fixtures can dispel the dullness typical of most halls. A night light in bedroom hallways is a good safety precaution.

Stairways are hazardous. Light that clearly differentiates the treads from the risers—such as ceiling or wall fixtures that send even, glare-free light downward—can lessen accidents. Spotty or distracting light is dangerous and best reserved for some other part of the house. Illuminate the first and last steps clearly—most falls occur there. Portable lamps at the foot of a stairway should be placed so that the bulb is not visible to anyone descending the stairs. It can momentarily blind the person.

Exterior lighting seldom gets the attention it deserves. The minimum—seldom met—would call for illuminating the entrance of a house so that it can be recognized and the house number read from the street. Visitor and host should be able to see each other clearly in a good light at the doorway. Walkways to the street and garage should also be illuminated for safe, secure passage. Light sources should be kept out of the direct line of sight, either above or below eye level.

Terraces, patios, and **gardens** can be enjoyed at night, even from inside, if they are lighted. This effect has become especially important with the increasing popularity of window walls and with landscape design that is integrated with the house. Seen from inside, lighted outdoor areas greatly expand the apparent size of the interior and bring some illumination into the house. Also, light outdoors eliminates the rather menacing black windows or mirror effect that results in the absence of balanced illumination. Typical solutions are weatherproof fixtures mounted on exterior walls or overhanging roofs. More elaborate installations have spotlights and floodlights concealed in the landscape. However, outdoor lighting must be handled with discretion, for high levels of illumination may seem unnatural and "stagy." A low glow will suffice to dispel the unwanted blackness.

It is relatively easy to focus sufficient light on work surfaces and to provide for some kind of general illumination. But a balanced combination of natural and artificial light throughout the home needs thoughtful planning.

Notes to the Text

1. Marjorie Branin Keiser, *Housing: An Environment for Living* (New York: Macmillan, 1978), p. 246.

References for Further Reading

Bedell, Ben. "Lighting: Watts the Matter," *Interiors*, April 1980, pp. 84–85, 102.

Caringer, Denise L. and Robert E. Dittmer. "Lighting: New Techniques, New Fixtures, New Looks," *Better Homes and Gardens*, September 1981, pp. 88–95.

"Choosing and Using Track Lighting," *Better Homes and Gardens*, October 1979, pp. 54, 56.

Design Criteria for Lighting Interior Living Spaces. New York: Illuminating Engineering Society of North America, 1980.

Faulkner, Sarah. *Planning a Home*. New York: Holt, Rinehart and Winston, 1979. Chap. 5, pp. 101–128.

Furnival, Lawrence. "Scattering Light," *Residential Interiors*, August 1980, pp. 54–57, 90.

Gilliatt, Mary and Douglas Baker. *Lighting Your Home: A Practical Guide*. New York: Pantheon, 1979.

Horn, Richard. "Task Lighting: Useful Hints for Lighting Up the Written Word," *Residential Interiors*, September–October 1979, pp. 114–115.

Kaufmann, John E. and Jack F. Christensen (eds.). *IES Lighting Handbook*, 5th ed. New York: Illuminating Engineering Society, 1972.

Keiser, Marjorie Branin. *Housing: An Environment for Living*. New York: Macmillan, 1978. Pp. 244–257.

Light and Color. Cleveland, OH: General Electric Company, 1974.

Light for Living. Chicago: American Home Lighting Institute, 1979.

"Lighting 1. Vertical Surfaces," *ASID Industry Foundation Bulletin*. New York: American Society of Interior Designers.

Marshall Editions Limited (ed.). *Color*. Los Angeles: Knapp Press, 1980. Pp. 10–23.

McDermott, Jeanne. "Closeup on an Energy Specialist," *Interiors*, October 1982, pp. 94, 112, 114.

Morgan, Jim. "Energy-Conscious Interior Design," *Residential Interiors*, August–September 1978, p. 30.

Nuckolls, James L. "Glare-Free Workstation," *Interiors*, August 1982, pp. 74-75.

Nuckolls, James L. *Interior Lighting for Environmental Designers*. New York: Wiley, 1976.

Pile, John. "The Lighting Direction for Health," *Interiors*, August 1982, pp. 34, 102.

Pile, John. "Getting On with the Task," *Interiors*, April 1980, pp. 86–87.

Raymond, Betty. "Interiors Report on Lighting: Making Every Lumen Count," *Interiors*, October 1979, pp. 14, 18, 22, 30.

Shapiro, Cecile, David Ulrich, and Neal DeLeo. *Better Kitchens*. Passaic, NJ: Creative Homeowner Press, 1980. Chap. 9, pp. 114–140.

Shemitz, Sylvan R. with Gladys Walker. "Designing with Light: Tools of the Trade," *Interior Design*, September 1982, pp. 224–227.

17

Furniture

Furniture provides the major transition between architecture and people. It exists to provide comfort in the things we do: working, eating, sleeping, and relaxing. We expect each piece of furniture to fulfill the specific functions we require of it. An easy chair and a dining chair, for instance, while meant basically for sitting, differ in design because they serve us in different situations. Moreover, furniture also performs as an architectural element by organizing the space within a room: defining conversation areas and traffic paths, suggesting separation of areas, and so forth. Finally, furniture enables us to impress our personal tastes on our lifespaces, even when they are architecturally the same as those of our neighbors. Very much as an expression of our lifestyles, we choose furniture that allows us to use various rooms as we see fit. We manipulate the character of the furnishings, and their arrangement, to define the type of living we expect a room to foster.

Furniture has been discussed and illustrated on many of the preceding pages. In the first part of the book furniture arrangement was considered as a factor in group and private spaces; the next chapters focused on design quality. In the third section, materials were considered for their impact on design and use. Keeping these earlier discussions in mind, we now approach the selection of furniture with particular emphasis on personal values.

Selecting Furniture

The vast array of furnishings currently available testifies to a wide divergence in the ways people live. There is so-called art furniture designed by craftsmen or designers, and there is mass-produced furniture that reflects and enhances every pattern and style of living. Furthermore, increasing numbers of people are finding satisfaction in constructing their own furnishings—either freely or from components—and in rehabilitating furniture others have discarded or no longer need.

In order to sort through the many types of furniture and find what will best fulfill the job, the designer should develop a scale of values that will allow evaluation of furniture as it relates to the particular necessities and aesthetics of the client. Deciding on physical requirements is the first step. Considerable thought should be given to how and in what situations the furniture will be used and who will use it. The single-person household will obviously have quite different needs than the family that includes, say, seven children and a dog.

Before selecting furniture, consideration should be given to how much space is available, what scale of furniture will relate well to the room, and possible arrangements. Stores, showrooms, catalogs, magazines, books, offices, and homes offer many kinds of chairs, tables, cabinets, and furniture systems—both new and old. These should be compared and contrasted, with the excellences and weaknesses of each noted. Very few are totally good or bad. When the opportunity presents itself, furniture should be sat on, looked at, and felt. Clients should be encouraged to "experience" it in this way, to enable the designer to find out what looks good and is comfortable to the people who will be using it.

The designer continues to look, think, and compare, consciously sharpening the ability to see and evaluate differences. At the same time, the designer decides which aspects are most important for the client's needs and personal scale of values. With some people, comfort or beauty may transcend all other considerations, although most people seek a balance.

below left: **17-1** "Strata," a table designed by Brian Faucheux, explores some of the possibilities of a new medium, ColorCore Formica. *(Courtesy Formica Corporation. Photograph: Hedrich-Blessing)*

below right: **17-2** An old Art Deco chair, discarded as trash by one owner, becomes—with the help of a little refurbishing—the focal point of a new owner's living room. *(Photograph: © Robert Perron)*

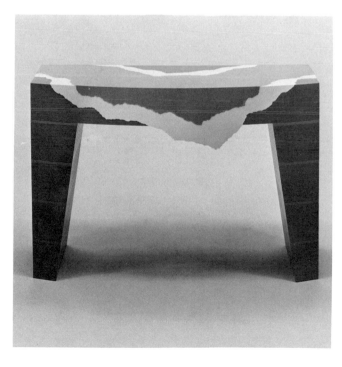

Utility and Economy

Whether furniture is for sleeping, sitting, eating, working, or playing, practical considerations should not be minimized. Important factors for function and economy are the following:

Convenience applies to efficient storage and to the ease with which often-moved furniture (such as dining chairs or beds that must be pulled out from the wall for making up) can be handled. Almost all furniture is moved from time to time, so it should be no heavier than necessary for use, strength, and appearance. Large pieces, especially if they are heavy, should be on casters or gliders.

Mobility is a fact of life in our society, and many households must cope with packing, shipping, and resettling at frequent intervals. Furniture that is lightweight, collapsible, or capable of being disassembled may provide the answer. Some people who move often find it easier either to rent furniture or to buy inexpensive or secondhand pieces that can be sold and left behind. While this expedient makes it more difficult to personalize a space, it does offer what for many individuals and designers is the exciting challenge of designing a new environment every few years.

Comfort relates to pieces on which we sit or sleep, as well as to the height of tables and desks and to the leg room under them. Sometimes comfort overrides every other factor in choosing a particular item of furniture (the classic example is the ugly, broken-down easy chair whose owner would never part with it). The age of household members becomes important here, for elderly and young people have definite but quite different requirements for comfort.

Flexibility pertains to furniture that can be used in more than one room or for more than one purpose. Until recently, most furniture was designed very specifically, like the typical dining sets of a few decades ago. Only the chairs could be moved about freely, but no matter where they were placed they carried a "dining room" character. Now many pieces are multipurpose.

Space required becomes increasingly important as homes grow smaller. Accordingly, many contemporary designers have eliminated protruding moldings and curved legs so pieces can be fitted together snugly; brought storage units to the floor or hung them on walls; designed cupboards and drawers to fit their contents flexibly; employed materials—metal, plywood, foam—that reduce size; developed folding, stacking, and nesting tables and chairs; and in some cases reduced both size and scale to a minimum.

above: 17-4 "Demetrio," small tables of lightweight but sturdy and colorful plastic can be set side by side to form a larger unit or stacked by fitting the ends of the legs into small depressions on the table tops. *(Courtesy Owens/Corning Fiberglas)*
right: 17-5 Built-in furniture makes the most of small spaces. Peter Stamberg, architect. *(Photograph: © Paul Warchol/ ESTO)*

The concept of modular and built-in furnishings has had great impact on the space in homes, as we have mentioned before. By eliminating the separate piece of furniture that must stand alone, designers utilize the in-between spaces, so that *more* furniture requires *less* floor area. Floor area is also freed when furniture is attached to walls.

Length of service depends on both physical and psychological durability. The physical life of furnishings, of course, is determined by materials, construction, finish, and use. Psychological longevity, while equally critical, can be harder to appraise. It makes no sense to buy a piece of furniture solid enough to last for generations if the homeowners are going to grow weary of it within a year or two. "Fad" styles have particularly short staying power. There is no reason why an inexpensive bit of whimsey cannot be bought occasionally to brighten the home, but when investing in basic articles of furniture, it is far better to choose well-made, well-proportioned items in which the materials have been honestly and suitably used. Some designs have an exceptional capacity for standing the test of time. They are "classics"—their beauty and character are as much appreciated today as when they were first designed, perhaps even more.

For some families, durability may no longer be the imperative it once was. When furnishing temporary quarters or anticipating a period of mobility, solid, expensive furnishings may actually be a handicap. Built-in furniture also has drawbacks in these situations, because it may be too large to move without tearing it apart, and the next tenants may find it objectionable. The length of service each article is capable of giving should depend somewhat on the length of service that will be required.

Cost of maintenance includes cleaning, repairing, refinishing, and reupholstering. The choice of appropriate materials can lighten cleaning burdens, while

strong materials and firm construction lessen the need for repairs. Durability of finish and ease of refinishing are important: painted furniture, whether wood or metal, needs new paint every few years; transparent finishes on wood, supplemented by wax or polish, last a long time, and some of the new synthetic finishes reportedly are almost indestructible. Such materials as aluminum and chromium can last indefinitely without being refinished. Upholstery fabrics may serve from one to twenty years or more depending on the material and the wear it is subjected to. Several factors govern the cost of reupholstering: the price of the fabric, the amount needed, and the labor involved. The use of zippered covers wherever possible facilitates both cleaning and recovering.

Beauty and Character

Whether furnishings have beauty and character depends on an entirely subjective appraisal, because individuals vary so markedly in their tastes. The concept of different standards of beauty has already been discussed. Insofar as furniture is concerned, some people consider beautiful only the most streamlined, ultramodern designs, while others prefer the grace and charm of antiques (Plate 53, p. 451). For those who cannot afford real antiques, there are many good contemporary reproductions of classic pieces—some available in kit form—that blend well with today's homes and lifestyles. Beyond this, other alternatives exist: the beauty of natural materials and that of man-made materials; the clarity of primary colors (Plate 54, p. 451) and the subtlety of neutrals; the precision of geometric order and the opulence of flowing curves. There are, indeed, many contrasting styles and tastes. In the end, each individual, and the household as a unit, must decide what types of furnishings are beautiful and have character (Plate 55, p. 452). At a time when more and more people live in architecturally similar spaces, it is more than ever important to choose furnishings that are personal, that will individualize a space and make people feel they are coming home—not to a hostile or indifferent environment but to their own lifespace, which gives them the freedom to expand mentally, psychologically, and spiritually.

top: 17-6 "Peacock," a chair designed by Hans J. Wegner in 1950, has become a modern classic and is still in production today. *(Courtesy Design Selections International, New York)*
bottom: 17-7 Good reproductions of 18th-century furniture grace many homes today. The original of this Queen Anne side chair (c. 1750) may be seen in the Winterthur Museum. *(Courtesy Kindel Furniture)*

17-8 Victorian furniture is at home in a 19th-century house restored by Nancy O'Neill with Thomas J. Tramont and Dan Somes, consulting architects; Timothy R. Wooldridge, interior designer; John Canning, paint restoration. *(Photograph: © Karen Bussolini)*

440

17-9 A media room has various levels of seating built in around the perimeter. Peter Wilson, architect. (*Photograph: © Norman McGrath*)

Furniture Types

The first furniture probably consisted of a natural rock ledge found in a protected spot and used for sitting or sleeping. Refinement of such existing surfaces led to recesses in the walls of the hut or cave occupied by primitive peoples. In effect, this was "built-in" furniture, the prototype of units integrated with the architectural shell we are accustomed to today. Historians theorize that the earliest individual pieces of furniture were hammocks and mats for sleeping, which in colder climates would have been made of skins, in warmer climates of grasses and reeds. From these ancestors all the myriad furniture articles we know evolved.

Once established, the preference for isolated furniture prevailed well into the nineteenth century. Even clothes closets were unknown, and people stored their garments in bulky wardrobes or chests. Then in the late 1800s home designers began to use walls more intensively, and by the early twentieth century built-in furniture had staged a revival that is still vigorous today. Combined with the interest in furniture that is at one with the architecture is the development of modular *unit* or *component* pieces, which in a sense offer a compromise between built-in and individual furnishings. Unit furniture organizes a variety of furniture elements into a cohesive structure.

Because it is at once ancient and up-to-the-minute, built-in furniture is considered first.

Built-in and Modular

More often than not, built-in furniture promotes flexible living, although this may seem like a contradiction. Because the furnishings take less room than movable pieces, they leave a maximum amount of free space around and between them. Built-in furniture can also minimize dust-catching crevices, give a feeling of permanence and security, and break up the boxiness of typical rooms. At the same time, it reduces the visual clutter brought by many isolated pieces of furniture, which have a tendency to get out of position. Many people trace the current interest in built-in furniture to Frank Lloyd Wright, who early in his career began thinking of the house as a unified whole, with storage, seating, and tables forming an integral part of the architecture (see Chapter 19). Built-in furniture may make it difficult to tell where architecture leaves off, so thoroughly may the two be integrated. This concept of total, unified design appeals to our sense of harmony and order.

Like built-in furniture, modular furniture answers a desire for coherence and spaciousness. Modular furniture, however, offers the added advantage of mobility and flexibility. The component pieces may be assembled into varying units, changed at will, and used wherever needed. Built-in and component furniture will be referred to again in relation to specific types of pieces.

Beds

Reducing physical strain to a minimum is the major purpose of beds. Individuals vary in their specific ideas about sleeping comfort, so the only real way to find out whether a bed is right for the intended user is to try it. We have been conditioned to believe that a bed should have a springy foundation and a resilient mattress. The typical foundation consists of either inexpensive, lightweight flat springs or more bulky, expensive coil springs, but a flat plywood foundation can also be comfortable if the mattress is thick enough, particularly for people who enjoy a very firm surface or find it necessary because of back trouble.

Mattresses have been filled with just about everything from straw to hair, even air and water. **Innerspring** mattresses are still the most popular, probably because people are familiar with them. They vary in the number of coils, their design, whether or not they are individually pocketed, and in the type or thickness of the padding that protects the user. All of this affects their conformity—the way in which they respond to a person's distributed body weight—and hence the individual's comfort, which can only be ascertained by trial.

Foam mattresses are lightweight in proportion to their size and harbor no insects or allergy producers. They seldom need to be turned and come in various degrees of resilience (as, of course, do innerspring mattresses). Foam mattresses can also be made to order, which allows them to be cut to size in the thickness and density desired or even built up of layers of foam in different densities for greater comfort. Today the least expensive are thin pads of polyurethane foam that can be rolled up and stored when not in use. The better grades have 4- to 6-inch cores of polyurethane or latex foam. For safety's sake, all mattresses should carry a label stating that they conform to the flammability standard established by the Consumer Product Safety Commission and any state laws that apply.

Box springs may be used with either innerspring or foam mattresses. Coordinated spring-and-mattress sets are recommended since they are matched in firmness and probable length of service. Springs can be supported on simple wood legs or the more convenient metal frames on casters that permit easy moving.

A **waterbed** consists of a heavy-duty plastic water bag, a solid frame that supports the bag, a watertight liner between the bed and frame to guard against leaks, and a special heating pad that warms the water to a comfortable temperature. (The heating pad should bear the Underwriters' Laboratories label of safety testing.) Waterbeds are firm and strongly supportive, because they can shape themselves exactly to body contours, but some people find disconcerting their quick reaction to changes in position. They also weigh a tremendous amount when filled (about 1600 pounds for a standard-size model), must be emptied for moving—distinctly not an easy task—and may require special sheets and bedcovers. They can be used only in buildings with strong foundations, and some landlords will not allow them at all. But for those who can overcome or overlook these obstacles, waterbeds do provide a new experience in sleeping comfort. Newer models have a smaller water bag encased in foam rubber, lightening the weight, easing bedmaking, and reducing the wavelike motion. The firm foam edge produces a more conventional look and feel while eliminating the necessity for a hard frame to support it and special bedding to fit it.

Built-in beds offer a certain reassuring protectiveness and bring many conveniences close to hand—lighting, possibly a slanted end for reading in bed, bookcases and stereo components or controls, surfaces on which to place things. The main difficulties lie in moving the bed and in making it.

In small quarters or for occasional guests, **sofabeds** make a sensible economy. Today, many of these are quite handsome. Also, the various types of **bunk beds, fold-down beds,** and **trundle beds** can be excellent space-savers.

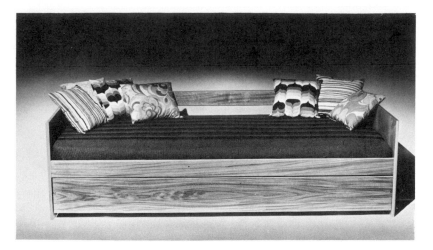

Sofas

The inclusive term *sofa* refers to a seat for two or more people, but many other names are or have been applied to such pieces of furniture. Some are used interchangeably, but the various terms may convey shades of meaning:

- **Chesterfield** refers to an overstuffed sofa with upholstered ends.
- **Couch** originally meant a long upholstered piece with a low back and one raised end for reclining.
- **Davenport** is used in the United States to describe an upholstered sofa often convertible into a bed, but originally the word designated a small writing desk named after its maker.
- **Divan** is a Turkish term for a large, low couch without arms or back that developed from piles of rugs for reclining.
- **Lounge** once referred to a type of couch with no back but with one high end for reclining. Today the term indicates either a flat padded surface on which to stretch out or any supercomfortable seating unit that invites relaxation.
- **Love seat** means a small sofa or "double chair" for two people.
- **Settee** refers to a light double seat with a back and sometimes with arms, often lightly upholstered.
- **Settles** are all-wood settees, used in Colonial days before a fire to trap heat with their high backs.
- **Sofa** comes from an Arabic word; in the United States it describes any long upholstered seat for more than one person. A **tuxedo** sofa has arms and back of the same height; a **Lawson** has arms lower than the back.
- **Convertible sofa, sofa-bed, sleeper,** or **studio couch** refers to a dual-purpose unit used for both sitting and sleeping.
- **Sectional units** or **modular sofas** have separate pieces easily assembled into various and changeable sizes and shapes or separated into individual chair units.
- **Seating platforms** often look built-in because they merge with the floor and wall.
- **Floor pads** are mattresses placed directly on the floor, often heaped with cushions, for relaxed lounging. If they can be folded over or rolled up to form seating units, they may be called **futons** after the traditional Japanese sleeping pads.

left: 17-12 "Champs," a post-modern sofa, is bulky but not heavy in weight because of the advances in foam cushioning. (*Courtesy Donghia Furniture*)

below: 17-13 A mattress and box spring on the floor serves for lounging among the pillows during social times, but it can be cleared for sleeping when desired. Peter Eisenman, architect. (*Photograph: Norman McGrath*)

17-14 Two Japanese futons on a movable platform are used as a bed at night in a studio/office 32 feet long but only 8 feet wide. *(Photograph: Gene Maggio/NYT Pictures)*

The variety of sofas is legion: straight, curved, or angled to fit a room; with or without arms; in one piece or sectional; long enough for a tall person to stretch out on or more modest in scale; heavy and massive, delicate and graceful, or light and simple. When shopping for a sofa, keep in mind the functions you will expect it to perform. In different situations individuals will need a sofa with one or more of the following characteristics:

- Long enough to stretch out on—6 feet or longer for most people
- Low and deep enough for relaxation but high and firm enough so that most people can get up under their own power
- Fitted with arms for comfort
- Convertible into a bed if extra sleeping space is required
- Sectional if flexibility or mobility is a necessity
- Upholstered for comfort in a material that combines beauty and durability

Chairs

For most people in the United States today, the greater part of our waking hours is spent sitting down. We work, study, relax, eat, and travel in a seated position. Leading such sedentary lives, we should be expert sitters; but we are not, because until recently no serious studies of sitting had been made. Now, however, we know from anthropometric data that maximum comfort results when weight and pressure are distributed and tension eased by having:

- The height of the seat somewhat less than the length of the sitter's lower legs, so that the feet rest on the floor and the legs can be relaxed

17-15 Charles Eames' swivel lounge chair of molded rosewood with cushioned leather upholstery adjusts to many positions; with the ottoman, it promises complete semi-reclining luxury. *(Museum of Modern Art, New York; gift of the manufacturer, Herman Miller, Inc.)*

- The depth of the seat a bit less than the length of the upper leg to avoid putting a pressure point under the knee
- The width of the seat ample enough to permit some movement
- The seat shaped or resilient, so that pressure is not concentrated on the small weight-bearing edge of the pelvis
- Both seat and back tilted backward slightly to buttress the weight
- The angle between seat and back 95 degrees or more
- The chair back in a position to provide lumbar support
- The position of the seat and back adjustable for different people (as in typists' chairs) or for different ways of relaxing (as in the old-fashioned Morris chairs and some of the new reclining chairs)
- A place to rest the head and relax the neck, plus supports for arms

The wing chair was one of the first types of seating devised for comfort. Over the years many variations have appeared. A contemporary design by Charles Eames (Fig. 17-15) resulted from a thorough exploration of new and old materials and techniques and a detailed study of sitting comfort, which showed that flexibility is essential. The Eames version has been so successful and has achieved such wide popularity that innumerable copies have appeared over the years.

Chairs must serve a number of purposes, and their forms should mirror their functions. The typical household needs chairs suitable to at least two categories of activity.

Furniture **447**

top left: 17-16 A reproduction of a chair designed by Josef Hoffmann in 1911 provides the padded comfort sought after today. *(Courtesy ICF Inc. Photograph: Peter Paige)*

top right: 17-17 Designer Shinya Okayama has taken advantage of the springiness of steel tubing for an eye-catching chair in which the arms become the back support but do not meet the back legs. *(Courtesy Gallery 91 Soho. Photograph: Mitsutaka Hashimoto)*

bottom left: 17-18 "Wink" can be changed from an armchair into a lounge chair or recliner by continuously adjustable controls in the steel frame. The fabric that covers the expanded polyurethane foam cushions can be removed for cleaning. Toshiyuki Kita, designer. *(Courtesy Atelier International, Ltd.)*

bottom right: 17-19 A spring base and frame of metal with overlapping leather upholstery straps makes a lightweight but comfortable chair. *(Courtesy Herman Miller, Inc.)*

Relaxed Activities

In the group space, in a study or seclusion room, and in bedrooms if possible, it is desirable to have seating that allows each person who regularly uses the room to relax completely for reading or simply for a brief "quiet time." The Eames chair and other types of reclining furniture meet this specification, as do sofas and most well-cushioned chairs, which adjust to varying individuals and are comfortable over long periods. Padded upholstered chairs and rocking chairs have long remained favorites for relaxing, but new designs expand the range of flexibility for supercomfortable chairs. Also, new types of springs and foams have greatly decreased weight and enable us to obtain pieces that are trim and neat, or even big and bulky but still movable.

Talking, listening to music, watching television, and similar pursuits can be enjoyed in the kinds of seating described above, but smaller side chairs that are fairly easy to move and give good support make helpful adjuncts. Such chairs can have shaped seats of wood, metal, or plastic, or they might be lightly upholstered, webbed, canvas-covered, or caned. Whatever the material, these chairs should be easy to grasp, light to lift, and strong enough to withstand frequent moving.

Alert Activities

Dining, working, and games require sturdy, easily moved chairs with relatively upright backs to keep the sitters alert; seats and backs that are shaped or lightly padded to lessen pressure; and upholstery that resists abrasion and soil. The most frequently used group dining space should have enough chairs or built-in seating always ready to accommodate the entire household, but it is helpful to have more of the same type of pull-up chairs (not necessarily identical) to bring out for larger gatherings.

Tables

The essence of table design calls for supporting a flat surface at a convenient level above the floor. This is reduced to its lowest common denominator when a home craftsman balances a piece of plywood or a flush door on prefabricated, easy-to-attach metal or wood legs or sometimes on a pair of sawhorses (which, incidentally, is an inexpensive way to get a striking table). There are problems, however, in all table design, and these include providing for:

- Necessary strength and stability
- Supports out of the way of feet and legs
- The right height, size, and shape for its use
- Durable materials

As with chairs, each home needs a variety of tables that differ in function and therefore in size, shape, height, and materials.

Dining Tables

Sit-down meals require a table that is sturdy enough not to be jarred by the unpredictable movements of children or the force of someone carving meat; that has a top large enough to give each person at least 2 feet of elbow room and high enough (usually 30 inches) to allow leg room between the chair and the table apron; that keeps supports out of the way of sitters' feet and knees; and that can be extended in size if necessary. Rather than extending a table, many people now use more than one for a larger crowd if the available space permits.

The surface of a dining table will be an important feature in its selection, because the table top—covered or uncovered—will form a background for china, crystal, silver, and linens. Tablecloths have become increasingly rare for daily

17-20 A favorite since its conception in 1925 by designer Josef Hoffmann, the "Prague" bentwood armchair is a comfortable and handsome pull-up chair for many uses. *(Courtesy Stendig, Inc.)*

17-21 A dining table of oak and rosewood expands with two 18-inch leaves to seat six to eight people. *(Courtesy Dunbar)*

17-22 The heavy glass top of the "Palasan" dining table exposes the tops of the bunched rattan pedestal as a striking design motif. *(Courtesy The McGuire Company. Photograph: Skelton Photography)*

meals, often being replaced by mats, so it pays to look closely at the durability, ease of maintenance, and beauty of the top surface (Plate 56, p. 452). Wood, plastic, and glass are commonly used materials; choice depends on use, effect desired, and price.

Shape is the other major consideration in choosing a dining table. Most are rectangular, because a basically squared shape harmonizes with rectangular rooms and can be pushed snugly against a wall or into a corner. In the right place, however, a round or oval table will give an inimitable friendly feeling. Many kinds of rectangular, round, or oval tables can be extended with leaves—the round thus becoming an oval. A polygonal or odd-shape table makes a refreshing change. *Drop-leaf tables*, in use since Elizabethan days, expand or contract with ease. Some contemporary *folding tables* can be compacted to 9 inches or stretched to 110 inches, the latter dimension providing space for fourteen people. *Extension tables* should be checked for ease of manipulation and stability when extended.

It is important to check dining chairs and tables together, because their legs often interfere with each other, the heights of the two are not coordinated, or the space between chair seat and table apron is insufficient for the sitters' comfort.

Coffee Tables

We have come to think that no sofa is complete unless faced with a long, low table on which ashtrays, books, magazines, newspapers, accessories, plants, flowers, and snacks abound. Most coffee tables, though, seem to have been designed

17-23 A coffee table, handcrafted by Gail Fredell Smith, contrasts cherry-wood with lacquered oak in a design that is beautiful as well as practical. *(Courtesy Norman Petersen & Associates)*

450

left: Plate 53 A beautifully crafted harpsichord occupies its own recess in this Cambridge, Massachusetts, home. While paying full respect to the piece as a musical instrument, the owner also focuses upon it as an elegant piece of furniture. Ben Thompson, designer. *(Photograph: © Ezra Stoller/ESTO)*

below: Plate 54 Red chairs around a glass-topped table add drama to a dining room in Brooklyn, New York. Alfredo De Vido, architect. *(Photograph: © Norman McGrath)*

top: Plate 55 Easy chairs designed by Michael Graves in the 1980s seem quite companionable in a setting from an earlier age. *(Courtesy SunarHauserman, Photograph: Bill Kontzias)*

bottom: Plate 56 Much of the light and color in this dining room come from the dining table itself—a Plexiglas case lit from within by fluorescent tubes. The translucent plastic "cloth" spreads yellow light through the whole area, and the color could be changed easily by switching to another hue in plastic. Joan Sprague and Chester Sprague, architects. *(Photograph: John T. Hill)*

only for the long, low, open look; they have no storage space for the things needed in a conversation area, are too low to be reached comfortably from the sofa and to give foot room, and if in scale with the sofa, usually block traffic, especially for the middle seating positions. The most useful coffee tables are about 20 inches high and offer some storage space. Their tops are durable and their supports strong, so they cannot be tipped easily.

Occasional Tables

Convenience seems to demand a horizontal surface, however small, within reach of every seat. Thus we often find a table at each end of the sofa and one for each group of chairs. Unlike coffee tables, occasional tables seldom interfere with the legs of sitters and may provide shelves or drawers for supplementary storage. They look better if they are of the same height as the arms of upholstered sofas and chairs, but a somewhat lower or higher level makes for greater convenience and diminishes spillage of beverages. Occasional tables often hold lamps. *Nests of tables*, the top one acting as an end or coffee table, greatly simplify entertaining, as do *stacking tables*. Clusters of cubes not only serve the same purpose but also double as extra seating. *Console* or *sofa tables* are higher (approximately 30 inches), longer, and designed to fit against a wall or sofa back.

Card and Game Tables

The folding or break-down card table is a wonderful invention. Most people find it more comfortable to play cards and other games at tables several inches lower than those meant for eating (27 inches is normal). Collapsible card tables are ideal for occasional games, bridge luncheons, buffet suppers, and supplementary serving at festive dinners. Space permitting, a permanent card table with at least two chairs always handy could be a fixture in any household where games or casual eating occur frequently.

Kitchen Tables

Once banished in the drive for compact efficiency, tables in kitchens or adjacent alcoves have again found popularity. Since they often serve for eating and meal preparation, they differ from dining tables only in having greater strength and durability.

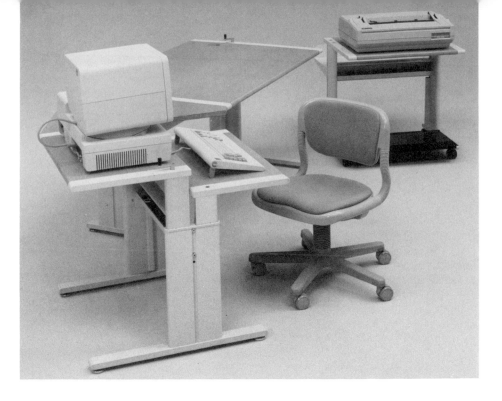

17-26 A desk or "work station" designed for the computer age is most comfortable if it is adjustable for the individual user as to height and tilt of the work surface. (*Courtesy CompuTech*)

Desks

An efficient desk has two essential properties: a suitable surface for writing and/or typing and computer use, and convenient and accessible storage for papers and supplies. It should be obvious that every household needs at least one good writing place, but the size, complexity, and location of the unit will depend on individual requirements. A desk can be a table with only one or two drawers, a compartment in a modular unit, or a piece of furniture designed for serious work such as a home computer desk. It may be located in the kitchen, study, bedroom, or any other room that provides the privacy and space needed. The surface should be steadily supported and at a convenient height for the person who uses it most often and the kind of use it receives. (Various work surface heights were detailed in Chapter 5.) A vertical file drawer or two is the most sensible place to store compactly all the pieces of paper related to household operation. Files can be part of a desk or purchased separately in units of one to four drawers. A two-drawer unit makes a good pedestal for an instant desk, with a piece of plywood or door for the top and a support of some kind at the other end.

Storage Units

Storage is a major problem today. Living quarters have steadily become smaller, while attics, spare rooms, and basements have all but disappeared. More people have more things to put away and apparently less time in which to do it. Yet many favor the uncluttered, clean-lined look, and having the proverbial "place for everything" does simplify housekeeping.

A total concept of household storage goes beyond what most of us call furniture, because efficient storage is part of the architectural design. This means giving at least as much thought to storage in all parts of the home as is typically devoted to the kitchen. Convenience, visibility, accessibility, flexibility, and maintenance are just as important in group spaces and bedrooms. The minimum one should

above: 17-27 A relatively small number of components can be fitted together in almost endless configurations to suit exacting storage requirements, with or without doors, in this furniture system. *(Courtesy ICF Inc.)*

right: 17-28 Storage systems can incorporate both open and closed sections to create an interesting design element in a room. *(Courtesy Interlübke)*

expect is empty space for cupboards and chests, for suitcases, strollers, bicycles, outdoor furniture, and the like. These facilities can be built into the house or added as modular units.

We store things by standing them on floors or shelves, by hanging them in closets, on walls or the backs of doors, by suspending them from ceilings, or by putting them in drawers or chests. Which of these solutions is best depends upon the use, size, shape, fragility, and value of the object to be stored.

Shelves

The simplest pieces of storage furniture are shelves. Despite the fact that books, stereo components, televisions, art objects, and miscellaneous items to be housed come in many different sizes and shapes, easily adjustable shelves can store them efficiently. Items on open shelves do get dusty, but they make a handsome display and can also absorb noise. Stability and flexibility are the critical factors in shelving. Home entertainment centers are available in ready-made units or modular systems, or they can be designed and assembled by household members themselves.

Nearly every room can profit by some book and magazine storage. In the kitchen a single shelf may store all the family's cookbooks, while a bookcase or a few shelves in the living area and in bedrooms suffice to hold current reading materials. The principal center for the household's collection of books could be the living room, dining area, study, family room, or even a separate library or gallery.

17-29 A simple, well-designed bookcase of Alaskan yellow cedar with clear lacquer would be a quiet but pleasing focus on an otherwise blank wall. Norman Petersen, designer. *(Courtesy Norman Petersen & Associates)*

456

Low bookcases double as tables and, if sufficiently long and well planned, can unify a wall. A bookcase that reaches to the ceiling often becomes a forceful architectural element. Shelves can frame and relate doors and windows or serve as partial or complete dividers between two rooms or parts of a single room.

Cabinets

Although they appear infrequently outside kitchens, dining spaces, and bathrooms, cabinets with doors and adjustable shelves or vertical dividers are welcome in every room.

Doors on cabinets present the same problems as doors between rooms. Swinging doors work easily and accept narrow storage racks on the back, but they get in the way when open. Sliding doors open only part of the cabinet at a time, sometimes jam, collect dust, and allow for no door-back shelves. When space in front of cabinets is at a premium—or when doors are left open while people move about—sliding doors offer a good solution, but in other places swinging doors have distinct advantages.

Cabinets for radios, stereo components, and television sets have no historical precedents, and the early ones were overly conspicuous. Today, audio-visual equipment is often integrated with cabinets and bookshelves or is built into the wall. Stereo components and television sets are highly engineered pieces of technology that lend themselves to visual expression of function. Too, we are growing less aware of the blank television screen, just as we accept the unlit fireplace.

17-30 Built-in storage facilities can house a media closet that can be opened or closed as needed. Eve Frankl, designer. (Photograph: © Peter Aaron/ESTO)

457

Chests and Drawers

The chest was the original piece of storage furniture, later divided into segments fitted with drawers. Although we take sliding drawers for granted, they were not widely used until the seventeenth century. Chests of drawers work best when they have strongly joined, dustproof drawers that slide easily on center guides, drawer stops to prevent them from falling out, and handles that can be grasped without difficulty. Shallow drawers at the top are a great convenience, and flexible dividers for them well justify their cost. Relatively small components that fit together increase flexibility of placement. Drawers combined with shelves and/or cabinets of different sizes can store a multitude of variously shaped items.

Outdoor Furniture

Interest in outdoor living has led to many kinds of weather-resistant furniture in a surprisingly wide range of materials. Redwood, cedar, and cypress are long-lasting and attractive. Aluminum never rusts, stays cool in the sun, and is light in weight. Wicker and rattan bring the charm of natural materials to an outdoor living area and are often used indoors as well. Some of the newer plastics stand weathering quite well and are also a good solution for use either indoors or out.

Tables present no special problems, nor do the frames of chairs and chaises, but it is not easy to make upholstery both weatherproof and resilient. Few springs, cushions, and pads remain unharmed by an excess of water, although some plastic materials can take moderate amounts. The seating most nearly approaching care-free comfort has metal frames with synthetic webbing for seats and backs. Then come the wood, plastic, or metal chairs and lounges with loose cushions, which should not be left out in the rain. For the latter, it is advisable to have a roofed outdoor living area or weathertight storage nearby.

top: 17-31 Made of carved and partly gilded walnut, painted bone, and wrought iron, this luxurious 17th-century *vargueno* and supporting cabinet are solidly fitted with drawers, and can be taken apart for traveling. (*Metropolitan Museum of Art, New York [gift of the Duchesse de Richelieu, 1960])*

bottom: 17-32 Outdoor furniture with a frame of square tubular aluminum and seat and back of a metal mesh called "Alumicane" is handsome, sturdy, and, above all, weather-resistant. Hall Bradley, designer. (*Courtesy Brown Jordan*)

17-33 Terrace furniture of welded steel wire is weather-resistant, easily moved to follow the sun or evade it, and has cushions that are removable in inclement weather. Harry Bertoia, designer. (*Courtesy Knoll International*)

Materials and Construction

There is no quick and easy way to size up furniture materials and construction. When buying new furniture much time and disappointment could be saved if the manufacturer's specifications were available for each line, a provision consumer groups have been advocating. Lacking these guidelines, it is advisable to look at every piece of furniture from literally every angle; to get all possible information from the salesperson; and to try to purchase only from manufacturers, wholesalers, or retailers who stand behind their merchandise. Furniture can be no better than the materials, the joinings, and the finishes that go into its makeup. Some preliminary test questions include the following:

- Does the piece stand firmly on the floor and resist efforts to make it wobble? This is particularly important in tables (even more so in expandable ones), as well as in desks and chairs.
- Do all movable parts, such as drawers and drop leaves, operate easily and steadily?
- Are all joints tightly and smoothly fitted together with some type of interlocking construction?
- Is the finish durable, smooth, and evenly applied? Is it composed of one or many coats properly applied or of one or two coats that look thick and gummy in any crevice or indentation?

Having answered these questions, the points of greatest wear and stress should be examined.

Flat surfaces—tops of tables, desks, counters, bookcases, cabinets, and chests—should resist scratching, denting, breaking, staining, and wetting. Properly finished hardwoods generally prove satisfactory if kept reasonably free from liquids. Plastic finishes on wood are durable, some exceedingly so; however, the problems of refinishing such surfaces have not been solved completely. Vinyl tiles or sheets provide quiet and good resistance to stains and cuts, while plastic laminates are even more durable but noisier. We have not yet come to the point of considering wear on plastics as a plus factor, as we may on wood that shows its age but has been lovingly cared for or restored. Glass is light and airy but presents a breakage hazard; it also requires almost constant cleaning. Marble, although rich and heavy, makes a noisy surface that can break and stain.

Edges of tables, doors, and drawers are the points most easily nicked and marred. All but the most durable materials will show wear, but hardwood or replaceable metal or plastic strips help. Bullnose edges soften the harshness of standard 90-degree-edge angles and, when made of solid wood, are more durable for vulnerable edges.

Runners of drawers should be made from hardwood, plastics, or noncorrosive metals since they receive the wear from sliding open and shut. Large and heavy drawers are best suspended on rollers and tracks.

Handles, knobs, and hinges show ample evidence of the use they get in the soil that collects on and around them. Hardwoods and matte-finish metals are still the most serviceable materials, but plastics now have taken over a portion of the field. Hinges should be of the best possible quality and securely fastened into a base material hard enough to hold screws under strain. Plastics have one important advantage in furniture manufacture in that functional devices can be part of the unit itself, rather than being applied, which makes them much more durable. Of course, if self-handles and hinges *should* be broken, repair might be difficult or impossible.

Legs and bases suffer assault from kicking feet, mops and brooms, vacuum cleaners, and children's toys. Damage can be reduced by minimizing the number of parts that touch the floor and then having these made of medium-dark wood, plastic, or metal, with finishes that do not scratch or chip readily. Indenting bases so they are not easily seen and covering them with upholstery or carpet are two other possibilities.

The following sections list the virtues and also the drawbacks of various materials for furniture and the ways in which these materials are fabricated.

Wood

The standard furniture material, wood should be thoroughly dry and of a variety that is stable in size and shape to minimize shrinking, swelling, and warping. Each wood has its own qualities, parts need not take a good finish but are best when of strong hardwood such as ash or birch. Exposed surfaces ought to wear well, be hard enough to resist scratching and denting, have a pleasant finish, and be beautiful in themselves; mahogany, walnut, oak, maple, and birch display these qualities. Redwood has a pleasant color and withstands weather, but it is soft and splintery. The qualities of various woods and finishes are presented in Tables 10–1 and 10–2 (pp. 239 and 251).

The term *solid* means that the furniture (at least all exposed parts of it) is made of whole wood, having no veneer. *Genuine* means that all exposed parts are made from a single kind of wood, with veneer on flat surfaces and solid wood structural supports such as legs. *Veneer* refers to a thin slice of finishing wood that is adhered to a body of less refined wood, perhaps even of several layers of wood, known as *plywood*. (The advantages of veneers and plywood are discussed in Chapter 10.) Some hard-pressed *composition boards*, manufactured from wood fibers, prove their value for table tops, backs of chests, and parts of drawers. The Federal Trade Commission prohibits misleading labeling regarding both construction and composition of furniture.

Wood in furniture can be joined in a number of ways:

- **Rebated** or rabbeted joints have a groove cut from the edge of one piece to receive the other member.
- **Dovetailed** joints have flaring tenons (or tongues) on one piece and mortises (or grooves) on the other. They are used in most good drawers.
- **Mortise-and-tenon** joints have a mortise (a hole or cavity) in one piece of wood into which a tenon (projecting piece) cut in the end of the other fits securely. They are usually stronger than doweled joints.
- **Tongue-and-groove** joints resemble mortise-and-tenon joints except that the tongue and groove extend the width of the boards.
- **Doweled** joints have wooden pegs (or dowels) inserted into holes in the two pieces of wood to be joined.

17-34 The way in which wood is joined critically affects the durability and appearance of furniture. The most typical joints are shown.

rebated   dovetailed   mortise-and-tenon   tongue-and-groove   doweled   butt

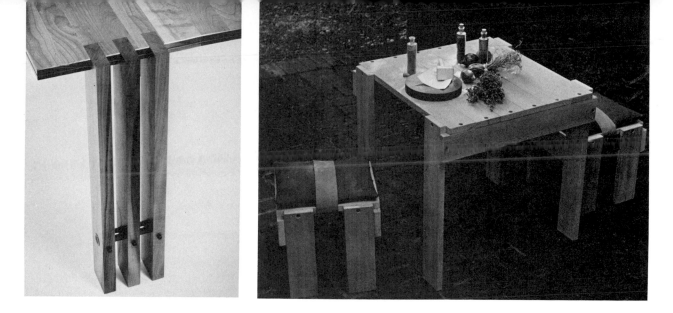

- **Butt** joints are the simplest and the weakest; they have no place in furniture unless reinforced with corner blocks.

Most joints need glue to reinforce them, and synthetic resins have joined the older vegetable and casein glues for this purpose. Frames of chairs, sofas, and case goods also require triangular wood or metal corner blocks tightly screwed and cemented in place for reinforcing. Screws strengthen joints much more than nails do.

Until a few decades ago wood joints were among the highlights of a fine piece of furniture—the sign of a master craftsman. After a period in which joinings declined in both interest and quality, we are now beginning to see again the emphasis on wood joints as things of beauty and structural design. Some of the newer knock-down furniture does away with rigid joints so that the pieces can be disassembled for moving.

Most *case* goods, which include chests, bookcases, cabinets, desks, tables, and chairs with no upholstered parts, are made of wood. However, other materials are becoming increasingly popular.

Metal

Mass-produced metal furniture is relatively inexpensive, which is a factor in its popularity. In recent years designers have begun to exploit metal for its inherent structural properties, finding it uniquely suitable for pieces that are strong and durable but not bulky. Steel with a baked enamel finish is familiar in kitchens and bathroom cabinets, as well as in indoor-outdoor chairs and tables. It is available in many colors, is easy to wash, and maintains its good appearance if not kicked or banged. Steel is also widely used for legs and frames of chairs, tables, and storage units. Rods and tubes of steel can be coated with any color, and some metallic enamels have a soft but rich glow. Chromium-plating gives lasting protection and surfaces that range visually from glittering hardness to pewterlike mellowness.

Notably different from the earlier "pipe and angle-iron" designs are those based on the sculptural potentialities of metal itself. In the hands of a sensitive designer steel wire becomes an inspirational, responsive medium for chairs that are both graceful and comfortable. Lightweight, rustproof, and cool to the touch, aluminum is particularly suitable for outdoor furniture. Some of the sculptured pieces are elegant far beyond their cost. Aluminum's natural color is pleasantly sympathetic, but it can be permanently treated with a wide range of hues.

above left: 17-35 Designer Gail Fredell Smith highlighted the beauty of wood joints in a table by allowing them to show on the top surface as part of the design. *(Courtesy Norman Petersen & Associates)*

above right: 17-36 Simple board furniture, the method of joining exposed, has an ingenuous but ingratiating quality. Roger Fleck, designer. *(Courtesy Bluepeter, Inc.)*

below: 17-37 Furniture made from interlocking metal legs and rails is very strong, demountable, and capable of being combined in many ways. The four-sided leg joint brings a sculptural quality to the plain structure. George Ciancimino, designer. *(Courtesy Jens Risom Design, Inc.)*

Metal can be joined by welding, riveting, bolting, or just shaping. Welding gives smooth, strong joints, but bolts and rivets suffice if seeing what holds the pieces together is not objectionable. Most metal furniture is so much stronger than normal household use demands that construction generally presents less of a problem to the consumer than does furniture made of wood. However, repairs are much more difficult.

Synthetics

Synthetic materials have affected furniture design and maintenance in three markedly different ways. Most obvious are the durable, easy-to-clean surfaces—vinyl and laminated melamine sheets for table and counter tops, vinyl upholstery for chairs and sofas. More striking is the use of molded plastics for chairs and tables. Thin and lightweight, amazingly strong yet slightly resilient, polyester resin reinforced with fiberglass, polypropylene, or acrylic can be molded so that the seat, back, and arms of the chair are one continuous piece, thus eliminating the need for joining. The plastic shell, much warmer and more pleasant to touch than metal, can be left as is, coated with vinyl, or upholstered with foam rubber and fabric. Finally, transparent or translucent plastics, such as Plexiglas or Lucite, offer designers opportunities for a new vocabulary in furniture design.

Foamed plastics represent an even newer development—one that has made possible a new type of furniture construction. Foams have revived the bulky look in furniture, although in this instance it is bulk without weight. These cellular plastics are quite versatile, since the density can be controlled to produce either rigid structural parts or soft cushioning. Certain of the foamed plastic units need no joining; they are simply blocks of the material, perhaps enclosed within a rigid frame. Others are built up of shaped slabs of foam in different densities held in place by contact cement with no rigid skeletal frame. Integral-skin foams on some pieces of furniture even eliminate the need for separate upholstery.

17-38 Transparent Lucite furniture seems to hover in a small greenhouse addition in a city apartment renovation. Paul Rudolph, architect. *(Photograph: Robert Levin)*

462

17-39 "Alanda" is made of molded polyurethane in which steel frames with springs are embedded. Arm and back cushions are of Dacron-wrapped molded polyurethane. Paolo Piva, designer. *(Courtesy B & B America/Stendig Inc.)*

Exciting as these developments are, the possibility exists for eventual dulling or discoloration, pitting or scratching, even breakage or breakdown of the material. To date, repair or refinishing ranges from difficult to impossible. Problems of flammability, including the release of toxic fumes, and ultimate solid-waste disposal have still to be worked out. Of course, these are common problems with wood and metal also, but the natural materials have been around longer, so their dangers, environmental problems, and recycling possibilities are fairly well known. With plastics, it becomes a matter of learning as we go along, of insisting on more thorough testing and disclosure.

Upholstered Furniture

The padding and covering put on chairs and sofas to make them conform to our contours can be of several degrees of comfort.

Fabric Stretched on a Frame

Until the Renaissance, upholstery consisted chiefly of textiles, rushes, or leather stretched over frames and often supplemented by loose cushions. Furniture with backs and seats of leather or fabric is still common today and provides lightweight, inexpensive resilience. The use of cane, rush, wicker, or rattan for furniture parts or whole pieces also prevails; in cost and extent it ranges from the cane seats familiar in bentwood and other occasional chairs through exotic imitations of Eastern furniture to elegant rattan pieces that would be at home in the most

17-40 Stretched leather seat and back on an X-frame folding chair of rattan is a modern version of a centuries-old design. Leonard Linden, designer. (*Courtesy The McGuire Company*)

formal setting. The latter two types often have upholstered cushions for greater comfort. In any event, the frame on which fabric is stretched should be strong as well as attractive, the upholstery durable and securely fastened to the frame but easily removable.

Simple Padding

The next step in comfortable seating would be a padding made from thin layers of resilient materials covered with fabric and secured to a frame. Since the seventeenth century this has been the standard method of making frequently moved chairs comfortable. Until recently, long curled hair was the best and most costly padding, with kapok, moss, and cotton relegated to less expensive pieces. But today, various types of foam padding are common. As a rule this arrangement takes the form of a foam cushion on a plywood base, on webbing, or on a sling of resilient material. Thicker foam pads have taken the place of springs and stuffing for many seating pieces. The pads are supported by plywood or webbing, and sometimes foam pads become furniture themselves, consisting of one piece or several held together by buckles or straps. Removable covers make cleaning easy, and in some cases the foam may have a plastic fabric laminated to it or an integral skin, which means it can be wiped clean with a damp sponge.

Stuffing and Springs

Although furniture designers began to place springs under stuffing during the eighteenth century, it was not until about 1914 that massively overstuffed pieces came into fashion. The materials and steps of this complicated process, a version of which is shown in Figure 17-41, may include:

- **Frame** of strong hardwood with secure joinings or of metal or plastic
- **Webbing** woven in a simple basket weave and tacked to the frame
- **Springs** usually coiled, tied to the webbing and frame and spaced closely enough to prevent sagging but not so closely that they rub against one another (twelve springs are needed in a good chair). Flat wire springs are used in slim-line furniture as well as many chair or sofa backs, and even seats today.
- **Burlap** covering the springs to protect the padding
- **Padding** or stuffing (similar to simple padding), which gives smooth, soft contours
- **Muslin** to cover the padding (only on better furniture)
- **Final fabric** hiding all of the above and presenting its finished appearance to the world

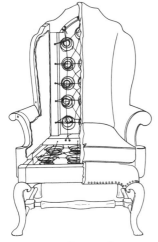

17-41 Stuffing-and-spring upholstery has several components, shown here in a cross-section drawing.

Cushions and Pillows

Once most upholstery was firmly fastened to the frame of the piece of furniture. Now separate cushions for the seat and pillows for the back and even the arms make furniture still more comfortable and adjustable to the human body.

Down (and feathers) remain the most luxurious stuffing but lack resilience and must be fluffed after each use. Newer types of cushions may have a core of coil springs or firm urethane foam covered by softer layers of foam and perhaps a wrap of polyester or even a layer of down encased in ticking. Different versions and densities may be used for sitting and support cushions. Back and arm pillows are often softer and perhaps filled with polyester fiberfill. One of the main benefits of man-made materials is that they spring back to their original contours. Sofa and chair arms should be adequately cushioned so that the wooden forms beneath cannot be felt.

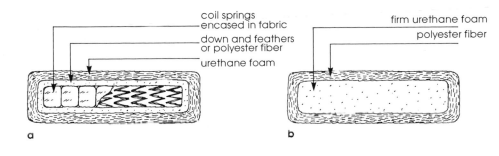

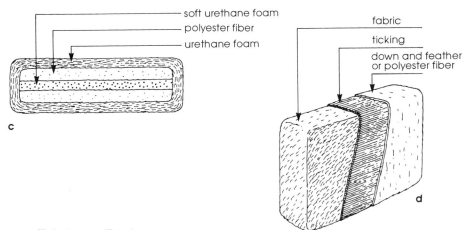

17-42 Seat and back furniture cushions can be made of springs encased in fabric, and covered with foam, down, and/or other stuffing (a).
Less expensive pillows are made of firm foam between two layers of soft foam (b), or dense foam with polyester fiberfill (c).
Back pillows may be down- and feather-filled or filled with polyester fiber or bits of foam (d).

Upholstery Fabrics

Fabrics become almost an integral part—and the most conspicuous part—of the furniture to which they are fastened, and they are what we touch. The least to expect is that they look comfortable to sit on, feel good to hands and arms, and resist abrasion and soil. Visual relationship to the shape they cover and the setting in which they are placed lifts them above mere utility. Beyond this are fabrics with their own distinctive character, used creatively.

Seeing identical pieces of furniture covered with varied fabrics alerts us to the forcefulness of color and design in altering the apparent shape, size, and character of any form. In rooms with several or many upholstered items, the whole effect can be changed with different furniture covers. Slipcovers can provide such a change, perhaps for different seasons. All that we know about the psychological effects of hue and value, emphasis and scale can be brought to bear in selecting upholstery.

Deciding on the fabric itself involves a knowledge of fibers and weaves as discussed in Chapter 12. Then it is a matter of searching for a textile that is aesthetically pleasing, assessing it for its intended use and cost. Tightly woven fabrics are more durable than loose, satin, or novelty weaves. Very dark and very light colors show lint and soil readily. Stain-resistant finishes are more durable when applied by the manufacturer than when sprayed on by a retailer.

The International Fabricare Institute has devised a voluntary code to be adopted by manufacturers to guide consumers in cleaning and caring for upholstered pieces. It suggests that a tag attached to each piece label the fabric as to type of cleaning product that should be used on it. All upholstered pieces should carry this information: manufacturer, fiber content, composition of fiberfill and cush-

above left: 17-43   The same piece of furniture can take on very different characteristics, depending on the upholstery fabric used. A wing chair upholstered in leather. *(Courtesy Drexel Heritage Furnishings, Inc.)*
above right: 17-44   The same chair upholstered in a patterned fabric. *(Courtesy Drexel Heritage Furnishings, Inc.)*

ioning, care instructions, colorfastness, shrinkage, and spot-stain resistance. In addition, commercial-grade fabrics (used more and more frequently in residential applications) must provide information on flammability and durability (wearability) and meet rigorous standards set by legislation.

The basic goal in all furniture selection (and arrangement) is a personal environment that works for its occupants rather than the other way around.

References for Further Reading

Abercrombie, Stanley. "Ergonomics—It's Not a New Exercise, It's the New Science of Comfort," *House and Garden*, February

Hennessey, James and Victor Papanek. *Nomadic Furniture.* New York: Random House, 1973.

Murphy, Dennis Grant. *The Materials of Interior Design.* Burbank, CA: Stratford House Publishing Company, 1978. Part III, Chaps. 7–9.

"Shopping for Upholstered Furniture," *Better Homes and Gardens*, October 1981, pp. 86–89.

Whiton, Sherrill. *Interior Design and Decoration*, 4th ed. Philadelphia: Lippincott, 1974. Pp. 585–592, 634–640.

"Why Comfort?," *House and Garden*, February 1980, p. 75.

Accessories

18

Human beings have an inherent desire for aesthetic enrichment. Almost as soon as primitive peoples learned to build shelters, to fabricate tools and useful objects, they began to add purely decorative touches. This of course is ornament, no different from the embellishments we are accustomed to seeing on a sofa or chair or even a wall. In a sense, enrichment does mean ornament—something that heightens the visual or textual interest of a piece, possibly a piece of furniture. But in the context of home design, accessories are usually considered from another point of view. Our homes abound with objects that are either purely decorative and serve no functional purpose or, if they are utilitarian, have been designed in such a way that they provide enrichment against a contrasting or simpler background (Plate 57, p. 485). These are the elements of primary concern in this chapter: the designs, arrangements, embellishments, and accessory objects that contribute a quality of richness to our daily lives and our personal lifespaces.

Depending upon one's interests and tastes, accessories can be approached in at least two ways: objects may serve as enhancement of the total design in architecture and furnishings or they may constitute the focus of the design, with other elements subordinated to them. In the latter treatment, accessories dominate

totally. The architectural elements, including wall, floor, and ceiling design may be extremely simple and straightforward, acting as background to cast the accessory collection in a central role. Upon entering such a room, the visitor's eye would be drawn immediately to the display of objects for its overall impact. Next, one could spend a pleasant time absorbing details, studying each individual piece as it competes for attention. The richness of interest and visual design may be so complex that each subsequent visit to such a home would be a new adventure, as previously undiscovered subtleties became apparent. If all the objects of enrichment were removed from the space—or a completely new set substituted—the room would take on a dramatically different character.

Basically the same approach might be followed by the household lucky enough to possess a treasured work of art. One extreme example of this is to subordinate everything else to the art. Most people would not be so single-minded; a subtler method of focusing attention on a painting is to repeat or recall its colors elsewhere in the room, so that the eye is inevitably drawn back to the source of the color.

Thoughtful use of accessories can also enhance the design of a home to bring out certain architectural or historical features. Three very different examples will illustrate this point.

The house shown in Figure 18-2 takes its character from the rustic architecture: thick masonry walls, deeply recessed windows, exposed rough-hewn beams. To emphasize the quality of an old country farmhouse, the owners have added several integral touches: a soft-hued painting in an antique frame, folk pottery and wood carvings, a wooden light fixture hanging from the ceiling, touches of wrought iron, an old butcher's block, and so on. The overall impression is one of harmony, warmth, and coziness, of lives enriched by the past through accessories.

18-2 Old artifacts, including an oval painting in an antique frame, seem appropriate enrichment for a renovated mill in Pennsylvania's Bucks County. Lilias Barger and Raymond Barger, designers. *(Photograph: John T. Hill)*

Figure 18-3 shows another traditional home, in this case a very formal one. The aura of nineteenth-century elegance is established by graceful paneled walls, an ornate carpet, and antique furnishings, but this effect would be incomplete without the enrichment provided by the crystal chandelier and candelabrum, the elaborate gold mirror frame, and porcelain ware on the table and sideboard. Period authenticity (or simply authenticity of feeling) is only one aspect of accessorizing, but it can be a very important one in certain situations.

18-3 Heavy crystal, fine porcelain, and an antique mirror in a gold-leaf frame enrich this formal, traditionally paneled dining room and foyer. *(Photograph: John T. Hill)*

18-4 Areas of concentrated enrichment, such as a grouping of plants, have long been used to heighten the effect of architecture. In this case the plants call attention to the high, sloping ceiling. James Caldwell, architect. *(Photograph: Philip L. Molten)*

The points to be emphasized in a particular home may have no clear relation to any style or period or type of design, but rather be a distinctive aspect of the architecture. One of the most striking features of the house illustrated in Figure 18-4 is its soaring height. To focus attention on the raised ceiling, the owners have added a unique form of accessories—a row of plants suspended near the roofline and illuminated by skylights. Set off against white walls, the plants naturally draw the eye upward, but they also refer back to plants massed around the fireplace to bring us down to ground level again.

These examples not only demonstrate how accessories can either carry a design or support it but also reveal a spectrum of tastes. We know much about the occupants of each of these homes without having met or seen them. Some people might empathize with the collector of charming native handcrafts, others with the person who cherishes classic accessories. This emphasizes an important aspect of home enrichment: a collection of objects without personal significance to those who live with them will never blend comfortably into a lifespace. Freedom of taste allows people to choose and combine what they like most, to express themselves in completing the design of a home.

So far accessories have been treated as something deliberately added with the conscious desire to "enrich." In so doing we overlook a very basic form of accessorizing—the kind that develops spontaneously or as a side effect from some other element. Because it is so fundamental, such incidental embellishment should be considered first.

18-5 A bookcase becomes a headboard for a bed and stores reading matter close by. Calvin Tsao, designer. *(Photograph: © Paul Warchol)*

Background Enrichment

The most obvious enrichment in any home is the one most likely forgotten about—people. No two people look alike or dress alike. Their varying personalities, changing moods, and different activities all affect the background against which they move. What a different quality a room has when it is populated and when it is not! Like actors bringing to life a stage setting, people enrich the lifespaces they inhabit.

Another basic form of enrichment may be provided by the architecture of the home itself. The patterns of ceiling beams, door and window frames, supporting columns, and wall panels often enrich otherwise unadorned surfaces. Windows and doors contribute two kinds of enrichment, in the patterns of light they admit and the vistas they allow of the outside environment.

Patterns in draperies and upholstery, in floor coverings and wall treatments, in furnishings and lighting fixtures all can provide a measure of enrichment. So too might the implements and materials of a profession or hobby, especially when they involve the visual arts. No space could be visually richer than the inside of a weaving studio, with its profusion of multicolored yarns, the satisfying form of the loom, and works in progress scattered about; a painting, sculpture, or ceramic studio creates the same kind of delightful image.

Books and magazines are not normally chosen for their physical appearance on a shelf, but it cannot be denied that a wall of books brings enrichment to any room. Personal involvement with certain books may add an emotional enrichment

18-6 The shapes and placement of beautiful objects here enhance the natural beauty of the environment and the strong architectural design to create a concentrated focal spot of permanent yet ever-changing enchantment. Wurster, Bernardi, and Emmons, architects. *(Photograph: © Morley Baer)*

to bolster the visual, but even without this attachment satisfaction can be taken in the rows of similarly shaped objects with their colorful bindings and dust jackets.

A special set of circumstances led to the very individual type of enrichment pictured in Figure 18-6: masonry walls that are 2 feet thick cut with a window offering an extraordinary view of mountains and coastline. The owner took advantage of the wide window ledge to create a still life of precious objects—a hot toddy maker, a tray and decanter, some elegant jars. The contrast between this precise, tranquil grouping and the turbulent vista beyond the window would bring endless fascination. This tableau represents a combination of enrichment—the inherent from the window and the deliberate in a placement of objects chosen for their beauty.

Functional Accessories

The typical household, over the years, will accumulate several—or several sets—of utilitarian objects, so that the possibility arises for altering the effect of accessories from day to day. All have a very specific functional purpose, but all come in a vast range of designs, so one can exercise a great deal of personal taste in selection.

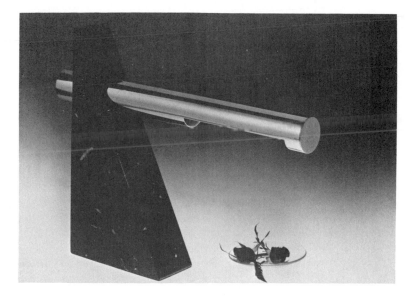

Portable Luminaires (Lamps)

Chapter 16 dealt with lighting in terms of architectural units and permanent fixtures. Here the concern is with portable luminaires, which often are chosen as much (or more) for their physical attractiveness as for the kind or amount of light they supply. There are several types: direct light, indirect light, a combination of direct and indirect light, luminous, structural-type, and accent fixtures.

Direct-light fixtures include gooseneck and apothecary types, bullet shades, and high-intensity luminaires. Because they concentrate light in one direction only, they are often used as task lighting but may also provide accent light for other accessories or even indirect light if aimed toward a wall or ceiling. Direct-light fixtures should not be used without sufficient general illumination, or they produce eye fatigue from glare resulting from contrast in light and shadow.

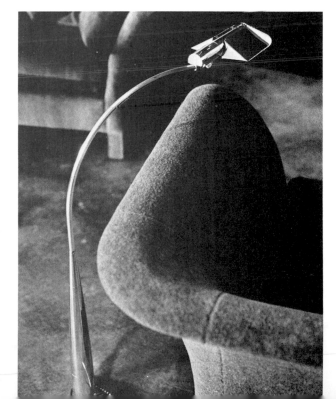

above left: 18-7 A lamp of black marble with a brass or chrome tube encasing the bulb would concentrate light on a desk or table. Robert Sonneman, designer. *(Courtesy George Kovacs Lighting, Inc.)*
above right: 18-8 The arm of an asymmetrically balanced halogen desk lamp called "Tizio" can be pivoted to cast high-intensity light where needed. Richard Sapper, designer. *(Photograph: Artemide, Inc.)*
left: 18-9 Cedric Hartman's floor lamp with a shallow pyramid reflector of brass or nickel is infinitely adjustable and provides a very wide beam spread at just below seated-eye-level height. *(Courtesy Cedric Hartman. Photograph: Vera Mercer, Paris)*

473

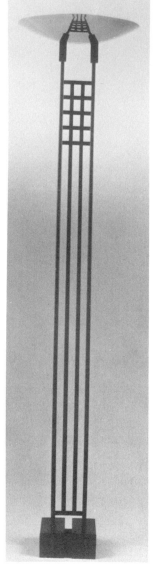

far left: 18-10 An indirect luminaire designed by Robert Sonneman of polished brass with black stem and base has a halogen bulb and a full-range dimmer. *(Courtesy George Kovacs Lighting, Inc.)*
left: 18-11 A canister lamp with the bulb in the base would throw light up to be reflected by the shade over a table or desk top. George Nelson, designer. *(Courtesy Koch & Lowy Inc.)*

Indirect luminaires include various torchère and urn types that aim light upward to be reflected from walls and ceilings. Their design is based upon the use of torches of flame to light interiors centuries ago and they have enjoyed a modern resurgence of popularity as ambient lighting.

The customary **table** or **floor fixture** provides a combination of direct and indirect light, for general room illumination as well as task performance. The shape of a fixture ought to grow from its function: the base supports the lamp bulb and shade; the lamp sends out light; the shade protects our eyes from glare and directs and diffuses light. The simplest base of a traditional table luminaire is a cylinder with a foot large enough for stability. The breadth-to-weight ratio is important in keeping a fixture upright, but materials also play a determining role; a support of metal, plastic, or wood can be more slender than a clay or glass one. Bases, lamps, and shades, although different in function and usually in material, comprise a unit when organized into a luminaire. This suggests a basic agreement among them—some qualities in common but seldom exact repetition.

Luminous fixtures might sometimes be described as light-as-object. Light is captured in a diffusing globe, column, panel, or sculptural form that in turn spreads the ambience of its glow in the immediate vicinity. A shaped lamp, usually frosted, may actually become the luminaire, supported by a compatible base. Such fixtures are primarily decorative although they may supply some ambient light as well. They must use low-wattage lamps in order to avoid annoying harshness.

Structural-type portable fixtures appear much like built-in brackets, strip lights, shelf lights, and tracks. But they are surface-mounted and plug into an outlet. They may be either decorative or functional but allow the flexibility and ease of installation often needed in rented living spaces.

Accent lighting uses exposed lamps to add sparkle and glitter to a room. It includes chandeliers, strips, sconces, clusters, and candles. Clear or tinted-glass lamps and chimneys may be used on these fixtures. They are purely decorative and use low wattages (up to 25-watt lamps).

left: 18-12 A floor lamp called "Chimera" diffuses light through a sculptured translucent column, providing a soft ambient glow. Vico Magistretti, designer. (*Courtesy Artemide, Inc.*)

below: 18-13 "Lesbo," a lamp designed by Angelo Mangiarotti, is an example of light-as-object, used more for its decorative effect than for the light it provides. (*Courtesy Artemide, Inc.*)

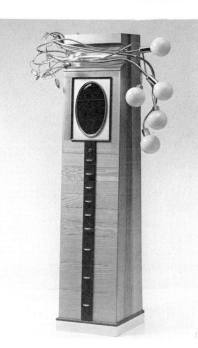

far left: 18-14 Track lighting provides a variety of fixtures to direct light on different places. The table and work surfaces are lit by green-shaded lamps hung from ceiling tracks. In addition, bare globe bulbs provide general lighting. Tom O'Toole, designer. (*Photograph: © Robert Perron*)

left: 18-15 A handcrafted chest of drawers with a tangle of low-wattage bulbs around the top is a startling piece of art furniture that is aesthetically challenging. Garry Knox Bennett, designer. (*Courtesy Norman Petersen & Associates*)

right: 18-16 Neon wall sconces would bring unexpected color as accent lighting in any room. Dan Chelsea, designer. (*Courtesy George Kovacs Lighting, Inc.*)

18-17 "Dafne" desk lamps with translucent shades thrust out on one side throw light on the working surface where it is needed. Orni Halloween, designer. *(Courtesy Artemide, Inc.)*

Shades

Shades generally take the form of drums, domes, or truncated cones to spread the light downward and sometimes upward as well. A tall, steep shade gives concentrated light, a low, wide one dispersed light. A 16-inch bottom diameter is recommended to spread light sufficiently and a 9-inch shade depth is needed for a single socket in a vertical position (6 to 8 inches for a multiple socket in a horizontal position with a top shield and diffusing disk below) to shield the lamp from view. If the lamp is positioned just above the lower edge of the shade, a wide downward spread of light results for reading and other tasks. Of course, shades can be square, triangular, or any other shape, but rounded forms seem more congenial to light, and we welcome their curves in our predominantly rectilinear homes.

Light transmittance is of importance in choosing shades. A translucent shade diffuses the light and provides attractive cross lighting, but if too transmittant "hot spots" revealing the lamp inside produce annoying glare. Opaque shades create heavy pools of light above and below and allow little light to reach vertical surfaces.

Color is important, especially in translucent shades but also in the whole ensemble, because lighted lamps are very conspicuous. A preference for warm, flattering incandescent light would tend to rule out translucent shades of blue, green, or violet. Opaque shades in colors may be used in rooms with the same colors in backgrounds; dark shades will be less conspicuous than light ones against dark walls. Translucent shades are mostly white or off-white; if colored, the light transmitted distorts the other colors in the room.

Shade linings should always be white to provide high reflectance. Medium-value colors have only 40 to 50 percent reflectance, meaning that much light is absorbed inside the shade, never reaching nearby surfaces.

Size

The optimum **size** of a luminaire will be determined by illumination requirements and by the size of the room and its furnishings. High fixtures with large spreading shades illumine broad areas and match large furniture in scale. Deliberately overscaled fixtures can create dramatic focal points, but unless they are sensitively used, they may crowd small spaces. The more fixtures a room has, the smaller each can be, but too many small luminaires may give the appearance of clutter. When several fixtures are used, they should be coordinated to give unity and order: pairs of fixtures with similar styling; shades of about the same brightness and color; and shade bottoms at the same approximate height throughout the room. Usually the bottom edge of the shade is kept at about the eye level of a seated person (38 to 42 inches) so the lamp is never visible.

Although many innovative luminaire designs have been introduced, most people would still think of the standard base-and-shade arrangement. To our grandchildren the word may conjure up quite a different image, while our grandparents might have envisioned something like a hurricane lamp. While hurricane and kerosene lamps rarely provide the only source of light in today's homes, they can be an attractive accessory, at the same time giving off their special warm glow as accent lighting.

Screens

With a venerable history as ornamental space dividers, screens are especially welcome in open-plan homes or in multipurpose rooms. Screens can be moved or adjusted to divide areas into comfortable units without completely shutting out what is beyond; or they can be folded inconspicuously against walls. There are no

limits to the possible materials: sheer silk and rice paper, clear or translucent glass and plastics, tapestry, brocades, leather, shutters and bamboo poles, curved or flat plywood, wallpaper or fabrics. Some screens are almost as heavy and substantial as walls, others are light and free-standing. Screens can be plain or ornamented, identical or different on the two sides, harmonious or contrasting with their surroundings.

Table Settings

The environment in which we eat can affect our health and happiness. Dining with companions, either family or friends, can be a pleasurable experience, and many elements go into enhancing that pleasure—the food served, the setting, and certainly the accouterments of eating. Meals are significant in any kind of group living, possibly being the only time the household congregates; they also play a significant role in entertaining guests, because the giving of food is a traditional gesture of hospitality. For these reasons, the atmosphere for dining deserves more than routine treatment.

Table settings represent a repeated experience, since they can be changed with relative ease. The same table set with different kinds of dishes, glassware, flatware, table coverings, and accessories will take on quite a different quality.

Tableware

Selecting tableware differs from most other aspects of home planning and furnishing in several important respects because of the ways in which it is typically accumulated and used. The household acquires pieces not only through planned (and occasional impulse) buying but also through unpredictable gifts and inheritances. Sets and individual objects can be variously combined and arranged with no cost other than imagination and a little time. The several kinds of tableware usually arrive in sets, and quick replacements may be indicated because of breakage, damage, or loss. Nothing else except cooking utensils will be handled, moved from place to place, and washed as frequently. Also, tableware requires easily accessible and specially planned storage to make the constant flow from cupboard to table to

18-21 A formal table setting sparkles with candles in high glass holders, tall wine glasses, and delicate dinnerware on a smooth table covering. *(Courtesy © Rosenthal Bilderdienst)*

sink or dishwasher and back to cupboard as convenient as possible. Finally, many families have everyday and guest tableware and linens, a distinction seldom made elsewhere in the home. Putting these factors together raises unique problems and, more significantly, great possibilities for enriching—and personalizing—the home.

The household's preferences in kind of food and method of serving, the present or planned dining and storage space as well as furniture, and the lifestyle all have direct bearing on the selection of tableware. Utility and economy are important, as always, but in this instance beauty and character may be more heavily weighted. Because tableware is seen only a few hours a day, there is much greater freedom to have patterns and colors that might be too demanding if always in view. Each piece can be used in different contexts, so it should have its own intrinsic beauty that is versatile yet affirmative. In few other phases of home life is change so easily and economically possible, and each change presents a new design challenge.

18-22 Heavy stoneware with a free asymmetrical pattern teams well with the bare wood of an old table and the casual arrangement. *(Courtesy Tiffany & Co.)*

479

Table Coverings

Comparatively inexpensive and easily stored, table coverings enhance variety and change. New fibers and weaves, easily cleaned plastics, strong or subtle colors are a challenge to those with self-reliant discrimination.

Incidental Accessories

The incidental pieces that further accessorize the table include serving pieces, centerpieces, salt and pepper shakers, candlesticks, napkin rings, and so on. All of these are available in the same materials as eating utensils—ceramic, metal, and glass. For more casual table settings, however, wood and plastic accessories offer a pleasant contrast of color and texture. Often it is the accessories, the most variable element of the setting, that most strongly underscore the table's theme.

The relation of centerpieces to the rest of the setting, as well as to the size of the table and the room, is all-important. If people sit or walk around the table, centerpieces should be attractive from all angles. Nearly always it is desirable that the centerpiece be low enough to permit those at the table to hold a conversation without interference.

Bed and Bath Accessories

Like table settings, bed and bath accessories are very flexible, since they are relatively inexpensive and easy to change. It seems hard to believe that until little over a quarter-century ago colored and patterned sheets and towels were almost unknown; pure white was standard. The extent of this revolution in design can be realized when we see world-famous textile and clothing designers applying their talents to bed coverings and bath accessories.

Since the bed will nearly always be the focus of any bedroom, the bed coverings that dominate the surface must strongly affect the room's overall design. Moreover, bedspreads and quilts allow an immediate kind of personal expression, and they are often the products of widely popular crafts and hobbies.

Bed coverings can also act to unify a room, as Figure 18-24 demonstrates. Here a graphic print by Victor Vasarely was the inspiration for a hand-crocheted

18-24 A crocheted wool bedspread is versatile and integral with the room's design; furthermore, it contributes warmth. Oxley & Landau, architects. *(Photograph: Julius Shulman)*

bedspread that picks up the colors and overall motif of the print without duplicating it exactly. An even simpler method of unifying a room depends on patterned sheets. Sheeting fabrics used on the bed can also cover a table or a scattering of pillows, become window curtains, canopies, or drapes, even become a self-headboard on the wall.

Functional bath accessories such as hardware, towels, shower curtains, hampers, and bath mats also provide a variety of colors and designs to enliven the bathroom. Most can be changed easily and inexpensively, even daily if desired.

18-25 The many handsome designs now available in patterned sheets have encouraged their migration to the tops of beds, as well as to other traditional fabric applications such as wall coverings. Maija Isola, designer, for Marimekko. *(Courtesy D/R International, Inc.)*

18-26 In a vacation home in Massachusetts, pillows help to make seating comfortable for people of all sizes and provide eye-catching interest in their variety. Charles A. Farrell of Short and Ford, architect. *(Photograph: © Sam Sweezy)*

Other Functional Accessories

The myriad of other functional accessories include such things as mirrors (which may also be purely decorative), clocks, fire tools, umbrella stands, and the many kinds of hardware used on doors, furniture pieces, and plumbing fixtures which can enhance spaces and provide personal expression.

Pillows covered in bright colors and patterns represent one of the most pervasive and versatile forms of enrichment. They are easy to make, lending themselves to all kinds of fabric arts. While nominally useful in providing comfort, pillows of this sort often take on a primarily decorative role, especially when intricately worked or heavily ornamented. This leads to consideration of objects that have no function whatsoever except just to be, for the sensuous delight they give us.

Decorative Accessories

In saying that the objects discussed here—plants and flowers, paintings, prints, and sculpture, handcrafted items and accessories—serve no useful purpose, the definition of "useful" is severely limited to a rigid, almost Puritan standard. Works of art, whether fabricated by nature or by human beings, enrich the very essence of our selves: our minds, our spirits, our sensibilities. A world—or a home—devoid of objects that exist purely for the joy of existing would be almost like a world without sounds.

Plants and Flowers

Live Plants

Plants are so much a fixture in today's homes that it seems difficult to imagine doing without them. A glance through the pages of this book will show that few rooms banish plants altogether and many enlist them as important design elements. Several factors explain this penchant for bringing part of the outdoors inside. The first is, of course, the widespread desire to introduce a natural touch in a controlled environment; this could be considered a psychological goal—to maintain touch with what has traditionally been an agrarian culture. In purely visual terms, plants contribute colors, textures, and ungoverned forms that contrast pleasantly with the human-controlled parts of an interior environment. Lastly, there remains the emotional satisfaction of watching something grow and change and develop. With reasonable care, plants get larger and in some cases may bloom (thus altering their physical appearances), which distinguishes them from any other element of home design.

As visual design, plants can play many roles. A single, strategically placed plant may be a dramatic, almost abstract, outline, whereas masses of plants filling a bay window, softening a garden room, or cascading from a balcony might create an effect ranging from a soft screen to a jungle. Big, bold plants are good for major effects or to fill a space where furniture does not fit; small ones, whose interesting foliage merits close study, could occupy a place of prominence on a table or window ledge.

18-27 A large and airy plant visually separates an open social space into living and dining areas. De Polo/Dunbar, designers. *(Photograph: © Peter Aaron/ESTO)*

Accessories **483**

Acquiring plants for their purely visual appeal can be a perilous adventure. If no one in the household has the slightest interest in gardening, the carefully chosen specimen that precisely fits one's design needs will inevitably wither and die, destroying the effect as well as the plant. Some plants, including cactus, philodendron, and certain members of the Dracaena family, seem to flourish in spite of being ignored, while others demand the most meticulous care merely to survive.

Flowering plants are a relatively inexpensive way of bringing color into the home. If chosen carefully and when the flowers are in bud or freshly open, many types will last far longer than cut flowers while giving more accent value than foliage plants.

Each type of plant has its own requirements of light, heat, soil, water, and humidity for best growth. Almost none like dark, hot, poorly ventilated rooms any more than humans do, but a few will survive even under such unfavorable conditions.

The containers in which plants are kept have much to do with both their ornamental value and their physical health. However, once the requirements for proper drainage, root spread, and soil aeration have been met, almost no container can be ruled out, the materials ranging from the classic unglazed pottery through glazed ceramics, metals, glass, and plastics. (Wood, unless lined, will split and rot from watering.)

18-28 A bay window, with its abundant light, is a natural spot for a cluster of plants, some flowering, some just with interesting leaves. Alfredo De Vido, architect. *(Photograph: © Norman McGrath)*

above: **Plate 57** A huge 19th-century pediment, rescued from a wrecker's ball, dominates the library of architect Charles Moore's house and holds in place the two-story wall of books behind it. *(Photograph: Tim Street-Porter)*

right: **Plate 58** A Victorian sofa with a bold wood frame balances a large-scale painting, while smaller accessories bring human scale to this living room. *(Photograph: © Norman McGrath)*

Plate 59 A restrained use of accessories allows each object to be appreciated individually yet blend into a coherent whole. Ronald and Victoria Borus, designers. *(Photograph: © Peter Aaron/ESTO)*

Fresh Flowers

Raised to the level of an eloquent art by the nature-loving Japanese and assiduously practiced by many in the United States, flower arrangement can mean anything from stuffing some blossoms into a vase to a fascinating art. The effects that can be produced are limitless. There are as many steps between symmetrical, strict formality and casual, spontaneous grouping as there are kinds of blossoms. Whether ingenuous or sophisticated, fresh flowers in the home bring a special kind of enrichment that cannot be duplicated with anything else.

The flowers, branches, and leaves obtainable play a decisive part in determining the kind of arrangement that is possible, because each plant has its own character and habit of growth. Arrangements that emphasize the distinctive personalities of the blossoms used are most likely to be successful.

The relation of flowers to their containers is important also but not dictated by rules. Usually, the container is subordinate to its contents, and simple glass, ceramic, or metal bowls or vases will happily hold varied flowers. Sometimes, though, a distinctive urn, cornucopia, or vase is almost as important as what it holds. Those who enjoy arranging flowers appreciate having varied containers, because it is stimulating to be able to select a vase or bowl just right in size, shape, color, and texture.

18-29 Even a few flowers, casually arranged, enhance a tea table set for two. *(Courtesy © Rosenthal Bilderdienst)*

487

18-30 A window becomes a still life with an arrangement of dried weeds, delicate against the heavy masonry wall. Wurster, Bernardi, and Emmons, architects. *(Photograph: © Morley Baer)*

Dry Arrangements

Dry arrangements are composed of everlasting flowers, weeds, and seedpods, leaves and bare branches, driftwood and rocks. They may cost little or nothing and require no care other than the somewhat tedious job of removing dust.

Often, though not always, dried flowers and weeds are subordinate to the containers they occupy, acting more as enhancements or complements than as statements in their own right. Spindly branches complement a solid round pot, or a bunch of feathery weeds may contrast with heavy masonry walls and the strict rectangularity of window frames.

Art

Works of art—paintings, drawings, prints, photographs, and sculpture—are as personal and emotionally charged as the books we read, the music we enjoy, the types of entertainment we pursue. Most people either have some objects of visual art that give them particular pleasure or are eager to seek them out. In terms of home enrichment, then, three factors must be considered: choosing works that evoke a special response; framing them appropriately; deciding where and how to display them to best advantage.

Two-Dimensional Art

The several categories of art differ substantially in medium, effect, content, and in cost.

Paintings are original, one-of-a-kind works done in oil, tempera, watercolor, acrylic, or other pigment bases on canvas or similar backing. Along with original sculptures, they are the most expensive works of art one can buy. Few people are in a position to purchase masterworks of a caliber visible in museums, but it must be remembered that the vast majority of paintings initially were sold to discerning collectors for a tiny fraction of their current value. Local art shows and galleries, art schools, even auctions can be the source of treasures that awaken particular responses and may, incidentally, have intrinsic value. A painting may suggest a general theme or color harmony but should provide an aesthetic appreciation on the part of the viewer rather than simply fill a void or coordinate with other furnishings (Plate 58, p. 485).

Drawings—in pencil, crayon, charcoal, or ink on paper—tend to be much less expensive than paintings, even when done by recognized artists. Because they are often preliminary sketches for other works, drawings may be more relaxed than paintings, a more direct revelation of the artist's concept; but they can also be precise delineations or full-bodied statements, as developed as a painting.

Prints, often known as multiples, are impressions on paper resulting from such processes as *woodcut*, *etching*, *drypoint*, *lithography*, and *silk screen*. They are considered original works of art when struck directly from plates made or supervised by the artist; numbered according to which impression in sequence each is from the initial print; signed or authorized by the artist. Prints are much less expensive than paintings or drawings; even works by established artists are usually within the range of average collectors and could represent a sound investment.

Photographs are a decorative medium of expression uniquely of this century. The content of a photograph can vary from the "art" subject—indistinguishable from that of paintings, drawings, or prints—to the picture that has only personal significance such as a snapshot of family and friends. Either is valid as an image for home accessories as long as it means something important to the individual.

Reproductions of artworks have no direct connection with the artist. They are inexpensive impressions on paper made photographically or by a commercial printing process. Such reproductions do not give the total impact of original works, for they lack the full range and brilliance of color, the special interests of texture and materials. Still, if one has particular empathy with a certain painting or drawing and reproductions are all that one can afford, they should not be scorned. High-quality reproductions, especially of drawings, are sometimes quite faithful to the originals.

Posters are a form of reproduction, often of works by well-known artists, that are frankly temporary. Brilliant or subtle in color, available in varying sizes, framed or unframed, they are an inexpensive and useful means of adding the personal touch to any home.

Framing and Hanging Pictures

Frames visually enclose pictures and contribute to their importance and effectiveness. Also, they form a boundary or transition between the free, intense expressiveness of pictures and the architectural backgrounds. Lastly, frames safeguard the edges, may hold protective glass, and facilitate moving and hanging. Their first duty is to enhance the pictures, their second to establish some kind of relationship with the setting. Generally this means that frames should either complement the size, scale, character, and color of what they enclose without overpowering it or simply be unobtrusive bands. Occasionally, marked contrast can accentuate the qualities of a painting. Only exceptionally should the frame dominate the picture. The wide, heavily carved and gilded frames of the past or any that project at the outer edges "set off" pictures from their backgrounds. Those of moderate width and simple design, harmonious in color with the walls and either flat or stepped back, relate to the walls, focusing attention on the individual artworks rather than the total composition. Today, much art is hung without frames, the impact of the boundary of a painting against its background being part of the total concept. These works may be supported by stretchers, the framework over which canvas, fabric, or even a photograph can be tautly attached. Some works may also be simply adhered to a rigid backing.

Mats and **glass** are typical accompaniments of watercolors, photographs, and graphic prints. Mats enlarge small pictures and surround them with rest space as a foil, especially important if the picture is delicate or if the background is competitive. They may also unify a group of pictures of various sizes. In color, mats are usually of white or pale-hued paper, because these tones concentrate attention on the picture, but they can be of textiles or patterned paper, cork, or metal, and have pronounced color.

In size, mats vary with the size and character of the picture as well as with the frame and the location. Heavy frames lessen the need for generous mats, while large or important locations increase it. To correct optical illusions and give satisfying up-and-down equilibrium, the width of the top, sides, and bottom of mats may be different. In matting a picture, as in creating one, the elusive interaction of form, line, and space—not a set formula—should determine the result. The discerning eye of the owner or framer will be the best judge of the correct mat for any particular picture in its intended location.

Glass is necessary for pictures that need to be protected from surface dirt, moisture, and abrasion. It also seems to intensify colors. But glass produces annoying reflections, a problem partially alleviated with the new nonreflective glass, as well as with Lucite, Plexiglas, and other plastics. Nonreflective coverings should be approached with care, however, for they tend to gray and soften what is underneath. Mats and glass generally go together on watercolors, prints, pastels, and photographs. Oil and acrylic paintings seldom have or need either.

18-31 Small and delicate engravings and drawings gain importance when arranged together on a wall over an 18th-century table. *(Photograph: Charles M. Nes IV)*

18-32 "Focal," a wall-size painting by Adolph Gottlieb, is so intense that it is the only wall accessory used in a living room designed by Robert Metzger. *(Photograph: © Wolfgang Hoyt/ESTO)*

Both aesthetic and prosaically physical considerations come into play in **hanging** a picture. Once the latter are dealt with and mastered, the former can be given free rein:

- Nails and hooks can be driven securely into some types of walls. In frame houses with interior walls of plaster or wallboard, it is necessary to find the wooden stud to anchor the nail. (Studs most often are 16 inches apart.)
- Some wall surfaces (and some landlords) will not permit nails to be driven in. For this purpose there exist picture hooks on superheavy tape that can be affixed to the wall.
- Concrete and similar walls may demand special plugs that expand on the other side to create a permanent, immovable projective for the picture. Similar bolts can be used between studs on wallboard.
- In general, pictures should be hung flat against the wall, with no wires or hooks showing, although sometimes the wires are decorative.

The location of paintings, drawings, photographs, and prints so that they interact pleasingly with each other and their setting involves using design principles. Since pictures help unify furniture and walls, they are often placed over something—a sofa or group of chairs, a desk, a table, a bookcase, a piano, or a fireplace. Keeping art at eye level lets it be viewed comfortably, relates it to furnishings, and emphasizes the room's horizontality. From time to time, though, it is refreshing to have a painting stand for what it is worth on an otherwise blank wall. Large, dominant paintings, by their forceful presence, almost demand this kind of treatment. Smaller, more modest works can be grouped successfully for greater impact if they are in scale with each other and provided each is in a position to invite leisurely study. Tight spacing emphasizes the total composition of a group of works while more generous spacing allows each work to be focused upon in turn. An odd number of works forms the most pleasing composition. Large bold works need space for the viewer to step back while smaller, more subtle, or detailed works need to be viewed at close range. Art should be hung in pleasing proportion to furnishings and walls and can be used to help create balance, rhythm, emphasis, and unity in interiors.

18-33 A display of drawings and watercolors all but fills the walls of this comfortable sitting room, but the effect is prevented from being "busy" or overpowering because of the subdued color scheme and regular pattern in which the works are hung. *(Photograph: John T. Hill)*

490

far left: 18-34 A sculptured head placed on a customized speaker designed by Mark Levenson that doubles as a pedestal brings life to a small, unused corner. *(Photograph: © Karen Bussolini)*
left: 18-35 Rufino Tamayo, an artist who designed his own house, made one wall into a honeycomb of display spaces for his collection of pre-Columbian art. *(Photograph: Julius Shulman)*

Sculpture

Bringing into three dimensions the intensity and expressiveness found in painting adds textural experience to art. An important piece of sculpture, regardless of its size, commands a place of importance and becomes the focus of attention. Large pieces that are free-standing can—from a purely organizational point of view—be treated as articles of furniture. That they will gather an aura of distinction about them depends as much upon their visual integrity as upon placement. Smaller pieces may occupy prominent positions on a shelf or table, on the wall, in a niche, or possibly suspended from the ceiling. The collector who is fortunate or diligent enough to amass many pieces of related sculpture will certainly want to create a display area particularly for them.

Crafts

Pottery, blown and stained glass, art fabrics, woodcraft, metalwork, basketry have all experienced a tremendous surge of popularity in the last several years. As collectors have increasingly turned their attention away from the "fine" arts toward an appreciation of the so-called applied arts, crafts have begun to throw off their "homey" image and assume their rightful place as serious expressive works. A beautiful ceramic object may be no less significant than a piece of sculpture, a handwoven tapestry no less important than an oil painting. Happily, craft objects are still much less expensive and much more readily accessible to the public than paintings and sculpture. In many homes such precious articles have begun to replace the traditional picture-on-the-wall as prized objects of enrichment.

Throughout this book many examples have been shown of the potter's and glass and fiber artists' work enriching contemporary interiors. Glass, whether stained or blown, combines color and light in a unique way. Although the glass itself is colored, it may depend upon the transmittance of light for its beauty, and must be hung or placed with natural or artificial light penetrating it. Baskets, when their design is sensitive and closely adapted to the materials, take the place of sculpture and make a pure aesthetic statement. While often divorced from their original utilitarian functions, such objects retain the suggestion of sturdy serviceability that relates them to the basic activities of everyday living.

Accessories **491**

above: **18-37** A wall hanging by Geraldine Millham is forceful enough to be placed by itself on a wall. *(Photograph: © Karen Bussolini)*

below: **18-38** A panel of recycled stained glass brings color and light together in a special way. Wong & Brocchini, architects. *(Photograph: Joshua Freiwald)*

above: **18-36** A magnificent tapestry becomes a wall in a remodeled barn, where its rich, strong detail equals the dominant setting. *(Photograph: John T. Hill)*

Mass-Produced Accessories

One major category has not yet been mentioned: objects that are not quite works of art or craft (since they are mass-produced) and not quite utilitarian (although they may perform some marginal task), but are simply kept about because they delight the eye or hand or intellect. A collection of such articles might include brass candlesticks, glass paperweights, a whimsical ceramic goose, a globe, or a collection of tools and implements pertaining to a trade. If we try to imagine a room stripped of these little islands of enrichment, it seems very dull indeed. That is because they delineate the very character of a room. Without them, a space would be impersonal and bland. In a sense, this sums up the underlying nature of accessorizing—that which personalizes a home, gives it its particular quality, and makes it peculiarly one's own.

18-39 This kitchen wall unit was designed by a person who collects dishes, has twelve sets in all, and likes to display them. *(Photograph: © Norman McGrath)*

Location and Background for Accessories

There are two logical types of location for accessories: those places where people normally look and those places where we want them to look with interest and pleasure.

People tend to look more or less straight ahead; through doors, windows, or wherever distance invites exploration; and at anything that is large, different, or well illumined. Thus it is reasonable to think about putting aesthetic interest opposite the home's entrance door, somewhere in the first view of the major group space, more or less opposite seating for conversation and dining, on the wall opposite a bed, in the space above a desk, and at the end of a hall. Outdoors, the major views from inside the house or from the terrace as well as the ends or turning points of garden paths are logical places on which to concentrate attention.

Entrance areas are introductions to the home. Usually they are small, which suggests something best seen at close range in a short period of time. A good table or chest with flowers, plants, or a small sculpture below a mirror is one possibility, if space permits. Or the accessory can be on the wall—a distinctive lighting fixture or mirror, an uncomplicated painting or print, a colorful art fabric.

The first view into the living room is another matter, for the opposite wall or window may be some distance away. In many contemporary homes this first view carries attention through the room out into the garden, which then becomes the place for interesting planting or fences, decorative urns or sculpture. In other houses, the fireplace wall is the first thing seen, and it may or may not need more than the architect has given in its design and materials. If the fireplace is small and simple, the wall above may have a painting or textile large enough and strong enough to balance the opening below and to make itself understood from across the room—and also with sufficient interest to be worth looking at over long periods of time. In still other quarters the initial view may end in a blank wall that, typically, has a group of furniture and accessories. Whatever the situation, it is gratifying to have something of interest greet the eyes. Changing the placement of accessories renews their appeal and freshens their impact. Most are quite easily moved and should be tried in a variety of locations and arrangements. Generally, acccessories chosen for group spaces should have aesthetic appeal beyond personal sentimental value. The selection of accessories should reinforce the atmosphere of each room: bedrooms are intended as restful places, living rooms and family rooms can be dramatic or subtle depending upon individual taste, and kitchens and baths may be light-hearted and cheerful.

Then there are the spots in most homes where we have to entice attention, such as uninteresting corners, long halls, or small wall spaces that must be used. A small, separate furniture group can be reinforced with congenial illumination; by having prints, paintings, or textiles on the wall; and by placing interesting objects on the table. Then, what was an unused corner becomes inhabited space, chiefly through appropriate furniture but to a surprising degree through distinctive accessories.

The effectiveness of any accessory can be increased or decreased markedly by its setting. Large, significant objects can proclaim their presence by being put in important positions, by being given backgrounds against which they can be readily seen, and by being built up with smaller objects. At the other extreme, some accessories can take their place unobtrusively, a little murmur in a harmonious setting (Plate 59, p. 486). Thus varying degrees of emphasis and subordination are achieved; balance and rhythm, scale, proportion, and harmony come into play, and accessories become important elements in the total home design.

References for Further Reading

Guide to Portable Lamps and Lighting. Washington, DC: Member Services Division, National Rural Electric Cooperative Association, April–May 1968.
Light for Living: Guidelines to Good Lighting. Chicago: American Home Lighting Institute, 1979.

V

Interior Design Today

Interior design today—minimal furnishings in a small New York City apartment. Joe D'Urso, designer. *(Photograph: © Peter Aaron/ESTO)*

The Modern Movement and Beyond

The appearance of today's homes reflects an evolution in architecture and design that began in the late nineteenth century, reached a critical turning point in the early twentieth, and has been refined and elaborated since.

During these two centuries, Western civilization underwent a transformation more rapid and comprehensive than any that had occurred in its previous history. Scientific discoveries and the theories of evolution and relativity challenged fundamental concepts of humanity and the universe. Conflicts between classes, nations, and ideologies culminated in the Russian Revolution and two World Wars. Perhaps the most important factor was the Industrial Revolution, which, in creating vast new sources of wealth and power, destroyed the old order of society, shifted international relations, and profoundly affected the lives of people everywhere. Transportation by railroad, steamship, automobile, and airplane, as well as communication by telegraph, telephone, radio, and the visual media brought individuals throughout the world into closer contact with each other, important events, and commercial products. In prosperous nations, improved material conditions changed living patterns and social structure, and the middle class became the predominant consumers of the products of industry.

The arts of the home naturally reflected these fundamental changes in culture and society. The domestic styles of the late nineteenth and twentieth centuries exhibit a broad variety of aims and achievements that cannot easily be summarized. In general, however, both architecture and furnishings gradually abandoned the imitation of past styles, whether in the form of archaeological reproduction, eclectic mixture, or free variation on past modes. Along with this development, both areas of design evolved a new formal language that took full advantage of the materials and methods introduced by industry. The aesthetic principle that the form of any object should express its function, materials, and process of construction became predominant, but this did not prevent architects and designers from creating distinct personal styles.

Perhaps the single most important innovation in house design during this period was the rejection of the enclosed box in favor of the fluid interpenetration of spaces expressed in the open plan. The strength of new materials, such as iron, steel, and concrete, facilitated the distinction between structural support and the devices used to separate interior spaces, while the development of central heating eliminated the need to contain heat in closed-off rooms.

Progressive Trends in the Nineteenth Century

The beginning stages of the modern movement took the form of a conscious revolt against popular taste, as expressed in the poor quality and stylistic confusion found in household objects mass-produced for commercial distribution. This reaction began in England, where early and rapid industrial progress had affected the crafts sooner than elsewhere. As early as the 1840s John Ruskin (1819–1900), popularizer of the Middle Ages and the undisputed arbiter of Victorian taste, condemned machine-made ornaments and the use of one material to simulate another as immoral "deceits." Similar sentiments were expressed by A. W. N. Pugin (1812–1852), who wrote in *Contrasts* (1836) that "the great test of beauty is the fitness of the design for the purpose for which it was intended."

The Arts and Crafts Movement: 1860–1900

Like Ruskin and Pugin, **William Morris** (1834–1896) identified art with morality, rejected modern civilization, and looked to the Middle Ages as a model for society and art. Ruskin and Morris both held that machine production destroyed the "joy in work" that had led medieval craftsmen to create objects of true beauty. Condemning both industry and the capitalistic system, Morris advocated a thorough reform of both art and society on a Utopian medieval model. Household furnishings, he argued, should offer honesty of construction and genuineness of materials rather than stylistic imitation, applied details, and illusionistic effects.

Morris went beyond his predecessors, however, by putting his theories to the test of reality. In 1861 he established a firm, later renamed Morris and Co., that produced textiles, wallpaper, and furnishings. Morris was aided by a number of artists and craftsmen in the design and execution of the firm's products.

The results of this collaboration appear in a room created in 1867. Architect Philip Webb designed the walls and ceiling with their painted and molded-plaster decorations, while painter Edward Burne-Jones provided stained-glass windows and the small painted panels in the wainscoting. Morris himself designed the carpet and, with his wife, painted the folding screen with figures from a tale by Chaucer. Morris and Co. produced all the furnishings, including a grand piano and several massively proportioned cabinets whose sturdy construction and hand-

painted, elegantly stylized decorations clearly identify each piece as the unique product of individual craftsmanship.

Morris dedicated much of his later life to the promulgation of his ideas in books and lectures, as well as through the example of his own pattern designs and the production of his firm. Unfortunately, the firm's handcrafted wares were inevitably more expensive than the debased products of industry and therefore failed to effect the broad reform on all levels of society that Morris had hoped to achieve. Nevertheless he attracted a wide following among artists, architects, and critics, including Charles Eastlake, whose *Hints on Household Taste* (1868) was especially influential in America. A number of guilds and associations were formed in the 1880s to consolidate the efforts of like-minded designers and attract public interest in their work. The Arts and Crafts Exhibition Society, founded in 1888, gave its name to the entire reform movement.

The general trend during the later nineteenth century, however, brought furnishings and interiors away from the heavy, rather medieval forms of Morris' circle toward lighter, simpler shapes with fewer historic references. A major factor in this development was the liberating influence of Japanese art, which became widely known, especially in the 1880s, through illustrated travel books and imported prints, scrolls, and pottery. Japanese homes typically contained no furniture as we know it, but their uncluttered spaciousness and refined detailing seemed like a breath of fresh air next to the dense clutter of the Victorian drawing room. The elegant linear patterns of Japanese prints contributed to the flatter, more stylized decorations applied to the later examples of Arts and Crafts furniture.

Charles F. A. Voysey (1857–1941) claims distinction as the most important of Morris' immediate successors. The houses he designed in the 1890s featured bright, uncluttered interiors, and his designs for wallpaper and textiles were the best of the day. Japanese influence contributed to the fresh, airy quality of Voysey's

19-2 An oak writing desk with a pierced copper hinge (1896) illustrates the work of Charles F. A. Voysey, whose simple, light designs were widely copied by commercial firms of the day. *(Victoria & Albert Museum, London [Crown Copyright])*

furniture. Voysey disliked ostentation, but the elegant flat patterns of his hinges and plaques revealed a unique talent for linear design.

The theories and achievements of the Arts and Crafts movement had a profound effect on the Continent by the turn of the century, but their earliest and most fruitful influence was in the United States.

Henry Hobson Richardson (1838–1886) developed a personal style of architecture using rough blocks of stone in thick courses, round arches, and towers recalling the Romanesque churches of medieval Europe. His houses featured exteriors of local stone or weathered wooden shingles that harmonized with the natu-

19-3 The staircase from the R. T. Paine house in Waltham, Massachusetts, was built between 1884 and 1886 by H. H. Richardson. *(Photograph: Wayne Andrews)*

501

19-4 This ebonized cherry desk belonged to a bedroom suite made by the Herter Brothers of New York between 1877 and 1882 for the American millionaire Jay Gould. The restrained dignity of the design follows the principles of Charles Eastlake and other English authors of the Arts and Crafts movement. *(Metropolitan Museum of Art, New York [gift of Paul Martini])*

19-5 A desk designed by Gustav Stickley circa 1901 shows the restraint and forthrightness he advocated. *(Photograph: The Brooklyn Museum, H. Randolph Lever Fund)*

ral setting. The size and placement of windows accommodated internal need rather than external regularity, and interiors followed an asymmetrical plan with a free flow of space around the entrance hall and stairway. His interiors reveal an emphasis on the warm attraction of expertly crafted woodwork. His interpenetration of spaces, as well as built-in furniture, anticipates the work of Frank Lloyd Wright.

Honesty of construction and a simple, rectilinear outline characterize the drop-front desk produced about 1880 by the **Herter Brothers** of New York. The flat surface pattern of stylized flowers, framed in rectangular panels, achieves the elegance and sophistication sought by later designers of the reform movement. Like the work of Morris and his associates, Herter Brothers' furniture emphasized qualities that could result only from individual handcrafting.

The reform movement in America gained widespread popularity among the middle classes through the designs and publications of **Gustav Stickley** (1848–1942). After a trip to Europe and England, where he met Voysey, Stickley introduced a line of "Craftsman" furniture whose severely rectilinear construction of thick pieces of wood, usually oak, emphasized honest joinery, simplicity, and massive solidity. From 1901 until 1916, Stickley published *The Craftsman*, a magazine that served as the forum of progressive design and gave its name to the American reform movement.

Currents outside the Mainstream

Even while Ruskin and Morris assailed the decline of quality in the household arts, at least two independent developments were taking place that in some degree fulfilled the ideals of the Arts and Crafts movement.

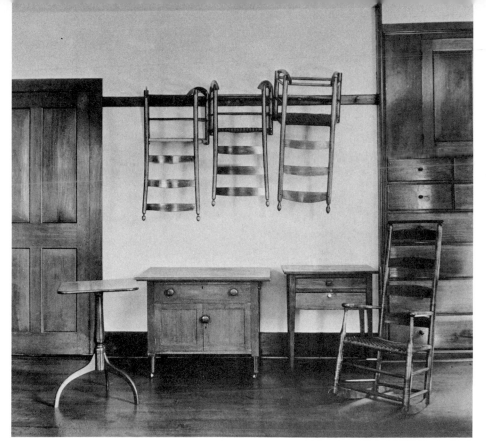

19-6 Austere simplicity and fine workmanship characterize a Shaker interior of the late 19th century in Hancock, Massachusetts. Ladderback rocking chairs recall the furniture of the early Colonial period. *(Courtesy Shaker Museum, Old Chatham, N.Y. Photograph: William Winter)*

19-7 Michael Thonet first mass-produced this version of the 33½" high "Vienna" café chair in 1876. A single section of bent wood forms the back and rear legs. With minor variations, it is still in production today. *(Collection Museum of Modern Art, New York. Purchase)*

Shaker Homes

The **Shakers,** a radical offshoot of the Quakers, came from England to the United States in the second half of the eighteenth century in order to pursue a communal, religious lifestyle. A strict but cheerful work ethic, a passion for cleanliness and order, and a compulsion for efficiency all contributed to an austere approach to design. Shaker homes were characteristically clean and uncluttered—especially through the use of built-in cabinets and strips of pegs, on which not only coats but also chairs and other pieces of furniture were hung when not in use. Shakers frowned on the luxury of superficial embellishments, preferring economy of means and fitness of purpose as the standards of design. Furniture designs were those of the eighteenth century, modified and pared down to their essentials to achieve maximum efficiency and lightness. Every piece was fabricated with utmost care by craftsmen who saw their task as a religious exercise.

The Shaker experience bears a surprising resemblance to Morris' Utopian vision of communal handcraft villages, and yet the results were very different—and in fact more modern in appearance than the solid furniture and densely patterned interiors created by Morris and Webb. The functional but personal quality of Shaker homes continues to inspire the design of contemporary interiors (Fig. 10-13).

Michael Thonet

In his zeal to correct the vulgarities of most furnishings produced by industry, Morris condemned the entire system. Yet during his lifetime the principles of honest construction and genuine materials (if not handcraftsmanship) had already been reconciled with mass production in the elegantly functional designs of **Michael Thonet** (1796–1871), the inventor of the bentwood chair. Born in a small town on the Rhine, Thonet moved to Vienna hoping to make cabinets for great palaces. Instead, in the 1830s he invented a process for steaming and bending solid lengths of beechwood into gently curved shapes. The result was a type of sturdy, lightweight, relatively inexpensive furniture whose unprecedented popularity brought it to cafés, ice-cream parlors, and homes of all social and economic levels throughout Europe and the United States. The Prague chair, introduced in 1851, featured rectangular lines with rounded corners, arms, and a cane seat. Thonet's rockers (Fig. 7-7, p. 163) fared less well with modern functionalists, who objected to the swirling arabesques that now seem wonderfully suited to the chair's swaying motion. Thonet's firm and others have produced numerous variations on all of the originals, but these nineteenth-century designs have stood up remarkably well and still grace many contemporary homes.

Art Nouveau: 1890–1905

The first truly original style since the French Rococo (1715–1774), **Art Nouveau** appeared almost simultaneously throughout Europe during the 1890s. Although it formed a transition between the nineteenth and twentieth centuries, the "Style 1900" bore little resemblance to the work that preceded or followed its brief popularity.

The explicit aim of Art Nouveau was to create a totally new formal language from which all traces of the past had been eliminated. The characteristic motif became the sinuous line, ending in a whiplash curve like the bud of a plant. Abstract but not geometric, the stylized forms expressed the process of natural growth without depending on literal representation.

All of these features appear in the *Tassel* house in Brussels, designed by the Belgian architect **Victor Horta** (1861–1947) and built between 1892 and 1893. Although probably influenced by Japanese prints and certain forward-looking English textile and book designs, Horta essentially created the style, in fully developed form, in a single building. In the stair hall, a slender iron column sprouting leaflike tendrils supports arched ceiling beams pierced by openwork. Sinuous, meandering ribbons in asymmetrical patterns appear everywhere: painted on walls, inlaid in floor mosaics, and molded in the iron handrail. Until now, iron had never been so frankly exposed except in bridges and engineering works. In Horta's hands, Art Nouveau combined industrial materials with handcraft uniqueness, and functional expression with rampant decoration.

Art Nouveau was primarily a style of interior decoration that its leading practitioners extended to everything in the house, including furniture, fixtures, lamps, and doorknobs. **Hector Guimard** (1867–1942), the leading Art Nouveau architect of France, even designed special nailheads as part of a totally unified environment. Long, sinuous lines interrupted by bulbous knots flow over Guimard's furniture, creating a dynamic unity out of deliberately asymmetrical designs.

Unaware of developments in Brussels and Paris, **Antoni Gaudí** (1852–1926) independently evolved a similar style of greater power and individuality in Spain. Gaudí's style is more plastic and sculptural than the linear elegance of his French and Belgian contemporaries. The swelling masses of Gaudí's exteriors seem to be in constant motion, pulling interior spaces askew and leaving strange kidney-shaped, round-cornered windows that seem hollowed out by the wind. The same fluid shapes reappear in furnishings and fixtures, but not always for purely aesthetic reasons: the saddle-seated chairs of the *Casa Battlo* are molded for human comfort, and the "ears" projecting from the chairbacks provide convenient, if quite unnecessary, handles for moving them about.

right: 19-8 A profusion of dynamic curvilinear patterns overwhelms the stair-hall of the Tassel House in Brussels (1892-1893), designed by Victor Horta. The earliest Art Nouveau building was also the first private residence to make use of iron, both as a structural material and as decoration. *(Photograph courtesy Museum of Modern Art, New York)*

above: 19-9 An angled cupboard of triangular section (1904–1907) illustrates Hector Guimard's talent for asymmetrical designs united by flowing, continuous lines. The pearwood cupboard formed part of Guimard's total design of a house for Léon Nozal in Paris. *(Musée des Arts Decoratifs, Paris)*

left: 19-10 Bulging, sinuous forms abound in the dining room and furnishings of the Casa Battló, built in Barcelona from 1904 to 1906 by the Catalan architect Antonio Gaudí. *(Photograph: MAS)*

19-11 Charles Rennie Macintosh collaborated with his wife in designing the drawing room of their Glasgow apartment in 1900. The light, airy quality and rectilinear discipline of the interior recalls the work of Voysey (see Fig. 19-2) and distinguishes Scottish Art Nouveau from the Continental movement. *(Photograph: T & R Annan & Sons, Ltd.)*

19-12 Louis Comfort Tiffany designed stained glass windows such as "View of Oyster Bay" in his own interpretation of Art Nouveau. *(Courtesy Metropolitan Museum of Art, from the McKean Collection, courtesy The Morse Gallery of Art, Winter Park, Florida)*

The most prophetic exponent of Art Nouveau (and the only major one in Britain) was **Charles Rennie Macintosh** (1868–1928), a Scots architect whose early interiors in Glasgow in the 1890s paralleled the work of Horta. With Macintosh, however, the delicate swirls of linear pattern are held in place by a framework of slender verticals and a few tempering horizontals, resulting in light, airy interiors with surfaces enlivened by evocative accents. His furniture was often built-in, but even his free-standing chairs defined spatial volumes through their tall, straight backs and lean, rectilinear shapes.

Art Nouveau had only two major practitioners in the United States. One was **Louis Sullivan** (1856–1924), the pioneer Chicago architect who developed a lush, florid brand of stylized naturalism in the ornament he applied to commercial structures. The other was **Louis Comfort Tiffany** (1848–1933). A leading designer and manufacturer of decorative art in metal and glass, Tiffany combined vibrant colors and asymmetrical decorative patterns in the lush trees and flowers of his lampshades and stained-glass windows, but he is equally well known for his exquisite Favrile glassware whose graceful, tapering shapes, translucent colors, and swirling forms seemed to arise naturally from the glass-blowing process.

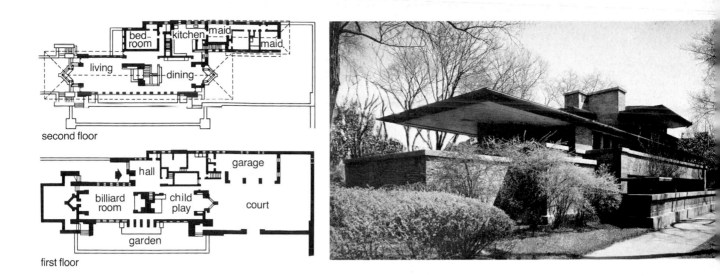

second floor

first floor

Frank Lloyd Wright

The series of houses built by **Frank Lloyd Wright** (1867–1959) during the first decade of the twentieth century represent the culmination of the craftsman movement as well as the beginning of modern home design. Wright's "Prairie" houses, as he called them, incorporated many features of Richardson's and contemporary craftsman-style homes—opening one room off another, for example, and the use of unpretentious materials, as well as covered verandas placed around the house—but he expanded, refined, and integrated these elements into a coherent, powerful style. Interior and exterior formed a single entity in the Prairie house, with which Wright hoped to express the freedom of movement and wide, open spaces of the American Midwest.

Trained in Chicago under Louis Sullivan, Wright developed the theory that architecture should be "organic," that a building should "grow" from the inside out, as determined by function, materials, and site. Thus the fireplace, traditionally the focus of family life, became the central feature around which interior

507

spaces were planned informally to allow free circulation within the house and between the interior and the outdoors. Unexpected light sources and variations in ceiling height—reaching two stories at least once in most of Wright's houses—gave each area a distinct atmosphere without interrupting the continuous flow of space. Voids and solid elements interacted to create a dynamic sense of movement throughout the interior. In addition to skylights and clerestories (often partially concealed), windows appeared in continuous horizontal bands held firmly in place between the ceiling and a common sill. Contrasting materials, the accentuation of structural features, and geometric detailing provided a decorative scheme fully integrated with the architecture. Much of the furniture was built-in, but Wright specially designed even the free-standing pieces for each house.

Wright's position as the bridge between the nineteenth-century reform movement and the twentieth-century acceptance of industrial technology was best expressed by the architect himself in the title of a lecture he delivered in 1901: "The Art and Craft of the Machine." "The machine is here to stay," Wright told his audience. "There is no more important work before the architect now than to use this normal tool of civilization to the best advantage." Unlike the Bauhaus leaders of the 1920s and 1930s (see pp. 509–510), however, Wright never *celebrated* the machine. Throughout his long career, which continued with great vitality and new innovations until his death in 1959, Wright maintained a romantic love of nature as strong as his hatred of the city. Even when responding to the Bauhaus-born International Style, he continued to exploit the varied colors and textures of natural materials and to integrate his houses with the contours of their natural settings. His *Falling Water*, built on the banks of a rushing stream, admirably fits his definition of a good building as "one that makes the landscape more beautiful than it was before."

19-16 *Falling Water*, the home built for Edgar J. Kaufmann in Mill Run, Pennsylvania, was designed by Frank Lloyd Wright in 1936. Cantilevered concrete balconies and thick, rough walls in local stone paraphrase the landscape below and around the house. *(Photograph: Hedrich-Blessing)*

Wright was too individualistic to become a teacher in the usual sense, but he trained many capable assistants who continued his principles in careers of their own, particularly in California and the Midwest. Followers and imitators spread the Master's influence far and wide—and sometimes rather thin, as in the "ranch-style" homes built by developers in the 1950s and 1960s. Many aspects of the Prairie houses passed into general currency during this period.

Design for the Machine Age: 1900–1930

The maturity of modern architecture in the 1920s grew directly from the functionalist trend that emerged in Europe, partly in reaction to Art Nouveau, during the early years of the twentieth century. This trend began in Austria, where Viennese architect Adolph Loos (1870–1933) succinctly expressed his attitude toward decoration in the title of his essay "Ornament and Crime" (1908). Other architects in France and Germany pioneered in the structural and expressive use of reinforced concrete, steel, and glass, creating several exteriors free of historic reminiscences.

De Stijl: 1917–1931

A decisive contribution to modern design issued from a group of Dutch artists and architects associated with the magazine *De Stijl* (Style), founded in 1917. Promising a "radical renewal of art," the painters of the group, which included Piet Mondrian, developed a totally nonrepresentational mode, restricting the elements of painting to an abstract arrangement of lines and geometric shapes on a flat surface, using only black, white, and the primary colors of red, blue, and yellow.

Gerrit Rietveld (1888–1964), a furniture designer turned architect, translated these principles into three-dimensional form as early as 1917 in his *Red-Blue Chair*. The chair's rectilinear structure, flat planes of wood, and simple joinery recall the furniture of Macintosh and Wright, but the emphasis here is very different. Paint and varnish conceal the natural grain of the wooden members, whose sharp edges suggest a machine aesthetic rather than the individual craftsmanship that actually produced the chair. Intersecting elements almost always continue beyond the point of intersection, as if they could be extended infinitely into the surrounding space. The slanting planes of the seat and back seem to be the only concession to human comfort. Yet for all its freshness and absolute renunciation of past modes, the Red-Blue Chair remains an overinvolved exercise—a rigid demonstration of an aesthetic doctrine. It was left to the Bauhaus to create a modern mode of design flexible enough for a complex, technological society.

19-17 Gerrit Rietveld, of the De Stijl group in Holland, created the 32½" high *Red-Blue Chair* in 1918 as a deliberate break with traditional furniture design. The back is painted red, the seat blue, and the remaining pieces black with white ends. *(Collection Museum of Modern Art, New York [gift of Philip Johnson])*

The Bauhaus: 1919–1933

Certainly the single most influential force in shaping all of modern architecture was the *Bauhaus*, the German state school of design. **Walter Gropius** (1883–1969) founded the school in Weimar in 1919 and later moved it to a new building complex of his own design in Dessau.

Initially devoted to arts and crafts in the tradition of the English reform movement, the Bauhaus curriculum was soon revised to place an emphasis on working with the machine in the design of buildings, furniture, textiles, and household articles. The chief aesthetic principle was to simplify the design of any object, so that no unnecessary elements would distract from the pure statement of function, material, and the process of industrial fabrication.

Attracting to its faculty artists, architects, craftsmen, industrial designers, and leaders of industry, the Bauhaus remained the center of European innovation

right: 19-18 The first tubular steel chair was designed in 1925 by Marcel Breuer, then the 23-year-old master of the Bauhaus furniture workshop. Breuer's 28″ high tubular armchair remains one of the most popular furnishings of contemporary homes. *(Collection Museum of Modern Art, New York [gift of Herbert Bayer])*

far right: 19-19 Slow, graceful curves and wide proportions characterize the earliest cantilever chair, designed by Ludwig Miës van der Rohe in 1926. The forthright clarity and refined elegance of the 32″ high design are paralleled in Miës' buildings. *(Collection Museum of Modern Art, New York [gift of Edgar J. Kaufmann, Jr.])*

until the Nazi regime forced its closing in 1933. After two generations of reform and debate, "Arts and Crafts" at last gave way to the "new unity" of art and technology.

One of the earliest expressions of this aim appeared in the invention of chairs made of tubular steel by the Hungarian architect-designer **Marcel Breuer** (1902–1981). Breuer's tubular armchair of 1925 reflects its inspiration in the handlebars of a bicycle as much as in the formal precedents of De Stijl, but its wholehearted exploitation of resilient, lightweight steel marks a pivotal moment in the history of design. Canvas or leather straps stretched across the metal tubes provide seat, back, and armrests; the wide stance of the chair ensures a stability surprising in a piece so easy to move. Chromium plating creates a gleaming, smooth surface that celebrates the precision of industrial production.

Breuer also designed a much simpler stool—an inverted U in tubular steel surmounted by stretched canvas or a block of wood—which was mass-produced in 1926 for Gropius' new Bauhaus buildings in Dessau. In the same year, another Bauhaus member, **Ludwig Miës van der Rohe** (see below) adopted Breuer's use of tubular steel in the first "cantilever chair," in which a single, continuous length of steel was arched upward from the floor to provide resilient support in a simple, graceful design. The excessive springiness of Miës' chair had to be corrected in later versions, however, and the leather or woven-cane seat and back could not be attached by machine. Breuer's more practical version of the cantilever chair, the *Cesca*, appeared in 1928 (Fig. 7-11). The rectilinear S shape of the tubular support offered less bounce and did not encumber the sitter's legs, while the separate attachment of seat and back allowed efficient mass production and clearly expressed a distinction between the parts. The lightness, clarity, and comfort of Breuer's chairs have ensured their continuing popularity.

Miës van der Rohe

The most innovative German architect of the 1920s was Ludwig Miës van der Rohe (1886–1969), who succeeded Gropius as director of the Bauhaus from 1930 to 1933. More than any other individual, Miës crystalized the machine-oriented aesthetic of the Bauhaus and spread its ideals throughout Europe and America in what came to be recognized as the *International Style*. As early as 1919, Miës designed a project for a thirty-story skyscraper with floors cantilevered from a central core and enclosed entirely in glass—a scheme boldly forecasting buildings of the 1950s.

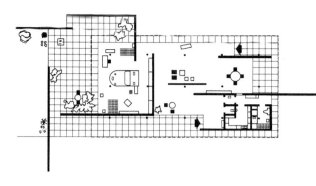

Miës van der Rohe's famous statement that "less is more" epitomized the architect's working method of reducing an object to its essentials and then refining the design through fastidious attention to every detail. Thus the expression of structure became the focus of Miës' architecture, with steel columns, slablike roofs, and nonsupporting walls all clearly distinguished and arranged on a rectangular grid plan.

Miës' early masterpiece was an exhibition pavilion in Barcelona (1929), which he adapted as a model house shown in Berlin in 1931. Under a low, flat roof resting on thin steel columns, free-standing walls divide the interior space into loosely defined areas. Those walls, parallel and perpendicular to each other, extend onto the flat site in an abstract arrangement recalling the compositions of De Stijl. The open plan also recalls Wright, but Miës strove to give his interiors a sense of static, classical repose rather than dynamic contrasts. The structure was meant to recede from view, to act as the neutral enclosure of a strictly ordered volume. Steel construction allowed supporting posts to be widely separated, so that interior spaces became broad, uncluttered, and infinitely adjustable. Wide, expansive windows, reaching to the logical boundaries of floor and ceiling, divided interior from exterior space with minimal emphasis. Living functions were sparsely defined by a single wall or a strategically placed carpet.

Miës designed every detail of his houses, including all the chairs and tables visible in Figure 19-21. In the foreground is his *Barcelona* chair, produced for the 1929 Barcelona pavilion. One meter square in plan, the chair's large scale reflects the ample proportions of Miës himself, but the gentle curves of its X-shaped supports are a perfect expression of luxurious comfort. No other chair designed since the Empire period of the 1800s rivals the Barcelona's monumental dignity, and it continues to hold a place of honor in today's homes.

Le Corbusier

Charles Edouard Jeanneret-Gris (1888–1965), commonly known as **Le Corbusier** or by the nickname Corbu, had the benefit of broad exposure to the work of many early twentieth-century masters. Although never a member of the Bauhaus, Le Corbusier participated directly in the creation of the International Style during the 1920s. Corbu possessed Gropius' and Miës' vision of the architect as a designer for all of society, as well as their concern for incorporating industrial technology in a new architecture. Moreover, he brought a painter's sense of abstract visual form to the creation of a monumental style of building.

In 1919 and 1920, contemporary with Miës' projects for glass skyscrapers, Le Corbusier developed a program for domestic architecture in what he called the *Citrohan* house, a prototype single-family dwelling planned as part of an urban settlement. The prototype had several specifications, including a two-story living area, lit by a tall "window-wall" and backed by a lower room under a balcony. This use of vertical space has returned to prominence in many contemporary homes.

Except for this feature, the salient characteristics of the Citrohan prototype appeared in the masterpiece of Corbu's early career, the *Villa Savoye*, built between 1929 and 1930 in the Paris suburb of Poissy. Constructed of reinforced concrete, the house is raised off the ground on stilts or *pilotis*, freeing the ground for circulation (Corbu explained) while a roof garden "recaptures" the open space covered by the structure. Frame construction frees the enclosing walls to be treated as geometric shapes dominated by long, horizontal "ribbon" windows. The wide spacing of concrete structural supports also allows for an open plan in the interior, here treated with living areas grouped around a sunken patio.

Le Corbusier called the modern house a "machine for living in." Equally opposed to Wright's romantic integration of house and landscape and Miës' rationalist ideal of neutral, reticulated space, he saw architecture as a heroic statement—an assertion of human will on the indifference of nature.

Le Corbusier's interiors were like hollow cubes, enclosed by geometric solids and sometimes enlivened by pastel colors and protruding sculptural shapes. He furnished several interiors with the aid of his brother, Pierre Jeanneret, and furniture designer Charlotte Perriand. Together they designed the elegant built-in storage walls and three very different chairs installed in a remodeled home (Fig. 19-23). The *Basculant* armchair (right) and form-fitting chaise longue (left) both had tension springs to provide resiliency, while the cube chair (rear) consisted entirely of stuffed leather pillows contained in a steel cage. Though less rational and more expensive than the chairs of Breuer and Miës, this sophisticated furniture remains perfectly at home in the most contemporary surroundings (Fig. 1-23, p. 26).

19-22 The Villa Savoye (1929–30) in Poissy-sur-Seine, near Paris, illustrates Le Corbusier's "heroic" approach to architecture. Raised by a dozen *pilotis* above the ground-level garage and foyer, the main part of the house is on one level, enclosed on three sides around an open patio. A ramp leads from the patio to a rooftop garden, which is partially protected by a curving windscreen. *(Photograph courtesy Museum of Modern Art, New York)*

Beginning in the 1930s, Le Corbusier turned away from the taut, white, planar surfaces of the Villa Savoye toward a more sculptural conception of architectural form, with an increasing interest in the plastic moldability and rough textures of exposed reinforced concrete. Although primarily concerned with city planning and large-scale projects, Corbu built a few smaller houses, in which vigorously shaped spaces and masses were enlivened by contrasting surfaces of concrete, brick, tile, and stone. Yet he did not abandon his original "heroic" approach in favor of a Wrightian integration with nature. Le Corbusier's exteriors emphasized the weight and mass of concrete in thick, heavy rectangles, protruding geometric shapes, and a balanced contrast between solids and voids that turned buildings into giant abstract sculptures.

Le Corbusier's sculptural manipulation of reinforced concrete represented an essential departure from the International Style of his earlier years, and this new approach was soon taken up by other architects.

19-23 The interior of an old home in Ville d'Avray, France, was remodeled in 1928–1929 by Le Corbusier, Pierre Jeanneret, and Charlotte Perriand, who together designed the chairs, glass-top table, and built-in storage wall. *(Photograph: Courtesy Museum of Modern Art, New York)*

19-24 Rough textures and vigorous sculptural forms energize the interior of the Maison Jaoul, designed by Le Corbusier in 1952 and built at Neuilly, outside Paris, between 1954 and 1957. Changing ceiling heights and vaults of unequal width dramatize the interior space; below, a long shelf is cantilevered from the wall and extended across the windows. *(Photograph: Lucien Hervé)*

Art Deco: 1925–1940

The popularization of modern trends in design took the form of the **Art Deco** style of the later 1920s and 1930s. Named after the Exposition Internationale des Arts Decoratifs, held in Paris in 1925, Art Deco quickly reached the general public through the efforts of department stores in Europe and America. On the whole, this "modernistic" style applied new materials and geometric decorations to traditional forms more acceptable to popular taste than the austere designs of the Bauhaus. Shiny metals, glossy lacquered woods, polished stone, glass, and some of the newly invented plastics were used in various, usually contrasting combinations. Geometric shapes, especially the triangle, appeared in dynamic patterns, including zigzags, thunderbolts, and sunbursts. During the 1930s, "airflow" patterns and "streamlining," suggesting the speed and power of modern machines, covered not only automobiles but everything from skyscrapers to easy chairs. Essentially a symbolic style, Art Deco celebrated mechanistic progress in much the same way that Art Nouveau had expressed organic growth. Although responsible for several stunning creations, the style lacked the theoretical foundation that allowed Bauhaus and later designers to integrate function, materials, and process in designs of more lasting value. The spread of "modernistic styling" also coincided with the introduction of planned obsolescence in the design of automobiles and home appliances. Interest in Art Deco design was revived during the 1960s when the influence of the past began to be recognized and adapted to current design.

19-25 Ceramic tile, glass, and gold plate create a dazzling display of Art Deco modernism in a private office bathroom, designed by Jacques Delamarre, in the Chanin Building, New York City (1929). A sunburst appears above the shower doors, which present a dynamic pattern of triangles, quadrants, and semicircles. *(Photograph: Angelo Hornak)*

514

Modern Design in Homes and Furnishings

The achievements of the early twentieth century were gradually refined, expanded, and popularized during the period after 1930. Despite the persistence of revivalistic modes, industrial materials, simple forms without applied ornament, and direct functional expression became standard features of architecture and household furnishings. Nevertheless, as modern concepts of design gained wider currency, the Bauhaus approach was moderated and made more flexible. Thus, in both architecture and furnishings, less geometrical shapes and more traditional materials such as wood and brick became accepted alongside the polished chrome and machine-like severity of the 1920s. The development of plastics provided new materials whose potentials were at first slow to be exploited, then widely used, and are still being explored today.

Furnishings

Renewed interest in wood and in less rectilinear shapes characterized furniture design after 1930. The persistence of strong craft traditions and the late arrival of industrialization contributed to the high quality of Scandinavian furniture, which became extremely popular throughout the world during the thirties, forties, and fifties. From the outset, first-rate designers collaborated with industry to create mass-produced furniture of almost handcrafted quality. Finnish architect **Alvar Aalto** (1898–1976) combined simplicity and lightness with the natural grain and color of laminated birch in a series of chairs and stacking stools designed from 1933. Native design traditions inspired new variations by a number of other designers in Denmark and Sweden such as Finn Juhl, Hans Wegner, and Karl Bruno Mathsson.

The polished metal frames and geometric forms of the Bauhaus lost their supremacy in other countries, too. Even Marcel Breuer turned to form-fitting bent plywood in a chair he designed in 1935.

American furniture design rose to prominence through the work of **Charles Eames** (1907–1978) and **Eero Saarinen** (1910–1961), who collaborated in a prize-winning chair design of 1940 in which back, seat, and arms formed a single, multicurved shell of bent plywood. Though produced only in a modified version, this prototype formed the basis for the later work of each individual. Eames' side chair of 1946 combined the best qualities of industrial and natural materials. Metal rods provide a strong, lightweight support, while seat and back are molded to human comfort in walnut plywood. Rubber disks joining the two elements add resilience. A similar combination of materials, together with thick upholstery, appeared in Eames' more recent lounge chair and ottoman (Fig. 17-15).

below left: 19-26 Alvar Aalto's lounge chair of laminated birch and webbing possesses the lyric simplicity that characterized his designs. *(Courtesy ICF Inc. Photograph: Peter Paige)*

below right: 19-27 Many of the characteristics of wood—such as tensile strength, slight resilience, and ability to be shaped and molded—are superbly demonstrated in this 29½" high chair designed by Charles Eames in 1946. *(Collection Museum of Modern Art, New York [gift of the Herman Miller Furniture Company])*

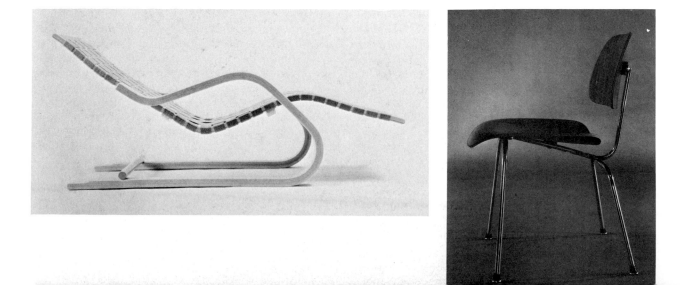

above: 19-28 A graceful continuity of line enhances the single-pedestal chair designed in 1958 by Eero Saarinen, an American born in Finland. Seat, back, and arms, made of molded plastic reinforced with fiberglass, rest on a base of cast aluminum. *(Courtesy Knoll International)*

right: 19-29 Charles Eames's home, built in 1949 near Los Angeles, has a light, intricate steel framework, probably the original use of high-tech components in domestic architecture. Walls, windows, doors, and even floors can be flexibly organized, and varied surfacing materials can be used as desired. *(Photograph by Julius Shulman)*

Saarinen developed his and Eames' original scheme into a set of single-pedestal tables and chairs, in which the seat, back, and arms all formed part of a unified, curving shape of molded plastic. As we have seen elsewhere, the almost infinite flexibility of plastic has made this material a major focus of contemporary design innovation. Plastic, fiberglass, and foam have been responsible for a number of new furniture designs since the late 1950s, ranging from Arne Jacobsen's *Egg* and *Swan* chairs to Eero Aarnio's *Gyro* chair, to the *Sacco* or bean-bag chair and soft structural foam furniture without rigid frames. With the advent of the home office and the high-tech electronic influence, anthropometrically designed office and industrial furnishings have found their way into the home as well.

Domestic Architecture

The closing of the Bauhaus in 1933 marked the end of the "classic" or definitive phase of the International Style. Of its creators, Corbu developed along different lines, while the former leaders of the Bauhaus were dispersed and temporarily cut off from major commissions. In the late 1930s, Miës, Gropius, and Breuer came to the United States, where they assumed academic positions and resumed their active careers. This artistic emigration from Germany accelerated the diffusion of the International Style throughout the world and contributed to the shift in architectural leadership from Europe to the New World after World War II. By the 1950s, transparent cubes of lightweight steel and glass could be found everywhere from Tokyo to Rio de Janeiro.

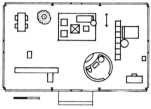

At the same time, the adoption of the new mode by increasing numbers of architects naturally led to greater diversity. The almost dogmatic unity of the 1920s gave way increasingly to personal and regional variations. And just as Wright and his followers responded to the European achievement, the International Style came to admit textured surfaces, natural materials, and greater variety in planning. This trend can be seen in the work of **Richard Neutra** (1892–1970), a Vienna-born architect who had worked briefly with Wright before establishing a practice in California. Neutra's houses of the 1940s exhibit the lean steel-frame construction, glass walls, and geometric composition of the International Style, but they also feature the warm textures of wood and brick and an open, informal integration with the immediate landscape. Similar combinations appeared in the buildings of Alvar Aalto and Marcel Breuer.

The sleek technological emphasis of the 1920s by no means disappeared, however. From 1940 until his death in 1969, Miës van der Rohe simplified and refined his basic concern with the metal frame and neutral, reticulated volumes. Perhaps the ultimate expression of his principles in domestic architecture was the *Glass House* designed in 1949 by Miës' foremost disciple, **Philip Johnson** (b. 1906). Except for an enclosed circular bathroom, the house is entirely surrounded by glass walls that all but eliminate the distinction between interior space and the carefully landscaped setting. Reduced to barest essentials, the structure has an obvious, self-evident quality that belies its originality.

19-33 A Michael Graves interior from 1981 illustrates his fresh approach to design, with allusions to the past but decidedly modern. *(Photograph: © Peter Aaron/ESTO)*

Post-Modern Design

A reaction to the modern movement in architecture and interior design became apparent in the 1970s. It sought to reestablish ornament and historic tradition in contemporary design, to reflect the rich heritage of the past in creative new forms that would evoke a more intimate response. Leading proponents included **Charles Moore, Richard Meier, Robert A. M. Stern, Michael Graves,** and **Robert Venturi.** Historical references were primarily classical in derivation: pediments, columns, and moldings used to ornament both exteriors and interiors.

Related to Post-modernism, regional vernacular styles have also evolved, resulting in eclectic interpretations of traditional styles, materials, and building types. The new traditional houses, like their antecedents, are usually designed in response to site and climate, but they stand out from rather than blend organically into the landscape.

19-34 Chairs reminiscent of the Queen Anne style but in a modern idiom suited to industrial processes were designed by Robert Venturi in the early 1980s. *(Courtesy Knoll International)*

518

In 1950 the history of modern architecture and design was seen in terms of a unitary progression, beginning with the reforming struggle of William Morris and culminating in the final mastery of technology in the machine style of the Bauhaus—whose enlightened gospel, the International Style, gradually reached to the farthest corners of the earth. Today's perspective is less doctrinaire. In a sense, we live in a new age of eclecticism, but the sources are not only the historic modes of a remote past; inspiration lies also in the immediate heritage of the postindustrial era.

Thus we find that the various phases of the modern period are all accessible to contemporary restatement, without the need for pointlessly literal imitation. The Arts and Crafts tradition lives on in the individual workmanship of hand-crafted furniture and many accessories and in the general emphasis on personality in the home environment. Distant echoes of Art Nouveau and Art Deco reverberate in some of the more imaginative furniture designed today. The International Style maintains its universal adaptability, economy, and elegance. The lesson of Frank Lloyd Wright is particularly relevant today, when ecological arguments bolster those of aesthetics for an integration of house and landscape. Both the smooth, white surfaces of Le Corbusier's early work and the sculptural plasticity of his later style reappear in contemporary homes.

The modern period thus provides not a single development of quickly outdated fashions but rather a rich and varied range of choices. Interiors as well as architecture may be traditional or modern, or a personal integration of old and new. No one approach can be accepted without question or without rethinking its suitability to the present day. Yet an awareness of the modern heritage enriches our experience and enables us to respond more effectively to contemporary life.

right: 19-36 An interest
in geometric order, some-
what similar to Art Deco,
is apparent in an apart-
ment designed by Calvin
Tsao. *(Photograph: © Paul
Warchol)*

below: 19-37 A desk of
Colorcore Formica, alumi-
num, rosewood, and 24K
gold plate by Garry Knox
Bennett illustrates the contemporary interest in ex-
ploring new pathways for
hand-crafted design. *(Courtesy The Workbench. Photograph: Si Chi Ko)*

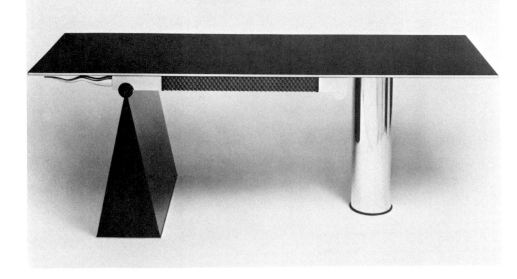

References for Further Reading

Architectural Record. *Record Houses of 19—*. New York: McGraw-Hill, annual.

Ball, Victoria Kloss. *Architecture and Interior Design: Europe and America from the Colonial Era to Today*. New York: Wiley, 1980.

Battersby, Martin, et al. (illus.) *History of Furniture*. New York: Morrow, 1976.

Bethany, Marilyn. "The Regional-Style Farmhouse," *The New York Times Magazine*, June 28, 1981, pp. 44–47.

Blake, Peter. *Frank Lloyd Wright*. Baltimore: Penguin, 1964.

Blake, Peter. *Mies van der Rohe*. Baltimore: Penguin, 1964.

Brown, Robert K. and Iris Weinstein. *Art Deco International*. New York: Quick Fox, 1978.

Clark, Robert Judson (ed.). *Arts and Crafts Movement in America 1876–1916*. Princeton, NJ: Princeton University Press, 1972.

Davern, Jeanne M. "A Conversation with Paul Rudolph," *Architectural Record*, March 1982, pp. 90–97.

Dean, Barry. "Architectural Ornamentation," *Residential Interiors*, September–October 1979, pp. 88–93.

Fitch, James Marsten. *Walter Gropius*. New York: Braziller, 1960.

Fitzgerald, Oscar P. *Three Centuries of American Furniture*. Englewood Cliffs, NJ: Prentice-Hall, 1982.

Giovannini, Joseph. "Regional Styles Enter the Architectural Mainstream," *New York Times*, September 22, 1983, pp. C1, C6.

Habitat VI: Contemporary Furniture. New York: Universe, 1978.

Harling, Robert (ed.). *Modern Furniture and Decoration*. New York: Viking, 1971.

Hatje, Gerd and Elke Kaspar (eds.). *New Furniture 10*. New York: Praeger, 1971.

Hennessey, James and Victor Papanek. *Nomadic Furniture*. New York: Random House, 1973.

Hennessey, James and Victor Papanek. *Nomadic Furniture 2*. New York: Random House, 1974.

Hitchcock, Henry Russell et al. *Architecture: Nineteenth and Twentieth Centuries*, 2nd ed. Baltimore: Penguin, 1963.

Hitchcock, Henry Russell and Philip Johnson. *International Style*. New York: Norton, 1966 reprint.

Jencks, Charles. *Le Corbusier and the Tragic View of Architecture*. Cambridge, MA: Harvard University Press, 1974.

Koch, Robert. *Louis C. Tiffany, Rebel in Glass*. New York: Crown, 1964.

Madsen, S. T. *Art Nouveau*. New York: McGraw-Hill, 1967.

McCoy, Esther. *Richard Neutra*. New York: Braziller, 1960.

Modern Chairs, 1918–1970. London: Whitechapel Art Gallery, Victoria and Albert Museum, 1970.

Pehnt, Wolfgang (ed.). *Encyclopedia of Modern Architecture*. New York: Abrams, 1964.

Pile, John F. *Modern Furniture*. New York: Wiley, 1978.

Pool, Mary Jane and Caroline Seebohm (eds.). *20th Century Decorating, Architecture and Gardens: 80 Years of Ideas and Pleasure from House and Garden*. New York: Holt, Rinehart and Winston, 1980.

Scully, Vincent J., Jr. *Modern Architecture*, rev. ed. New York: Braziller, 1974.

Stickley, Gustav. *Craftsman Homes*. New York: Craftsman, 1909.

Straub, Calvin C. *The Man-Made Environment: An Introduction to World Architecture and Design*. Dubuque, IA: Kendall/Hunt Publishing Company, 1983.

Thompson, P. (ed.). *Work of William Morris*. London: Heinemann, 1967.

Whiton, Sherrill. *Interior Design and Decoration*, 4th ed. Philadelphia: Lippincott, 1974. Pp. 374–415.

20 Interior Design as a Profession

History of Interior Design
Role of the Interior Designer
Interior Design Career Options
Educational Requirements

Future of the Profession
Professional Organizations
    Notes to the Text
    References for Further Reading

There have been many changes in the interior design profession in recent years, broadening the scope of the industry, increasing the career opportunities, and constantly striving for higher professional standards. The Career Guidance Committee of the Interior Design Educators Council has best defined the profession in "Interior Design as a Profession," which is reprinted with their permission below.[1]

History of Interior Design

The desire to create a pleasant, functional interior environment is as old as human existence itself. However, the career we now know as interior design is a relatively new discipline.

Interior "decoration" as we know it in America started late in the nineteenth century and received its initial impetus from Candace Wheeler, whose article entitled "Interior Decoration as a Profession for Women" was published in 1890. At the turn of the century Elsie de Wolfe, a famous actress of the era, established herself as the first decorator in America and it is she who is recognized as having the greatest influence on the early development of the profession.

top: 20-1 In 1896 Elsie de Wolfe designed a dining room in New York in the prevailing dark and somber style of that decade. *(Photograph by Byron. The Byron Collection, Museum of the City of New York)*

bottom: 20-2 Two years later, in 1898, she redecorated the same room in the lighter and brighter style that she espoused, and started interior design on a new pathway. *(Photograph by Byron. The Byron Collection, Museum of the City of New York)*

The early twentieth century was primarily concerned with the selection of furniture, draperies, floor coverings, and other interior furnishings and the decorators' services were available only to the well-to-do until the 1950s.

After World War II the demand for well-trained professional interior designers grew rapidly. With the great commercial growth of the 1950s–1970s, the population explosion, building boom, and increased affluence of middle-class Americans, the emphasis of the profession shifted from the decoration of interior spaces to the creation of spaces that function well for the occupants. The profession of interior design ceased serving only high-income residential clients and expanded to meet the needs of people in all areas of their lives. The designer's influence is now felt in all physical spaces with which we come in contact.

The extent of this influence can be seen in the definition of the interior designer endorsed by the Interior Design Educators Council:

> The professional interior designer is a person qualified by education, experience, and examination, who
>
> I   identifies, researches, and creatively solves problems pertaining to the function and quality of the interior environment;
>
> II   performs services relative to interior spaces, including programming, design analysis, space planning, and aesthetics, using specialized knowledge of interior construction, building codes, equipment, materials, and furnishings; and
>
> III prepares drawings and documents relative to the design of interior spaces in order to enhance and protect the health, safety, and welfare of the public.[2]

Role of the Interior Designer

The scope of the interior designer's role has changed dramatically in the last thirty years from that of "merchant-decorator" whose primary concern was producing fashionable interiors to that of a skilled professional who is qualified to handle all aspects of the design and execution of an interior.

Such changes in the field of interior design have not always been recognized by the public. Many people still think of the interior designer as simply a person with artistic talent and "good taste." Young people who seek to enter the field because they have been told they have a "flair for decorating" often find themselves sadly disillusioned when they realize that interior design is not the glamorous career they anticipated.

The decorating of interior spaces is just one aspect of the profession. A professional interior designer's responsibilities also include problem definition and analysis, space planning, selection and specifications of all interior furnishings and finishes, and coordination of installation. This requires technical knowledge of construction, codes, zoning laws, fire regulations, product technology, and product sources.

Although artistic talent is important, it is only one of a wide range of abilities needed by the successful interior designer. In addition to a sensitivity to beauty, the interior designer should also possess the following characteristics:

- Psychological insight
- Ability to approach a problem analytically
- Flexibility
- Ability to communicate visually
- Ability to meet necessary deadlines
- Ability to work well with diverse personalities
- Business ability

- Organizational and record-keeping skills
- Ability to budget time
- Ability to pay close attention to detail and accuracy
- Enthusiasm

Interior Design Career Options

A wide range of career opportunities are available to the professional interior designer.

Designers specializing in **residential** interiors may work in a design studio, department store, furniture store, or other types of retail outlets. Although there are still retailers labeling salespeople as designers, the more professionally responsible firms are showing increasing recognition of the scope of the designer's skills, responsibilities, and services beyond simply the sale of merchandise.

Residential design specialists may also be employed by contractors, architects, and the mobile-home industry.

Interior designers who specialize in nonresidential interiors may be involved in the planning of hotels, motels, and resorts; restaurants and clubs; school and university facilities; hospitals and other medical facilities; offices; stores and shopping malls; government buildings; factories; and civic centers.

Commercial and **institutional** design specialists may be employed by architectural firms, space planning firms, design studios, and contract furnishings dealers and manufacturers as well as the contract design department of furniture stores and department stores. Others are employed by government, industry, and institutions as in-house corporate designers.

Other designers choose to specialize in one aspect of interior design. Such specialized or related areas would include:

- Transportation interior design
- Set design
- Lighting design
- Model home or room design
- Space planning
- Color consultation
- Interior design education
- Design journalism
- Display design
- Kitchen design
- Historic preservation
- Rendering

The working conditions of the interior designer are varied. Business may be transacted in the client's home or office, in the designer's office, or in a variety of other locations. Designer's work hours are sometimes long and irregular and may involve nights or weekends.

Starting salaries can range from minimum wage plus a small commission to a fixed salary comparable to that of beginning teachers, depending on special skills. Incomes of experienced designers vary greatly depending on location, volume of business, and their professional reputation. The greatest number of job opportunities and highest wages generally exist in larger cities.

As the level of professionalism in the practice of interior design is raised, there is a greater recognition that designers, like other professionals such as attorneys and doctors, should be paid for their time and expertise.

20-3 The home office of Russota & Cama Design Associates, interior designers. (*Photograph: © Karen Bussolini*)

Educational Requirements

Formal education at an accredited college or university or professional school of interior design is necessary today for entry into this field. The Foundation for Interior Design Education Research (FIDER) recognizes undergraduate programs in three categories:

- **Baccalaureate Degree Programs** of at least four years' duration with major emphasis on education for professional interior design combined with general education in the liberal arts.
- **Certificate or Diploma Programs** of no less than three years' duration with emphasis on intensive training for professional interior design. (Such programs are generally offered by specialized design schools with less emphasis on liberal arts subject matter.)
- **Certificate or Associate Degree Programs** of at least two years' duration with emphasis on either preprofessional (preparatory) education or technical paraprofessional (terminal education) training for interior design aides. (Such programs are generally given through community and junior colleges or technical institutes.)

Interior design is being taught in one form or another in more than 350 programs in the United States. Interior design courses may be found in departments and schools of art, architecture, design, and home economics, with each type of program having a somewhat different emphasis.

The interior design curriculum should offer specialized courses in principles of design, history of art, architecture and interiors, freehand and mechanical drawing or architectural drafting, visual presentation techniques, space planning, residential and contract design, interior materials and systems, product design and construction, human factors, and business practices and principles.

A list of schools with accredited interior design programs and a general overview of required courses and education needed can be obtained from FIDER.

In addition to a professional education, it is recommended that persons starting in interior design obtain a minimum of one to three years of practical experience as an "apprentice" or assistant to a professional interior designer before assuming the full responsibility of an interior design position.

The National Council for Interior Design Qualification (NCIDQ) administers an interior design examination that is prerequisite for professional membership in most professional organizations whose members practice interior design.

The examination consists of two parts. The first part is a written academic section, testing the candidate's knowledge of history, modern design, technical information, business practices and ethics.

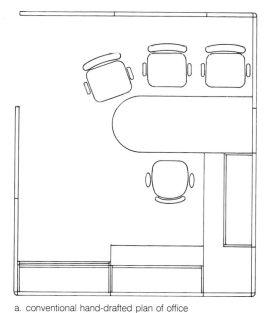

a. conventional hand-drafted plan of office

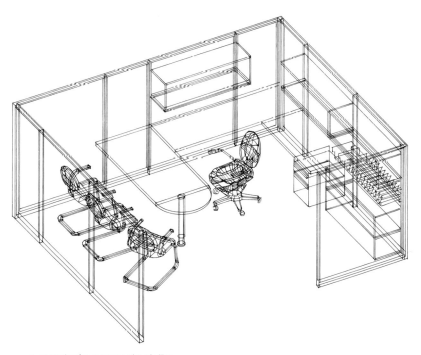

b. computer drawing of office plan

c. computer-drawn perspective of office

20-4 (a,b,c) The computer will transform the workload of the interior designer by drawing and redrawing in a few seconds work that previously took hours. Here an office plan is quickly transformed into a perspective. *(Courtesy Haworth, Inc., Holland, Michigan.)*

The second part, a practical examination, tests the candidate's ability to arrive at a conceptual solution of a realistic design problem involving space allocation, furniture arrangement and selection, lighting and electrical plans, finish selection, schedules, elevations and a perspective.

Future of the Profession

Future directions in interior design will be influenced by technological advances as well as an increasing emphasis on professionalism. The computer, already an important design tool, will continue to play a stronger role in analysis of client needs, project coordination, graphic communication, and information retrieval. Microfiche has begun to supplement, and may eventually replace, bulky catalogs.

Designers will be called upon to have more technical knowledge in specialized design areas such as energy-efficient design, interiors for the handicapped and aged, adaptive reuse of buildings, and environmental safety.

As the practice of interior design becomes more complex and the technical aspects more demanding, there is increasing pressure both within and from outside the profession for the legal recognition of interior designers. The designers of the future must be prepared to accept greater responsibility and accountability for the environments they shape.

Professional Organizations

Please refer to the following organizations for further information:

- Foundation for Interior Design Education Research (FIDER)
  322 Eighth Avenue
  New York, NY 10001
- National Council for Interior Design Qualification (NCIDQ)
  118 East 25th Street
  New York, NY 10010
- American Society of Interior Designers (ASID)
  1430 Broadway
  New York, NY 10018
- Institute of Business Designers (IBD)
  1155 Merchandise Mart
  Chicago, IL 60654
- Interior Designers of Canada (IDC)
  P.O. Box 752, Station B
  Ottawa, Ontario
  Canada K1P 5P8
- Interior Design Educators Council (IDEC)
  P.O. Box 8744
  Richmond, VA 23226

Notes to the Text

1. "Interior Design as a Profession" (Richmond, VA: Interior Design Educators Council, 1982).
2. This definition of an interior designer is a revision of the original definition published by

the Interior Design Educators Council. The current definition of an interior designer was formulated by the National Council for Interior Design Qualification (NCIDQ), has been endorsed by the American Society of Interior Designers (ASID) and the Interior Design Educators Council (IDEC), and has been approved by the Foundation for Interior Design Education Research (FIDER).

References for Further Reading

Alderman, Robert L. *How to Make More Money at Interior Design*. New York: Whitney Communications Corporation, 1982.

Jones, Gerre L. *How to Market Professional Design Services*. New York: McGraw-Hill, 1973.

Kliment, Stephen A. *Creative Communications for a Successful Design Practice*. New York: Whitney Library of Design, 1977.

Knackstedt, Mary V. *Interior Design for Profit*. New York: Kobro Publications, Inc., 1980.

Siegel, Harry. *Business Guide for Interior Designers*. New York: Whitney Library of Design, 1976.

Siegel, Harry, with Alan Siegel. *A Guide to Business Principles and Practices for Interior Designers*, new rev. ed. New York: Whitney Library of Design, 1982.

An Appendix of Designer Symbols

Architectural Symbols

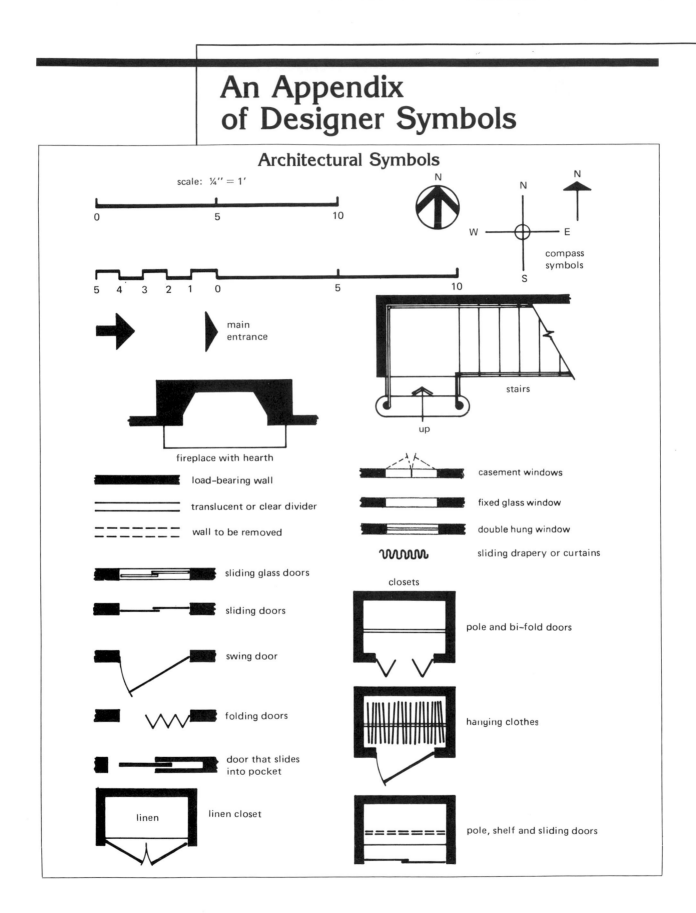

scale: ¼" = 1'

0   5   10

5 4 3 2 1 0   5   10

compass symbols

N / W E / S

main entrance

stairs

up

fireplace with hearth

load-bearing wall

translucent or clear divider

wall to be removed

sliding glass doors

sliding doors

swing door

folding doors

door that slides into pocket

linen   linen closet

casement windows

fixed glass window

double hung window

sliding drapery or curtains

closets

pole and bi-fold doors

hanging clothes

pole, shelf and sliding doors

Architectural Symbols

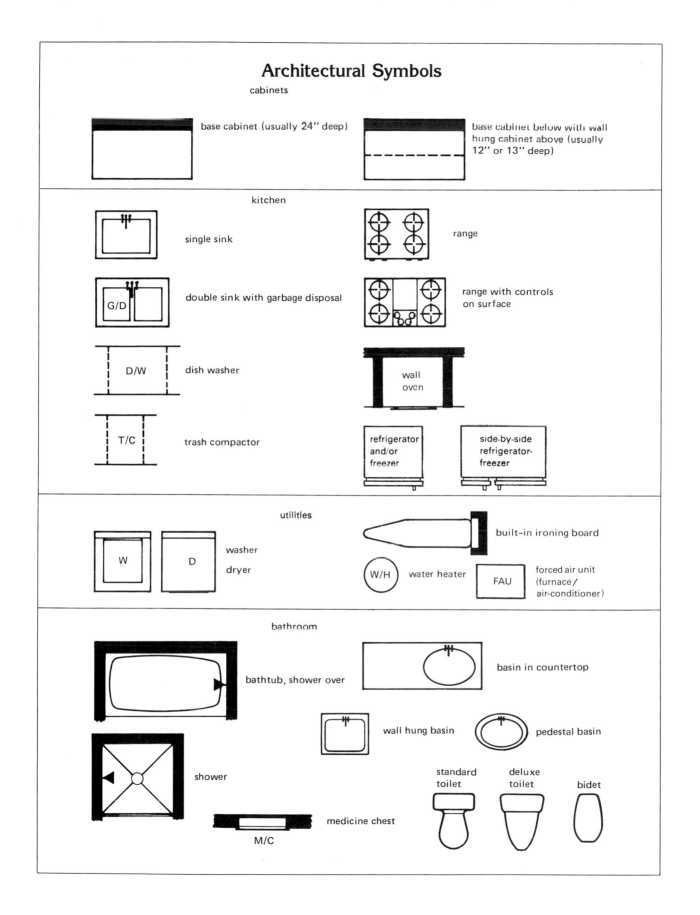

cabinets

base cabinet (usually 24" deep)

base cabinet below with wall hung cabinet above (usually 12" or 13" deep)

kitchen

single sink

range

double sink with garbage disposal

G/D

range with controls on surface

D/W

dish washer

wall oven

T/C

trash compactor

refrigerator and/or freezer

side-by-side refrigerator-freezer

utilities

W

D

washer

dryer

built-in ironing board

W/H   water heater

FAU

forced air unit (furnace/ air-conditioner)

bathroom

bathtub, shower over

basin in countertop

wall hung basin

pedestal basin

shower

standard toilet

deluxe toilet

bidet

medicine chest

M/C

Electrical Symbols

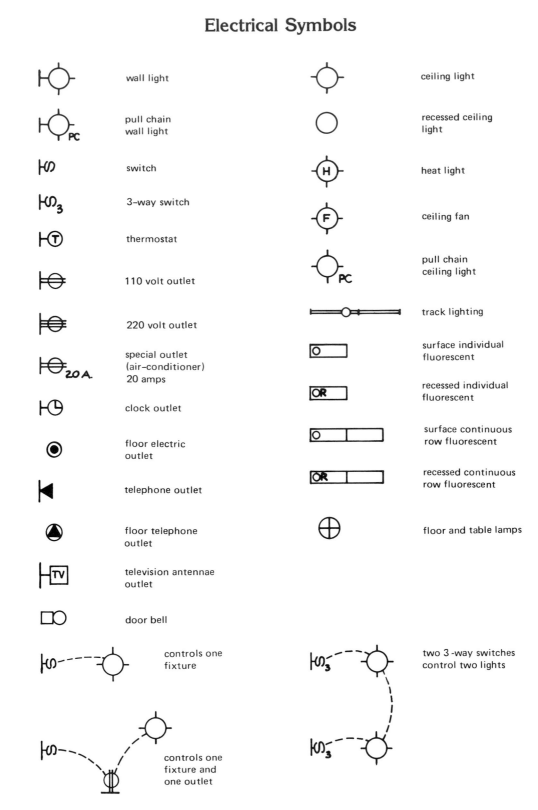

wall light

pull chain
wall light

switch

3-way switch

thermostat

110 volt outlet

220 volt outlet

special outlet
(air-conditioner)
20 amps

clock outlet

floor electric
outlet

telephone outlet

floor telephone
outlet

television antennae
outlet

door bell

controls one
fixture

controls one
fixture and
one outlet

ceiling light

recessed ceiling
light

heat light

ceiling fan

pull chain
ceiling light

track lighting

surface individual
fluorescent

recessed individual
fluorescent

surface continuous
row fluorescent

recessed continuous
row fluorescent

floor and table lamps

two 3-way switches
control two lights

Furniture Symbols

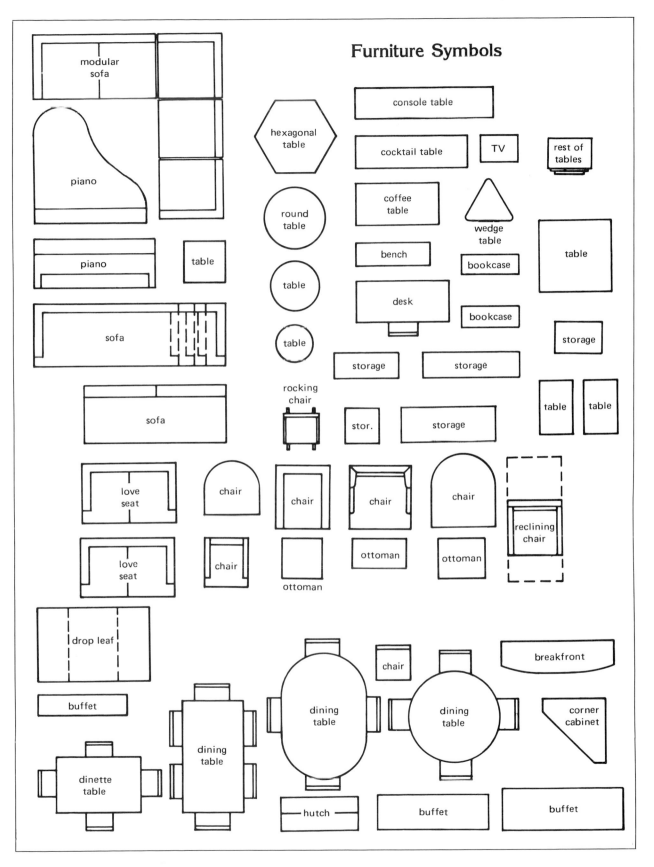

Furniture Symbols

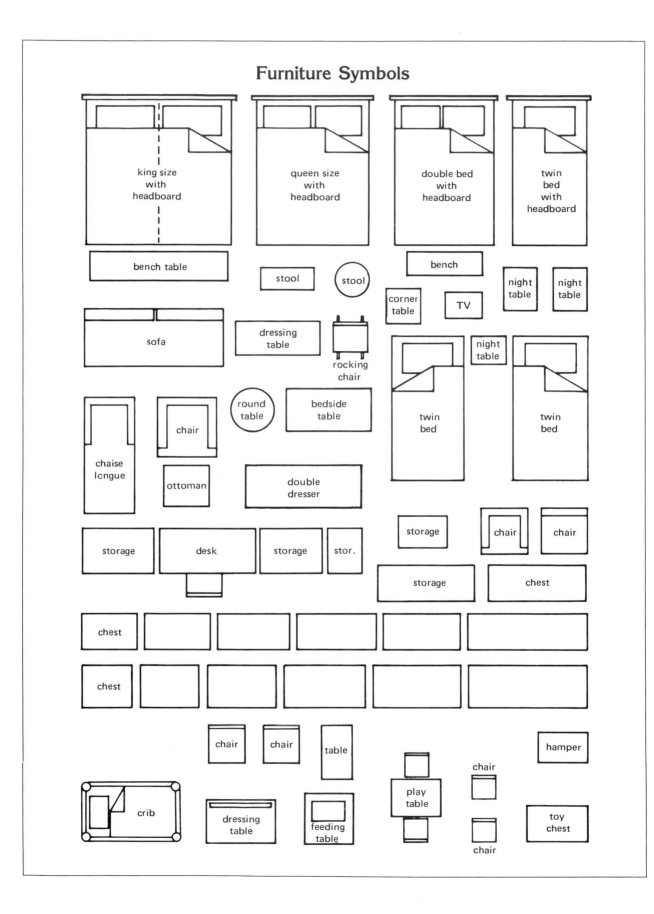

Glossary

Terms italicized within definitions are also defined separately in the glossary.

ABS (acrylonitrile, butadiene, styrene) A tough, lightweight, highly moldable *plastic* compound especially suited to fitted parts and interlocking components; major uses include *modular* furniture, luggage, plumbing systems.

achromatic Neutral color, lacking in chroma or intensity: black, white, or gray

acoustics A science dealing with sound as it is produced, transmitted, and controlled. Often refers specifically to the optimum quality of musical sounds.

acrylics Rigid, durable *plastics* that are very clear and transparent and have the unique ability to "pipe" light. Common trade names include Lucite, Plexiglas, and Perspex.

active solar system A system of specially designed equipment that requires additional energy to collect, store, and especially to distribute solar heat.

adaptive reuse Recycling of older and historic buildings.

adobe brick *Brick* composed of sun-dried clay with a *cement* or asphalt stabilizer; a traditional building material in the southwestern United States and other hot, dry climates.

aerial perspective The effect of the atmosphere on distant colors, diminishing contrasts, lowering intensities, and lightening values.

afterimage A visual sensation that occurs after exposure to the external stimulus has ceased; often the appearance of a complementary hue after intense visual stimulation by strong color.

ambient light General illumination.

American Society of Interior Designers (ASID) The largest national professional interior design organization in the world. Membership is based on educational and practical experience as well as a competency exam. The organization focuses on professionalism in design.

amplification The effect of color intensification due to the interreflection of light from one colored surface to another; also an increase in the volume of sound.

anthropometrics The measurement of the size and proportions of the human body and its application to the design of furnishings, equipment, and spaces.

area The two-dimensional measure of a surface; in home design, usually the square measure of large planar elements—walls, floors, or the whole enclosure.

ASA (acrylonitrile, styrene, acrylic elastomer) A *plastic* compound with properties similar to those of ABS.

ashlar *Masonry* construction in rectangular stones or *bricks*.

atrium plan An architectural *plan* in which all major rooms open directly upon an atrium or central courtyard, which may be glass-enclosed.

awning windows Windows hinged at the top or occasionally at the bottom that swing in or out to open.

balloon frame See *skeletal frame construction*.

balustrade A series of turned vertical supports for a stair rail.

banquette An upholstered bench-type seat.

batten A thin narrow strip of wood used to cover a joint.

Bauhaus A school of design begun in Germany in 1919 advocating the union of art and technology that led to the development of the *International Style*.

bay window A window set in a frame projecting outward from a wall to create an interior recess. Usually of fixed glass but may have movable sections.

beam The horizontal member of a structure's support skeleton resting on vertical *posts*; usually a heavy timber or metal bar.

bidet A bathroom fixture designed for water-cleansing of the perineal area of both males and females after using the toilet.

binuclear plan An architectural *plan* that divides a structure into two separated *wings*. In home design, such a plan often sets aside one wing for group living, the other for bedrooms.

biodegradable Capable of being broken down into innocuous products by the action of living beings.

blister (1) A bulge in a *veneer*ed surface; (2) an irregular-shaped growth ring in wood.

board-and-batten construction A type of wall surfacing in which wide vertical boards are sealed at their junctures by narrow strips of wood, the *battens*.

bow window A *bay window* in the form of an unbroken curve.

braced frame See *skeletal frame construction*.

brick A clay block hardened by heat, often used as a building material. See also *adobe brick*, *firebrick*.

broadloom Floor *textiles* woven on looms more than 36 inches wide.

burl A wartlike growth on a tree that is the source of a *veneer* with a mottled pattern.

cabriole A furniture leg of double curvature, tapering gradually to an ornamental foot, often in the form of an animal's paw.

candela The unit of measure of *candlepower*.

candlepower The luminous intensity of a light source in a specific direction.

cantilever In architecture, any horizontal member—a *beam*, floor, or other surface—projecting beyond its support.

carpet A soft-surface floor covering available by the yard and blanketing the entire floor. Increasingly, the term is used to embrace partial floor coverings or *rugs*.

casement window A window hinged at one side to swing inward or outward.

cast To mold a substance while it is in a malleable, usually liquid state, allowing it afterward to set or harden. Also, the result of such a process.

cavity-wall construction A building technique that provides hollow space within a wall to afford room for pipe and wiring as well as *insulation* in the form of thermal materials or simply trapped air.

cement A finely powdered composition of alumina, silica, lime, iron oxide, and magnesia that, when combined with water, sets to a hard, durable mass; the binding agent for *concrete*.

ceramics Objects shaped from clay and heated (fired) in a kiln to make them hard and durable.

chaise longue An elongated seat for reclining with a raised backrest and sometimes arms.

china Fine white *ceramic* ware fired at a very high temperature; used for figurines and much expensive dinnerware.

clapboard A wood *siding* composed of narrow boards each with one thinner edge to facilitate horizontal overlapping;

also, an individual board of this type.

clerestory A window or bank of windows inserted between two roof levels to bring light high into a room.

closed plan An architectural *plan* that divides the internal space of a structure into separate, discrete rooms.

coffered ceiling Ceiling with ornamental sunken panels between beams that are closely spaced and placed at right angles to one another.

commode A low chest of two or more drawers resting on legs.

concrete A material consisting of *cement* mixed in varying proportions with sand and gravel or other aggregates. With the addition of water, the mixture becomes moldable, capable of assuming almost any shape. Concrete dries to a heavy, stonelike mass of great strength. Pre*cast* blocks and slabs offer particular convenience for building. See also *reinforced concrete*.

concrete blocks Large, generally hollow, bricklike blocks composed of *concrete*. Widely used in building, especially for walls.

condominium A multiunit living complex—usually of the apartment-house type but sometimes organized as a group of separate dwellings—in which residents own their individual units. Services and maintenance are provided by a management company, which charges a fee to residents.

conduction heater A heating system whereby radiators circulating hot water or steam warm the air in an enclosure.

console table A table placed against, or whose top is affixed to, a wall.

convection heater A heating system whereby air warmed in a furnace is blown out through registers; a forced-air unit.

cornice The topmost horizontal member of any structure. In interior design, a horizontal band at a window top or ceiling that conceals curtain or *drapery* tops and rods.

coved ceiling A ceiling that curves into the supporting walls rather than meets them at right angles.

crotch The junction of a tree trunk and limb that produces a V-shaped figure in *veneers*.

crown molding Topmost *molding*.

cruciform In the shape of a cross.

crystal In common usage, *glass* of superior quality containing lead.

dado The specially finished lower portion of an interior wall defined by a continuous horizontal *molding* that is normally waist-high; also, the molding itself.

daybed An elongated chair or *chaise longue*; more generally, a convertible couch in which the mattresses serve as the seating surface.

dead storage Holding space either beyond unaided human reach or otherwise inconveniently situated.

decibel A unit for expressing the relative intensity of sounds on a scale from zero for the least perceptible sound to about 130 for the average pain level.

dome A hemispherical roof or vault. In theory, the result of rotating an arch about its vertical axis.

dormer A window structure projecting outward from a sloped roof.

double-glazed window A window with two glass panes, having a dead-air space between them to provide insulation and prevent condensation on the inside pane.

double-glazing The process of providing windows with two thin sheets of *glass* hermetically sealed together and trapping air between them; often used for window walls because of the superior cold insulation.

double-hung windows Windows having two vertically movable *sashes*.

down light Lighting directed downward from *luminaires* attached to or recessed in the ceiling.

draperies Loosely hung, often heavy *fabric* curtains.

drop-leaf table A table whose top has one or more hinged "leaves" that can be folded down.

dropped ceiling That portion of a ceiling lowered below the actual functional level or below other sections of the ceiling within the same space. Often, a dropped ceiling serves to articulate specific segments of a room, such as a dining area.

earth berm A mound of earth used to partially cover and insulate exterior walls.

earthenware A relatively coarse red or brown *ceramic* ware fired at a low temperature; typically brittle and fragile, porous if *unglazed*.

electric discharge lamp A lamp that contains a gas or mixture of gases such as mercury, sodium, or neon and produces light by either a high-pressure or low-pressure arc.

ell A right-angled building extension.

ergofit The relationship between people and their environment.

ergonomics The science that seeks to adapt the environment to its users.

fabric Cloth; more specifically, a construction of *fibers*, not necessarily woven.

facade The face or front of a building or article, frequently applied rather than natural.

fenestration The arrangement and design of windows and other openings in a building.

fiber A material of natural or synthetic derivation capable of forming a continuous filament such as *yarn* or thread.

fiberglass Any number of *plastic* resins, such as polyesters, polypropylene, or *nylon* reinforced with segments of *glass fibers*.

figure As applied to wood, the overall pattern and character, including all irregularities of *grain*, *burls*, *knots*, and so forth.

film As applied to *textiles*, an extremely thin sheet of *plastic* produced by extrusion, *casting*, or calendering (compression between rollers or plates). Films are used as *fabrics* or as bonding *laminates*.

firebrick Very hard *brick* capable of withstanding the intense heat of a kiln or fireplace interior.

flatware The implements of eating and serving food—knives, forks, and spoons.

fluorescent lighting Artificial lighting that results when electrical current activates a gaseous mixture of mercury and argon within a sealed *glass* tube to create invisible radiation which is then absorbed by the tube's interior surface coating of fluorescent material to yield visible luminescence.

footlambert The unit of measure of reflected light.

footcandle A measure of *incident illumination*.

Foundation for Interior Design Education Research (FIDER) The national accrediting body for interior design educational programs.

fretwork Ornamental openwork or relief arranged as a network of small, usually straight bars; often carved.

FRP *Fiberglass*-reinforced *plastics* in thin, translucent sheets; often used for patio roofs, light-transmitting walls and ceilings, and furniture.

gabled roof A double-pitched roof; a roof that comes to a point and forms a tri-angle; also describes the interior ceiling.

galvanized iron Iron coated with zinc or paint to retard rust.

gateleg table A *drop-leaf* table with legs that rotate outward to support collapsible leaves.

geodesic dome Developed by R. Buckminster Fuller, a self-supporting rigid network of steel or paper rods joined in triangular patterns and covered with a membrane of *glass*, *plastic*, or other material.

glare Uncomfortably brilliant light.

glass A mixture of silicates, alkalies, and lime that is extremely moldable when heated to high temperatures—permitting blown, molded, pressed, and stretched forms—and cools to a rigid, nonabsorbent, transparent or translucent substance.

glass blocks Hollow, bricklike forms of *glass* available in a variety of shapes and sizes. They can be set together or joined to other materials with *mortar*.

glaze A protective and/or decorative glassy coating bonded to a *ceramic* piece by firing.

grain Disposition of the vertical *fibers* and pores in a piece of wood. More generally, *texture*, from fine to coarse, resulting from the particle composition of the material. See also *hardwood*, *softwood*.

gypsum board Also known as *wallboard* or plasterboard, an interior wall surfacing consisting of thin panels of a *plaster*-like material. The boards are not decorative, so they must be painted, wallpapered, or covered with another material.

half-timbered Constructed of exposed wood *beams* and *posts* with remaining spaces filled by *masonry*, *brick*, or wattle and daub.

hardwood Finely *grained* wood types from broadleaf deciduous trees such as maple, oak, and walnut. Hardwoods are for the most part (although not always) harder than *softwoods*; they are also more expensive and accept fine finishes and intricate shapes more readily.

highboy A tall chest of drawers, usually divided to simulate a chest-on-chest, with the lower section most often resting on short legs.

high intensity discharge lamp (HID) *Electric discharge lamp* which produces light when a high-pressure electric arc passes through a gas vapor.

historic preservation The saving of architecturally significant buildings from destruction.

holistic Emphasizing the relationship between the whole and its parts and that the whole is greater than the mere sum of its parts.

incandescent lighting Artificial radiant lighting created by heating a filament—usually of tungsten—to a temperature at which it glows.

incident illumination The amount of light that reaches a surface.

inlay A general term for techniques of decoration whereby pieces of wood, metal, ivory, or shell combine in patterns of contrasting color and/or *texture*, either as insertions in a background material or applications to a solid backing, to result in a continuous surface. See also *intarsia*, *marquetry*, *parquetry*.

insulation The prevention, by means of certain materials, of an excessive transfer of electricity, cold, heat, or sound between the inside and the outside of a structure or between portions of a structure; also, the materials themselves.

intarsia A type of *inlay* in which shaped pieces (usually of wood) are fitted and glued into a flat surface of solid wood.

intensity (chroma) The purity or saturation of color as contrasted with grayness or neutrality.

Interior Design Educators Council (IDEC) An international organization for interior design educators.

International Style Twentieth-century style of architecture and design emphasizing function, structure, and material, and lacking a specific national identity.

jalousie windows Louvered window units of narrow, adjustable *glass*, *plastic*, or wood slats, most often arranged horizontally.

joining The method of assembling furniture by fitting together pieces of wood.

kiln An oven or furnace used to fire ceramic ware.

knot A round or oval figure interrupting the regular grain in wood; caused by the growth of a branch.

lamination The process of bonding together, generally with glue, thin sheets or small pieces of material to create a substance having properties the material would not otherwise possess, such as

strength, durability, or intricate form.

lamp An artificial light source consisting of bulb and base.

lath A framework of thin wood or metal ribs integral with a building skeleton for the support of *tiles*, *plaster*, *reinforced concrete*, *plastic* foams, or the like.

lathe A machine on which wood or metal is turned to shape and carve it.

law of chromatic distribution The traditional use of predominantly neutralized hues with intensity increasing as the size of areas decreases.

leno An open, gauzelike fabric woven with paired warp yarns twined between insertions of the filling yarn which prevents the filling yarns from slipping.

line Technically, the extension of a point in a single dimension. More generally, the outline of a form or shape. In the language of design, the general disposition and dominant direction of elements.

load-bearing wall construction A structural system in which thick, solid walls of stone, *brick*, *adobe*, *concrete-block masonry*, or poured *concrete* carry the weight of the roof to the foundations.

loft An upper floor, normally of a commercial building or warehouse, converted into a home or studio. Also, a raised platform or projecting balcony used for sleeping.

lowboy A low chest of drawers resting on short legs; the Colonial American term for a *commode*.

lumen A measure of light output or quantity of light produced by a *lamp*.

luminaire Light fixture.

luminescence Visible light produced by friction or by electrical or chemical action, as opposed to *incandescence* produced by heat.

mansard roof A roof sloped in two planes, the lower slope being the steeper. A mansard roof provides more attic space than a conventional pitched or *gabled* roof.

marquetry An elaborate *inlay* technique in which pieces of wood, shell, and ivory are set in a wood *veneer* that is then glued to a firm backing.

masonry Architectural construction of stones, *bricks*, *tiles*, *concrete blocks*, or *glass blocks* joined together with *mortar*. In broader usage, construction, as of a wall, from *plaster* or *concrete*.

matte Dull.

medullary rays Lines radiating from the heart of a tree trunk.

melamines High-melting, transparent-to-translucent *plastics* noted for the exceptional durability they bring to *laminated* counters and table tops and molded dinnerware. Common trade names are Formica, Micarta, and Melmac.

melon bulb A large bulbous turned support typical of English Elizabethan and Jacobean furniture.

metamerism The visual matching of colors under one kind of illumination but not under another.

mezzanine A low-ceilinged story between two main floor levels, usually placed over the ground floor; an intermediate story that projects as a balcony.

mobile home Originally, a small, compact dwelling capable of being towed by an automobile or truck. Today the term applies to any *prefabricated* home equipped with axles. The basic *module* can be no more than 12 feet wide, although frequently two sections are bolted together.

modular Built of *modules* or according to standardized sets of measurements.

module One of a series of units designed and scaled to integrate with each other in many different combinations to form, for example, a set of furnishings, a system of construction, or whole buildings. In current usage, the term is most often applied to mass-produced *prefabricated* units.

molding An ornamental strip of wood or plaster that protrudes from a ceiling or wall surface.

monolithic construction A building system in which the major part of the structure consists of a single, self-supporting mass, usually of *reinforced concrete*, *plastic*, or *fiberglass*.

mortar *Cement*, lime, or *plaster* combined with sand and water. When wet, the substance is moldable; it hardens to form the binding agent of *masonry* construction.

mottle A dappled or blotched color or grain.

National Council for Interior Design Qualification (NCIDQ) The organization responsible for testing minimum professional competencies and establishing guidelines for legal licensing of interior designers.

National Home Fashions League (NHFL) A national organization for executive-level women in the interior furnishings industry and related fields.

nosing The projection of the *tread* of a stair beyond the *riser*, usually 1⅛".

nylon The generic term (as well as trade name) for a family of *plastics* exhibiting high tensile strength in *fiber* or sheet form.

open plan An architectural *plan* organized with few fixed partitions to provide maximum flexibility in the use of interior space.

orientation Arrangement, alignment, or position in relation to other factors or elements.

paneling Thin, flat wood boards or other similarly rectangular pieces of construction material joined side by side to form the interior and usually decorative surface for walls or ceilings.

panelized housing Dwelling structures assembled from *modular*, *prefabricated* panels or sheets that serve as walls, floors, and ceilings.

PAR lamp A parabolic aluminized reflector lamp with good beam control; made of heavy glass that can be used outside.

parquetry *Inlay* of wood that takes the form of geometric patterns; used primarily for floors and sometimes for table tops.

passive solar system A technique of solar heating that uses parts of the building structure to collect, store, and distribute solar heat without pumps or fans.

patina The sheen, color, and texture on furniture, produced by age, use, waxing, and/or polishing. On metal, patina is the film that develops from long exposure to the atmosphere.

pitched roof A sloped roof.

plan The configuration of spaces and rooms, walls and openings in an architectural structure; also, the graphic representation of such an arrangement.

plane A two-dimensional expanse; a flat surface.

plaster A paste, usually of lime, sand, and water, which hardens as it dries. Often used as a finish for interior wall and ceiling surfaces.

plastic Describing a malleable, ductile material. More specifically, a member of any of the several families of synthetic polymer substances.

plate glass Ground and polished *glass* sheets formed by spreading molten material on an iron table mold with rollers.

plugmold strips Long tracks with numerous electrical outlets that permit flexible spacing of lighting fixtures and bulbs.

plywood A composite sheet of *laminated veneers*, some or all made of wood, with the *grain* of adjacent strata arranged at different angles to each other for increased strength.

polyethylenes A group of lightweight, flexible *plastics* characterized by a waxy surface and resistance to chemicals and moisture but not high temperatures; popular for household containers.

polystyrenes A family of rigid, transparent-to-opaque *plastics* that are durable, capable of accepting varied finishes, and possessed of good *insulation* properties.

polyurethanes See *urethanes*.

porcelain High-grade, translucent white *ceramic* ware fired at extremely high temperatures; most familiar in fine dishes and ornaments, but with many industrial applications, such as plumbing fixtures and electrical *insulators*.

post In architecture, a vertical member that supports horizontal *beams* to create a structure framework.

prefabricate To mass-produce standardized construction parts or *modules* for later assembly and/or combination.

printing As applied to *textiles*, the application of dyes according to a selective pattern to create a design by such methods as woodcut, silk screen, and tie-dye.

proportion The relation in terms of magnitude, quantity, or degree of parts to each other or to the whole. See also *scale*.

proxemics The study of human interaction with space and of personal and cultural spatial needs.

radiation A type of heating in which the heat is transmitted by radiant panels—installed in the architectural shell and warmed by air or water heated in a furnace or by electrical current—to solid masses within the area.

ranch style Descriptive of a single-story dwelling often of *open plan* and having a low-pitched roof.

reflectance The amount of incident light falling upon a surface that is reflected, expressed as a percentage.

refraction The bending or deflection of light rays from their original path as they pass through different media.

rehabilitate To *restore* to usefulness.

reinforced concrete Concrete embedded before hardening with steel rods that lend the material a tensile strength far beyond its original capacity.

renovate To *restore* to a better previous condition by rebuilding, repairing, or cleaning.

restore To renew or return to an original state or condition.

retrofit To fit with new parts or equipment not available at the time of initial construction or production.

reverberation A sound effect that resembles an echo.

riser The vertical distance from one *tread* top to another in a flight of stairs.

R lamp A *reflector* lamp that directs a beam of light; usually restricted to interior use.

Rococo A style of eighteenth-century French decoration using profuse asymmetrical ornamentation based on natural forms.

row house See *townhouse*.

rubble masonry *Masonry* construction of rough, irregularly shaped stones joined with *mortar*.

rug A heavy *fabric* floor covering made or cut to standard sizes; also, a floor covering that covers only a portion of the surface. See also *carpeting*.

run The total horizontal distance of the entire stairway (*tread* minus *nosing*).

R value The thermal resistance of a material.

saltbox A *skeletal-frame*, two-story dwelling with a double-pitched roof whose rear slope is continued over a one-story extension at the rear.

sash A window frame holding panes of glass; the movable part of the window.

scale Size relative to a standard or to a familiar size.

secretary A tall writing desk with drawers for storage below and a set of shelves enclosed by doors above a hinged writing surface.

shade A low-value or dark color produced by adding black to a hue.

shape The measurable, identifiable contours of an object.

shed ceiling A single-slope, lean-to ceiling.

shingle A thin slab of wood or other material, slightly thinner at one end. Laid in overlapping rows, shingles form a building's *siding* or roof covering.

siding The exterior surfacing of a building; boards, metal slabs, *shingles*, or other materials providing protective covering for the exposed outer walls of frame buildings.

simultaneous contrast The accentuation of differences between the *hue*, *value*, and *intensity* of colors due to adjacent or background colors.

site The actual groundspace on which a house is constructed.

skeletal frame construction A building system consisting of a supporting framework of *posts* and *beams*, to which walls and roof are attached as a shell or skin. If junctures of the support skeleton are strengthened by diagonal crosspieces, the arrangement is termed a braced frame or, in small wooden-frame homes, a balloon frame.

skylight A window in a roof admitting natural light through reinforced *glass* or some other transparent or translucent material.

soffit The underside of a projecting structural part of a ceiling, *cornice*, or *beam*.

softwood Coarse-*grain*ed, fibrous wood primarily from trees with needle-type leaves that they do not shed, such as pine, cedar, and redwood. Although they may actually be harder than some *hardwoods*, softwoods are less expensive and cannot be given as high a finish.

specular reflection The reflection of bright light from a mirror or other highly polished surface.

split-level Descriptive of a house in which the floor level of one portion lies approximately midway between floors of the adjoining two-story section.

spur wall A free-standing wall projecting from an adjoining wall at one end.

stainless steel Durable, blue-gray steel made rust- and stain-resistant by the inclusion of chromium.

stoneware A relatively fine, durable, and waterproof *ceramic* ware made from gray or light brown clays fired at medium temperatures, often used for medium-price dinnerware.

stucco A weather-resistant *plaster* for exterior use.

studio A one-room apartment; a combined living/working space.

stump or **butt wood** The lowest part or root end of a log of wood, the source of crinkly or rippling-patterned decorative *veneers*.

suspension A variation of *skeletal-frame construction* in which horizontal *beams*, floors, or roofs are hung from the supporting vertical *posts*.

synthetic fiber A man-made fiber synthesized from chemical substances in the laboratory; nylon, polyester, acrylic, modacrylic, olefin, and saran.

task light The light needed for the performance of a specific activity.

tensile strength Capacity to resist breaking or tearing apart under longitudinal stress.

terra cotta Fired clay, usually low-fire *earthenware*; also, the reddish-brown color associated with this ware.

terrazzo A polished concrete flooring made of crushed marble and cement.

textile A *fiber* construction; technically, a woven *fabric*.

texture Tactile surface quality, perceived directly through touch or indirectly through vision.

thermoplastic A material that softens with heat and hardens again when cooled.

thermoset An irreversible property of a substance that is attained by heat softening to change the chemistry of the substance, making it firm.

tile Stone, *concrete*, or *ceramic* pieces, flattened and/or curved, used for roofing and as wall and floor covering. Also, thin *modules* of cork, *vinyl*, or other resilient material used primarily to protect and enhance interior walls, floors, and ceilings.

tint A high-value or light color produced by adding white to the hue.

tone The *intensity* of a color.

topography The configuration of physical features of the surface of the land, including position and elevation.

total rise The vertical distance from one finished floor to the next.

townhouse Once termed a "row house," a structure two to five stories high that directly abuts the buildings adjacent on either side. Interior space tends to be long and narrow, with doors and windows only at the front and back.

track light A movable *luminaire* mounted on a recessed or surface-mounted electrical raceway (track).

tract development A residential community planned with detached single-family dwellings, each on its own plot of land. Lots and houses typically are arranged in a tight grid pattern.

tread *Run* or the horizontal distance from the face of one *riser* to the next in a flight of stairs. There will always be one less *tread* than *riser*.

trombe wall A glass-covered, dark-painted *masonry* wall which provides the three-fold functions of collection, storage, and distribution of heat in a *passive solar system*.

trompe-l'oeil "Deceive the eye" in French; skillful rendering of objects or scenes in three-dimensional effect through the use of perspective, foreshortening, and shadows.

tungsten-halogen lamp A small, long-life incandescent light source (also called quartz or quartz-iodine lamp).

turning The art of shaping decorative wooden cylindrical forms—furniture parts, columns, utensils—through the cutting action of a fixed tool upon a piece of wood as it rotates rapidly on a *lathe*. Also, the result of this technique.

Uniform Building Code A set of specifications regulating materials and methods used in construction and maintaining consistent standards to assure healthy, safe, and sanitary conditions.

upholstery A soft covering of *fabric* on seating units, sometimes but not necessarily over padding, stuffing, and possibly springs.

urethanes Lightweight, cellular *plastics* capable of assuming nearly any density and thus any hardness from resilient to rigid. Urethane foams can be sprayed as surface coating or preformed as cushioning and *insulation*.

utility core A central space or a unit, sometimes *prefabricated*, that contains all a home's service elements, including bathrooms, heating, air conditioning, and the like.

valance A decorative *fabric* heading at the top of a window that may conceal lighting.

value The relative lightness or darkness of color.

vaulted ceiling A ceiling constructed as an extended arch, often semicylindrical in form (a barrel vault). Intersecting arches produce a groin vault; a ribbed vault reveals the framework of arched ribs.

veneer A thin facing of decorative or protective material attached to another material that is usually of inferior quality.

ventilator A mechanism such as a louver designed to admit fresh air to the interior.

vernacular architecture The characteristic design of buildings that is sensitive to and makes use of daily and seasonal temperature fluctuations in a given place.

vinyls A versatile family of strong, lightweight *plastics* available in flexible and rigid, molded and *film*, foam and cellular forms.

visible spectrum The small segment of visible light energy that enables us to see; the wavelengths of light that contain visible color.

vista View through an opening or along an avenue.

visual weight The effect of visual impact regardless of actual weight, determined in part by color, texture, and pattern.

volume Mass or space expressed in cubic units (length × width × height = cubic volume).

wallboard See *gypsum board*.

wall washer *Luminaire* used to illumine a wall for *ambient lighting*.

wavelength The distance between corresponding points on successive waves (of light); colors at the red end of the spectrum have long wavelengths while the violet end of the spectrum has short wavelengths.

weaving The process of interlacing two or more sets of *yarns*, usually set at right angles to each other, to make *textiles*.

wing A building portion that extends from or is subordinate to the major central area.

work triangle The path formed by connecting the three major appliances (refrigerator, sink, and range) in the kitchen; used for efficient design.

yarn A long strand, either of *fibers* twisted together or of extruded synthetic material, used in *fabric* construction.

Index

cathedral ceilings, 350
ceiling luminaires, 426–427 (Fig. 16–19), 428 (Fig. 16–22)
ceilings, 60, 61, 316, 348–353 (Figs. 13–28—13–38), 355 (Fig. 14–2); color and texture of, 206, 352–353; height of, 348–349; materials for, 351–352 (Figs. 13–37, 13–38); shape and direction of, 349–351 (Figs. 13–34—13–36)
cellulosic fibers, 289–292, 294, 370–371
centerpieces, 480
ceramic glazes, 265, 267, 268, 269
ceramics, 264–269 (Figs. 11–1—11–5); clay bodies in, 265–266; form in, 267; in home, 269; ornament in, 267–268
ceramic tiles, 259, 268 (Fig. 11–3), 269, 333 (Fig. 13–13); for flooring, 359 (Fig. 14–5), 360 (Fig. 14–6)
chairs, 437 (Fig. 17–2), 440 (Figs. 17–6, 17–7), 446–449 (Figs. 17–15—17–20), 451 (Pl. 54), 452 (Pl. 55); materials for, 162–163 (Figs. 7–4—7–8); modern design and, 510 (Figs. 19–18, 19–19), 511 (Fig. 19–21), 512, 513 (Fig. 19–23), 515–516 (Figs. 19–26—19–28), 518 (Fig. 19–34)
character, 22, 27, 28, 33
chests, 458
chests of drawers, 458 (Fig. 17–31)
children: bedrooms of, 115 (Fig. 5–11); safety considerations and, 42, 44; small, dining spaces for, 83; spaces for activities of, 78, 79 (Figs. 3–20, 3–21)
china, 266
chintz, 309 (Fig. 12–24)
Christmas lights, 416 (Fig. 16–14)
chroma, *see* intensity of color
chromatic distribution, law of, 192
circles, 171–172, 177
circulation, 41–42 (Fig. 2–16), 44, 57, 69 (Fig. 3–7), 73 (Pl. 5)
clays, *see* ceramics
client profile, 13
climate, 18, 20, 131 (Figs. 6–1, 6–2), 146–147, 382
closed plans, 31 (Fig. 2–2), 48 (Fig. 2–19), 49 (Fig. 2–20), 51 (Fig. 2–22)
closets, 42, 65
coffee tables, 450–453 (Fig. 17–23)
coffered ceilings, 350
color(s), 186–207 (Figs. 8–1—8–16); applied to fabrics, 303–304; in bathrooms, 120, 121; of ceilings, 206, 352–353; climate and, 18, 20; cool, 92 (Pl. 16), 189; of curtains and draperies, 397; economies with, 207; effects of, 186, 192–199 (Figs. 8–4, 8–5) (Table 8–1); geared to furniture or accessories, 205; household members' preferences and, 204–205; hue of, 188–189, 193 (Pl. 21); intensity of, 188, 191–192, 194 (Pl. 24); in kitchens, 91 (Pls. 9, 10); Munsell system of, 199–201 (Figs. 8–6, 8–7) (Table 8.2), 421; Ostwald system of, 199–200, 201, 202 (Fig. 8–8); in room design, 206–207;

color(s) (*cont.*)
value of, 188, 189–191 (Figs. 8–2, 8–3), 193–194 (Pls. 22—24); warm, 92 (Pl. 15), 189
color harmonies, 202–204 (Figs. 8–9—8–15)
color wheel, 188, 193 (Pl. 21), 201
complementary color schemes, 196 (Pl. 27), 203–204 (Figs. 8–11, 8–13)
complementary hues, 188–189, 192, 194 (Pl. 24), 201
composition boards, 460
computers, 527–528 (Fig. 20–4); home, 77 (Fig. 3–17), 116 (Fig. 5–13), 127 (Fig. 5–29)
concrete, 260, 261 (Fig. 10–30); for flooring, 356 (Fig. 14–3), 360
concrete blocks, 247 (Pl. 32), 259, 333 (Fig. 13–12)
Con Edison's Conservation House, Briarcliff, N.Y., 139 (Fig. 6–9), 140 (Fig. 6–11)
cones, 178
construction, 28, 324–325
contrast, 219 (Fig. 9–11), 229 (Pl. 29)
contrasting color schemes, 202
conversation areas, 10, 11 (Fig. 1–7), 12 (Fig. 1–8), 66–69 (Fig. 3–2), 73 (Pl. 5); furniture arrangement in, 67–69 (Figs. 3–3—3–7); lighting of, 431
cook centers, 94–95 (Figs. 4–7, 4–8)
cool hues, 92 (Pl. 16), 189
coolness, atmosphere of, 20, 21 (Fig. 1–19)
cord yarns, 296
cork, 330
cornices (luminaires), 427
cornices (window treatment), 395
costs, 22, 25, 33–35 (Fig. 2–3), 59
cotton, 289, 295, 371
cotton brocade, 310 (Fig. 12–27)
counters, in kitchen, 90, 93, 94, 95, 96
coved ceilings, 350
cove lighting, 414 (Fig. 16–10), 428
crafts, 491, 492 (Figs. 18–36—18–38); work spaces for, 128 (Figs. 5–30, 5–31)
crimp, 289
crowding, 8, 11–12
crystal, 270
cultural influences, 5–7
curtains, 387, 395, 396–397, 399 (Pl. 47), 401, 404
curved forms, 173, 177–179 (Figs. 7–30—7–34)
cushions, 464, 465 (Fig. 17–42)
cut glass, 272–273
cutouts, 389
cut pile, 369
cylinders, 178

damask, 311 (Fig. 12–28)
Davis, Sam, 38 (Fig. 2–12), 136
decks, 77 (Fig. 3–19)
decorative lighting, 415 (Fig. 16–13), 416 (Fig. 16–14)

design, 28, 156–157; balance principle in, 209, 210–215 (Figs. 9–1—9–5); emphasis principle in, 209, 219–221 (Figs. 9–12—9–14), 230 (Pl. 9–3); form and shape in, 172–179 (Figs. 7–20—7–34), 180 (Fig. 7–36); function and, 157–161; harmony principle in, 225–228 (Figs. 9–19—9–23); line in, 179–180 (Figs. 7–35, 7–36); materials and, 161–163 (Figs. 7–3—7–8); rhythm principle in, 209, 216–219 (Figs. 9–6—9–11); scale and proportion in, 222–225 (Figs. 9–15—9–18); space element in, 168–172 (Figs. 7–14—7–19); style and, 166–167; technology and, 164–165 (Figs. 7–9—7–11); texture, ornament, and pattern in, 180–184 (Figs. 7–37—7–44)
desks, 454 (Fig. 17–26)
De Stijl, 509 (Fig. 19–17), 510, 511
de Wolfe, Elsie, 522, 523 (Figs. 20–1, 20–2)
dimmers, rheostatic, 421
dining areas, 14 (Fig. 1–9), 41, 73 (Pl. 6), 74 (Pl. 7), 78, 79–83 (Figs. 3–22—3–33), 97 (Fig. 4–13), 149; lighting of, 80, 433 (Fig. 16–30); space required in, 67 (Table 3–1), 80 (Figs. 3–22—3–25, 3–27)
dining patterns, 81–83
dining tables, 438 (Fig. 17–3), 449–450 (Figs. 17–21, 17–22), 452 (Pl. 56); space required for, 80 (Figs. 3–22—3–25, 3–27); standard sizes of, 67 (Table 3–1), 81 (Figs. 3–28, 3–29)
direct-light fixtures, 473 (Figs. 18–7—18–9)
dishwashers, 94
doors, 65, 144, 378, 400 (Pl. 49), 401–405 (Figs. 15–27—15–29); in bathrooms, 118; in bedrooms, 113; design of, 404; functional aspects of, 403–404; in kitchens, 101; types of, 402–403; wheelchair access and, 45 (Fig. 2–18)
double complementary color schemes, 203–204 (Fig. 8–12)
draperies, 395–401 (Figs. 15–24—15–26) (Pl. 48); draw, 396–398 (Fig. 15–25); yardage needed for, 401
draw curtains and draperies, 395, 396–398 (Fig. 15–25)
drawings, 488, 489 (Fig. 18–31), 490 (Fig. 18–33)
dressing areas, 110–111 (Figs. 5–3, 5–4)
duplexes, 54
Dutch doors, 400 (Pl. 49), 401, 402
dyes, 303–304

Eames, Charles, 447 (Fig. 17–15), 448, 516 (Fig. 19–27), 517 (Fig. 19–29)
earthenware, 265–266 (Fig. 11–1), 268 (Fig. 11–3)
earth-sheltered housing, 145 (Fig. 6–19)
Eastlake, Charles, 500
ecological concerns, 5, 25–26